KEYBOARD SCAN COD

The following keyboard scan codes may be retrieved either by calling INT 16h or by calling INT 21h for keyboard input a second time (the first keyboard read returns 0). All codes are in hexadecimal:

FUNCTION KEYS

Key	Normal	With Shift	With Ctrl	With Alt
F1	3B	54	5E	68
F2	3C	55	5F	69
F3	3D	56	60	6A
F4	3E	57	61	6B
F5	3F	58	62	6C
F6	40	59	63	6D
F7	41	5A	64	6E
F8	42	5B	65	6F
F9	43	5C	66	70
F10	44	5D	67	71
F11	85	87	89	8B
F12	86	88	8A	8C

Key	Alone	With Ctrl Key
Home	47	77
End	4F	75
PgUp	49	84
PgDn	51	76
PrtSc	37	72
Left arrow	4B	73
Rt arrow	4D	74
Up arrow	48	8D
Dn arrow	50	91
Ins	52	92
Del	53	93
Back tab	0F	94
Gray +	4E	90
Gray –	4A	8E

CONTENTS

Preface   xix

1   Basic Concepts   1

1.1   Welcome to Assembly Language   1
1.1.1   Good Questions to Ask   2
1.1.2   Assembly Language Applications   5
1.1.3   Section Review   6

1.2   Virtual Machine Concept   7
1.2.1   Section Review   9

1.3   Data Representation   9
1.3.1   Binary Integers   9
1.3.2   Binary Addition   11
1.3.3   Integer Storage Sizes   12
1.3.4   Hexadecimal Integers   13
1.3.5   Signed Integers   15
1.3.6   Character Storage   17
1.3.7   Section Review   19

1.4   Boolean Operations   22
1.4.1   Truth Tables for Boolean Functions   24
1.4.2   Section Review   26

1.5   Chapter Summary   26

1.6   Exercises   27
1.6.1   Programming Tasks   27
1.6.2   Nonprogramming Tasks   27

2   x86 Processor Architecture   29

2.1   General Concepts   29
2.1.1   Basic Microcomputer Design   30
2.1.2   Instruction Execution Cycle   31
2.1.3   Reading from Memory   33
2.1.4   How Programs Run   34
2.1.5   Section Review   35

2.2   x86 Architecture Details   36
2.2.1   Modes of Operation   36
2.2.2   Basic Execution Environment   36
2.2.3   Floating-Point Unit   39
2.2.4   Overview of Intel Microprocessors   39
2.2.5   Section Review   42

2.3   x86 Memory Management   43
2.3.1   Real-Address Mode   43
2.3.2   Protected Mode   45
2.3.3   Section Review   47

2.4   Components of a Typical x86 Computer   48
2.4.1   Motherboard   48
2.4.2   Video Output   50
2.4.3   Memory   50
2.4.4   Input-Output Ports and Device Interfaces   50
2.4.5   Section Review   52

2.5   Input-Output System   52
2.5.1   Levels of I/O Access   52
2.5.2   Section Review   55

2.6   Chapter Summary   55

2.7   Chapter Exercises   57

3   Assembly Language Fundamentals   58

3.1   Basic Elements of Assembly Language   58
3.1.1   Integer Constants   59
3.1.2   Integer Expressions   60
3.1.3   Real Number Constants   61
3.1.4   Character Constants   61
3.1.5   String Constants   61
3.1.6   Reserved Words   62
3.1.7   Identifiers   62
3.1.8   Directives   62
3.1.9   Instructions   63
3.1.10   The NOP (No Operation) Instruction   65
3.1.11   Section Review   66

3.2   Example: Adding and Subtracting Integers   66
3.2.1   Alternative Version of AddSub   69
3.2.2   Program Template   70
3.2.3   Section Review   70

3.3   Assembling, Linking, and Running Programs   71
3.3.1   The Assemble-Link-Execute Cycle   71
3.3.2   Section Review   77

3.4   Defining Data   77

3.4.1   Intrinsic Data Types   77
3.4.2   Data Definition Statement   77
3.4.3   Defining BYTE and SBYTE Data   78
3.4.4   Defining WORD and SWORD Data   80
3.4.5   Defining DWORD and SDWORD Data   81
3.4.6   Defining QWORD Data   81
3.4.7   Defining Packed Binary Coded Decimal (TBYTE) Data   82
3.4.8   Defining Real Number Data   83
3.4.9   Little Endian Order   83
3.4.10 Adding Variables to the AddSub Program   84
3.4.11 Declaring Uninitialized Data   85
3.4.12 Section Review   85

3.5   Symbolic Constants   86

3.5.1   Equal-Sign Directive   86
3.5.2   Calculating the Sizes of Arrays and Strings   87
3.5.3   EQU Directive   88
3.5.4   TEXTEQU Directive   89
3.5.5   Section Review   90

3.6   Real-Address Mode Programming (Optional)   90

3.6.1   Basic Changes   90

3.7   Chapter Summary   91

3.8   Programming Exercises   92

4   Data Transfers, Addressing, and Arithmetic   94

4.1   Data Transfer Instructions   94

4.1.1   Introduction   94
4.1.2   Operand Types   95
4.1.3   Direct Memory Operands   96
4.1.4   MOV Instruction   96
4.1.5   Zero/Sign Extension of Integers   98
4.1.6   LAHF and SAHF Instructions   100
4.1.7   XCHG Instruction   100
4.1.8   Direct-Offset Operands   101
4.1.9   Example Program (Moves)   102
4.1.10 Section Review   103

4.2   Addition and Subtraction   104

4.2.1   INC and DEC Instructions   104
4.2.2   ADD Instruction   104
4.2.3   SUB Instruction   105
4.2.4   NEG Instruction   105

4.2.5   Implementing Arithmetic Expressions   106
4.2.6   Flags Affected by Addition and Subtraction   106
4.2.7   Example Program (AddSub3)   110
4.2.8   Section Review   111

4.3   Data-Related Operators and Directives   112
4.3.1   OFFSET Operator   112
4.3.2   ALIGN Directive   113
4.3.3   PTR Operator   114
4.3.4   TYPE Operator   115
4.3.5   LENGTHOF Operator   115
4.3.6   SIZEOF Operator   116
4.3.7   LABEL Directive   116
4.3.8   Section Review   117

4.4   Indirect Addressing   117
4.4.1   Indirect Operands   118
4.4.2   Arrays   119
4.4.3   Indexed Operands   120
4.4.4   Pointers   121
4.4.5   Section Review   123

4.5   JMP and LOOP Instructions   124
4.5.1   JMP Instruction   124
4.5.2   LOOP Instruction   124
4.5.3   Summing an Integer Array   126
4.5.4   Copying a String   126
4.5.5   Section Review   127

4.6   Chapter Summary   128

4.7   Programming Exercises   129

5   Procedures   132

5.1   Introduction   132

5.2   Linking to an External Library   132
5.2.1   Background Information   133
5.2.2   Section Review   134

5.3   The Book's Link Library   134
5.3.1   Overview   136
5.3.2   Individual Procedure Descriptions   137
5.3.3   Library Test Programs   149
5.3.4   Section Review   157

5.4   Stack Operations   157
5.4.1   Runtime Stack   158
5.4.2   PUSH and POP Instructions   160
5.4.3   Section Review   162

5.5   Defining and Using Procedures   163

    5.5.1   PROC Directive   163

    5.5.2   CALL and RET Instructions   165

    5.5.3   Example: Summing an Integer Array   168

    5.5.4   Flowcharts   169

    5.5.5   Saving and Restoring Registers   170

    5.5.6   Section Review   171

5.6   Program Design Using Procedures   172

    5.6.1   Integer Summation Program (Design)   173

    5.6.2   Integer Summation Implementation   175

    5.6.3   Section Review   177

5.7   Chapter Summary   177

5.8   Programming Exercises   178

6   Conditional Processing   180

6.1   Introduction   180

6.2   Boolean and Comparison Instructions   181

    6.2.1   The CPU Flags   182

    6.2.2   AND Instruction   182

    6.2.3   OR Instruction   183

    6.2.4   Bit-Mapped Sets   184

    6.2.5   XOR Instruction   186

    6.2.6   NOT Instruction   187

    6.2.7   TEST Instruction   187

    6.2.8   CMP Instruction   188

    6.2.9   Setting and Clearing Individual CPU Flags   189

    6.2.10   Section Review   189

6.3   Conditional Jumps   190

    6.3.1   Conditional Structures   190

    6.3.2   *Jcond* Instruction   191

    6.3.3   Types of Conditional Jump Instructions   192

    6.3.4   Conditional Jump Applications   195

    6.3.5   Section Review   199

6.4   Conditional Loop Instructions   200

    6.4.1   LOOPZ and LOOPE Instructions   200

    6.4.2   LOOPNZ and LOOPNE Instructions   201

    6.4.3   Section Review   201

6.5   Conditional Structures   202

    6.5.1   Block-Structured IF Statements   202

    6.5.2   Compound Expressions   204

    6.5.3   WHILE Loops   206

    6.5.4   Table-Driven Selection   208

    6.5.5   Section Review   210

6.6   Application: Finite-State Machines   211
6.6.1   Validating an Input String   211
6.6.2   Validating a Signed Integer   212
6.6.3   Section Review   216

6.7   Conditional Control Flow Directives   217
6.7.1   Creating IF Statements   218
6.7.2   Signed and Unsigned Comparisons   219
6.7.3   Compound Expressions   220
6.7.4   Creating Loops with .REPEAT and .WHILE   223

6.8   Chapter Summary   224

6.9   Programming Exercises   225

7   Integer Arithmetic   229

7.1   Introduction   229

7.2   Shift and Rotate Instructions   230
7.2.1   Logical Shifts and Arithmetic Shifts   230
7.2.2   SHL Instruction   231
7.2.3   SHR Instruction   232
7.2.4   SAL and SAR Instructions   233
7.2.5   ROL Instruction   234
7.2.6   ROR Instruction   235
7.2.7   RCL and RCR Instructions   235
7.2.8   Signed Overflow   236
7.2.9   SHLD/SHRD Instructions   236
7.2.10   Section Review   238

7.3   Shift and Rotate Applications   239
7.3.1   Shifting Multiple Doublewords   240
7.3.2   Binary Multiplication   241
7.3.3   Displaying Binary Bits   242
7.3.4   Isolating MS-DOS File Date Fields   242
7.3.5   Section Review   243

7.4   Multiplication and Division Instructions   243
7.4.1   MUL Instruction   243
7.4.2   IMUL Instruction   245
7.4.3   Measuring Program Execution Times   247
7.4.4   DIV Instruction   249
7.4.5   Signed Integer Division   250
7.4.6   Implementing Arithmetic Expressions   253
7.4.7   Section Review   255

7.5   Extended Addition and Subtraction   256
7.5.1   ADC Instruction   256
7.5.2   Extended Addition Example   257

7.5.3 SBB Instruction 258
7.5.4 Section Review 259

7.6 ASCII and Unpacked Decimal Arithmetic 260

7.6.1 AAA Instruction 261
7.6.2 AAS Instruction 262
7.6.3 AAM Instruction 263
7.6.4 AAD Instruction 263
7.6.5 Section Review 264

7.7 Packed Decimal Arithmetic 264

7.7.1 DAA Instruction 264
7.7.2 DAS Instruction 266
7.7.3 Section Review 266

7.8 Chapter Summary 266

7.9 Programming Exercises 267

8 Advanced Procedures 270

8.1 Introduction 270

8.2 Stack Frames 271

8.2.1 Stack Parameters 272
8.2.2 Accessing Stack Parameters 273
8.2.3 Local Variables 281
8.2.4 ENTER and LEAVE Instructions 285
8.2.5 LOCAL Directive 286
8.2.6 Section Review 289

8.3 Recursion 290

8.3.1 Recursively Calculating a Sum 291
8.3.2 Calculating a Factorial 292
8.3.3 Section Review 298

8.4 INVOKE, ADDR, PROC, and PROTO 299

8.4.1 INVOKE Directive 299
8.4.2 ADDR Operator 300
8.4.3 PROC Directive 301
8.4.4 PROTO Directive 304
8.4.5 Parameter Classifications 307
8.4.6 Example: Exchanging Two Integers 307
8.4.7 Debugging Tips 308
8.4.8 WriteStackFrame Procedure 309
8.4.9 Section Review 310

8.5 Creating Multimodule Programs 311

8.5.1 Hiding and Exporting Procedure Names 311
8.5.2 Calling External Procedures 312

8.5.3   Using Variables and Symbols across Module Boundaries   313
8.5.4   Example: ArraySum Program   314
8.5.5   Creating the Modules Using Extern   314
8.5.6   Creating the Modules Using INVOKE and PROTO   318
8.5.7   Section Review   321

8.6   Java Bytecodes   321
8.6.1   Java Virtual Machine   321
8.6.2   Instruction Set   322
8.6.3   Java Disassembly Examples   323

8.7   Chapter Summary   328

8.8   Programming Exercises   329

9   Strings and Arrays   332

9.1   Introduction   332

9.2   String Primitive Instructions   333
9.2.1   MOVSB, MOVSW, and MOVSD   334
9.2.2   CMPSB, CMPSW, and CMPSD   335
9.2.3   SCASB, SCASW, and SCASD   336
9.2.4   STOSB, STOSW, and STOSD   336
9.2.5   LODSB, LODSW, and LODSD   337
9.2.6   Section Review   337

9.3   Selected String Procedures   338
9.3.1   Str_compare Procedure   338
9.3.2   Str_length Procedure   339
9.3.3   Str_copy Procedure   340
9.3.4   Str_trim Procedure   340
9.3.5   Str_ucase Procedure   343
9.3.6   String Library Demo Program   344
9.3.7   Section Review   346

9.4   Two-Dimensional Arrays   346
9.4.1   Ordering of Rows and Columns   346
9.4.2   Base-Index Operands   347
9.4.3   Base-Index-Displacement Operands   349
9.4.4   Section Review   350

9.5   Searching and Sorting Integer Arrays   350
9.5.1   Bubble Sort   350
9.5.2   Binary Search   352
9.5.3   Section Review   359

9.6   Java Bytecodes: String Processing   359

9.7   Chapter Summary   360

9.8   Programming Exercises   361

10 Structures and Macros   366

10.1   Structures   366

10.1.1 Defining Structures   367
10.1.2 Declaring Structure Variables   368
10.1.3 Referencing Structure Variables   370
10.1.4 Example: Displaying the System Time   372
10.1.5 Structures Containing Structures   375
10.1.6 Example: Drunkard's Walk   375
10.1.7 Declaring and Using Unions   378
10.1.8 Section Review   381

10.2   Macros   382

10.2.1 Overview   382
10.2.2 Defining Macros   382
10.2.3 Invoking Macros   383
10.2.4 Additional Macro Features   384
10.2.5 Using the Book's Macro Library   388
10.2.6 Example Program: Wrappers   394
10.2.7 Section Review   395

10.3   Conditional-Assembly Directives   396

10.3.1 Checking for Missing Arguments   397
10.3.2 Default Argument Initializers   398
10.3.3 Boolean Expressions   399
10.3.4 IF, ELSE, and ENDIF Directives   399
10.3.5 The IFIDN and IFIDNI Directives   400
10.3.6 Example: Summing a Matrix Row   401
10.3.7 Special Operators   404
10.3.8 Macro Functions   407
10.3.9 Section Review   409

10.4   Defining Repeat Blocks   410

10.4.1 WHILE Directive   410
10.4.2 REPEAT Directive   410
10.4.3 FOR Directive   411
10.4.4 FORC Directive   412
10.4.5 Example: Linked List   412
10.4.6 Section Review   414

10.5   Chapter Summary   415

10.6   Programming Exercises   416

11 MS-Windows Programming   419

11.1   Win32 Console Programming   419

11.1.1 Background Information   420
11.1.2 Win32 Console Functions   424
11.1.3 Displaying a Message Box   426

11.1.4   Console Input   429
11.1.5   Console Output   435
11.1.6   Reading and Writing Files   437
11.1.7   File I/O in the Irvine32 Library   442
11.1.8   Testing the File I/O Procedures   444
11.1.9   Console Window Manipulation   447
11.1.10 Controlling the Cursor   450
11.1.11 Controlling the Text Color   451
11.1.12 Time and Date Functions   453
11.1.13 Section Review   456

11.2 Writing a Graphical Windows Application   457
11.2.1   Necessary Structures   458
11.2.2   The MessageBox Function   459
11.2.3   The WinMain Procedure   460
11.2.4   The WinProc Procedure   460
11.2.5   The ErrorHandler Procedure   461
11.2.6   Program Listing   461
11.2.7   Section Review   465

11.3 Dynamic Memory Allocation   466
11.3.1   HeapTest Programs   469
11.3.2   Section Review   473

11.4 x86 Memory Management   473
11.4.1   Linear Addresses   473
11.4.2   Page Translation   477
11.4.3   Section Review   479

11.5 Chapter Summary   479

11.6 Programming Exercises   481

12 Floating-Point Processing and Instruction Encoding   483

12.1 Floating-Point Binary Representation   483
12.1.1   IEEE Binary Floating-Point Representation   484
12.1.2   The Exponent   485
12.1.3   Normalized Binary Floating-Point Numbers   486
12.1.4   Creating the IEEE Representation   486
12.1.5   Converting Decimal Fractions to Binary Reals   488
12.1.6   Section Review   490

12.2 Floating-Point Unit   490
12.2.1   FPU Register Stack   491
12.2.2   Rounding   493
12.2.3   Floating-Point Exceptions   495
12.2.4   Floating-Point Instruction Set   495

12.2.5   Arithmetic Instructions   498
12.2.6   Comparing Floating-Point Values   502
12.2.7   Reading and Writing Floating-Point Values   504
12.2.8   Exception Synchronization   506
12.2.9   Code Examples   507
12.2.10 Mixed-Mode Arithmetic   508
12.2.11 Masking and Unmasking Exceptions   509
12.2.12 Section Review   511

12.3 x86 Instruction Encoding   512
12.3.1   Instruction Format   512
12.3.2   Single-Byte Instructions   513
12.3.3   Move Immediate to Register   514
12.3.4   Register-Mode Instructions   514
12.3.5   Processor Operand-Size Prefix   515
12.3.6   Memory-Mode Instructions   516
12.3.7   Section Review   519

12.4 Chapter Summary   520

12.5 Programming Exercises   521

13 High-Level Language Interface   525

13.1 Introduction   525
13.1.1   General Conventions   526
13.1.2   .MODEL Directive   527
13.1.3   Section Review   529

13.2 Inline Assembly Code   529
13.2.1   __asm Directive in Microsoft Visual C++   529
13.2.2   File Encryption Example   532
13.2.3   Section Review   535

13.3 Linking to C/C++ in Protected Mode   535
13.3.1   Using Assembly Language to Optimize C++ Code   536
13.3.2   Calling C and C++ Functions   542
13.3.3   Multiplication Table Example   544
13.3.4   Calling C Library Functions   547
13.3.5   Directory Listing Program   550
13.3.6   Section Review   552

13.4 Linking to C/C++ in Real-Address Mode   552
13.4.1   Linking to Borland C++   553
13.4.2   ReadSector Example   554
13.4.3   Example: Large Random Integers   558
13.4.4   Section Review   559

13.5 Chapter Summary   560

13.6 Programming Exercises   560

14   16-Bit MS-DOS Programming   562

14.1   MS-DOS and the IBM-PC   562
14.1.1   Memory Organization   563
14.1.2   Redirecting Input-Output   564
14.1.3   Software Interrupts   565
14.1.4   INT Instruction   565
14.1.5   Coding for 16-Bit Programs   567
14.1.6   Section Review   568

14.2   MS-DOS Function Calls (INT 21h)   568
14.2.1   Selected Output Functions   570
14.2.2   Hello World Program Example   572
14.2.3   Selected Input Functions   573
14.2.4   Date/Time Functions   577
14.2.5   Section Review   581

14.3   Standard MS-DOS File I/O Services   581
14.3.1   Create or Open File (716Ch)   583
14.3.2   Close File Handle (3Eh)   584
14.3.3   Move File Pointer (42h)   584
14.3.4   Get File Creation Date and Time   585
14.3.5   Selected Library Procedures   585
14.3.6   Example: Read and Copy a Text File   586
14.3.7   Reading the MS-DOS Command Tail   588
14.3.8   Example: Creating a Binary File   591
14.3.9   Section Review   594

14.4   Chapter Summary   594

14.5   Programming Exercises   596

Chapters are available from the Companion Web site

15   Disk Fundamentals

16   BIOS-Level Programming

17   Expert MS-DOS Programming

Appendix A   MASM Reference   598
Appendix B   The x86 Instruction Set   620
Appendix C   Answers to Review Questions   655

Appendices are available from the Companion Web site

Appendix D   BIOS and MS-DOS Interrupts

Appendix E   Answers to Review Questions
(Chapters 15–17)

Index   699

Preface

Assembly Language for x86 Processors, Sixth Edition, teaches assembly language programming and architecture for Intel and AMD processors. It is an appropriate text for the following types of college courses:

- Assembly Language Programming
- Fundamentals of Computer Systems
- Fundamentals of Computer Architecture

Students use Intel or AMD processors and program with **Microsoft Macro Assembler (MASM),** running on Windows 98, XP, Vista, and Windows 7. Although this book was originally designed as a programming textbook for college students, it serves as an effective supplement to computer architecture courses. As a testament to its popularity, previous editions have been translated into Spanish, Korean, Chinese, French, Russian, and Polish.

Emphasis of Topics   This edition includes topics that lead naturally into subsequent courses in computer architecture, operating systems, and compiler writing:

- Virtual machine concept
- Instruction set architecture
- Elementary Boolean operations
- Instruction execution cycle
- Memory access and handshaking
- Interrupts and polling
- Hardware-based I/O
- Floating-point binary representation

Other topics relate specially to Intel and AMD architecture:

- Protected memory and paging
- Memory segmentation in real-address mode
- 16-bit interrupt handling
- MS-DOS and BIOS system calls (interrupts)
- Floating-point unit architecture and programming
- Instruction encoding

Certain examples presented in the book lend themselves to courses that occur later in a computer science curriculum:

- Searching and sorting algorithms
- High-level language structures

- Finite-state machines
- Code optimization examples

What's New in the Sixth Edition

In this revision, we have placed a strong emphasis on improving the descriptions of important programming concepts and relevant program examples.

- We have added numerous step-by-step descriptions of sample programs, particularly in Chapters 1–8.
- Many new illustrations have been inserted into the chapters to improve student comprehension of concepts and details.
- **Java Bytecodes:** The Java Virtual Machine (JVM) provides an excellent real-life example of a stack-oriented architecture. It provides an excellent contrast to x86 architecture. Therefore, in Chapters 8 and 9, the author explains the basic operation of Java bytecodes with short illustrative examples. Numerous short examples are shown in disassembled bytecode format, followed by detailed step-by-step explanations.
- Selected programming exercises have been replaced in the first 8 chapters. Programming exercises are now assigned stars to indicate their difficulty. One star is the easiest, four stars indicate the most difficult level.
- Tutorial videos by the author are available on the Companion Web site (www.pearsonhighered.com/ irvine) to explain worked-out programming exercises.
- The order of chapters in the second half of the book has been revised to form a more logical sequence of topics, and selected chapters are supplied in electronic form for easy searching.

This book is still focused on its primary goal, to teach students how to write and debug programs at the machine level. It will never replace a complete book on computer architecture, but it does give students the first-hand experience of writing software in an environment that teaches them how a computer works. Our premise is that students retain knowledge better when theory is combined with experience. In an engineering course, students construct prototypes; in a computer architecture course, students should write machine-level programs. In both cases, they have a memorable experience that gives them the confidence to work in any OS/machine-oriented environment.

Real Mode and Protected Mode   This edition emphasizes 32-bit protected mode, but it still has three electronic chapters devoted to real-mode programming. For example, there is an entire chapter on BIOS programming for the keyboard, video display (including graphics), and mouse. Another chapter covers MS-DOS programming using interrupts (system calls). Students can benefit from programming directly to hardware and the BIOS.

The examples in the first half of the book are nearly all presented as 32-bit text-oriented applications running in protected mode using the flat memory model. This approach is wonderfully simple because it avoids the complications of segment-offset addressing. Specially marked paragraphs and popup boxes point out occasional differences between protected mode and real-mode programming. Most differences are abstracted by the book's parallel link libraries for real-mode and protected mode programming.

Link Libraries We supply two versions of the link library that students use for basic input-output, simulations, timing, and other useful stuff. The 32-bit version (Irvine32.lib) runs in protected mode, sending its output to the Win32 console. The 16-bit version (Irvine16.lib) runs in real-address mode. Full source code for the libraries is supplied on the Companion Web site. The link libraries are available only for convenience, not to prevent students from learning how to program input-output themselves. Students are encouraged to create their own libraries.

Included Software and Examples All the example programs were tested with Microsoft Macro Assembler Version 10.0, running in Microsoft Visual Studio 2010. In addition, batch files are supplied that permit students to assemble and run applications from the Windows command prompt. The 32-bit C++ applications in Chapter 14 were tested with Microsoft Visual C++ .NET.

Web Site Information Updates and corrections to this book may be found at the Companion Web site, including additional programming projects for instructors to assign at the ends of chapters.

Overall Goals

The following goals of this book are designed to broaden the student's interest and knowledge in topics related to assembly language:

- Intel and AMD processor architecture and programming
- Real-address mode and protected mode programming
- Assembly language directives, macros, operators, and program structure
- Programming methodology, showing how to use assembly language to create system-level software tools and application programs
- Computer hardware manipulation
- Interaction between assembly language programs, the operating system, and other application programs

One of our goals is to help students approach programming problems with a machine-level mind set. It is important to think of the CPU as an interactive tool, and to learn to monitor its operation as directly as possible. A debugger is a programmer's best friend, not only for catching errors, but as an educational tool that teaches about the CPU and operating system. We encourage students to look beneath the surface of high-level languages and to realize that most programming languages are designed to be portable and, therefore, independent of their host machines. In addition to the short examples, this book contains hundreds of ready-to-run programs that demonstrate instructions or ideas as they are presented in the text. Reference materials, such as guides to MS-DOS interrupts and instruction mnemonics, are available at the end of the book.

Required Background The reader should already be able to program confidently in at least one high-level programming language such as Python, Java, C, or C++. One chapter covers C++ interfacing, so it is very helpful to have a compiler on hand. I have used this book in the classroom with majors in both computer science and management information systems, and it has been used elsewhere in engineering courses.

Features

Complete Program Listings The Companion Web site contains supplemental learning materials, study guides, and all the source code from the book's examples. An extensive link library is supplied with the book, containing more than 30 procedures that simplify user input-output, numeric processing, disk and file handling, and string handling. In the beginning stages of the course, students can use this library to enhance their programs. Later, they can create their own procedures and add them to the library.

Programming Logic   Two chapters emphasize Boolean logic and bit-level manipulation. A conscious attempt is made to relate high-level programming logic to the low-level details of the machine. This approach helps students to create more efficient implementations and to better understand how compilers generate object code.

Hardware and Operating System Concepts   The first two chapters introduce basic hardware and data representation concepts, including binary numbers, CPU architecture, status flags, and memory mapping. A survey of the computer's hardware and a historical perspective of the Intel processor family helps students to better understand their target computer system.

Structured Programming Approach   Beginning with Chapter 5, procedures and functional decomposition are emphasized. Students are given more complex programming exercises, requiring them to focus on design before starting to write code.

Java Bytecodes and the Java Virtual Machine   In Chapters 8 and 9, the author explains the basic operation of Java bytecodes with short illustrative examples. Numerous short examples are shown in disassembled bytecode format, followed by detailed step-by-step explanations.

Disk Storage Concepts   Students learn the fundamental principles behind the disk storage system on MS-Windows–based systems from hardware and software points of view.

Creating Link Libraries   Students are free to add their own procedures to the book's link library and create new libraries. They learn to use a toolbox approach to programming and to write code that is useful in more than one program.

Macros and Structures   A chapter is devoted to creating structures, unions, and macros, which are essential in assembly language and systems programming. Conditional macros with advanced operators serve to make the macros more professional.

Interfacing to High-Level Languages   A chapter is devoted to interfacing assembly language to C and C++. This is an important job skill for students who are likely to find jobs programming in high-level languages. They can learn to optimize their code and see examples of how C++ compilers optimize code.

Instructional Aids   All the program listings are available on the Web. Instructors are provided a test bank, answers to review questions, solutions to programming exercises, and a Microsoft PowerPoint slide presentation for each chapter.

VideoNotes   VideoNotes are Pearson's new visual tool designed to teach students key programming concepts and techniques. These short step-by-step videos demonstrate how to solve problems from design through coding. VideoNotes allow for self-paced instruction with easy navigation including the ability to select, play, rewind, fast-forward, and stop within each VideoNote exercise. A note appears within the text to designate that a VideoNote is available.

VideoNotes are free with the purchase of a new textbook. To *purchase* access to VideoNotes, go to www.pearsonhighered.com/irvine and click on the VideoNotes under *Student Resources*.

Chapter Descriptions

Chapters 1 to 8 contain core concepts of assembly language and should be covered in sequence. After that, you have a fair amount of freedom. The following chapter dependency graph shows how later chapters depend on knowledge gained from other chapters.

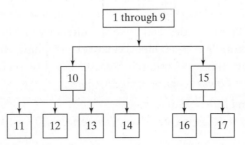

1. **Basic Concepts:** Applications of assembly language, basic concepts, machine language, and data representation.
2. **x86 Processor Architecture:** Basic microcomputer design, instruction execution cycle, x86 processor architecture, x86 memory management, components of a microcomputer, and the input-output system.
3. **Assembly Language Fundamentals:** Introduction to assembly language, linking and debugging, and defining constants and variables.
4. **Data Transfers, Addressing, and Arithmetic:** Simple data transfer and arithmetic instructions, assemble-link-execute cycle, operators, directives, expressions, JMP and LOOP instructions, and indirect addressing.
5. **Procedures:** Linking to an external library, description of the book's link library, stack operations, defining and using procedures, flowcharts, and top-down structured design.
6. **Conditional Processing:** Boolean and comparison instructions, conditional jumps and loops, high-level logic structures, and finite-state machines.
7. **Integer Arithmetic:** Shift and rotate instructions with useful applications, multiplication and division, extended addition and subtraction, and ASCII and packed decimal arithmetic.
8. **Advanced Procedures:** Stack parameters, local variables, advanced PROC and INVOKE directives, and recursion.
9. **Strings and Arrays:** String primitives, manipulating arrays of characters and integers, two-dimensional arrays, sorting, and searching.
10. **Structures and Macros:** Structures, macros, conditional assembly directives, and defining repeat blocks.
11. **MS-Windows Programming:** Protected mode memory management concepts, using the Microsoft-Windows API to display text and colors, and dynamic memory allocation.
12. **Floating-Point Processing and Instruction Encoding:** Floating-point binary representation and floating-point arithmetic. Learning to program the IA-32 floating-point unit. Understanding the encoding of IA-32 machine instructions.

13. **High-Level Language Interface:** Parameter passing conventions, inline assembly code, and linking assembly language modules to C and C++ programs.

14. **16-Bit MS-DOS Programming:** Calling MS-DOS interrupts for console and file input-output.

   • **Appendix A:** MASM Reference
   • **Appendix B:** The x86 Instruction Set
   • **Appendix C:** Answers to Review Questions

The following chapters and appendices are supplied online at the Companion Web site:

15. **Disk Fundamentals:** Disk storage systems, sectors, clusters, directories, file allocation tables, handling MS-DOS error codes, and drive and directory manipulation.

16. **BIOS-Level Programming:** Keyboard input, video text, graphics, and mouse programming.

17. **Expert MS-DOS Programming:** Custom-designed segments, runtime program structure, and Interrupt handling. Hardware control using I/O ports.

   • **Appendix D:** BIOS and MS-DOS Interrupts
   • **Appendix E:** Answers to Review Questions (Chapters 15–17)

Instructor and Student Resources

Instructor Resource Materials

The following protected instructor material is available on the Companion Web site:

www.pearsonhighered.com/irvine

For username and password information, please contact your Pearson Representative.

   • Lecture PowerPoint Slides
   • Instructor Solutions Manual

Student Resource Materials

The student resource materials can be accessed through the publisher's Web site located at www.pearsonhighered.com/irvine. These resources include:

   • VideoNotes
   • Online Chapters and Appendices
      • Chapter 15: *Disk Fundamentals*
      • Chapter 16: *BIOS-Level Programming*
      • Chapter 17: *Expert MS-DOS Programming*
      • Appendix D: *BIOS and MS-DOS Interrupts*
      • Appendix E: *Answers to Review Questions (Chapters 15–17)*

Students must use the access card located in the front of the book to register and access the online chapters and VideoNotes. If there is no access card in the front of this textbook, students can purchase access by going to www.pearsonhighered.com/irvine and selecting "purchase access to premium content." Instructors must also register on the site to access this material. Students will also find a link to the author's Web site. An access card is not required for the following materials:

   • *Getting Started*, a comprehensive step-by-step tutorial that helps students customize Visual Studio for assembly language programming.
   • Supplementary articles on assembly language programming topics.

- Complete source code for all example programs in the book, as well as the source code for the author's supplementary library.
- *Assembly Language Workbook*, an interactive workbook covering number conversions, addressing modes, register usage, debug programming, and floating-point binary numbers. Content pages are HTML documents to allow for customization. Help File in Windows Help Format.
- Debugging Tools: Tutorials on using Microsoft CodeView, MS-DOS Debug, and Microsoft Visual Studio.

Acknowledgments

Many thanks are due to Tracy Dunkelberger, Executive Editor for Computer Science at Pearson Education, who has provided friendly, helpful guidance over the past few years. Maheswari Pon-Saravanan of TexTech International did an excellent job on the book production, along with Jane Bonnell as the production editor at Pearson. Many thanks to Scott Disanno, the book's managing editor, and Melinda Haggerty, the assistant editor.

Sixth Edition

Many thanks are due to Professor James Brink of Pacific Lutheran University, Professor David Topham of Ohlone College, and Professor W. A. Barrett of San Jose State University. All have contributed excellent code examples and debugging suggestions to this book. In addition, I give grateful acknowledgment to the reviewers of the Sixth edition:

- Hisham Al-Mubaid, University of Houston, Clearlake
- John-Thones Amenyo, York College of CUNY
- John F. Doyle, Indiana University, Southeast
- Nicole Jiao, South Texas Community College
- Remzi Seker, University of Arkansas, Little Rock

Previous Editions

I offer my special thanks to the following individuals who were most helpful during the development of earlier editions of this book:

- William Barrett, San Jose State University
- Scott Blackledge
- James Brink, Pacific Lutheran University
- Gerald Cahill, Antelope Valley College
- John Taylor

About the Author

Kip Irvine has written five computer programming textbooks, for Intel Assembly Language, C++, Visual Basic (beginning and advanced), and COBOL. His book *Assembly Language for Intel-Based Computers* has been translated into six languages. His first college degrees (B.M., M.M., and doctorate) were in Music Composition, at University of Hawaii and University of Miami. He began programming computers for music synthesis around 1982 and taught programming at Miami-Dade Community College for 17 years. Kip earned an M.S. degree in Computer Science from the University of Miami, and he has been a full-time member of the faculty in the School of Computing and Information Sciences at Florida International University since 2000.

1

BASIC CONCEPTS

1.1 **Welcome to Assembly Language**
    1.1.1 Good Questions to Ask
    1.1.2 Assembly Language Applications
    1.1.3 Section Review

1.2 **Virtual Machine Concept**
    1.2.1 Section Review

1.3 **Data Representation**
    1.3.1 Binary Integers
    1.3.2 Binary Addition
    1.3.3 Integer Storage Sizes
    1.3.4 Hexadecimal Integers

    1.3.5 Signed Integers
    1.3.6 Character Storage
    1.3.7 Section Review

1.4 **Boolean Operations**
    1.4.1 Truth Tables for Boolean Functions
    1.4.2 Section Review

1.5 **Chapter Summary**

1.6 **Exercises**
    1.6.1 Programming Tasks
    1.6.2 Nonprogramming Tasks

1.1 Welcome to Assembly Language

Assembly Language for x86 Processors focuses on programming microprocessors compatible with the Intel IA-32 and AMD x86 processors running under Microsoft Windows. The x86 processor type first appeared in the Intel 80386 processor, and continued with processors such as the Intel Pentium, Intel Pentium 4, Intel Pentium Core Duo, and the Advanced Micro Devices (AMD) Athlon.

Microsoft Macro Assembler 8.0, 9.0, or 10.0 can be used with this book. This assembler is commonly known by its nickname: MASM. There are other good assemblers for Intel-based computers, including TASM (*Turbo Assembler*), NASM (*Netwide Assembler*), and the GNU assembler. Of these, TASM has the most similar syntax to MASM, and you could (with some help from your instructor) assemble and run most of the programs in this book. The NASM assembler is next closest in similarity to MASM. Finally, the GNU assembler has a completely different syntax.

Assembly language is the oldest programming language, and of all languages, bears the closest resemblance to native machine language. It provides direct access to computer hardware, requiring you to understand much about your computer's architecture and operating system.

Educational Value   Why read this book? Perhaps you're taking a college course whose name is similar to one of these:

• Microcomputer Assembly Language
• Assembly Language Programming
• Introduction to Computer Architecture
• Fundamentals of Computer Systems
• Embedded Systems Programming

These are names of courses at colleges and universities using previous editions of this book. This book covers basic principles about computer architecture, machine language, and low-level programming. You will learn enough assembly language to test your knowledge on today's most widely used microprocessor family. You won't be learning to program a "toy" computer using a simulated assembler; MASM is an industrial-strength assembler, used by practicing professionals. You will learn the architecture of the x86 processor family from a programmer's point of view.

If you are planning to be a C or C++ developer, you need to develop an understanding of how memory, address, and instructions work at a low level. A lot of programming errors are not easily recognized at the high-level language level. You will often find it necessary to "drill down" into your program's internals to find out why it isn't working.

If you doubt the value of low-level programming and studying details of computer software and hardware, take note of the following quote from a leading computer scientist, Donald Knuth, in discussing his famous book series, *The Art of Computer Programming:*

> Some people [say] that having machine language, at all, was the great mistake that I made. I really don't think you can write a book for serious computer programmers unless you are able to discuss low-level detail.[1]

Visit this book's Web site to get lots of supplemental information, tutorials, and exercises at **www.asmirvine.com**

1.1.1 Good Questions to Ask

What Background Should I Have?   Before reading this book, you should have programmed in at least one structured high-level language, such as Java, C, Python, or C++. You should know how to use IF statements, arrays, and functions to solve programming problems.

What Are Assemblers and Linkers?   An *assembler* is a utility program that converts source code programs from assembly language into machine language. A *linker* is a utility program that combines individual files created by an assembler into a single executable program. A related utility, called a *debugger*, lets you to step through a program while it's running and examine registers and memory.

What Hardware and Software Do I Need?   You need a computer with an x86 processor. Intel Pentium and AMD processors are good examples.

MASM is compatible with all versions of Microsoft Windows, beginning with Windows 95. A few of the advanced programs relating to direct hardware access and disk sector programming will only run under MS-DOS, Windows 95, or 98, because of tight security restrictions imposed by later versions of Windows.

In addition, you will need the following:

- *Editor:* Use a text editor or programmer's editor to create assembly language source files. We recommend the latest version of Microsoft Visual Studio.
- *32-Bit Debugger:* Strictly speaking, you don't need a debugger, but you will probably want one. The debugger supplied with Microsoft Visual Studio is excellent.

What Types of Programs Will I Create?   This book shows how to create two general classes of programs:

- *16-Bit Real-Address Mode:* 16-bit real-address mode programs run under MS-DOS and in the console window under MS-Windows. Also known as *real mode* programs, they use a segmented memory model required of programs written for the Intel 8086 and 8088 processors. There are notes throughout the book with tips about programming in real-address mode, and two chapters are exclusively devoted to programming in real mode.
- *32-Bit Protected Mode:* 32-bit protected mode programs run under all 32-bit versions of Microsoft Windows. They are usually easier to write and understand than real mode programs.

What Supplements Are Supplied with This Book?   The book's Web site (*www.asmirvine.com*) has the following:

- *Online Help File* detailing the book's library procedures and essential Windows API structures.
- *Assembly Language Workbook,* a collection of tutorials.
- *Irvine32 and Irvine16 link libraries* for real-address mode and protected mode programming, with complete source code.
- *Example programs* with all source code from the book.
- *Corrections* to the book and example programs.
- *Getting Started,* a detailed tutorial designed to help you set up Visual Studio to use the Microsoft assembler.
- *Articles* on advanced topics not included in the printed book for lack of space.
- *An online discussion forum,* where you can get help from other experts who use the book.

What Will I Learn?   This book should make you better informed about data representation, debugging, programming, and hardware manipulation. Here's what you will learn:

- Basic principles of computer architecture as applied to x86 processors
- Basic boolean logic and how it applies to programming and computer hardware
- How x86 processors manage memory, using real mode, protected mode, and virtual mode
- How high-level language compilers (such as C++) translate statements from their language into assembly language and native machine code
- How high-level languages implement arithmetic expressions, loops, and logical structures at the machine level

- Data representation, including signed and unsigned integers, real numbers, and character data
- How to debug programs at the machine level. The need for this skill is vital when you work in languages such as C and C++, which provide access to low-level data and hardware
- How application programs communicate with the computer's operating system via interrupt handlers, system calls, and common memory areas
- How to interface assembly language code to C++ programs
- How to create assembly language application programs

How Does Assembly Language Relate to Machine Language?

Machine language is a numeric language specifically understood by a computer's processor (the CPU). All x86 processors understand a common machine language. *Assembly language* consists of statements written with short mnemonics such as ADD, MOV, SUB, and CALL. Assembly language has a *one-to-one* relationship with machine language: Each assembly language instruction corresponds to a single machine-language instruction.

How Do C++ and Java Relate to Assembly Language?

High-level languages such as C++ and Java have a *one-to-many* relationship with assembly language and machine language. A single statement in C++ expands into multiple assembly language or machine instructions. We can show how C++ statements expand into machine code. Most people cannot read raw machine code, so we will use its closest relative, assembly language. The following C++ code carries out two arithmetic operations and assigns the result to a variable. Assume X and Y are integers:

```
int    Y;
int    X = (Y + 4) * 3;
```

Following is the equivalent translation to assembly language. The translation requires multiple statements because assembly language works at a detailed level:

```
mov    eax,Y          ; move Y to the EAX register
add    eax,4          ; add 4 to the EAX register
mov    ebx,3          ; move 3 to the EBX register
imul   ebx            ; multiply EAX by EBX
mov    X,eax          ; move EAX to X
```

(*Registers* are named storage locations in the CPU that hold intermediate results of operations.) The point in this example is not to claim that C++ is superior to assembly language or vice versa, but to show their relationship.

Is Assembly Language Portable?

A language whose source programs can be compiled and run on a wide variety of computer systems is said to be *portable*. A C++ program, for example, should compile and run on just about any computer, unless it makes specific references to library functions that exist under a single operating system. A major feature of the Java language is that compiled programs run on nearly any computer system.

Assembly language is not portable because it is designed for a specific processor family. There are a number of different assembly languages widely used today, each based on a processor family. Some well-known processor families are Motorola 68x00, x86, SUN Sparc, Vax, and IBM-370. The instructions in assembly language may directly match the computer's architecture or they may be translated during execution by a program inside the processor known as a *microcode interpreter*.

Why Learn Assembly Language?   If you're still not convinced that you should learn assembly language, consider the following points:

- If you study computer engineering, you may likely be asked to write *embedded* programs. They are short programs stored in a small amount of memory in single-purpose devices such as telephones, automobile fuel and ignition systems, air-conditioning control systems, security systems, data acquisition instruments, video cards, sound cards, hard drives, modems, and printers. Assembly language is an ideal tool for writing embedded programs because of its economical use of memory.

- Real-time applications dealing with simulation and hardware monitoring require precise timing and responses. High-level languages do not give programmers exact control over machine code generated by compilers. Assembly language permits you to precisely specify a program's executable code.

- Computer game consoles require their software to be highly optimized for small code size and fast execution. Game programmers are experts at writing code that takes full advantage of hardware features in a target system. They use assembly language as their tool of choice because it permits direct access to computer hardware, and code can be hand optimized for speed.

- Assembly language helps you to gain an overall understanding of the interaction between computer hardware, operating systems, and application programs. Using assembly language, you can apply and test theoretical information you are given in computer architecture and operating systems courses.

- Some high-level languages abstract their data representation to the point that it becomes awkward to perform low-level tasks such as bit manipulation. In such an environment, programmers will often call subroutines written in assembly language to accomplish their goal.

- Hardware manufacturers create device drivers for the equipment they sell. *Device drivers* are programs that translate general operating system commands into specific references to hardware details. Printer manufacturers, for example, create a different MS-Windows device driver for each model they sell. The same is true for Mac OS, Linux, and other operating systems.

Are There Rules in Assembly Language?   Most rules in assembly language are based on physical limitations of the target processor and its machine language. The CPU, for example, requires two instruction operands to be the same size. Assembly language has fewer rules than C++ or Java because the latter use syntax rules to reduce unintended logic errors at the expense of low-level data access. Assembly language programmers can easily bypass restrictions characteristic of high-level languages. Java, for example, does not permit access to specific memory addresses. One can work around the restriction by calling a C function using JNI (Java Native Interface) classes, but the resulting program can be awkward to maintain. Assembly language, on the other hand, can access any memory address. The price for such freedom is high: Assembly language programmers spend a lot of time debugging!

1.1.2   Assembly Language Applications

In the early days of programming, most applications were written partially or entirely in assembly language. They had to fit in a small area of memory and run as efficiently as possible on slow processors. As memory became more plentiful and processors dramatically increased in speed, programs became more complex. Programmers switched to high-level languages such as C, FORTRAN, and COBOL that contained a certain amount of structuring capability. More recently, object-oriented languages such as C++, C#, and Java have made it possible to write complex programs containing millions of lines of code.

It is rare to see large application programs coded completely in assembly language because they would take too much time to write and maintain. Instead, assembly language is used to optimize certain sections of application programs for speed and to access computer hardware. Table 1-1 compares the adaptability of assembly language to high-level languages in relation to various types of applications.

Table 1-1   Comparison of Assembly Language to High-Level Languages.

Type of Application	High-Level Languages	Assembly Language
Commercial or scientific application, written for single platform, medium to large size.	Formal structures make it easy to organize and maintain large sections of code.	Minimal formal structure, so one must be imposed by programmers who have varying levels of experience. This leads to difficulties maintaining existing code.
Hardware device driver.	The language may not provide for direct hardware access. Even if it does, awkward coding techniques may be required, resulting in maintenance difficulties.	Hardware access is straightforward and simple. Easy to maintain when programs are short and well documented.
Commercial or scientific application written for multiple platforms (different operating systems).	Usually portable. The source code can be recompiled on each target operating system with minimal changes.	Must be recoded separately for each platform, using an assembler with a different syntax. Difficult to maintain.
Embedded systems and computer games requiring direct hardware access.	Produces too much executable code, and may not run efficiently.	Ideal, because the executable code is small and runs quickly.

The C and C++ languages have the unique quality of offering a compromise between high-level structure and low-level details. Direct hardware access is possible but completely nonportable. Most C and C++ compilers have the ability to generate assembly language source code, which the programmer can customize and refine before assembling into executable code.

1.1.3 Section Review

1. How do assemblers and linkers work together?
2. How will studying assembly language enhance your understanding of operating systems?
3. What is meant by a *one-to-many relationship* when comparing a high-level language to machine language?
4. Explain the concept of *portability* as it applies to programming languages.
5. Is the assembly language for x86 processors the same as those for computer systems such as the Vax or Motorola 68x00?

6. Give an example of an *embedded systems* application.

7. What is a device driver?

8. Do you suppose type checking on pointer variables is stronger (stricter) in assembly language or in C and C++?

9. Name two types of applications that would be better suited to assembly language than a high-level language.

10. Why would a high-level language not be an ideal tool for writing a program that directly accesses a particular brand of printer?

11. Why is assembly language not usually used when writing large application programs?

12. *Challenge:* Translate the following C++ expression to assembly language, using the example presented earlier in this chapter as a guide: X = (Y * 4) + 3.

1.2   Virtual Machine Concept

An effective way to explain how a computer's hardware and software are related is called the *virtual machine concept*. A well-known explanation of this model can be found in Andrew Tanenbaum's book, *Structured Computer Organization*. To explain this concept, let us begin with the most basic function of a computer, executing programs.

A computer can usually execute programs written in its native *machine language*. Each instruction in this language is simple enough to be executed using a relatively small number of electronic circuits. For simplicity, we will call this language **L0**.

Programmers would have a difficult time writing programs in L0 because it is enormously detailed and consists purely of numbers. If a new language, **L1**, could be constructed that was easier to use, programs could be written in L1. There are two ways to achieve this:

- *Interpretation:* As the L1 program is running, each of its instructions could be decoded and executed by a program written in language L0. The L1 program begins running immediately, but each instruction has to be decoded before it can execute.
- *Translation:* The entire L1 program could be converted into an L0 program by an L0 program specifically designed for this purpose. Then the resulting L0 program could be executed directly on the computer hardware.

Virtual Machines   Rather than using only languages, it is easier to think in terms of a hypothetical computer, or *virtual machine*, at each level. Informally, we can define a virtual machine as a software program that emulates the functions of some other physical or virtual computer. The virtual machine **VM1**, as we will call it, can execute commands written in language L1. The virtual machine **VM0** can execute commands written in language L0:

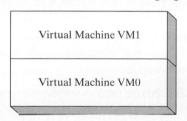

Virtual Machine VM1

Virtual Machine VM0

Each virtual machine can be constructed of either hardware or software. People can write programs for virtual machine VM1, and if it is practical to implement VM1 as an actual computer, programs can be executed directly on the hardware. Or programs written in VM1 can be interpreted/translated and executed on machine VM0.

Machine VM1 cannot be radically different from VM0 because the translation or interpretation would be too time-consuming. What if the language VM1 supports is still not programmer-friendly enough to be used for useful applications? Then another virtual machine, VM2, can be designed that is more easily understood. This process can be repeated until a virtual machine VMn can be designed to support a powerful, easy-to-use language.

The Java programming language is based on the virtual machine concept. A program written in the Java language is translated by a Java compiler into *Java byte code*. The latter is a low-level language quickly executed at runtime by a program known as a *Java virtual machine (JVM)*. The JVM has been implemented on many different computer systems, making Java programs relatively system independent.

Specific Machines   Let us relate this to actual computers and languages, using names such as **Level 2** for VM2 and **Level 1** for VM1, shown in Figure 1–1. A computer's digital logic hardware represents machine Level 1. Above this is Level 2, called the *instruction set architecture (ISA)*. This is the first level at which users can typically write programs, although the programs consist of binary values called *machine language*.

FIGURE 1–1   Virtual Machine Levels.

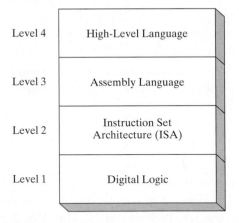

Level 4	High-Level Language
Level 3	Assembly Language
Level 2	Instruction Set Architecture (ISA)
Level 1	Digital Logic

Instruction Set Architecture (Level 2)   Computer chip manufacturers design into the processor an instruction set to carry out basic operations, such as move, add, or multiply. This set of instructions is also referred to as *machine language*. Each machine-language instruction is executed either directly by the computer's hardware or by a program embedded in the microprocessor chip called a *microprogram*. A discussion of microprograms is beyond the scope of this book, but you can refer to Tanenbaum for more details.

Assembly Language (Level 3)   Above the ISA level, programming languages provide translation layers to make large-scale software development practical. Assembly language, which appears at Level 3, uses short mnemonics such as ADD, SUB, and MOV, which are easily translated to the ISA level. Assembly language programs are translated (assembled) in their entirety into machine language before they begin to execute.

High-Level Languages (Level 4)   At Level 4 are high-level programming languages such as C, C++, and Java. Programs in these languages contain powerful statements that translate into multiple assembly language instructions. You can see such a translation, for example, by examining the listing file output created by a C++ compiler. The assembly language code is automatically assembled by the compiler into machine language.

1.2.1   Section Review

1. In your own words, describe the *virtual machine* concept.
2. Why don't programmers write application programs in machine language?
3. (*True/False*): When an interpreted program written in language L1 runs, each of its instructions is decoded and executed by a program written in language L0.
4. Explain the technique of translation when dealing with languages at different virtual machine levels.
5. At which level does assembly language appear in the virtual machine example shown in this section?
6. What software permits compiled Java programs to run on almost any computer?
7. Name the four virtual machine levels named in this section, from lowest to highest.
8. Why don't programmers write applications in machine language?
9. Machine language is used at which level of the virtual machine shown in Figure 1–1?
10. Statements at the assembly language level of a virtual machine are translated into statements at which other level?

1.3   Data Representation

Assembly language programmers deal with data at the physical level, so they must be adept at examining memory and registers. Often, binary numbers are used to describe the contents of computer memory; at other times, decimal and hexadecimal numbers are used. You must develop a certain fluency with number formats, so you can quickly translate numbers from one format to another.

Each numbering format, or system, has a *base*, or maximum number of symbols that can be assigned to a single digit. Table 1-2 shows the possible digits for the numbering systems used most commonly in hardware and software manuals. In the last row of the table, hexadecimal numbers use the digits 0 through 9 and continue with the letters A through F to represent decimal values 10 through 15. It is quite common to use hexadecimal numbers when showing the contents of computer memory and machine-level instructions.

1.3.1   Binary Integers

A computer stores instructions and data in memory as collections of electronic charges. Representing these entities with numbers requires a system geared to the concepts of *on* and *off* or *true* and *false*. *Binary numbers* are base 2 numbers, in which each binary digit (called a *bit*) is either 0 or 1. **Bits** are numbered sequentially starting at zero on the right side and increasing toward the left. The bit on the left is called the *most significant bit* (MSB), and the bit on the right is the *least significant bit* (LSB). The MSB and LSB bit numbers of a 16-bit binary number are shown in the following figure:

```
MSB                          LSB
1 0 1 1 0 0 1 0 1 0 0 1 1 1 0 0
15                            0   bit number
```

Table 1-2   Binary, Octal, Decimal, and Hexadecimal Digits.

System	Base	Possible Digits
Binary	2	0 1
Octal	8	0 1 2 3 4 5 6 7
Decimal	10	0 1 2 3 4 5 6 7 8 9
Hexadecimal	16	0 1 2 3 4 5 6 7 8 9 A B C D E F

Binary integers can be signed or unsigned. A signed integer is positive or negative. An unsigned integer is by default positive. Zero is considered positive. When writing down large binary numbers, many people like to insert a dot every 4 bits or 8 bits to make the numbers easier to read. Examples are 1101.1110.0011.1000.0000 and 11001010.10101100.

Unsigned Binary Integers

Starting with the LSB, each bit in an unsigned binary integer represents an increasing power of 2. The following figure contains an 8-bit binary number, showing how powers of two increase from right to left:

```
1 1 1 1 1 1 1 1
2^7 2^6 2^5 2^4 2^3 2^2 2^1 2^0
```

Table 1-3 lists the decimal values of 2^0 through 2^{15}.

Table 1-3   Binary Bit Position Values.

2^n	Decimal Value	2^n	Decimal Value
2^0	1	2^8	256
2^1	2	2^9	512
2^2	4	2^{10}	1024
2^3	8	2^{11}	2048
2^4	16	2^{12}	4096
2^5	32	2^{13}	8192
2^6	64	2^{14}	16384
2^7	128	2^{15}	32768

Translating Unsigned Binary Integers to Decimal

Weighted positional notation represents a convenient way to calculate the decimal value of an unsigned binary integer having *n* digits:

$$dec = (D_{n-1} \times 2^{n-1}) + (D_{n-2} \times 2^{n-2}) + \cdots + (D_1 \times 2^1) + (D_0 \times 2^0)$$

D indicates a binary digit. For example, binary 00001001 is equal to 9. We calculate this value by leaving out terms equal to zero:

$$(1 \times 2^3) + (1 \times 2^0) = 9$$

The same calculation is shown by the following figure:

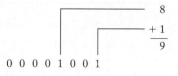

Translating Unsigned Decimal Integers to Binary

To translate an unsigned decimal integer into binary, repeatedly divide the integer by 2, saving each remainder as a binary digit. The following table shows the steps required to translate decimal 37 to binary. The remainder digits, starting from the top row, are the binary digits D_0, D_1, D_2, D_3, D_4, and D_5:

Division	Quotient	Remainder
37 / 2	18	1
18 / 2	9	0
9 / 2	4	1
4 / 2	2	0
2 / 2	1	0··
1 / 2	0	1

We can just concatenate the binary bits from the remainder column of the table in reverse order (D5, D4, . . .) to produce binary 100101. Because x86 computer storage always consists of binary numbers whose lengths are multiples of 8, we fill the remaining two digit positions on the left with zeros, producing 00100101.

1.3.2   Binary Addition

When adding two binary integers, proceed bit by bit, starting with the low-order pair of bits (on the right) and add each subsequent pair of bits. There are four ways to add two binary digits, as shown here:

0 + 0 = 0	0 + 1 = 1
1 + 0 = 1	1 + 1 = 10

When adding 1 to 1, the result is 10 binary (think of it as the decimal value 2). The extra digit generates a carry to the next-highest bit position. In the following figure, we add binary 00000100 to 00000111:

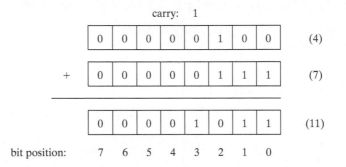

Beginning with the lowest bit in each number (bit position 0), we add $0 + 1$, producing a 1 in the bottom row. The same happens in the next highest bit (position 1). In bit position 2, we add $1 + 1$, generating a sum of zero and a carry of 1. In bit position 3, we add the carry bit to $0 + 0$, producing 1. The rest of the bits are zeros. You can verify the addition by adding the decimal equivalents shown on the right side of the figure ($4 + 7 = 11$).

Sometimes a carry is generated out of the highest bit position. When that happens, the size of the storage area set aside becomes important. If we add 11111111 to 00000001, for example, a 1 carries out of the highest bit position, and the lowest 8 bits of the sum equal all zeros. If the storage location for the sum is at least 9 bits long, we can represent the sum as 100000000. But if the sum can only store 8 bits, it will equal to 00000000, the lowest 8 bits of the calculated value.

1.3.3 Integer Storage Sizes

The basic storage unit for all data in an x86 computer is a *byte*, containing 8 bits. Other storage sizes are *word* (2 bytes), *doubleword* (4 bytes), and *quadword* (8 bytes). In the following figure, the number of bits is shown for each size:

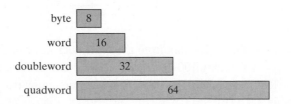

Table 1-4 shows the range of possible values for each type of unsigned integer.

Large Measurements   A number of large measurements are used when referring to both memory and disk space:

- One *kilobyte* is equal to 2^{10}, or 1024 bytes.
- One *megabyte* (1 MByte) is equal to 2^{20}, or 1,048,576 bytes.
- One *gigabyte* (1 GByte) is equal to 2^{30}, or 1024^3, or 1,073,741,824 bytes.
- One *terabyte* (1 TByte) is equal to 2^{40}, or 1024^4, or 1,099,511,627,776 bytes.

Table 1-4   Ranges of Unsigned Integers.

Storage Type	Range (Low to High)	Powers of 2	Byte Measurements
Unsigned byte	0 to 255	0 to $(2^8 - 1)$	1 byte
Unsigned word	0 to 65,535	0 to $(2^{16} - 1)$	2 bytes
Unsigned doubleword	0 to 4,294,967,295	0 to $(2^{32} - 1)$	4 bytes
Unsigned quadword	0 to 18,446,744,073,709,551,615	0 to $(2^{64} - 1)$	8 bytes

- One *petabyte* is equal to 2^{50}, or 1,125,899,906,842,624 bytes.
- One *exabyte* is equal to 2^{60}, or 1,152,921,504,606,846,976 bytes.
- One *zettabyte* is equal to 2^{70} bytes.
- One *yottabyte* is equal to 2^{80} bytes.

1.3.4   Hexadecimal Integers

Large binary numbers are cumbersome to read, so hexadecimal digits offer a convenient way to represent binary data. Each digit in a hexadecimal integer represents four binary bits, and two hexadecimal digits together represent a byte. A single hexadecimal digit represents decimal 0 to 15, so letters A to F represent decimal values in the range 10 through 15. Table 1-5 shows how each sequence of four binary bits translates into a decimal or hexadecimal value.

Table 1-5   Binary, Decimal, and Hexadecimal Equivalents.

Binary	Decimal	Hexadecimal	Binary	Decimal	Hexadecimal
0000	0	0	1000	8	8
0001	1	1	1001	9	9
0010	2	2	1010	10	A
0011	3	3	1011	11	B
0100	4	4	1100	12	C
0101	5	5	1101	13	D
0110	6	6	1110	14	E
0111	7	7	1111	15	F

The following example shows how binary 0001.0110.1010.0111.1001.0100 is equivalent to hexadecimal 16A794:

1	6	A	7	9	4
0001	0110	1010	0111	1001	0100

Converting Unsigned Hexadecimal to Decimal

In hexadecimal, each digit position represents a power of 16. This is helpful when calculating the decimal value of a hexadecimal integer. Suppose we number the digits in a four-digit hexadecimal integer with subscripts as $D_3D_2D_1D_0$. The following formula calculates the integer's decimal value:

$$dec = (D_3 \times 16^3) + (D_2 \times 16^2) + (D_1 \times 16^1) + (D_0 \times 16^0)$$

The formula can be generalized for any n-digit hexadecimal integer:

$$dec = (D_{n-1} \times 16^{n-1}) + (D_{n-2} \times 16^{n-2}) + \cdots + (D_1 \times 16^1) + (D_0 \times 16^0)$$

> In general, you can convert an n-digit integer in any base B to decimal using the following formula: $dec = (D_{n-1} \times B^{n-1}) + (D_{n-2} \times B^{n-2}) + \cdots + (D_1 \times B^1) + (D_0 \times B^0)$.

For example, hexadecimal 1234 is equal to $(1 \times 16^3) + (2 \times 16^2) + (3 \times 16^1) + (4 \times 16^0)$, or decimal 4660. Similarly, hexadecimal 3BA4 is equal to $(3 \times 16^3) + (11 \times 16^2) + (10 \times 16^1) + (4 \times 16^0)$, or decimal 15,268. The following figure shows this last calculation:

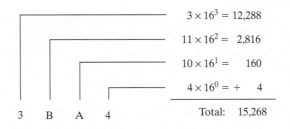

Table 1-6 lists the powers of 16 from 16^0 to 16^7.

TABLE 1-6   Powers of 16 in Decimal.

16^n	Decimal Value	16^n	Decimal Value
16^0	1	16^4	65,536
16^1	16	16^5	1,048,576
16^2	256	16^6	16,777,216
16^3	4096	16^7	268,435,456

Converting Unsigned Decimal to Hexadecimal

To convert an unsigned decimal integer to hexadecimal, repeatedly divide the decimal value by 16 and retain each remainder as a hexadecimal digit. For example, the following table lists the steps when converting decimal 422 to hexadecimal:

Division	Quotient	Remainder
422 / 16	26	6
26 / 16	1	A
1 / 16	0	1

The resulting hexadecimal number is assembled from the digits in the remainder column, starting from the last row and working upward to the top row. In this example, the hexadecimal representation is **1A6**. The same algorithm was used for binary integers in Section 1.3.1. To convert from decimal into some other number base other than hexadecimal, replace the divisor (16) in each calculation with the desired number base.

1.3.5   Signed Integers

Signed binary integers are positive or negative. For x86 processors, the MSB indicates the sign: 0 is positive and 1 is negative. The following figure shows examples of 8-bit negative and positive integers:

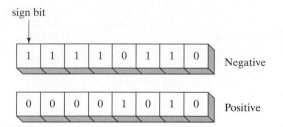

Two's-Complement Notation

Negative integers use *two's-complement* representation, using the mathematical principle that the two's complement of an integer is its additive inverse. (If you add a number to its additive inverse, the sum is zero.)

Two's-complement representation is useful to processor designers because it removes the need for separate digital circuits to handle both addition and subtraction. For example, if presented with the expression $A - B$, the processor can simply convert it to an addition expression: $A + (-B)$.

The two's complement of a binary integer is formed by inverting (complementing) its bits and adding 1. Using the 8-bit binary value 00000001, for example, its two's complement turns out to be 11111111, as can be seen as follows:

Starting value	00000001
Step 1: Reverse the bits	11111110
Step 2: Add 1 to the value from Step 1	11111110 +00000001
Sum: Two's-complement representation	11111111

11111111 is the two's-complement representation of -1. The two's-complement operation is reversible, so the two's complement of 11111111 is 00000001.

Two's Complement of Hexadecimal   To create the two's complement of a hexadecimal integer, reverse all bits and add 1. An easy way to reverse the bits of a hexadecimal digit is to subtract the digit from 15. Here are examples of hexadecimal integers converted to their two's complements:

```
6A3D --> 95C2 + 1 --> 95C3
95C3 --> 6A3C + 1 --> 6A3D
```

Converting Signed Binary to Decimal   Use the following algorithm to calculate the decimal equivalent of a signed binary integer:

- If the highest bit is a 1, the number is stored in two's-complement notation. Create its two's complement a second time to get its positive equivalent. Then convert this new number to decimal as if it were an unsigned binary integer.
- If the highest bit is a 0, you can convert it to decimal as if it were an unsigned binary integer.

For example, signed binary 11110000 has a 1 in the highest bit, indicating that it is a negative integer. First we create its two's complement, and then convert the result to decimal. Here are the steps in the process:

Starting value	11110000
Step 1: Reverse the bits	00001111
Step 2: Add 1 to the value from Step 1	00001111 + 1
Step 3: Create the two's complement	00010000
Step 4: Convert to decimal	16

Because the original integer (11110000) was negative, we know that its decimal value is −**16**.

Converting Signed Decimal to Binary   To create the binary representation of a signed decimal integer, do the following:

1. Convert the absolute value of the decimal integer to binary.
2. If the original decimal integer was negative, create the two's complement of the binary number from the previous step.

For example, −43 decimal is translated to binary as follows:

1. The binary representation of unsigned 43 is 00101011.
2. Because the original value was negative, we create the two's complement of 00101011, which is 11010101. This is the representation of −43 decimal.

Converting Signed Decimal to Hexadecimal   To convert a signed decimal integer to hexadecimal, do the following:

1. Convert the absolute value of the decimal integer to hexadecimal.
2. If the decimal integer was negative, create the two's complement of the hexadecimal number from the previous step.

Converting Signed Hexadecimal to Decimal   To convert a signed hexadecimal integer to decimal, do the following:

1. If the hexadecimal integer is negative, create its two's complement; otherwise, retain the integer as is.
2. Using the integer from the previous step, convert it to decimal. If the original value was negative, attach a minus sign to the beginning of the decimal integer.

You can tell whether a hexadecimal integer is positive or negative by inspecting its most significant (highest) digit. If the digit is ≥ 8, the number is negative; if the digit is ≤ 7, the number is positive. For example, hexadecimal 8A20 is negative and 7FD9 is positive.

Maximum and Minimum Values

A signed integer of n bits uses only $n - 1$ bits to represent the number's magnitude. Table 1-7 shows the minimum and maximum values for signed bytes, words, doublewords, and quadwords.

Table 1-7   Storage Sizes and Ranges of Signed Integers.

Storage Type	Range (Low to High)	Powers of 2
Signed byte	-128 to $+127$	-2^7 to $(2^7 - 1)$
Signed word	$-32,768$ to $+32,767$	-2^{15} to $(2^{15} - 1)$
Signed doubleword	$-2,147,483,648$ to $2,147,483,647$	-2^{31} to $(2^{31} - 1)$
Signed quadword	$-9,223,372,036,854,775,808$ to $+9,223,372,036,854,775,807$	-2^{63} to $(2^{63} - 1)$

1.3.6   Character Storage

If computers only store binary data, how do they represent characters? They use a *character set*, which is a mapping of characters to integers. Until a few years ago, character sets used only 8 bits. Even now, when running in character mode (such as MS-DOS), IBM-compatible microcomputers use the *ASCII* (pronounced "askey") character set. ASCII is an acronym for *American Standard Code for Information Interchange*. In ASCII, a unique 7-bit integer is assigned to each character. Because ASCII codes use only the lower 7 bits of every byte, the extra bit is used on various computers to create a proprietary character set. On IBM-compatible microcomputers, for example, values 128 through 255 represent graphics symbols and Greek characters.

ANSI Character Set   American National Standards Institute (ANSI) defines an 8-bit character set that represents up to 256 characters. The first 128 characters correspond to the letters and symbols on a standard U.S. keyboard. The second 128 characters represent special characters such as letters in international alphabets, accents, currency symbols, and fractions. MS-Windows Millennium, 98, and 95 used the ANSI character set. To increase the number of available characters, MS-Windows switches between character tables known as *code pages*.

Unicode Standard   There has been a need for some time to represent a wide variety of international languages in computer software. As a result, the *Unicode* standard was created as a universal way of defining characters and symbols. It defines codes for characters, symbols, and punctuation used in all major languages, as well as European alphabetic scripts, Middle Eastern right-to-left scripts, and many scripts of Asia. Three encoding forms are available in Unicode, permitting data to be transmitted in byte, word, or doubleword formats:

- **UTF-8** is used in HTML, and has the same byte values as ASCII (American Standard Code for Information Interchange). It can be incorporated into a variable-length encoding system for all Unicode characters.

- **UTF-16** is used in environments that balance efficient access to characters with economical use of storage. Recent versions of Microsoft Windows, for example, use UTF-16 encoding. Each character is encoded in 16 bits.
- **UTF-32** is used in environments where space is no concern and fixed-width characters are required. Each character is encoded in 32 bits.

You can copy a smaller Unicode value (byte, for example) into a larger one (word or double-word) without losing any data.

ASCII Strings   A sequence of one or more characters is called a *string*. More specifically, an *ASCII string* is stored in memory as a succession of bytes containing ASCII codes. For example, the numeric codes for the string "ABC123" are 41h, 42h, 43h, 31h, 32h, and 33h. A *null-terminated* string is a string of characters followed by a single byte containing zero. The C and C++ languages use null-terminated strings, and many DOS and Windows functions require strings to be in this format.

Using the ASCII Table   A table on the inside back cover of this book lists ASCII codes used when running in MS-DOS mode. To find the hexadecimal ASCII code of a character, look along the top row of the table and find the column containing the character you want to translate. The most significant digit of the hexadecimal value is in the second row at the top of the table; the least significant digit is in the second column from the left. For example, to find the ASCII code of the letter **a**, find the column containing the **a** and look in the second row: The first hexadecimal digit is 6. Next, look to the left along the row containing **a** and note that the second column contains the digit 1. Therefore, the ASCII code of **a** is 61 hexadecimal. This is shown as follows in simplified form:

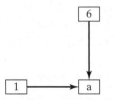

ASCII Control Characters   Character codes in the range 0 through 31 are called *ASCII control characters*. If a program writes these codes to standard output (as in C++), the control characters will carry out predefined actions. Table 1-8 lists the most commonly used characters in this range, and a complete list may be found in the inside front cover of this book.

Table 1-8   ASCII Control Characters.

ASCII Code (Decimal)	Description
8	Backspace (moves one column to the left)
9	Horizontal tab (skips forward *n* columns)
10	Line feed (moves to next output line)
12	Form feed (moves to next printer page)
13	Carriage return (moves to leftmost output column)
27	Escape character

Terminology for Numeric Data Representation   It is important to use precise terminology when describing the way numbers and characters are represented in memory and on the display screen. Decimal 65, for example, is stored in memory as a single binary byte as 01000001. A debugging program would probably display the byte as "41," which is the number's hexadecimal representation. If the byte were copied to video memory, the letter **"A"** would appear on the screen because 01000001 is the ASCII code for the letter **A**. Because a number's interpretation can depend on the context in which it appears, we assign a specific name to each type of data representation to clarify future discussions:

- A *binary integer* is an integer stored in memory in its raw format, ready to be used in a calculation. Binary integers are stored in multiples of 8 bits (8, 16, 32, 48, or 64).
- An *ASCII digit string* is a string of ASCII characters, such as "123" or "65," which is made to look like a number. This is simply a representation of the number and can be in any of the formats shown for the decimal number 65 in Table 1-9:

Table 1-9   Types of Numeric Strings.

Format	Value
ASCII binary	"01000001"
ASCII decimal	"65"
ASCII hexadecimal	"41"
ASCII octal	"101"

1.3.7   Section Review

1. Explain the term Least Significant Bit (LSB).

2. Explain the term Most Significant Bit (MSB).

3. What is the decimal representation of each of the following unsigned binary integers?
    a. 11111000
    b. 11001010
    c. 11110000

4. What is the decimal representation of each of the following unsigned binary integers?
    a. 00110101
    b. 10010110
    c. 11001100

5. What is the sum of each pair of binary integers?
    a. 00001111 + 00000010
    b. 11010101 + 01101011
    c. 00001111 + 00001111

6. What is the sum of each pair of binary integers?

   a. 10101111 + 11011011
   b. 10010111 + 11111111
   c. 01110101 + 10101100

7. How many bytes are contained in each of the following data types?

   a. word
   b. doubleword
   c. quadword

8. How many bits are contained in each of the following data types?

   a. word
   b. doubleword
   c. quadword

9. What is the minimum number of binary bits needed to represent each of the following unsigned decimal integers?

   a. 65
   b. 256
   c. 32768

10. What is the minimum number of binary bits needed to represent each of the following unsigned decimal integers?

    a. 4095
    b. 65534
    c. 2134657

11. What is the hexadecimal representation of each of the following binary numbers?

    a. 1100 1111 0101 0111
    b. 0101 1100 1010 1101
    c. 1001 0011 1110 1011

12. What is the hexadecimal representation of each of the following binary numbers?

    a. 0011 0101 1101 1010
    b. 1100 1110 1010 0011
    c. 1111 1110 1101 1011

13. What is the binary representation of the following hexadecimal numbers?

    a. E5B6AED7
    b. B697C7A1
    c. 234B6D92

14. What is the binary representation of the following hexadecimal numbers?

    a. 0126F9D4
    b. 6ACDFA95
    c. F69BDC2A

15. What is the unsigned decimal representation of each hexadecimal integer?

   a. 3A
   b. 1BF
   c. 4096

16. What is the unsigned decimal representation of each hexadecimal integer?

   a. 62
   b. 1C9
   c. 6A5B

17. What is the 16-bit hexadecimal representation of each signed decimal integer?

   a. −26
   b. −452

18. What is the 16-bit hexadecimal representation of each signed decimal integer?

   a. −32
   b. −62

19. The following 16-bit hexadecimal numbers represent signed integers. Convert to decimal.

   a. 7CAB
   b. C123

20. The following 16-bit hexadecimal numbers represent signed integers. Convert to decimal.

   a. 7F9B
   b. 8230

21. What is the decimal representation of the following signed binary numbers?

   a. 10110101
   b. 00101010
   c. 11110000

22. What is the decimal representation of the following signed binary numbers?

   a. 10000000
   b. 11001100
   c. 10110111

23. What is the 8-bit binary (two's-complement) representation of each of the following signed decimal integers?

   a. −5
   b. −36
   c. −16

24. What is the 8-bit binary (two's-complement) representation of each of the following signed decimal integers?

   a. −72
   b. −98
   c. −26

25. What are the hexadecimal and decimal representations of the ASCII character capital X?

26. What are the hexadecimal and decimal representations of the ASCII character capital M?

27. Why was Unicode invented?

28. *Challenge:* What is the largest value you can represent using a 256-bit *unsigned* integer?

29. *Challenge:* What is the largest positive value you can represent using a 256-bit *signed* integer?

1.4 Boolean Operations

Boolean algebra defines a set of operations on the values **true** and **false.** It was invented by George Boole, a mid–nineteenth-century mathematician. When early digital computers were invented, it was found that Boole's algebra could be used to describe the design of digital circuits. At the same time, boolean expressions are used in computer programs to express logical operations.

Boolean Expression   A boolean expression involves a boolean operator and one or more operands. Each boolean expression implies a value of true or false. The set of operators includes the folllowing:

- NOT: notated as ¬ or ~ or '
- AND: notated as ∧ or •
- OR: notated as ∨ or +

The NOT operator is unary, and the other operators are binary. The operands of a boolean expression can also be boolean expressions. The following are examples:

Expression	Description
¬X	NOT X
X ∧ Y	X AND Y
X ∨ Y	X OR Y
¬X ∨ Y	(NOT X) OR Y
¬(X ∧ Y)	NOT (X AND Y)
X ∧ ¬Y	X AND (NOT Y)

NOT   The NOT operation reverses a boolean value. It can be written in mathematical notation as ¬X, where X is a variable (or expression) holding a value of true (T) or false (F). The following truth table shows all the possible outcomes of NOT using a variable **X**. Inputs are on the left side and outputs (shaded) are on the right side:

X	¬X
F	T
T	F

A truth table can use 0 for false and 1 for true.

AND   The Boolean AND operation requires two operands, and can be expressed using the notation X ∧ Y. The following truth table shows all the possible outcomes (shaded) for the values of X and Y:

X	Y	X ∧ Y
F	F	F
F	T	F
T	F	F
T	T	T

The output is true only when both inputs are true. This corresponds to the logical AND used in compound boolean expressions in C++ and Java.

The AND operation is often carried out at the bit level in assembly language. In the following example, each bit in X is ANDed with its corresponding bit in Y:

```
X:          11111111
Y:          00011100
X ∧ Y:      00011100
```

As Figure 1–2 shows, each bit of the resulting value, 00011100, represents the result of ANDing the corresponding bits in X and Y.

Figure 1–2   ANDing the Bits of Two Binary Integers.

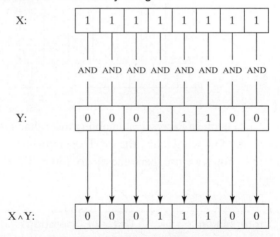

OR   The Boolean OR operation requires two operands, and is often expressed using the notation **X ∨ Y**. The following truth table shows all the possible outcomes (shaded) for the values of X and Y:

X	Y	X ∨ Y
F	F	F
F	T	T
T	F	T
T	T	T

The output is false only when both inputs are false. This truth table corresponds to the logical OR used in compound boolean expressions in C++ and Java.

The OR operation is often carried out at the bit level. In the following example, each bit in X is ORed with its corresponding bit in Y, producing 11111100:

```
X:          11101100
Y:          00011100
X ∨ Y:      11111100
```

As shown in Figure 1–3, the bits are ORed individually, producing a corresponding bit in the result.

FIGURE 1–3   ORing the Bits in Two Binary Integers.

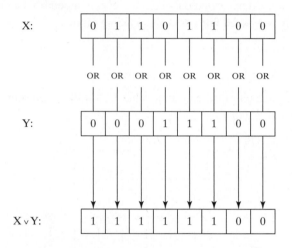

Operator Precedence   In a boolean expression involving more than one operator, precedence is important. As shown in the following table, the NOT operator has the highest precedence, followed by AND and OR. You can use parentheses to force the initial evaluation of an expression:

Expression	Order of Operations
¬X ∨ Y	NOT, then OR
¬(X ∨ Y)	OR, then NOT
X ∨ (Y ∧ Z)	AND, then OR

1.4.1 Truth Tables for Boolean Functions

A *boolean function* receives boolean inputs and produces a boolean output. A truth table can be constructed for any boolean function, showing all possible inputs and outputs. The following are truth tables representing boolean functions having two inputs named X and Y. The shaded column on the right is the function's output:

Example 1: ¬X ∨ Y

X	¬X	Y	¬X ∨ Y
F	T	F	T
F	T	T	T
T	F	F	F
T	F	T	T

Example 2: X ∧ ¬Y

X	Y	¬Y	X ∧ ¬Y
F	F	T	F
F	T	F	F
T	F	T	T
T	T	F	F

Example 3: (Y ∧ S) ∨ (X ∧ ¬S)

X	Y	S	Y ∧ S	¬S	X ∧ ¬S	(Y ∧ S) ∨ (X ∧ ¬S)
F	F	F	F	T	F	F
F	T	F	F	T	F	F
T	F	F	F	T	T	T
T	T	F	F	T	T	T
F	F	T	F	F	F	F
F	T	T	T	F	F	T
T	F	T	F	F	F	F
T	T	T	T	F	F	T

This boolean function describes a *multiplexer*, a digital component that uses a selector bit (S) to select one of two outputs (X or Y). If S = false, the function output (Z) is the same as X. If S = true, the function output is the same as Y. Here is a block diagram of a multiplexer:

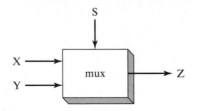

1.4.2   Section Review

1. Describe the following boolean expression: ¬X ∨ Y.
2. Describe the following boolean expression: (X ∧ Y).
3. What is the value of the boolean expression (T ∧ F) ∨ T ?
4. What is the value of the boolean expression ¬(F ∨ T) ?
5. What is the value of the boolean expression ¬F ∨ ¬T ?
6. Create a truth table to show all possible inputs and outputs for the boolean function described by ¬(A ∨ B).
7. Create a truth table to show all possible inputs and outputs for the boolean function described by (¬A ∧ ¬B).
8. If a boolean function has four inputs, how many rows are required for its truth table?
9. How many selector bits are required for a four-input multiplexer?

1.5   Chapter Summary

This book focuses on programming x86 processors, using the MS-Windows platform. We cover basic principles about computer architecture, machine language, and low-level programming. You will learn enough assembly language to test your knowledge on today's most widely used microprocessor family.

Before reading this book, you should have completed a single college course or equivalent in computer programming.

An assembler is a program that converts source-code programs from assembly language into machine language. A companion program, called a linker, combines individual files created by an assembler into a single executable program. A third program, called a debugger, provides a way for a programmer to trace the execution of a program and examine the contents of memory.

You will create two basic types of programs: 16-bit real-address mode programs and 32-bit protected mode programs.

You will learn the following concepts from this book: basic computer architecture applied to x86 processors; elementary boolean logic; how x86 processors manage memory; how high-level language compilers translate statements from their language into assembly language and native machine code; how high-level languages implement arithmetic expressions, loops, and logical structures at the machine level; and the data representation of signed and unsigned integers, real numbers, and character data.

Assembly language has a *one-to-one* relationship with machine language, in which a single assembly language instruction corresponds to one machine language instruction. Assembly language is not portable because it is tied to a specific processor family.

Programming languages are tools that you can use to create individual applications or parts of applications. Some applications, such as device drivers and hardware interface routines, are more suited to assembly language. Other applications, such as multiplatform commercial and scientific applications, are more easily written in high-level languages.

The *virtual machine* concept is an effective way of showing how each layer in a computer architecture represents an abstraction of a machine. Layers can be constructed of hardware or software, and programs written at any layer can be translated or interpreted by the next-lowest layer. The virtual machine concept can be related to real-world computer layers, including digital logic, instruction set architecture, assembly language, and high-level languages.

Binary and hexadecimal numbers are essential notational tools for programmers working at the machine level. For this reason, you must understand how to manipulate and translate between number systems and how character representations are created by computers.

The following boolean operators were presented in this chapter: NOT, AND, and OR. A boolean expression combines a boolean operator with one or more operands. A truth table is an effective way to show all possible inputs and outputs of a boolean function.

1.6 Exercises

1.6.1 Programming Tasks

Use any high-level programming language you wish for the following programming exercises. Do not call built-in library functions that accomplish these tasks automatically. (Examples are *sprintf* and *sscanf* from the Standard C library.)

1. Write a function that receives a string containing a 16-bit binary integer. The function must return the decimal integer value of the binary integer.

2. Write a function that receives a string containing a 32-bit hexadecimal integer. The function must return the decimal integer value of the hexadecimal integer.

3. Write a function that receives an integer. The function must return a string containing the binary representation of the integer.

4. Write a function that receives an integer. The function must return a string containing the hexadecimal representation of the integer.

1.6.2 Nonprogramming Tasks

1. Write a Java program that contains the following calculation. Then, use the *javap –c* command to disassemble your code. Then, add comments to each line that provide your best guess as to its purpose.

```
int Y;
int X = (Y + 4) * 3;
```

2. Devise a way of subtracting unsigned binary integers. Test your technique by subtracting binary 0000101 from binary 10001000, producing 10000011. Test your technique with at least two other sets of integers, in which a smaller value is always subtracted from a larger one.

End Notes

1. Donald Knuth, *MMIX, A RISC Computer for the New Millennium,* Transcript of a lecture given at the Massachusetts Institute of Technology, December 30, 1999.

2

x86 Processor Architecture

2.1 **General Concepts**
    2.1.1 Basic Microcomputer Design
    2.1.2 Instruction Execution Cycle
    2.1.3 Reading from Memory
    2.1.4 How Programs Run
    2.1.5 Section Review

2.2 **x86 Architecture Details**
    2.2.1 Modes of Operation
    2.2.2 Basic Execution Environment
    2.2.3 Floating-Point Unit
    2.2.4 Overview of Intel Microprocessors
    2.2.5 Section Review

2.3 **x86 Memory Management**
    2.3.1 Real-Address Mode

2.3.2 Protected Mode
2.3.3 Section Review

2.4 **Components of a Typical x86 Computer**
    2.4.1 Motherboard
    2.4.2 Video Output
    2.4.3 Memory
    2.4.4 Input-Output Ports and Device Interfaces
    2.4.5 Section Review

2.5 **Input-Output System**
    2.5.1 Levels of I/O Access
    2.5.2 Section Review

2.6 **Chapter Summary**

2.7 **Chapter Exercises**

2.1 General Concepts

This chapter describes the architecture of the x86 processor family and its host computer system from a programmer's point of view. Included in this group are all Intel IA-32 processors, such as the Intel Pentium and Core-Duo, as well as the Advanced Micro Devices (AMD) Athlon, Phenom, and Opteron processors. Assembly language is a great tool for learning how a computer works, and it requires you to have a working knowledge of computer hardware. To that end, the concepts and details in this chapter will help you to understand the assembly language code you write.

We strike a balance between concepts applying to all microcomputer systems and specifics about x86 processors. You may work on various processors in the future, so we expose you to broad concepts. To avoid giving you a superficial understanding of machine architecture, we focus on specifics of the x86, which will give you a solid grounding when programming in assembly language.

> If you want to learn more about the Intel IA-32 architecture, read *the Intel 64 and IA-32 Architectures Software Developer's Manual, Volume 1: Basic Architecture.* It's a free download from the Intel Web site (www.intel.com).

2.1.1 Basic Microcomputer Design

Figure 2–1 shows the basic design of a hypothetical microcomputer. The *central processor unit* (CPU), where calculations and logic operations take place, contains a limited number of storage locations named *registers*, a high-frequency clock, a control unit, and an arithmetic logic unit.

- The *clock* synchronizes the internal operations of the CPU with other system components.
- The *control unit* (CU) coordinates the sequencing of steps involved in executing machine instructions.
- The *arithmetic logic unit* (ALU) performs arithmetic operations such as addition and subtraction and logical operations such as AND, OR, and NOT.

The CPU is attached to the rest of the computer via pins attached to the CPU socket in the computer's motherboard. Most pins connect to the data bus, the control bus, and the address bus. The *memory storage unit* is where instructions and data are held while a computer program is running. The storage unit receives requests for data from the CPU, transfers data from random access memory (RAM) to the CPU, and transfers data from the CPU into memory. All processing of data takes place within the CPU, so programs residing in memory must be copied into the CPU before they can execute. Individual program instructions can be copied into the CPU one at a time, or groups of instructions can be copied together.

A *bus* is a group of parallel wires that transfer data from one part of the computer to another. A computer system usually contains four bus types: data, I/O, control, and address. The *data bus*

Figure 2–1   Block Diagram of a Microcomputer.

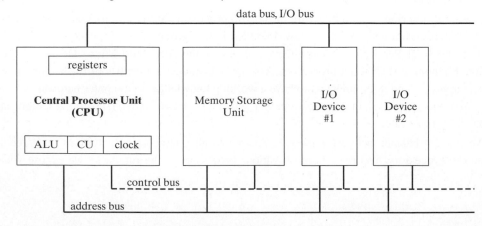

transfers instructions and data between the CPU and memory. The I/O bus transfers data between the CPU and the system input/output devices. The *control bus* uses binary signals to synchronize actions of all devices attached to the system bus. The *address bus* holds the addresses of instructions and data when the currently executing instruction transfers data between the CPU and memory.

Clock   Each operation involving the CPU and the system bus is synchronized by an internal clock pulsing at a constant rate. The basic unit of time for machine instructions is a *machine cycle* (or *clock cycle*). The length of a clock cycle is the time required for one complete clock pulse. In the following figure, a clock cycle is depicted as the time between one falling edge and the next:

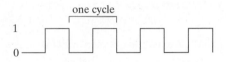

The duration of a clock cycle is calculated as the reciprocal of the clock's speed, which in turn is measured in oscillations per second. A clock that oscillates 1 billion times per second (1 GHz), for example, produces a clock cycle with a duration of one billionth of a second (1 nanosecond).

A machine instruction requires at least one clock cycle to execute, and a few require in excess of 50 clocks (the multiply instruction on the 8088 processor, for example). Instructions requiring memory access often have empty clock cycles called *wait states* because of the differences in the speeds of the CPU, the system bus, and memory circuits.

2.1.2   Instruction Execution Cycle

The execution of a single machine instruction can be divided into a sequence of individual operations called the *instruction execution cycle*. Before executing, a program is loaded into memory. The *instruction pointer* contains the address of the next instruction. The *instruction queue* holds a group of instructions about to be executed. Executing a machine instruction requires three basic steps: *fetch, decode,* and *execute.* Two more steps are required when the instruction uses a memory operand: *fetch operand* and *store output operand.* Each of the steps is described as follows:

- *Fetch:* The control unit fetches the next instruction from the instruction queue and increments the instruction pointer (IP). The IP is also known as the *program counter.*
- *Decode:* The control unit decodes the instruction's function to determine what the instruction will do. The instruction's input operands are passed to the ALU, and signals are sent to the ALU indicating the operation to be performed.
- *Fetch operands:* If the instruction uses an input operand located in memory, the control unit uses a *read* operation to retrieve the operand and copy it into internal registers. Internal registers are not visible to user programs.

- **Execute:** The ALU executes the instruction using the named registers and internal registers as operands and sends the output to named registers and/or memory. The ALU updates status flags providing information about the processor state.
- **Store output operand:** If the output operand is in memory, the control unit uses a write operation to store the data.

The sequence of steps can be expressed neatly in pseudocode:

```
loop
    fetch next instruction
    advance the instruction pointer (IP)
    decode the instruction
    if memory operand needed, read value from memory
    execute the instruction
    if result is memory operand, write result to memory
continue loop
```

A block diagram showing data flow within a typical CPU is shown in Figure 2–2. The diagram helps to show relationships between components that interact during the instruction execution cycle. In order to read program instructions from memory, an address is placed on the address bus. Next, the memory controller places the requested code on the data bus, making the code available inside the code cache. The instruction pointer's value determines which instruction will be executed next. The instruction is analyzed by the instruction decoder, causing the appropriate

Figure 2–2   Simplified CPU Block Diagram.

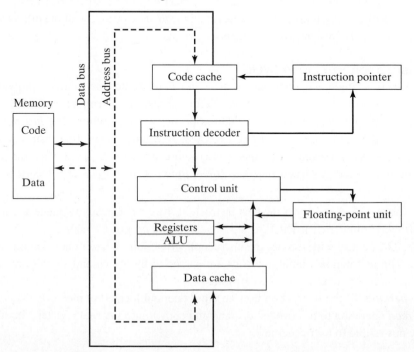

digital signals to be sent to the control unit, which coordinates the ALU and floating-point unit. Although the control bus is not shown in this figure, it carries signals that use the system clock to coordinate the transfer of data between the different CPU components.

2.1.3   Reading from Memory

Program throughput is often dependent on the speed of memory access. CPU clock speed might be several gigahertz, whereas access to memory occurs over a system bus running at a much slower speed. The CPU must wait one or more clock cycles until operands have been fetched from memory before the current instruction can complete its execution. The wasted clock cycles are called *wait states*.

Several steps are required when reading instructions or data from memory, controlled by the processor's internal clock. Figure 2–3 shows the processor clock (CLK) rising and falling at regular time intervals. In the figure, a clock cycle begins as the clock signal changes from high to low. The changes are called *trailing edges,* and they indicate the time taken by the transition between states.

FIGURE 2–3   Memory Read Cycle.

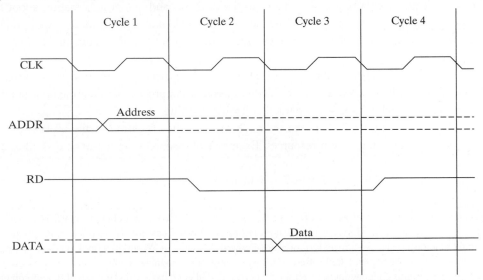

The following is a simplified description of what happens during each clock cycle during a memory read:

Cycle 1: The address bits of the memory operand are placed on the *address bus* (ADDR). The address lines in the diagram cross, showing that some bits equal 1 and others equal 0.

Cycle 2: The *read line* (RD) is set low (0) to notify memory that a value is to be read.

Cycle 3: The CPU waits one cycle to give memory time to respond. During this cycle, the memory controller places the operand on the *data bus* (DATA).

Cycle 4: The read line goes to 1, signaling the CPU to read the data on the data bus.

Cache Memory   Because conventional memory is so much slower than the CPU, computers use high-speed *cache memory* to hold the most recently used instructions and data. The first time a program reads a block of data, it leaves a copy in the cache. If the program needs to read the same data a second time, it looks for the data in cache. A *cache hit* indicates the data is in cache; a *cache miss* indicates the data is not in cache and must be read from conventional memory. In general, cache memory has a noticeable effect on improving access to data, particularly when the cache is large.

2.1.4   How Programs Run

Load and Execute Process

The following steps describe, in sequence, what happens when a computer user runs a program at a command prompt:

- The operating system (OS) searches for the program's filename in the current disk directory. If it cannot find the name there, it searches a predetermined list of directories (called *paths*) for the filename. If the OS fails to find the program filename, it issues an error message.
- If the program file is found, the OS retrieves basic information about the program's file from the disk directory, including the file size and its physical location on the disk drive.
- The OS determines the next available location in memory and loads the program file into memory. It allocates a block of memory to the program and enters information about the program's size and location into a table (sometimes called a *descriptor table*). Additionally, the OS may adjust the values of pointers within the program so they contain addresses of program data.
- The OS begins execution of the program's first machine instruction. As soon as the program begins running, it is called a *process*. The OS assigns the process an identification number (*process ID*), which is used to keep track of it while running.
- The *process* runs by itself. It is the OS's job to track the execution of the process and to respond to requests for system resources. Examples of resources are memory, disk files, and input-output devices.
- When the process ends, it is removed from memory.

If you're using any version of Microsoft Windows, press *Ctrl-Alt-Delete* and click on the *Task Manager* button. There are tabs labeled *Applications* and *Processes*. Applications are the names of complete programs currently running, such as Windows Explorer or Microsoft Visual C++. When you click on the *Processes* tab, you see 30 or 40 names listed, often some you might not recognize. Each of those processes is a small program running independent of all the others. Note that each has a PID (process ID), and you can continuously track the amount of CPU time and memory it uses. Most processes run in the background. You can shut down a process somehow left running in memory by mistake. Of course, if you shut down the wrong process, your computer may stop running, and you'll have to reboot.

Multitasking

A *multitasking* operating system is able to run multiple tasks at the same time. A *task* is defined as either a program (a process) or a thread of execution. A process has its own memory area and may contain multiple threads. A thread shares its memory with other threads belonging to the same process. Game programs, for example, often use individual threads to simultaneously control multiple graphic objects. Web browsers use separate threads to simultaneously load graphic images and respond to user input.

Most modern operating systems simultaneously execute tasks that communicate with hardware, display user interfaces, perform background file processing, and so on. A CPU can really execute only one instruction at a time, so a component of the operating system named the *scheduler* allocates a slice of CPU time (called a *time slice*) to each task. During a single time slice, the CPU executes a block of instructions, stopping when the time slice has ended.

By rapidly switching tasks, the processor creates the illusion they are running simultaneously. One type of scheduling used by the OS is called *round-robin scheduling*. In Figure 2–4, nine tasks are active. Suppose the *scheduler* arbitrarily assigned 100 milliseconds to each task, and switching between tasks consumed 8 milliseconds. One full circuit of the task list would require 972 milliseconds $(9 \times 100) + (9 \times 8)$ to complete.

FIGURE 2–4   Round-Robin Scheduler.

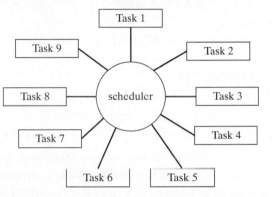

A multitasking OS runs on a processor (such as the x86) that supports *task switching*. The processor saves the state of each task before switching to a new one. A task's *state* consists of the contents of the processor registers, program counter, and status flags, along with references to the task's memory segments. A multitasking OS will usually assign varying priorities to tasks, giving them relatively larger or smaller time slices. A *preemptive* multitasking OS (such as Windows XP or Linux) permits a higher-priority task to interrupt a lower-priority one, leading to better system stability. Suppose an application program is locked in loop and has stopped responding to input. The keyboard handler (a high-priority OS task) can respond to the user's Ctrl-Alt-Del command and shut down the buggy application program.

2.1.5 Section Review

1. The central processor unit (CPU) contains registers and what other basic elements?
2. The central processor unit is connected to the rest of the computer system using what three buses?
3. Why does memory access take more machine cycles than register access?
4. What are the three basic steps in the instruction execution cycle?
5. Which two additional steps are required in the instruction execution cycle when a memory operand is used?

6. During which stage of the instruction execution cycle is the program counter incremented?

7. When a program runs, what information does the OS read from the filename's disk directory entry?

8. After a program has been loaded into memory, how does it begin execution?

9. Define *multitasking*.

10. What is the function of the OS scheduler?

11. When the processor switches from one task to another, what values in the first task's state must be preserved?

12. What is the duration of a single clock cycle in a 3-GHz processor?

2.2   x86 Architecture Details

In this section, we focus on the basic architectural features of the x86 processor family, which includes both Intel IA-32 and 32-bit AMD processors.

2.2.1   Modes of Operation

x86 processors have three primary modes of operation: protected mode, real-address mode, and system management mode. A sub-mode, named *virtual-8086*, is a special case of protected mode. Here are short descriptions of each:

Protected Mode   Protected mode is the native state of the processor, in which all instructions and features are available. Programs are given separate memory areas named *segments*, and the processor prevents programs from referencing memory outside their assigned segments.

Virtual-8086 Mode   While in protected mode, the processor can directly execute real-address mode software such as MS-DOS programs in a safe multitasking environment. In other words, if an MS-DOS program crashes or attempts to write data into the system memory area, it will not affect other programs running at the same time. Windows XP can execute multiple separate virtual-8086 sessions at the same time.

Real-Address Mode   Real-address mode implements the programming environment of the Intel 8086 processor with a few extra features, such as the ability to switch into other modes. This mode is available in Windows 98, and can be used to run an MS-DOS program that requires direct access to system memory and hardware devices. Programs running in real-address mode can cause the operating system to crash (stop responding to commands).

System Management Mode   System Management mode (SMM) provides an operating system with a mechanism for implementing functions such as power management and system security. These functions are usually implemented by computer manufacturers who customize the processor for a particular system setup.

2.2.2   Basic Execution Environment

Address Space

In 32-bit protected mode, a task or program can address a linear address space of up to 4 GBytes. Beginning with the P6 processor, a technique called Extended Physical Addressing allows a total of 64 GBytes of physical memory to be addressed. Real-address mode programs, on the other hand, can only address a range of 1 MByte. If the processor is in protected mode and running multiple programs in virtual-8086 mode, each program has its own 1-MByte memory area.

Basic Program Execution Registers

Registers are high-speed storage locations directly inside the CPU, designed to he accessed at much higher speed than conventional memory. When a processing loop is optimized for speed, for example, loop counters are held in registers rather than variables. Figure 2–5 shows the *basic program execution registers*. There are eight general-purpose registers, six segment registers, a processor status flags register (EFLAGS), and an instruction pointer (EIP).

FiGURE 2–5   Basic Program Execution Registers.

32-bit General-Purpose Registers

EAX
EBX
ECX
EDX

EBP
ESP
ESI
EDI

EFLAGS

EIP

16-bit Segment Registers

CS
SS
DS

ES
FS
GS

General-Purpose Registers   The *general-purpose registers* are primarily used for arithmetic and data movement. As shown in Figure 2–6, the lower 16 bits of the EAX register can be referenced by the name AX.

FiGURE 2–6   General-Purpose Registers.

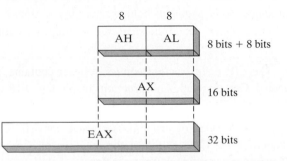

Portions of some registers can be addressed as 8-bit values. For example, the AX register, has an 8-bit upper half named AH and an 8-bit lower half named AL. The same overlapping relationship exists for the EAX, EBX, ECX, and EDX registers:

32-Bit	16-Bit	8-Bit (High)	8-Bit (Low)
EAX	AX	AH	AL
EBX	BX	BH	BL
ECX	CX	CH	CL
EDX	DX	DH	DL

The remaining general-purpose registers can only be accessed using 32-bit or 16-bit names, as shown in the following table:

32-Bit	16-Bit
ESI	SI
EDI	DI
EBP	BP
ESP	SP

Specialized Uses   Some general-purpose registers have specialized uses:

- EAX is automatically used by multiplication and division instructions. It is often called the *extended accumulator* register.
- The CPU automatically uses ECX as a loop counter.
- ESP addresses data on the stack (a system memory structure). It is rarely used for ordinary arithmetic or data transfer. It is often called the *extended stack pointer* register.
- ESI and EDI are used by high-speed memory transfer instructions. They are sometimes called the *extended source index* and *extended destination index* registers.
- EBP is used by high-level languages to reference function parameters and local variables on the stack. It should not be used for ordinary arithmetic or data transfer except at an advanced level of programming. It is often called the *extended frame pointer* register.

Segment Registers   In real-address mode, 16-bit segment registers indicate base addresses of preassigned memory areas named *segments*. In protected mode, segment registers hold pointers to segment descriptor tables. Some segments hold program instructions (code), others hold variables (data), and another segment named the *stack segment* holds local function variables and function parameters.

Instruction Pointer   The EIP, or *instruction pointer*, register contains the address of the next instruction to be executed. Certain machine instructions manipulate EIP, causing the program to branch to a new location.

EFLAGS Register   The EFLAGS (or just *Flags*) register consists of individual binary bits that control the operation of the CPU or reflect the outcome of some CPU operation. Some instructions test and manipulate individual processor flags.

A flag is *set* when it equals 1; it is *clear* (or reset) when it equals 0.

Control Flags   Control flags control the CPU's operation. For example, they can cause the CPU to break after every instruction executes, interrupt when arithmetic overflow is detected, enter virtual-8086 mode, and enter protected mode.

Programs can set individual bits in the EFLAGS register to control the CPU's operation. Examples are the *Direction* and *Interrupt* flags.

Status Flags   The Status flags reflect the outcomes of arithmetic and logical operations performed by the CPU. They are the Overflow, Sign, Zero, Auxiliary Carry, Parity, and Carry flags. Their abbreviations are shown immediately after their names:

- The **Carry** flag (CF) is set when the result of an *unsigned* arithmetic operation is too large to fit into the destination.
- The **Overflow** flag (OF) is set when the result of a *signed* arithmetic operation is too large or too small to fit into the destination.
- The **Sign** flag (SF) is set when the result of an arithmetic or logical operation generates a negative result.
- The **Zero** flag (ZF) is set when the result of an arithmetic or logical operation generates a result of zero.
- The **Auxiliary Carry** flag (AC) is set when an arithmetic operation causes a carry from bit 3 to bit 4 in an 8-bit operand.
- The **Parity** flag (PF) is set if the least-significant byte in the result contains an even number of 1 bits. Otherwise, PF is clear. In general, it is used for error checking when there is a possibility that data might be altered or corrupted.

MMX Registers

MMX technology was added onto the Pentium processor by Intel to improve the performance of advanced multimedia and communications applications. The eight 64-bit MMX registers support special instructions called SIMD (*Single-Instruction, Multiple-Data*). As the name implies, MMX instructions operate in parallel on the data values contained in MMX registers. Although they appear to be separate registers, the MMX register names are in fact aliases to the same registers used by the floating-point unit.

XMM Registers

The x86 architecture also contains eight 128-bit registers called XMM registers. They are used by streaming SIMD extensions to the instruction set.

2.2.3   Floating-Point Unit

The *floating-point unit* (FPU) performs high-speed floating-point arithmetic. At one time a separate coprocessor chip was required for this. From the Intel486 onward, the FPU has been integrated into the main processor chip. There are eight floating-point data registers in the FPU, named ST(0), ST(1), ST(2), ST(3), ST(4), ST(5), ST(6), and ST(7). The remaining control and pointer registers are shown in Figure 2–7.

2.2.4   Overview of Intel Microprocessors

Let's take a short trip down memory lane, starting when the IBM-PC was first released, when PC's had 64 KByte of RAM and no hard drives.

FIGURE 2–7   Floating-Point Unit Registers.

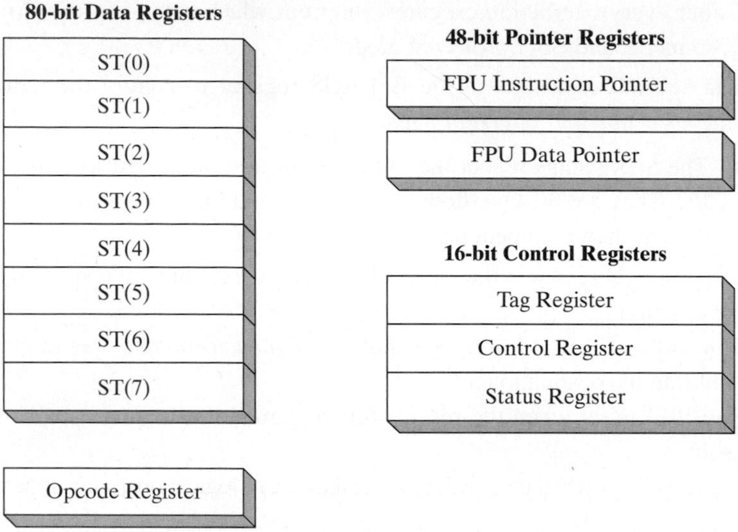

80-bit Data Registers

| ST(0) |
| ST(1) |
| ST(2) |
| ST(3) |
| ST(4) |
| ST(5) |
| ST(6) |
| ST(7) |

| Opcode Register |

48-bit Pointer Registers

| FPU Instruction Pointer |
| FPU Data Pointer |

16-bit Control Registers

| Tag Register |
| Control Register |
| Status Register |

When discussing processor evolution, references to the data bus size are significant because they affect system performance. When a processor uses an 8-bit data bus to transfer a 32-bit integer to memory, for example, the integer must be broken into four parts, and four separate data transfer operations are required to complete the operation. Given that there is a significant delay (called *latency*) involved in each data transfer operation, an 8-bit data bus transfers data at one-fourth the speed of a 32-bit data bus.

Intel 8086   The Intel 8086 processor (1978) marked the beginning of the modern Intel architecture family. The primary innovations of the 8086 over earlier processors were that it had 16-bit registers and a 16-bit data bus and used a segmented memory model permitting programs to address up to 1 MByte of RAM. Greater access to memory made it possible to write complex business applications. The IBM-PC (1980) contained an Intel 8088 processor, which was identical to the 8086, except it had an 8-bit data bus that made it slightly less expensive to produce. Today, the Intel 8088 is used in low-cost microcontrollers.

Backward Compatibility. Each processor introduced into the Intel family since the 8086 has been backward-compatible with earlier processors. This approach enables older software to run (without recompilation) on newer computers without modification. Newer software eventually appeared, requiring features of more advanced processors.

Intel 80286   The Intel 80286 processor, first used in the IBM-PC/AT computer, set a new standard of speed and power. It was the first Intel processor to run in protected mode. The 80286 addresses up to 16 MByte of RAM using a 24-bit address bus.

IA-32 Processor Family (x86)

The Intel 80386 processor (1985) introduced 32-bit data registers and a 32-bit address bus and external data path. Here, we can distinguish between an internal data path, which is a bus that moves data within the processor itself, and an external data path, which is the bus that moves data to and from memory and I/O devices. As such, it was the first member of the IA-32 family. IA-32 processors can address virtual memory larger than the computer's physical memory. Each program is assigned a 4-GByte (gigabyte) linear address space.

Intel i486   Continuing the IA-32 family, the Intel i486 processor (1989) featured an instruction set microarchitecture using pipelining techniques that permitted multiple instructions to be processed at the same time.

Pentium   The Intel Pentium processor (1993) added many performance improvements, including a superscalar design with two parallel execution pipelines. Two instructions could be decoded and executed simultaneously. The Pentium used a 32-bit address bus and a 64-bit internal data path (inside the processor itself), and introduced MMX technology to the IA-32 family.

Intel64 for 64-bit Processing

Intel64 is the name given to Intel's implementation of the *x86-64 specification*, originally developed by AMD. Intel64 provides a 64-bit linear address space, although individual processors generally implement less than 64 bits. Their physical address space can be greater than 64 GBytes. Intel64 provides backward compatibility to run 32-bit programs with no performance penalty.

Intel64 was first used in the *Pentium Extreme* processor, and has continued in the Intel Xeon, Celeron D, Pentium D, Core 2, Core i7, and Atom processors, as well as newer generations of the Pentium 4. In addition to the Protected mode, Real-address mode, and System management modes of the IA-32 processor family, Intel64 processors support the *IA-32e mode*, designed for 64-bit processing.

IA-32e Mode   IA-32e Mode has two sub-modes, designed to benefit users of 64-bit operating systems such as Windows Vista and Linux: Compatibility mode and 64-bit mode.

1. **Compatibility mode** permits legacy 16-bit and 32-bit applications to run without recompilation under a 64-bit operating system. Operand sizes are 16 and 32 bits, and the addressable range of memory is 4 GByte.
2. **64-bit mode** uses 64-bit addresses, 64-bit (and 32-bit) operands, a greater number of registers, and extensions to the instruction set to improve the processing of massive amounts of data. Memory segmentation is disabled, creating a flat 64-bit linear-address space.

Individual applications running at the same time can run in either Compatibility mode or 64-bit mode. But an application running in 64-bit mode cannot use the segmented or real-address modes.

Processor Families   At the time of this book's publication, the following Intel processor families were currently the most widely used. To give you an idea of their relative power, some specifications are listed. These statistics become obsolete quickly, so consult the intel.com Web site for the latest information:

Intel Celeron—dual-core, 512 KByte L2 cache, up to 2.2 GHz, 800 MHz bus

Intel Pentium—dual-core, 2 MByte L2 cache, 1.6 to 2.7 GHz, 800 MHz bus

Core 2 Duo—2 processor cores, 1.8–3.33 GHz, 64 bit, 6 MByte L2 cache

Core 2 Quad—4 processor cores, up to 12 MByte L2 cache, 1333 MHz front side bus

Core i7—4 processor cores, (up to 2.93 GHz), 8 processing threads, 8 MByte smart cache, 3 channels DDR3 memory

Hyperthreading and Multi-core Processing

A *dual processor* system contains two separate physical computer processors, usually attached to the same motherboard with its own socket. The computer's operating system will schedule two separate tasks (processes or threads) to run at the same time, in parallel.

Intel *Hyper-Threading (HT)* technology allows two tasks to execute on a traditional single processor at the same time. This approach is less expensive than a dual processor system, and it makes efficient use of the processor's resources. In effect, a single physical processor is divided into two logical processors. The shared resources include cache, registers, and execution units. The Intel Xeon processor and some Pentium 4 processors use HT technology.

The term *Dual Core* refers to integrated circuit (IC) chips that contain two complete physical computer processor chips in the same IC package. Each processor has its own resources, and each has its own communication path to the computer system's front-side bus. Sometimes, dual-core processors also incorporate HT technology, causing them to appear as four logical processors, running four tasks simultaneously. Intel also offers packages containing more than two processors, called *multi core*.

CISC and RISC

The Intel 8086 processor was the first in a line of processors using a *Complex Instruction Set Computer* (CISC) design. The instruction set is large, and includes a wide variety of memory-addressing, shifting, arithmetic, data movement, and logical operations. Complex instruction sets permit compiled programs to contain a relatively small number of instructions. A major disadvantage to CISC design is that complex instructions require a relatively long time to decode and execute. An interpreter inside the CPU written in a language called *microcode* decodes and executes each machine instruction. Once Intel released the 8086, it became necessary for all subsequent Intel processors to be backward-compatible with the first one.

A completely different approach to microprocessor design is called *Reduced Instruction Set* (RISC). A RISC consists of a relatively small number of short, simple instructions that execute relatively quickly. Rather than using a microcode interpreter to decode and execute machine instructions, a RISC processor directly decodes and executes instructions using hardware. High-speed engineering and graphics workstations have been built using RISC processors for many years.

Because of the huge popularity of IBM-PC–compatible computers, Intel was able to lower the price of its processors and dominate the microprocessor market. At the same time, Intel recognized many advantages to the RISC approach and found a way to use RISC-like features, such as overlapping execution in the Pentium series. The x86 instruction set continues to expand and improve.

2.2.5 Section Review

1. What are the x86 processor's three basic modes of operation?
2. Name all eight 32-bit general-purpose registers.
3. Name all six segment registers.
4. What special purpose does the ECX register serve?

5. Besides the stack pointer (ESP), what other register points to variables on the stack?

6. Name at least four CPU status flags.

7. Which flag is set when the result of an *unsigned* arithmetic operation is too large to fit into the destination?

8. Which flag is set when the result of a *signed* arithmetic operation is either too large or too small to fit into the destination?

9. Which flag is set when an arithmetic or logical operation generates a negative result?

10. Which part of the CPU performs floating-point arithmetic?

11. How many bits long are the FPU data registers?

12. Which Intel processor was the first member of the IA-32 family?

13. Which Intel processor first introduced superscalar execution?

14. Which Intel processor first used MMX technology?

15. Describe the CISC design approach.

16. Describe the RISC design approach.

2.3 x86 Memory Management

x86 processors manage memory according to the basic modes of operation discussed in Section 2.2.1. Protected mode is the most robust and powerful, but it does restrict application programs from directly accessing system hardware.

In *real-address* mode, only 1 MByte of memory can be addressed, from hexadecimal 00000 to FFFFF. The processor can run only one program at a time, but it can momentarily interrupt that program to process requests (called *interrupts*) from peripherals. Application programs are permitted to access any memory location, including addresses that are linked directly to system hardware. The MS-DOS operating system runs in real-address mode, and Windows 95 and 98 can be booted into this mode.

In *protected* mode, the processor can run multiple programs at the same time. It assigns each process (running program) a total of 4 GByte of memory. Each program can be assigned its own reserved memory area, and programs are prevented from accidentally accessing each other's code and data. MS-Windows and Linux run in protected mode.

In *virtual-8086* mode, the computer runs in protected mode and creates a virtual 8086 machine with its own 1-MByte address space that simulates an 80x86 computer running in real-address mode. Windows NT and 2000, for example, create a virtual 8086 machine when you open a *Command* window. You can run many such windows at the same time, and each is protected from the actions of the others. Some MS-DOS programs that make direct references to computer hardware will not run in this mode under Windows NT, 2000, and XP.

In Sections 2.3.1 and 2.3.2 we will explain details of both real-address mode and protected mode.

2.3.1 Real-Address Mode

In real-address mode, an x86 processor can access 1,048,576 bytes of memory (1 MByte) using 20-bit addresses in the range 0 to FFFFF hexadecimal. Intel engineers had to solve a basic problem: The 16-bit registers in the Intel 8086 processor could not hold 20-bit addresses. They came up with a scheme known as *segmented memory*. All of memory is divided into 64-kilobyte (64-KByte) units called *segments*, shown in Figure 2–8. An analogy is a large building, in which *segments* represent the building's floors. A person can ride the elevator to a particular floor, get off, and begin following the room numbers to locate a room. The *offset* of a room can be thought of as the distance from the elevator to the room.

Again in Figure 2–8, each segment begins at an address having a zero for its last hexadecimal digit. Because the last digit is always zero, it is omitted when representing segment values. A segment value of C000, for example, refers to the segment at address C0000. The same figure shows an expansion of the segment at 80000. To reach a byte in this segment, add a 16-bit offset (0 to FFFF) to the segment's base location. The address 8000:0250, for example, represents an offset of 250 inside the segment beginning at address 80000. The linear address is 80250h.

FIGURE 2–8   Segmented Memory Map, Real-Address Mode.

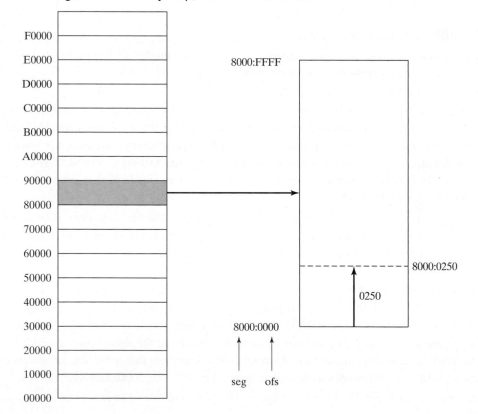

20-Bit Linear Address Calculation   An *address* refers to a single location in memory, and x86 processors permit each byte location to have a separate address. The term for this is *byte-addressable memory*. In real-address mode, the *linear* (or *absolute*) address is 20 bits, ranging from 0 to FFFFF hexadecimal. Programs cannot use linear addresses directly, so addresses are expressed using two 16-bit integers. A *segment-offset* address includes the following:

- A 16-bit **segment** value, placed in one of the segment registers (CS, DS, ES, SS)
- A 16-bit **offset** value

The CPU automatically converts a segment-offset address to a 20-bit linear address. Suppose a variable's hexadecimal segment-offset address is 08F1:0100. The CPU multiplies the segment value by 16 (10 hexadecimal) and adds the product to the variable's offset:

```
08F1h X 10h = 08F10h          (adjusted segment value)
Adjusted Segment value:       0  8  F  1  0
Add the offset:                  0  1  0  0
Linear address:               0  9  0  1  0
```

A typical program has three segments: code, data, and stack. Three segment registers, CS, DS, and SS, contain the segments' base locations:

- CS contains the 16-bit **code** segment address
- DS contains the 16-bit **data** segment address
- SS contains the 16-bit **stack** segment address
- ES, FS, and GS can point to alternate data segments, that is, segments that supplement the default data segment

2.3.2   Protected Mode

Protected mode is the more powerful "native" processor mode. When running in protected mode, a program's linear address space is 4 GBytes, using addresses 0 to FFFFFFFF hexadecimal. In the context of the Microsoft Assembler, the **flat** segmentation model is appropriate for protected mode programming. The flat model is easy to use because it requires only a single 32-bit integer to hold the address of an instruction or variable. The CPU performs address calculation and translation in the background, all of which are transparent to application programmers. Segment registers (CS, DS, SS, ES, FS, GS) point to *segment descriptor tables,* which the operating system uses to keep track of locations of individual program segments. A typical protected-mode program has three segments: code, data, and stack, using the CS, DS, and SS segment registers:

- CS references the descriptor table for the code segment
- DS references the descriptor table for the data segment
- SS references the descriptor table for the stack segment

Flat Segmentation Model

In the flat segmentation model, all segments are mapped to the entire 32-bit physical address space of the computer. At least two segments are required, one for code and one for data. Each segment is defined by a *segment descriptor,* a 64-bit integer stored in a table known as the *global descriptor table* (GDT). Figure 2–9 shows a segment descriptor whose *base address* field points to the first available location in memory (00000000). In this figure, the segment limit is 0040. The *access* field contains bits that determine how the segment can be used. All modern operating systems based on x86 architecture use the flat segmentation model.

FIGURE 2–9   Flat Segmentation Model.

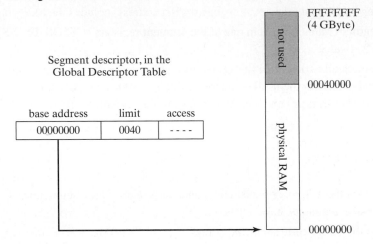

Multi-Segment Model

In the multi-segment model, each task or program is given its own table of segment descriptors, called a *local descriptor table* (LDT). Each descriptor points to a segment, which can be distinct from all segments used by other processes. Each segment has its own address space. In Figure 2–10, each entry in the LDT points to a different segment in memory. Each segment descriptor specifies the exact size of its segment. For example, the segment beginning at 3000 has size 2000 hexadecimal, which is computed as (0002 × 1000 hexadecimal). The segment beginning at 8000 has size A000 hexadecimal.

FIGURE 2–10   Multi-Segment Model.

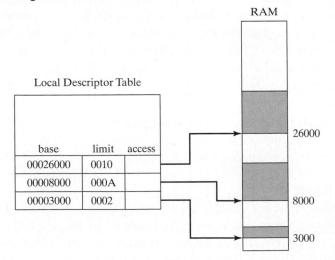

Paging

x86 processors support *paging*, a feature that permits segments to be divided into 4,096-byte blocks of memory called *pages*. Paging permits the total memory used by all programs running at the same time to be much larger than the computer's physical memory. The complete collection of pages mapped by the operating system is called *virtual memory*. Operating systems have utility programs named *virtual memory managers*.

Paging is an important solution to a vexing problem faced by software and hardware designers. A program must be loaded into main memory before it can run, but memory is expensive. Users want to be able to load numerous programs into memory and switch among them at will. Disk storage, on the other hand, is cheap and plentiful. Paging provides the illusion that memory is almost unlimited in size. Disk access is much slower than main memory access, so the more a program relies on paging, the slower it runs.

When a task is running, parts of it can be stored on disk if they are not currently in use. Parts of the task are *paged* (swapped) to disk. Other actively executing pages remain in memory. When the processor begins to execute code that has been paged out of memory it issues a *page fault*, causing the page or pages containing the required code or data to be loaded back into memory. To see how this works, find a computer with somewhat limited memory and run many large applications at the same time. You should notice a delay when switching from one program to another because the operating system must transfer paged portions of each program into memory from disk. A computer runs faster when more memory is installed because large application files and programs can be kept entirely in memory, reducing the amount of paging.

2.3.3 Section Review

1. What is the range of addressable memory in protected mode?
2. What is the range of addressable memory in real-address mode?
3. The two ways of describing an address in real-address mode are segment-offset and

   _____.

4. In real-address mode, convert the following hexadecimal segment-offset address to a linear address: 0950:0100.
5. In real-address mode, convert the following hexadecimal segment-offset address to a linear address: 0CD1:02E0.
6. In MASM's flat segmentation model, how many bits hold the address of an instruction or variable?
7. In protected mode, which register references the descriptor for the stack segment?
8. In protected mode, which table contains pointers to memory segments used by a single program?
9. In the flat segmentation model, which table contains pointers to at least two segments?
10. What is the main advantage to using the paging feature of x86 processors?
11. *Challenge:* Can you think of a reason why MS-DOS was not designed to support protected-mode programming?
12. *Challenge:* In real-address mode, demonstrate two segment-offset addresses that point to the same linear address.

2.4   Components of a Typical x86 Computer

Let us look at how the x86 integrates with other components by examining a typical mother-board configuration and the set of chips that surround the CPU. Then we will discuss memory, I/O ports, and common device interfaces. Finally, we will show how assembly language programs can perform I/O at different levels of access by tapping into system hardware, firmware, and by calling functions in the operating system.

2.4.1   Motherboard

The heart of a microcomputer is its *motherboard*, a flat circuit board onto which are placed the computer's CPU, supporting processors (*chipset*), main memory, input-output connectors, power supply connectors, and expansion slots. The various components are connected to each other by a *bus*, a set of wires etched directly on the motherboard. Dozens of motherboards are available on the PC market, varying in expansion capabilities, integrated components, and speed. The following components have traditionally been found on PC motherboards:

- A CPU socket. Sockets are different shapes and sizes, depending on the type of processor they support.
- Memory slots (SIMM or DIMM) holding small plug-in memory boards
- BIOS (*basic input-output system*) computer chips, holding system software
- CMOS RAM, with a small circular battery to keep it powered
- Connectors for mass-storage devices such as hard drives and CD-ROMs
- USB connectors for external devices
- Keyboard and mouse ports
- PCI bus connectors for sound cards, graphics cards, data acquisition boards, and other input-output devices

The following components are optional:

- Integrated sound processor
- Parallel and serial device connectors
- Integrated network adapter
- AGP bus connector for a high-speed video card

Following are some important support processors in a typical system:

- The *Floating-Point Unit* (FPU) handles floating-point and extended integer calculations.
- The 8284/82C284 *Clock Generator*, known simply as the *clock,* oscillates at a constant speed. The clock generator synchronizes the CPU and the rest of the computer.
- The 8259A *Programmable Interrupt Controller* (PIC) handles external interrupts from hardware devices, such as the keyboard, system clock, and disk drives. These devices interrupt the CPU and make it process their requests immediately.
- The 8253 *Programmable Interval Timer/Counter* interrupts the system 18.2 times per second, updates the system date and clock, and controls the speaker. It is also responsible for constantly refreshing memory because RAM memory chips can remember their data for only a few milliseconds.
- The 8255 *Programmable Parallel Port* transfers data to and from the computer using the IEEE Parallel Port interface. This port is commonly used for printers, but it can be used with other input-output devices as well.

PCI and PCI Express Bus Architectures

The **PCI** (*Peripheral Component Interconnect*) bus provides a connecting bridge between the CPU and other system devices such as hard drives, memory, video controllers, sound cards, and network controllers. More recently, the *PCI Express* bus provides two-way serial connections between devices, memory, and the processor. It carries data in packets, similar to networks, in separate "lanes." It is widely supported by graphics controllers, and can transfer data at about 4 GByte per second.

Motherboard Chipset

A motherboard chipset is a collection of processor chips designed to work together on a specific type of motherboard. Various chipsets have features that increase processing power, multimedia capabilities, or reduce power consumption. The *Intel P965 Express Chipset* can be used as an example. It is used in desktop PCs, with either an Intel Core 2 Duo or Pentium D processor. Here are some of its features:

- Intel *Fast Memory Access* uses an updated Memory Controller Hub (MCH). It can access dual-channel DDR2 memory, at an 800 MHz clock speed.
- An I/O Controller Hub (Intel ICH8/R/DH) uses Intel Matrix Storage Technology (MST) to support six Serial ATA devices (disk drives).
- Support for 10 USB ports, six PCI express slots, networking, Intel Quiet System technology.
- A high definition audio chip provides digital sound capabilities.

A diagram may be seen in Figure 2–11. Motherboard manufacturers will build products around specific chipsets. For example, the P5B-E P965 motherboard by Asus Corporation uses the P965 chipset.

FIGURE 2–11   Intel 965 Express Chipset Block Diagram.

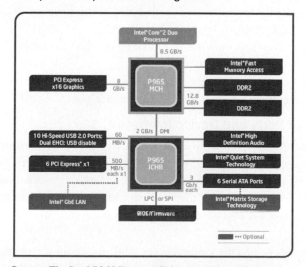

Source: The Intel P965 Express Chipset (product brief),
© 2006 by Intel Corporation, used by permission.
http://www.intcl.com/Assets/PDF/prodbrief/P965-prodbrief.pdf

2.4.2 Video Output

The video adapter controls the display of text and graphics. It has two components: the video controller and video display memory. All graphics and text displayed on the monitor are written into video display RAM, where it is then sent to the monitor by the video controller. The video controller is itself a special-purpose microprocessor, relieving the primary CPU of the job of controlling video hardware.

Older Cathode-ray tube (CRT) video displays used a technique called *raster scanning* to display images. A beam of electrons illuminates phosphorus dots on the screen called *pixels*. Starting at the top of the screen, the gun fires electrons from the left side to the right in a horizontal row, briefly turns off, and returns to the left side of the screen to begin a new row. *Horizontal retrace* refers to the time period when the gun is off between rows. When the last row is drawn, the gun turns off (called the *vertical retrace*) and moves to the upper left corner of the screen to start over.

A direct digital Liquid Crystal Display (LCD) panel, considered standard today, receives a digital bit stream directly from the video controller and does not require raster scanning. Digital displays generally display sharper text than analog displays.

2.4.3 Memory

Several basic types of memory are used in Intel-based systems: read-only memory (ROM), erasable programmable read-only memory (EPROM), dynamic random-access memory (DRAM), static RAM (SRAM), video RAM (VRAM), and complimentary metal oxide semiconductor (CMOS) RAM:

- **ROM** is permanently burned into a chip and cannot be erased.
- **EPROM** can be erased slowly with ultraviolet light and reprogrammed.
- **DRAM**, commonly known as main memory, is where programs and data are kept when a program is running. It is inexpensive, but must be refreshed every millisecond to avoid losing its contents. Some systems use ECC (error checking and correcting) memory.
- **SRAM** is used primarily for expensive, high-speed cache memory. It does not have to be refreshed. CPU cache memory is comprised of SRAM.
- **VRAM** holds video data. It is dual ported, allowing one port to continuously refresh the display while another port writes data to the display.
- **CMOS RAM** on the system motherboard stores system setup information. It is refreshed by a battery, so its contents are retained when the computer's power is off.

2.4.4 Input-Output Ports and Device Interfaces

Universal Serial Bus (USB)   The Universal Serial Bus port provides intelligent, high-speed connection between a computer and USB-supported devices. USB Version 2.0 supports data transfer speeds of 480 megabits per second. You can connect single-function units (mice, printers) or compound devices having more than one peripheral sharing the same port. A USB hub, shown in Figure 2–12, is a compound device connected to several other devices, including other USB hubs.

When a device is attached to the computer via USB, the computer queries (enumerates) the device to get its name, device type, and the type of device driver it supports. The computer can suspend power to individual devices, putting them in a suspended state.

Parallel Port   Printers have traditionally been connected to computers using *parallel ports*. The term *parallel* indicates that the bits in a data byte or word travel simultaneously from the computer to the device, each on a separate wire. Data is transferred at high speed (1 MByte per second) over short distances, usually no more than 10 feet. DOS automatically recognizes three parallel ports: LPT1, LPT2, and LPT3. Parallel ports can be *bidirectional*, allowing the computer to both send data to and receive information from a device. Although many printers now use USB connectors, parallel ports are useful for high-speed connections to laboratory instruments and custom hardware devices.

Figure 2–12   USB Hub Configuration.

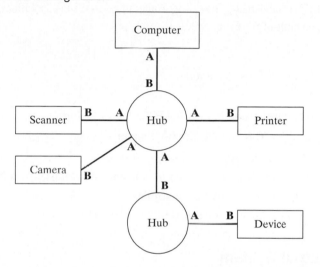

ATA Host Adapters   Known as *intelligent drive electronics* or *integrated drive electronics*, ATA host adapters connect computers to mass-storage devices such as hard drives and CD-ROMs. The letters ATA stand for *advanced technology attachment*, referring to the way the drive controller hardware and firmware are located on the drive itself. ATA adapters use a common interface named IDE (*integrated drive electronics*) found on all motherboards.

SATA Host Adapters   SATA (*serial ATA*) host adapters have become the most common storage interface for laptop and desktop computers, replacing IDE and ATA interfaces. With only four signal lines, serial ATA uses an inexpensive high-speed cable that permits reading and writing data in both directions simultaneously.

FireWire   FireWire is a high-speed external bus standard supporting data transfer speeds up to 800 MByte per second. A large number of devices can be attached to a single FireWire bus, and data can be delivered at a guaranteed rate (*isochronous data transfer*).

Serial Port   An *RS-232 serial interface* sends binary bits one at a time, more slowly than parallel and USB ports, but with the ability to send over larger distances. The highest data transfer rate is 19,200 bits per second. Laboratory acquisition devices often use serial interfaces, as do telephone modems. The 16550 UART (*Universal Asynchronous Receiver Transmitter*) chip controls serial data transfer.

Bluetooth   Bluetooth is a wireless communication protocol for exchanging small amounts of data over short distances. It is commonly used with mobile devices such as cell phones and PDAs. It features low power consumption and can be implemented using low-cost microchips.

Wi-Fi   Wi-Fi, sometimes known as *wireless Ethernet*, describes a certification asserting that a device can send data wirelessly to another Wi-Fi enabled device. Wi-Fi is based on industry-standard IEEE 802.11 standards. Wi-Fi devices operate at a greater speed and capacity than Bluetooth. Wi-Fi devices often communicate with each other when in range of a wireless network. For example, a wireless network can be established by a network router that has Wi-Fi capabilities. Most laptop computers sold today have built-in Wi-Fi capabilities.

2.4.5   Section Review

1. Describe SRAM and its most common use.
2. Describe VRAM.
3. List at least two features found in the Intel P965 Express chipset.
4. Name four types of RAM mentioned in this chapter.
5. Which type of RAM is used for Level 2 cache memory?
6. What advantages does a USB device offer over a standard serial or parallel device?
7. What is the purpose of the 8259A PIC controller?
8. What are the main differences between Wi-Fi and Bluetooth?

2.5   Input-Output System

Tip: Because computer games are so memory and I/O intensive, they push computer performance to the max. Programmers who excel at game programming often know a lot about video and sound hardware, and optimize their code for hardware features.

2.5.1   Levels of I/O Access

Application programs routinely read input from keyboard and disk files and write output to the screen and to files. I/O need not be accomplished by directly accessing hardware—instead, you can call functions provided by the operating system. I/O is available at different access levels, similar to the virtual machine concept shown in Chapter 1. There are three primary levels:

- **High-level language functions:** A high-level programming language such as C++ or Java contains functions to perform input-output. These functions are portable because they work on a variety of different computer systems and are not dependent on any one operating system.
- **Operating system:** Programmers can call operating system functions from a library known as the API (*application programming interface*). The operating system provides high-level operations such as writing strings to files, reading strings from the keyboard, and allocating blocks of memory.

- **BIOS:** The Basic Input-Output System is a collection of low-level subroutines that communicate directly with hardware devices. The BIOS is installed by the computer's manufacturer and is tailored to fit the computer's hardware. Operating systems typically communicate with the BIOS.

Device Drivers   *Device drivers* are programs that permit the operating system to communicate directly with hardware devices. For example, a device driver might receive a request from the OS to read some data; the device driver satisfies the request by executing code in the device firmware that reads data in a way that is unique to the device. Device drivers are usually installed one of two ways: (1) before a specific hardware device is attached to a computer, or (2) after a device has been attached and identified. In the latter case, the OS recognizes the device name and signature; it then locates and installs the device driver software onto the computer.

We can put the I/O hierarchy into perspective by showing what happens when an application program displays a string of characters on the screen in (Figure 2–13). The following steps are involved:

1. A statement in the application program calls an HLL library function that writes the string to standard output.
2. The library function (Level 3) calls an operating system function, passing a string pointer.
3. The operating system function (Level 2) uses a loop to call a BIOS subroutine, passing it the ASCII code and color of each character. The operating system calls another BIOS subroutine to advance the cursor to the next position on the screen.
4. The BIOS subroutine (Level 1) receives a character, maps it to a particular system font, and sends the character to a hardware port attached to the video controller card.
5. The video controller card (Level 0) generates timed hardware signals to the video display that control the raster scanning and displaying of pixels.

FIGURE 2–13   Access Levels for Input-Output Operations.

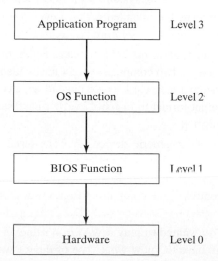

Application Program	Level 3
OS Function	Level 2
BIOS Function	Level 1
Hardware	Level 0

Programming at Multiple Levels   Assembly language programs have power and flexibility in the area of input-output programming. They can choose from the following access levels (Figure 2–14):

• Level 3: Call library functions to perform generic text I/O and file-based I/O. We supply such a library with this book, for instance.
• Level 2: Call operating system functions to perform generic text I/O and file-based I/O. If the OS uses a graphical user interface, it has functions to display graphics in a device-independent way.
• Level 1: Call BIOS functions to control device-specific features such as color, graphics, sound, keyboard input, and low-level disk I/O.
• Level 0: Send and receive data from hardware ports, having absolute control over specific devices. This approach cannot be used with a wide variety of hardware devices, so we say that it is *not portable*. Different devices often use different hardware ports, so the program code must be customized for each specific type of device.

Figure 2–14   Assembly Language Access Levels.

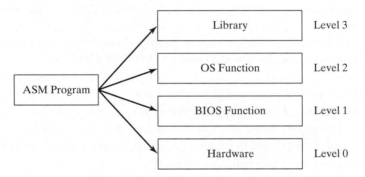

What are the tradeoffs? Control versus portability is the primary one. Level 2 (OS) works on any computer running the same operating system. If an I/O device lacks certain capabilities, the OS will do its best to approximate the intended result. Level 2 is not particularly fast because each I/O call must go through several layers before it executes.

Level 1 (BIOS) works on all systems having a standard BIOS, but will not produce the same result on all systems. For example, two computers might have video displays with different resolution capabilities. A programmer at Level 1 would have to write code to detect the user's hardware setup and adjust the output format to match. Level 1 runs faster than Level 2 because it is only one level above the hardware.

Level 0 (hardware) works with generic devices such as serial ports and with specific I/O devices produced by known manufacturers. Programs using this level must extend their coding logic to handle variations in I/O devices. Real-mode game programs are prime examples because they usually take control of the computer. Programs at this level execute as quickly as the hardware will permit.

Suppose, for example, you wanted to play a WAV file using an audio controller device. At the OS level, you would not have to know what type of device was installed, and you would not be concerned with nonstandard features the card might have. At the BIOS level, you would query the sound card (using its installed device driver software) and find out whether it belonged to a certain class of sound cards having known features. At the hardware level, you would fine tune the program for certain models of audio cards, taking advantage of each card's special features.

Finally, not all operating systems permit user programs to directly access system hardware. Such access is reserved for the operating system itself and specialized device driver programs. This is the case with all versions of Microsoft Windows beyond Windows 95, in which vital system resources are shielded from application programs. MS-DOS, on the other hand, has no such restrictions.

2.5.2   Section Review

1. Of the four levels of input/output in a computer system, which is the most universal and portable?

2. What characteristics distinguish BIOS-level input/output?

3. Why are device drivers necessary, given that the BIOS already has code that communicates with the computer's hardware?

4. In the example regarding displaying a string of characters, which level exists between the operating system and the video controller card?

5. At which level(s) can an assembly language program manipulate input/output?

6. Why do game programs often send their sound output directly to the sound card's hardware ports?

7. *Challenge:* Is it likely that the BIOS for a computer running MS-Windows would be different from that used by a computer running Linux?

2.6   Chapter Summary

The central processor unit (CPU) is where calculations and logic processing occur. It contains a limited number of storage locations called *registers*, a high-frequency clock to synchronize its operations, a control unit, and the arithmetic logic unit. The memory storage unit is where instructions and data are held while a computer program is running. A *bus* is a series of parallel wires that transmit data among various parts of the computer.

The execution of a single machine instruction can be divided into a sequence of individual operations called the *instruction execution cycle*. The three primary operations are fetch, decode, and execute. Each step in the instruction cycle takes at least one tick of the system clock, called a *clock cycle*. The *load and execute* sequence describes how a program is located by the operating system, loaded into memory, and executed by the operating system.

A *multitasking* operating system can run multiple tasks at the same time. It runs on a processor that supports *task switching*, the ability to save the current task state and transfer control to a different task.

x86 processors have three basic modes of operation: *protected* mode, *real-address* mode, and *system management* mode. In addition, *virtual-8086* mode is a special case of protected mode.

Intel64 processors have two basic modes of operation: Compatibility mode and 64-bit mode. In Compatibility mode they can run 16-bit and 32-bit applications.

Registers are named locations within the CPU that can be accessed much more quickly than conventional memory. Following are brief descriptions of register types:

- The *general-purpose* registers are primarily used for arithmetic, data movement, and logical operations.
- The *segment registers* are used as base locations for preassigned memory areas called segments.
- The EIP (*instruction pointer*) register contains the address of the next instruction to be executed.
- The EFLAGS (*extended flags*) register consists of individual binary bits that control the operation of the CPU and reflect the outcome of ALU operations.

The x86 has a floating-point unit (FPU) expressly used for the execution of high-speed floating-point instructions.

The Intel 8086 processor marked the beginning of the modern Intel architecture family. The Intel 80386 processor, the first of the IA-32 family, featured 32-bit registers and a 32-bit address bus and external data path. More recent processors, such as the Core 2 Duo, have multiple processor cores. They employ Intel Hyper-Threading technology to execute multiple tasks in parallel on the same processor core.

x86 processors are based on the *complex instruction set* (CISC) approach. The instruction set includes powerful ways to address data and instructions that are relatively high level complex operations. A completely different approach to microprocessor design is the *reduced instruction set* (RISC). A RISC machine language consists of a relatively small number of short, simple instructions that can be executed quickly by the processor.

In real-address mode, only 1 MByte of memory can be addressed, using hexadecimal addresses 00000 to FFFFF. In protected mode, the processor can run multiple programs at the same time. It assigns each process (running program) a total of 4 GByte of virtual memory. In virtual-8086 mode, the processor runs in protected mode and creates a virtual 8086 machine with its own 1-MByte address space that simulates an Intel 8086 computer running in real-address mode.

In the flat segmentation model, all segments are mapped to the entire physical address space of the computer. In the multi-segment model, each task is given its own table of segment descriptors, called a local descriptor table (LDT). x86 processors support a feature called *paging*, which permits a segment to be divided into 4096-byte blocks of memory called pages. Paging permits the total memory used by all programs running at the same time to be much larger than the computer's actual (physical) memory.

The heart of any microcomputer is its motherboard, holding the computer's CPU, supporting processors, main memory, input-output connectors, power supply connectors, and expansion slots. The PCI (Peripheral Component Interconnect) bus provides a convenient upgrade path for Pentium processors. Most motherboards contain an integrated set of several microprocessors and controllers, called a chipset. The chipset largely determines the capabilities of the computer.

The video adapter controls the display of text and graphics on IBM-compatibles. It has two components: the video controller and video display memory.

Several basic types of memory are used in PCs: ROM, EPROM, Dynamic RAM (DRAM), Static RAM (SRAM), Video RAM (VRAM), and CMOS RAM.

The Universal Serial Bus (USB) port provides an intelligent, high-speed connection between a computer and USB-supported devices. A parallel port transmits 8 or 16 data bits simultaneously from one device to another. An RS-232 serial port sends binary bits one at a time, resulting in slower speeds than the parallel and USB ports.

Input-output is accomplished via different access levels, similar to the virtual machine concept. Library functions are at the highest level, and the operating system is at the next level below. The BIOS (Basic Input-Output System) is a collection of functions that communicate directly with hardware devices. Programs can also directly access input-output devices.

A simple instruction set can be designed in such a way that each instruction is the same length, it carries out most operations within registers, and only reads and writes memory from a single register. The RISC (reduced instruction set architecture) is modeled along these principles.

2.7   Chapter Exercises

The following exercises require you to look in Intel's online manuals relating to the Intel64 and IA-32 processor architecture.

1. What are some of the innovative characteristics of the P6 processor architecture?
2. Locate a description of the Intel NetBurst Microarchitecture in one of the Intel64 and IA-32 processor manuals. Read about and summarize the functions of the *Front End Pipeline*.
3. Briefly explain the meaning of *out of order execution*. Why is it useful?
4. In processors that use Intel's *Hyperthreading Technology*, what components are coupled with each logical processor?
5. What is the size of the physical address space in a processor that implements the Intel64 architecture?
6. What are the Intel *Virtual Machine Extensions*? Why are virtual machines useful today?

3

Assembly Language Fundamentals

3.1 Basic Elements of Assembly Language
    3.1.1 Integer Constants
    3.1.2 Integer Expressions
    3.1.3 Real Number Constants
    3.1.4 Character Constants
    3.1.5 String Constants
    3.1.6 Reserved Words
    3.1.7 Identifiers
    3.1.8 Directives
    3.1.9 Instructions
    3.1.10 The NOP (No Operation) Instruction
    3.1.11 Section Review

3.2 Example: Adding and Subtracting Integers
    3.2.1 Alternative Version of AddSub
    3.2.2 Program Template
    3.2.3 Section Review

3.3 Assembling, Linking, and Running Programs
    3.3.1 The Assemble-Link-Execute Cycle
    3.3.2 Section Review

3.4 Defining Data
    3.4.1 Intrinsic Data Types
    3.4.2 Data Definition Statement

3.4.3 Defining BYTE and SBYTE Data
3.4.4 Defining WORD and SWORD Data
3.4.5 Defining DWORD and SDWORD Data
3.4.6 Defining QWORD Data
3.4.7 Defining Packed Binary Coded Decimal (TBYTE) Data
3.4.8 Defining Real Number Data
3.4.9 Little Endian Order
3.4.10 Adding Variables to the AddSub Program
3.4.11 Declaring Uninitialized Data
3.4.12 Section Review

3.5 Symbolic Constants
    3.5.1 Equal-Sign Directive
    3.5.2 Calculating the Sizes of Arrays and Strings
    3.5.3 EQU Directive
    3.5.4 TEXTEQU Directive
    3.5.5 Section Review

3.6 Real-Address Mode Programming (Optional)
    3.6.1 Basic Changes

3.7 Chapter Summary

3.8 Programming Exercises

3.1 Basic Elements of Assembly Language

Chapter 1 introduced number concepts and virtual machines. Chapter 2 introduced hardware basics. Now you're ready to begin programming. There is an element of truth in saying "*Assembly language is simple.*" It was designed to run in little memory and consists of mainly low-level, simple operations. Then why does it have the reputation of being difficult to learn? After all, how hard can it be to move data between registers and do a calculation? Here's a proof of concept— a simple program in assembly language that adds two numbers and displays the result:

```
main PROC
     mov   eax,5            ; move 5 to the EAX register
     add   eax,6            ; add 6 to the EAX register
     call  WriteInt         ; display value in EAX
     exit                   ; quit
main ENDP
```

We simplified things a bit by calling a library subroutine named **WriteInt**, which itself contains a fair amount of code. But in general, assembly language is not hard to learn if you're happy writing short programs that do practically nothing.

Details, Details   Becoming a skilled assembly language programmer requires a love of details. You will find it helpful to build a foundation of basic information and gradually fill in the details. If you were a cook, we would show you around the kitchen and explain how to use mixers, grinders, knives, stoves, and saucepans. Similarly, we will identify the ingredients of assembly language, mix them together, and cook up a few tasty programs.

Next, we describe basic elements of Microsoft Macro Assembler (MASM) syntax. Knowing these elements will help you to write your first programs in assembly language.

3.1.1   Integer Constants

An *integer constant* (or integer literal) is made up of an optional leading sign, one or more digits, and an optional suffix character (called a *radix*) indicating the number's base:

```
[{+|-}] digits [radix]
```

> Microsoft syntax notation is used throughout this chapter. Elements within square brackets [..] are optional and elements within braces {..} require a choice of one of the enclosed elements (separated by the | character). Elements in *italics* denote items that have known definitions or descriptions.

Radix may be one of the following (uppercase or lowercase):

h	Hexadecimal	r	Encoded real
q/o	Octal	t	Decimal *(alternate)*
d	Decimal	y	Binary *(alternate)*
b	Binary		

If no radix is given, the integer constant is assumed to be decimal. Here are some examples using different radixes:

26	Decimal	42o	Octal
26d	Decimal	1Ah	Hexadecimal
11010011b	Binary	0A3h	Hexadecimal
42q	Octal		

A hexadecimal constant beginning with a letter must have a leading zero to prevent the assembler from interpreting it as an identifier.

3.1.2 Integer Expressions

An *integer expression* is a mathematical expression involving integer values and arithmetic operators. The expression must evaluate to an integer, which can be stored in 32 bits (0 through FFFFFFFFh). The arithmetic operators are listed in Table 3-1 according to their precedence order, from highest (1) to lowest (4). The important thing to realize about integer expressions is that they can only be evaluated at assembly time. These are not runtime expressions.

Table 3-1   Arithmetic Operators.

Operator	Name	Precedence Level
( )	Parentheses	1
+, −	Unary plus, minus	2
*, /	Multiply, divide	3
MOD	Modulus	3
+, −	Add, subtract	4

Precedence refers to the implied order of operations when an expression contains two or more operators. The order of operations is shown for the following expressions:

```
4 + 5 * 2                    Multiply, add
12 - 1 MOD 5                 Modulus, subtract
-5 + 2                       Unary minus, add
(4 + 2) * 6                  Add, multiply
```

The following are examples of valid expressions and their values:

Expression	Value
16 / 5	3
−(3 + 4) * (6 − 1)	−35
−3 + 4 * 6 − 1	20
25 mod 3	1

Use parentheses in expressions to clarify the order of operations so you don't have to remember precedence rules.

3.1.3   Real Number Constants

Real number constants are represented as decimal reals or encoded (hexadecimal) reals. A *decimal real* contains an optional sign followed by an integer, a decimal point, an optional integer that expresses a fraction, and an optional exponent:

```
[sign] integer. [integer] [exponent]
```

Following are the syntax for the sign and exponent:

```
sign       {+,-}
exponent   E[{+,-}]integer
```

Following are examples of valid real number constants:

```
2.
+3.0
-44.2E+05
26.E5
```

At least one digit and a decimal point are required.

Encoded Reals   An encoded real represents a real number in hexadecimal, using the IEEE floating-point format for short reals (see Chapter 12). The binary representation of decimal +1.0, for example, is

```
0011 1111 1000 0000 0000 0000 0000 0000
```

The same value would be encoded as a short real in assembly language as

```
3F800000r
```

3.1.4   Character Constants

A *character constant* is a single character enclosed in single or double quotes. MASM stores the value in memory as the character's binary ASCII code. Examples are

```
'A'
"d"
```

A complete list of ASCII codes is printed on the inside back cover of this book.

3.1.5   String Constants

A *string constant* is a sequence of characters (including spaces) enclosed in single or double quotes:

```
'ABC'
'X'
"Good night, Gracie"
'4096'
```

Embedded quotes are permitted when used in the manner shown by the following examples:

```
"This isn't a test"
'Say "Good night," Gracie'
```

3.1.6 Reserved Words

Reserved words have special meaning in MASM and can only be used in their correct context. There are different types of reserved words:

- Instruction mnemonics, such as MOV, ADD, and MUL
- Register names
- Directives, which tell MASM how to assemble programs
- Attributes, which provide size and usage information for variables and operands. Examples are BYTE and WORD
- Operators, used in constant expressions
- Predefined symbols, such as @data, which return constant integer values at assembly time

A common list of MASM reserved words can be found in Appendix A.

3.1.7 Identifiers

An *identifier* is a programmer-chosen name. It might identify a variable, a constant, a procedure, or a code label. Keep the following in mind when creating identifiers:

- They may contain between 1 and 247 characters.
- They are not case sensitive.
- The first character must be a letter (A..Z, a..z), underscore (_), @ , ?, or $. Subsequent characters may also be digits.
- An identifier cannot be the same as an assembler reserved word.

> You can make all keywords and identifiers case sensitive by adding the –Cp command line switch when running the assembler.

The @ symbol is used extensively by the assembler as a prefix for predefined symbols, so avoid it in your own identifiers. Make identifier names descriptive and easy to understand. Here are some valid identifiers:

```
var1            Count           $first
_main           MAX             open_file
myFile          xVal            _12345
```

3.1.8 Directives

A *directive* is a command embedded in the source code that is recognized and acted upon by the assembler. Directives do not execute at runtime. Directives can define variables, macros, and procedures. They can assign names to memory segments and perform many other housekeeping tasks related to the assembler. In MASM, directives are case insensitive. For example, it recognizes **.data**, **.DATA**, and **.Data** as equivalent.

The following example helps to show the difference between directives and instructions. The DWORD directive tells the assembler to reserve space in the program for a doubleword variable. The MOV instruction, on the other hand, executes at runtime, copying the contents of **myVar** to the EAX register:

```
myVar   DWORD 26                        ; DWORD directive
mov     eax,myVar                       ; MOV instruction
```

Although all assemblers for Intel processors share the same instruction set, they have completely different sets of directives. The Microsoft assembler's REPT directive, for example, is not recognized by some other assemblers.

Defining Segments   One important function of assembler directives is to define program sections, or *segments*. The .DATA directive identifies the area of a program containing variables:

```
.data
```

The .CODE directive identifies the area of a program containing executable instructions:

```
.code
```

The .STACK directive identifies the area of a program holding the runtime stack, setting its size:

```
.stack 100h
```

Appendix A contains a useful reference for MASM directives and operators.

3.1.9   Instructions

An *instruction* is a statement that becomes executable when a program is assembled. Instructions are translated by the assembler into machine language bytes, which are loaded and executed by the CPU at runtime. An instruction contains four basic parts:

- Label (optional)
- Instruction mnemonic (required)
- Operand(s) (usually required)
- Comment (optional)

This is the basic syntax:

```
[label:] mnemonic [operands] [;comment]
```

Let's explore each part separately, beginning with the *label* field.

Label

A *label* is an identifier that acts as a place marker for instructions and data. A label placed just before an instruction implies the instruction's address. Similarly, a label placed just before a variable implies the variable's address.

Data Labels   A data label identifies the location of a variable, providing a convenient way to reference the variable in code. The following, for example, defines a variable named count:

```
count  DWORD 100
```

The assembler assigns a numeric address to each label. It is possible to define multiple data items following a label. In the following example, array defines the location of the first number (1024). The other numbers following in memory immediately afterward:

```
array DWORD 1024, 2048
      DWORD 4096, 8192
```

Variables will be explained in Section 3.4.2, and the MOV instruction will be explained in Section 4.1.4.

Code Labels   A label in the code area of a program (where instructions are located) must end with a colon (:) character. Code labels are used as targets of jumping and looping instructions. For example, the following JMP (jump) instruction transfers control to the location marked by the label named **target**, creating a loop:

```
target:
     mov    ax,bx
     . . .
     jmp    target
```

A code label can share the same line with an instruction, or it can be on a line by itself:

```
L1:  mov    ax,bx
L2:
```

Label names are created using the rules for identifiers discussed in Section 3.1.7. You can use the same code label more than once in a program as long as each label is unique within its enclosing procedure. (A procedure is like a function.)

Instruction Mnemonic

An *instruction mnemonic* is a short word that identifies an instruction. In English, a *mnemonic* is a device that assists memory. Similarly, assembly language instruction mnemonics such as mov, add, and sub provide hints about the type of operation they perform. Following are examples of instruction mnemonics:

```
mov     Move (assign) one value to another
add     Add two values
sub     Subtract one value from another
mul     Multiply two values
jmp     Jump to a new location
call    Call a procedure
```

Operands   Assembly language instructions can have between zero and three operands, each of which can be a register, memory operand, constant expression, or input-output port. We discussed register names in Chapter 2, and we discussed constant expressions in Section 3.1.2. A *memory operand* is specified by the name of a variable or by one or more registers containing the address of a variable. A variable name implies the address of the variable and instructs the computer to reference the contents of memory at the given address. The following table contains several sample operands:

Example	Operand Type
96	Constant (*immediate value*)
2 + 4	Constant expression
eax	Register
count	Memory

Following are examples of assembly language instructions having varying numbers of operands. The STC instruction, for example, has no operands:

```
stc                          ; set Carry flag
```

The INC instruction has one operand:

```
inc   eax                        ; add 1 to EAX
```

The MOV instruction has two operands:

```
mov count,ebx                    ; move EBX to count
```

In a two-operand instruction, the first operand is called the *destination*. The second operand is the *source*. In general, the contents of the destination operand are modified by the instruction. In a MOV instruction, for example, data is copied from the source to the destination.

The IMUL instruction has 3 operands, in which the first operand is the destination, and the following 2 operands are source operands:

```
imul eax,ebx,5
```

In this case, EBX is multiplied by 5, and the product is stored in the EAX register.

Comments

Comments are an important way for the writer of a program to communicate information about the program's design to a person reading the source code. The following information is typically included at the top of a program listing:

- Description of the program's purpose
- Names of persons who created and/or revised the program
- Program creation and revision dates
- Technical notes about the program's implementation

Comments can be specified in two ways:

- Single-line comments, beginning with a semicolon character (;). All characters following the semicolon on the same line are ignored by the assembler.
- Block comments, beginning with the COMMENT directive and a user-specified symbol. All subsequent lines of text are ignored by the assembler until the same user-specified symbol appears. For example,

```
COMMENT    !
     This line is a comment.
     This line is also a comment.
!
```

We can also use any other symbol:

```
COMMENT &
     This line is a comment.
     This line is also a comment.
&
```

Of course, it is important to provide comments throughout your program, particularly where the intent of your code is not obvious.

3.1.10   The NOP (No Operation) Instruction

The safest (and the most useless) instruction you can write is called NOP (no operation). It takes up 1 byte of program storage and doesn't do any work. It is sometimes used by compilers and assemblers to align code to even-address boundaries. In the following example, the first MOV instruction generates three machine code bytes. The NOP instruction aligns the address of the third instruction to a doubleword boundary (even multiple of 4):

```
00000000  66 8B C3    mov ax,bx
00000003  90          nop                ; align next instruction
00000004  8B D1       mov edx,ecx
```

x86 processors are designed to load code and data more quickly from even doubleword addresses.

3.1.11   Section Review

1. Identify valid suffix characters used in integer constants.

2. *(Yes/No):* Is A5h a valid hexadecimal constant?

3. *(Yes/No):* Does the multiplication operator (*) have a higher precedence than the division operator (/) in integer expressions?

4. Write a constant expression that divides 10 by 3 and returns the integer remainder.

5. Show an example of a valid real number constant with an exponent.

6. *(Yes/No):* Must string constants be enclosed in single quotes?

7. Reserved words can be instruction mnemonics, attributes, operators, predefined symbols, and _____.

8. What is the maximum length of an identifier?

9. *(True/False):* An identifier cannot begin with a numeric digit.

10. *(True/False):* Assembly language identifiers are (by default) case insensitive.

11. *(True/False):* Assembler directives execute at runtime.

12. *(True/False):* Assembler directives can be written in any combination of uppercase and lowercase letters.

13. Name the four basic parts of an assembly language instruction.

14. *(True/False):* MOV is an example of an instruction mnemonic.

15. *(True/False):* A code label is followed by a colon (:), but a data label does not have a colon.

16. Show an example of a block comment.

17. Why would it not be a good idea to use numeric addresses when writing instructions that access variables?

3.2   Example: Adding and Subtracting Integers

We now introduce a short assembly language program that adds and subtracts integers. Registers are used to hold the intermediate data, and we call a library subroutine to display the contents of the registers on the screen. Here is the program source code:

```
TITLE Add and Subtract             (AddSub.asm)

; This program adds and subtracts 32-bit integers.

INCLUDE Irvine32.inc
```

```
.code
main PROC

        mov    eax,10000h              ; EAX = 10000h
        add    eax,40000h              ; EAX = 50000h
        sub    eax,20000h              ; EAX = 30000h
        call   DumpRegs                ; display registers

        exit
main ENDP
END main
```

Let's go through the program line by line. Each line of program code will appear before its explanation.

```
    TITLE Add and Subtract                (AddSub.asm)
```

The TITLE directive marks the entire line as a comment. You can put anything you want on this line.

```
    ; This program adds and subtracts 32-bit integers.
```

All text to the right of a semicolon is ignored by the assembler, so we use it for comments.

```
    INCLUDE Irvine32.inc
```

The INCLUDE directive copies necessary definitions and setup information from a text file named *Irvine32.inc*, located in the assembler's INCLUDE directory. (The file is described in Chapter 5.)

```
    .code
```

The **.code** directive marks the beginning of the *code segment*, where all executable statements in a program are located.

```
    main PROC
```

The PROC directive identifies the beginning of a procedure. The name chosen for the only procedure in our program is **main**.

```
    mov    eax,10000h                   ; EAX = 10000h
```

The MOV instruction moves (copies) the integer 10000h to the EAX register. The first operand (EAX) is called the *destination operand,* and the second operand is called the *source operand.* The comment on the right side shows the expected new value in the EAX register.

```
    add    eax,40000h                   ; EAX = 50000h
```

The ADD instruction adds 40000h to the EAX register. The comment shows the expected new value in EAX.

```
    sub    eax,20000h                   ; EAX = 30000h
```

The SUB instruction subtracts 20000h from the EAX register.

```
    call DumpRegs                       ; display registers
```

The CALL statement calls a procedure that displays the current values of the CPU registers. This can be a useful way to verify that a program is working correctly.

```
        exit
    main ENDP
```

The **exit** statement (indirectly) calls a predefined MS-Windows function that halts the program. The ENDP directive marks the end of the **main** procedure. Note that **exit** is not a MASM keyword; instead, it's a macro command defined in the *Irvine32.inc* include file that provides a simple way to end a program.

```
    END main
```

The END directive marks the last line of the program to be assembled. It identifies the name of the program's *startup* procedure (the procedure that starts the program execution).

Program Output   The following is a snapshot of the program's output, generated by the call to DumpRegs:

```
EAX=00030000   EBX=7FFDF000   ECX=00000101   EDX=FFFFFFFF
ESI=00000000   EDI=00000000   EBP=0012FFF0   ESP=0012FFC4
EIP=00401024   EFL=00000206   CF=0  SF=0  ZF=0  OF=0  AF=0  PF=1
```

The first two rows of output show the hexadecimal values of the 32-bit general-purpose registers. EAX equals 00030000h, the value produced by the ADD and SUB instructions in the program. The values in the other general-purpose registers are unimportant, since their values were not set by our program. The third row shows the values of the EIP (extended instruction pointer) and EFL (extended flags) registers, as well as the values of the Carry, Sign, Zero, Overflow, Auxiliary Carry, and Parity flags.

Segments   Programs are organized around segments, which are usually named code, data, and stack. The *code* segment contains all of a program's executable instructions. Ordinarily, the code segment contains one or more procedures, with one designated as the *startup* procedure. In the **AddSub** program, the startup procedure is **main**. Another segment, the *stack* segment, holds procedure parameters and local variables. The *data* segment holds variables.

Coding Styles   Because assembly language is case insensitive, there is no fixed style rule regarding capitalization of source code. In the interest of readability, you should be consistent in your approach to capitalization, as well as the naming of identifiers. Following are some approaches to capitalization you may want to adopt:

• Use lowercase for keywords, mixed case for identifiers, and all capitals for constants. This approach follows the general model of C, C++, and Java.
• Capitalize everything. This approach was used in pre-1980 software when many computer terminals did not support lowercase letters. It has the advantage of overcoming the effects of poor-quality printers and less-than-perfect eyesight, but seems a bit old-fashioned.
• Use capital letters for assembler reserved words, including instruction mnemonics, and register names. This approach makes it easy to distinguish between identifiers and reserved words.

• Capitalize assembly language directives and operators, use mixed case for identifiers, and lowercase for everything else. This approach is used in this book, except that lowercase is used for the .code, .stack, .model, and .data directives.

3.2.1   Alternative Version of AddSub

Our first version of the **AddSub** program used the *Irvine32.inc* file, which hides a few details. Eventually you will understand everything in that file, but we're just getting started in assembly language. If you prefer full disclosure of information from the start, here is a version of AddSub that does not depend on include files. A bold font is used to highlight the portions of the program that are different from the previous version:

```
TITLE Add and Subtract                        (AddSubAlt.asm)

; This program adds and subtracts 32-bit integers.
.386
.model flat,stdcall
.stack 4096
ExitProcess PROTO, dwExitCode:DWORD
DumpRegs PROTO

.code
main PROC
        mov   eax,10000h                    ; EAX = 10000h
        add   eax,40000h                    ; EAX = 50000h
        sub   eax,20000h                    ; EAX = 30000h
        call  DumpRegs

        INVOKE ExitProcess,0
main ENDP
END main
```

Let's discuss the lines that have changed. As before, we show each line of code followed by its explanation.

```
.386
```

The .386 directive identifies the minimum CPU required for this program (Intel386, the first x86 processor).

```
.model flat,stdcall
```

The .MODEL directive is used in our sample for two purposes: it identifies the segmentation model used by the program and it identifies the convention used for passing parameters to procedures. In the current .model directive, the **flat** keyword tells the assembler to generate code for a protected mode program, and the **stdcall** keyword enables the calling of MS-Windows functions.

```
ExitProcess PROTO, dwExitCode:DWORD
DumpRegs PROTO
```

Two PROTO directives declare prototypes for procedures used by this program: **ExitProcess** is an MS-Windows function that halts the current program (called a *process*), and **DumpRegs** is a procedure from the Irvine32 link library that displays registers.

```
INVOKE ExitProcess,0
```

The program ends by calling the **ExitProcess** function, passing it a return code of zero. INVOKE is an assembler directive that calls a procedure or function.

3.2.2 Program Template

Assembly language programs have a simple structure, with small variations. When you begin a new program, it helps to start with an empty shell program with all basic elements in place. You can avoid redundant typing by filling in the missing parts and saving the file under a new name. The following protected-mode program (*Template.asm*) can easily be customized. Note that comments have been inserted, marking the points where your own code should be added:

```
TITLE Program Template               (Template.asm)

; Program Description:
; Author:
; Creation Date:
; Revisions:
; Date:

INCLUDE Irvine32.inc
.data
     ; (insert variables here)

.code
main PROC
     ; (insert executable instructions here)

   exit
main ENDP

     ; (insert additional procedures here)
END main
```

Use Comments   Several comment fields have been inserted at the beginning of the program. It's a very good idea to include a program description, the name of the program's author, creation date, and information about subsequent modifications.

Documentation of this kind is useful to anyone who reads the program listing (including you, months or years from now). Many programmers have discovered, years after writing a program, that they must become reacquainted with their own code before they can modify it. If you're taking a programming course, your instructor may insist on additional information.

3.2.3 Section Review

1. In the AddSub program (Section 3.2), what is the meaning of the INCLUDE directive?
2. In the AddSub program, what does the .CODE directive identify?
3. What are the names of the segments in the AddSub program?
4. In the AddSub program, how are the CPU registers displayed?

5. In the AddSub program, which statement halts the program?

6. Which directive begins a procedure?

7. Which directive ends a procedure?

8. What is the purpose of the identifier in the END statement?

9. What does the PROTO directive do?

3.3   Assembling, Linking, and Running Programs

A source program written in assembly language cannot be executed directly on its target computer. It must be translated, or *assembled* into executable code. In fact, an assembler is very similar to a *compiler*, the type of program you would use to translate a C++ or Java program into executable code.

The assembler produces a file containing machine language called an *object file*. This file isn't quite ready to execute. It must be passed to another program called a *linker*, which in turn produces an *executable file*. This file is ready to execute from the MS-DOS/Windows command prompt.

3.3.1   The Assemble-Link-Execute Cycle

The process of editing, assembling, linking, and executing assembly language programs is summarized in Figure 3–1. Following is a detailed description of each step.

Step 1: A programmer uses a **text editor** to create an ASCII text file named the *source file*.

Step 2: The **assembler** reads the source file and produces an *object file,* a machine-language translation of the program. Optionally, it produces a *listing file*. If any errors occur, the programmer must return to Step 1 and fix the program.

Step 3: The **linker** reads the object file and checks to see if the program contains any calls to procedures in a link library. The **linker** copies any required procedures from the link library, combines them with the object file, and produces the *executable file*.

Step 4: The operating system **loader** utility reads the executable file into memory and branches the CPU to the program's starting address, and the program begins to execute.

See the topic "Getting Started" on the author's Web site (www.asmirvine.com) for detailed instructions on assembling, linking, and running assembly language programs using Microsoft Visual Studio.

FIGURE 3–1   Assemble-Link-Execute Cycle.

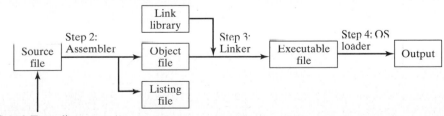

Listing File

A *listing file* contains a copy of the program's source code, suitable for printing, with line numbers, offset addresses, translated machine code, and a symbol table. Let's look at the listing file for the AddSub program from Section 3.2, with some lines omitted to save printing space:

```
Microsoft (R) Macro Assembler Version 9.00.30729.01     05/07/09
16:43:07
Add and Subtract      (AddSub.asm)          Page 1 - 1

TITLE Add and Subtract               (AddSub.asm)

; This program adds and subtracts 32-bit integers.
INCLUDE Irvine32.inc
C .NOLIST
C .LIST

00000000                        .code
00000000                        main PROC

00000000  B8 00010000   mov     eax,10000h     ; EAX = 10000h
00000005  05 00040000   add     eax,40000h     ; EAX = 50000h
0000000A  2D 00020000   sub     eax,20000h     ; EAX = 30000h
0000000F  E8 00000000 E call     DumpRegs

0000001B                        main ENDP
                                END main
```

```
Structures and Unions:
          Name                      Size
                                    Offset        Type

CONSOLE_CURSOR_INFO . . . . . .     00000008
   dwSize . . . . . . . . . . .     00000000      DWord
   bVisible . . . . . . . . . .     00000004      DWord
CONSOLE_SCREEN_BUFFER_INFO . . .    00000016
   dwSize . . . . . . . . . . .     00000000      DWord
   dwCursorPosition . . . . . .     00000004      DWord
   wAttributes  . . . . . . . .     00000008      Word
   srWindow . . . . . . . . . .     0000000A      QWord
   dwMaximumWindowSize  . . . . .   00000012      DWord
   .
(lines omitted to save space)

Segments and Groups:
```

Name	Size	Length	Align	Combine	Class
FLAT	GROUP				
STACK	32 Bit	00001000	Para	Stack	'STACK'
_DATA	32 Bit	00000000	Para	Public	'DATA'
_TEXT	32 Bit	0000001B	Para	Public	'CODE'

Procedures, parameters, and locals:

Name	Type	Value	Attr
CloseFile	P Near 00000000	FLAT	Length= 00000000 External STDCALL
CloseHandle	P Near 00000000	FLAT	Length= 00000000 External STDCALL
Clrscr	P Near 00000000	FLAT	Length= 00000000 External STDCALL
CreateFileA	P Near 00000000	FLAT	Length= 00000000 External STDCALL
CreateOutputFile . .	P Near 00000000	FLAT	Length= 00000000 External STDCALL
Crlf	P Near 00000000	FLAT	Length= 00000000 External STDCALL
Delay	P Near 00000000	FLAT	Length= 00000000 External STDCALL
DumpMem	P Near 00000000	FLAT	Length= 00000000 External STDCALL
DumpRegs	P Near 00000000	FLAT	Length= 00000000 External STDCALL

.

(lines omitted to save space)

.

Name	Type	Value	Attr
WriteToFile	P Near 00000000	FLAT	Length= 00000000 External STDCALL
WriteWindowsMsg . .	P Near 00000000	FLAT	Length= 00000000 External STDCALL
main	P Near 00000000	_TEXT	Length= 0000001B Public STDCALL
printf	P Near 00000000	FLAT	Length= 00000000 External C
scanf	P Near 00000000	FLAT	Length= 00000000 External C
wsprintfA	P Near 00000000	FLAT	Length= 00000000 External C

Symbols:

Name	Type	Value	Attr
@CodeSize	Number	00000000h	
@DataSize	Number	00000000h	

```
@Interface . . . . . . . . . . . Number        00000003h
@Model . . . . . . . . . . . . . Number        00000007h
.
(lines omitted to save space)
   0 Warnings
   0 Errors
```

Let's look more closely at individual lines from the listing file. The first two lines are a section heading. The first line identifies the assembler, its version number, and the date and time when the listing file was generated (the line wraps around on the printed page):

```
Microsoft (R) Macro Assembler Version 9.00.30729.01     05/07/09
16:43:07
```

The second line identifies the program title, filename, and listing file page number:

```
Add and Subtract              (AddSub.asm)     Page 1 - 1
```

Next, a few lines are copied from the source file, up to the INCLUDE directive. The two lines following INCLUDE start with a letter C, indicating that they were copied from the include file (named *Irvine32.inc*) into the assembly stream:

```
TITLE Add and Subtract                    (AddSub.asm)

; This program adds and subtracts 32-bit integers.

INCLUDE Irvine32.inc
C .NOLIST
C .LIST
```

In fact, *Irvine32.inc* contains a great many lines, but it begins with a .NOLIST directive that disables listing of the program's source code until a corresponding .LIST directive is reached. Generally, there is no point in listing all the lines of an include file unless you suspect that it contains errors.

Next, we see lines taken directly from the *AddSub.asm* program file. Along the left side are 32-bit addresses that indicate the relative byte distance of each statement from the beginning of the program's code area:

```
00000000                    .code
00000000                    main PROC

00000000  B8 00010000    mov    eax,10000h    ; EAX = 10000h
00000005  05 00040000    add    eax,40000h    ; EAX = 50000h
0000000A  2D 00020000    sub    eax,20000h    ; EAX = 30000h
0000000F  E8 00000000 E  call   DumpRegs
```

The first two lines, because they are directives, contain no executable instructions. But the subsequent lines are assembly language instructions, each 5 bytes long. The hexadecimal values in the second column, such as B8 00010000 are the actual instruction bytes.

The last two lines of the source code file appear next, containing the exit statement and the ENDP directive:

```
0000001B                              main ENDP
                                      END main
```

The next section of the listing file contains a list of structures and unions. Although the AddSub program does not explicitly contain any structures or unions, there are quite a few of them inside the *Irvine32.inc* file. Each structure name is followed by a list of fields within the structure:

```
Structures and Unions:

                    Name                Size
                                        Offset           Type

CONSOLE_CURSOR_INFO  . . . . . .        00000008
    dwSize . . . . . . . .  . . . .     00000000         DWord
    bVisible . . . . . . . .  . . .     00000004         DWord
CONSOLE_SCREEN_BUFFER_INFO . . .        00000016
    dwSize . . . . . . . .  . . . .     00000000         DWord
    dwCursorPosition . . . . . .        00000004         DWord
    wAttributes  . . . . . . . .       00000008         Word
    srWindow . . . . . . . .  . .        0000000A         QWord
    dwMaximumWindowSize  . . . . .       00000012         DWord
(etc.)
```

The list of structures has been shortened to save space. Next, the listing file contains a list of Segments and Groups (of segments):

```
Segments and Groups:

        Name            Size      Length      Align      Combine      Class

FLAT . . . . . .        GROUP

STACK  . . . . .        32 Bit    00001000    Para       Stack        'STACK'

_DATA  . . . . .        32 Bit    00000000    Para       Public       'DATA'

_TEXT  . . . . .        32 Bit    0000001B    Para       Public       'CODE'
```

The AddSub program uses a flat segmentation model, which causes the definition of a group named FLAT. Notice that each segment has a name, size, length, and other attributes. Unless you're doing real-mode programming, you don't have to think about segments. Chapter 16 covers real-mode programming and explains in detail how segments are defined.

Next, the listing file contains a list of procedures, parameters, and local variables. To save space, we will show some of the more interesting entries:

```
Procedures, parameters, and locals:

            Name                Type        Value           Attr

CloseFile  . . . . .    P Near 00000000     FLAT       Length= 00000000
                                                       External STDCALL

CloseHandle  . . . .    P Near 00000000     FLAT       Length= 00000000
                                                       External STDCALL

Clrscr . . . . . .      P Near 00000000     FLAT       Length= 00000000
                                                       External STDCALL
```

```
    CreateFileA  .  .  .  .     P Near 00000000     FLAT        Length= 00000000
                                                                External  STDCALL

    CreateOutputFile . .        P Near 00000000     FLAT        Length= 00000000
                                                                External  STDCALL

    Crlf .  .  .  .  .  .  .     P Near 00000000     FLAT        Length= 00000000
                                                                External  STDCALL

    Delay  .  .  .  .  .  .      P Near 00000000     FLAT        Length= 00000000
                                                                External  STDCALL

    DumpMem  .  .  .  .  .       P Near 00000000     FLAT        Length= 00000000
                                                                External  STDCALL

    DumpRegs .  .  .  .  .       P Near 00000000     FLAT        Length= 00000000
                                                                External  STDCALL

    .

    .

    WriteToFile  .  .  .  .     P Near 00000000     FLAT        Length= 00000000
                                                                External  STDCALL

    WriteWindowsMsg  .  .        P Near 00000000     FLAT        Length= 00000000
                                                                External  STDCALL

    main .  .  .  .  .  .  .     P Near 00000000     _TEXT       Length= 0000001B
                                                                 Public  STDCALL

    printf .  .  .  .  .  .      P Near 00000000     FLAT        Length= 00000000
                                                                   External  C

    scanf  .  .  .  .  .  .      P Near 00000000     FLAT        Length= 00000000
                                                                   External  C

    wsprintfA  .  .  .  .  .     P Near 00000000     FLAT        Length= 00000000
                                                                   External  C
```

The AddSub program defines only a single procedure named main, and it calls a single procedure named DumpRegs. The rest of the procedures are here only because they are defined in the Irvine32.inc file (or one of the files that it includes).

Finally, the listing file contains a long list of symbols, such as constants, labels, and variable names. We show only the first few rows here:

```
    Symbols:

                    Name                  Type        Value        Attr

    @CodeSize  .  .  .  .  .  .  .  .  .  .  .  Number      00000000h
    @DataSize  .  .  .  .  .  .  .  .  .  .  .  Number      00000000h
    @Interface .  .  .  .  .  .  .  .  .  .  .  Number      00000003h
    @Model  .  .  .  .  .  .  .  .  .  .  .  .  Number      00000007h
    (etc.)
```

Symbols beginning with @ are predefined by MASM. Finally, at the end of the file are counts of the numbers of warnings and errors produced by the assembler:

```
0 Warnings
0 Errors
```

3.3.2 Section Review

1. What types of files are produced by the assembler?
2. *(True/False):* The linker extracts assembled procedures from the link library and inserts them in the executable program.
3. *(True/False):* When a program's source code is modified, it must be assembled and linked again before it can be executed with the changes.
4. Which operating system component reads and executes programs?
5. What types of files is produced by the linker?

3.4   Defining Data

3.4.1 Intrinsic Data Types

MASM defines *intrinsic data types,* each of which describes a set of values that can be assigned to variables and expressions of the given type. The essential characteristic of each type is its size in bits: 8, 16, 32, 48, 64, and 80. Other characteristics (such as signed, pointer, or floating-point) are optional and are mainly for the benefit of programmers who want to be reminded about the type of data held in the variable. A variable declared as DWORD, for example, logically holds an unsigned 32-bit integer. In fact, it could hold a signed 32-bit integer, a 32-bit single precision real, or a 32-bit pointer. The assembler is not case sensitive, so a directive such as DWORD can be written as **dword**, **Dword**, **dWord**, and so on.

In Table 3-2, all data types pertain to integers except the last three. In those, the notation IEEE refers to standard real number formats published by the IEEE Computer Society.

3.4.2 Data Definition Statement

A *data definition statement* sets aside storage in memory for a variable, with an optional name. Data definition statements create variables based on intrinsic data types (Table 3-2). A data definition has the following syntax:

```
[name] directive initializer [,initializer]...
```

This is an example of a data definition statement:

```
count DWORD 12345
```

Name   The optional name assigned to a variable must conform to the rules for identifiers (Section 3.1.7).

Directive   The directive in a data definition statement can be BYTE, WORD, DWORD, SBYTE, SWORD, or any of the types listed in Table 3-2. In addition, it can be any of the legacy data definition directives shown in Table 3-3, supported also by the Netwide Assembler (NASM) and Turbo Assembler (TASM).

TABLE 3-2   Intrinsic Data Types.

Type	Usage
BYTE	8-bit unsigned integer. B stands for byte
SBYTE	8-bit signed integer. S stands for signed
WORD	16-bit unsigned integer (can also be a Near pointer in real-address mode)
SWORD	16-bit signed integer
DWORD	32-bit unsigned integer (can also be a Near pointer in protected mode). D stands for double
SDWORD	32-bit signed integer. SD stands for signed double
FWORD	48-bit integer (Far pointer in protected mode)
QWORD	64-bit integer. Q stands for quad
TBYTE	80-bit (10-byte) integer. T stands for Ten-byte
REAL4	32-bit (4-byte) IEEE short real
REAL8	64-bit (8-byte) IEEE long real
REAL10	80-bit (10-byte) IEEE extended real

TABLE 3-3   Legacy Data Directives.

Directive	Usage
DB	8-bit integer
DW	16-bit integer
DD	32-bit integer or real
DQ	64-bit integer or real
DT	define 80-bit (10-byte) integer

Initializer   At least one *initializer* is required in a data definition, even if it is zero. Additional initializers, if any, are separated by commas. For integer data types, *initializer* is an integer constant or expression matching the size of the variable's type, such as BYTE or WORD. If you prefer to leave the variable uninitialized (assigned a random value), the **?** symbol can be used as the initializer. All initializers, regardless of their format, are converted to binary data by the assembler. Initializers such as 00110010b, 32h, and 50d all end up being having the same binary value.

3.4.3   Defining BYTE and SBYTE Data

The BYTE (define byte) and SBYTE (define signed byte) directives allocate storage for one or more unsigned or signed values. Each initializer must fit into 8 bits of storage. For example,

```
value1 BYTE   'A'              ; character constant
value2 BYTE    0               ; smallest unsigned byte
value3 BYTE   255              ; largest unsigned byte
value4 SBYTE -128              ; smallest signed byte
value5 SBYTE +127              ; largest signed byte
```

A question mark (?) initializer leaves the variable uninitialized, implying it will be assigned a value at runtime:

```
value6 BYTE ?
```

The optional name is a label marking the variable's offset from the beginning of its enclosing segment. For example, if **value1** is located at offset 0000 in the data segment and consumes 1 byte of storage, **value2** is automatically located at offset 0001:

```
value1 BYTE 10h
value2 BYTE 20h
```

The DB directive can also define an 8-bit variable, signed or unsigned:

```
val1 DB 255                    ; unsigned byte
val2 DB -128                   ; signed byte
```

Multiple Initializers

If multiple initializers are used in the same data definition, its label refers only to the offset of the first initializer. In the following example, assume **list** is located at offset 0000. If so, the value 10 is at offset 0000, 20 is at offset 0001, 30 is at offset 0002, and 40 is at offset 0003:

```
list BYTE 10,20,30,40
```

Figure 3–2 shows **list** as a sequence of bytes, each with its own offset.

Figure 3–2   Memory Layout of a Byte Sequence.

Offset	Value
0000:	10
0001:	20
0002:	30
0003:	40

Not all data definitions require labels. To continue the array of bytes begun with **list**, for example, we can define additional bytes on the next lines:

```
list BYTE 10,20,30,40
     BYTE 50,60,70,80
     BYTE 81,82,83,84
```

Within a single data definition, its initializers can use different radixes. Character and string constants can be freely mixed. In the following example, **list1** and **list2** have the same contents:

```
list1 BYTE 10, 32, 41h, 00100010b
list2 BYTE 0Ah, 20h, 'A', 22h
```

Defining Strings

To define a string of characters, enclose them in single or double quotation marks. The most common type of string ends with a null byte (containing 0). Called a *null-terminated* string, strings of this type are used in many programming languages:

```
greeting1 BYTE "Good afternoon",0
greeting2 BYTE 'Good night',0
```

Each character uses a byte of storage. Strings are an exception to the rule that byte values must be separated by commas. Without that exception, **greeting1** would have to be defined as

```
greeting1 BYTE 'G','o','o','d'....etc.
```

which would be exceedingly tedious. A string can be divided between multiple lines without having to supply a label for each line:

```
greeting1 BYTE "Welcome to the Encryption Demo program "
   BYTE "created by Kip Irvine.",0dh,0ah
   BYTE "If you wish to modify this program, please "
   BYTE "send me a copy.",0dh,0ah,0
```

The hexadecimal codes 0Dh and 0Ah are alternately called CR/LF (carriage-return line-feed) or *end-of-line characters*. When written to standard output, they move the cursor to the left column of the line following the current line.

The line continuation character (\) concatenates two source code lines into a single statement. It must be the last character on the line. The following statements are equivalent:

```
greeting1 BYTE "Welcome to the Encryption Demo program "
```

and

```
greeting1 \
BYTE "Welcome to the Encryption Demo program "
```

DUP Operator

The *DUP operator* allocates storage for multiple data items, using a constant expression as a counter. It is particularly useful when allocating space for a string or array, and can be used with initialized or uninitialized data:

```
BYTE 20 DUP(0)                ; 20 bytes, all equal to zero
BYTE 20 DUP(?)                ; 20 bytes, uninitialized
BYTE  4 DUP("STACK")          ; 20 bytes: "STACKSTACKSTACKSTACK"
```

3.4.4   Defining WORD and SWORD Data

The WORD (define word) and SWORD (define signed word) directives create storage for one or more 16-bit integers:

```
word1  WORD   65535           ; largest unsigned value
word2  SWORD  -32768          ; smallest signed value
word3  WORD   ?               ; uninitialized, unsigned
```

The legacy DW directive can also be used:

```
val1  DW 65535                ; unsigned
val2  DW -32768               ; signed
```

Array of Words   Create an array of words by listing the elements or using the DUP operator. The following array contains a list of values:

```
myList  WORD 1,2,3,4,5
```

Figure 3–3 shows a diagram of the array in memory, assuming **myList** starts at offset 0000. The addresses increment by 2 because each value occupies 2 bytes.

Figure 3–3   Memory Layout, 16-bit Word Array.

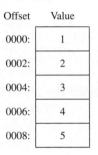

```
Offset    Value
0000:      1
0002:      2
0004:      3
0006:      4
0008:      5
```

The DUP operator provides a convenient way to initialize multiple words:

```
array WORD 5 DUP(?)              ; 5 values, uninitialized
```

3.4.5   Defining DWORD and SDWORD Data

The DWORD (define doubleword) and SDWORD (define signed doubleword) directives allocate storage for one or more 32-bit integers:

```
val1 DWORD   12345678h          ; unsigned
val2 SDWORD −2147483648         ; signed
val3 DWORD   20 DUP(?)          ; unsigned array
```

The legacy DD directive can also be used:

```
val1 DD 12345678h               ; unsigned
val2 DD −2147483648             ; signed
```

The DWORD can be used to declare a variable that contains the 32-bit offset of another variable. Below, **pVal** contains the offset of **val3**:

```
pVal DWORD val3
```

Array of Doublewords   Create an array of doublewords by explicitly initializing each element, or use the DUP operator. Here is an array containing specific unsigned values:

```
myList DWORD 1,2,3,4,5
```

Figure 3–4 shows a diagram of the array in memory, assuming **myList** starts at offset 0000. The offsets increment by 4.

3.4.6   Defining QWORD Data

The QWORD (define quadword) directive allocates storage for 64-bit (8-byte) values:

```
quad1 QWORD 1234567812345678h
```

The legacy DQ directive can also be used:

```
quad1 DQ 1234567812345678h
```

Figure 3–4   Memory Layout, 32-bit Doubleword Array.

Offset	Value
0000:	1
0004:	2
0008:	3
000C:	4
0010:	5

3.4.7   Defining Packed Binary Coded Decimal (TBYTE) Data

Intel stores a packed *binary coded decimal* (BCD) integers in a 10-byte package. Each byte (except the highest) contains two decimal digits. In the lower 9 storage bytes, each half-byte holds a single decimal digit. In the highest byte, the highest bit indicates the number's sign. If the highest byte equals 80h, the number is negative; if the highest byte equals 00h, the number is positive. The integer range is $-999,999,999,999,999,999$ to $+999,999,999,999,999,999$.

Example   The hexadecimal storage bytes for positive and negative decimal 1234 are shown in the following table, from the least significant byte to the most significant byte:

Decimal Value	Storage Bytes
+1234	34 12 00 00 00 00 00 00 00 00
−1234	34 12 00 00 00 00 00 00 00 80

MASM uses the TBYTE directive to declare packed BCD variables. Constant initializers must be in hexadecimal because the assembler does not automatically translate decimal constants to BCD. The following two examples demonstrate both valid and invalid ways of representing decimal -1234:

```
intVal TBYTE 800000000000001234h        ; valid
intVal TBYTE -1234                       ; invalid
```

The reason the second example is invalid is that MASM encodes the constant as a binary integer rather than a packed BCD integer.

If you want to encode a real number as packed BCD, you can first load it onto the floating-point register stack with the FLD instruction and then use the FBSTP instruction to convert it to packed BCD. This instruction rounds the value to the nearest integer:

```
.data
posVal REAL8 1.5
bcdVal TBYTE ?

.code
fld posVal               ; load onto floating-point stack
fbstp bcdVal             ; rounds up to 2 as packed BCD
```

If posVal were equal to 1.5, the resulting BCD value would be 2. In Chapter 7, you will learn how to do arithmetic with packed BCD values.

3.4.8   Defining Real Number Data

REAL4 defines a 4-byte single-precision real variable. REAL8 defines an 8-byte double-precision real, and REAL10 defines a 10-byte double extended-precision real. Each requires one or more real constant initializers:

```
rVal1       REAL4  -1.2
rVal2       REAL8  3.2E-260
rVal3       REAL10 4.6E+4096
ShortArray REAL4  20 DUP(0.0)
```

Table 3-4 describes each of the standard real types in terms of their minimum number of significant digits and approximate range:

Table 3-4   Standard Real Number Types.

Data Type	Significant Digits	Approximate Range
Short real	6	1.18×10^{-38} to 3.40×10^{38}
Long real	15	2.23×10^{-308} to 1.79×10^{308}
Extended-precision real	19	3.37×10^{-4932} to 1.18×10^{4932}

The DD, DQ, and DT directives can define real numbers:

```
rVal1 DD  -1.2                    ; short real
rVal2 DQ  3.2E-260                ; long real
rVal3 DT  4.6E+4096              ; extended-precision real
```

3.4.9   Little Endian Order

x86 processors store and retrieve data from memory using *little endian* order (low to high). The least significant byte is stored at the first memory address allocated for the data. The remaining bytes are stored in the next consecutive memory positions. Consider the doubleword 12345678h. If placed in memory at offset 0000, 78h would be stored in the first byte, 56h would be stored in the second byte, and the remaining bytes would be at offsets 0002 and 0003, as shown in Figure 3–5.

Figure 3–5   Little Endian Representation of 12345678h.

0000:	78
0001:	56
0002:	34
0003:	12

Some other computer systems use *big endian* order (high to low). Figure 3–6 shows an example of 12345678h stored in big endian order at offset 0:

Figure 3–6   Big Endian Representation of 12345678h.

0000:	12
0001:	34
0002:	56
0003:	78

3.4.10   Adding Variables to the AddSub Program

Using the **AddSub** program from Section 3.2, we can add a data segment containing several doubleword variables. The revised program is named **AddSub2**:

```
TITLE Add and Subtract, Version 2          (AddSub2.asm)

; This program adds and subtracts 32-bit unsigned
; integers and stores the sum in a variable.

INCLUDE Irvine32.inc
.data
val1  DWORD 10000h
val2  DWORD 40000h
val3  DWORD 20000h
finalVal DWORD ?

.code
main PROC
    mov   eax,val1              ; start with 10000h
    add   eax,val2              ; add 40000h
    sub   eax,val3              ; subtract 20000h
    mov   finalVal,eax          ; store the result (30000h)
    call  DumpRegs              ; display the registers
    exit
main ENDP
END main
```

How does it work? First, the integer in **val1** is moved to EAX:

```
mov  eax,val1                   ; start with 10000h
```

Next, **val2** is added to EAX:

```
add  eax,val2                   ; add 40000h
```

Next, **val3** is subtracted from EAX:

```
sub  eax,val3                   ; subtract 20000h
```

EAX is copied to **finalVal**:

```
mov  finalVal,eax               ; store the result (30000h)
```

3.4.11   Declaring Uninitialized Data

The .DATA? directive declares uninitialized data. When defining a large block of uninitialized data, the .DATA? directive reduces the size of a compiled program. For example, the following code is declared efficiently:

```
.data
smallArray DWORD 10 DUP(0)        ; 40 bytes
.data?
bigArray DWORD 5000 DUP(?)        ; 20,000 bytes, not initialized
```

The following code, on the other hand, produces a compiled program 20,000 bytes larger:

```
.data
smallArray DWORD 10 DUP(0)        ; 40 bytes
bigArray DWORD 5000 DUP(?)        ; 20,000 bytes
```

Mixing Code and Data   The assembler lets you switch back and forth between code and data in your programs. You might, for example, want to declare a variable used only within a localized area of a program. The following example inserts a variable named **temp** between two code statements:

```
.code
mov eax,ebx
.data
temp DWORD ?
.code
mov temp,eax
  . . .
```

Although the declaration of **temp** appears to interrupt the flow of executable instructions, MASM places **temp** in the data segment, separate from the segment holding compiled code. At the same time, intermixing .code and .data directives can cause a program to become hard to read.

3.4.12   Section Review

1. Create an uninitialized data declaration for a 16-bit signed integer.
2. Create an uninitialized data declaration for an 8-bit unsigned integer.
3. Create an uninitialized data declaration for an 8-bit signed integer.
4. Create an uninitialized data declaration for a 64-bit integer.
5. Which data type can hold a 32-bit signed integer?
6. Declare a 32-bit signed integer variable and initialize it with the smallest possible negative decimal value. (*Hint:* Refer to integer ranges in Chapter 1.)
7. Declare an unsigned 16-bit integer variable named **wArray** that uses three initializers.
8. Declare a string variable containing the name of your favorite color. Initialize it as a null-terminated string.
9. Declare an uninitialized array of 50 unsigned doublewords named **dArray**.
10. Declare a string variable containing the word "TEST" repeated 500 times.
11. Declare an array of 20 unsigned bytes named **bArray** and initialize all elements to zero.

12. Show the order of individual bytes in memory (lowest to highest) for the following double-word variable:

```
val1 DWORD 87654321h
```

3.5 Symbolic Constants

A *symbolic constant* (or *symbol definition*) is created by associating an identifier (a symbol) with an integer expression or some text. Symbols do not reserve storage. They are used only by the assembler when scanning a program, and they cannot change at runtime. The following table summarizes their differences:

	Symbol	Variable
Uses storage?	No	Yes
Value changes at runtime?	No	Yes

We will show how to use the equal-sign directive (=) to create symbols representing integer expressions. We will use the EQU and TEXTEQU directives to create symbols representing arbitrary text.

3.5.1 Equal-Sign Directive

The *equal-sign directive* associates a symbol name with an integer expression (see Section 3.1.2). The syntax is

```
name = expression
```

Ordinarily, expression is a 32-bit integer value. When a program is assembled, all occurrences of *name* are replaced by *expression* during the assembler's preprocessor step. Suppose the following statement occurs near the beginning of a source code file:

```
COUNT = 500
```

Further, suppose the following statement should be found in the file 10 lines later:

```
mov eax, COUNT
```

When the file is assembled, MASM will scan the source file and produce the corresponding code lines:

```
mov eax, 500
```

Why Use Symbols?   We might have skipped the COUNT symbol entirely and simply coded the MOV instruction with the literal 500, but experience has shown that programs are easier to read and maintain if symbols are used. Suppose COUNT were used many times throughout a program. At a later time, we could easily redefine its value:

```
COUNT = 600
```

Assuming that the source file was assembled again, all instances of COUNT would be automatically replaced by the value 600.

Current Location Counter   One of the most important symbols of all, shown as $, is called the *current location counter*. For example, the following declaration declares a variable named **selfPtr** and initializes it with its own location counter:

```
selfPtr DWORD $
```

Keyboard Definitions   Programs often define symbols that identify commonly used numeric keyboard codes. For example, 27 is the ASCII code for the Esc key:

```
Esc_key = 27
```

Later in the same program, a statement is more self-describing if it uses the symbol rather than an immediate value. Use

```
mov  al,Esc_key                       ; good style
```

rather than

```
mov  al,27                            ; poor style
```

Using the DUP Operator   Section 3.4.3 showed how to use the DUP operator to create storage for arrays and strings. The counter used by DUP should be a symbolic constant, to simplify program maintenance. In the next example, if COUNT has been defined, it can be used in the following data definition:

```
array DWORD COUNT DUP(0)
```

Redefinitions   A symbol defined with = can be redefined within the same program. The following example shows how the assembler evaluates COUNT as it changes value:

```
COUNT = 5
mov al,COUNT                          ; AL = 5
COUNT = 10
mov al,COUNT                          ; AL = 10
COUNT = 100
mov al,COUNT                          ; AL = 100
```

The changing value of a symbol such as COUNT has nothing to do with the runtime execution order of statements. Instead, the symbol changes value according to the assembler's sequential processing of the source code during the assembler's preprocessing stage.

3.5.2   Calculating the Sizes of Arrays and Strings

When using an array, we usually like to know its size. The following example uses a constant named **ListSize** to declare the size of **list**:

```
list BYTE 10,20,30,40
ListSize = 4
```

Explicitly stating an array's size can lead to a programming error, particularly if you should later insert or remove array elements. A better way to declare an array size is to let the assembler calculate its value for you. The $ operator (*current location counter*) returns the offset associated with the current program statement. In the following example, **ListSize** is calculated by subtracting the offset of **list** from the current location counter ($):

```
list BYTE 10,20,30,40
ListSize = ($ - list)
```

ListSize must follow immediately after **list**. The following, for example, produces too large a value (24) for **ListSize** because the storage used by **var2** affects the distance between the current location counter and the offset of **list**:

```
list BYTE 10,20,30,40
var2 BYTE 20 DUP(?)
ListSize = ($ - list)
```

Rather than calculating the length of a string manually, let the assembler do it:

```
myString  BYTE "This is a long string, containing"
          BYTE "any number of characters"
myString_len = ($ – myString)
```

Arrays of Words and DoubleWords   When calculating the number of elements in an array containing values other than bytes, you should always divide the total array size (in bytes) by the size of the individual array elements. The following code, for example, divides the address range by 2 because each word in the array occupies 2 bytes (16 bits):

```
list  WORD  1000h,2000h,3000h,4000h
ListSize = ($ – list) / 2
```

Similarly, each element of an array of doublewords is 4 bytes long, so its overall length must be divided by four to produce the number of array elements:

```
list  DWORD  10000000h,20000000h,30000000h,40000000h
ListSize = ($ –list) / 4
```

3.5.3   EQU Directive

The *EQU directive* associates a symbolic name with an integer expression or some arbitrary text. There are three formats:

```
name EQU expression
name EQU symbol
name EQU <text>
```

In the first format, *expression* must be a valid integer expression (see Section 3.1.2). In the second format, *symbol* is an existing symbol name, already defined with = or EQU. In the third format, any text may appear within the brackets <. . .>. When the assembler encounters *name* later in the program, it substitutes the integer value or text for the symbol.

EQU can be useful when defining a value that does not evaluate to an integer. A real number constant, for example, can be defined using EQU:

```
PI EQU <3.1416>
```

Example   The following example associates a symbol with a character string. Then a variable can be created using the symbol:

```
pressKey EQU <"Press any key to continue...",0>
  .
  .
  .
.data
prompt  BYTE    pressKey
```

Example   Suppose we would like to define a symbol that counts the number of cells in a 10-by-10 integer matrix. We will define symbols two different ways, first as an integer expression and second as a text expression. The two symbols are then used in data definitions:

```
matrix1  EQU    10 * 10
matrix2  EQU    <10 * 10>
.data
M1 WORD matrix1
M2 WORD matrix2
```

The assembler produces different data definitions for **M1** and **M2**. The integer expression in **matrix1** is evaluated and assigned to **M1**. On the other hand, the text in **matrix2** is copied directly into the data definition for **M2**:

```
M1 WORD   100
M2 WORD   10 * 10
```

No Redefinition   Unlike the = directive, a symbol defined with EQU cannot be redefined in the same source code file. This restriction prevents an existing symbol from being inadvertently assigned a new value.

3.5.4   TEXTEQU Directive

The *TEXTEQU directive*, similar to EQU, creates what is known as a *text macro*. There are three different formats: the first assigns text, the second assigns the contents of an existing text macro, and the third assigns a constant integer expression:

```
name TEXTEQU <text>
name TEXTEQU textmacro
name TEXTEQU %constExpr
```

For example, the **prompt1** variable uses the **continueMsg** text macro:

```
continueMsg TEXTEQU <"Do you wish to continue (Y/N)?">
.data
prompt1 BYTE continueMsg
```

Text macros can build on each other. In the next example, **count** is set to the value of an integer expression involving **rowSize**. Then the symbol **move** is defined as **mov**. Finally, **setupAL** is built from **move** and **count**:

```
rowSize = 5
count    TEXTEQU    %(rowSize * 2)
move     TEXTEQU    <mov>
setupAL  TEXTEQU    <move al,count>
```

Therefore, the statement

```
setupAL
```

would be assembled as

```
mov al,10
```

A symbol defined by TEXTEQU can be redefined at any time.

3.5.5   Section Review

1. Declare a symbolic constant using the equal-sign directive that contains the ASCII code (08h) for the Backspace key.

2. Declare a symbolic constant named **SecondsInDay** using the equal-sign directive and assign it an arithmetic expression that calculates the number of seconds in a 24-hour period.

3. Write a statement that causes the assembler to calculate the number of bytes in the following array, and assign the value to a symbolic constant named **ArraySize**:

   ```
   myArray WORD 20 DUP(?)
   ```

4. Show how to calculate the number of elements in the following array, and assign the value to a symbolic constant named **ArraySize**:

   ```
   myArray DWORD 30 DUP(?)
   ```

5. Use a TEXTEQU expression to redefine "PROC" as "PROCEDURE."

6. Use TEXTEQU to create a symbol named **Sample** for a string constant, and then use the symbol when defining a string variable named **MyString**.

7. Use TEXTEQU to assign the symbol **SetupESI** to the following line of code:

   ```
   mov esi,OFFSET myArray
   ```

3.6   Real-Address Mode Programming (Optional)

Programs designed for MS-DOS must be 16-bit applications running in real-address mode. Real-address mode applications use 16-bit segments and follow the segmented addressing scheme described in Section 2.3.1. If you're using an x86 processor, you can still use the 32-bit general-purpose registers for data.

3.6.1   Basic Changes

There are a few changes you must make to the 32-bit programs presented in this chapter to transform them into real-address mode programs:

- The INCLUDE directive references a different library:

  ```
  INCLUDE Irvine16.inc
  ```

- Two additional instructions are inserted at the beginning of the startup procedure (main). They initialize the DS register to the starting location of the data segment, identified by the predefined MASM constant **@data**:

  ```
  mov ax,@data
  mov ds,ax
  ```

- See the book's Web site (www.asmirvine.com) for instructions on assembling 16-bit programs.

- Offsets (addresses) of data and code labels are 16 bits.

You cannot move @data directly into DS and ES because the MOV instruction does not permit a constant to be moved directly to a segment register.

The AddSub2 Program

Here is a listing of the *AddSub2.asm* program, revised to run in real-address mode. New lines are marked by comments:

```
TITLE Add and Subtract, Version 2    (AddSub2.asm)

; This program adds and subtracts 32-bit integers
; and stores the sum in a variable.
; Target: real-address mode.

INCLUDE Irvine16.inc              ; changed *
.data
val1      DWORD 10000h
val2      DWORD 40000h
val3      DWORD 20000h
finalVal DWORD ?

.code
main PROC
      mov   ax,@data              ; new *
      mov   ds,ax                 ; new *

      mov   eax,val1              ; get first value
      add   eax,val2              ; add second value
      sub   eax,val3              ; subtract third value
      mov   finalVal,eax          ; store the result
      call  DumpRegs              ; display registers

      exit
main ENDP
END main
```

3.7 Chapter Summary

An integer expression is a mathematical expression involving integer constants, symbolic constants, and arithmetic operators. *Precedence* refers to the implied order of operations when an expression contains two or more operators.

A *character constant* is a single character enclosed in quotes. The assembler converts a character to a byte containing the character's binary ASCII code. A *string constant* is a sequence of characters enclosed in quotes, optionally ending with a null byte.

Assembly language has a set of *reserved words* with special meanings that may only be used in the correct context. An *identifier* is a programmer-chosen name identifying a variable, a symbolic constant, a procedure, or a code label. Identifiers cannot be reserved words.

A *directive* is a command embedded in the source code and interpreted by the assembler. An *instruction* is a source code statement that is executed by the processor at runtime. An *instruction mnemonic* is a short keyword that identifies the operation carried out by an instruction. A *label* is an identifier that acts as a place marker for instructions or data.

Operands are values passed to instructions. An assembly language instruction can have between zero and three operands, each of which can be a register, memory operand, constant expression, or input-output port number.

Programs contain *logical segments* named code, data, and stack. The code segment contains executable instructions. The stack segment holds procedure parameters, local variables, and return addresses. The data segment holds variables.

A *source file* contains assembly language statements. A *listing file* contains a copy of the program's source code, suitable for printing, with line numbers, offset addresses, translated machine code, and a symbol table. A source file is created with a text editor. An *assembler* is a program that reads the source file, producing both object and listing files. The *linker* is a program that reads one or more object files and produces an executable file. The latter is executed by the operating system loader.

MASM recognizes intrinsic data types, each of which describes a set of values that can be assigned to variables and expressions of the given type:

• BYTE and SBYTE define 8-bit variables.
• WORD and SWORD define 16-bit variables.
• DWORD and SDWORD define 32-bit variables.
• QWORD and TBYTE define 8-byte and 10-byte variables, respectively.
• REAL4, REAL8, and REAL10 define 4-byte, 8-byte, and 10-byte real number variables, respectively.

A data definition statement sets aside storage in memory for a variable, and may optionally assign it a name. If multiple initializers are used in the same data definition, its label refers only to the offset of the first initializer. To create a string data definition, enclose a sequence of characters in quotes. The DUP operator generates a repeated storage allocation, using a constant expression as a counter. The current location counter operator ($) is used in address-calculation expressions.

x86 processors store and retrieve data from memory using *little endian* order: The least significant byte of a variable is stored at its starting (lowest) address value.

A *symbolic constant* (or symbol definition) associates an identifier with an integer or text expression. Three directives create symbolic constants:

• The equal-sign directive (=) associates a symbol name with an integer expression.
• The EQU and TEXTEQU directives associate a symbolic name with an integer expression or some arbitrary text.

You can convert almost any program from 32-bit protected mode to 16-bit real-address mode. This book is supplied with two link libraries containing the same procedure names for both types of programs.

3.8   Programming Exercises

The following exercises can be done in protected mode or real-address mode.

★ **1.   Subtracting Three Integers**

Using the **AddSub** program from Section 3.2 as a reference, write a program that subtracts three integers using only 16-bit registers. Insert a **call DumpRegs** statement to display the register values.

★ **2.   Data Definitions**

Write a program that contains a definition of each data type listed in Table 3-2 in Section 3.4. Initialize each variable to a value that is consistent with its data type.

★ **3.   Symbolic Integer Constants**

Write a program that defines symbolic constants for all of the days of the week. Create an array variable that uses the symbols as initializers.

★ **4.   Symbolic Text Constants**

Write a program that defines symbolic names for several string literals (characters between quotes). Use each symbolic name in a variable definition.

4

Data Transfers, Addressing, and Arithmetic

4.1 Data Transfer Instructions
    4.1.1 Introduction
    4.1.2 Operand Types
    4.1.3 Direct Memory Operands
    4.1.4 MOV Instruction
    4.1.5 Zero/Sign Extension of Integers
    4.1.6 LAHF and SAHF Instructions
    4.1.7 XCHG Instruction
    4.1.8 Direct-Offset Operands
    4.1.9 Example Program (Moves)
    4.1.10 Section Review

4.2 Addition and Subtraction
    4.2.1 INC and DEC Instructions
    4.2.2 ADD Instruction
    4.2.3 SUB Instruction
    4.2.4 NEG Instruction
    4.2.5 Implementing Arithmetic Expressions
    4.2.6 Flags Affected by Addition and Subtraction
    4.2.7 Example Program (AddSub3)
    4.2.8 Section Review

4.3 Data-Related Operators and Directives
    4.3.1 OFFSET Operator

4.3.2 ALIGN Directive
4.3.3 PTR Operator
4.3.4 TYPE Operator
4.3.5 LENGTHOF Operator
4.3.6 SIZEOF Operator
4.3.7 LABEL Directive
4.3.8 Section Review

4.4 Indirect Addressing
    4.4.1 Indirect Operands
    4.4.2 Arrays
    4.4.3 Indexed Operands
    4.4.4 Pointers
    4.4.5 Section Review

4.5 JMP and LOOP Instructions
    4.5.1 JMP Instruction
    4.5.2 LOOP Instruction
    4.5.3 Summing an Integer Array
    4.5.4 Copying a String
    4.5.5 Section Review

4.6 Chapter Summary

4.7 Programming Exercises

4.1 Data Transfer Instructions

4.1.1 Introduction

This chapter introduces a great many details, highlighting a fundamental difference between assembly language and high-level languages: In assembly language, one must be aware of data storage and machine-specific details. High-level language compilers such as C++ and Java perform strict type checking on variables and assignment statements. Compilers do this to help programmers avoid logic errors relating to mismatched data. Assemblers, on the other hand, provide enormous freedom when declaring and moving data. They perform little error checking, and supply a wide variety of operators and address expressions. What price must you pay for this freedom? You must master a significant number of details before writing meaningful programs.

If you take the time to thoroughly learn the material presented in this chapter, the rest of the reading in this book will be easier to understand. As the example programs become more complicated, you must rely on mastery of fundamental tools presented in this chapter.

4.1.2   Operand Types

Chapter 3 introduced x86 instruction formats:

```
[label:] mnemonic [operands][ ; comment ]
```

Because the number of operands may vary, we can further subdivide the formats to have zero, one, two, or three operands. Here, we omit the label and comment fields for clarity:

```
mnemonic
mnemonic [destination]
mnemonic [destination],[source]
mnemonic [destination],[source-1],[source-2]
```

To give added flexibility to the instruction set, x86 assembly language uses different types of instruction operands. The following are the easiest to use:

• Immediate—uses a numeric literal expression
• Register—uses a named register in the CPU
• Memory—references a memory location

Table 4-1 lists a simple notation for operands freely adapted from the Intel manuals. We will use it from this point on to describe the syntax of individual instructions.

Table 4-1   Instruction Operand Notation.

Operand	Description
reg8	8-bit general-purpose register: AH, AL, BH, BL, CH, CL, DH, DL
reg16	16-bit general-purpose register: AX, BX, CX, DX, SI, DI, SP, BP
reg32	32-bit general-purpose register: EAX, EBX, ECX, EDX, ESI, EDI, ESP, EBP
reg	Any general-purpose register
sreg	16-bit segment register: CS, DS, SS, ES, FS, GS
imm	8-, 16-, or 32-bit immediate value
imm8	8-bit immediate byte value
imm16	16-bit immediate word value
imm32	32-bit immediate doubleword value
reg/mem8	8-bit operand, which can be an 8-bit general register or memory byte
reg/mem16	16-bit operand, which can be a 16-bit general register or memory word
reg/mem32	32-bit operand, which can be a 32-bit general register or memory doubleword
mem	An 8-, 16-, or 32-bit memory operand

4.1.3 Direct Memory Operands

Section 3.4 explained that variable names are references to offsets within the data segment. For example, the following declaration indicates that a byte containing the number 10h has been allocated in the data segment:

```
.data
var1 BYTE 10h
```

Program code contains instructions that dereference (look up) memory operands using their addresses. Suppose **var1** were located at offset 10400h. An assembly language instruction moving it to the AL register would be

```
mov  AL,var1
```

Microsoft Macro Assembler (MASM) would assemble it into the following machine instruction:

```
A0 00010400
```

The first byte in the machine instruction is the opcode. The remaining part is the 32-bit hexadecimal address of **var1**. Although it might be possible to write programs using only numeric addresses, symbolic names such as **var1** make it easier to reference memory.

Alternative Notation. Some programmers prefer to use the following notation with direct operands because the brackets imply a dereference operation:

```
mov  al,[var1]
```

MASM permits this notation, so you can use it in your own programs if you want. Because so many programs (including those from Microsoft) are printed without the brackets, we will only use them in this book when an arithmetic expression is involved:

```
mov  al,[var1 + 5]
```

(This is called a direct-offset operand, a subject discussed at length in Section 4.1.8.)

4.1.4 MOV Instruction

The MOV instruction copies data from a source operand to a destination operand. Known as a *data transfer* instruction, it is used in virtually every program. Its basic format shows that the first operand is the destination and the second operand is the source:

```
MOV destination,source
```

The destination operand's contents change, but the source operand is unchanged. The right to left movement of data is similar to the assignment statement in C++ or Java:

```
dest = source;
```

(In nearly all assembly language instructions, the left-hand operand is the destination and the right-hand operand is the source.)

MOV is very flexible in its use of operands, as long as the following rules are observed:

• Both operands must be the same size.
• Both operands cannot be memory operands.
• CS, EIP, and IP cannot be destination operands.
• An immediate value cannot be moved to a segment register.

Here is a list of the general variants of MOV, excluding segment registers:

```
MOV  reg,reg
MOV  mem,reg
MOV  reg,mem
MOV  mem,imm
MOV  reg,imm
```

Segment registers should not be directly modified by programs running in protected mode. The following options are available when running in real mode, with the exception that CS cannot be a target operand:

```
MOV  reg/mem16,sreg
MOV  sreg,reg/mem16
```

Memory to Memory   A single MOV instruction cannot be used to move data directly from one memory location to another. Instead, you must move the source operand's value to a register before moving its value to a memory operand:

```
.data
var1 WORD ?
var2 WORD ?
.code
mov  ax,var1
mov  var2,ax
```

You must consider the minimum number of bytes required by an integer constant when copying it to a variable or register. For unsigned integer constants, refer to Table 1-4 in Chapter 1. For signed integer constants, refer to Table 1-7.

Overlapping Values

The following code example shows how the same 32-bit register can be modified using differently sized data. When **oneWord** is moved to AX, it overwrites the existing value of AL. When **oneDword** is moved to EAX, it overwrites AX. Finally, when 0 is moved to AX, it overwrites the lower half of EAX.

```
.data
oneByte BYTE 78h
oneWord WORD 1234h
oneDword DWORD 12345678h

.code
    mov  eax,0           ; EAX = 00000000h
    mov  al,oneByte      ; EAX = 00000078h
    mov  ax,oneWord      ; EAX = 00001234h
    mov  eax,oneDword    ; EAX = 12345678h
    mov  ax,0            ; EAX = 12340000h
```

4.1.5 Zero/Sign Extension of Integers

Copying Smaller Values to Larger Ones

Although MOV cannot directly copy data from a smaller operand to a larger one, programmers can create workarounds. Suppose **count** (unsigned, 16 bits) must be moved to ECX (32 bits). We can set ECX to zero and move **count** to CX:

```
.data
count WORD 1
.code
mov ecx,0
mov cx,count
```

What happens if we try the same approach with a signed integer equal to −16?

```
.data
signedVal SWORD -16                 ; FFF0h (-16)
.code
mov ecx,0
mov cx,signedVal                    ; ECX = 0000FFF0h (+65,520)
```

The value in ECX (+65,520) is completely different from −16. On the other hand, if we had filled ECX first with FFFFFFFFh and then copied **signedVal** to CX, the final value would have been correct:

```
mov ecx,0FFFFFFFFh
mov cx,signedVal                    ; ECX = FFFFFFF0h (-16)
```

The effective result of this example was to use the highest bit of the source operand (1) to fill the upper 16 bits of the destination operand, ECX. This technique is called *sign extension*. Of course, we cannot always assume that the highest bit of the source is a 1. Fortunately, the engineers at Intel anticipated this problem when designing the Intel386 processor and introduced the MOVZX and MOVSX instructions to deal with both unsigned and signed integers.

MOVZX Instruction

The MOVZX instruction (*move with zero-extend*) copies the contents of a source operand into a destination operand and zero-extends the value to 16 or 32 bits. This instruction is only used with unsigned integers. There are three variants:

```
MOVZX   reg32,reg/mem8
MOVZX   reg32,reg/mem16
MOVZX   reg16,reg/mem8
```

(Operand notation was explained in Table 4-1.) In each of the three variants, the first operand (a register) is the destination and the second is the source. The following example zero-extends binary 10001111 into AX:

```
.data
byteVal BYTE 10001111b
.code
movzx  ax,byteVal                   ; AX = 0000000010001111b
```

Figure 4–1 shows how the source operand is zero-extended into the 16-bit destination.

FIGURE 4–1   Using MOVZX to copy a byte into a 16-bit destination.

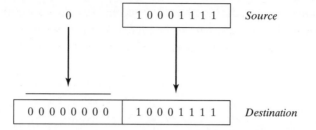

The following examples use registers for all operands, showing all the size variations:

```
mov     bx,0A69Bh
movzx   eax,bx                        ; EAX = 0000A69Bh
movzx   edx,bl                        ; EDX = 0000009Bh
movzx   cx,bl                         ; CX  = 009Bh
```

The following examples use memory operands for the source and produce the same results:

```
.data
byte1   BYTE 9Bh
word1   WORD 0A69Bh
.code
movzx   eax,word1                     ; EAX = 0000A69Bh
movzx   edx,byte1                     ; EDX = 0000009Bh
movzx   cx,byte1                      ; CX  = 009Bh
```

> If you want to run and test examples from this chapter in real-address mode, use INCLUDE with
> Irvine16.lib and insert the following lines at the beginning of the main procedure:
>
> ```
> mov ax,@data
> mov ds,ax
> ```

MOVSX Instruction

The MOVSX instruction (move with sign-extend) copies the contents of a source operand into a destination operand and sign-extends the value to 16 or 32 bits. This instruction is only used with signed integers. There are three variants:

```
MOVSX   reg32,reg/mem8
MOVSX   reg32,reg/mem16
MOVSX   reg16,reg/mem8
```

An operand is sign-extended by taking the smaller operand's highest bit and repeating (replicating) the bit throughout the extended bits in the destination operand. The following example sign-extends binary 10001111b into AX:

```
.data
byteVal BYTE 10001111b
.code
movsx   ax,byteVal                    ; AX = 1111111110001111b
```

The lowest 8 bits are copied as in Figure 4–2. The highest bit of the source is copied into each of the upper 8 bit positions of the destination.

A hexadecimal constant has its highest bit set if its most significant hexadecimal digit is greater than 7. In the following example, the hexadecimal value moved to BX is A69B, so the leading "A" digit tells us that the highest bit is set. (The leading zero appearing before A69B is just a notational convenience so the assembler does not mistake the constant for the name of an identifier.)

```
mov     bx,0A69Bh
movsx   eax,bx                     ; EAX = FFFFA69Bh
movsx   edx,bl                     ; EDX = FFFFFF9Bh
movsx   cx,bl                      ; CX  = FF9Bh
```

Figure 4–2   Using MOVSX to copy a byte into a 16-bit destination.

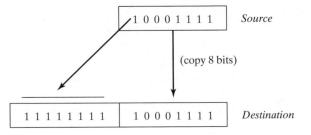

4.1.6   LAHF and SAHF Instructions

The LAHF (load status flags into AH) instruction copies the low byte of the EFLAGS register into AH. The following flags are copied: Sign, Zero, Auxiliary Carry, Parity, and Carry. Using this instruction, you can easily save a copy of the flags in a variable for safekeeping:

```
.data
saveflags BYTE ?
.code
lahf                      ; load flags into AH
mov saveflags,ah          ; save them in a variable
```

The SAHF (store AH into status flags) instruction copies AH into the low byte of the EFLAGS register. For example, you can retrieve the values of flags saved earlier in a variable:

```
mov  ah,saveflags         ; load saved flags into AH
sahf                      ; copy into Flags register
```

4.1.7   XCHG Instruction

The XCHG (exchange data) instruction exchanges the contents of two operands. There are three variants:

```
XCHG    reg,reg
XCHG    reg,mem
XCHG    mem,reg
```

The rules for operands in the XCHG instruction are the same as those for the MOV instruction (Section 4.1.4), except that XCHG does not accept immediate operands. In array sorting applications, XCHG provides a simple way to exchange two array elements. Here are a few examples using XCHG:

```
xchg    ax,bx                   ; exchange 16-bit regs
xchg    ah,al                   ; exchange 8-bit regs
xchg    var1,bx                 ; exchange 16-bit mem op with BX
xchg    eax,ebx                 ; exchange 32-bit regs
```

To exchange two memory operands, use a register as a temporary container and combine MOV with XCHG:

```
mov     ax,val1
xchg    ax,val2
mov     val1,ax
```

4.1.8   Direct-Offset Operands

You can add a displacement to the name of a variable, creating a direct-offset operand. This lets you access memory locations that may not have explicit labels. Let's begin with an array of bytes named **arrayB**:

```
arrayB  BYTE 10h,20h,30h,40h,50h
```

If we use MOV with **arrayB** as the source operand, we automatically move the first byte in the array:

```
mov  al,arrayB                  ; AL = 10h
```

We can access the second byte in the array by adding 1 to the offset of **arrayB**:

```
mov  al,[arrayB+1]              ; AL = 20h
```

The third byte is accessed by adding 2:

```
mov  al,[arrayB+2]              ; AL = 30h
```

An expression such as **arrayB+1** produces what is called an *effective address* by adding a constant to the variable's offset. Surrounding an effective address with brackets indicates the expression is dereferenced to obtain the contents of memory at the address. The brackets are not required by MASM, so the following statements are equivalent:

```
mov  al,[arrayB+1]
mov  al,arrayB+1
```

Range Checking   MASM has no built-in range checking for effective addresses. If we execute the following statement, the assembler just retrieves a byte of memory outside the array. The result is a sneaky logic bug, so be extra careful when checking array references:

```
mov  al,[arrayB+20]            ; AL = ??
```

Word and Doubleword Arrays   In an array of 16-bit words, the offset of each array element is 2 bytes beyond the previous one. That is why we add 2 to **ArrayW** in the next example to reach the second element:

```
.data
arrayW WORD 100h,200h,300h
```

```
.code
mov  ax,arrayW                          ; AX = 100h
mov  ax,[arrayW+2]                       ; AX = 200h
```

Similarly, the second element in a doubleword array is 4 bytes beyond the first one:

```
.data
arrayD DWORD 10000h,20000h
.code
mov  eax,arrayD                         ; EAX = 10000h
mov  eax,[arrayD+4]                      ; EAX = 20000h
```

4.1.9 Example Program (Moves)

The following program demonstrates most of the data transfer examples from Section 4.1:

```
TITLE Data Transfer Examples            (Moves.asm)

INCLUDE Irvine32.inc
.data
val1 WORD 1000h
val2 WORD 2000h
arrayB BYTE 10h,20h,30h,40h,50h
arrayW WORD 100h,200h,300h
arrayD DWORD 10000h,20000h

.code
main PROC

;   Demonstrating MOVZX instruction:
    mov   bx,0A69Bh
    movzx eax,bx                        ; EAX = 0000A69Bh
    movzx edx,bl                        ; EDX = 0000009Bh
    movzx cx,bl                         ; CX  = 009Bh

;   Demonstrating MOVSX instruction:
    mov   bx,0A69Bh
    movsx eax,bx                        ; EAX = FFFFA69Bh
    movsx edx,bl                        ; EDX = FFFFFF9Bh
    mov   bl,7Bh
    movsx cx,bl                         ; CX  = 007Bh

;   Memory-to-memory exchange:
    mov   ax,val1                       ; AX = 1000h
    xchg  ax,val2                       ; AX=2000h, val2=1000h
    mov   val1,ax                       ; val1 = 2000h

;   Direct-Offset Addressing (byte array):
    mov   al,arrayB                     ; AL = 10h
    mov   al,[arrayB+1]                 ; AL = 20h
    mov   al,[arrayB+2]                 ; AL = 30h

;   Direct-Offset Addressing (word array):
    mov   ax,arrayW                     ; AX = 100h
    mov   ax,[arrayW+2]                 ; AX = 200h
```

```
;   Direct-Offset Addressing (doubleword array):
        mov   eax,arrayD                    ; EAX = 10000h
        mov   eax,[arrayD+4]                ; EAX = 20000h
        mov   eax,[arrayD+4]                ; EAX = 20000h

        exit
main ENDP
END main
```

This program generates no screen output, but you can (and should) run it using a debugger. Please refer to tutorials on the book's Web site showing how to use the Microsoft Visual Studio debugger. Section 5.3 explains how to display integers using a function library supplied with this book.

4.1.10 Section Review

1. What are the three basic types of operands?
2. *(True/False):* The destination operand of a MOV instruction cannot be a segment register.
3. *(True/False):* In a MOV instruction, the second operand is known as the *destination* operand.
4. *(True/False):* The EIP register cannot be the destination operand of a MOV instruction.
5. In the operand notation used by Intel, what does *reg/mem32* indicate?
6. In the operand notation used by Intel, what does *imm16* indicate?

Use the following variable definitions for the remaining questions in this section:

```
.data
var1 SBYTE -4,-2,3,1
var2 WORD 1000h,2000h,3000h,4000h
var3 SWORD -16,-42
var4 DWORD 1,2,3,4,5
```

7. For each of the following statements, state whether or not the instruction is valid:

```
a. mov   ax,var1
b. mov   ax,var2
c. mov   eax,var3
d. mov   var2,var3
e. movzx ax,var2
f. movzx var2,al
g. mov   ds,ax
h. mov   ds,1000h
```

8. What will be the hexadecimal value of the destination operand after each of the following instructions execute in sequence?

```
mov  al,var1                   ; a.
mov  ah,[var1+3]               ; b.
```

9. What will be the value of the destination operand after each of the following instructions execute in sequence?

```
mov  ax,var2                   ; a.
mov  ax,[var2+4]               ; b.
mov  ax,var3                   ; c.
mov  ax,[var3-2]               ; d.
```

10. What will be the value of the destination operand after each of the following instructions execute in sequence?

```
mov    edx,var4              ; a.
movzx  edx,var2              ; b.
mov    edx,[var4+4]          ; c.
movsx  edx,var1              ; d.
```

4.2 Addition and Subtraction

Arithmetic is a fairly big subject in assembly language, so we will approach it in steps. For the moment, we will focus on integer addition and subtraction. Chapter 7 introduces integer multiplication and division. Chapter 12 shows how to do floating-point arithmetic with a completely different instruction set. Let's begin with INC (increment), DEC (decrement), ADD (add), SUB (subtract), and NEG (negate). The question of how status flags (Carry, Sign, Zero, etc.) are affected by these instructions is important, and will be discussed in Section 4.2.6.

4.2.1 INC and DEC Instructions

The INC (increment) and DEC (decrement) instructions, respectively, add 1 and subtract 1 from a single operand. The syntax is

```
INC reg/mem
DEC reg/mem
```

Following are some examples:

```
.data
myWord WORD 1000h
.code
inc  myWord                  ; myWord = 1001h
mov  bx,myWord
dec  bx                      ; BX = 1000h
```

The Overflow, Sign, Zero, Auxiliary Carry, and Parity flags are changed according to the value of the destination operand. The INC and DEC instructions do not affect the Carry flag (which is something of a surprise).

4.2.2 ADD Instruction

The ADD instruction adds a source operand to a destination operand of the same size. The syntax is

```
ADD dest,source
```

Source is unchanged by the operation, and the sum is stored in the destination operand. The set of possible operands is the same as for the MOV instruction (Section 4.1.4). Here is a short code example that adds two 32-bit integers:

```
.data
var1 DWORD 10000h
var2 DWORD 20000h
.code
mov  eax,var1                ; EAX = 10000h
add  eax,var2                ; EAX = 30000h
```

Flags   The Carry, Zero, Sign, Overflow, Auxiliary Carry, and Parity flags are changed according to the value that is placed in the destination operand.

4.2.3   SUB Instruction

The SUB instruction subtracts a source operand from a destination operand. The set of possible operands is the same as for the ADD and MOV instructions (see Section 4.1.4). The syntax is

```
SUB dest,source
```

Here is a short code example that subtracts two 32-bit integers:

```
.data
var1 DWORD 30000h
var2 DWORD 10000h
.code
mov eax,var1                     ; EAX = 30000h
sub eax,var2                     ; EAX = 20000h
```

Internally, the CPU can implement subtraction as a combination of negation and addition. Figure 4–3 shows how the expression $4 - 1$ can be rewritten as $4 + (-1)$. Two's-complement notation is used for negative numbers, so -1 is represented by 11111111.

Figure 4–3   Adding the Value -1 to 4.

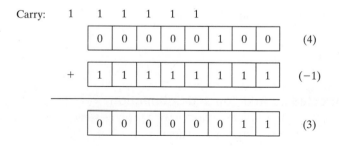

Flags   The Carry, Zero, Sign, Overflow, Auxiliary Carry, and Parity flags are changed according to the value that is placed in the destination operand.

4.2.4   NEG Instruction

The NEG (negate) instruction reverses the sign of a number by converting the number to its two's complement. The following operands are permitted:

```
NEG reg
NEG mem
```

(Recall that the two's complement of a number can be found by reversing all the bits in the destination operand and adding 1.)

Flags   The Carry, Zero, Sign, Overflow, Auxiliary Carry, and Parity flags are changed according to the value that is placed in the destination operand.

4.2.5 Implementing Arithmetic Expressions

Armed with the ADD, SUB, and NEG instructions, you have the means to implement arithmetic expressions involving addition, subtraction, and negation in assembly language. In other words, one can simulate what a C++ compiler might do when reading an expression such as

```
Rval = -Xval + (Yval - Zval);
```

The following signed 32-bit variables will be used:

```
Rval SDWORD ?
Xval SDWORD 26
Yval SDWORD 30
Zval SDWORD 40
```

When translating an expression, evaluate each term separately and combine the terms at the end. First, we negate a copy of **Xval**:

```
; first term: -Xval
mov  eax,Xval
neg  eax                        ; EAX = -26
```

Then **Yval** is copied to a register and **Zval** is subtracted:

```
; second term: (Yval - Zval)
mov  ebx,Yval
sub  ebx,Zval                   ; EBX = -10
```

Finally, the two terms (in EAX and EBX) are added:

```
; add the terms and store:
add  eax,ebx
mov  Rval,eax                   ; -36
```

4.2.6 Flags Affected by Addition and Subtraction

When executing arithmetic instructions, we often want to know something about the result. Is it negative, positive, or zero? Is it too large or too small to fit into the destination operand? Answers to such questions can help us detect calculation errors that might otherwise cause erratic program behavior. We use the values of CPU status flags to check the outcome of arithmetic operations. We also use status flag values to activate conditional branching instructions, the basic tools of program logic. Here's a quick overview of the status flags.

- The Carry flag indicates unsigned integer overflow. For example, if an instruction has an 8-bit destination operand but the instruction generates a result larger than 11111111 binary, the Carry flag is set.
- The Overflow flag indicates signed integer overflow. For example, if an instruction has a 16-bit destination operand but it generates a negative result smaller than −32,768 decimal, the Overflow flag is set.
- The Zero flag indicates that an operation produced zero. For example, if an operand is subtracted from another of equal value, the Zero flag is set.
- The Sign flag indicates that an operation produced a negative result. If the most significant bit (MSB) of the destination operand is set, the Sign flag is set.

- The Parity flag indicates whether or not an even number of 1 bits occurs in the least significant byte of the destination operand, immediately after an arithmetic or boolean instruction has executed.
- The Auxiliary Carry flag is set when a 1 bit carries out of position 3 in the least significant byte of the destination operand.

To display CPU status flag values in programs, call **DumpRegs** from the book's link library. Following is an example:

```
EAX=76D448FF  EBX=7FFDE000  ECX=00000000  EDX=00401005
ESI=00000000  EDI=00000000  EBP=0012FF94  ESP=0012FF8C
EIP=0040101A  EFL=00000246  CF=0  SF=0  ZF=1  OF=0  AF=0  PF=1
```

Unsigned Operations: Zero, Carry, and Auxiliary Carry

The Zero flag is set when the result of an arithmetic operation is zero. The following examples show the state of the destination register and Zero flag after executing the SUB, INC, and DEC instructions:

```
mov   ecx,1
sub   ecx,1                  ; ECX = 0, ZF = 1
mov   eax,0FFFFFFFFh
inc   eax                    ; EAX = 0, ZF = 1
inc   eax                    ; EAX = 1, ZF = 0
dec   eax                    ; EAX = 0, ZF = 1
```

Addition and the Carry Flag   The Carry flag's operation is easiest to explain if we consider addition and subtraction separately. When adding two unsigned integers, the Carry flag is a copy of the carry out of the MSB of the destination operand. Intuitively, we can say CF = 1 when the sum exceeds the storage size of its destination operand. In the next example, ADD sets the Carry flag because the sum (100h) is too large for AL:

```
mov   al,0FFh
add   al,1                   ; AL = 00, CF = 1
```

Figure 4-4 shows what happens at the bit level when 1 is added to 0FFh. The carry out of the highest bit position of AL is copied into the Carry flag.

FIGURE 4-4   Adding 1 to 0FFh Sets the Carry Flag.

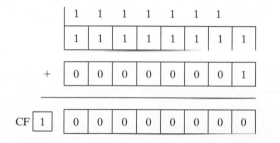

On the other hand, if 1 is added to 00FFh in AX, the sum easily fits into 16 bits and the Carry flag is clear:

```
mov  ax,00FFh
add  ax,1                          ; AX = 0100h, CF = 0
```

But adding 1 to FFFFh in the AX register generates a Carry out of the high bit position of AX:

```
mov  ax,0FFFFh
add  ax,1                          ; AX = 0000, CF = 1
```

Subtraction and the Carry Flag A subtract operation sets the Carry flag when a larger unsigned integer is subtracted from a smaller one. It's easiest to consider subtraction's effect on the Carry flag from a hardware point of view. Let's assume, for a moment, that the CPU can negate a positive unsigned integer by forming its two's complement:

1. The source operand is negated and added to the destination.
2. The carry out of MSB is inverted and copied to the Carry flag.

Figure 4–5 shows what happens when we subtract 2 from 1, using 8-bit operands. First, we negate 2 and then perform addition. The sum (FF hexadecimal) is not valid. The carry out of bit 7 is inverted and placed in the Carry flag, so CF = 1. Here is the corresponding assembly code:

```
mov  al,1
sub  al,2                          ; AL = FFh, CF = 1
```

The INC and DEC instructions do not affect the Carry flag. Applying the NEG instruction to a nonzero operand always sets the Carry flag.

FIGURE 4–5   Subtracting 2 from 1 Sets the Carry Flag.

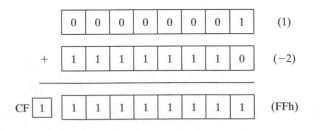

Auxiliary Carry The Auxiliary Carry (AC) flag indicates a carry or borrow out of bit 3 in the destination operand. It is primarily used in binary coded decimal (BCD) arithmetic (Section 7.6), but can be used in other contexts. Suppose we add 1 to 0Fh. The sum (10h) contains a 1 in bit position 4 that was carried out of bit position 3:

```
mov  al,0Fh
add  al,1                          ; AC = 1
```

Here is the arithmetic:

```
  0 0 0 0 1 1 1 1
+ 0 0 0 0 0 0 0 1
------------------
  0 0 0 1 0 0 0 0
```

Parity   The Parity flag (PF) is set when the least significant byte of the destination has an even number of 1 bits. The following ADD and SUB instructions alter the parity of AL:

```
mov  al,10001100b
add  al,00000010b          ; AL = 10001110, PF = 1
sub  al,10000000b          ; AL = 00001110, PF = 0
```

After the ADD, AL contains binary 10001110 (four 0 bits and four 1 bits), and PF = 1. After the SUB, AL contains an odd number of 1 bits, so PF = 0.

Signed Operations: Sign and Overflow Flags

Sign Flag   The Sign flag is set when the result of a signed arithmetic operation is negative. The next example subtracts a larger integer (5) from a smaller one (4):

```
mov  eax,4
sub  eax,5                 ; EAX = -1, SF = 1
```

From a mechanical point of view, the Sign flag is a copy of the destination operand's high bit. The next example shows the hexadecimal values of BL when a negative result is generated:

```
mov  bl,1                  ; BL = 01h
sub  bl,2                  ; BL = FFh (-1), SF = 1
```

Overflow Flag   The Overflow flag is set when the result of a signed arithmetic operation overflows or underflows the destination operand. For example, from Chapter 1 we know that the largest possible integer signed byte value is +127; adding 1 to it causes overflow:

```
mov  al,+127
add  al,1                  ; OF = 1
```

Similarly, the smallest possible negative integer byte value is −128. Subtracting 1 from it causes underflow. The destination operand value does not hold a valid arithmetic result, and the Overflow flag is set:

```
mov  al,-128
sub  al,1                  ; OF = 1
```

The Addition Test   There is a very easy way to tell whether signed overflow has occurred when adding two operands. Overflow occurs when

- two positive operands generate a negative sum,
- two negative operands generate a positive sum.

Overflow never occurs when the signs of two addition operands are different.

How the Hardware Detects Overflow   The CPU uses an interesting mechanism to determine the state of the Overflow flag after an addition or subtraction operation. The Carry flag is exclusive ORed with the high bit of the result. The resulting value is placed in the Overflow flag.

In Figure 4–6, we show that adding the 8-bit binary integers 10000000 and 11111110 produces CF = 1 and a resulting MSB = 0. In other words, 1 XOR 0 produces OF = 1.

FIGURE 4–6   Demonstration of how the Overflow Flag Is Set.

	1 0 0 0 0 0 0 0
+	1 1 1 1 1 1 1 0
CF 1	0 1 1 1 1 1 1 0

NEG Instruction   The NEG instruction produces an invalid result if the destination operand cannot be stored correctly. For example, if we move −128 to AL and try to negate it, the correct value (+128) will not fit into AL. The Overflow flag is set, indicating that AL contains an invalid value:

```
mov  al,-128                ; AL = 10000000b
neg  al                     ; AL = 10000000b, OF = 1
```

On the other hand, if +127 is negated, the result is valid and the Overflow flag is clear:

```
mov  al,+127                ; AL = 01111111b
neg  al                     ; AL = 10000001b, OF = 0
```

> How does the CPU know whether an arithmetic operation is signed or unsigned? We can only give what seems a dumb answer: It doesn't! The CPU sets all status flags after an arithmetic operation using a set of boolean rules, regardless of which flags are relevant. You (the programmer) decide which flags to interpret and which to ignore, based on your knowledge of the type of operation performed.

4.2.7 Example Program (AddSub3)

The following program implements various arithmetic expressions using the ADD, SUB, INC, DEC, and NEG instructions, and shows how certain status flags are affected:

```
TITLE Addition and Subtraction        (AddSub3.asm)

INCLUDE Irvine32.inc
.data
Rval    SDWORD ?
Xval    SDWORD 26
Yval    SDWORD 30
Zval    SDWORD 40

.code
main PROC
      ; INC and DEC
      mov  ax,1000h
      inc  ax                 ; 1001h
      dec  ax                 ; 1000h

      ; Expression: Rval = -Xval + (Yval - Zval)
      mov  eax,Xval
      neg  eax                ; -26
      mov  ebx,Yval
```

```
          sub    ebx,Zval                ; -10
          add    eax,ebx
          mov    Rval,eax                ; -36

          ; Zero flag example:
          mov    cx,1
          sub    cx,1                     ; ZF = 1
          mov    ax,0FFFFh
          inc    ax                       ; ZF = 1

          ; Sign flag example:
          mov    cx,0
          sub    cx,1                     ; SF = 1
          mov    ax,7FFFh
          add    ax,2                     ; SF = 1

          ; Carry flag example:
          mov    al,0FFh
          add    al,1                     ; CF = 1,   AL = 00

          ; Overflow flag example:
          mov    al,+127
          add    al,1                     ; OF = 1
          mov    al,-128
          sub    al,1                     ; OF = 1

          exit
      main ENDP
      END main
```

4.2.8   Section Review

Use the following data for the next several questions:

```
      .data
      val1 BYTE   10h
      val2 WORD   8000h
      val3 DWORD  0FFFFh
      val4 WORD   7FFFh
```

1. Write an instruction that increments **val2**.

2. Write an instruction that subtracts **val3** from EAX.

3. Write instructions that subtract **val4** from **val2**.

4. If **val2** is incremented by 1 using the ADD instruction, what will be the values of the Carry and Sign flags?

5. If **val4** is incremented by 1 using the ADD instruction, what will be the values of the Overflow and Sign flags?

6. Where indicated, write down the values of the Carry, Sign, Zero, and Overflow flags after each instruction has executed:

```
      mov  ax,7FF0h
      add  al,10h                ; a. CF =    SF =    ZF =    OF =
      add  ah,1                  ; b. CF =    SF =    ZF =    OF =
      add  ax,2                  ; c. CF =    SF =    ZF =    OF =
```

7. Implement the following expression in assembly language: AX = (−val2 + BX) − val4.

8. *(Yes/No):* Is it possible to set the Overflow flag if you add a positive integer to a negative integer?

9. *(Yes/No):* Will the Overflow flag be set if you add a negative integer to a negative integer and produce a positive result?

10. *(Yes/No):* Is it possible for the NEG instruction to set the Overflow flag?

11. *(Yes/No):* Is it possible for both the Sign and Zero flags to be set at the same time?

12. Write a sequence of two instructions that set both the Carry and Overflow flags at the same time.

13. Write a sequence of instructions showing how the Zero flag could be used to indicate unsigned overflow after executing INC and DEC instructions.

14. In our discussion of the Carry flag we subtracted unsigned 2 from 1 by negating the 2 and adding it to 1. The Carry flag was the inversion of the carry out of the MSB of the sum. Demonstrate this process by subtracting 3 from 4 and show how the Carry flag value is produced.

4.3 Data-Related Operators and Directives

Operators and directives are not executable instructions; instead, they are interpreted by the assembler. You can use a number of MASM directives to get information about the addresses and size characteristics of data:

- The OFFSET operator returns the distance of a variable from the beginning of its enclosing segment.
- The PTR operator lets you override an operand's default size.
- The TYPE operator returns the size (in bytes) of an operand or of each element in an array.
- The LENGTHOF operator returns the number of elements in an array.
- The SIZEOF operator returns the number of bytes used by an array initializer.

In addition, the LABEL directive provides a way to redefine the same variable with different size attributes. The operators and directives in this chapter represent only a small subset of the operators supported by MASM. You may want to view the complete list in Appendix D.

> MASM continues to support the legacy directives LENGTH (rather than LENGTHOF) and SIZE (rather than SIZEOF).

4.3.1 OFFSET Operator

The OFFSET operator returns the offset of a data label. The offset represents the distance, in bytes, of the label from the beginning of the data segment. To illustrate, Figure 4–7 shows a variable named **myByte** inside the data segment.

Figure 4–7   A Variable Named myByte.

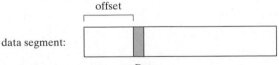

OFFSET Example

In the next example, we declare three different types of variables:

```
.data
bVal   BYTE   ?
wVal   WORD   ?
dVal   DWORD ?
dVal2 DWORD ?
```

If **bVal** were located at offset 00404000 (hexadecimal), the OFFSET operator would return the following values:

```
mov  esi,OFFSET bVal                       ; ESI = 00404000
mov  esi,OFFSET wVal                       ; ESI = 00404001
mov  esi,OFFSET dVal                       ; ESI = 00404003
mov  esi,OFFSET dVal2                      ; ESI = 00404007
```

OFFSET can also be applied to a direct-offset operand. Suppose **myArray** contains five 16-bit words. The following MOV instruction obtains the offset of **myArray**, adds 4, and moves the resulting address to ESI. We can say that ESI points to the third integer in the array:

```
.data
myArray WORD 1,2,3,4,5
.code
mov  esi,OFFSET myArray + 4
```

You can initialize a doubleword variable with the offset of another variable, effectively creating a pointer. In the following example, **pArray** points to the beginning of **bigArray**:

```
.data
bigArray DWORD 500 DUP(?)
pArray DWORD bigArray
```

The following statement loads the pointer's value into ESI, so the register can point to the beginning of the array:

```
mov esi,pArray
```

4.3.2   ALIGN Directive

The ALIGN directive aligns a variable on a byte, word, doubleword, or paragraph boundary. The syntax is

ALIGN *bound*

Bound can be 1, 2, 4, or 16. A value of 1 aligns the next variable on a 1-byte boundary (the default). If bound is 2, the next variable is aligned on an even-numbered address. If bound is 4, the next address is a multiple of 4. If bound is 16, the next address is a multiple of 16, a paragraph boundary. The assembler can insert one or more empty bytes before the variable to fix the alignment. Why bother aligning data? Because the CPU can process data stored at even-numbered addresses more quickly than those at odd-numbered addresses.

In the following revision of an example from Section 4.3.1, **bVal** is arbitrarily located at offset 00404000. Inserting the ALIGN 2 directive before **wVal** causes it to be assigned an even-numbered offset:

```
bVal  BYTE  ?                    ; 00404000
ALIGN 2
wVal  WORD  ?                    ; 00404002
bVal2 BYTE  ?                    ; 00404004
ALIGN 4
dVal  DWORD ?                    ; 00404008
dVal2 DWORD ?                    ; 0040400C
```

Note that **dVal** would have been at offset 00404005, but the ALIGN 4 directive bumped it up to offset 00404008.

4.3.3 PTR Operator

You can use the PTR operator to override the declared size of an operand. This is only necessary when you're trying to access the variable using a size attribute that's different from the one used to declare the variable.

Suppose, for example, that you would like to move the lower 16 bits of a doubleword variable named **myDouble** into AX. The assembler will not permit the following move because the operand sizes do not match:

```
.data
myDouble  DWORD  12345678h
.code
mov ax,myDouble                 ; error
```

But the WORD PTR operator makes it possible to move the low-order word (5678h) to AX:

```
mov ax,WORD PTR myDouble
```

Why wasn't 1234h moved into AX? x86 processors use the *little endian* storage format (Section 3.4.9), in which the low-order byte is stored at the variable's starting address. In Figure 4–8, the memory layout of **myDouble** is shown three ways: first as a doubleword, then as two words (5678h, 1234h), and finally as four bytes (78h, 56h, 34h, 12h).

Figure 4–8 Memory Layout of myDouble.

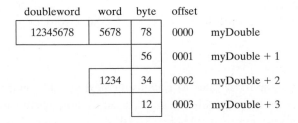

The CPU can access memory in any of these three ways, independent of the way a variable was defined. For example, if **myDouble** begins at offset 0000, the 16-bit value stored at that address is 5678h. We could also retrieve 1234h, the word at location **myDouble+2,** using the following statement:

```
mov   ax,WORD PTR [myDouble+2]            ; 1234h
```

Similarly, we could use the BYTE PTR operator to move a single byte from **myDouble** to BL:

```
mov    bl,BYTE PTR myDouble              ; 78h
```

Note that PTR must be used in combination with one of the standard assembler data types, BYTE, SBYTE, WORD, SWORD, DWORD, SDWORD, FWORD, QWORD, or TBYTE.

Moving Smaller Values into Larger Destinations   We might want to move two smaller values from memory to a larger destination operand. In the next example, the first word is copied to the lower half of EAX and the second word is copied to the upper half. The DWORD PTR operator makes this possible:

```
.data
wordList WORD 5678h,1234h
.code
mov eax,DWORD PTR wordList              ; EAX = 12345678h
```

4.3.4   TYPE Operator

The TYPE operator returns the size, in bytes, of a single element of a variable. For example, the TYPE of a byte equals 1, the TYPE of a word equals 2, the TYPE of a doubleword is 4, and the TYPE of a quadword is 8. Here are examples of each:

```
.data
var1  BYTE   ?
var2  WORD   ?
var3  DWORD  ?
var4  QWORD  ?
```

The following table shows the value of each TYPE expression.

Expression	Value
TYPE var1	1
TYPE var2	2
TYPE var3	4
TYPE var4	8

4.3.5   LENGTHOF Operator

The LENGTHOF operator counts the number of elements in an array, defined by the values appearing on the same line as its label. We will use the following data as an example:

```
.data
byte1     BYTE   10,20,30
array1    WORD   30 DUP(?),0,0
array2    WORD   5 DUP(3 DUP(?))
array3    DWORD  1,2,3,4
digitStr  BYTE   "12345678",0
```

When nested DUP operators are used in an array definition, LENGTHOF returns the product of the two counters. The following table lists the values returned by each LENGTHOF expression:

Expression	Value
LENGTHOF byte1	3
LENGTHOF array1	30 + 2
LENGTHOF array2	5 * 3
LENGTHOF array3	4
LENGTHOF digitStr	9

If you declare an array that spans multiple program lines, LENGTHOF only regards the data from the first line as part of the array. Given the following data, LENGTHOF myArray would return the value 5:

```
myArray BYTE 10,20,30,40,50
        BYTE 60,70,80,90,100
```

Alternatively, you can end the first line with a comma and continue the list of initializers onto the next line. Given the following data, LENGTHOF myArray would return the value 10:

```
myArray BYTE 10,20,30,40,50,
        60,70,80,90,100
```

4.3.6 SIZEOF Operator

The SIZEOF operator returns a value that is equivalent to multiplying LENGTHOF by TYPE. In the following example, **intArray** has TYPE = 2 and LENGTHOF = 32. Therefore, SIZEOF **intArray** equals 64:

```
.data
intArray WORD 32 DUP(0)
.code
mov eax,SIZEOF intArray      ; EAX = 64
```

4.3.7 LABEL Directive

The LABEL directive lets you insert a label and give it a size attribute without allocating any storage. All standard size attributes can be used with LABEL, such as BYTE, WORD, DWORD, QWORD or TBYTE. A common use of LABEL is to provide an alternative name and size attribute for the variable declared next in the data segment. In the following example, we declare a label just before **val32** named **val16** and give it a WORD attribute:

```
.data
val16 LABEL WORD
val32 DWORD 12345678h
.code
mov ax,val16                 ; AX = 5678h
mov dx,[val16+2]             ; DX = 1234h
```

val16 is an alias for the same storage location as **val32.** The LABEL directive itself allocates no storage.

Sometimes we need to construct a larger integer from two smaller integers. In the next example, a 32-bit value is loaded into EAX from two 16-bit variables:

```
.data
LongValue LABEL DWORD
val1  WORD  5678h
val2  WORD  1234h
.code
mov eax,LongValue                   ; EAX = 12345678h
```

4.3.8   Section Review

1. *(True/False):* The OFFSET operator always returns a 16-bit value.
2. *(True/False):* The PTR operator returns the 32-bit address of a variable.
3. *(True/False):* The TYPE operator returns a value of 4 for doubleword operands.
4. *(True/False):* The LENGTHOF operator returns the number of bytes in an operand.
5. *(True/False):* The SIZEOF operator returns the number of bytes in an operand.

Use the following data definitions for the next seven exercises:

```
.data
myBytes   BYTE 10h,20h,30h,40h
myWords   WORD 3 DUP(?),2000h
myString BYTE "ABCDE"
```

6. Insert a directive in the given data that aligns **myBytes** to an even-numbered address.
7. What will be the value of EAX after each of the following instructions execute?

```
mov  eax,TYPE myBytes          ; a.
mov  eax,LENGTHOF myBytes      ; b.
mov  eax,SIZEOF myBytes        ; c.
mov  eax,TYPE myWords          ; d.
mov  eax,LENGTHOF myWords      ; e.
mov  eax,SIZEOF myWords        ; f.
mov  eax,SIZEOF myString       ; g.
```

8. Write a single instruction that moves the first two bytes in **myBytes** to the DX register. The resulting value will be 2010h.
9. Write an instruction that moves the second byte in **myWords** to the AL register.
10. Write an instruction that moves all four bytes in **myBytes** to the EAX register.
11. Insert a LABEL directive in the given data that permits **myWords** to be moved directly to a 32-bit register.
12. Insert a LABEL directive in the given data that permits **myBytes** to be moved directly to a 16-bit register.

4.4   Indirect Addressing

Direct addressing is impractical for array processing because it is not practical to use constant offsets to address more than a few array elements. Instead, we use a register as a pointer (called *indirect addressing*) and manipulate the register's value. When an operand uses indirect addressing, it is called an *indirect operand*.

4.4.1 Indirect Operands

Protected Mode   In protected mode, an indirect operand can be any 32-bit general-purpose register (EAX, EBX, ECX, EDX, ESI, EDI, EBP, and ESP) surrounded by brackets. The register is assumed to contain the address of some data. In the next example, ESI contains the offset of **byteVal**. The MOV instruction uses the indirect operand as the source, the offset in ESI is dereferenced, and a byte is moved to AL:

```
.data
byteVal BYTE 10h
.code
mov  esi,OFFSET byteVal
mov  al,[esi]                    ; AL = 10h
```

If the destination operand uses indirect addressing, a new value is placed in memory at the location pointed to by the register. In the following example, the contents of the BL register are copied to the memory location addressed by ESI.

```
mov  [esi],bl
```

Real-Address Mode   In real-address mode, a 16-bit register holds the offset of a variable. If the register is used as an indirect operand, it may only be SI, DI, BX, or BP. Avoid BP unless you are using it to index into the stack. In the next example, SI references **byteVal**:

```
.data
byteVal BYTE 10h
.code
main PROC
    startup
    mov   si,OFFSET byteVal
    mov   al,[si]               ; AL = 10h
```

General Protection Fault   In protected mode, if the effective address points to an area outside your program's data segment, the CPU executes a *general protection (GP) fault*. This happens even when an instruction does not modify memory. For example, if ESI were uninitialized, the following instruction would probably generate a GP fault:

```
mov  ax,[esi]
```

Always initialize registers before using them as indirect operands. The same applies to high-level language programming with subscripts and pointers. General protection faults do not occur in real-address mode, which makes uninitialized indirect operands difficult to detect.

Using PTR with Indirect Operands   The size of an operand may not be evident from the context of an instruction. The following instruction causes the assembler to generate an "operand must have size" error message:

```
inc [esi]                       ; error: operand must have size
```

The assembler does not know whether ESI points to a byte, word, doubleword, or some other size. The PTR operator confirms the operand size:

```
inc BYTE PTR [esi]
```

4.4.2 Arrays

Indirect operands are ideal tools for stepping through arrays. In the next example, **arrayB** contains 3 bytes. As ESI is incremented, it points to each byte, in order:

```
.data
arrayB  BYTE 10h,20h,30h
.code
mov  esi,OFFSET arrayB
mov  al,[esi]              ; AL = 10h
inc  esi
mov  al,[esi]              ; AL = 20h
inc  esi
mov  al,[esi]              ; AL = 30h
```

If we use an array of 16-bit integers, we add 2 to ESI to address each subsequent array element:

```
.data
arrayW  WORD 1000h,2000h,3000h
.code
mov  esi,OFFSET arrayW
mov  ax,[esi]              ; AX = 1000h
add  esi,2
mov  ax,[esi]              ; AX = 2000h
add  esi,2
mov  ax,[esi]              ; AX = 3000h
```

Suppose **arrayW** is located at offset 10200h. The following illustration shows the initial value of ESI in relation to the array data:

Offset	Value
10200	1000h ←——[esi]
10202	2000h
10204	3000h

Example: Adding 32-Bit Integers The following code example adds three doublewords. A displacement of 4 must be added to ESI as it points to each subsequent array value because doublewords are 4 bytes long:

```
.data
arrayD DWORD 10000h,20000h,30000h
.code
mov  esi,OFFSET arrayD
mov  eax,[esi]         ; first number
add  esi,4
add  eax,[esi]         ; second number
add  esi,4
add  eax,[esi]         ; third number
```

Suppose **arrayD** is located at offset 10200h. Then the following illustration shows the initial value of ESI in relation to the array data:

```
        Offset      Value
        10200     ┌──────────┐
                  │  10000h  │  ◄── [esi]
        10204     ├──────────┤
                  │  20000h  │  ◄── [esi] + 4
        10208     ├──────────┤
                  │  30000h  │  ◄── [esi] + 8
                  └──────────┘
```

4.4.3 Indexed Operands

An *indexed operand* adds a constant to a register to generate an effective address. Any of the 32-bit general-purpose registers may be used as index registers. There are different notational forms permitted by MASM (the brackets are part of the notation):

```
constant[reg]
[constant + reg]
```

The first notational form combines the name of a variable with a register. The variable name is translated by the assembler into a constant that represents the variable's offset. Here are examples that show both notational forms:

arrayB[esi]	[arrayB + esi]
arrayD[ebx]	[arrayD + ebx]

Indexed operands are ideally suited to array processing. The index register should be initialized to zero before accessing the first array element:

```
.data
arrayB BYTE 10h,20h,30h
.code
mov esi,0
mov al,[arrayB + esi]          ; AL = 10h
```

The last statement adds ESI to the offset of **arrayB**. The address generated by the expression **[arrayB + ESI]** is dereferenced and the byte in memory is copied to AL.

Adding Displacements   The second type of indexed addressing combines a register with a constant offset. The index register holds the base address of an array or structure, and the constant identifies offsets of various array elements. The following example shows how to do this with an array of 16-bit words:

```
.data
arrayW  WORD 1000h,2000h,3000h
.code
mov esi,OFFSET arrayW
mov ax,[esi]                    ; AX = 1000h
mov ax,[esi+2]                  ; AX = 2000h
mov ax,[esi+4]                  ; AX = 3000h
```

Using 16-Bit Registers   It is usual to use 16-bit registers as indexed operands in real-address mode. In that case, you are limited to using SI, DI, BX, or BP:

```
mov  al,arrayB[si]
mov  ax,arrayW[di]
mov  eax,arrayD[bx]
```

As is the case with indirect operands, avoid using BP except when addressing data on the stack.

Scale Factors in Indexed Operands

Indexed operands must take into account the size of each array element when calculating offsets. Using an array of doublewords, as in the following example, we multiply the subscript (3) by 4 (the size of a doubleword) to generate the offset of the array element containing 400h:

```
.data
arrayD  DWORD 100h, 200h, 300h, 400h
.code
mov esi,3 * TYPE arrayD               ; offset of arrayD[3]
mov eax,arrayD[esi]                   ; EAX = 400h
```

Intel designers wanted to make a common operation easier for compiler writers, so they provided a way for offsets to be calculated, using a *scale factor*. The scale factor is the size of the array component (word = 2, doubleword = 4, or quadword = 8). Let's revise our previous example by setting ESI to the array subscript (3) and multiplying ESI by the scale factor (4) for doublewords:

```
.data
arrayD  DWORD 1,2,3,4
.code
mov esi,3                             ; subscript
mov eax,arrayD[esi*4]                 ; EAX = 4
```

The TYPE operator can make the indexing more flexible should arrayD be redefined as another type in the future:

```
mov esi,3                             ; subscript
mov eax,arrayD[esi*TYPE arrayD]       ; EAX = 4
```

4.4.4 Pointers

A variable containing the address of another variable is called a *pointer*. Pointers are a great tool for manipulating arrays and data structures, and they make dynamic memory allocation possible. x86 programs use two basic types of pointers, NEAR and FAR. Their sizes are affected by the processor's current mode (16-bit real or 32-bit protected), as shown in Table 4-2:

Table 4-2   Pointer Types in 16- and 32-Bit Modes.

	16-Bit Mode	**32-Bit Mode**
NEAR pointer	16-bit offset from the beginning of the data segment	32-bit offset from the beginning of the data segment
FAR pointer	32-bit segment-offset address	48-bit segment selector-offset address

The 32-bit mode programs in this book use near pointers, so they are stored in doubleword variables. Here are two examples: **ptrB** contains the offset of **arrayB**, and **ptrW** contains the offset of **arrayW**:

```
arrayB    BYTE    10h,20h,30h,40h
arrayW    WORD    1000h,2000h,3000h
ptrB      DWORD   arrayB
ptrW      DWORD   arrayW
```

Optionally, you can use the OFFSET operator to make the relationship clearer:

```
ptrB    DWORD OFFSET arrayB
ptrW    DWORD OFFSET arrayW
```

> High-level languages purposely hide physical details about pointers because their implementations vary among different machine architectures. In assembly language, because we deal with a single implementation, we examine and use pointers at the physical level. This approach helps to remove some of the mystery surrounding pointers.

Using the TYPEDEF Operator

The TYPEDEF operator lets you create a user-defined type that has all the status of a built-in type when defining variables. TYPEDEF is ideal for creating pointer variables. For example, the following declaration creates a new data type PBYTE that is a pointer to bytes:

```
PBYTE TYPEDEF PTR BYTE
```

This declaration would usually be placed near the beginning of a program, before the data segment. Then, variables could be defined using PBYTE:

```
.data
arrayB BYTE 10h,20h,30h,40h
ptr1   PBYTE ?                      ; uninitialized
ptr2   PBYTE arrayB                 ; points to an array
```

Example Program: Pointers   The following program (*pointers.asm*) uses TYPDEF to create three pointer types (PBYTE, PWORD, PDWORD). It creates several pointers, assigns several array offsets, and dereferences the pointers:

```
TITLE Pointers                              (Pointers.asm)

INCLUDE Irvine32.inc

; Create user-defined types.
PBYTE   TYPEDEF PTR BYTE            ; pointer to bytes
PWORD   TYPEDEF PTR WORD            ; pointer to words
PDWORD  TYPEDEF PTR DWORD           ; pointer to doublewords

.data
arrayB BYTE  10h,20h,30h
arrayW WORD  1,2,3
arrayD DWORD 4,5,6

; Create some pointer variables.
ptr1 PBYTE   arrayB
ptr2 PWORD   arrayW
ptr3 PDWORD  arrayD
```

```
        .code
    main PROC
    ; Use the pointers to access data.
            mov    esi,ptr1
            mov    al,[esi]                          ; 10h
            mov    esi,ptr2
            mov    ax,[esi]                          ; 1
            mov    esi,ptr3
            mov    eax,[esi]                         ; 4
            exit
    main ENDP
    END main
```

4.4.5 Section Review

1. *(True/False):* Any 16-bit general-purpose register can be used as an indirect operand.

2. *(True/False):* Any 32-bit general-purpose register can be used as an indirect operand.

3. *(True/False):* The BX register is usually reserved for addressing the stack.

4. *(True/False):* A general protection fault occurs in real-address mode when an array subscript is out of range.

5. *(True/False):* The following instruction is invalid: inc [esi]

6. *(True/False):* The following is an indexed operand: array[esi]

Use the following data definitions for the remaining questions in this section:

```
    myBytes    BYTE  10h,20h,30h,40h
    myWords    WORD  8Ah,3Bh,72h,44h,66h
    myDoubles  DWORD 1,2,3,4,5
    myPointer  DWORD myDoubles
```

7. Fill in the requested register values on the right side of the following instruction sequence:

```
    mov  esi,OFFSET myBytes
    mov  al,[esi]                      ; a. AL =
    mov  al,[esi+3]                    ; b. AL =
    mov  esi,OFFSET myWords + 2
    mov  ax,[esi]                      ; c. AX =
    mov  edi,8
    mov  edx,[myDoubles + edi]         ; d. EDX =
    mov  edx,myDoubles[edi]            ; e. EDX =
    mov  ebx,myPointer
    mov  eax,[ebx+4]                   ; f. EAX =
```

8. Fill in the requested register values on the right side of the following instruction sequence:

```
    mov  esi,OFFSET myBytes
    mov  ax,[esi]                      ; a. AX =
    mov  eax,DWORD PTR myWords         ; b. EAX =
    mov  esi,myPointer
    mov  ax,[esi+2]                    ; c. AX =
    mov  ax,[esi+6]                    ; d. AX =
    mov  ax,[esi-4]                    ; e. AX =
```

4.5 JMP and LOOP Instructions

By default, the CPU loads and executes programs sequentially. But the current instruction might be *conditional*, meaning that it transfers control to a new location in the program based on the values of CPU status flags (Zero, Sign, Carry, etc.). Assembly language programs use conditional instructions to implement high-level statements such as IF statements and loops. Each of the conditional statements involves a possible transfer of control (jump) to a different memory address. A *transfer of control*, or *branch*, is a way of altering the order in which statements are executed. There are two basic types of transfers:

- **Unconditional Transfer:** Control is transferred to a new location in all cases; a new address is loaded into the instruction pointer, causing execution to continue at the new address. The JMP instruction does this.
- **Conditional Transfer:** The program branches if a certain condition is true. A wide variety of conditional transfer instructions can be combined to create conditional logic structures. The CPU interprets true/false conditions based on the contents of the ECX and Flags registers.

4.5.1 JMP Instruction

The JMP instruction causes an unconditional transfer to a destination, identified by a code label that is translated by the assembler into an offset. The syntax is

```
JMP destination
```

When the CPU executes an unconditional transfer, the offset of *destination* is moved into the instruction pointer, causing execution to continue at the new location.

Creating a Loop   The JMP instruction provides an easy way to create a loop by jumping to a label at the top of the loop:

```
top:
    .
    .
    .
    jmp top                        ; repeat the endless loop
```

JMP is unconditional, so a loop like this will continue endlessly unless another way is found to exit the loop.

4.5.2 LOOP Instruction

The LOOP instruction, formally known as *Loop According to ECX Counter*, repeats a block of statements a specific number of times. ECX is automatically used as a counter and is decremented each time the loop repeats. Its syntax is

```
LOOP destination
```

The loop destination must be within −128 to +127 bytes of the current location counter. The execution of the LOOP instruction involves two steps: First, it subtracts 1 from ECX. Next, it compares ECX to zero. If ECX is not equal to zero, a jump is taken to the label identified by *destination*. Otherwise, if ECX equals zero, no jump takes place, and control passes to the instruction following the loop.

In real-address mode, CX is the default loop counter for the LOOP instruction. On the other hand, the LOOPD instruction uses ECX as the loop counter, and the LOOPW instruction uses CX as the loop counter.

In the following example, we add 1 to AX each time the loop repeats. When the loop ends, AX = 5 and ECX = 0:

```
        mov   ax,0
        mov   ecx,5
  L1:
        inc   ax
        loop L1
```

A common programming error is to inadvertently initialize ECX to zero before beginning a loop. If this happens, the LOOP instruction decrements ECX to FFFFFFFFh, and the loop repeats 4,294,967,296 times! If CX is the loop counter (in real-address mode), it repeats 65,536 times.

Occasionally, you might create a loop that is large enough to exceed the allowed relative jump range of the LOOP instruction. Following is an example of an error message generated by MASM because the target label of a LOOP instruction was too far away:

```
error A2075: jump destination too far : by 14 byte(s)
```

Rarely should you explicitly modify ECX inside a loop. If you do, the LOOP instruction may not work as expected. In the following example, ECX is incremented within the loop. It never reaches zero, so the loop never stops:

```
  top:
        .
        .
        .
        inc   ecx
        loop top
```

If you need to modify ECX inside a loop, you can save it in a variable at the beginning of the loop and restore it just before the LOOP instruction:

```
        .data
        count DWORD ?
        .code
        mov   ecx,100           ; set loop count
  top:
        mov   count,ecx         ; save the count
        .
        mov   ecx,20            ; modify ECX
        .
        mov   ecx,count         ; restore loop count
        loop  top
```

Nested Loops   When creating a loop inside another loop, special consideration must be given to the outer loop counter in ECX. You can save it in a variable:

```
        .data
        count DWORD ?
        .code
        mov   ecx,100           ; set outer loop count
```

```
L1:
        mov    count,ecx            ; save outer loop count
        mov    ecx,20              ; set inner loop count
L2:
        .
        .
        .
        loop  L2                   ; repeat the inner loop

        mov    ecx,count           ; restore outer loop count
        loop  L1                   ; repeat the outer loop
```

As a general rule, nested loops more than two levels deep are difficult to write. If the algorithm you're using requires deep loop nesting, move some of the inner loops into subroutines.

4.5.3 Summing an Integer Array

There's hardly any task more common in beginning programming than calculating the sum of the elements in an array. In assembly language, you would follow these steps:

1. Assign the array's address to a register that will serve as an indexed operand.
2. Initialize the loop counter to the length of the array.
3. Assign zero to the register that accumulates the sum.
4. Create a label to mark the beginning of the loop.
5. In the loop body, add a single array element to the sum.
6. Point to the next array element.
7. Use a LOOP instruction to repeat the loop.

Steps 1 through 3 may be performed in any order. Here's a short program that sums an array of 16-bit integers.

```
TITLE Summing an Array                    (SumArray.asm)
INCLUDE Irvine32.inc
.data
intarray DWORD 10000h,20000h,30000h,40000h

.code
main PROC
        mov    edi,OFFSET intarray     ; 1: EDI = address of intarray
        mov    ecx,LENGTHOF intarray   ; 2: initialize loop counter
        mov    eax,0                   ; 3: sum = 0
L1:                                    ; 4: mark beginning of loop
        add   eax,[edi]                ; 5: add an integer
        add   edi,TYPE intarray        ; 6: point to next element
        loop L1                        ; 7: repeat until ECX = 0

        exit
main ENDP
END main
```

4.5.4 Copying a String

Programs often copy large blocks of data from one location to another. The data may be arrays or strings, but they can contain any type of objects. Let's see how this can be done in assembly

language, using a loop that copies a string, represented as an array of bytes with a null terminator value. Indexed addressing works well for this type of operation because the same index register references both strings. The target string must have enough available space to receive the
copied characters, including the null byte at the end:

```
TITLE Copying a String                      (CopyStr.asm)

INCLUDE Irvine32.inc
.data
source  BYTE   "This is the source string",0
target  BYTE   SIZEOF source DUP(0)

.code
main PROC
        mov   esi,0                ; index register
        mov   ecx,SIZEOF source    ; loop counter
L1:
        mov   al,source[esi]       ; get a character from source
        mov   target[esi],al       ; store it in the target
        inc   esi                  ; move to next character
        loop L1                    ; repeat for entire string

        exit
main ENDP
END main
```

The MOV instruction cannot have two memory operands, so each character is moved from the
source string to AL, then from AL to the target string.

When programming in C++ or Java, beginning programmers often do not realize how often background copy operations take place. In Java, for example, if you exceed the existing capacity of
an ArrayList when adding a new element, the runtime system allocates a block of new storage, copies
the existing data to a new location, and deletes the old data. (The same is true when using a C++
vector.) If a large number of copy operations take place, they have a significant effect on a program's
execution speed.

4.5.5   Section Review

1. *(True/False):* A JMP instruction can only jump to a label inside the current procedure.

2. *(True/False):* JMP is a conditional transfer instruction.

3. If ECX is initialized to zero before beginning a loop, how many times will the LOOP
   instruction repeat? (Assume ECX is not modified by any other instructions inside the loop.)

4. *(True/False):* The LOOP instruction first checks to see whether ECX is not equal to zero;
   then LOOP decrements ECX and jumps to the destination label.

5. *(True/False):* The LOOP instruction does the following: It decrements ECX; then, if ECX is
   not equal to zero, LOOP jumps to the destination label.

6. In real-address mode, which register is used as the counter by the LOOP instruction?

7. In real-address mode, which register is used as the counter by the LOOPD instruction?

8. *(True/False):* The target of a LOOP instruction must be within 256 bytes of the current location.

9. *(Challenge):* What will be the final value of EAX in this example?

```
        mov    eax,0
        mov    ecx,10                   ; outer loop counter
    L1:
        mov    eax,3
        mov    ecx,5                    ; inner loop counter
    L2:
        add    eax,5
        loop   L2                       ; repeat inner loop
        loop   L1                       ; repeat outer loop
```

10. Revise the code from the preceding question so the outer loop counter is not erased when the inner loop starts.

4.6 Chapter Summary

MOV, a data transfer instruction, copies a source operand to a destination operand. The MOVZX instruction zero-extends a smaller operand into a larger one. The MOVSX instruction sign-extends a smaller operand into a larger register. The XCHG instruction exchanges the contents of two operands. At least one operand must be a register.

Operand Types   The following types of operands are presented in this chapter:

• A *direct* operand is the name of a variable, and represents the variable's address.

• A *direct-offset* operand adds a displacement to the name of a variable, generating a new offset. This new offset can be used to access data in memory.

• An *indirect* operand is a register containing the address of data. By surrounding the register with brackets (as in [esi]), a program dereferences the address and retrieves the memory data.

• An *indexed* operand combines a constant with an indirect operand. The constant and register value are added, and the resulting offset is dereferenced. For example, [array+esi] and array[esi] are indexed operands.

The following arithmetic instructions are important:

• The INC instruction adds 1 to an operand.

• The DEC instruction subtracts 1 from an operand.

• The ADD instruction adds a source operand to a destination operand.

• The SUB instruction subtracts a source operand from a destination operand.

• The NEG instruction reverses the sign of an operand.

When converting simple arithmetic expressions to assembly language, use standard operator precedence rules to select which expressions to evaluate first.

Status Flags   The following CPU status flags are affected by arithmetic operations:

• The Sign flag is set when the outcome of an arithmetic operation is negative.

• The Carry flag is set when the result of an unsigned arithmetic operation is too large for the destination operand.

- The Parity flag indicates whether or not an even number of 1 bits occurs in the least significant byte of the destination operand immediately after an arithmetic or boolean instruction has executed.
- The Auxiliary Carry flag is set when a carry or borrow occurs in bit position 3 of the destination operand.
- The Zero flag is set when the outcome of an arithmetic operation is zero.
- The Overflow flag is set when the result of an signed arithmetic operation is too large for the destination operand. In a byte operation, for example, the CPU detects overflow by exclusive-ORing the carry out of bit 6 with the carry out of bit 7.

Operators   The following operators are common in assembly language:
- The OFFSET operator returns the distance of a variable from the beginning of its enclosing segment.
- The PTR operator overrides a variable's declared size.
- The TYPE operator returns the size (in bytes) of a single variable or of a single element in an array.
- The LENGTHOF operator returns the number of elements in an array.
- The SIZEOF operator returns the number bytes used by an array initializer.
- The TYPEDEF operator creates a user-defined type.

Loops   The JMP (Jump) instruction unconditionally branches to another location. The LOOP (Loop According to ECX Counter) instruction is used in counting-type loops. In 32-bit mode, LOOP uses ECX as the counter; in 16-bit mode, CX is the counter. In both 16- and 32-bit modes, LOOPD uses ECX as the counter, and LOOPW uses CX as the counter.

4.7 Programming Exercises

The following exercises can be done in protected mode or real-address mode.

★ **1.   Carry Flag**

Write a program that uses addition and subtraction to set and clear the Carry flag. After each instruction, insert the **call DumpRegs** statement to display the registers and flags. Using comments, explain how (and why) the Carry flag was affected by each instruction.

★ **2.   Zero and Sign Flags**

Write a program that uses addition and subtraction to set and clear the Zero and Sign flags. After each addition or subtraction instruction, insert the **call DumpRegs** statement (see Section 3.2) to display the registers and flags. Using comments, explain how (and why) the Zero and Sign flags were affected by each instruction.

★ **3.   Overflow Flag**

Write a program that uses addition and subtraction to set and clear the Overflow flag. After each addition or subtraction instruction, insert the **call DumpRegs** statement (see Section 3.2) to display the registers and flags. Using comments, explain how (and why) the Overflow flag was affected by each instruction. Include an ADD instruction that sets both the Carry and Overflow flags.

★ **4. Direct-Offset Addressing**

Insert the following variables in your program:

```
.data
Uarray WORD 1000h,2000h,3000h,4000h
Sarray SWORD -1,-2,-3,-4
```

Write instructions that use direct-offset addressing to move the four values in **Uarray** to the EAX, EBX, ECX, and EDX registers. When you follow this with a **call DumpRegs** statement (see Section 3.2), the following register values should display:

```
EAX=00001000   EBX=00002000   ECX=00003000   EDX=00004000
```

Next, write instructions that use direct-offset addressing to move the four values in **Sarray** to the EAX, EBX, ECX, and EDX registers. When you follow this with a **call DumpRegs** statement, the following register values should display:

```
EAX=FFFFFFFF   EBX=FFFFFFFE   ECX=FFFFFFFD   EDX=FFFFFFFC
```

★★★ **5. Reverse an Array**

Use a loop with indirect or indexed addressing to reverse the elements of an integer array in place. Do not copy the elements to any other array. Use the SIZEOF, TYPE, and LENGTHOF operators to make the program as flexible as possible if the array size and type should be changed in the future. Optionally, you may display the modified array by calling the DumpMem method from the Irvine32 library. See Chapter 5 for details. *(A VideoNote for this exercise is posted on the Web site.)*

★★ **6. Fibonacci Numbers**

Write a program that uses a loop to calculate the first seven values of the *Fibonacci* number sequence, described by the following formula: $Fib(1) = 1$, $Fib(2) = 1$, $Fib(n) = Fib(n-1) + Fib(n-2)$. Place each value in the EAX register and display it with a **call DumpRegs** statement (see Section 3.2) inside the loop.

★★ **7. Arithmetic Expression**

Write a program that implements the following arithmetic expression:

```
EAX = -val2 + 7 - val3 + val1
```

Use the following data definitions:

```
val1 SDWORD 8
val2 SDWORD -15
val3 SDWORD 20
```

In comments next to each instruction, write the hexadecimal value of EAX. Insert a **call DumpRegs** statement at the end of the program.

★★★ **8. Copy a String Backwards**

Write a program using the LOOP instruction with indirect addressing that copies a string from **source** to **target**, reversing the character order in the process. Use the following variables:

```
source  BYTE "This is the source string",0
target  BYTE  SIZEOF source DUP('#')
```

Insert the following statements immediately after the loop to display the hexadecimal contents of the target string:

```
mov   esi,OFFSET target    ; offset of variable
mov   ebx,1                ; byte format
mov   ecx,SIZEOF target    ; counter
call  DumpMem
```

If your program works correctly, it will display the following sequence of hexadecimal bytes:

```
67 6E 69 72 74 73 20 65 63 72 75 6F 73 20 65 68
74 20 73 69 20 73 69 68 54
```

(The DumpMem procedure is explained in Section 5.3.2.) *(A VideoNote for this exercise is posted on the Web site.)*

5

•——•

PROCEdUReS

5.1   Introduction

5.2   Linking to an External Library
    5.2.1   Background Information
    5.2.2   Section Review

5.3   The Book's Link Library
    5.3.1   Overview
    5.3.2   Individual Procedure Descriptions
    5.3.3   Library Test Programs
    5.3.4   Section Review

5.4   Stack Operations
    5.4.1   Runtime Stack
    5.4.2   PUSH and POP Instructions
    5.4.3   Section Review

5.5   Defining and Using Procedures
    5.5.1   PROC Directive
    5.5.2   CALL and RET Instructions
    5.5.3   Example: Summing an Integer Array
    5.5.4   Flowcharts
    5.5.5   Saving and Restoring Registers
    5.5.6   Section Review

5.6   Program Design Using Procedures
    5.6.1   Integer Summation Program (Design)
    5.6.2   Integer Summation Implementation
    5.6.3   Section Review

5.7   Chapter Summary

5.8   Programming Exercises

5.1   Introduction

This chapter introduces you to a convenient and powerful library that you can use to simplify tasks related to input-output and string handling. You will also explore two essential concepts in this chapter: (1) how to divide programs into manageable units by calling subroutines; (2) how programming languages use the runtime stack to track subroutine calls. A concrete understanding of the runtime stack is also a great help when you debug programs written in high-level languages such as C and C++.

5.2   Linking to an External Library

If you spend the time, you can write detailed code for input-output in assembly language. It's a lot like building your own automobile from scratch so that you can drive somewhere.

The work is both interesting and time consuming. In Chapter 11 you will get a chance to see how input-output is handled in MS-Windows protected mode. It is great fun, and a new world opens up when you see the available tools. For now, however, input-output should be easy while you are learning assembly language basics. Section 5.3 shows how to call procedures from the book's link libraries, named **Irvine32.lib** and **Irvine16.lib**. The complete library source code is available at the publisher's support Web site (listed in the Preface).

The Irvine32 library is for programs written in 32-bit protected mode. It contains procedures that link to the MS-Windows API when they generate input-output. The Irvine16 library is for programs written in 16-bit real-address mode. It contains procedures that execute MS-DOS Interrupts when they generate input-output.

5.2.1   Background Information

A *link library* is a file containing procedures (subroutines) that have been assembled into machine code. A link library begins as one or more source files, which are assembled into object files. The object files are inserted into a specially formatted file recognized by the linker utility. Suppose a program displays a string in the console window by calling a procedure named **WriteString**. The program source must contain a PROTO directive identifying the WriteString procedure:

```
WriteString PROTO
```

Next, a CALL instruction executes **WriteString**:

```
call WriteString
```

When the program is assembled, the assembler leaves the target address of the CALL instruction blank, knowing that it will be filled in by the linker. The linker looks for **WriteString** in the link library and copies the appropriate machine instructions from the library into the program's executable file. In addition, it inserts **WriteString's** address into the CALL instruction. If a procedure you're calling is not in the link library, the linker issues an error message and does not generate an executable file.

Linker Command Options   The linker utility combines a program's object file with one or more object files and link libraries. The following command, for example, links hello.obj to the irvine32.lib and kernel32.lib libraries:

```
link hello.obj irvine32.lib kernel32.lib
```

Linking 32-Bit Programs   Let's go into more detail regarding linking 32-bit programs. The kernel32.lib file, part of the Microsoft Windows Platform *Software Development Kit*, contains linking information for system functions located in a file named kernel32.dll. The latter is a fundamental part of MS-Windows, and is called a *dynamic link library*. It contains executable functions that perform character-based input-output. Figure 5–1 shows how kernel32.lib is a bridge to kernel32.dll.

FIGURE 5–1   Linking 32-bit programs.

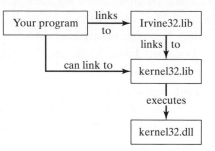

In Chapters 1 through 10, our programs link to Irvine32.lib. Chapter 11 shows how to link programs directly to kernel32.lib.

5.2.2   Section Review

1. *(True/False):* A link library consists of assembly language source code.

2. Use the PROTO directive to declare a procedure named **MyProc** in an external link library.

3. Write a CALL statement that calls a procedure named **MyProc** in an external link library.

4. What is the name of the 32-bit link library supplied with this book?

5. Which library contains functions called from **Irvine32.lib**?

6. What type of file is **kernel32.dll**?

5.3   The Book's Link Library

Table 5-1 contains a complete list of procedures in the Irvine32 and Irvine16 libraries. Any procedure found only in the Irvine32 library has a * at the end of its description.

TABLE 5-1   Procedures in the Link Library.

Procedure	Description
CloseFile	Closes a disk file that was previously opened.*
Clrscr	Clears the console window and locates the cursor at the upper left corner.
CreateOutputFile	Creates a new disk file for writing in output mode.*
Crlf	Writes an end-of-line sequence to the console window.
Delay	Pauses the program execution for a specified *n*-millisecond interval.
DumpMem	Writes a block of memory to the console window in hexadecimal.
DumpRegs	Displays the EAX, EBX, ECX, EDX, ESI, EDI, EBP, ESP, EFLAGS, and EIP registers in hexadecimal. Also displays the most common CPU status flags.
GetCommandTail	Copies the program's command-line arguments (called the *command tail*) into an array of bytes.
GetDateTime	Gets the current date and time from the system.

Table 5-1   *(Continued)*

Procedure	Description
GetMaxXY	Gets the number of columns and rows in the console window's buffer.*
GetMseconds	Returns the number of milliseconds elapsed since midnight.
GetTextColor	Returns the active foreground and background text colors in the console window.*
Gotoxy	Locates the cursor at a specific row and column in the console window.
IsDigit	Sets the Zero flag if the AL register contains the ASCII code for a decimal digit (0–9).
MsgBox	Displays a popup message box.*
MsgBoxAsk	Display a yes/no question in a popup message box.*
OpenInputFile	Opens an existing disk file for input.*
ParseDecimal32	Converts an unsigned decimal integer string to 32-bit binary.
ParseInteger32	Converts a signed decimal integer string to 32-bit binary.
Random32	Generates a 32-bit pseudorandom integer in the range 0 to FFFFFFFFh.
Randomize	Seeds the random number generator with a unique value.
RandomRange	Generates a pseudorandom integer within a specified range.
ReadChar	Waits for a single character to be typed at the keyboard and returns the character.
ReadDec	Reads an unsigned 32-bit decimal integer from the keyboard, terminated by the Enter key.
ReadFromFile	Reads an input disk file into a buffer.*
ReadHex	Reads a 32-bit hexadecimal integer from the keyboard, terminated by the Enter key.
ReadInt	Reads a 32-bit signed decimal integer from the keyboard, terminated by the Enter key.
ReadKey	Reads a character from the keyboard's input buffer without waiting for input.
ReadString	Reads a string from the keyboard, terminated by the Enter key.
SetTextColor	Sets the foreground and background colors of all subsequent text output to the console.*
Str_compare	Compares two strings.
Str_copy	Copies a source string to a destination string.
Str_length	Returns the length of a string in EAX.
Str_trim	Removes unwanted characters from a string.
Str_ucase	Converts a string to uppercase letters.
WaitMsg	Displays a message and waits for a key to be pressed.
WriteBin	Writes an unsigned 32-bit integer to the console window in ASCII binary format.
WriteBinB	Writes a binary integer to the console window in byte, word, or doubleword format.
WriteChar	Writes a single character to the console window.
WriteDec	Writes an unsigned 32-bit integer to the console window in decimal format.
WriteHex	Writes a 32-bit integer to the console window in hexadecimal format.
WriteHexB	Writes a byte, word, or doubleword integer to the console window in hexadecimal format.

Table 5-1   *(Continued)*

Procedure	Description
WriteInt	Writes a signed 32-bit integer to the console window in decimal format.
WriteStackFrame	Writes the current procedure's stack frame to the console.
WriteStackFrameName	Writes the current procedure's name and stack frame to the console.
WriteString	Writes a null-terminated string to the console window.
WriteToFile	Writes a buffer to an output file.*
WriteWindowsMsg	Displays a string containing the most recent error generated by MS-Windows.*

* Procedure not available in the Irvine16 library.

5.3.1 Overview

Console Window   The *console window* (or *command window*) is a text-only window created by MS-Windows when a command prompt is displayed.

There are two ways to display a console window, depending on which version of Windows you use: In Windows Vista, click the Start button on the desktop, type *cmd* into the *Start Search field*, and press Enter. In Windows XP, click the Start button on the desktop, select *Run,* type the name *cmd*, and press Enter. Once a console window is open, you can resize the console window buffer by right-clicking on the system menu in the window's upper-left corner, selecting *Properties* from the popup menu, and then modifying the values, as shown in Figure 5–2.

You can also select various font sizes and colors. The console window defaults to 25 rows by 80 columns. You can use the mode command to change the number of columns and lines. The following, typed at the command prompt, sets the console window to 40 columns by 30 lines:

```
mode con cols=40 lines=30
```

Redirecting Standard Input-Output

The Irvine32 and Irvine16 libraries both write output to the console window, but the Irvine16 library has one additional feature named *redirection of standard input-output*. For example, its output can be redirected at the DOS or Windows command prompt to write to a disk file rather than the console window. Here's how it works: Suppose a program named *sample.exe* writes to standard output; then we can use the following command (at the DOS prompt) to redirect its output to a file named *output.txt:*

```
sample > output.txt
```

Similarly, if the same program reads input from the keyboard (*standard input*), we can tell it to read its input from a file named *input.txt:*

```
sample < input.txt
```

We can redirect both input and output with a single command:

```
sample < input.txt > output.txt
```

Figure 5–2   Modifying the Console Window Properties.

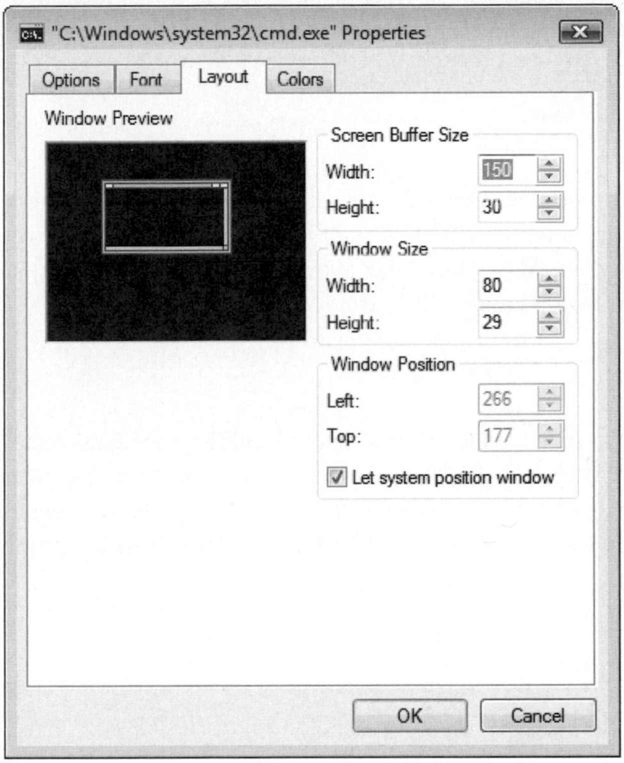

We can send the standard output from *prog1.exe* to the standard input of *prog2.exe* using the pipe (|) symbol:

```
prog1 | prog2
```

We can send the standard output from *prog1.exe* to the standard input of *prog2.exe*, and send the output of *prog2.exe* to a file named *output.txt:*

```
prog1 | prog2 > output.txt
```

Prog1.exe can read input from *input.txt*, send its output to *prog2.exe*, which in turn can send its output to *output.txt:*

```
prog1 < input.txt | prog2 > output.txt
```

The filenames input.txt and output.txt are arbitrary, so you can choose different filenames.

5.3.2   Individual Procedure Descriptions

In this section, we describe how each of the procedures in the Irvine16 and Irvine32 libraries is used. We will omit a few of the more advanced procedures, which will be explained in later chapters. In the descriptions, references to the console window are appropriate for the Irvine32 library, but would more correctly be termed standard output in the Irvine16 library.

CloseFile   *(Irvine32 only)* The CloseFile procedure closes a file that was previously created or opened (see CreateOutputFile and OpenInputFile). The file is identified by a 32-bit integer *handle*, which is passed in EAX. If the file is closed successfully, the value returned in EAX will be nonzero. Sample call:

```
mov    eax,fileHandle
call   CloseFile
```

Clrscr   The Clrscr procedure clears the console window. This procedure is typically called at the beginning and end of a program. If you call it at other times, you may need to pause the program by first calling WaitMsg. Doing this allows the user to view information already on the screen before it is erased. Sample call:

```
call   WaitMsg                        ; "Press any key..."
call   Clrscr
```

CreateOutputFile   *(Irvine32 only)* The CreateOutputFile procedure creates a new disk file and opens it for writing. When you call the procedure, place the offset of a filename in EDX. When the procedure returns, EAX will contain a valid file handle (32-bit integer) if the file was created successfully. Otherwise, EAX equals INVALID_HANDLE_VALUE (a predefined constant). Sample call:

```
.data
filename BYTE "newfile.txt",0
.code
mov   edx,OFFSET filename
call CreateOutputFile
```

The following pseudocode describes the possible outcomes after calling CreateOutputFile:

```
if EAX = INVALID_FILE_HANDLE
    the file was not created successfully
else
    EAX = handle for the open file
endif
```

Crlf   The Crlf procedure advances the cursor to the beginning of the next line in the console window. It writes a string containing the ASCII character codes 0Dh and 0Ah. Sample call:

```
call   Crlf
```

Delay   The Delay procedure pauses the program for a specified number of milliseconds. Before calling Delay, set EAX to the desired interval. Sample call:

```
mov    eax,1000                       ; 1 second
call   Delay
```

(The Irvine16.lib version does not work under Windows NT, 2000, XP, or Vista.)

DumpMem   The DumpMem procedure writes a range of memory to the console window in hexadecimal. Pass it the starting address in ESI, the number of units in ECX, and the unit size in EBX

(1 = byte, 2 = word, 4 = doubleword). The following sample call displays an array of 11 doublewords in hexadecimal:

```
.data
array DWORD 1,2,3,4,5,6,7,8,9,0Ah,0Bh
.code
main PROC
      mov    esi,OFFSET array                ; starting OFFSET
      mov    ecx,LENGTHOF array              ; number of units
      mov    ebx,TYPE array                  ; doubleword format
      call   DumpMem
```

The following output is produced:

```
00000001   00000002   00000003   00000004   00000005   00000006
00000007   00000008   00000009   0000000A   0000000B
```

DumpRegs   The DumpRegs procedure displays the EAX, EBX, ECX, EDX, ESI, EDI, EBP, ESP, EIP, and EFL (EFLAGS) registers in hexadecimal. It also displays the values of the Carry, Sign, Zero, Overflow, Auxiliary Carry, and Parity flags. Sample call:

```
call DumpRegs
```

Sample output:

```
EAX=00000613   EBX=00000000   ECX=000000FF   EDX=00000000
ESI=00000000   EDI=00000100   EBP=0000091E   ESP=000000F6
EIP=00401026   EFL=00000286   CF=0   SF=1   ZF=0   OF=0   AF=0   PF=1
```

The displayed value of EIP is the offset of the instruction following the call to DumpRegs. DumpRegs can be useful when debugging programs because it displays a snapshot of the CPU. It has no input parameters and no return value.

GetCommandTail   The GetCommandTail procedure copies the program's command line into a null-terminated string. If the command line was found to be empty, the Carry flag is set; otherwise, the Carry flag is cleared. This procedure is useful because it permits the user of a program to pass parameters on the command line. Suppose a program named **Encrypt.exe** reads an input file named **file1.txt** and produces an output file named **file2.txt**. The user can pass both filenames on the command line when running the program:

```
Encrypt file1.txt file2.txt
```

When it starts up, the Encrypt program can call GetCommandTail and retrieve the two filenames. When calling Get_Commandtail, EDX must contain the offset of an array of at least 129 bytes. Sample call:

```
.data
cmdTail BYTE 129 DUP(0)           ; empty buffer
.code
mov    edx,OFFSET cmdTail
call   GetCommandTail             ; fills the buffer
```

There is a way to pass command-line arguments when running an application in Visual Studio. From the Project menu, select *<projectname> Properties*. In the Property Pages window, expand the entry under *Configuration Properties*, and select *Debugging*. Then enter your command arguments into the edit line on the right panel named *Command Arguments*.

GetMaxXY   *(Irvine32 only)* The GetMaxXY procedure gets the size of the console window's buffer. If the console window buffer is larger than the visible window size, scroll bars appear automatically. GetMaxXY has no input parameters. When it returns, the DX register contains the number of buffer columns and AX contains the number of buffer rows. The possible range of each value can be no greater than 255, which may be smaller than the actual window buffer size. Sample call:

```
.data
rows  BYTE ?
cols  BYTE ?
.code
call  GetMaxXY
mov   rows,al
mov   cols,dl
```

GetMseconds   The GetMseconds procedure gets the number of milliseconds elapsed since midnight on the host computer, and returns the value in the EAX register. The procedure is a great tool for measuring the time between events. No input parameters are required. The following example calls GetMseconds, storing its return value. After the loop executes, the code call GetMseconds a second time and subtract the two time values. The difference is the approximate execution time of the loop:

```
.data
startTime DWORD ?
.code
call GetMseconds
mov  startTime,eax
L1:
  ; (loop body)
loop L1
call GetMseconds
sub  eax,startTime            ; EAX = loop time, in milliseconds
```

GetTextColor *(Irvine32 only)* The GetTextColor procedure gets the current foreground and background colors of the console window. It has no input parameters. It returns the background color in the upper four bits of AL and the foreground color in the lower four bits. Sample call:

```
.data
color BYTE ?
.code
call  GetTextColor
mov   color,AL
```

Gotoxy   The Gotoxy procedure locates the cursor at a given row and column in the console window. By default, the console window's X-coordinate range is 0 to 79 and the Y-coordinate range is

0 to 24. When you call Gotoxy, pass the Y-coordinate (row) in DH and the X-coordinate (column) in DL. Sample call:

```
mov   dh,10                    ; row 10
mov   dl,20                    ; column 20
call  Gotoxy                   ; locate cursor
```

The user may have resized the console window, so you can call GetMaxXY to find out the current number of rows and columns.

IsDigit   The IsDigit procedure determines whether the value in AL is the ASCII code for a valid decimal digit. When calling it, pass an ASCII character in AL. The procedure sets the Zero flag if AL contains a valid decimal digit; otherwise, it clears Zero flag. Sample call:

```
mov   AL,somechar
call  IsDigit
```

MsgBox   *(Irvine32 only)* The MsgBox procedure displays a graphical popup message box with an optional caption. (This works when the program is running in a console window.) Pass it the offset of a string in EDX, which will appear in the inside the box. Optionally, pass the offset of a string for the box's title in EBX. To leave the title blank, set EBX to zero. Sample call:

```
.data
caption db "Dialog Title", 0
HelloMsg BYTE "This is a pop-up message box.", 0dh,0ah
       BYTE "Click OK to continue...", 0
.code
mov   ebx,OFFSET caption
mov   edx,OFFSET HelloMsg
call  MsgBox
```

Sample output:

MsgBoxAsk   *(Irvine32 only)* The MsgBoxAsk procedure displays a graphical popup message box with Yes and No buttons. (This works when the program is running in a console window.) Pass it the offset of a question string in EDX, which will appear in the inside the box. Optionally, pass the offset of a string for the box's title in EBX. To leave the title blank, set EBX to zero. MsgBoxAsk returns an integer in EAX that tells you which button was selected by the user. The value will be one of two predefined Windows constants: IDYES (equal to 6) or IDNO (equal to 7). Sample call:

```
.data
caption BYTE "Survey Completed",0
question BYTE "Thank you for completing the survey."
  BYTE 0dh,0ah
```

```
    BYTE "Would you like to receive the results?",0
.code
mov    ebx,OFFSET caption
mov    edx,OFFSET question
call   MsgBoxAsk
;(check return value in EAX)
```

Sample output:

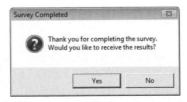

OpenInputFile *(Irvine32 only)* The OpenInputFile procedure opens an existing file for input. Pass it the offset of a filename in EDX. When it returns, if the file was opened successfully, EAX will contain a valid file handle. Otherwise, EAX will equal INVALID_HANDLE_VALUE (a predefined constant).

Sample call:

```
.data
filename BYTE "myfile.txt",0
.code
mov edx,OFFSET filename
call OpenInputFile
```

The following pseudocode describes the possible outcomes after calling OpenInputFile:

```
if EAX = INVALID_FILE_HANDLE
    the file was not opened successfully
else
    EAX = handle for the open file
endif
```

ParseDecimal32 The ParseDecimal32 procedure converts an unsigned decimal integer string to 32-bit binary. All valid digits occurring before a nonnumeric character are converted. Leading spaces are ignored. Pass it the offset of a string in EDX and the string's length in ECX. The binary value is returned in EAX. Sample call:

```
.data
buffer BYTE "8193"
bufSize = ($ - buffer)
.code
mov    edx,OFFSET buffer
mov    ecx,bufSize
call   ParseDecimal32              ; returns EAX
```

- If the integer is blank, EAX = 0 and CF = 1
- If the integer contains only spaces, EAX = 0 and CF = 1

- If the integer is larger than $2^{32}-1$, EAX = 0 and CF = 1
- Otherwise, EAX contains the converted integer and CF = 0

See the description of the **ReadDec** procedure for details about how the Carry flag is affected.

ParseInteger32   The ParseInteger32 procedure converts a signed decimal integer string to 32-bit binary. All valid digits from the beginning of the string to the first nonnumeric character are converted. Leading spaces are ignored. Pass it the offset of a string in EDX and the string's length in ECX. The binary value is returned in EAX. Sample call:

```
.data
buffer BYTE "-8193"
bufSize = ($ - buffer)
.code
mov    edx,OFFSET buffer
mov    ecx,bufSize
call   ParseInteger32              ; returns EAX
```

The string may contain an optional leading plus or minus sign, followed only by decimal digits. The Overflow flag is set and an error message is displayed on the console if the value cannot be represented as a 32-bit signed integer (range: $-2,147,483,648$ to $+2,147,483,647$).

Random32   The Random32 procedure generates and returns a 32-bit random integer in EAX. When called repeatedly, Random32 generates a simulated random sequence. The numbers are created using a simple function having an input called a *seed*. The function uses the seed in a formula that generates the random value. Subsequent random values are generated using each previously generated random value as their seeds. The following code snippet shows a sample call to Random32:

```
.data
randVal DWORD ?
.code
call   Random32
mov    randVal,eax
```

Random32 is also available in the Irvine16 library, returning its value in EAX.

Randomize   The Randomize procedure initializes the starting seed value of the Random32 and RandomRange procedures. The seed equals the time of day, accurate to 1/100 of a second. Each time you run a program that calls Random32 and RandomRange, the generated sequence of random numbers will be unique. You need only to call Randomize once at the beginning of a program. The following example produces 10 random integers:

```
        call   Randomize
        mov    ecx,10
L1:     call   Random32

        ; use or display random value in EAX here...

        loop   L1
```

RandomRange   The RandomRange procedure produces a random integer within the range of 0 to $n - 1$, where n is an input parameter passed in the EAX register. The random integer is returned in EAX. The following example generates a single random integer between 0 and 4999 and places it in a variable named *randVal*.

```
.data
randVal DWORD ?
.code
mov   eax,5000
call  RandomRange
mov   randVal,eax
```

ReadChar   The ReadChar procedure reads a single character from the keyboard and returns the character in the AL register. The character is not echoed in the console window. Sample call:

```
.data
char BYTE ?
.code
call ReadChar
mov  char,al
```

If the user presses an extended key such as a function key, arrow key, Ins, or Del, the procedure sets AL to zero, and AH contains a keyboard scan code. A list of scan codes is shown on the page facing the book's inside front cover. The upper half of EAX is not preserved. The following pseudocode describes the possible outcomes after calling ReadChar:

```
if an extended key was pressed
     AL = 0
     AH = keyboard scan code
else
     AL = ASCII key value
endif
```

ReadDec   The ReadDec procedure reads a 32-bit unsigned decimal integer from the keyboard and returns the value in EAX. Leading spaces are ignored. The return value is calculated from all valid digits found until a nondigit character is encountered. For example, if the user enters 123ABC, the value returned in EAX is 123. Following is a sample call:

```
.data
intVal DWORD ?
.code
call ReadDec
mov  intVal,eax
```

ReadDec affects the Carry flag in the following ways:

• If the integer is blank, EAX = 0 and CF = 1
• If the integer contains only spaces, EAX = 0 and CF = 1
• If the integer is larger than $2^{32} - 1$, EAX = 0 and CF = 1
• Otherwise, EAX holds the converted integer and CF = 0

ReadFromFile   (*Irvine32 only*) The ReadFromFile procedure reads an input disk file into a memory buffer. When you call ReadFromFile, pass it an open file handle in EAX, the offset of a buffer in EDX, and the maximum number of bytes to read in ECX. When ReadFromFile returns, check the value of the Carry flag: If CF is clear, EAX contains a count of the number of bytes read from the file. But if CF is set, EAX contains a numeric system error code. You can call the WriteWindowsMsg procedure to get a text representation of the error. In the following example, as many as 5000 bytes are copied from the file into the buffer variable:

```
.data
BUFFER_SIZE = 5000
buffer BYTE BUFFER_SIZE DUP(?)
bytesRead DWORD ?

.code
mov    edx,OFFSET buffer        ; points to buffer
mov    ecx,BUFFER_SIZE          ; max bytes to read
call   ReadFromFile             ; read the file
```

If the Carry flag were clear at this point, you could execute the following instruction:

```
mov  bytesRead,eax                  ; count of bytes actually read
```

But if the Carry flag were set, you would call WriteWindowsMsg procedure, which displays a string that contains the error code and description of the most recent error generated by the application:

```
call   WriteWindowsMsg
```

ReadHex   The ReadHex procedure reads a 32-bit hexadecimal integer from the keyboard and returns the corresponding binary value in EAX. No error checking is performed for invalid characters. You can use both uppercase and lowercase letters for the digits A through F. A maximum of eight digits may be entered (additional characters are ignored). Leading spaces are ignored. Sample call:

```
.data
hexVal DWORD ?
.code
call ReadHex
mov   hexVal,eax
```

ReadInt   The ReadInt procedure reads a 32-bit signed integer from the keyboard and returns the value in EAX. The user can type an optional leading plus or minus sign, and the rest of the number may only consist of digits. ReadInt sets the Overflow flag and display an error message if the value entered cannot be represented as a 32-bit signed integer (range: $-2{,}147{,}483{,}648$ to $+2{,}147{,}483{,}647$). The return value is calculated from all valid digits found until a nondigit character is encountered. For example, if the user enters $+123ABC$, the value returned is $+123$. Sample call:

```
.data
intVal SDWORD ?
.code
call   ReadInt
mov    intVal,eax
```

ReadKey The ReadKey procedure performs a no-wait keyboard check. In other words, it inspects the keyboard input buffer to see if a key has been pressed by the user. If no keyboard data is found, the Zero flag is set. If a keypress is found by ReadKey, the Zero flag is cleared and AL is assigned either zero or an ASCII code. If AL contains zero, the user may have pressed a special key (function key, arrow key, etc.) The AH register contains a virtual scan code, DX contains a virtual key code, and EBX contains the keyboard flag bits. The following pseudocode describes the various outcomes when calling ReadKey:

```
if no_keyboard_data then
   ZF = 1
else
   ZF = 0
   if AL = 0 then
     extended key was pressed, and AH = scan code, DX = virtual
        key code, and EBX =  keyboard flag bits
   else
     AL = the key's ASCII code
   endif
endif
```

The upper halves of EAX and EDX are overwritten when ReadKey is called.

ReadString The ReadString procedure reads a string from the keyboard, stopping when the user presses the Enter key. Pass the offset of a buffer in EDX and set ECX to the maximum number of characters the user can enter, plus 1 (to save space for the terminating null byte). The procedure returns the count of the number of characters typed by the user in EAX. Sample call:

```
.data
buffer BYTE 21 DUP(0)            ; input buffer
byteCount DWORD ?                ; holds counter
.code
mov   edx,OFFSET buffer          ; point to the buffer
mov   ecx,SIZEOF buffer          ; specify max characters
call  ReadString                 ; input the string
mov   byteCount,eax              ; number of characters
```

ReadString automatically inserts a null terminator in memory at the end of the string. The following is a hexadecimal and ASCII dump of the first 8 bytes of **buffer** after the user has entered the string "ABCDEFG":

41 42 43 44 45 46 47 00	ABCDEFG

The variable **byteCount** equals 7.

SetTextColor The SetTextColor procedure *(Irvine32 library only)* sets the foreground and background colors for text output. When calling SetTextColor, assign a color attribute to EAX.

The following predefined color constants can be used for both foreground and background:

black = 0	red = 4	gray = 8	lightRed = 12
blue = 1	magenta = 5	lightBlue = 9	lightMagenta = 13
green = 2	brown = 6	lightGreen = 10	yellow = 14
cyan = 3	lightGray = 7	lightCyan = 11	white = 15

Color constants are defined in the include files named *Irvine32.inc* and *Irvine16.inc*. Multiply the background color by 16 and add it to the foreground color. The following constant, for example, indicates yellow characters on a blue background:

```
yellow + (blue * 16)
```

The following statements set the color to white on a blue background:

```
mov    eax,white + (blue * 16)   ; white on blue
call   SetTextColor
```

An alternative way to express color constants is to use the SHL operator. You shift the background color leftward by 4 bits before adding it to the foreground color.

```
yellow + (blue SHL 4)
```

The bit shifting is performed at assembly time, so it can only be used with constants. In Chapter 7, you will learn how to shift integers at runtime. You can find a detailed explanation of video attributes in Section 16.3.2. The Irvine16 version of SetTextColor clears the console window with the selected colors.

StrLength   The StrLength procedure returns the length of a null-terminated string. Pass the string's offset in EDX. The procedure returns the string's length in EAX. Sample call:

```
.data
buffer BYTE "abcde",0
bufLength DWORD ?
.code
mov    edx,OFFSET buffer        ; point to string
call   StrLength                ; EAX = 5
mov    bufLength,eax            ; save length
```

WaitMsg   The WaitMsg procedure displays the message "Press any key to continue. . ." and waits for the user to press a key. This procedure is useful when you want to pause the screen display before data scrolls off and disappears. It has no input parameters. Sample call:

```
call   WaitMsg
```

WriteBin   The WriteBin procedure writes an integer to the console window in ASCII binary format. Pass the integer in EAX. The binary bits are displayed in groups of four for easy reading. Sample call:

```
mov    eax,12346AF9h
call   WriteBin
```

The following output would be displayed by our sample code:

```
0001 0010 0011 0100 0110 1010 1111 1001
```

WriteBinB   The WriteBinB procedure writes a 32-bit integer to the console window in ASCII binary format. Pass the value in the EAX register and let EBX indicate the display size in bytes (1, 2, or 4). The bits are displayed in groups of four for easy reading. Sample call:

```
mov    eax,00001234h
mov    ebx,TYPE WORD          ; 2 bytes
call   WriteBinB              ; displays 0001 0010 0011 0100
```

WriteChar   The WriteChar procedure writes a single character to the console window. Pass the character (or its ASCII code) in AL. Sample call:

```
mov    al,'A'
call   WriteChar             ; displays: "A"
```

WriteDec   The WriteDec procedure writes a 32-bit unsigned integer to the console window in decimal format with no leading zeros. Pass the integer in EAX. Sample call:

```
mov    eax,295
call   WriteDec              ; displays: "295"
```

WriteHex   The WriteHex procedure writes a 32-bit unsigned integer to the console window in 8-digit hexadecimal format. Leading zeros are inserted if necessary. Pass the integer in EAX. Sample call:

```
mov    eax,7FFFh
call   WriteHex             ; displays: "00007FFF"
```

WriteHexB   The WriteHexB procedure writes a 32-bit unsigned integer to the console window in hexadecimal format. Leading zeros are inserted if necessary. Pass the integer in EAX and let EBX indicate the display format in bytes (1, 2, or 4). Sample call:

```
mov    eax,7FFFh
mov    ebx,TYPE WORD          ; 2 bytes
call   WriteHexB             ; displays: "7FFF"
```

WriteInt   The WriteInt procedure writes a 32-bit signed integer to the console window in decimal format with a leading sign and no leading zeros. Pass the integer in EAX. Sample call:

```
mov    eax,216543
call   WriteInt             ; displays: "+216543"
```

WriteString   The WriteString procedure writes a null-terminated string to the console window. Pass the string's offset in EDX. Sample call:

```
.data
prompt BYTE "Enter your name: ",0
.code
mov    edx,OFFSET prompt
call   WriteString
```

WriteToFile   *(Irvine32 only)* The WriteToFile procedure writes the contents of a buffer to an output file. Pass it a valid file handle in EAX, the offset of the buffer in EDX, and the number of bytes to write in ECX. When the procedure returns, if EAX is greater than zero, it contains a count of the number of bytes written; otherwise, an error occurred. The following code calls WriteToFile:

```
BUFFER_SIZE = 5000
.data
fileHandle    DWORD ?
buffer        BYTE BUFFER_SIZE DUP(?)

.code
mov   eax,fileHandle
mov   edx,OFFSET buffer
mov   ecx,BUFFER_SIZE
call  WriteToFile
```

The following pseudocode describes how to handle the value returned in EAX after calling WriteToFile:

```
if EAX = 0 then
    error occurred when writing to file
    call WriteWindowsMessage to see the error
else
    EAX = number of bytes written to the file
endif
```

WriteWindowsMsg   *(Irvine32 only)* The WriteWindowsMsg procedure displays a string containing the most recent error generated by your application when executing a call to a system function. Sample call:

```
call WriteWindowsMsg
```

The following is an example of a message string:

```
Error 2: The system cannot find the file specified.
```

5.3.3   Library Test Programs

Tutorial: Library Test #1
In this hands-on tutorial, you will write a program that demonstrates integer input-output with screen colors.

Step 1: Begin the program with a standard heading:

```
TITLE Library Test #1: Integer I/O (InputLoop.asm)

; Tests the Clrscr, Crlf, DumpMem, ReadInt, SetTextColor,
; WaitMsg, WriteBin, WriteHex, and WriteString procedures
INCLUDE Irvine32.inc
```

Step 2: Declare a **COUNT** constant that will determine the number of times the program's loop repeats later on. Then two constants, **BlueTextOnGray** and **DefaultColor**, are defined here so they can be used later on when we change the console window colors. The color byte stores the background color in the upper 4 bits, and the foreground (text) color in the lower 4 bits. We have not yet discussed bit shifting instructions, but you can multiply the background color by 16 to shift it into the high 4 bits of the color attribute byte:

```
.data
COUNT = 4
BlueTextOnGray = blue + (lightGray * 16)
DefaultColor = lightGray + (black * 16)
```

Step 3: Declare an array of signed doubleword integers, using hexadecimal constants. Also, add a string that will be used as prompt when the program asks the user to input an integer:

```
arrayD SDWORD 12345678h,1A4B2000h,3434h,7AB9h
prompt BYTE "Enter a 32-bit signed integer: ",0
```

Step 4: In the code area, declare the main procedure and write code that initializes ECX to blue text on a light gray background. The **SetTextColor** method changes the foreground and background color attributes of all text written to the window from this point onward in the program's execution:

```
.code
main PROC
    mov    eax,BlueTextOnGray
    call   SetTextColor
```

In order to set the background of the console window to the new color, you must use the Clrscr procedure to clear the screen:

```
    call   Clrscr                              ; clear the screen
```

Next, the program will display a range of doubleword values in memory, identified by the variable named **arrayD***. The DumpMem procedure requires parameters to be passed in the ESI, EBX, and ECX registers.*

Step 5: Assign to ESI the offset of **arrayD,** which marks the beginning of the range we wish to display:

```
    mov    esi,OFFSET arrayD
```

Step 6: EBX is assigned an integer value that specifies the size of each array element. Since we are displaying an array of doublewords, EBX equals 4. This is the value returned by the expression TYPE arrayD:

```
    mov    ebx,TYPE arrayD                     ; doubleword = 4 bytes
```

Step 7: ECX must be set to the number of units that will be displayed, using the LENGTHOF operator. Then, when DumpMem is called, it has all the information it needs:

```
    mov    ecx,LENGTHOF arrayD    ; number of units in arrayD
    call   DumpMem                ; display memory
```

The following figure shows the type of output that would be generated by DumpMem:

```
Dump of offset 00405000
-------------------------------
12345678  1A4B2000  00003434  00007AB9
```

Next, the user will be asked to input a sequence of four signed integers. After each integer is entered, it is redisplayed in signed decimal, hexadecimal, and binary.

Step 8: Output a blank line by calling the Crlf procedure. Then, initialize ECX to the constant value COUNT so ECX can be the counter for the loop that follows:

```
call   Crlf
mov    ecx,COUNT
```

Step 9: We need to display a string that asks the user to enter an integer. Assign the offsct of the string to EDX, and call the WriteString procedure. Then, call the ReadInt procedure to receive input from the user. The value the user enters will be automatically stored in EAX:

```
L1: mov    edx,OFFSET prompt
    call   WriteString
    call   ReadInt                    ; input integer into EAX
    call   Crlf                       ; display a newline
```

Step 10: Display the integer stored in EAX in signed decimal format by calling the WriteInt procedure. Then call Crlf to move the cursor to the next output line:

```
    call   WriteInt                   ; display in signed decimal
    call   Crlf
```

Step 11: Display the same integer (still in EAX) in hexadecimal and binary formats, by calling the WriteHex and WriteBin procedures:

```
    call   WriteHex                   ; display in hexadecimal
    call   Crlf
    call   WriteBin                   ; display in binary
    call   Crlf
    call   Crlf
```

Step 12: You will insert a Loop instruction that allows the loop to repeat at Label L1. This instruction first decrements ECX, and then jumps to label L1 only if ECX is not equal to zero:

```
    Loop  L1                          ; repeat the loop
```

Step 13: After the loop ends, we want to display a "Press any key…" message and then pause the output and wait for a key to be pressed by the user. To do this, we call the WaitMsg procedure:

```
    call   WaitMsg                    ; "Press any key..."
```

Step 14: Just before the program ends, the console window attributes are returned to the default colors (light gray characters on a black background).

```
    mov    eax, DefaultColor
    call   SetTextColor
    call   Clrscr
```

Here are the closing lines of the program:

```
    exit
main ENDP
END main
```

The remainder of the program's output is shown in the following figure, using four sample integers entered by the user:

```
Enter a 32-bit signed integer: -42

-42
FFFFFFD6
1111 1111 1111 1111 1111 1111 1101 0110

Enter a 32-bit signed integer: 36

+36
00000024
0000 0000 0000 0000 0000 0000 0010 0100

Enter a 32-bit signed integer: 244324

+244324
0003BA64
0000 0000 0000 0011 1011 1010 0110 0100

Enter a 32-bit signed integer: -7979779

-7979779
FF863CFD
1111 1111 1000 0110 0011 1100 1111 1101
```

A complete listing of the program appears below, with a few added comment lines:

```
TITLE Library Test #1: Integer I/O   (InputLoop.asm)

; Tests the Clrscr, Crlf, DumpMem, ReadInt, SetTextColor,
; WaitMsg, WriteBin, WriteHex, and WriteString procedures.
INCLUDE Irvine32.inc
.data
COUNT = 4
BlueTextOnGray = blue + (lightGray * 16)
DefaultColor = lightGray + (black * 16)
arrayD SDWORD 12345678h,1A4B2000h,3434h,7AB9h
prompt BYTE "Enter a 32-bit signed integer: ",0

.code
main PROC

; Select blue text on a light gray background

    mov   eax,BlueTextOnGray
    call  SetTextColor
    call  Clrscr                    ; clear the screen

    ; Display an array using DumpMem.

    mov   esi,OFFSET arrayD         ; starting OFFSET
    mov   ebx,TYPE arrayD           ; doubleword = 4 bytes
    mov   ecx,LENGTHOF arrayD       ; number of units in arrayD
```

```
        call    DumpMem                          ; display memory

        ; Ask the user to input a sequence of signed integers

        call    Crlf                             ; new line
        mov     ecx,COUNT
L1:     mov     edx,OFFSET prompt
        call    WriteString
        call    ReadInt                          ; input integer into EAX
        call    Crlf                             ; new line

    ; Display the integer in decimal, hexadecimal, and binary

        call    WriteInt                         ; display in signed decimal
        call    Crlf
        call    WriteHex                         ; display in hexadecimal
        call    Crlf
        call    WriteBin                         ; display in binary
        call    Crlf
        call    Crlf
        Loop    L1                               ; repeat the loop

    ; Return the console window to default colors

        call    WaitMsg                          ; "Press any key..."
        mov     eax,DefaultColor
        call    SetTextColor
        call    Clrscr

        exit
main ENDP
END main
```

Library Test #2: Random Integers

Let's look at a second library test program that demonstrates random-number-generation capabilities of the link library, and introduces the CALL instruction (to be covered fully in Section 5.5). First, it randomly generates 10 unsigned integers in the range 0 to 4,294,967,294. Next, it generates 10 signed integers in the range −50 to +49:

```
TITLE Link Library Test #2 (TestLib2.asm)

; Testing the Irvine32 Library procedures.

INCLUDE Irvine32.inc

TAB = 9                         ; ASCII code for Tab
.code
main PROC
    call    Randomize           ; init random generator
    call    Rand1
    call    Rand2
    exit
main ENDP

Rand1 PROC
; Generate ten pseudo-random integers.
```

```
            mov     ecx,10                      ; loop 10 times
    L1: call    Random32                    ; generate random int
        call    WriteDec                    ; write in unsigned decimal
        mov     al,TAB                      ; horizontal tab
        call    WriteChar                   ; write the tab
        loop    L1

        call    Crlf
        ret
    Rand1 ENDP

    Rand2 PROC
    ; Generate ten pseudo-random integers from -50 to +49
            mov     ecx,10                      ; loop 10 times

    L1: mov     eax,100                     ; values 0-99
        call    RandomRange                 ; generate random int
        sub     eax,50                      ; values -50 to +49
        call    WriteInt                    ; write signed decimal
        mov     al,TAB                      ; horizontal tab
        call    WriteChar                   ; write the tab
        loop    L1

        call    Crlf
        ret
    Rand2 ENDP
    END main
```

Here is sample output from the program:

```
    3221236194      2210931702      974700167      367494257     2227888607

    926772240       506254858      1769123448    2288603673    736071794

    -34     +27     +38     -34     +31     -13     -29     +44     -48     -43
```

Library Test #3: Performance Timing

Assembly language is often used to optimize sections of code seen as critical to a program's performance. The *GetMseconds* procedure from the book's library returns the number of milliseconds elapsed since midnight. In our third library test program, we call *GetMseconds*, execute a nested loop, and call *GetMSeconds* a second time. The difference between the two values returned by these procedure calls gives us the elapsed time of the nested loop:

```
    TITLE Link Library Test #3       (TestLib3.asm)

    ; Calculate the elapsed execution time of a nested loop
    INCLUDE Irvine32.inc

    .data
    OUTER_LOOP_COUNT = 3
    startTime DWORD ?
    msg1 BYTE "Please wait...",0dh,0ah,0
    msg2 BYTE "Elapsed milliseconds: ",0
```

```
        .code
main PROC
        mov    edx,OFFSET msg1        ; "Please wait..."
        call   WriteString

; Save the starting time

        call   GetMSeconds
        mov    startTime,eax

; Start the outer loop

        mov    ecx,OUTER_LOOP_COUNT

L1: call   innerLoop
        loop   L1

; Calculate the elapsed time

        call   GetMSeconds
        sub    eax,startTime

; Display the elapsed time

        mov    edx,OFFSET msg2        ; "Elapsed milliseconds: "
        call   WriteString
        call   WriteDec               ; write the milliseconds
        call   Crlf

        exit
main ENDP

innerLoop PROC
        push   ecx                    ; save current ECX value

        mov    ecx,0FFFFFFFh          ; set the loop counter
L1: mul    eax                    ; use up some cycles
        mul    eax
        mul    eax
        loop   L1                     ; repeat the inner loop

        pop    ecx                    ; restore ECX's saved value
        ret
innerLoop ENDP

END main
```

Here is sample output from the program running on an Intel Core Duo processor:

```
    Please wait....
    Elapsed milliseconds: 4974
```

Detailed Analysis of the Program

Let us study Library Test #3 in greater detail. The *main* procedure displays the string "Please wait…" in the console window:

```
main PROC
        mov    edx,OFFSET msg1        ; "Please wait..."
        call   WriteString
```

When *GetMSeconds* is called, it returns the number of milliseconds that have elapsed since midnight into the EAX register. This value is saved in a variable for later use:

```
call   GetMSeconds
mov    startTime,eax
```

Next, we create a loop that executes based on the value of the OUTER_LOOP_COUNT constant. That value is moved to ECX for use later in the LOOP instruction:

```
mov    ecx,OUTER_LOOP_COUNT
```

The loop begins with label L1, where the *innerLoop* procedure is called. This CALL instruction repeats until ECX is decremented down to zero:

```
L1: call   innerLoop
    loop   L1
```

The **innerLoop** procedure uses an instruction named PUSH to save ECX on the stack before setting it to a new value. (We will discuss PUSH and POP in the upcoming Section 5.4.) Then, the loop itself has a few instructions designed to use up clock cycles:

```
innerLoop PROC
    push  ecx                           ; save current ECX value

    mov   ecx,0FFFFFFFh                  ; set the loop counter
L1: mul   eax                           ; use up some cycles
    mul   eax
    mul   eax
    loop  L1                            ; repeat the inner loop
```

The LOOP instruction will have decremented ECX down to zero at this point, so we pop the saved value of ECX off the stack. It will now have the same value on leaving this procedure that it had when entering. The PUSH and POP sequence is necessary because the *main* procedure was using ECX as a loop counter when it called the *innerLoop* procedure. Here are the last few lines of *innerLoop:*

```
    pop   ecx                           ; restore ECX's saved value
    ret
innerLoop ENDP
```

Back in the *main* procedure, after the loop finishes, we call GetMSeconds, which returns its result in EAX. All we have to do is subtract the starting time from this value to get the number of milliseconds that elapsed between the two calls to GetMSeconds:

```
call   GetMSeconds
sub    eax,startTime
```

The program displays a new string message, and then displays the integer in EAX that represents the number of elapsed milliseconds:

```
mov    edx,OFFSET msg2                  ; "Elapsed milliseconds: "
call   WriteString
call   WriteDec                         ; display the value in EAX
call   Crlf
exit
main ENDP
```

5.3.4   Section Review

1. Which procedure in the link library generates a random integer within a selected range?

2. Which procedure in the link library displays "Press [Enter] to continue. . ." and waits for the user to press the Enter key?

3. Write statements that cause a program to pause for 700 milliseconds.

4. Which procedure from the link library writes an unsigned integer to the console window in decimal format?

5. Which procedure from the link library places the cursor at a specific console window location?

6. Write the INCLUDE directive that is required when using the Irvine32 library.

7. What types of statements are inside the *Irvine32.inc* file?

8. What are the required input parameters for the DumpMem procedure?

9. What are the required input parameters for the ReadString procedure?

10. Which processor status flags are displayed by the DumpRegs procedure?

11. *Challenge:* Write statements that prompt the user for an identification number and input a string of digits into an array of bytes.

5.4   Stack Operations

If we place 10 plates on each other as in the following diagram, the result can be called a stack. While it might be possible to remove a dish from the middle of the stack, it is much more common to remove from the top. New plates can be added to the top of the stack, but never to the bottom or middle (Figure 5–3):

Figure 5–3   Stack of Plates.

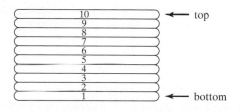

A *stack data structure* follows the same principle as a stack of plates: New values are added to the top of the stack, and existing values are removed from the top. Stacks in general are useful structures for a variety of programming applications, and they can easily be implemented using object-oriented programming methods. If you have taken a programming course that used data structures, you have worked with the *stack abstract data type*. A stack is also called a LIFO structure (*Last-In, First-Out*) because the last value put into the stack is always the first value taken out.

In this chapter, we concentrate specifically on the *runtime stack*. It is supported directly by hardware in the CPU, and it is an essential part of the mechanism for calling and returning from procedures. Most of the time, we just call it *the stack*.

5.4.1 Runtime Stack

The *runtime stack* is a memory array managed directly by the CPU, using the ESP register, known as the *stack pointer register*. The ESP register holds a 32-bit offset into some location on the stack. We rarely manipulate ESP directly; instead, it is indirectly modified by instructions such as CALL, RET, PUSH, and POP.

ESP always points to the last value to be added to, or *pushed* on, the top of stack. To demonstrate, let's begin with a stack containing one value. In Figure 5–4, the ESP (extended stack pointer) contains hexadecimal 00001000, the offset of the most recently pushed value (00000006). In our diagrams, the top of the stack moves downward when the stack pointer decreases in value:

FIGURE 5–4   A Stack Containing a Single Value.

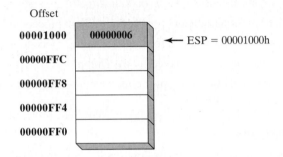

Each stack location in this figure contains 32 bits, which is the case when a program is running in 32-bit mode. In 16-bit real-address mode, the SP register points to the most recently pushed value and stack entries are typically 16 bits long.

The runtime stack discussed here is not the same as the *stack abstract data type* (ADT) discussed in data structures courses. The runtime stack works at the system level to handle subroutine calls. The stack ADT is a programming construct typically written in a high-level programming language such as C++ or Java. It is used when implementing algorithms that depend on last-in, first-out operations.

Push Operation

A 32-bit push operation decrements the stack pointer by 4 and copies a value into the location in the stack pointed to by the stack pointer. Figure 5–5 shows the effect of pushing 000000A5 on a

FIGURE 5–5   Pushing Integers on the Stack

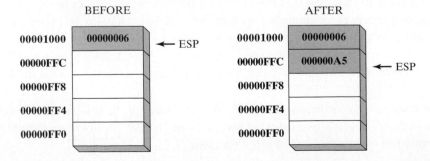

stack that already contains one value (00000006). Notice that the ESP register always points to the top of the stack. The figure shows the stack ordering opposite to that of the stack of plates we saw earlier, because the runtime stack grows downward in memory, from higher addresses to lower addresses. Before the push, ESP = 00001000h; after the push, ESP = 00000FFCh. Figure 5–6 shows the same stack after pushing a total of four integers.

Figure 5–6   Stack, after Pushing 00000001 and 00000002.

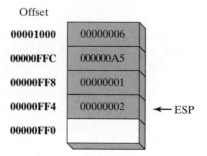

Pop Operation

A *pop* operation removes a value from the stack. After the value is popped from the stack, the stack pointer is incremented (by the stack element size) to point to the next-highest location in the stack. Figure 5–7 shows the stack before and after the value 00000002 is popped.

Figure 5–7   Popping a Value from the Runtime Stack.

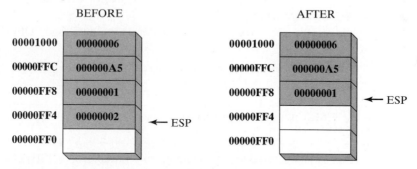

The area of the stack below ESP is *logically empty*, and will be overwritten the next time the current program executes any instruction that pushes a value on the stack.

Stack Applications

There are several important uses of runtime stacks in programs:

- A stack makes a convenient temporary save area for registers when they are used for more than one purpose. After they are modified, they can be restored to their original values.
- When the CALL instruction executes, the CPU saves the current subroutine's return address on the stack.
- When calling a subroutine, you pass input values called *arguments* by pushing them on the stack.
- The stack provides temporary storage for local variables inside subroutines.

5.4.2 PUSH and POP Instructions

PUSH Instruction

The PUSH instruction first decrements ESP and then copies a source operand into the stack. A 16-bit operand causes ESP to be decremented by 2. A 32-bit operand causes ESP to be decremented by 4. There are three instruction formats:

```
PUSH reg/mem16
PUSH reg/mem32
PUSH imm32
```

> If your program calls procedures in the Irvine32 library, you must push 32-bit values; if you do not, the Win32 Console functions used by the library will not work correctly. If your program calls procedures from the Irvine16 library (in real-address mode), you can push both 16-bit and 32-bit values.

Immediate values are always 32 bits in 32-bit mode. In real-address mode, immediate values default to 16 bits, unless the .386 processor (or higher) directive is used. (The .386 directive was explained in Section 3.2.1).

POP Instruction

The POP instruction first copies the contents of the stack element pointed to by ESP into a 16- or 32-bit destination operand and then increments ESP. If the operand is 16 bits, ESP is incremented by 2; if the operand is 32 bits, ESP is incremented by 4:

```
POP reg/mem16
POP reg/mem32
```

PUSHFD and POPFD Instructions

The PUSHFD instruction pushes the 32-bit EFLAGS register on the stack, and POPFD pops the stack into EFLAGS:

```
pushfd
popfd
```

> 16-bit programs use the PUSHF instruction to push the 16-bit FLAGS register on the stack and POPF to pop the stack into FLAGS.

The MOV instruction cannot be used to copy the flags to a variable, so PUSHFD may be the best way to save the flags. There are times when it is useful to make a backup copy of the flags so you can restore them to their former values later. Often, we enclose a block of code within PUSHFD and POPFD:

```
pushfd                              ; save the flags
;
; any sequence of statements here...
;
popfd                               ; restore the flags
```

When using pushes and pops of this type, be sure the program's execution path does not skip over the POPFD instruction. When a program is modified over time, it can be tricky to remember where all the pushes and pops are located. The need for precise documentation is critical!

A less error-prone way to save and restore the flags is to push them on the stack and immediately pop them into a variable:

```
.data
saveFlags DWORD ?
.code
pushfd                          ; push flags on stack
pop  saveFlags                  ; copy into a variable
```

The following statements restore the flags from the same variable:

```
push saveFlags                  ; push saved flag values
popfd                           ; copy into the flags
```

PUSHAD, PUSHA, POPAD, and POPA

The PUSHAD instruction pushes all of the 32-bit general-purpose registers on the stack in the following order: EAX, ECX, EDX, EBX, ESP (value before executing PUSHAD), EBP, ESI, and EDI. The POPAD instruction pops the same registers off the stack in reverse order. Similarly, the PUSHA instruction, introduced with the 80286 processor, pushes the 16-bit general-purpose registers (AX, CX, DX, BX, SP, BP, SI, DI) on the stack in the order listed. The POPA instruction pops the same registers in reverse order.

If you write a procedure that modifies a number of 32-bit registers, use PUSHAD at the beginning of the procedure and POPAD at the end to save and restore the registers. The following code fragment is an example:

```
MySub PROC
        pushad                          ; save general-purpose registers
        .
        .
        mov eax,...
        mov edx,...
        mov ecx,...
        .
        .
        popad                           ; restore general-purpose registers
        ret
MySub ENDP
```

An important exception to the foregoing example must be pointed out; procedures returning results in one or more registers should not use PUSHA and PUSHAD. Suppose the following **ReadValue** procedure returns an integer in EAX; the call to POPAD overwrites the return value from EAX:

```
ReadValue PROC
        pushad                          ; save general-purpose registers
        .
        .
        mov   eax,return_value
        .
        .
        popad                           ; overwrites EAX!
        ret
ReadValue ENDP
```

Example: Reversing a String

The *RevStr.asm* program loops through a string and pushes each character on the stack. It then pops the letters from the stack (in reverse order) and stores them back into the same string variable. Because the stack is a LIFO (*last-in, first-out*) structure, the letters in the string are reversed:

```
TITLE Reversing a String              (RevStr.asm)

INCLUDE Irvine32.inc
.data
aName BYTE "Abraham Lincoln",0
nameSize = ($ - aName) - 1

.code
main PROC
; Push the name on the stack.
    mov    ecx,nameSize
    mov    esi,0

L1: movzx eax,aName[esi]                ; get character
    push  eax                           ; push on stack
    inc   esi
    loop  L1

; Pop the name from the stack, in reverse,
; and store in the aName array.
    mov    ecx,nameSize
    mov    esi,0

L2: pop    eax                          ; get character
    mov    aName[esi],al                ; store in string
    inc    esi
    loop   L2

; Display the name.
    mov    edx,OFFSET aName
    call   WriteString
    call   Crlf
    exit
main ENDP
END main
```

5.4.3 Section Review

1. Which register (in protected mode) manages the stack?

2. How is the runtime stack different from the stack abstract data type?

3. Why is the stack called a LIFO structure?

4. When a 32-bit value is pushed on the stack, what happens to ESP?

5. (*True/False*) Only 32-bit values should be pushed on the stack when using the Irvine32 library.

6. (*True/False*) Only 16-bit values should be pushed on the stack when using the Irvine16 library.

7. (*True/False*) Local variables in procedures are created on the stack.

8. *(True/False)* The PUSH instruction cannot have an immediate operand.

9. Which instruction pushes all of the 32-bit general-purpose registers on the stack?

10. Which instruction pushes the 32-bit EFLAGS register on the stack?

11. Which instruction pops the stack into the EFLAGS register?

12. *Challenge:* Another assembler (called NASM) permits the PUSH instruction to list multiple specific registers. Why might this approach be better than the PUSHAD instruction in MASM? Here is a NASM example:

```
PUSH EAX EBX ECX
```

13. *Challenge:* Suppose there were no PUSH instruction. Write a sequence of two other instructions that would accomplish the same as PUSH EAX.

5.5   Defining and Using Procedures

If you've already studied a high-level programming language, you know how useful it can be to divide programs into *subroutines*. A complicated problem is usually divided into separate tasks before it can be understood, implemented, and tested effectively. In assembly language, we typically use the term *procedure* to mean a subroutine. In other languages, subroutines are called methods or functions.

In terms of object-oriented programming, the functions or methods in a single class are roughly equivalent to the collection of procedures and data encapsulated in an assembly language module. Assembly language was created long before object-oriented programming, so it doesn't have the formal structure found in object-oriented languages. Assembly programmers must impose their own formal structure on programs.

5.5.1   PROC Directive

Defining a Procedure

Informally, we can define a *procedure* as a named block of statements that ends in a return statement. A procedure is declared using the PROC and ENDP directives. It must be assigned a name (a valid identifier). Each program we've written so far contains a procedure named **main**, for example,

```
main PROC
 .
 .
main ENDP
```

When you create a procedure other than your program's startup procedure, end it with a RET instruction. RET forces the CPU to return to the location from where the procedure was called:

```
sample PROC
   .
   .
     ret
sample ENDP
```

The startup procedure (**main**) is a special case because it ends with the **exit** statement. When you use the INCLUDE *Irvine32.inc* statement, **exit** is an alias for a call to **ExitProcess**, a system procedure that terminates the program:

```
INVOKE ExitProcess,0
```

(In Section 8.5.1 we introduce the INVOKE directive, which can call a procedure and pass arguments.)

If you use the INCLUDE *Irvine16.inc* statement, **exit** is translated to the **.EXIT** assembler directive. The latter causes the assembler to generate the following two instructions:

```
mov ah,4C00h      ; call MS-DOS function 4Ch
int 21h           ; terminate program
```

Labels in Procedures

By default, labels are visible only within the procedure in which they are declared. This rule often affects jump and loop instructions. In the following example, the label named *Destination* must be located in the same procedure as the JMP instruction:

```
jmp Destination
```

It is possible to work around this limitation by declaring a global label, identified by a double colon (::) after its name:

```
Destination::
```

In terms of program design, it's not a good idea to jump or loop outside of the current procedure. Procedures have an automated way of returning and adjusting the runtime stack. If you directly transfer out of a procedure, the runtime stack can easily become corrupted. For more information about the runtime stack, see Section 8.2.

Example: Sum of Three Integers

Let's create a procedure named **SumOf** that calculates the sum of three 32-bit integers. We will assume that relevant integers are assigned to EAX, EBX, and ECX before the procedure is called. The procedure returns the sum in EAX:

```
SumOf PROC
      add   eax,ebx
      add   eax,ecx
      ret
SumOf ENDP
```

Documenting Procedures

A good habit to cultivate is that of adding clear and readable documentation to your programs. The following are a few suggestions for information that you can put at the beginning of each procedure:

- A description of all tasks accomplished by the procedure.
- A list of input parameters and their usage, labeled by a word such as **Receives**. If any input parameters have specific requirements for their input values, list them here.
- A description of any values returned by the procedure, labeled by a word such as **Returns**.
- A list of any special requirements, called *preconditions*, that must be satisfied before the procedure is called. These can be labeled by the word **Requires**. For example, for a procedure

that draws a graphics line, a useful precondition would be that the video display adapter must already be in graphics mode.

> The descriptive labels we've chosen, such as Receives, Returns, and Requires, are not absolutes; other useful names are often used.

With these ideas in mind, let's add appropriate documentation to the **SumOf** procedure:

```
;-------------------------------------------------------
Sumof PROC
;
; Calculates and returns the sum of three 32-bit integers.
; Receives: EAX, EBX, ECX, the three integers. May be
;           signed or unsigned.
; Returns:  EAX = sum
;-------------------------------------------------------
    add   eax,ebx
    add   eax,ecx
    ret
SumOf ENDP
```

Functions written in high-level languages like C and C++ typically return 8-bit values in AL, 16-bit values in AX, and 32-bit values in EAX.

5.5.2 CALL and RET Instructions

The CALL instruction calls a procedure by directing the processor to begin execution at a new memory location. The procedure uses a RET (return from procedure) instruction to bring the processor back to the point in the program where the procedure was called. Mechanically speaking, the CALL instruction pushes its return address on the stack and copies the called procedure's address into the instruction pointer. When the procedure is ready to return, its RET instruction pops the return address from the stack into the instruction pointer. In 32-bit mode, the CPU executes the instruction in memory pointed to by EIP (instruction pointer register). In 16-bit mode, IP points to the instruction.

Call and Return Example

Suppose that in **main**, a CALL statement is located at offset 00000020. Typically, this instruction requires 5 bytes of machine code, so the next statement (a MOV in this case) is located at offset 00000025:

```
              main PROC
00000020        call MySub
00000025        mov  eax,ebx
```

Next, suppose that the first executable instruction in **MySub** is located at offset 00000040:

```
              MySub PROC
00000040        mov eax,edx
                .
                .
                .
                ret
              MySub ENDP
```

When the CALL instruction executes (Figure 5–8), the address following the call (00000025) is pushed on the stack and the address of **MySub** is loaded into EIP. All instructions in **MySub** execute up to its RET instruction. When the RET instruction executes, the value in the stack pointed to by ESP is popped into EIP (step 1 in Figure 5–9). In step 2, ESP is incremented so it points to the previous value on the stack (step 2).

Figure 5–8   Executing a CALL Instruction.

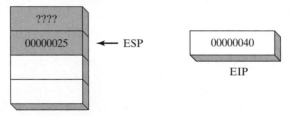

Figure 5–9   Executing the RET Instruction.

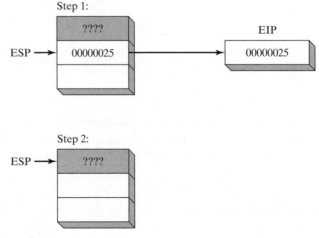

Nested Procedure Calls

A *nested procedure call* occurs when a called procedure calls another procedure before the first procedure returns. Suppose that **main** calls a procedure named **Sub1**. While **Sub1** is executing, it calls the **Sub2** procedure. While **Sub2** is executing, it calls the **Sub3** procedure. The process is shown in Figure 5–10.

When the RET instruction at the end of **Sub3** executes, it pops the value at stack[ESP] into the instruction pointer. This causes execution to resume at the instruction following the call **Sub3** instruction. The following diagram shows the stack just before the return from **Sub3** is executed:

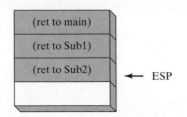

Figure 5–10   Nested Procedure Calls.

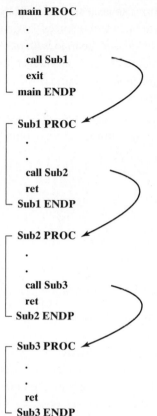

After the return, ESP points to the next-highest stack entry. When the RET instruction at the end of **Sub2** is about to execute, the stack appears as follows:

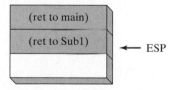

Finally, when **Sub1** returns, stack[ESP] is popped into the instruction pointer, and execution resumes in **main**:

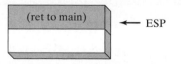

Clearly, the stack proves itself a useful device for remembering information, including nested procedure calls. Stack structures, in general, are used in situations where programs must retrace their steps in a specific order.

Passing Register Arguments to Procedures

If you write a procedure that performs some standard operation such as calculating the sum of an integer array, it's not a good idea to include references to specific variable names inside the procedure. If you did, the procedure could only be used with one array. A better approach is to pass the offset of an array to the procedure and pass an integer specifying the number of array elements. We call these *arguments* (or *input parameters*). In assembly language, it is common to pass arguments inside general-purpose registers.

In the preceding section we created a simple procedure named **SumOf** that added the integers in the EAX, EBX, and ECX registers. In **main**, before calling **SumOf**, we assign values to EAX, EBX, and ECX:

```
.data
theSum  DWORD  ?
.code
main PROC
    mov   eax,10000h                    ; argument
    mov   ebx,20000h                    ; argument
    mov   ecx,30000h                    ; argument
    call  Sumof                         ; EAX = (EAX + EBX + ECX)
    mov   theSum,eax                    ; save the sum
```

After the CALL statement, we have the option of copying the sum in EAX to a variable.

5.5.3 Example: Summing an Integer Array

A very common type of loop that you may have already coded in C++ or Java is one that calculates the sum of an integer array. This is very easy to implement in assembly language, and it can be coded in such a way that it will run as fast as possible. For example, one can use registers rather than variables inside a loop.

Let's create a procedure named **ArraySum** that receives two parameters from a calling program: a pointer to an array of 32-bit integers, and a count of the number of array values. It calculates and returns the sum of the array in EAX:

```
;----------------------------------------------------
ArraySum PROC
;
; Calculates the sum of an array of 32-bit integers.
; Receives: ESI = the array offset
;           ECX = number of elements in the array
; Returns:  EAX = sum of the array elements
;----------------------------------------------------
    push  esi                     ; save ESI, ECX
    push  ecx
    mov   eax,0                   ; set the sum to zero

L1: add   eax,[esi]               ; add each integer to sum
    add   esi,TYPE DWORD          ; point to next integer
    loop  L1                      ; repeat for array size

    pop   ecx                     ; restore ECX, ESI
```

```
       pop    esi
       ret                              ; sum is in EAX
    ArraySum ENDP
```

Nothing in this procedure is specific to a certain array name or array size. It could be used in any program that needs to sum an array of 32-bit integers. Whenever possible, you should also create procedures that are flexible and adaptable.

Calling ArraySum   Following is an example of calling **ArraySum**, passing the address of **array** in ESI and the array count in ECX. After the call, we copy the sum in EAX to a variable:

```
    .data
    array  DWORD  10000h,20000h,30000h,40000h,50000h
    theSum DWORD  ?
    .code
    main PROC
         mov   esi,OFFSET array            ; ESI points to array
         mov   ecx,LENGTHOF array          ; ECX = array count
         call  ArraySum                    ; calculate the sum
         mov   theSum,eax                   ; returned in EAX
```

5.5.4 Flowcharts

A *flowchart* is a well-established way of diagramming program logic. Each shape in a flowchart represents a single logical step, and lines with arrows connecting the shapes show the ordering of the logical steps. Figure 5–11 shows the most common flowchart shapes. The same shape is used for begin/end connectors, as well as labels that are the targets of jump instructions.

FIGURE 5–11   Basic Flowchart Shapes.

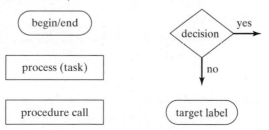

Text notations such as *yes* and *no* are added next to *decision* symbols to show branching directions. There is no required position for each arrow connected to a decision symbol. Each process symbol can contain one or more closely related instructions. The instructions need not be syntactically correct. For example, we could add 1 to CX using either of the following process symbols:

Let's use the **ArraySum** procedure from the preceding section to design a simple flowchart, shown in Figure 5–12. It uses a decision symbol for the LOOP instruction because LOOP must determine whether or not to transfer control to a label (based on the value of CX). A code insert shows the original procedure listing.

FIGURE 5-12   Flowchart for the **ArraySum** Procedure.

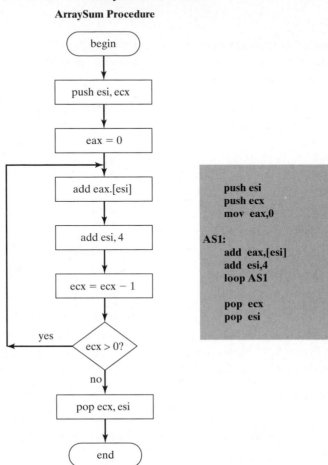

ArraySum Procedure

5.5.5   Saving and Restoring Registers

In the **ArraySum** example, ECX and ESI were pushed on the stack at the beginning of the procedure and popped at the end. This action is typical of most procedures that modify registers. Always save and restore registers that are modified by a procedure so the calling program can be sure that none of its own register values will be overwritten. The exception to this rule pertains to registers used as return values, usually EAX. Do not push and pop them.

USES Operator

The USES operator, coupled with the PROC directive, lets you list the names of all registers modified within a procedure. USES tells the assembler to do two things: First, generate PUSH instructions that save the registers on the stack at the beginning of the procedure. Second, generate POP instructions that restore the register values at the end of the procedure. The USES operator immediately follows PROC, and is itself followed by a list of registers on the same line separated by spaces or tabs (not commas).

The ArraySum procedure from Section 5.5.3 used PUSH and POP instructions to save and restore ESI and ECX. The USES operator can more easily do the same:

```
ArraySum PROC USES esi ecx
       mov    eax,0                  ; set the sum to zero
L1:
       add    eax,[esi]             ; add each integer to sum
       add    esi,TYPE DWORD        ; point to next integer
       loop   L1                    ; repeat for array size

       ret                          ; sum is in EAX
ArraySum ENDP
```

The corresponding code generated by the assembler shows the effect of USES:

```
ArraySum PROC
       push   esi
       push   ecx
       mov    eax,0                  ; set the sum to zero

L1:
       add    eax,[esi]             ; add each integer to sum
       add    esi,TYPE DWORD        ; point to next integer
       loop   L1                    ; repeat for array size

       pop    ecx
       pop    esi
       ret
ArraySum ENDP
```

> *Debugging Tip:* When using the Microsoft Visual Studio debugger, you can view the hidden machine instructions generated by MASM's advanced operators and directives. Select *Debug Windows* from the *View* menu, and select *Disassembly*. This window displays your program's source code along with hidden machine instructions generated by the assembler.

Exception There is an important exception to our standing rule about saving registers that applies when a procedure returns a value in a register (usually EAX). In this case, the return register should not be pushed and popped. For example, in the SumOf procedure in the following example, it pushes and pops EAX, causing the procedure's return value to be lost:

```
SumOf PROC                          ; sum of three integers
       push   eax                   ; save EAX
       add    eax,ebx              ; calculate the sum
       add    eax,ecx              ; of EAX, EBX, ECX
       pop    eax                   ; lost the sum!
       ret
SumOf ENDP
```

5.5.6 Section Review

1. *(True/False):* The PROC directive begins a procedure and the ENDP directive ends a procedure.

2. *(True/False):* It is possible to define a procedure inside an existing procedure.

3. What would happen if the RET instruction was omitted from a procedure?

4. How are the words *Receives* and *Returns* used in the suggested procedure documentation?

5. *(True/False):* The CALL instruction pushes the offset of the CALL instruction on the stack.

6. *(True/False):* The CALL instruction pushes the offset of the instruction following the CALL on the stack.

7. *(True/False):* The RET instruction pops the top of the stack into the instruction pointer.

8. *(True/False):* Nested procedure calls are not permitted by the Microsoft assembler unless the NESTED operator is used in the procedure definition.

9. *(True/False):* In protected mode, each procedure call uses a minimum of 4 bytes of stack space.

10. *(True/False):* The ESI and EDI registers cannot be used when passing parameters to procedures.

11. *(True/False):* The ArraySum procedure (Section 5.5.3) receives a pointer to any array of doublewords.

12. *(True/False):* The USES operator lets you name all registers that are modified within a procedure.

13. *(True/False):* The USES operator only generates PUSH instructions, so you must code POP instructions yourself.

14. *(True/False):* The register list in the USES directive must use commas to separate the register names.

15. Which statement(s) in the ArraySum procedure (Section 5.5.3) would have to be modified so it could accumulate an array of 16-bit words? Create such a version of ArraySum and test it.

5.6 Program Design Using Procedures

Any programming application beyond the trivial tends to involve a number of different tasks. One could code all tasks in a single procedure, but the program would be difficult to read and maintain. Instead, it's best to dedicate a separate procedure for each task.

When creating a program, create a set of specifications that list exactly what the program is supposed to do. The specifications should be the result of careful analysis of the problem you're trying to solve. Then design the program based on the specifications. A standard design approach is to divide an overall problem into discrete tasks, a process known as *functional decomposition, or top-down design*. It relies on some basic principles:

• A large problem may be more easily divided into small tasks.

• A program is easier to maintain if each procedure is tested separately.

• A top-down design lets you see how procedures are related to each other.

• When you are sure of the overall design, you can more easily concentrate on details, writing code that implements each procedure.

In the next section, we demonstrate the top-down design approach for a program that inputs integers and calculates their sum. Although the program is simple, the same approach can be applied to programs of almost any size.

5.6.1 Integer Summation Program (Design)

The following are specifications for a simple program that we will call **Integer Summation**:

> Write a program that prompts the user for three 32-bit integers, stores them in an array, calculates the sum of the array, and displays the sum on the screen.

The following pseudocode shows how we might divide the specifications into tasks:

```
Integer Summation Program
     Prompt user for three integers
     Calculate the sum of the array
     Display the sum
```

In preparation for writing a program, let's assign a procedure name to each task:

```
Main
      PromptForIntegers
      ArraySum
      DisplaySum
```

In assembly language, input-output tasks often require detailed code to implement. To reduce some of this detail, we can call procedures that clear the screen, display a string, input an integer, and display an integer:

```
Main
      Clrscr                         ; clear screen
      PromptForIntegers
         WriteString                 ; display string
          ReadInt                    ; input integer
      ArraySum                       ; sum the integers
      DisplaySum
         WriteString                 ; display string
         WriteInt                    ; display integer
```

Structure Chart The diagram in Figure 5–13, called a *structure chart*, describes the program's structure. Procedures from the link library are shaded.

Figure 5–13   Structure Chart for the Summation Program.

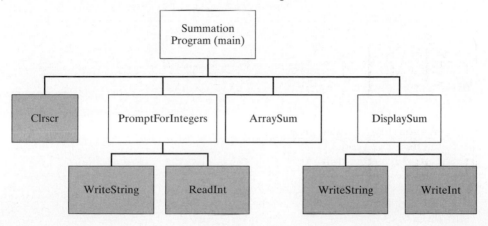

Stub Program   Let's create a minimal version of the program called a *stub program*. It contains only empty (or nearly empty) procedures. The program assembles and runs, but does not actually do anything useful:

```
TITLE Integer Summation Program          (Sum1.asm)

; This program prompts the user for three integers,
; stores them in an array, calculates the sum of the
; array, and displays the sum.

INCLUDE Irvine32.inc
.code
main PROC
; Main program control procedure.
; Calls: Clrscr, PromptForIntegers,
;         ArraySum, DisplaySum

     exit
main ENDP

;-------------------------------------------------------
PromptForIntegers PROC
;
; Prompts the user for three integers, inserts
; them in an array.
; Receives: ESI points to an array of
;    doubleword integers, ECX = array size.
; Returns: nothing
; Calls: ReadInt, WriteString
;-------------------------------------------------------
     ret
PromptForIntegers ENDP

;-------------------------------------------------------
ArraySum PROC
;
; Calculates the sum of an array of 32-bit integers.
; Receives: ESI points to the array, ECX = array size
; Returns:  EAX = sum of the array elements
;-------------------------------------------------------
     ret
ArraySum ENDP

;-------------------------------------------------------
DisplaySum PROC
;
; Displays the sum on the screen.
; Receives: EAX = the sum
; Returns: nothing
; Calls: WriteString, WriteInt
;-------------------------------------------------------
     ret
DisplaySum ENDP
END main
```

A stub program gives you the chance to map out all procedure calls, study the dependencies between procedures, and possibly improve the structural design before coding the details. Use comments in each procedure to explain its purpose and parameter requirements.

5.6.2   Integer Summation Implementation

Let's complete the summation program. We will declare an array of three integers and use a defined constant for the array size in case we want to change it later:

```
INTEGER_COUNT = 3
array DWORD  INTEGER_COUNT DUP(?)
```

A couple of strings are used as screen prompts:

```
str1  BYTE  "Enter a signed integer: ",0
str2  BYTE  "The sum of the integers is: ",0
```

The **main** procedure clears the screen, passes an array pointer to the **PromptForIntegers** procedure, calls **ArraySum**, and calls **DisplaySum**:

```
call  Clrscr
mov   esi,OFFSET array
mov   ecx,INTEGER_COUNT
call  PromptForIntegers
call  ArraySum
call  DisplaySum
```

- **PromptForIntegers** calls **WriteString** to prompt the user for an integer. It then calls ReadInt to input the integer from the user, and stores the integer in the array pointed to by ESI. A loop executes these steps multiple times.
- **ArraySum** calculates and returns the sum of an array of integers.
- **DisplaySum** displays a message on the screen ("The sum of the integers is:") and calls WriteInt to display the integer in EAX.

Finished Program Listing   The following listing shows the completed Summation program:

```
TITLE Integer Summation Program     (Sum2.asm)

; This program prompts the user for three integers,
; stores them in an array, calculates the sum of the
; array, and displays the sum.
INCLUDE Irvine32.inc
INTEGER_COUNT = 3
.data
str1  BYTE  "Enter a signed integer: ",0
str2  BYTE  "The sum of the integers is: ",0
array DWORD  INTEGER_COUNT DUP(?)

.code
main PROC
    call  Clrscr
    mov   esi,OFFSET array
    mov   ecx,INTEGER_COUNT
    call  PromptForIntegers
```

```
        call   ArraySum
        call   DisplaySum
        exit
main ENDP

;-------------------------------------------------------
PromptForIntegers PROC USES ecx edx esi
;
; Prompts the user for an arbitrary number of integers
; and inserts the integers into an array.
; Receives: ESI points to the array, ECX = array size
; Returns:  nothing
;-------------------------------------------------------
        mov    edx,OFFSET str1      ; "Enter a signed integer"
L1:     call   WriteString          ; display string
        call   ReadInt              ; read integer into EAX
        call   Crlf                 ; go to next output line
        mov    [esi],eax            ; store in array
        add    esi,TYPE DWORD       ; next integer
        loop   L1
        ret
PromptForIntegers ENDP

;-------------------------------------------------------
ArraySum PROC USES esi ecx
;
; Calculates the sum of an array of 32-bit integers.
; Receives: ESI points to the array, ECX = number
;   of array elements
; Returns:  EAX = sum of the array elements
;-------------------------------------------------------
        mov    eax,0                ; set the sum to zero
L1:     add    eax,[esi]            ; add each integer to sum
        add    esi,TYPE DWORD       ; point to next integer
        loop   L1                   ; repeat for array size
        ret                         ; sum is in EAX
ArraySum ENDP

;-------------------------------------------------------
DisplaySum PROC USES edx
;
; Displays the sum on the screen
; Receives: EAX = the sum
; Returns:  nothing
;-------------------------------------------------------
        mov    edx,OFFSET str2      ; "The sum of the..."
        call   WriteString
        call   WriteInt             ; display EAX
        call   Crlf
        ret
DisplaySum ENDP
END main
```

5.6.3 Section Review

1. What is the name given to the process of dividing up large tasks into smaller ones?

2. Which procedures in the Summation program design (Section 5.6.1) are located in the Irvine32 library?

3. What is a *stub program*?

4. *(True/False):* The **ArraySum** procedure of the Summation program (Section 5.6.1) directly references the name of an array variable.

5. Which lines in the **PromptForIntegers** procedure of the Summation program (Section 5.6.1) would have to be modified so it could handle an array of 16-bit words? Create such a version and test it.

6. Draw a flowchart for the **PromptForIntegers** procedure of the Summation program (flowcharts were introduced in Section 5.5.4).

5.7 Chapter Summary

This chapter introduces the book's link library to make it easier for you to process input-output in assembly language applications.

Table 5–1 lists most of the procedures from the Irvine32 link library. The most up-to-date listing of all procedures is available on the book's Web site (www.asmirvine.com).

The *library test program* in Section 5.3.3 demonstrates a number of input-output functions from the Irvine32 library. It generates and displays a list of random numbers, a register dump, and a memory dump. It displays integers in various formats and demonstrates string input-output.

The *runtime stack* is a special array that is used as a temporary holding area for addresses and data. The ESP register holds a 32-bit OFFSET into some location on the stack. The stack is called a LIFO structure (*last-in, first-out*) because the last value placed in the stack is the first value taken out. A *push* operation copies a value into the stack. A *pop* operation removes a value from the stack and copies it to a register or variable. Stacks often hold procedure return addresses, procedure parameters, local variables, and registers used internally by procedures.

The PUSH instruction first decrements the stack pointer and then copies a source operand into the stack. The POP instruction first copies the contents of the stack pointed to by ESP into a 16- or 32-bit destination operand and then increments ESP.

The PUSHAD instruction pushes the 32-bit general-purpose registers on the stack, and the PUSHA instruction does the same for the 16-bit general-purpose registers. The POPAD instruction pops the stack into the 32-bit general-purpose registers, and the POPA instruction does the same for the 16-bit general-purpose registers.

The PUSHFD instruction pushes the 32-bit EFLAGS register on the stack, and POPFD pops the stack into EFLAGS. PUSHF and POPF do the same for the 16-bit FLAGS register.

The *RevStr* program (Section 5.4.2) uses the stack to reverse a string of characters.

A *procedure* is a named block of code declared using the PROC and ENDP directives. A procedure's execution ends with the RET instruction. The SumOf procedure, shown in Section 5.5.1, calculates the sum of three integers. The CALL instruction executes a procedure by inserting the procedure's address into the instruction pointer register. When the procedure finishes, the RET (return from procedure) instruction brings the processor back to the point in the program from where the procedure was called. A *nested procedure call* occurs when a called procedure calls another procedure before it returns.

A code label followed by a single colon is only visible within its enclosing procedure. A code label followed by :: is a global label, making it accessible from any statement in the same source code file.

The ArraySum procedure, shown in Section 5.5.3, calculates and returns the sum of the elements in an array.

The USES operator, coupled with the PROC directive, lets you list all registers modified by a procedure. The assembler generates code that pushes the registers at the beginning of the procedure and pops the registers before returning.

A program of any size should be carefully designed from a set of clear specifications. A standard approach is to use functional decomposition (top-down design) to divide the program into procedures (functions). First, determine the ordering and connections between procedures, and later fill in the procedure details.

5.8 Programming Exercises

When you write programs to solve the programming exercises, use multiple procedures when possible. Follow the style and naming conventions used in this book, unless instructed otherwise by your instructor. Use explanatory comments in your programs at the beginning of each procedure and next to nontrivial statements. As a bonus, your instructor may ask you to provide flowcharts and/or pseudocode for solution programs.

★ **1.   Draw Text Colors**

Write a program that displays the same string in four different colors, using a loop. Call the **SetTextColor** procedure from the book's link library. Any colors may be chosen, but you may find it easiest to change the foreground color.

★★★ **2.   File of Fibonacci Numbers**

Using Programming Exercise 6 in Chapter 4 as a starting point, write a program that generates the first 47 values in the *Fibonacci* series, stores them in an array of doublewords, and writes the doubleword array to a disk file. You need not perform any error checking on the file input-output because conditional processing has not been covered yet. Your output file size should be 188 bytes because each doubleword is 4 bytes. Use debug.exe or Visual Studio to open and inspect the file contents, shown here in hexadecimal:

```
00000000   01 00 00 00 01 00 00 00   02 00 00 00 03 00 00 00
00000010   05 00 00 00 08 00 00 00   0D 00 00 00 15 00 00 00
00000020   22 00 00 00 37 00 00 00   59 00 00 00 90 00 00 00
00000030   E9 00 00 00 79 01 00 00   62 02 00 00 DB 03 00 00
00000040   3D 06 00 00 18 0A 00 00   55 10 00 00 6D 1A 00 00
00000050   C2 2A 00 00 2F 45 00 00   F1 6F 00 00 20 B5 00 00
00000060   11 25 01 00 31 DA 01 00   42 FF 02 00 73 D9 04 00
00000070   B5 D8 07 00 28 B2 0C 00   DD 8A 14 00 05 3D 21 00
00000080   E2 C7 35 00 E7 04 57 00   C9 CC 8C 00 B0 D1 E3 00
00000090   79 9E 70 01 29 70 54 02   A2 0E C5 03 CB 7E 19 06
000000a0   6D 8D DE 09 38 0C F8 0F   A5 99 D6 19 DD A5 CE 29
000000b0   82 3F A5 43 5F E5 73 6D   E1 24 19 B1
```

(A VideoNote for this exercise is posted on the Web site.)

★ **3.   Simple Addition (1)**

Write a program that clears the screen, locates the cursor near the middle of the screen, prompts the user for two integers, adds the integers, and displays their sum.

★★ **4.   Simple Addition (2)**

Use the solution program from the preceding exercise as a starting point. Let this new program repeat the same steps three times, using a loop. Clear the screen after each loop iteration.

★ **5.   BetterRandomRange Procedure**

The RandomRange procedure from the Irvine32 library generates a pseudorandom integer between 0 and $N - 1$. Your task is to create an improved version that generates an integer between M and $N - 1$. Let the caller pass M in EBX and N in EAX. If we call the procedure *BetterRandomRange*, the following code is a sample test:

```
mov   ebx,-300          ; lower bound
mov   eax,100           ; upper bound
call  BetterRandomRange
```

Write a short test program that calls BetterRandomRange from a loop that repeats 50 times. Display each randomly generated value.

★★ **6.   Random Strings**

Write a program that generates and displays 20 random strings, each consisting of 10 capital letters {A..Z}. *(A VideoNote for this exercise is posted on the Web site.)*

★ **7.   Random Screen Locations**

Write a program that displays a single character at 100 random screen locations, using a timing delay of 100 milliseconds. *Hint:* Use the GetMaxXY procedure to determine the current size of the console window.

★★ **8.   Color Matrix**

Write a program that displays a single character in all possible combinations of foreground and background colors ($16 \times 16 = 256$). The colors are numbered from 0 to 15, so you can use a nested loop to generate all possible combinations.

★ **9.   Summation Program**

Modify the Summation program in Section 5.6.1 as follows: Select an array size using a constant:

```
ARRAY_SIZE = 20
array DWORD  ARRAY_SIZE DUP(?)
```

Write a new procedure that prompts the user for the number of integers to be processed. Pass the same value to the PromptForIntegers procedure. For example,

```
How many integers will be added? 5
```

6

Conditional Processing

6.1 Introduction

6.2 Boolean and Comparison Instructions
    6.2.1 The CPU Flags
    6.2.2 AND Instruction
    6.2.3 OR Instruction
    6.2.4 Bit-Mapped Sets
    6.2.5 XOR Instruction
    6.2.6 NOT Instruction
    6.2.7 TEST Instruction
    6.2.8 CMP Instruction
    6.2.9 Setting and Clearing Individual CPU Flags
    6.2.10 Section Review

6.3 Conditional Jumps
    6.3.1 Conditional Structures
    6.3.2 Jcond Instruction
    6.3.3 Types of Conditional Jump Instructions
    6.3.4 Conditional Jump Applications
    6.3.5 Section Review

6.4 Conditional Loop Instructions
    6.4.1 LOOPZ and LOOPE Instructions
    6.4.2 LOOPNZ and LOOPNE Instructions

6.4.3 Section Review

6.5 Conditional Structures
    6.5.1 Block-Structured IF Statements
    6.5.2 Compound Expressions
    6.5.3 WHILE Loops
    6.5.4 Table-Driven Selection
    6.5.5 Section Review

6.6 Application: Finite-State Machines
    6.6.1 Validating an Input String
    6.6.2 Validating a Signed Integer
    6.6.3 Section Review

6.7 Conditional Control Flow Directives
    6.7.1 Creating IF Statements
    6.7.2 Signed and Unsigned Comparisons
    6.7.3 Compound Expressions
    6.7.4 Creating Loops with .REPEAT and .WHILE

6.8 Chapter Summary

6.9 Programming Exercises

6.1 Introduction

A programming language that permits decision making lets you alter the flow of control, using a technique known as *conditional branching*. Every IF statement, switch statement, or conditional loop found in high-level languages has built-in branching logic. Assembly language, as primitive as it is, provides all the tools you need for decision-making logic. In this chapter, we will see how the translation works, from high-level conditional statements to low-level implementation code.

Programs that deal with hardware devices must be able to manipulate individual bits in numbers. Individual bits must be tested, cleared, and set. Data encryption and compression also rely on bit manipulation. We will show how to perform these operations in assembly language.

This chapter should answer some basic questions:

- How can I use the boolean operations introduced in Chapter 1 (AND, OR, NOT)?
- How do I write an IF statement in assembly language?
- How are nested-IF statements translated by compilers into machine language?
- How can I set and clear individual bits in a binary number?
- How can I perform simple binary data encryption?
- How are signed numbers differentiated from unsigned numbers in boolean expressions?

This chapter follows a *bottom-up* approach, starting with the binary foundations behind programming logic. Next, you will see how the CPU compares instruction operands, using the CMP instruction and the processor status flags. Finally, we put it all together and show how to use assembly language to implement logic structures characteristic of high-level languages.

6.2 Boolean and Comparison Instructions

In Chapter 1, we introduced the four basic operations of boolean algebra: AND, OR, XOR, and NOT. These operations can be carried at the binary bit level, using assembly language instructions. These operations are also important at the boolean expression level, in IF statements, for example. First, we will look at the bitwise instructions. The techniques used here could be used to manipulate control bits for hardware devices, implement communication protocols, or encrypt data, just to name a few applications. The Intel instruction set contains the AND, OR, XOR, and NOT instructions, which directly implement boolean operations on binary bits, shown in Table 6-1. In addition, the TEST instruction is a nondestructive AND operation, and the BT (including BTC, BTR, and BTS) provides a combined bitwise operation.

Table 6-1 Selected Boolean Instructions.

Operation	Description
AND	Boolean AND operation between a source operand and a destination operand.
OR	Boolean OR operation between a source operand and a destination operand.
XOR	Boolean exclusive-OR operation between a source operand and a destination operand.
NOT	Boolean NOT operation on a destination operand.
TEST	Implied boolean AND operation between a source and destination operand, setting the CPU flags appropriately.
BT, BTC, BTR, BTS	Copy bit n from the source operand to the Carry flag and complement/reset/set the same bit in the destination operand (covered in Section 6.3.5).

6.2.1   The CPU Flags

Boolean instructions affect the Zero, Carry, Sign, Overflow, and Parity flags. Here's a quick review of their meanings:

- The Zero flag is set when the result of an operation equals zero.
- The Carry flag is set when an operation generates a carry out of the highest bit of the destination operand.
- The Sign flag is a copy of the high bit of the destination operand, indicating that it is negative if *set* and positive if *clear*. (Zero is assumed to be positive.)
- The Overflow flag is set when an instruction generates an invalid signed result.
- The Parity flag is set when an instruction generates an even number of 1 bits in the low byte of the destination operand.

6.2.2   AND Instruction

The AND instruction performs a boolean (bitwise) AND operation between each pair of matching bits in two operands and places the result in the destination operand:

```
AND    destination,source
```

The following operand combinations are permitted:

```
AND reg,reg
AND reg,mem
AND reg,imm
AND mem,reg
AND mem,imm
```

The operands can be 8, 16, or 32 bits, and they must be the same size. For each matching bit in the two operands, the following rule applies: If both bits equal 1, the result bit is 1; otherwise, it is 0. The following truth table from Chapter 1 labels the input bits x and y. The third column shows the value of the expression $\mathbf{x} \wedge \mathbf{y}$:

x	y	$\mathbf{x} \wedge \mathbf{y}$
0	0	0
0	1	0
1	0	0
1	1	1

The AND instruction lets you clear 1 or more bits in an operand without affecting other bits. The technique is called bit *masking*, much as you might use masking tape when painting a house to cover areas (such as windows) that should not be painted. Suppose, for example, that a control byte is about to be copied from the AL register to a hardware device. Further, we will assume that the device resets itself when bits 0 and 3 are cleared in the control byte. Assuming that we want to reset the device without modifying any other bits in AL, we can write the following:

```
and AL,11110110b    ; clear bits 0 and 3, leave others unchanged
```

For example, suppose AL is initially set to 10101110 binary. After ANDing it with 11110110, AL equals 10100110:

```
mov al,10101110b
and al,11110110b                    ; result in AL = 10100110
```

Flags   The AND instruction always clears the Overflow and Carry flags. It modifies the Sign, Zero, and Parity flags in a way that is consistent with the value assigned to the destination operand. For example, suppose the following instruction results in a value of Zero in the EAX register. In that case, the Zero flag will be set:

```
and eax,1Fh
```

Converting Characters to Upper Case

The AND instruction provides an easy way to translate a letter from lowercase to uppercase. If we compare the ASCII codes of capital **A** and lowercase **a**, it becomes clear that only bit 5 is different:

```
0 1 1 0 0 0 0 1 = 61h ('a')
0 1 0 0 0 0 0 1 = 41h ('A')
```

The rest of the alphabetic characters have the same relationship. If we AND any character with 11011111 binary, all bits are unchanged except for bit 5, which is cleared. In the following example, all characters in an array are converted to uppercase:

```
.data
array BYTE 50 "This Sentence is in Mixed Case",0
.code
      mov    ecx,LENGTHOF array
      mov    esi,OFFSET array
L1:   and    BYTE PTR [esi],11011111b    ; clear bit 5
      inc    esi
      loop   L1
```

6.2.3   OR Instruction

The OR instruction performs a boolean OR operation between each pair of matching bits in two operands and places the result in the destination operand:

```
OR   destination,source
```

The OR instruction uses the same operand combinations as the AND instruction:

```
OR reg,reg
OR reg,mem
OR reg,imm
OR mem,reg
OR mem,imm
```

The operands can be 8, 16, or 32 bits, and they must be the same size. For each matching bit in the two operands, the output bit is 1 when at least one of the input bits is 1. The following truth table (from Chapter 1) describes the boolean expression **x** ∨ **y**:

x	y	x ∨ y
0	0	0
0	1	1
1	0	1
1	1	1

The OR instruction is particularly useful when you need to set 1 or more bits in an operand without affecting any other bits. Suppose, for example, that your computer is attached to a servo motor, which is activated by setting bit 2 in its control byte. Assuming that the AL register contains a control byte in which each bit contains some important information, the following code only sets the bit in position 2.

```
or AL,00000100b                  ; set bit 2, leave others unchanged
```

For example, if AL is initially equal to 11100011 binary and then we OR it with 00000100, the result equals 11100111:

```
mov al,11100011b
and al,00000100b                 ; result in AL = 11100111
```

Flags   The OR instruction always clears the Carry and Overflow flags. It modifies the Sign, Zero, and Parity flags in a way that is consistent with the value assigned to the destination operand. For example, you can OR a number with itself (or zero) to obtain certain information about its value:

```
or  al,al
```

The values of the Zero and Sign flags indicate the following about the contents of AL:

Zero Flag	Sign Flag	Value in AL Is . . .
Clear	Clear	Greater than zero
Set	Clear	Equal to zero
Clear	Set	Less than zero

6.2.4   Bit-Mapped Sets

Some applications manipulate sets of items selected from a limited-sized universal set. Examples might be employees within a company, or environmental readings from a weather monitoring station. In such cases, binary bits can indicate set membership. Rather than holding pointers or references to objects in a container such as a Java HashSet, an application can use a *bit vector* (or bit map) to map the bits in a binary number to an array of objects, shown in Figure 6–1.

For example, the following binary number uses bit positions numbered from 0 on the right to 31 on the left to indicate that array elements 0, 1, 2, and 31 are members of the set named SetX:

```
SetX = 10000000 00000000 00000000 00000111
```

Figure 6–1 Mapping Binary Bits to an Array.

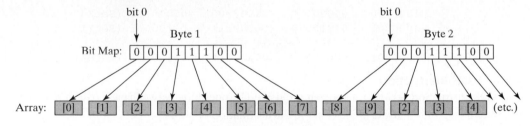

(The bytes have been separated to improve readability.) We can easily check for set membership by ANDing a particular member's bit position with a 1:

```
mov   eax,SetX
and   eax,10000b                  ; is element[16] a member of SetX?
```

If the AND instruction in this example clears the Zero flag, we know that element [16] is a member of SetX.

Set Complement

The complement of a set can be generated using the NOT instruction, which reverses all bits. Therefore, the complement of the SetX that we introduced is generated in EAX using the following instructions:

```
mov  eax,SetX
not  eax                          ; complement of SetX
```

Set Intersection

The AND instruction produces a bit vector that represents the intersection of two sets. The following code generates and stores the intersection of SetX and SetY in EAX:

```
mov   eax,SctX
and   eax,SetY
```

This is how the intersection of SetX and SetY is produced:

```
        1000000    00000000    00000000    00000111 (SetX)
(AND)   1000001    01010000    00000111    01100011 (SetY)
----------------------------------------------------
        1000000    00000000    00000000    00000011 (intersection)
```

It is hard to imagine any faster way to generate a set intersection. A larger domain would require more bits than could be held in a single register, making it necessary to use a loop to AND all of the bits together.

Set Union

The OR instruction produces a bit map that represents the union of two sets. The following code generates the union of SetX and SetY in EAX:

```
mov   eax,SetX
or    eax,SetY
```

This is how the union of SetX and SetY is generated by the OR instruction:

```
             1000000   00000000   00000000   00000111 (SetX)
    (OR)     1000001   01010000   00000111   01100011 (SetY)
    --------------------------------------------------
             1000001   01010000   00000111   01100111 (union)
```

6.2.5 XOR Instruction

The XOR instruction performs a boolean exclusive-OR operation between each pair of matching bits in two operands and stores the result in the destination operand:

```
    XOR   destination,source
```

The XOR instruction uses the same operand combinations and sizes as the AND and OR instructions. For each matching bit in the two operands, the following applies: If both bits are the same (both 0 or both 1), the result is 0; otherwise, the result is 1. The following truth table describes the boolean expression $x \oplus y$:

x	y	$x \oplus y$
0	0	0
0	1	1
1	0	1
1	1	0

A bit exclusive-ORed with 0 retains its value, and a bit exclusive-ORed with 1 is toggled (complemented). XOR reverses itself when applied twice to the same operand. The following truth table shows that when bit x is exclusive-ORed with bit y twice, it reverts to its original value:

x	y	$x \oplus y$	$(x \oplus y) \oplus y$
0	0	0	0
0	1	1	0
1	0	1	1
1	1	0	1

As you will find out in Section 6.3.4, this "reversible" property of XOR makes it an ideal tool for a simple form of symmetric encryption.

Flags   The XOR instruction always clears the Overflow and Carry flags. XOR modifies the Sign, Zero, and Parity flags in a way that is consistent with the value assigned to the destination operand.

Checking the Parity Flag   Parity checking is a function performed on a binary number that counts the number of 1 bits contained in the number; if the resulting count is even, we say that the data has even parity; if the count is odd, the data has odd parity. In an IA-32 processor, the Parity flag is set when the lowest byte of the destination operand of a bitwise or arithmetic operation has even parity. Conversely, when the operand has odd parity, the flag is cleared. An effective way to check the parity of a number without changing its value is to exclusive-OR the number with zero:

```
mov  al,10110101b              ; 5 bits = odd parity
xor  al,0                      ; Parity flag clear (PO)
mov  al,11001100b              ; 4 bits = even parity
xor  al,0                      ; Parity flag set (PE)
```

(Debuggers often use PE to indicate even parity and PO to indicate odd parity.)

16-Bit Parity   You can check the parity of a 16-bit register by performing an exclusive-OR between the upper and lower bytes:

```
mov  ax,64C1h                  ; 0110 0100 1100 0001
xor  ah,al                     ; Parity flag set (PE)
```

Imagine the set bits (bits equal to 1) in each register as being members of an 8-bit set. The XOR instruction zeroes all bits belonging to the intersection of the sets. XOR also forms the union between the remaining bits. The parity of this union will be the same as the parity of the entire 16-bit integer.

What about 32-bit values? If we number the bytes from B_0 through B_3, we can calculate the parity as B_0 XOR B_1 XOR B_2 XOR B_3.

6.2.6   NOT Instruction

The NOT instruction toggles (inverts) all bits in an operand. The result is called the *one's complement*. The following operand types are permitted:

```
NOT reg
NOT mem
```

For example, the one's complement of F0h is 0Fh:

```
mov  al,11110000b
not  al                        ; AL = 00001111b
```

Flags   No flags are affected by the NOT instruction.

6.2.7   TEST Instruction

The TEST instruction performs an implied AND operation between each pair of matching bits in two operands and sets the Sign, Zero, and Parity flags based on the value assigned to the destination operand. The only difference between TEST and AND is that TEST does not modify the destination operand. The TEST instruction permits the same operand combinations as the AND instruction. TEST is particularly valuable for finding out whether individual bits in an operand are set.

Example: Testing Multiple Bits   The TEST instruction can check several bits at once. Suppose we want to know whether bit 0 or bit 3 is set in the AL register. We can use the following instruction to find this out:

```
test al,00001001b              ; test bits 0 and 3
```

(The value 00001001 in this example is called a *bit mask*.) From the following example data sets, we can infer that the Zero flag is set only when all tested bits are clear:

```
0 0 1 0 0 1 0 1  <- input value
0 0 0 0 1 0 0 1  <- test value
0 0 0 0 0 0 0 1  <- result: ZF = 0

0 0 1 0 0 1 0 0  <- input value
0 0 0 0 1 0 0 1  <- test value
0 0 0 0 0 0 0 0  <- result: ZF = 1
```

Flags   The TEST instruction always clears the Overflow and Carry flags. It modifies the Sign, Zero, and Parity flags in the same way as the AND instruction.

6.2.8 CMP Instruction

Having examined all of the bitwise instructions, let's now turn to instructions used in logical (boolean) expressions. At the heart of any boolean expression is some type of comparison. The following pseudocode examples support this idea:

```
if A > B then ...
while X > 0 and X < 200  ...
if check_for_error( N ) = true then
```

In Intel assembly language we use the CMP instruction to compare integers. Character codes are also integers, so they work with CMP as well. Floating-point values require specialized comparison instructions, which we cover in Section 12.2.

The CMP (compare) instruction performs an implied subtraction of a source operand from a destination operand. Neither operand is modified:

```
CMP destination,source
```

CMP uses the same operand combinations as the AND instruction.

Flags   The CMP instruction changes the Overflow, Sign, Zero, Carry, Auxiliary Carry, and Parity flags according to the value the destination operand would have had if actual subtraction had taken place. When two unsigned operands are compared, the Zero and Carry flags indicate the following relations between operands:

CMP Results	ZF	CF
Destination < source	0	1
Destination > source	0	0
Destination = source	1	0

When two signed operands are compared, the Sign, Zero, and Overflow flags indicate the following relations between operands:

CMP Results	Flags
Destination < source	SF ≠ OF
Destination > source	SF = OF
Destination = source	ZF = 1

CMP is a valuable tool for creating conditional logic structures. When you follow CMP with a conditional jump instruction, the result is the assembly language equivalent of an IF statement.

Examples Let's look at three code fragments showing how flags arc affected by the CMP instruction. When AX equals 5 and is compared to 10, the Carry flag is set because subtracting 10 from 5 requires a borrow:

```
mov  ax,5
cmp  ax,10                          ; ZF = 0 and CF = 1
```

Comparing 1000 to 1000 sets the Zero flag because subtracting the source from the destination produces zero:

```
mov  ax,1000
mov  cx,1000
cmp  cx,ax                          ; ZF = 1 and CF = 0
```

Comparing 105 to 0 clears both the Zero and Carry flags because subtracting 0 from 105 would generate a positive, nonzero value.

```
mov  si,105
cmp  si,0                           ; ZF = 0 and CF = 0
```

6.2.9   Setting and Clearing Individual CPU Flags

How can you easily set or clear the Zero, Sign, Carry, and Overflow flags? There are several ways, most of which require modifying the destination operand. To set the Zero flag, TEST or AND an operand with Zero; to clear the Zero flag, OR an operand with 1:

```
test  al,0                          ; set Zero flag
and   al,0                          ; set Zero flag
or    al,1                          ; clear Zero flag
```

TEST does not modify the operand, whereas AND does. To set the Sign flag, OR the highest bit of an operand with 1. To clear the sign flag, AND the highcst bit with 0:

```
or    al,80h                        ; set Sign flag
and   al,7Fh                        ; clear Sign flag
```

To set the Carry flag, use the STC instruction; to clear the Carry flag, use CLC:

```
stc                                 ; set Carry flag
clc                                 ; clear Carry flag
```

To set the Overflow flag, add two positive values that produce a negative sum. To clear the Overflow flag, OR an operand with 0:

```
mov  al,7Fh                         ; AL = +127
inc  al                             ; AL = 80h (-128), OF=1
or   eax,0                          ; clear Overflow flag
```

6.2.10   Section Review

1. In the following instruction sequence, show the resulting value of AL where indicated, in binary:

```
mov  al,01101111b
and  al,00101101b           ; a.
mov  al,6Dh
```

```
and  al,4Ah                         ; b.
mov  al,00001111b
or   al,61h                         ; c.
mov  al,94h
xor  al,37h                         ; d.
```

2. In the following instruction sequence, show the resulting value of AL where indicated, in hexadecimal:

```
mov  al,7Ah
not  al                             ; a.
mov  al,3Dh
and  al,74h                         ; b.
mov  al,9Bh
or   al,35h                         ; c.
mov  al,72h
xor  al,0DCh                        ; d.
```

3. In the following instruction sequence, show the values of the Carry, Zero, and Sign flags where indicated:

```
mov   al,00001111b
test  al,00000010b                  ; a.  CF=    ZF=    SF=
mov   al,00000110b
cmp   al,00000101b                  ; b.  CF=    ZF=    SF=
mov   al,00000101b
cmp   al,00000111b                  ; c.  CF=    ZF=    SF=
```

4. Write a single instruction using 16-bit operands that clears the high 8 bits of AX and does not change the low 8 bits.

5. Write a single instruction using 16-bit operands that sets the high 8 bits of AX and does not change the low 8 bits.

6. Write a single instruction (other than NOT) that reverses all the bits in EAX.

7. Write instructions that set the Zero flag if the 32-bit value in EAX is even and clear the Zero flag if EAX is odd.

8. Write a single instruction that converts an uppercase character in AL to lowercase but does not modify AL if it already contains a lowercase letter.

9. Write a single instruction that converts an ASCII digit in AL to its corresponding binary value. If AL already contains a binary value (00h to 09h), leave it unchanged.

10. Write instructions that calculate the parity of the 32-bit memory operand. *Hint:* Use the formula presented earlier in this section: B_0 XOR B_1 XOR B_2 XOR B_3.

11. Given two bit-mapped sets named SetX and SetY, write a sequence of instructions that generate a bit string in EAX that represents members in SetX that are not members of SetY.

6.3 Conditional Jumps

6.3.1 Conditional Structures

There are no explicit high-level logic structures in the x86 instruction set, but you can implement them using a combination of comparisons and jumps. Two steps are involved in executing a conditional statement: First, an operation such as CMP, AND, or SUB modifies the CPU status flags. Second, a conditional jump instruction tests the flags and causes a branch to a new address. Let's look at a couple of examples.

Example 1   The CMP instruction in the following example compares EAX to Zero. The JZ (jump if Zero) instruction jumps to label **L1** if the Zero flag was set by the CMP instruction:

```
        cmp    eax,0
        jz     L1                        ; jump if ZF = 1
        .
        .
L1:
```

Example 2   The AND instruction in the following example performs a bitwise AND on the DL register, affecting the Zero flag. The JNZ (jump if not Zero) instruction jumps if the Zero flag is clear:

```
        and    dl,10110000b
        jnz    L2                        ; jump if ZF = 0
        .
        .
L2:
```

6.3.2   J*cond* Instruction

A conditional jump instruction branches to a destination label when a status flag condition is true. Otherwise, if the flag condition is false, the instruction immediately following the conditional jump is executed. The syntax is as follows:

```
    Jcond destination
```

cond refers to a flag condition identifying the state of one or more flags. The following examples are based on the Carry and Zero flags:

jc	Jump if carry (Carry flag set)
jnc	Jump if not carry (Carry flag clear)
jz	Jump if zero (Zero flag set)
jnz	Jump if not zero (Zero flag clear)

CPU status flags are most commonly set by arithmetic, comparison, and boolean instructions. Conditional jump instructions evaluate the flag states, using them to determine whether or not jumps should be taken.

Using the CMP Instruction   Suppose you want to jump to label L1 when EAX equals 5. In the next example, if EAX equals 5, the CMP instruction sets the Zero flag; then, the JE instruction jumps to L1 because the Zero flag is set:

```
    cmp    eax,5
    je     L1                            ; jump if equal
```

(The JE instruction always jumps based on the value of the Zero flag.) If EAX were not equal to 5, CMP would clear the Zero flag, and the JE instruction would not jump.

In the following example, the JL instruction jumps to label L1 because AX is less than 6:

```
mov   ax,5
cmp   ax,6
jl    L1                             ; jump if less
```

In the following example, the jump is taken because AX is greater than 4:

```
mov   ax,5
cmp   ax,4
jg    L1                             ; jump if greater
```

6.3.3 Types of Conditional Jump Instructions

The x86 instruction set has a large number of conditional jump instructions. They are able to compare signed and unsigned integers and perform actions based on the values of individual CPU flags. The conditional jump instructions can be divided into four groups:

- Jumps based on specific flag values
- Jumps based on equality between operands or the value of (E)CX
- Jumps based on comparisons of unsigned operands
- Jumps based on comparisons of signed operands

Table 6-2 shows a list of jumps based on the Zero, Carry, Overflow, Parity, and Sign flags.

Table 6-2   Jumps Based on Specific Flag Values.

Mnemonic	Description	Flags / Registers
JZ	Jump if zero	ZF = 1
JNZ	Jump if not zero	ZF = 0
JC	Jump if carry	CF = 1
JNC	Jump if not carry	CF = 0
JO	Jump if overflow	OF = 1
JNO	Jump if not overflow	OF = 0
JS	Jump if signed	SF = 1
JNS	Jump if not signed	SF = 0
JP	Jump if parity (even)	PF = 1
JNP	Jump if not parity (odd)	PF = 0

Equality Comparisons

Table 6-3 lists jump instructions based on evaluating equality. In some cases, two operands are compared; in other cases, a jump is taken based on the value of CX or ECX. In the table, the notations *leftOp* and *rightOp* refer to the left (destination) and right (source) operands in a CMP instruction:

```
CMP leftOp,rightOp
```

The operand names reflect the ordering of operands for relational operators in algebra. For example, in the expression X < Y, X is called *leftOp* and Y is called *rightOp*.

Table 6-3 Jumps Based on Equality.

Mnemonic	Description
JE	Jump if equal (*leftOp* = *rightOp*)
JNE	Jump if not equal (*leftOp* ≠ *rightOp*)
JCXZ	Jump if CX = 0
JECXZ	Jump if ECX = 0

Although the JE instruction is equivalent to JZ (jump if Zero) and JNE is equivalent to JNZ (jump if not Zero), it's best to select the mnemonic (JE or JZ) that best indicates your intention to either compare two operands or examine a specific status flag.

Following are code examples that use the JE, JNE, JCXZ, and JECXZ instructions. Examine the comments carefully to be sure that you understand why the conditional jumps were (or were not) taken.

Example 1:

```
mov  edx,0A523h
cmp  edx,0A523h
jne  L5                        ; jump not taken
je   L1                        ; jump is taken
```

Example 2:

```
mov  bx,1234h
sub  bx,1234h
jne  L5                        ; jump not taken
je   L1                        ; jump is taken
```

Example 3:

```
mov  cx,0FFFFh
inc  cx
jcxz L2                        ; jump is taken
```

Example 4:

```
xor  ecx,ecx
jecxz L2                       ; jump is taken
```

Unsigned Comparisons

Jumps based on comparisons of unsigned numbers are shown in Table 6-4. The operand names reflect the order of operands, as in the expression (*leftOp* < *rightOp*). The jumps in Table 6-4 are only meaningful when comparing unsigned values. Signed operands use a different set of jumps.

Signed Comparisons

Table 6-5 displays a list of jumps based on signed comparisons. The following instruction sequence demonstrates the comparison of two signed values:

```
mov  al,+127                   ; hexadecimal value is 7Fh
cmp  al,-128                   ; hexadecimal value is 80h
ja   IsAbove                   ; jump not taken, because 7Fh < 80h
jg   IsGreater                 ; jump taken, because +127 > -128
```

Table 6-4   Jumps Based on Unsigned Comparisons.

Mnemonic	Description
JA	Jump if above (if *leftOp* > *rightOp*)
JNBE	Jump if not below or equal (same as JA)
JAE	Jump if above or equal (if *leftOp* ≥ *rightOp*)
JNB	Jump if not below (same as JAE)
JB	Jump if below (if *leftOp* < *rightOp*)
JNAE	Jump if not above or equal (same as JB)
JBE	Jump if below or equal (if *leftOp* ≤ *rightOp*)
JNA	Jump if not above (same as JBE)

The JA instruction, which is designed for unsigned comparisons, does not jump because unsigned 7Fh is smaller than unsigned 80h. The JG instruction, on the other hand, is designed for signed comparisons—it jumps because +127 is greater than −128.

Table 6-5   Jumps Based on Signed Comparisons.

Mnemonic	Description
JG	Jump if greater (if *leftOp* > *rightOp*)
JNLE	Jump if not less than or equal (same as JG)
JGE	Jump if greater than or equal (if *leftOp* ≥ *rightOp*)
JNL	Jump if not less (same as JGE)
JL	Jump if less (if *leftOp* < *rightOp*)
JNGE	Jump if not greater than or equal (same as JL)
JLE	Jump if less than or equal (if *leftOp* ≤ *rightOp*)
JNG	Jump if not greater (same as JLE)

In the following code examples, examine the comments to be sure you understand why the jumps were (or were not) taken.

Example 1

```
mov     edx,-1
cmp     edx,0
jnl     L5                      ; jump not taken (-1 >= 0 is false)
jnle    L5                      ; jump not taken (-1 > 0 is false)
jl      L1                      ; jump is taken (-1 < 0 is true)
```

Example 2

```
mov     bx,+32
cmp     bx,-35
jng     L5                      ; jump not taken (+32 <= -35 is false)
jnge    L5                      ; jump not taken (+32 < -35 is false)
jge     L1                      ; jump is taken (+32 >= -35 is true)
```

Example 3

```
mov  ecx,0
cmp  ecx,0
jg   L5                        ; jump not taken (0 > 0 is false)
jnl  L1                        ; jump is taken (0 >= 0 is true)
```

Example 4

```
mov  ecx,0
cmp  ecx,0
jl   L5                        ; jump not taken (0 < 0 is false)
jng  L1                        ; jump is taken (0 <= 0 is true)
```

6.3.4 Conditional Jump Applications

Testing Status Bits

Bitwise instructions that examine groups of bits in binary data usually modify the values of certain CPU status flags. Conditional jump instructions often use these status flags to determine whether or not to transfer control to code labels. Suppose, for example, that an 8-bit memory operand named **status** contains status information about an external device attached to the computer. The following instructions jump to a label if bit 5 is set, indicating that the device is offline:

```
mov   al,status
test  al,00100000b             ; test bit 5
jnz   EquipOffline
```

The following statements jump to a label if any of the bits 0, 1, or 4 are set:

```
mov   al,status
test  al,00010011b             ; test bits 0,1,4
jnz   InputDataByte
```

Jumping to a label if bits 2, 3, and 7 are all set requires both the AND and CMP instructions:

```
mov   al,status
and   al,10001100b             ; mask bits 2,3,7
cmp   al,10001100b             ; all bits set?
je    ResetMachine             ; yes: jump to label
```

Larger of Two Integers The following code compares the unsigned integers in EAX and EBX and moves the larger of the two to EDX:

```
    mov  edx,eax               ; assume EAX is larger
    cmp  eax,ebx               ; if EAX is >= EBX then
    jae  L1                    ;    jump to L1
    mov  edx,ebx               ; else move EBX to EDX
L1:                            ; EDX contains the larger integer
```

Smallest of Three Integers The following instructions compare the unsigned 16-bit values in the variables V1, V2, and V3 and move the smallest of the three to AX:

```
.data
V1 WORD ?
V2 WORD ?
```

```
V3 WORD ?
.code
     mov    ax,V1             ; assume V1 is smallest
     cmp    ax,V2             ; if AX <= V2 then
     jbe    L1                ;    jump to L1
     mov    ax,V2             ; else move V2 to AX
L1:  cmp    ax,V3             ; if AX <= V3 then
     jbe    L2                ;    jump to L2
     mov    ax,V3             ; else move V3 to AX
L2:
```

Loop until Key Pressed   In the following 32-bit code, a loop runs continuously until the user presses a standard alphanumeric key. The *ReadKey* method from the Irvine32 library sets the Zero flag if no key is present in the input buffer:

```
.data
char BYTE ?
.code
L1: mov  eax,10              ; create 10ms delay
    call Delay
    call ReadKey             ; check for key
    jz   L1                  ; repeat if no key
    mov  char,AL             ; save the character
```

The foregoing code inserts a 10-millisecond delay in the loop to give MS-Windows time to process event messages. If you omit the delay, keystrokes may be ignored. In a 16-bit application, on the other hand, you can omit the delay. The following code calls ReadKey from the Irvine16 library:

```
.data
char BYTE ?
.code
L1: call ReadKey             ; check for key
    jz   L1                  ; repeat if no key
    mov  char,AL             ; save the character
```

Application: Sequential Search of an Array

A common programming task is to search for values in an array that meet some criteria. For example, the following program looks for the first nonzero value in an array of 16-bit integers. If it finds one, it displays the value; otherwise, it displays a message stating that a nonzero value was not found:

```
TITLE Scanning an Array                    (ArryScan.asm)
; Scan an array for the first nonzero value.

INCLUDE Irvine32.inc

.data
intArray  SWORD  0,0,0,0,1,20,35,-12,66,4,0
;intArray SWORD  1,0,0,0                    ; alternate test data
;intArray SWORD  0,0,0,0                    ; alternate test data
;intArray SWORD  0,0,0,1                    ; alternate test data
noneMsg   BYTE "A non-zero value was not found",0
```

> This program contains alternate test data that are currently commented out. Uncomment these lines to
> test the program with different data configurations.

```
.code
main PROC
        mov    ebx,OFFSET intArray   ; point to the array
        mov    ecx,LENGTHOF intArray; loop counter

L1:     cmp    WORD PTR [cbx],0      ; compare value to zero
        jnz    found                ; found a value
        add    ebx,2                ; point to next
        loop   L1                   ; continue the loop
        jmp    notFound             ; none found

found:                              ; display the value
        movsx eax,WORD PTR[ebx]     ; sign-extend into EAX
        call   WriteInt
        jmp    quit

notFound:                           ; display "not found" message
        mov    edx,OFFSET noneMsg
        call   WriteString

quit:
        call Crlf
        exit
main ENDP
END main
```

Application: Simple String Encryption

Section 6.2.5 showed that the XOR instruction has an interesting property. If an integer X is
XORed with Y and the resulting value is XORed with Y again, the value produced is X:

$$((X \otimes Y) \otimes Y) = X$$

This "reversible" property of XOR provides an easy way to perform a simple form of data
encryption: A *plain text* message is transformed into an encrypted string called *cipher text by*
XORing each of its characters with a character from a third string called a *key*. The intended
viewer can use the key to decrypt the cipher text and produce the original plain text.

Example Program   We will demonstrate a simple program that uses *symmetric encryption*,
a process by which the same key is used for both encryption and decryption. The following steps
occur in order at runtime:

1. The user enters the plain text.
2. The program uses a single-character key to encrypt the plain text, producing the cipher text,
   which is displayed on the screen.
3. The program decrypts the cipher text, producing and displaying the original plain text.

Here is sample output from the program:

Program Listing   Here is a complete program listing:

```
TITLE Encryption Program                    (Encrypt.asm)

INCLUDE Irvine32.inc
KEY = 239                           ; any value between 1-255
BUFMAX = 128                        ; maximum buffer size

.data
sPrompt  BYTE "Enter the plain text:",0
sEncrypt BYTE "Cipher text:      ",0
sDecrypt BYTE "Decrypted:        ",0
buffer   BYTE   BUFMAX+1 DUP(0)
bufSize  DWORD  ?

.code
main PROC
     call  InputTheString      ; input the plain text
     call  TranslateBuffer      ; encrypt the buffer
     mov   edx,OFFSET sEncrypt  ; display encrypted message
     call  DisplayMessage
     call  TranslateBuffer      ; decrypt the buffer
     mov   edx,OFFSET sDecrypt  ; display decrypted message
     call  DisplayMessage
     exit
main ENDP

;-----------------------------------------------------
InputTheString PROC
;
; Prompts user for a plaintext string. Saves the string
; and its length.
; Receives: nothing
; Returns: nothing
;-----------------------------------------------------
     pushad                     ; save 32-bit registers
     mov   edx,OFFSET sPrompt   ; display a prompt
     call  WriteString
     mov   ecx,BUFMAX           ; maximum character count
     mov   edx,OFFSET buffer    ; point to the buffer
     call  ReadString           ; input the string
     mov   bufSize,eax          ; save the length
```

```
            call   Crlf
            popad
            ret
    InputTheString ENDP

    ;----------------------------------------------------
    DisplayMessage PROC
    ;
    ; Displays the encrypted or decrypted message.
    ; Receives: EDX points to the message
    ; Returns:  nothing
    ;----------------------------------------------------
            pushad
            call   WriteString
            mov    edx,OFFSET buffer    ; display the buffer
            call   WriteString
            call   Crlf
            call   Crlf
            popad
            ret
    DisplayMessage ENDP

    ;----------------------------------------------------
    TranslateBuffer PROC
    ;
    ; Translates the string by exclusive-ORing each
    ; byte with the encryption key byte.
    ; Receives: nothing
    ; Returns:  nothing
    ;----------------------------------------------------
            pushad
            mov    ecx,bufSize          ; loop counter
            mov    esi,0                ; index 0 in buffer
    L1:
            xor    buffer[esi],KEY      ; translate a byte
            inc    esi                  ; point to next byte
            loop   L1
            popad
            ret
    TranslateBuffer ENDP
    END main
```

You should never encrypt important data with a single-character encryption key, because it can be too easily decoded. Instead, the chapter exercises suggest that you use an encryption key containing multiple characters to encrypt and decrypt the plain text.

6.3.5 Section Review

1. Which jump instructions follow unsigned integer comparisons?
2. Which jump instructions follow signed integer comparisons?
3. Which conditional jump instruction branches based on the contents of ECX?

4. *(Yes/No):* Are the JA and JNBE instructions equivalent? Explain your answer.

5. Suppose the CMP instruction compares the integers 7FFFh and 8000h. Show how the JB and JL instructions would generate different results if used after comparing these values.

6. Which conditional jump instruction is equivalent to the JNA instruction?

7. Which conditional jump instruction is equivalent to the JNGE instruction?

8. *(Yes/No):* Will the following code jump to the label named **Target**?

```
mov ax,8109h
cmp ax,26h
jg  Target
```

9. *(Yes/No):* Will the following code jump to the label named **Target**?

```
mov ax,-30
cmp ax,-50
jg  Target
```

10. *(Yes/No):* Will the following code jump to the label named **Target**?

```
mov ax,-42
cmp ax,26
ja  Target
```

11. Write instructions that jump to label L1 when the unsigned integer in DX is less than or equal to the integer in CX.

12. Write instructions that jump to label L2 when the signed integer in AX is greater than the integer in CX.

13. Write instructions that first clear bits 0 and 1 in AL. Then, if the destination operand is equal to zero, the code should jump to label L3. Otherwise, it should jump to label L4.

6.4   Conditional Loop Instructions

6.4.1   LOOPZ and LOOPE Instructions

The LOOPZ (loop if zero) instruction works just like the LOOP instruction except that it has one additional condition: the Zero flag must be set in order for control to transfer to the destination label. The syntax is

```
LOOPZ destination
```

The LOOPE (loop if equal) instruction is equivalent to LOOPZ and they share the same opcode. They perform the following tasks:

```
ECX = ECX - 1
if ECX > 0 and ZF = 1, jump to destination
```

Otherwise, no jump occurs, and control passes to the next instruction. LOOPZ and LOOPE do not affect any of the status flags.

In 32-bit mode, ECX is the loop counter register. In 16-bit real-address mode, CX is the counter, and in 64-bit mode, RCX is the counter.

6.4.2   LOOPNZ and LOOPNE Instructions

The LOOPNZ (loop if not zero) instruction is the counterpart of LOOPZ. The loop continues while the unsigned value of ECX is greater than zero (after being decremented) and the Zero flag is clear. The syntax is

```
LOOPNZ destination
```

The LOOPNE (loop if not equal) instruction is equivalent to LOOPNZ and they share the same opcode. They perform the following tasks:

```
ECX = ECX - 1
if ECX > 0 and ZF = 0, jump to destination
```

Otherwise, nothing happens, and control passes to the next instruction.

Example   The following code excerpt (from *Loopnz.asm*) scans each number in an array until a nonnegative number is found (when the sign bit is clear). Notice that we push the flags on the stack before the ADD instruction because ADD will modify the flags. Then the flags are restored by POPFD just before the LOOPNZ instruction executes:

```
.data
array   SWORD   -3,-6,-1,-10,10,30,40,4
sentinel SWORD  0
.code
        mov     esi,OFFSET array
        mov     ecx,LENGTHOF array

L1: test    WORD PTR [esi],8000h         ; test sign bit
    pushfd                               ; push flags on stack
    add     esi,TYPE array               ; move to next position
    popfd                                ; pop flags from stack
    loopnz  L1                           ; continue loop
    jnz     quit                         ; none found
    sub     esi,TYPE array               ; ESI points to value
quit:
```

If a nonnegative value is found, ESI is left pointing at it. If the loop fails to find a positive number, it stops when ECX equals zero. In that case, the JNZ instruction jumps to label **quit**, and ESI points to the sentinel value (0), located in memory immediately following the array.

6.4.3   Section Review

1. *(True/False):* The LOOPE instruction jumps to a label when (and only when) the Zero flag is clear.

2. *(True/False):* The LOOPNZ instruction jumps to a label when ECX is greater than zero and the Zero flag is clear.

3. *(True/False):* The destination label of a LOOPZ instruction must be no farther than -128 or $+127$ bytes from the instruction immediately following LOOPZ.

4. Modify the LOOPNZ example in Section 6.4.2 so that it scans for the first negative value in the array. Change the array initializers so they begin with positive values.

5. *Challenge:* The LOOPNZ example in Section 6.4.2 relies on a sentinel value to handle the possibility that a positive value might not be found. What might happen if we removed the sentinel?

6.5 Conditional Structures

We define a *conditional structure* to be one or more conditional expressions that trigger a choice between different logical branches. Each branch causes a different sequence of instructions to execute. No doubt you have already used conditional structures in a high-level programming language. But you may not know how language compilers translate conditional structures into low-level machine code. Let's find out how that is done.

6.5.1 Block-Structured IF Statements

An IF structure implies that a boolean expression is followed by two lists of statements; one performed when the expression is true, and another performed when the expression is false:

```
if( boolean-expression )
  statement-list-1
else
  statement-list-2
```

The **else** portion of the statement is optional. In assembly language, we code this structure in steps. First, we evaluate the boolean expression in such a way that one of the CPU status flags is affected. Second, we construct a series of jumps that transfer control to the two lists of statements, based on the value of the relevant CPU status flag.

Example 1 In the following C++ code, two assignment statements are executed if **op1** is equal to **op2**:

```
if( op1 == op2 ) then
{
    X = 1;
    Y = 2;
}
```

We translate this IF statement into assembly language with a CMP instruction followed by conditional jumps. Because **op1** and **op2** are memory operands (variables), one of them must be moved to a register before executing CMP. The following code implements the IF statement as efficiently as possible by allowing the code to "fall through" to the two MOV instructions that we want to execute when the boolean condition is true:

```
        mov    eax,op1
        cmp    eax,op2            ; op1 == op2?
        jne    L1                 ; no: skip next
        mov    X,1                ; yes: assign X and Y
        mov    Y,2
    L1:
```

If we implemented the == operator using JE, the resulting code would be slightly less compact (six instructions rather than five):

```
        mov    eax,op1
        cmp    eax,op2            ; op1 == op2?
        je     L1                 ; yes: jump to L1
        jmp    L2                 ; no: skip assignments
    L1: mov    X,1                ; assign X and Y
        mov    Y,2
    L2:
```

> As you see from the foregoing example, the same conditional structure can be translated into assembly language in multiple ways. When examples of compiled code are shown in this chapter, they represent only what a hypothetical compiler might produce.

Example 2   In the FAT32 file storage system, the size of a disk cluster depends on the disk's overall capacity. In the following pseudocode, we set the cluster size to 4,096 if the disk size (in the variable named **gigabytes**) is less than 8 GBytes. Otherwise, we set the cluster size to 8,192:

```
clusterSize = 8192;
if gigabytes < 8
  clusterSize = 4096;
```

Here's a way to implement the same statement in assembly language:

```
        mov     clusterSize,8192    ; assume larger cluster
        cmp     gigabytes,8         ; larger than 8 GB?
        jae     next
        mov     clusterSize,4096    ; switch to smaller cluster
next:
```

(Disk clusters are described in Section 15.2.)

Example 3   The following pseudocode statement has two branches:

```
if op1 > op2 then
    call Routine1
else
    call Routine2
end if
```

In the following assembly language translation of the pseudocode, we assume that **op1** and **op2** are signed doubleword variables. When comparing variables, one must be moved to a register:

```
        mov   eax,op1           ; move op1 to a register
        cmp   eax,op2           ; op1 > op2?
        jg    A1                ; yes: call Routine1
        call  Routine2          ; no: call Routine2
        jmp   A2                ; exit the IF statement
A1:     call  Routine1
A2:
```

White Box Testing

Complex conditional statements may have multiple execution paths, making them hard to debug by inspection (looking at the code). Programmers often implement a technique known as *white box testing*, which verifies a subroutine's inputs and corresponding outputs. White box testing requires you to have a copy of the source code. You assign a variety of values to the input variables. For each combination of inputs, you manually trace through the source code and verify the execution path and outputs produced by the subroutine. Let's see how this is done in assembly language by implementing the following nested-IF statement:

```
if op1 == op2 then
  if X > Y then
     call Routine1
  else
     call Routine2
  end if
else
  call Routine3
end if
```

Following is a possible translation to assembly language, with line numbers added for reference. It reverses the initial condition (op1 == op2) and immediately jumps to the ELSE portion. All that is left to translate is the inner IF-ELSE statement:

```
1:          mov     eax,op1
2:          cmp     eax,op2        ; op1 == op2?
3:          jne     L2             ; no: call Routine3

; process the inner IF-ELSE statement.
4:          mov     eax,X
5:          cmp     eax,Y          ; X > Y?
6:          jg      L1             ; yes: call Routine1
7:          call    Routine2       ; no: call Routine2
8:          jmp     L3             ; and exit
9:   L1: call      Routine1       ; call Routine1
10:         jmp     L3             ; and exit
11:  L2: call      Routine3
12:  L3:
```

Table 6-6 shows the results of white box testing of the sample code. In the first four columns, test values have been assigned to op1, op2, X, and Y. The resulting execution paths are verified in columns 5 and 6.

Table 6-6   Testing the Nested IF Statement.

op1	op2	X	Y	Line Execution Sequence	Calls
10	20	30	40	1, 2, 3, 11, 12	Routine3
10	20	40	30	1, 2, 3, 11, 12	Routine3
10	10	30	40	1, 2, 3, 4, 5, 6, 7, 8, 12	Routine2
10	10	40	30	1, 2, 3, 4, 5, 6, 9, 10, 12	Routine1

6.5.2 Compound Expressions

Logical AND Operator

Assembly language easily implements compound boolean expressions containing AND operators. Consider the following pseudocode, in which the values being compared are assumed to be unsigned integers:

```
if (al > bl) AND (bl > cl) then
    X = 1
end if
```

Short-Circuit Evaluation   The following is a straightforward implementation using *short-circuit* evaluation, in which the second expression is not evaluated if the first expression is false. This is the norm for high-level languages:

```
        cmp    al,bl                 ; first expression...
        ja     L1
        jmp    next
L1:     cmp    bl,cl                 ; second expression...
        ja     L2
        jmp    next
L2:     mov    X,1                   ; both true: set X to 1
    next:
```

We can reduce the code to five instructions by changing the initial JA instruction to JBE:

```
        cmp    al,bl                 ; first expression...
        jbe    next                  ; quit if false
        cmp    bl,cl                 ; second expression
        jbe    next                  ; quit if false
        mov    X,1                   ; both are true
    next:
```

The 29% reduction in code size (seven instructions down to five) results from letting the CPU fall through to the second CMP instruction if the first JBE is not taken.

Logical OR Operator

When a compound expression contains subexpressions joined by the OR operator, the overall expression is true if any of the subexpressions is true. Let's use the following pseudocode as an example:

```
if (al > bl) OR (bl > cl) then
    X = 1
```

In the following implementation, the code branches to L1 if the first expression is true; otherwise, it falls through to the second CMP instruction. The second expression reverses the > operator and uses JBE instead:

```
        cmp    al,bl                 ; 1: compare AL to BL
        ja     L1                    ; if true, skip second expression
        cmp    bl,cl                 ; 2: compare BL to CL
        jbe    next                  ; false: skip next statement
L1:     mov    X,1                   ; true: set X = 1
    next:
```

For a given compound expression, there are multiple ways the expression can be implemented in assembly language.

6.5.3 WHILE Loops

A WHILE loop tests a condition first before performing a block of statements. As long as the loop condition remains true, the statements are repeated. The following loop is written in C++:

```
while( val1 < val2 )
{
    val1++;
    val2--;
}
```

When implementing this structure in assembly language, it is convenient to reverse the loop condition and jump to **endwhile** if a condition becomes true. Assuming that **val1** and **val2** are variables, we must copy one of them to a register at the beginning and restore the variable's value at the end:

```
        mov     eax,val1            ; copy variable to EAX
beginwhile:
        cmp     eax,val2            ; if not (val1 < val2)
        jnl     endwhile            ;    exit the loop
        inc     eax                 ; val1++;
        dec     val2                ; val2--;
        jmp     beginwhile          ; repeat the loop
endwhile:
        mov     val1,eax            ; save new value for val1
```

EAX is a proxy (substitute) for **val1** inside the loop. References to **val1** must be through EAX. JNL is used, implying that **val1** and **val2** are signed integers.

Example: IF statement Nested in a Loop

High-level languages are particularly good at representing nested control structures. In the following C++ code, an IF statement is nested inside a WHILE loop. It calculates the sum of all array elements greater than the value in **sample**:

```
int array[] = {10,60,20,33,72,89,45,65,72,18};
int sample = 50;
int ArraySize = sizeof array / sizeof sample;
int index = 0;
int sum = 0;
while( index < ArraySize )
{
    if( array[index] > sample )
    {
        sum += array[index];
    }
    index++;
}
```

Before coding this loop in assembly language, let's use the flowchart in Figure 6–2 to describe the logic. To simplify the translation and speed up execution by reducing the number of memory accesses, registers have been substituted for variables. EDX = sample, EAX = sum, ESI = index, and ECX = ArraySize (a constant). Label names have been added to the shapes.

Figure 6–2   Loop Containing IF Statement.

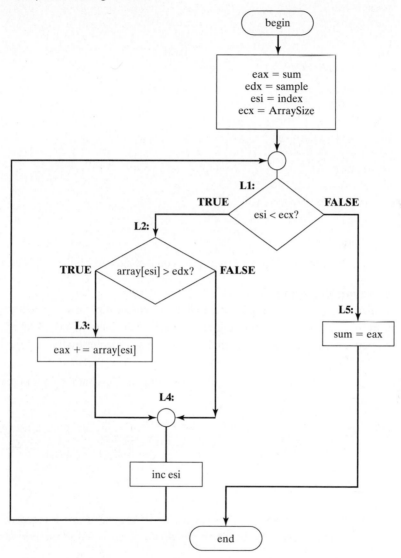

Assembly Code   The easiest way to generate assembly code from a flowchart is to implement separate code for each flowchart shape. Note the direct correlation between the flowchart labels and labels used in the following source code (see *Flowchart.asm*):

```
.data
sum DWORD 0
sample DWORD 50
array DWORD 10,60,20,33,72,89,45,65,72,18
ArraySize = ($ - Array) / TYPE array
```

```
        .code
        main PROC
                mov     eax,0                   ; sum
                mov     edx,sample
                mov     esi,0                   ; index
                mov     ecx,ArraySize

        L1:     cmp     esi,ecx                 ; if esi < ecx
                jl      L2
                jmp     L5

        L2:     cmp     array[esi*4], edx       ; if array[esi] > edx
                jg      L3
                jmp     L4
        L3:     add     eax,array[esi*4]

        L4:     inc     esi
                jmp     L1

        L5:     mov     sum,eax
```

A review question at the end of Section 6.5 will give you a chance to improve this code.

6.5.4 Table-Driven Selection

Table-driven selection is a way of using a table lookup to replace a multiway selection structure. To use it, you must create a table containing lookup values and the offsets of labels or procedures, and then you must use a loop to search the table. This works best when a large number of comparisons are made.

For example, the following is part of a table containing single-character lookup values and addresses of procedures:

```
        .data
        CaseTable BYTE   'A'              ; lookup value
            DWORD Process_A               ; address of procedure
            BYTE  'B'
            DWORD Process_B
            (etc.)
```

Let's assume Process_A, Process_B, Process_C, and Process_D are located at addresses 120h, 130h, 140h, and 150h, respectively. The table would be arranged in memory as shown in Figure 6–3.

FIGURE 6–3   Table of Procedure Offsets.

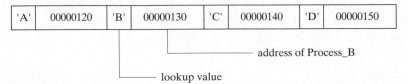

Example Program   In the following example program (*ProcTble.asm*), the user inputs a character from the keyboard. Using a loop, the character is compared to each entry in a lookup table. The first match found in the table causes a call to the procedure offset stored immediately after the lookup value. Each procedure loads EDX with the offset of a different string, which is displayed during the loop:

```
TITLE Table of Procedure Offsets              (ProcTble.asm)

; This program contains a table with offsets of procedures.
; It uses the table to execute indirect procedure calls.

INCLUDE Irvine32.inc
.data
CaseTable BYTE 'A'                       ; lookup value
          DWORD    Process_A             ; address of procedure
EntrySize = ($ - CaseTable)
          BYTE 'B'
          DWORD    Process_B
          BYTE 'C'
          DWORD    Process_C
          BYTE 'D'
          DWORD    Process_D
NumberOfEntries = ($ - CaseTable) / EntrySize
prompt BYTE "Press capital A,B,C,or D: ",0
```

Define a separate message string for each procedure:

```
msgA BYTE "Process_A",0
msgB BYTE "Process_B",0
msgC BYTE "Process_C",0
msgD BYTE "Process_D",0

.code
main PROC
        mov   edx,OFFSET prompt          ; ask user for input
        call  WriteString
        call  ReadChar                   ; read character into AL
        mov   ebx,OFFSET CaseTable       ; point EBX to the table
        mov   ecx,NumberOfEntries        ; loop counter
L1:
        cmp   al,[ebx]                    ; match found?
        jne   L2                          ; no: continue
        call  NEAR PTR [ebx + 1]          ; yes: call the procedure
```

This CALL instruction calls the procedure whose address is stored in the memory location referenced by EBX+1. An indirect call such as this requires the NEAR PTR operator.

```
        call  WriteString                ; display message
        call  Crlf
        jmp   L3                          ; exit the search
L2:
        add   ebx,EntrySize              ; point to the next entry
        loop  L1                          ; repeat until ECX = 0
```

```
L3:
     exit
main ENDP
```

> Each of the following procedures moves a different string offset to EDX:

```
Process_A PROC
     mov    edx,OFFSET msgA
     ret
Process_A ENDP

Process_B PROC
     mov    edx,OFFSET msgB
     ret
Process_B ENDP

Process_C PROC
     mov    edx,OFFSET msgC
     ret
Process_C ENDP

Process_D PROC
     mov    edx,OFFSET msgD
     ret
Process_D ENDP
END main
```

The table-driven selection method involves some initial overhead, but it can reduce the amount of code you write. A table can handle a large number of comparisons, and it can be more easily modified than a long series of compare, jump, and CALL instructions. A table can even be reconfigured at runtime.

6.5.5 Section Review

Notes: In all compound expressions, use short-circuit evaluation. Assume that val1 and X are 32-bit variables.

1. Implement the following pseudocode in assembly language:

```
if ebx > ecx then
   X = 1
```

2. Implement the following pseudocode in assembly language:

```
if edx <= ecx then
   X = 1
else
   X = 2
```

3. Implement the following pseudocode in assembly language:

```
if( val1 > ecx ) AND ( ecx > edx ) then
   X = 1
else
   X = 2;
```

4. Implement the following pseudocode in assembly language:

```
if( ebx > ecx ) OR ( ebx > val1 ) then
    X = 1
else
    X = 2
```

5. Implement the following pseudocode in assembly language:

```
if( ebx > ecx AND ebx > edx) OR ( edx > eax ) then
    X = 1
else
    X = 2
```

6. In the program from Section 6.5.4, why is it better to let the assembler calculate NumberOfEntries rather than assigning a constant such as NumberOfEnteries = 4?

7. *Challenge:* Rewrite the code from Section 6.5.3 so it is functionally equivalent, but uses fewer instructions.

6.6   Application: Finite-State Machines

A *finite-state machine* (FSM) is a machine or program that changes state based on some input. It is fairly simple to use a graph to represent an FSM, which contains squares (or circles) called *nodes* and lines with arrows between the circles called *edges (or arcs)*.

A simple example is shown in Figure 6–4. Each node represents a program state, and each edge represents a transition from one state to another. One node is designated as the *start state*, shown in our diagram with an incoming arrow. The remaining states can be labeled with numbers or letters. One or more states are designated as *terminal states*, shown by a thick border around the square. A terminal state represents a state in which the program might stop without producing an error. A FSM is a specific instance of a more general type of structure called a *directed graph*. The latter is a set of nodes connected by edges having specific directions.

FIGURE 6–4   Simple Finite-State Machine.

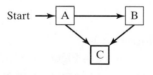

Directed graphs have many useful applications in computer science related to dynamic data structures and advanced searching techniques.

6.6.1   Validating an Input String

Programs that read input streams often must validate their input by performing a certain amount of error checking. A programming language compiler, for instance, can use a FSM to scan source programs and convert words and symbols into *tokens*, which are usually keywords, arithmetic operators, and identifiers.

When using a FSM to check the validity of an input string, you usually read the input character by character. Each character is represented by an edge (transition) in the diagram. A FSM detects illegal input sequences in one of two ways:

• The next input character does not correspond to any transitions from the current state.
• The end of input is reached and the current state is a nonterminal state.

Character String Example   Let's check the validity of an input string according to the following two rules:

• The string must begin with the letter 'x' and end with the letter 'z.'
• Between the first and last characters, there can be zero or more letters within the range {'a'..'y'}.

The FSM diagram in Figure 6–5 describes this syntax. Each transition is identified with a particular type of input. For example, the transition from state A to state B can only be accomplished if the letter **x** is read from the input stream. A transition from state B to itself is accomplished by the input of any letter of the alphabet except **z**. A transition from state B to state C occurs only when the letter **z** is read from the input stream.

FIGURE 6–5   FSM for String.

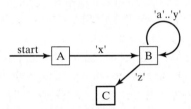

If the end of the input stream is reached while the program is in state A or B, an error condition results because only state C is marked as a terminal state. The following input strings would be recognized by this FSM:

```
xaabcdefgz
xz
xyyqqrrstuvz
```

6.6.2   Validating a Signed Integer

A FSM for parsing a signed integer is shown in Figure 6–6. Input consists of an optional leading sign followed by a sequence of digits. There is no maximum number of digits implied by the diagram.

FIGURE 6–6   Signed Decimal Integer FSM.

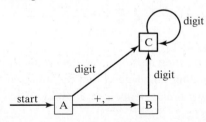

Finite-state machines are easily translated into assembly language code. Each state in the diagram (A, B, C, . . .) is represented in the program by a label. The following actions are performed at each label:

1. A call to an input procedure reads the next character from input.
2. If the state is a terminal state, check to see whether the user has pressed the Enter key to end the input.
3. One or more compare instructions check for each possible transition leading away from the state. Each comparison is followed by a conditional jump instruction.

For example, at state A, the following code reads the next input character and checks for a possible transition to state B:

```
StateA:
    call  Getnext            ; read next char into AL
    cmp   al,'+'             ; leading + sign?
    je    StateB             ; go to State B
    cmp   al,'-'             ; leading - sign?
    je    StateB             ; go to State B
    call  IsDigit            ; ZF = 1 if AL contains a digit
    jz    StateC             ; go to State C
    call  DisplayErrorMsg    ; invalid input found
    jmp   Quit
```

Let's examine this code in more detail. First, it calls *Getnext* to read the next character from the console input into the AL register. The code will check for a leading + or – sign. It begins by comparing the value in AL to a '+' character. If the character matches, a jump is taken to the label named *StateB:*

```
StateA:
    call  Getnext            ; read next char into AL
    cmp   al,'+'             ; leading + sign?
    je    StateB             ; go to State B
```

At this point, we should look again at Figure 6–6, and see that the transition from state A to state B can only be made if a + or – character is read from input. Therefore, the code must also check for the minus sign:

```
    cmp   al,'-'             ; leading - sign?
    je    StateB             ; go to State B
```

If a transition to state B is not possible, we can check the AL register for a digit, which would cause a transition to state C. The call to the *IsDigit* procedure (from the book's link library) sets the Zero flag if AL contains a digit:

```
    call  IsDigit            ; ZF = 1 if AL contains a digit
    jz    StateC             ; go to State C
```

Finally, there are no other possible transitions away from state A. If the character in AL has not been found to be a leading sign or digit, the program calls *DisplayErrorMsg* (which displays an error message on the console) and then jumps to the label named Quit:

```
    call  DisplayErrorMsg    ; invalid input found
    jmp   Quit
```

The label *Quit* marks the exit point of the program, at the end of the main procedure:

```
Quit:
     call  Crlf
     exit
main ENDP
```

Complete Finite State Machine Program The following program implements the signed integer FSM from Figure 6–5.

```
TITLE Finite State Machine               (Finite.asm)

INCLUDE Irvine32.inc

ENTER_KEY = 13
.data
InvalidInputMsg BYTE "Invalid input",13,10,0

.code
main PROC
     call Clrscr

StateA:
     call  Getnext          ; read next char into AL
     cmp   al,'+'           ; leading + sign?
     je    StateB           ; go to State B
     cmp   al,'-'           ; leading - sign?
     je    StateB           ; go to State B
     call  IsDigit          ; ZF = 1 if AL contains a digit
     jz    StateC           ; go to State C
     call  DisplayErrorMsg  ; invalid input found
     jmp   Quit

StateB:
     call  Getnext          ; read next char into AL
     call  IsDigit          ; ZF = 1 if AL contains a digit
     jz    StateC
     call  DisplayErrorMsg  ; invalid input found
     jmp   Quit

StateC:
     call  Getnext          ; read next char into AL
     call  IsDigit          ; ZF = 1 if AL contains a digit
     jz    StateC
     cmp   al,ENTER_KEY     ; Enter key pressed?
     je    Quit             ; yes: quit
     call  DisplayErrorMsg  ; no: invalid input found
     jmp   Quit

Quit:
     call  Crlf
     exit
main ENDP

;------------------------------------------------
```

```
Getnext PROC
;
; Reads a character from standard input.
; Receives: nothing
; Returns: AL contains the character
;------------------------------------------------
    call  ReadChar            ; input from keyboard
    call  WriteChar           ; echo on screen
    ret
Getnext ENDP

;------------------------------------------------
DisplayErrorMsg PROC
;
; Displays an error message indicating that
; the input stream contains illegal input.
; Receives: nothing.
; Returns: nothing
;------------------------------------------------
    push  edx
    mov   edx,OFFSET InvalidInputMsg
    call  WriteString
    pop   edx
    ret
DisplayErrorMsg ENDP
    END main
```

IsDigit Procedure   The Finite State Machine sample program calls the *IsDigit* procedure, which belongs to the book's link library. Let's look at the source code for IsDigit. It receives the AL register as input, and the value it returns is the setting of the Zero flag:

```
;--------------------------------------------------------------------
IsDigit PROC
;
; Determines whether the character in AL is a valid decimal digit.
; Receives: AL = character
; Returns: ZF = 1 if AL contains a valid decimal digit; otherwise, ZF = 0.
;--------------------------------------------------------------------
    cmp   al,'0'
    jb    ID1                 ; ZF = 0 when jump taken
    cmp   al,'9'
    ja    ID1                 ; ZF = 0 when jump taken
    test  ax,0                ; set ZF = 1
ID1: ret
IsDigit ENDP
```

Before examining the code in IsDigit, we can review the set of ASCII codes for decimal digits, shown in the following table. Because the values are contiguous, we need only to check for the starting and ending range values:

Character	'0'	'1'	'2'	'3'	'4'	'5'	'6'	'7'	'8'	'9'
ASCII code (hex)	30	31	32	33	34	35	36	37	38	39

In the IsDigit procedure, the first two instructions compare the character in the AL register to the ASCII code for the digit 0. If the numeric ASCII code of the character is less than the ASCII code for 0, the program jumps to the label ID1:

```
cmp  al,'0'
jb   ID1                              ; ZF = 0 when jump taken
```

But one may ask, if JB transfers control to the label named ID1, how do we know the state of the Zero flag? The answer lies in the way CMP works—it carries out an implied subtraction of the ASCII code for Zero (30h) from the character in the AL register. If the value in AL is smaller, the Carry flag is set, and the Zero flag is clear. (You may want to step through this code with a debugger to verify this fact.) The JB instruction is designed to transfer control to a label when CF = 1 and ZF = 0.

Next, the code in the IsDigit procedure compares AL to the ASCII code for the digit 9. If the value is greater, the code jumps to the same label:

```
cmp  al,'9'
ja   ID1                              ; ZF = 0 when jump taken
```

If the ASCII code for the character in AL is larger than the ASCII code of the digit 9 (39h), the Carry flag and Zero flag are cleared. That is exactly the flag combination that causes the JA instruction to transfer control to its target label.

If neither jump is taken (JA or JB), we assume that the character in AL is indeed a digit. Therefore, we insert an instruction that is guaranteed to set the Zero flag. To test any value with zero means to perform an implied AND with all zero bits. The result must be zero:

```
test  ax,0                            ; set ZF = 1
```

The JB and JA instructions we looked at earlier in IsDigit jumped to a label that was just beyond the TEST instruction. So if those jumps are taken, the Zero flag will be clear. Here is the complete procedure one more time:

```
Isdigit PROC
    cmp  al,'0'
    jb   ID1                          ; ZF = 0 when jump taken
    cmp  al,'9'
    ja   ID1                          ; ZF = 0 when jump taken
    test ax,0                         ; set ZF = 1
ID1: ret
Isdigit ENDP
```

In real-time or high-performance applications, programmers often take advantage of hardware characteristics to fully optimize their code. The IsDigit procedure is an example of this approach because it uses the flag settings of JB, JA, and TEST to return what is essentially a Boolean result.

6.6.3 Section Review

1. A finite-state machine is a specific application of what type of data structure?
2. In a finite-state machine diagram, what do the nodes represent?
3. In a finite-state machine diagram, what do the edges represent?

4. In the signed integer finite-state machine (Section 6.6.2), which state is reached when the input consists of "+5"?

5. In the signed integer finite-state machine (Section 6.6.2), how many digits can occur after a minus sign?

6. What happens in a finite-state machine when no more input is available and the current state is a nonterminal state?

7. Would the following simplification of a signed decimal integer finite-state machine work just as well as the one shown in Section 6.6.2? If not, why not?

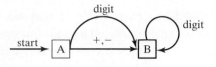

6.7 Conditional Control Flow Directives

MASM includes a number of high-level *conditional control flow directives* that help to simplify the coding of conditional statements. (The printed MASM manuals from 1992 used the term *Decision Directives*.) Before assembling your code, the assembler performs a preprocessing step. In this step, it recognizes directives such as .CODE, .DATA, as well as directives that can be used for conditional control flow. Table 6-7 lists the directives.

Table 6-7   Conditional Control Flow Directives.

Directive	Description
.BREAK	Generates code to terminate a .WHILE or .REPEAT block
.CONTINUE	Generates code to jump to the top of a .WHILE or .REPEAT block
.ELSE	Begins block of statements to execute when the .IF condition is false
.ELSEIF *condition*	Generates code that tests *condition* and executes statements that follow, until an .ENDIF directive or another .ELSEIF directive is found
.ENDIF	Terminates a block of statements following an .IF, .ELSE, or .ENDIF directive
.ENDW	Terminates a block of statements following a .WHILE directive
.IF *condition*	Generates code that executes the block of statements if *condition* is true.
.REPEAT	Generates code that repeats execution of the block of statements until condition becomes true
.UNTIL *condition*	Generates code that repeats the block of statements between .REPEAT and .UNTIL until *condition* becomes true
.UNTILCXZ	Generates code that repeats the block of statements between .REPEAT and .UNTIL until *CX* equals zero
.WHILE *condition*	Generates code that executes the block of statements between .WHILE and .ENDW as long as *condition* is true

6.7.1 Creating IF Statements

The .IF, .ELSE, .ELSEIF, and .ENDIF directives make it easy for you to code multiway branching logic. They cause the assembler to generate CMP and conditional jump instructions in the background, which appear in the output listing file (*progname*.lst). This is the syntax:

```
.IF condition1
    statements
[.ELSEIF condition2
    statements ]
[.ELSE
    statements ]
.ENDIF
```

The square brackets show that .ELSEIF and .ELSE are optional, whereas .IF and .ENDIF are required. A *condition* is a boolean expression involving the same operators used in C++ and Java (such as $<$, $>$, $==$, and $!=$). The expression is evaluated at runtime. The following are examples of valid conditions, using 32-bit registers and variables:

```
eax > 10000h
val1 <= 100
val2 == eax
val3 != ebx
```

The following are examples of compound conditions:

```
(eax > 0) && (eax > 10000h)
(val1 <= 100) || (val2 <= 100)
(val2 != ebx) && !CARRY?
```

A complete list of relational and logical operators is shown in Table 6-8.

Table 6-8   Runtime Relational and Logical Operators.

Operator	Description
expr1 $==$ *expr2*	Returns true when *expr1* is equal to *expr2*.
expr1 $!=$ *expr2*	Returns true when *expr1* is not equal to *expr2*.
expr1 $>$ *expr2*	Returns true when *expr1* is greater than *expr2*.
expr1 $\geq$ *expr2*	Returns true when *expr1* is greater than or equal to *expr2*.
expr1 $<$ *expr2*	Returns true when *expr1* is less than *expr2*.
expr1 $\leq$ *expr2*	Returns true when *expr1* is less than or equal to *expr2*.
! expr	Returns true when *expr* is false.
expr1 && *expr2*	Performs logical AND between *expr1* and *expr2*.
expr1 ‖ *expr2*	Performs logical OR between *expr1* and *expr2*.
expr1 & *expr2*	Performs bitwise AND between *expr1* and *expr2*.
CARRY?	Returns true if the Carry flag is set.
OVERFLOW?	Returns true if the Overflow flag is set.
PARITY?	Returns true if the Parity flag is set.
SIGN?	Returns true if the Sign flag is set.
ZERO?	Returns true if the Zero flag is set.

> Before using MASM conditional directives, be sure you thoroughly understand how to implement conditional branching instructions in pure assembly language. In addition, when a program containing decision directives is assembled, inspect the listing file to make sure the code generated by MASM is what you intended.

Generating ASM Code   When you use high-level directives such as .IF and .ELSE, the assembler writes code for you. For example, let's write an .IF directive that compares EAX to the variable **val1**:

```
mov eax,6
.IF eax > val1
  mov result,1
.ENDIF
```

val1 and **result** are assumed to be 32-bit unsigned integers. When the assembler reads the foregoing lines, it expands them into the following assembly language instructions, which you can view if you run the program with debugging and view the Disassembly window:

```
mov     eax,6
cmp     eax,val1
jbe     @C0001              ; jump on unsigned comparison
mov     result,1
@C0001:
```

The label name @C0001 was created by the assembler. This is done in a way that guarantees that all labels within same procedure are unique.

> To control whether or not MASM-generated code appears in the source listing file, you can configure the Project properties in Visual Studio. Here's how: from the Project menu, select *Project Properties*, select *Microsoft Macro Assembler*, select *Listing File*, and set *Enable Assembly Generated Code Listing* to Yes.

6.7.2 Signed and Unsigned Comparisons

When you use the .IF directive to compare values, you must be aware of how MASM generates conditional jumps. If the comparison involves an unsigned variable, an unsigned conditional jump instruction is inserted in the generated code. This is a repeat of a previous example that compares EAX to **val1**, an unsigned doubleword:

```
.data
val1 DWORD    5
result DWORD  ?
.code
    mov eax,6
    .IF eax > val1
      mov result,1
    .ENDIF
```

The assembler expands this using the JBE (unsigned jump) instruction:

```
mov eax,6
cmp eax,val1
jbe @C0001                  ; jump on unsigned comparison
mov result,1
@C0001:
```

Comparing a Signed Integer If an .IF directive compares a signed variable, however, a signed conditional jump instruction is inserted into the generated code. For example, **val2**, is a signed doubleword:

```
.data
val2 SDWORD -1
result DWORD ?
.code
    mov eax,6
    .IF eax > val2
      mov result,1
    .ENDIF
```

Consequently, the assembler generates code using the JLE instruction, a jump based on signed comparisons:

```
    mov eax,6
    cmp eax,val2
    jle @C0001               ; jump on signed comparison
    mov result,1
@C0001:
```

Comparing Registers The question we might then ask is, what happens if two registers are compared? Clearly, the assembler cannot determine whether the values are signed or unsigned:

```
    mov eax,6
    mov ebx,val2
    .IF eax > ebx
        mov result,1
    .ENDIF
```

The following code is generated, showing that the assembler defaults to an unsigned comparison (note the use of the JBE instruction).

```
    mov    eax,6
    mov    ebx,val2
    cmp    eax, ebx
    jbe    @C0001
    mov    result,1
@C0001:
```

6.7.3 Compound Expressions

Many compound boolean expressions use the logical OR and AND operators. When using the .IF directive, the ‖ symbol is the logical OR operator:

```
.IF expression1 || expression2
    statements
.ENDIF
```

Similarly, the && symbol is the logical AND operator:

```
.IF expression1 && expression2
    statements
.ENDIF
```

The logical OR operator will be used in the next program example.

SetCursorPosition Example

The **SetCursorPosition** procedure, shown in the next example, performs range checking on its two input parameters, DH and DL (see *SetCur.asm*). The Y-coordinate (DH) must be between 0 and 24. The X-coordinate (DL) must be between 0 and 79. If either is found to be out of range, an error message is displayed:

```
SetCursorPosition PROC
; Sets the cursor position.
; Receives: DL = X-coordinate, DH = Y-coordinate.
; Checks the ranges of DL and DH.
; Returns: nothing
;-----------------------------------------------
.data
BadXCoordMsg BYTE "X-Coordinate out of range!",0Dh,0Ah,0
BadYCoordMsg BYTE "Y-Coordinate out of range!",0Dh,0Ah,0
.code
    .IF (dl < 0) || (dl > 79)
        mov   edx,OFFSET BadXCoordMsg
        call  WriteString
        jmp   quit
    .ENDIF

    .IF (dh < 0) || (dh > 24)
        mov   edx,OFFSET BadYCoordMsg
        call  WriteString
        jmp   quit

    .ENDIF

    call Gotoxy
quit:
    ret
SetCursorPosition ENDP
```

The following code is generated by MASM when it preprocesses SetCursorPosition:

```
.code
; .IF (dl < 0) || (dl > 79)
    cmp   dl, 000h
    jb    @C0002
    cmp   dl, 04Fh
    jbe   @C0001
@C0002:
    mov   edx,OFFSET BadXCoordMsg
    call  WriteString
    jmp   quit
; .ENDIF
@C0001:
```

```
; .IF (dh < 0) || (dh > 24)

    cmp    dh, 000h
    jb     @C0005
    cmp    dh, 018h
    jbe    @C0004

@C0005:
    mov    edx,OFFSET BadYCoordMsg
    call   WriteString
    jmp    quit

; .ENDIF

@C0004:
    call  Gotoxy
quit:
    ret
```

College Registration Example

Suppose a college student wants to register for courses. We will use two criteria to determine whether or not the student can register: The first is the person's grade average, based on a 0 to 400 scale, where 400 is the highest possible grade. The second is the number of credits the person wants to take. A multiway branch structure can be used, involving .IF, .ELSEIF, and .ENDIF. The following shows an example (see *Regist.asm*):

```
.data
TRUE = 1
FALSE = 0
gradeAverage   WORD 275            ; test value
credits        WORD 12             ; test value
OkToRegister   BYTE ?
.code
    mov OkToRegister,FALSE
    .IF gradeAverage > 350
      mov OkToRegister,TRUE
    .ELSEIF (gradeAverage > 250) && (credits <= 16)
      mov OkToRegister,TRUE
    .ELSEIF (credits <= 12)
      mov OkToRegister,TRUE
    .ENDIF
```

Table 6-9 lists the corresponding code generated by the assembler, which you can view by looking at the *Dissassembly* window of the Microsoft Visual Studio debugger. (It has been cleaned up here a bit to make it easier to read.) MASM-generated code will appear in the source listing file if you use the /Sg command-line option when assembling programs. The size of a defined constants (such as TRUE or FALSE in the current code example) is 32-bits. Therefore, when a constant is moved to a BYTE address, MASM inserts the BYTE PTR operator.

Table 6-9   Registration Example, MASM-Generated Code.

```
          mov   byte ptr OkToRegister,FALSE
          cmp   word ptr gradeAverage,350
          jbe   @C0006
          mov   byte ptr OkToRegister,TRUE
          jmp   @C0008
    @C0006:
          cmp   word ptr gradeAverage,250
          jbe   @C0009
          cmp   word ptr credits,16
          ja    @C0009
          mov   byte ptr OkToRegister,TRUE
          jmp   @C0008
    @C0009:
          cmp   word ptr credits,12
          ja    @C0008
          mov   byte ptr OkToRegister,TRUE
    @C0008:
```

6.7.4   Creating Loops with .REPEAT and .WHILE

The .REPEAT and .WHILE directives offer alternatives to writing your own loops with CMP and conditional jump instructions. They permit the conditional expressions listed earlier in Table 6-8. The .REPEAT directive executes the loop body before testing the runtime condition following the .UNTIL directive:

```
.REPEAT
    statements
.UNTIL condition
```

The .WHILE directive tests the condition before executing the loop:

```
.WHILE condition
    statements
.ENDW
```

Examples: The following statements display the values 1 through 10 using the .WHILE directive. The counter register (EAX) is initialized to zero before the loop. Then, in the first statement inside the loop, EAX is incremented. The .WHILE directive branches out of the loop when EAX equals 10.

```
mov eax,0
.WHILE eax < 10
    inc   eax
    call  WriteDec
    call  Crlf
.ENDW
```

The following statements display the values 1 through 10 using the .REPEAT directive:

```
mov eax,0
.REPEAT
    inc   eax
    call WriteDec
    call Crlf
.UNTIL eax == 10
```

Example: Loop Containing an IF Statement

Earlier in this chapter, in Section 6.5.3, we showed how to write assembly language code for an IF statement nested inside a WHILE loop. Here is the pseudocode:

```
while( op1 < op2 )
{
    op1++;
    if( op1 == op3 )
      X = 2;
    else
      X = 3;
}
```

The following is an implementation of the pseudocode using the .WHILE and .IF directives. Because **op1**, **op2**, and **op3** are variables, they are moved to registers to avoid having two memory operands in any one instruction:

```
.data
X    DWORD 0
op1 DWORD 2                          ; test data
op2 DWORD 4                          ; test data
op3 DWORD 5                          ; test data
.code
    mov eax,op1
    mov ebx,op2
    mov ecx,op3
    .WHILE eax < ebx
      inc eax
      .IF eax == ecx
         mov X,2
      .ELSE
         mov X,3
      .ENDIF
    .ENDW
```

6.8   Chapter Summary

The AND, OR, XOR, NOT, and TEST instructions are called *bitwise instructions* because they work at the bit level. Each bit in a source operand is matched to a bit in the same position of the destination operand:

• The AND instruction produces 1 when both input bits are 1.
• The OR instruction produces 1 when at least one of the input bits is 1.
• The XOR instruction produces 1 only when the input bits are different.

- The TEST instruction performs an implied AND operation on the destination operand, setting the flags appropriately. The destination operand is not changed.
- The NOT instruction reverses all bits in a destination operand.

The CMP instruction compares a destination operand to a source operand. It performs an implied subtraction of the source from the destination and modifies the CPU status flags accordingly. CMP is usually followed by a conditional jump instruction that transfers control to a code label.

Four types of conditional jump instructions are shown in this chapter:

- Table 6-2 contains examples of jumps based on specific flag values, such as JC (jump carry), JZ (jump zero), and JO (jump overflow).
- Table 6-3 contains examples of jumps based on equality, such as JE (jump equal), JNE (jump not equal), and JECXZ (jump if ECX = 0).
- Table 6-4 contains examples of conditional jumps based on comparisons of unsigned integers, such as JA (jump if above), JB (jump if below), and JAE (jump if above or equal).
- Table 6-5 contains examples of jumps based on signed comparisons, such as JL (jump if less) and JG (jump if greater).

In 32-bit mode, the LOOPZ (LOOPE) instruction repeats when the Zero flag is set and ECX is greater than Zero. The LOOPNZ (LOOPNE) instruction repeats when the Zero flag is clear and ECX is greater than zero.

Encryption is a process that encodes data, and *decryption* is a process that decodes data. The XOR instruction can be used to perform simple encryption and decryption.

Flowcharts are an effective tool for visually representing program logic. You can easily write assembly language code, using a flowchart as a model. It is helpful to attach a label to each flowchart symbol and use the same label in your assembly source code.

A *finite-state machine* (FSM) is an effective tool for validating strings containing recognizable characters such as signed integers. It is relatively easy to implement a FSM in assembly language if each state is represented by a label.

The .IF, .ELSE, .ELSEIF, and .ENDIF directives evaluate runtime expressions and greatly simplify assembly language coding. They are particularly useful when coding complex compound boolean expressions. You can also create conditional loops, using the .WHILE and .REPEAT directives.

6.9   Programming Exercises

★ **1.   Counting Array Values**

Write an application that does the following: (1) fill an array with 50 random integers; (2) loop through the array, displaying each value, and count the number of negative values; (3) after the loop finishes, display the count. Note: The Random32 procedure from the Irvine32 library generates random integers.

★ **2.   Selecting Array Elements**

Implement the following C++ code in assembly language, using the block-structured .IF and .WHILE directives. Assume that all variables are 32-bit signed integers:

```
int array[] = {10,60,20,33,72,89,45,65,72,18};
int sample = 50;
```

```
    int ArraySize = sizeof array / sizeof sample;
    int index = 0;
    int sum = 0;
    while( index < ArraySize )
    {
        if( array[index] <= sample )
        {
            sum += array[index];
        }
        index++;
    }
```

Optional: Draw a flowchart of your code.

★ **3.   Test Score Evaluation (1)**

Using the following table as a guide, write a program that asks the user to enter an integer test score between 0 and 100. The program should display the appropriate letter grade:

Score Range	Letter Grade
90 to 100	A
80 to 89	B
70 to 79	C
60 to 69	D
0 to 59	F

★★ **4.   Test Score Evaluation (2)**

Using the solution program from the preceding exercise as a starting point, add the following features:

- Run in a loop so that multiple test scores can be entered.
- Accumulate a counter of the number of test scores.
- Perform range checking on the user's input: Display an error message if the test score is less than 0 or greater than 100. *(A VideoNote for this exercise is posted on the Web site.)*

★★ **5.   College Registration (1)**

Using the College Registration example from Section 6.7.3 as a starting point, do the following:

- Recode the logic using CMP and conditional jump instructions (instead of the .IF and .ELSEIF directives).
- Perform range checking on the **credits** value; it cannot be less than 1 or greater than 30. If an invalid entry is discovered, display an appropriate error message.
- Prompt the user for the grade average and credits values.
- Display a message that shows the outcome of the evaluation, such as "The student can register" or "The student cannot register".

★★★ 6.   College Registration (2)

Using the solution program from the preceding exercise as a starting point, write a complete program that does the following:

1. Use a loop that lets the user continue entering grade averages and credits, and seeing the evaluation results. If the user enters 0 as the grade average, stop the loop.

2. Perform range checking when the user inputs credits and GradeAverage. Credits must be between 1 and 30. GradeAverage must be between 0 and 400. If either value is out of range, display an appropriate error message.

★★ 7.   Boolean Calculator (1)

Create a program that functions as a simple boolean calculator for 32-bit integers. It should display a menu that asks the user to make a selection from the following list:

1. x AND y
2. x OR y
3. NOT x
4. x XOR y
5. Exit program

When the user makes a choice, call a procedure that displays the name of the operation about to be performed. (We will implement the operations in the exercise following this one.)

★★★ 8.   Boolean Calculator (2)

Continue the solution program from the preceding exercise by implementing the following procedures:

- AND_op: Prompt the user for two hexadecimal integers. AND them together and display the result in hexadecimal.
- OR_op: Prompt the user for two hexadecimal integers. OR them together and display the result in hexadecimal.
- NOT_op: Prompt the user for a hexadecimal integer. NOT the integer and display the result in hexadecimal.
- XOR_op: Prompt the user for two hexadecimal integers. Exclusive-OR them together and display the result in hexadecimal.

★★★ 9.   Probabilities and Colors

Write a program that randomly chooses among three different colors for displaying text on the screen. Use a loop to display 20 lines of text, each with a randomly chosen color. The probabilities for each color are to be as follows: white = 30%, blue = 10%, green = 60%. *Hint:* Generate a random integer between 0 and 9. If the resulting integer is in the range 0 to 2, choose white. If the integer equals 3, choose blue. If the integer is in the range 4 to 9, choose green. *(A VideoNote for this exercise is posted on the Web site.)*

★ 10.   Print Fibonacci until Overflow

Write a program that calculates and displays the Fibonacci number sequence {1, 1, 2, 3, 5, 8, 13, . . .}, stopping only when the Carry flag is set. Display each unsigned decimal integer value on a separate line.

★★★ **11. Message Encryption**

Revise the encryption program in Section 6.3.4 in the following manner: Let the user enter an encryption key consisting of multiple characters. Use this key to encrypt and decrypt the plaintext by XORing each character of the key against a corresponding byte in the message. Repeat the key as many times as necessary until all plain-text bytes are translated. Suppose, for example the key equals "ABXmv#7". This is how the key would align with the plain-text bytes:

Plain text	T	h	i	s		i	s		a		P	l	a	i	n	t	e	x	t		m	e	s	s	a	g	e	(etc.)
Key	A	B	X	m	v	#	7	A	B	X	m	v	#	7	A	B	X	m	v	#	7	A	8	X	m	v	#	7

(The key repeats until it equals the length of the plain text...)

(A VideoNote for this exercise is posted on the Web site.)

★★ **12. Weighted Probabilities**

Create a procedure that receives a value N between 0 and 100. When the procedure is called, there should be a probability of $N/100$ that it clears the Zero flag. Write a program that asks the user to enter a probability value between 0 and 100. The program should call your procedure 30 times, passing it the same probability value and displaying the value of the Zero flag after the procedure returns.

7

Integer Arithmetic

7.1 Introduction

7.2 Shift and Rotate Instructions
  7.2.1 Logical Shifts and Arithmetic Shifts
  7.2.2 SHL Instruction
  7.2.3 SHR Instruction
  7.2.4 SAL and SAR Instructions
  7.2.5 ROL Instruction
  7.2.6 ROR Instruction
  7.2.7 RCL and RCR Instructions
  7.2.8 Signed Overflow
  7.2.9 SHLD/SHRD Instructions
  7.2.10 Section Review

7.3 Shift and Rotate Applications
  7.3.1 Shifting Multiple Doublewords
  7.3.2 Binary Multiplication
  7.3.3 Displaying Binary Bits
  7.3.4 Isolating MS-DOS File Date Fields
  7.3.5 Section Review

7.4 Multiplication and Division Instructions
  7.4.1 MUL Instruction
  7.4.2 IMUL Instruction
  7.4.3 Measuring Program Execution Times

7.4.4 DIV Instruction
7.4.5 Signed Integer Division
7.4.6 Implementing Arithmetic Expressions
7.4.7 Section Review

7.5 Extended Addition and Subtraction
  7.5.1 ADC Instruction
  7.5.2 Extended Addition Example
  7.5.3 SBB Instruction
  7.5.4 Section Review

7.6 ASCII and Unpacked Decimal Arithmetic
  7.6.1 AAA Instruction
  7.6.2 AAS Instruction
  7.6.3 AAM Instruction
  7.6.4 AAD Instruction
  7.6.5 Section Review

7.7 Packed Decimal Arithmetic
  7.7.1 DAA Instruction
  7.7.2 DAS Instruction
  7.7.3 Section Review

7.8 Chapter Summary

7.9 Programming Exercises

7.1 Introduction

Assembly language has instructions that move bits around inside operands. *Shift and rotate* instructions, as they are called, are particularly useful when controlling hardware devices, encrypting data, and implementing high-speed graphics. This chapter explains how to perform shift and rotate operations and how to carry out efficient integer multiplication and division using shift operations.

Next, we explore the integer multiplication and division instructions. Intel classifies the instructions according to signed and unsigned operations. Using these instructions, we show how to translate mathematical expressions from C++ into assembly language. Compilers divide complex expressions into discrete sequences of machine instructions. If you learn to translate mathematical expressions into assembly language, you can gain a better understanding of how compilers work, and you will be better able to hand optimize assembly language code. You will learn how operator precedence rules and register optimization work at the machine level.

Arithmetic with arbitrary-length integers (also known as *bignums*) is not supported by all high-level languages. But in assembly language, you can use instructions such as ADC (*add with carry*) and SBB (*subtract with borrow*) that work on integers of any size. In this chapter, we also present specialized instructions for performing arithmetic on packed decimal integers and integer strings.

7.2   Shift and Rotate Instructions

Along with bitwise instructions introduced in Chapter 6, shift instructions are among the most characteristic of assembly language. *Shifting* means to move bits right and left inside an operand. x86 processors provide a particularly rich set of instructions in this area (Table 7-1), all affecting the Overflow and Carry flags.

Table 7-1   Shift and Rotate Instructions.

SHL	Shift left
SHR	Shift right
SAL	Shift arithmetic left
SAR	Shift arithmetic right
ROL	Rotate left
ROR	Rotate right
RCL	Rotate carry left
RCR	Rotate carry right
SHLD	Double-precision shift left
SHRD	Double-precision shift right

7.2.1   Logical Shifts and Arithmetic Shifts

There are two ways to shift an operand's bits. The first, *logical shift*, fills the newly created bit position with zero. In the following illustration, a byte is logically shifted one position to the right. In other words, each bit is moved to the next lowest bit position. Note that bit 7 is assigned 0:

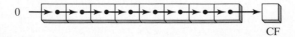

CF

The following illustration shows a single logical right shift on the binary value 11001111, producing 01100111. The lowest bit is shifted into the Carry flag:

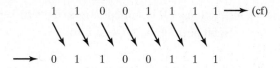

Another type of shift is called an *arithmetic shift*. The newly created bit position is filled with a copy of the original number's sign bit:

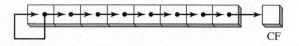

Binary 11001111, for example, has a 1 in the sign bit. When shifted arithmetically 1 bit to the right, it becomes 11100111:

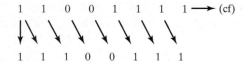

7.2.2   SHL Instruction

The SHL (shift left) instruction performs a logical left shift on the destination operand, filling the lowest bit with 0. The highest bit is moved to the Carry flag, and the bit that was in the Carry flag is discarded:

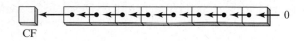

If you shift 11001111 left by 1 bit, it becomes 10011110:

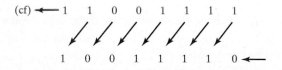

The first operand in SHL is the destination and the second is the shift count:

```
SHL  destination,count
```

The following lists the types of operands permitted by this instruction:

```
SHL  reg,imm8
SHL  mem,imm8
SHL  reg,CL
SHL  mem,CL
```

x86 processors permit *imm8* to be any integer between 0 and 255. Alternatively, the CL register can contain a shift count. Formats shown here also apply to the SHR, SAL, SAR, ROR, ROL, RCR, and RCL instructions.

Example   In the following instructions, BL is shifted once to the left. The highest bit is copied into the Carry flag and the lowest bit position is assigned zero:

```
mov  bl,8Fh                       ; BL = 10001111b
shl  bl,1                         ; CF = 1, BL = 00011110b
```

Multiple Shifts   When a value is shifted leftward multiple times, the Carry flag contains the last bit to be shifted out of the most significant bit (MSB). In the following example, bit 7 does not end up in the Carry flag because it is replaced by bit 6 (a zero):

```
mov  al,10000000b
shl  al,2                         ; CF = 0, AL = 00000000b
```

Similarly, when a value is shifted rightward multiple times, the Carry flag contains the last bit to be shifted out of the least significant bit (LSB).

Bitwise Multiplication   SHL can perform multiplication by powers of 2. Shifting any operand left by *n* bits multiplies the operand by 2^n. For example, shifting the integer 5 left by 1 bit yields the product of $5 \times 2^1 = 10$:

```
mov  dl,5
shl  dl,1
```

Before: | 0 0 0 0 0 1 0 1 | = 5

After: | 0 0 0 0 1 0 1 0 | = 10

If binary 00001010 (decimal 10) is shifted left by 2 bits, the result is the same as multiplying 10 by 2^2:

```
mov  dl,10                        ; before:  00001010
shl  dl,2                         ; after:   00101000
```

7.2.3   SHR Instruction

The SHR (shift right) instruction performs a logical right shift on the destination operand, replacing the highest bit with a 0. The lowest bit is copied into the Carry flag, and the bit that was previously in the Carry flag is lost:

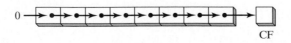

SHR uses the same instruction formats as SHL. In the following example, the 0 from the lowest bit in AL is copied into the Carry flag, and the highest bit in AL is filled with a zero:

```
mov  al,0D0h                      ; AL = 11010000b
shr  al,1                         ; AL = 01101000b, CF = 0
```

Multiple Shifts   In a multiple shift operation, the last bit to be shifted out of position 0 (the LSB) ends up in the Carry flag:

```
mov  al,00000010b
shr  al,2                              ; AL = 00000000b, CF = 1
```

Bitwise Division   Logically shifting an unsigned integer right by n bits divides the operand by 2^n. In the following statements, we divide 32 by 2^1, producing 16:

```
mov  dl,32
shr  dl,1
```

In the following example, 64 is divided by 2^3:

```
mov  al,01000000b                      ; AL = 64
shr  al,3                              ; divide by 8, AL = 00001000b
```

Division of signed numbers by shifting is accomplished using the SAR instruction because it preserves the number's sign bit.

7.2.4   SAL and SAR Instructions

The SAL (shift arithmetic left) instruction works the same as the SHL instruction. For each shift count, SAL shifts each bit in the destination operand to the next highest bit position. The lowest bit is assigned 0. The highest bit is moved to the Carry flag, and the bit that was in the Carry flag is discarded:

If you shift binary 11001111 to the left by one bit, it becomes 10011110:

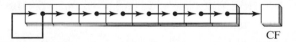

The SAR (shift arithmetic right) instruction performs a right arithmetic shift on its destination operand:

The operands for SAL and SAR are identical to those for SHL and SHR. The shift may be repeated, based on the counter in the second operand:

```
SAR destination,count
```

The following example shows how SAR duplicates the sign bit. AL is negative before and after it is shifted to the right:

```
mov  al,0F0h                      ; AL = 11110000b (-16)
sar  al,1                         ; AL = 11111000b (-8), CF = 0
```

Signed Division   You can divide a signed operand by a power of 2, using the SAR instruction. In the following example, −128 is divided by 2^3. The quotient is −16:

```
mov  dl,-128                      ; DL = 10000000b
sar  dl,3                         ; DL = 11110000b
```

Sign-Extend AX into EAX   Suppose AX contains a signed integer and you want to extend its sign into EAX. First shift EAX 16 bits to the left, then shift it arithmetically 16 bits to the right:

```
mov  ax,-128                      ; EAX = ????FF80h
shl  eax,16                       ; EAX = FF800000h
sar  eax,16                       ; EAX = FFFFFF80h
```

7.2.5 ROL Instruction

The ROL (rotate left) instruction shifts each bit to the left. The highest bit is copied into the Carry flag and the lowest bit position. The instruction format is the same as for SHL:

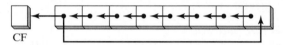

CF

Bit rotation does not lose bits. A bit rotated off one end of a number appears again at the other end. Note in the following example how the high bit is copied into both the Carry flag and bit position 0:

```
mov  al,40h                       ; AL = 01000000b
rol  al,1                         ; AL = 10000000b, CF = 0
rol  al,1                         ; AL = 00000001b, CF = 1
rol  al,1                         ; AL = 00000010b, CF = 0
```

Multiple Rotations   When using a rotation count greater than 1, the Carry flag contains the last bit rotated out of the MSB position:

```
mov  al,00100000b
rol  al,3                         ; CF = 1, AL = 00000001b
```

Exchanging Groups of Bits   You can use ROL to exchange the upper (bits 4–7) and lower (bits 0–3) halves of a byte. For example, 26h rotated four bits in either direction becomes 62h:

```
mov  al,26h
rol  al,4                         ; AL = 62h
```

When rotating a multibyte integer by 4 bits, the effect is to rotate each hexadecimal digit one position to the right or left. Here, for example, we repeatedly rotate 6A4Bh left 4 bits, eventually ending up with the original value:

```
mov  ax,6A4Bh
rol  ax,4                         ; AX = A4B6h
rol  ax,4                         ; AX = 4B6Ah
rol  ax,4                         ; AX = B6A4h
rol  ax,4                         ; AX = 6A4Bh
```

7.2.6   ROR Instruction

The ROR (rotate right) instruction shifts each bit to the right and copies the lowest bit into the Carry flag and the highest bit position. The instruction format is the same as for SHL:

In the following examples, note how the lowest bit is copied into both the Carry flag and the highest bit position of the result:

```
mov  al,01h                 ; AL = 00000001b
ror  al,1                   ; AL = 10000000b, CF = 1
ror  al,1                   ; AL = 01000000b, CF = 0
```

Multiple Rotations   When using a rotation count greater than 1, the Carry flag contains the last bit rotated out of the LSB position:

```
mov  al,00000100b
ror  al,3                   ; AL = 10000000b, CF = 1
```

7.2.7   RCL and RCR Instructions

The RCL (rotate carry left) instruction shifts each bit to the left, copies the Carry flag to the LSB, and copies the MSB into the Carry flag:

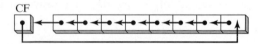

If we imagine the Carry flag as an extra bit added to the high end of the operand, RCL looks like a rotate left operation. In the following example, the CLC instruction clears the Carry flag. The first RCL instruction moves the high bit of BL into the Carry flag and shifts the other bits left. The second RCL instruction moves the Carry flag into the lowest bit position and shifts the other bits left:

```
clc                         ; CF = 0
mov  bl,88h                 ; CF,BL = 0 10001000b
rcl  bl,1                   ; CF,BL = 1 00010000b
rcl  bl,1                   ; CF,BL = 0 00100001b
```

Recover a Bit from the Carry Flag   RCL can recover a bit that was previously shifted into the Carry flag. The following example checks the lowest bit of **testval** by shifting its lowest bit into the Carry flag. If the lowest bit of testval is 1, a jump is taken; if the lowest bit is 0, RCL restores the number to its original value:

```
.data
testval BYTE  01101010b
.code
shr testval,1               ; shift LSB into Carry flag
jc  exit                    ; exit if Carry flag set
rcl testval,1               ; else restore the number
```

RCR Instruction. The RCR (rotate carry right) instruction shifts each bit to the right, copies the Carry flag into the MSB, and copies the LSB into the Carry flag:

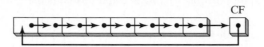

As in the case of RCL, it helps to visualize the integer in this figure as a 9-bit value, with the Carry flag to the right of the LSB.

The following code example uses STC to set the Carry flag; then, it performs a Rotate Carry Right operation on the AH register:

```
stc                              ; CF = 1
mov  ah,10h                      ; AH, CF = 00010000 1
rcr  ah,1                        ; AH, CF = 10001000 0
```

7.2.8 Signed Overflow

The Overflow flag is set when shifting or rotating a signed integer by one bit position generates a value outside the signed integer range of the destination operand. To put it another way, the number's sign is reversed. In the following example, a positive integer ($+127$) stored in an 8-bit register becomes negative (-2) when rotated left:

```
mov  al,+127                     ; AL = 01111111b
rol  al,1                        ; OF = 1, AL = 11111110b
```

Similarly, when –128 is shifted one position to the right, the Overflow flag is set. The result in AL (+64) has the opposite sign:

```
mov  al,-128                     ; AL = 10000000b
shr  al,1                        ; OF = 1, AL = 01000000b
```

The value of the Overflow flag is undefined when the shift or rotation count is greater than 1.

7.2.9 SHLD/SHRD Instructions

The SHLD (shift left double) instruction shifts a destination operand a given number of bits to the left. The bit positions opened up by the shift are filled by the most significant bits of the source operand. The source operand is not affected, but the Sign, Zero, Auxiliary, Parity, and Carry flags are affected:

```
SHLD  dest, source, count
```

The following illustration shows the execution of SHLD with a shift count of 1. The highest bit of the source operand is copied into the lowest bit of the destination operand. All the destination operand bits are shifted left:

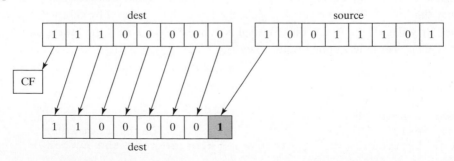

The SHRD (shift right double) instruction shifts a destination operand a given number of bits to the right. The bit positions opened up by the shift are filled by the least significant bits of the source operand:

```
SHRD    dest, source, count
```

The following illustration shows the execution of SHRD with a shift count of 1:

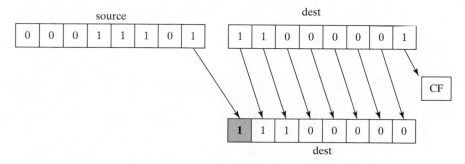

The following instruction formats apply to both SHLD and SHRD. The destination operand can be a register or memory operand, and the source operand must be a register. The count operand can be the CL register or an 8-bit immediate operand:

```
SHLD    reg16,reg16,CL/imm8
SHLD    mem16,reg16,CL/imm8
SHLD    reg32,reg32,CL/imm8
SHLD    mem32,reg32,CL/imm8
```

Example 1   The following statements shift **wval** to the left 4 bits and insert the high 4 bits of AX into the low 4 bit positions of **wval:**

```
.data
wval WORD 9BA6h
.code
mov    ax,0AC36h
shld   wval,ax,4                    ; wval = BA6Ah
```

The data movement is shown in the following figure:

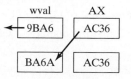

Example 2   In the following example, AX is shifted to the right 4 bits, and the low 4 bits of DX are shifted into the high 4 positions of AX:

```
mov    ax,234Bh
mov    dx,7654h
shrd   ax,dx,4                        ; AX = 4234h
```

SHLD and SHRD can be used to manipulate bit-mapped images, when groups of bits must be shifted left and right to reposition images on the screen. Another potential application is data encryption, in which the encryption algorithm involves the shifting of bits. Finally, the two instructions can be used when performing fast multiplication and division with very long integers.

The following code example demonstrates SHRD by shifting an array of doublewords to the right by 4 bits:

```
.data
array DWORD 648B2165h,8C943A29h,6DFA4B86h,91F76C04h,8BAF9857h

.code
        mov    bl,4                          ; shift count
        mov    esi,OFFSET array              ; offset of the array
        mov    ecx,(LENGTHOF array) - 1      ; number of array elements

L1:     push   ecx                           ; save loop counter
        mov    eax,[esi + TYPE DWORD]
        mov    cl,bl                         ; shift count
        shrd   [esi],eax,cl                  ; shift EAX into high bits of
                                             ;  [ESI]
        add    esi,TYPE DWORD                ; point to next doubleword pair
        pop    ecx                           ; restore loop counter
        loop   L1

        shr DWORD PTR [esi],COUNT            ; shift the last doubleword
```

7.2.10 Section Review

1. Which instruction shifts each bit in an operand to the left and copies the highest bit into both the Carry flag and the lowest bit position?

2. Which instruction shifts each bit to the right, copies the lowest bit into the Carry flag, and copies the Carry flag into the highest bit position?

3. Write a sequence of shift instructions that cause AX to be sign-extended into EAX. In other words, the sign bit of AX is copied into the upper 16 bits of EAX. (*Note: Do not use the CWD instruction, which is covered later in this chapter.*)

4. Which instruction performs the following operation (CF = Carry flag)?

```
Before:   CF,AL = 1 11010101
After:    CF,AL = 1 10101011
```

5. Suppose the instruction set contained no rotate instructions. Show how we might use SHR and a conditional jump instruction to rotate the contents of the AL register one position to the right.

6. What happens to the Carry flag when the SHR AX,1 instruction is executed?

7. Write a logical shift instruction that multiplies the contents of EAX by 16.

8. Write a logical shift instruction that divides EBX by 4.

9. Write a single rotate instruction that exchanges the high and low halves of the DL register.

10. Write a SHLD instruction that shifts the highest bit of the AX register into the lowest bit position of DX and shifts DX one bit to the left.

11. In the following code sequence, show the value of AL after each shift or rotate instruction has executed:

```
mov   al,0D4h
shr   al,1                              ; a.
mov   al,0D4h
sar   al,1                              ; b.
mov   al,0D4h
sar   al,4                              ; c.
mov   al,0D4h
rol   al,1                              ; d.
```

12. In the following code sequence, show the value of AL after each shift or rotate instruction has executed:

```
mov   al,0D4h
ror   al,3                              ; a.
mov   al,0D4h
rol   al,7                              ; b.
stc
mov   al,0D4h
rcl   al,1                              ; c.
stc
mov   al,0D4h
rcr   al,3                              ; d.
```

13. *Challenge:* Write a series of instructions that shift the lowest bit of AX into the highest bit of BX without using the SHRD instruction. Next, perform the same operation using SHRD.

14. *Challenge:* One way to calculate the parity of a 32-bit number in EAX is to use a loop that shifts each bit into the Carry flag and accumulates a count of the number of times the Carry flag was set. Write a code that does this, and set the Parity flag accordingly.

15. *Challenge:* Using only SUB, MOV, and AND instructions, show how to calculate $x = n$ *mod* y, assuming that you are given the values of n and y. You can assume that n is any 32-bit unsigned integer, and y is a power of 2.

16. *Challenge:* Using only SAR, ADD, and XOR instructions (but no conditional jumps), write code that calculates the absolute value of the signed integer in the EAX register. Hint: A number can be negated by adding -1 to it and then forming its one's complement. Also, if you XOR an integer with all 1's, the integer's bits are reversed. On the other hand, if you XOR an integer with all zeros, the integer is unchanged.

7.3   Shift and Rotate Applications

When a program needs to move bits from one part of an integer to another, assembly language is a great tool for the job. Sometimes, we move a subset of a number's bits to position 0 to make it easier to isolate the value of the bits. In this section, we show a few common bit shift and rotate applications that are easy to implement. More applications will be found in the chapter exercises.

7.3.1   Shifting Multiple Doublewords

You can shift an extended-precision integer that has been divided into an array of bytes, words, or doublewords. Before doing this, you must know how the array elements are stored. A common way to store the integer is called *little-endian order*. It works like this: Place the low-order byte at the array's starting address. Then, working your way up from that byte to the high-order byte, store each in the next sequential memory location. Instead of storing the array as a series of bytes, you could store it as a series of words or doublewords. If you did so, the individual bytes would still be in little-endian order, because x86 machines store words and doublewords in little-endian order.

The following steps show how to shift array of bytes one bit to the right:

Step 1: Shift the highest byte at [ESI+2] to the right, automatically copying its lowest bit into the Carry flag.

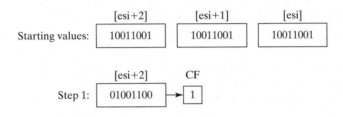

Step 2: Rotate the value at [ESI+1] to the right, filling the highest bit with the value of the Carry flag, and shifting the lowest bit into the Carry flag:

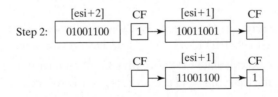

Step 3: Rotate the value at [ESI] to the right, filling the highest bit with the value of the Carry flag, and shifting the lowest bit into the Carry flag:

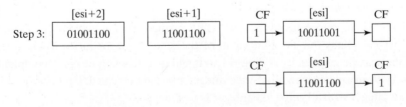

When finished, all bits have been shifted 1 position to the right:

[esi+2]	[esi+1]	[esi]
01001100	11001100	11001100

The following code excerpt from the *Multishift.asm* program implements the steps we just outlined.

```
.data
ArraySize = 3
array BYTE ArraySize DUP(99h)    ; 1001 pattern in each nybble
.code
main PROC
     mov esi,0
     shr array[esi+2],1          ; high byte
     rcr array[esi+1],1          ; middle byte, include Carry flag
     rcr array[esi],1            ; low byte, include Carry flag
```

Although our current example only shifts 3 bytes, the example could easily be modified to shift an array of words or doublewords. Using a loop, you could shift an array of arbitrary size.

7.3.2 Binary Multiplication

In earlier Intel processors, the binary multiplication instructions (MUL and IMUL) are considered slow relative to other machine instructions. As a result, programmers found that multiplication could be performed more efficiently by using bit shifting techniques. The SHL instruction performs unsigned multiplication efficiently when the multiplier is a power of 2. Shifting an unsigned integer n bits to the left multiplies it by 2^n. Any other multiplier can be expressed as the sum of powers of 2. For example, to multiply unsigned EAX by 36, we can write 36 as $2^5 + 2^2$ and use the distributive property of multiplication:

$$
\begin{aligned}
\text{EAX} * 36 &= \text{EAX} * (2^5 + 2^2) \\
&= \text{EAX} * (32 + 4) \\
&= (\text{EAX} * 32) + (\text{EAX} * 4)
\end{aligned}
$$

The following figure shows the multiplication 123 * 36, producing 4428, the product:

```
              01111011        123
    ×         00100100         36
              01111011        123 SHL 2
 +        01111011            123 SHL 5
       0001000101001100       4428
```

It is rather remarkable to discover that bits 2 and 5 are set in the multiplier (36), and the integers 2 and 5 are also the required shift counters. Using this information, the following code excerpt multiplies 123 by 36, using SHL and ADD instructions:

```
.code
mov  eax,123
mov  ebx,eax
shl  eax,5                     ; mult by 2^5
shl  ebx,2                     ; mult by 2^2
add  eax,ebx                   ; add the products
```

As a chapter exercise, you will be asked to generalize this example and create a procedure that multiplies any two 32-bit unsigned integers using shifting and addition.

7.3.3 Displaying Binary Bits

A common programming task is converting a binary integer to an ASCII binary string, allowing the latter to be displayed. The SHL instruction is useful in this regard because it copies the highest bit of an operand into the Carry flag each time the operand is shifted left. The following Bin-ToAsc procedure is a simple implementation:

```
;---------------------------------------------------------
BinToAsc PROC
;
; Converts 32-bit binary integer to ASCII binary.
; Receives: EAX = binary integer, ESI points to buffer
; Returns: buffer filled with ASCII binary digits
;---------------------------------------------------------
        push  ecx
        push  esi

        mov   ecx,32                ; number of bits in EAX

L1:  shl   eax,1                  ; shift high bit into Carry flag
        mov   BYTE PTR [esi],'0'    ; choose 0 as default digit
        jnc   L2                    ; if no Carry, jump to L2
        mov   BYTE PTR [esi],'1'    ; else move 1 to buffer

L2:  inc   esi                    ; next buffer position
        loop  L1                    ; shift another bit to left

        pop   esi
        pop   ecx
        ret
BinToAsc ENDP
```

7.3.4 Isolating MS-DOS File Date Fields

When storage space is at a premium, system-level software often packs multiple data fields into a single integer. To uncover this data, applications often need to extract sequences of bits called *bit strings*. For example, in real-address mode, MS-DOS function 57h returns the date stamp of a file in DX. (The date stamp shows the date on which the file was last modified.) Bits 0 through 4 represent a day number between 1 and 31, bits 5 through 8 are the month number, and bits 9 through 15 hold the year number. If a file was last modified on March 10, 1999, the file's date stamp would appear as follows in the DX register (the year number is relative to 1980):

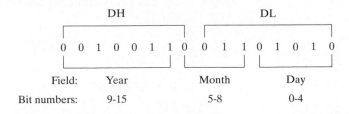

To extract a single bit string, shift its bits into the lowest part of a register and clear the irrelevant bit positions. The following code example extracts the day number field of a date stamp integer by making a copy of DL and masking off bits not belonging to the field:

```
mov  al,dl              ; make a copy of DL
and  al,00011111b       ; clear bits 5-7
mov  day,al             ; save in day
```

To extract the month number field, we shift bits 5 through 8 into the low part of AL before masking off all other bits. AL is then copied into a variable:

```
mov  ax,dx              ; make a copy of DX
shr  ax,5               ; shift right 5 bits
and  al,00001111b       ; clear bits 4-7
mov  month,al           ; save in month
```

The year number (bits 9 through 15) field is completely within the DH register. We copy it to AL and shift right by 1 bit:

```
mov  al,dh              ; make a copy of DH
shr  al,1               ; shift right one position
mov  ah,0               ; clear AH to zeros
add  ax,1980            ; year is relative to 1980
mov  year,ax            ; save in year
```

7.3.5   Section Review

1. Write a sequence of instructions that shift three memory bytes to the right by 1 bit position. Use the following data definition:

   ```
   byteArray BYTE 81h,20h,33h
   ```

2. Write a sequence of instructions that shift three memory words to the left by 1 bit position. Use the following data definition:

   ```
   byteArray WORD 810Dh, 0C064h,93ABh
   ```

3. Write ASM instructions that calculate EAX * 24 using binary multiplication.

4. Write ASM instructions that calculate EAX * 21 using binary multiplication. *Hint:* $21 = 2^4 + 2^2 + 2^0$.

5. What change would you make to the BinToAsc procedure in Section 7.3.3 in order to display the binary bits in reverse order?

6. The time stamp field of a file directory entry uses bits 0 through 4 for the seconds, bits 5 through 10 for the minutes, and bits 11 through 15 for the hours. Write instructions that extract the minutes and copy the value to a byte variable named **bMinutes**.

7.4   Multiplication and Division Instructions

Integer multiplication in x86 assembly language can be performed as a 32-bit, 16-bit, or 8-bit operation. In many cases, it revolves around EAX or one of its subsets (AX, AL). The MUL and IMUL instructions perform unsigned and signed integer multiplication, respectively. The DIV instruction performs unsigned integer division, and IDIV performs signed integer division.

7.4.1   MUL Instruction

The MUL (unsigned multiply) instruction comes in three versions: the first version multiplies an 8-bit operand by the AL register. The second version multiplies a 16-bit operand by the AX register, and the third version multiplies a 32-bit operand by the EAX register. The multiplier and multiplicand must always be the same size, and the product is twice their size. The three formats accept register and memory operands, but not immediate operands:

```
MUL   reg/mem8
MUL   reg/mem16
MUL   reg/mem32
```

The single operand in the MUL instruction is the multiplier. Table 7-2 shows the default multiplicand and product, depending on the size of the multiplier. Because the destination operand is twice the size of the multiplicand and multiplier, overflow cannot occur. MUL sets the Carry and Overflow flags if the upper half of the product is not equal to zero. The Carry flag is ordinarily used for unsigned arithmetic, so we'll focus on it here. When AX is multiplied by a 16-bit operand, for example, the product is stored in the combined DX and AX registers. That is, the high 16 bits of the product are stored in DX, and the low 16 bits are stored in AX. The Carry flag is set if DX is not equal to zero, which lets us know that the product will not fit into the lower half of the implied destination operand.

Table 7-2   MUL Operands.

Multiplicand	Multiplier	Product
AL	reg/mem8	AX
AX	reg/mem16	DX:AX
EAX	reg/mem32	EDX:EAX

A good reason for checking the Carry flag after executing MUL is to know whether the upper half of the product can safely be ignored.

MUL Examples
The following statements multiply AL by BL, storing the product in AX. The Carry flag is clear (CF = 0) because AH (the upper half of the product) equals zero:

```
mov   al,5h
mov   bl,10h
mul   bl                         ; AX = 0050h, CF = 0
```

```
    AL        BL            AX     CF
  ┌────┐   ┌────┐        ┌──────┐ ┌───┐
  │ 05 │ × │ 10 │ ────→  │ 0050 │ │ 0 │
  └────┘   └────┘        └──────┘ └───┘
```

The following statements multiply the 16-bit value 2000h by 0100h. The Carry flag is set because the upper part of the product (located in DX) is not equal to zero:

```
.data
val1   WORD   2000h
val2   WORD   0100h
.code
mov ax,val1                      ; AX = 2000h
mul val2                         ; DX:AX = 00200000h, CF = 1
```

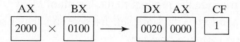

The following statements multiply 12345h by 1000h, producing a 64-bit product in the combined EDX and EAX registers. The Carry flag is clear because the upper half of the product in EDX equals zero:

```
mov   eax,12345h
mov   ebx,1000h
mul   ebx               ; EDX:EAX = 0000000012345000h, CF = 0
```

7.4.2 IMUL Instruction

The IMUL (signed multiply) instruction performs signed integer multiplication. Unlike the MUL instruction, IMUL preserves the sign of the product. It does this by sign extending the highest bit of the lower half of the product into the upper bits of the product. The x86 instruction set supports three formats for the IMUL instruction: one operand, two operands, and three operands. In the one-operand format, the multiplier and multiplicand are the same size and the product is twice their size.

One-Operand Formats The one-operand formats store the product in AX, DX:AX, or EDX:EAX:

```
IMUL   reg/mem8            ; AX = AL * reg/mem8
IMUL   reg/mem16           ; DX:AX = AX * reg/mem16
IMUL   reg/mem32           ; EDX:EAX = EAX * reg/mem32
```

As in the case of MUL, the storage size of the product makes overflow impossible. Also, the Carry and Overflow flags are set if the upper half of the product is not a sign extension of the lower half. You can use this information to decide whether to ignore the upper half of the product.

Two-Operand Formats The two-operand version of the IMUL instruction stores the product in the first operand, which must be a register. The second operand (the multiplier) can be a register, memory operand, or immediate value. Following are the 16-bit formats:

```
IMUL   reg16,reg/mem16
IMUL   reg16,imm8
IMUL   reg16,imm16
```

Following are the 32-bit operand types showing that the multiplier can be a 32-bit register, 32-bit memory operand, or immediate value (8 or 32 bits):

```
IMUL   reg32,reg/mem32
IMUL   reg32,imm8
IMUL   reg32,imm32
```

The two-operand formats truncate the product to the length of the destination. If significant digits are lost, the Overflow and Carry flags are set. Be sure to check one of these flags after performing an IMUL operation with two operands.

Three-Operand Formats   The three-operand formats store the product in the first operand. The second operand can be a 16-bit register or memory operand, which is multiplied by the third operand, an 8- or 16-bit immediate value:

```
IMUL   reg16,reg/mem16,imm8
IMUL   reg16,reg/mem16,imm16
```

A 32-bit register or memory operand can be multiplied by an 8- or 32-bit immediate value:

```
IMUL   reg32,reg/mem32,imm8
IMUL   reg32,reg/mem32,imm32
```

If significant digits are lost when IMUL executes, the Overflow and Carry flags are set. Be sure to check one of these flags after performing an IMUL operation with three operands.

Unsigned Multiplication   The two-operand and three-operand IMUL formats may also be used for unsigned multiplication because the lower half of the product is the same for signed and unsigned numbers. There is a small disadvantage to doing so: The Carry and Overflow flags will not indicate whether the upper half of the product is Zero.

IMUL Examples
The following instructions multiply 48 by 4, producing +192 in AX. Although the product is correct, AH is not a sign extension of AL, so the Overflow flag is set:

```
mov   al,48
mov   bl,4
imul  bl                        ; AX = 00C0h, OF = 1
```

The following instructions multiply −4 by 4, producing −16 in AX. AH is a sign extension of AL so the Overflow flag is clear:

```
mov   al,-4
mov   bl,4
imul  bl                        ; AX = FFF0h, OF = 0
```

The following instructions multiply 48 by 4, producing +192 in DX:AX. DX is a sign extension of AX, so the Overflow flag is clear:

```
mov   ax,48
mov   bx,4
imul  bx                        ; DX:AX = 000000C0h, OF = 0
```

The following instructions perform 32-bit signed multiplication (4,823,424 * −423), producing −2,040,308,352 in EDX:EAX. The Overflow flag is clear because EDX is a sign extension of EAX:

```
mov   eax,+4823424
mov   ebx,-423
imul  ebx                       ; EDX:EAX = FFFFFFFF86635D80h, OF = 0
```

The following instructions demonstrate two-operand formats:

```
.data
word1    SWORD  4
dword1   SDWORD 4
.code
mov   ax,-16                        ; AX = -16
mov   bx,2                          ; BX = 2
imul  bx,ax                         ; BX = -32
imul  bx,2                          ; BX = -64
imul  bx,word1                      ; BX = -256
mov   eax,-16                       ; EAX = -16
mov   ebx,2                         ; EBX = 2
imul  ebx,eax                       ; EBX = -32
imul  ebx,2                         ; EBX = -64
imul  ebx,dword1                    ; EBX = -256
```

The two-operand and three-operand IMUL instructions use a destination operand that is the same size as the multiplier. Therefore, it is possible for signed overflow to occur. Always check the Overflow flag after executing these types of IMUL instructions. The following two-operand instructions demonstrate signed overflow because $-64,000$ cannot fit within the 16-bit destination operand:

```
mov   ax,-32000
imul  ax,2                          ; OF = 1
```

The following instructions demonstrate three-operand formats, including an example of signed overflow:

```
.data
word1  SWORD  4
dword1 SDWORD 4
.code
imul  bx,word1,-16                  ; BX = -64
imul  ebx,dword1,-16               ; EBX = -64
imul  ebx,dword1,-2000000000       ; OF = 1
```

7.4.3   Measuring Program Execution Times

Programmers often find it useful to compare the performance of one code implementation to another by measuring their performance times. The Microsoft Windows API library provides the necessary tools to do this, which we have made even more accessible with the GetMseconds procedure in the Irvine32 library. The procedure gets the number of system milliseconds that have elapsed since midnight. In the following code example, GetMSeconds is called first, so we can record the system starting time. Then we call the procedure whose execution time we wish to measure (*FirstProcedureToTest*). Finally, GetMseconds is called a second time, and the difference between the current milliseconds value and the starting time is calculated:

```
.data
startTime DWORD ?
procTime1 DWORD ?
procTime2 DWORD ?
```

```
.code
call GetMseconds                 ; get start time
mov   startTime,eax
    .
call FirstProcedureToTest
    .
call GetMseconds                 ; get stop time
sub   eax,startTime              ; calculate the elapsed time
mov   procTime1,eax              ; save the elapsed time
```

There is, of course, a small amount of execution time used up by calling GetMseconds twice. But this overhead is insignificant when we measure the ratio of performance times between one code implementation and another. Here, we call the other procedure we wish to test, and save its execution time (*procTime2*):

```
call GetMseconds                 ; get start time
mov   startTime,eax
    .
call SecondProcedureToTest
    .
call GetMseconds                 ; get stop time
sub   eax,startTime              ; calculate the elapsed time
mov   procTime2,eax              ; save the elapsed time
```

Now, the ratio of *procTime1* to *procTime2* indicates the relative performance of the two procedures.

Comparing MUL and IMUL to Bit Shifting

In older x86 processors, there was a significant difference in performance between multiplication by bit shifting versus multiplication using the MUL and IMUL instructions. We can use the GetMseconds procedure to compare the execution time of the two types of multiplication. The following two procedures perform multiplication repeatedly using a LOOP_COUNT constant to determine the amount of repetition:

```
mult_by_shifting PROC
;
; Multiplies EAX by 36 using SHL, LOOP_COUNT times.
;
    mov   ecx,LOOP_COUNT
L1: push eax                     ; save original EAX
    mov   ebx,eax
    shl   eax,5
    shl   ebx,2
    add   eax,ebx
    pop   eax                    ; restore EAX
    loop L1
    ret
mult_by_shifting ENDP

mult_by_MUL PROC
;
```

```
; Multiplies EAX by 36 using MUL, LOOP_COUNT times.
;
       mov   ecx,LOOP_COUNT
L1:    push  eax                      ; save original EAX
       mov   ebx,36
       mul   ebx
       pop   eax                      ; restore EAX
       loop  L1
       ret
mult_by_MUL ENDP
```

The following code calls *mult_by_shifting* and displays the timing results. See the *Compare-Mult.asm* program from the book's Chapter 7 examples for the complete implementation:

```
.data
LOOP_COUNT = 0FFFFFFFFh
.data
intval DWORD 5
startTime DWORD ?
.code
call  GetMseconds                     ; get start time
mov   startTime,eax
mov   eax,intval                      ; multiply now
call  mult_by_shifting
call  GetMseconds                     ; get stop time
sub   eax,startTime
call  WriteDec                        ; display elapsed time
```

After calling *mult_by_MUL* in the same manner, the resulting timings on a legacy 4-GHz Pentium 4 showed that the SHL approach executed in 6.078 seconds and the MUL approach executed in 20.718 seconds. In other words, using MUL instruction was 241 percent slower. However, when running the same program on an Intel Duo-core processor, the timings of both function calls were exactly the same. This example shows that Intel has managed to greatly optimize the MUL and IMUL instructions in recent processors.

7.4.4   DIV Instruction

The DIV (unsigned divide) instruction performs 8-bit, 16-bit, and 32-bit unsigned integer division. The single register or memory operand is the divisor. The formats are

```
DIV   reg/mem8
DIV   reg/mem16
DIV   reg/mem32
```

The following table shows the relationship between the dividend, divisor, quotient, and remainder:

Dividend	Divisor	Quotient	Remainder
AX	reg/mem8	AL	AH
DX:AX	reg/mem16	AX	DX
EDX:EAX	reg/mem32	EAX	EDX

DIV Examples

The following instructions perform 8-bit unsigned division (83h / 2), producing a quotient of 41h and a remainder of 1:

```
mov  ax,0083h                    ; dividend
mov  bl,2                        ; divisor
div  bl                          ; AL = 41h,  AH = 01h
```

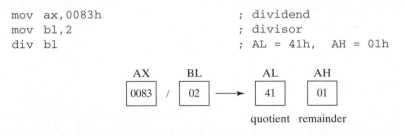

The following instructions perform 16-bit unsigned division (8003h / 100h), producing a quotient of 80h and a remainder of 3. DX contains the high part of the dividend, so it must be cleared before the DIV instruction executes:

```
mov  dx,0                        ; clear dividend, high
mov  ax,8003h                    ; dividend, low
mov  cx,100h                     ; divisor
div  cx                          ; AX = 0080h,  DX = 0003h
```

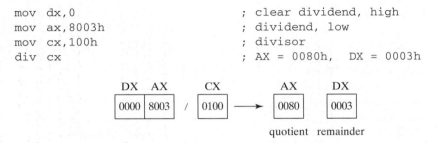

The following instructions perform 32-bit unsigned division using a memory operand as the divisor:

```
.data
dividend QWORD 0000000800300020h
divisor  DWORD 00000100h
.code
mov  edx,DWORD PTR dividend + 4 ; high doubleword
mov  eax,DWORD PTR dividend     ; low doubleword
div  divisor                    ; EAX = 08003000h, EDX = 00000020h
```

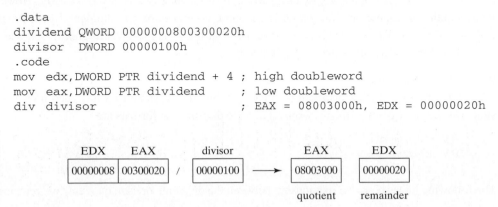

7.4.5 Signed Integer Division

Signed integer division is nearly identical to unsigned division, with one important difference: The dividend must be fully sign-extended before the division takes place. First we will look at sign extension instructions. Then we will apply them to the signed integer divide instruction, IDIV.

Sign Extension Instructions (CBW, CWD, CDQ)

Dividends of signed integer division instructions must often be sign-extended before the division takes place. (Sign extension was described in Section 4.1.5.) Intel provides three useful sign extension instructions: CBW, CWD, and CDQ. The CBW instruction (convert byte to word) extends the sign bit of AL into AH, preserving the number's sign. In the next example, 9Bh (in AL) and FF9Bh (in AX) both equal −101 decimal:

```
.data
byteVal SBYTE -101              ; 9Bh
.code
mov  al,byteVal                 ; AL = 9Bh
cbw                             ; AX = FF9Bh
```

The CWD (convert word to doubleword) instruction extends the sign bit of AX into DX:

```
.data
wordVal SWORD -101              ; FF9Bh
.code
mov  ax,wordVal                 ; AX = FF9Bh
cwd                             ; DX:AX = FFFFFF9Bh
```

The CDQ (convert doubleword to quadword) instruction extends the sign bit of EAX into EDX:

```
.data
dwordVal SDWORD -101            ; FFFFFF9Bh
.code
mov  eax,dwordVal
cdq                             ; EDX:EAX = FFFFFFFFFFFFFF9Bh
```

The IDIV Instruction

The IDIV (signed divide) instruction performs signed integer division, using the same operands as DIV. Before executing 8-bit division, the dividend (AX) must be completely sign-extended. The remainder always has the same sign as the dividend.

Example 1 The following instructions divide −48 by 5. After IDIV executes, the quotient in AL is −9 and the remainder in AH is −3:

```
.data
byteVal SBYTE -48               ; D0 hexadecimal
.code
mov  al,byteVal                 ; lower half of dividend
cbw                             ; extend AL into AH
mov  bl,+5                      ; divisor
idiv bl                         ; AL = -9, AH = -3
```

The following illustration shows how AL is sign-extended into AX by the CBW instruction:

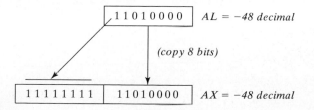

To understand why sign extension of the dividend is necessary, let's repeat the previous example without using sign extension. The following code initializes AH to zero so it has a known value, and then divides without using CBW to prepare the dividend:

```
.data
byteVal SBYTE -48              ; D0 hexadecimal
.code
mov  ah,0                      ; upper half of dividend
mov  al,byteVal                ; lower half of dividend
mov  bl,+5                     ; divisor
idiv bl                        ; AL = 41, AH = 3
```

Before the division, AX = 00D0h (208 decimal). IDIV divides this by 5, producing a quotient of 41 decimal, and a remainder of 3. That is certainly not the correct answer.

Example 2   16-bit division requires AX to be sign-extended into DX. The next example divides −5000 by 256:

```
.data
wordVal SWORD -5000
.code
mov  ax,wordVal                ; dividend, low
cwd                            ; extend AX into DX
mov  bx,+256                   ; divisor
idiv bx                        ; quotient AX = -19, rem DX = -136
```

Example 3   32-bit division requires EAX to be sign-extended into EDX. The next example divides 50,000 by −256:

```
.data
dwordVal SDWORD +50000
.code
mov  eax,dwordVal              ; dividend, low
cdq                            ; extend EAX into EDX
mov  ebx,-256                  ; divisor
idiv ebx                       ; quotient EAX = -195, rem EDX = +80
```

> All arithmetic status flag values are undefined after executing DIV and IDIV.

Divide Overflow

If a division operand produces a quotient that will not fit into the destination operand, a *divide overflow* condition results. This causes a CPU interrupt, and the current program halts. The following instructions, for example, generate a divide overflow because the quotient (100h) will not fit into the AL register:

```
mov  ax,1000h
mov  bl,10h
div  bl                        ; AL cannot hold 100h
```

When this code executes under MS-Windows, Figure 7–1 shows the resulting error dialog produced by Windows. A similar dialog window appears when you write instructions that attempt to divide by zero.

Figure 7–1   Divide Overflow Error Example.

Use a 32-bit divisor and 64-bit dividend to reduce the probability of a divide overflow condition. In the following code, the divisor is EBX, and the dividend is placed in the 64-bit combined EDX and EAX registers:

```
mov  eax,1000h
cdq
mov  ebx,10h
div  ebx                    ; EAX = 00000100h
```

To prevent division by zero, test the divisor before dividing:

```
mov  ax,dividend
mov  bl,divisor
cmp  bl,0                   ; check the divisor
je   NoDivideZero           ; zero? display error
div  bl                     ; not zero: continue
.
.
NoDivideZero:               ;(display "Attempt to divide by zero")
```

7.4.6   Implementing Arithmetic Expressions

Section 4.2.5 showed how to implement arithmetic expressions using addition and subtraction. We can now include multiplication and division. Implementing arithmetic expressions at first seems to be an activity best left for compiler writers, but there is much to be gained by hands-on study. You can learn how compilers optimize code. Also, you can implement better error checking than a typical compiler by checking the size of the product following multiplication operations. Most high-level language compilers ignore the upper 32 bits of the product when multiplying two 32-bit operands. In assembly language, however, you can use the Carry and Overflow flags to tell you when the product does not fit into 32 bits. The use of these flags was explained in Sections 7.4.1 and 7.4.2.

There are two easy ways to view assembly code generated by a C++ compiler: Open a disassembly window while debugging a C++ program or generate an assembly language listing file. In Microsoft Visual C++, for example, the /FA command-line switch generates an assembly language listing file.

Example 1 Implement the following C++ statement in assembly language, using unsigned 32-bit integers:

```
var4 = (var1 + var2) * var3;
```

This is a straightforward problem because we can work from left to right (addition, then multiplication). After the second instruction, EAX contains the sum of **var1** and **var2**. In the third instruction, EAX is multiplied by **var3** and the product is stored in EAX:

```
        mov   eax,var1
        add   eax,var2
        mul   var3              ; EAX = EAX * var3
        jc    tooBig            ; unsigned overflow?
        mov   var4,eax
        jmp   next
tooBig:                         ; display error message
```

If the MUL instruction generates a product larger than 32 bits, the JC instruction jumps to a label that handles the error.

Example 2 Implement the following C++ statement, using unsigned 32-bit integers:

```
var4 = (var1 * 5) / (var2 - 3);
```

In this example, there are two subexpressions within parentheses. The left side can be assigned to EDX:EAX, so it is not necessary to check for overflow. The right side is assigned to EBX, and the final division completes the expression:

```
mov   eax,var1              ; left side
mov   ebx,5
mul   ebx                   ; EDX:EAX = product
mov   ebx,var2              ; right side
sub   ebx,3
div   ebx                   ; final division
mov   var4,eax
```

Example 3 Implement the following C++ statement, using signed 32-bit integers:

```
var4 = (var1 * -5) / (-var2 % var3);
```

This example is a little trickier than the previous ones. We can begin with the expression on the right side and store its value in EBX. Because the operands are signed, it is important to sign-extend the dividend into EDX and use the IDIV instruction:

```
mov   eax,var2              ; begin right side
neg   eax
cdq                         ; sign-extend dividend
idiv  var3                  ; EDX = remainder
mov   ebx,edx               ; EBX = right side
```

Next, we calculate the expression on the left side, storing the product in EDX:EAX:

```
mov   eax,-5                        ; begin left side
imul  var1                         ; EDX:EAX = left side
```

Finally, the left side (EDX:EAX) is divided by the right side (EBX):

```
idiv  ebx                          ; final division
mov   var4,eax                     ; quotient
```

7.4.7 Section Review

 1. Explain why overflow cannot occur when the MUL and one-operand IMUL instructions execute.

 2. How is the one-operand IMUL instruction different from MUL in the way it generates a multiplication product?

 3. What has to happen in order for the one-operand IMUL to set the Carry and Overflow flags?

 4. When EBX is the operand in a DIV instruction, which register holds the quotient?

 5. When BX is the operand in a DIV instruction, which register holds the quotient?

 6. When BL is the operand in a MUL instruction, which registers hold the product?

 7. Show an example of sign extension before calling the IDIV instruction with a 16-bit operand.

 8. What will be the contents of AX and DX after the following operation?

```
mov  dx,0
mov  ax,222h
mov  cx,100h
mul  cx
```

 9. What will be the contents of AX after the following operation?

```
mov  ax,63h
mov  bl,10h
div  bl
```

10. What will be the contents of EAX and EDX after the following operation?

```
mov  eax,123400h
mov  edx,0
mov  ebx,10h
div  ebx
```

11. What will be the contents of AX and DX after the following operation?

```
mov  ax,4000h
mov  dx,500h
mov  bx,10h
div  bx
```

12. Write instructions that multiply −5 by 3 and store the result in a 16-bit variable **val1**.

13. Write instructions that divide −276 by 10 and store the result in a 16-bit variable **val1**.

14. Implement the following C++ expression in assembly language, using 32-bit unsigned operands: val1 = (val2 * val3) / (val4 − 3)

15. Implement the following C++ expression in assembly language, using 32-bit signed operands: val1 = (val2 / val3) * (val1 + val2)

7.5 Extended Addition and Subtraction

Extended precision addition and subtraction is adding and subtracting numbers having an almost unlimited size. In C++, writing a program that adds two 1024-bit integers would not be easy. But in assembly language, the ADC (add with carry) and SBB (subtract with borrow) instructions are well suited to this type of problem.

7.5.1 ADC Instruction

The ADC (add with carry) instruction adds both a source operand and the contents of the Carry flag to a destination operand. The instruction formats are the same as for the ADD instruction, and the operands must be the same size:

```
ADC   reg,reg
ADC   mem,reg
ADC   reg,mem
ADC   mem,imm
ADC   reg,imm
```

For example, the following instructions add two 8-bit integers (FFh + FFh), producing a 16-bit sum in DL:AL, which is 01FEh:

```
mov  dl,0
mov  al,0FFh
add  al,0FFh                    ; AL = FEh
adc  dl,0                       ; DL/AL = 01FEh
```

The following illustration shows the movement of data during the two addition steps. First, FFh is added to AL, producing FEh in the AL register and setting the Carry flag. Next, both 0 and the contents of the Carry flag are added to the DL register:

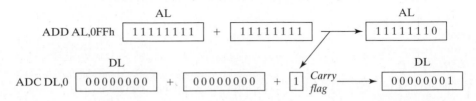

Similarly, the following instructions add two 32-bit integers (FFFFFFFFh + FFFFFFFFh), producing a 64-bit sum in EDX:EAX: 00000001FFFFFFFEh:

```
mov   edx,0
mov   eax,0FFFFFFFFh
add   eax,0FFFFFFFFh
adc   edx,0
```

7.5.2   Extended Addition Example

The following Extended_Add procedure adds two extended integers of the same size. Using a loop, it works its way through the two extended integers as if they were parallel arrays. As it adds each matching pair of values in the arrays, it includes the value of the carry from the addition that was performed during the previous iteration of the loop. Our implementation assumes that the integers are stored as arrays of bytes, but the example could easily be modified to add arrays of doublewords:

```
;------------------------------------------------------------
Extended_Add PROC
;
; Calculates the sum of two extended integers stored
; as arrays of bytes.
; Receives: ESI and EDI point to the two integers,
;    EBX points to a variable that will hold the sum,
;    and ECX indicates the number of bytes to be added.
; Storage for the sum must be one byte longer than the
; input operands.
; Returns: nothing
;------------------------------------------------------------
      pushad
      clc                             ; clear the Carry flag

L1:   mov    al,[esi]                 ; get the first integer
      adc    al,[edi]                 ; add the second integer
      pushfd                          ; save the Carry flag
      mov    [ebx],al                 ; store partial sum
      add    esi,1                    ; advance all three pointers
      add    edi,1
      add    ebx,1
      popfd                           ; restore the Carry flag
      loop   L1                       ; repeat the loop

      mov    byte ptr [ebx],0         ; clear high byte of sum
      adc    byte ptr [ebx],0         ; add any leftover carry
      popad
      ret
Extended_Add ENDP
```

The following excerpt from *ExtAdd.asm* calls **Extended_Add,** passing it two 8-byte integers. We are careful to allocate an extra byte for the sum, in case a carry is generated when adding the two high-order bytes of the integers.

```
.data
op1 BYTE 34h,12h,98h,74h,06h,0A4h,0B2h,0A2h
op2 BYTE 02h,45h,23h,00h,00h,87h,10h,80h
sum BYTE 9 dup(0)

.code
main PROC
```

```
        mov    esi,OFFSET op1              ; first operand
        mov    edi,OFFSET op2              ; second operand
        mov    ebx,OFFSET sum              ; sum operand
        mov    ecx,LENGTHOF op1            ; number of bytes
        call   Extended_Add

; Display the sum.

        mov    esi,OFFSET sum
        mov    ecx,LENGTHOF sum
        call   Display_Sum
        call   Crlf
```

The following output is produced by the program. The addition produces a carry:

```
    0122C32B0674BB5736
```

The **Display_Sum** procedure (from the same program) displays the sum in its proper order, starting with the high-order byte, and working its way down to the low-order byte:

```
Display_Sum PROC
    pushad
    ; point to the last array element
    add  esi,ecx
    sub  esi,TYPE BYTE
    mov  ebx,TYPE BYTE

L1: mov  al,[esi]              ; get an array byte
    call WriteHexB             ; display it
    sub  esi,TYPE BYTE         ; point to previous byte
    loop L1

    popad
    ret
Display_Sum ENDP
```

7.5.3 SBB Instruction

The SBB (subtract with borrow) instruction subtracts both a source operand and the value of the Carry flag from a destination operand. The possible operands are the same as for the ADC instruction. The following example code performs 64-bit subtraction. It sets EDX:EAX to 0000000700000001h and subtracts 2 from this value. The lower 32 bits are subtracted first, setting the Carry flag. Then the upper 32 bits are subtracted, including the Carry flag:

```
    mov  edx,7                     ; upper half
    mov  eax,1                     ; lower half
    sub  eax,2                     ; subtract 2
    sbb  edx,0                     ; subtract upper half
```

Figure 7–2 demonstrates the movement of data during the two subtraction steps. First, the value 2 is subtracted from EAX, producing FFFFFFFFh in EAX. The Carry flag is set because a borrow is required when subtracting a larger number from a smaller one. Next the SBB instruction subtracts both 0 and the contents of the Carry flag from EDX.

Figure 7–2 Subtracting from a 64-bit Integer Using SBB.

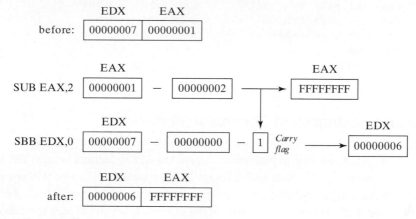

7.5.4 Section Review

1. Describe the ADC instruction.

2. Describe the SBB instruction.

3. What will be the values of EDX:EAX after the following instructions execute?

```
mov  edx,10h
mov  eax,0A0000000h
add  eax,20000000h
adc  edx,0
```

4. What will be the values of EDX:EAX after the following instructions execute?

```
mov  edx,100h
mov  eax,80000000h
sub  eax,90000000h
sbb  edx,0
```

5. What will be the contents of DX after the following instructions execute (STC sets the Carry flag)?

```
mov  dx,5
stc                          ; set Carry flag
mov  ax,10h
adc  dx,ax
```

6. *Challenge:* The following program is supposed to subtract **val2** from **val1**. Find and correct all logic errors (CLC clears the Carry flag):

```
.data
val1 QWORD  20403004362047A1h
val2 QWORD  055210304A2630B2h
result QWORD  0
.code
    mov  cx,8                ; loop counter
    mov  esi,val1            ; set index to start
    mov  edi,val2
    clc                      ; clear Carry flag
```

```
top:
        mov     al,BYTE PTR[esi]        ; get first number
        sbb     al,BYTE PTR[edi]        ; subtract second
        mov     BYTE PTR[esi],al        ; store the result
        dec     esi
        dec     edi
        loop    top
```

7.6   ASCII and Unpacked Decimal Arithmetic

The integer arithmetic shown so far in this book has dealt only with binary values. The CPU calculates in binary, but is also able to perform arithmetic on ASCII decimal strings. The latter can be conveniently entered by the user and displayed in the console window, without requiring them to be converted to binary. Suppose a program is to input two numbers from the user and add them together. The following is a sample of the output, in which the user has entered 3402 and 1256:

```
Enter first number:    3402
Enter second number:   1256
The sum is:            4658
```

We have two options when calculating and displaying the sum:

1. Convert both operands to binary, add the binary values, and convert the sum from binary to ASCII digit strings.
2. Add the digit strings directly by successively adding each pair of ASCII digits ($2 + 6, 0 + 5$, $4 + 2$, and $3 + 1$). The sum is an ASCII digit string, so it can be directly displayed on the screen.

The second option requires the use of specialized instructions that adjust the sum after adding each pair of ASCII digits. Four instructions that deal with ASCII addition, subtraction, multiplication, and division are as follows:

AAA	(ASCII adjust after addition)
AAS	(ASCII adjust after subtraction)
AAM	(ASCII adjust after multiplication)
AAD	(ASCII adjust before division)

ASCII Decimal and Unpacked Decimal   The high 4 bits of an unpacked decimal integer are always zeros, whereas the same bits in an ASCII decimal number are equal to 0011b. In any case, both types of integers store one digit per byte. The following example shows how 3402 would be stored in both formats:

ASCII format: | 33 | 34 | 30 | 32 | Unpacked: | 03 | 04 | 00 | 02 |

(all values are in hexadecimal)

Although ASCII arithmetic executes more slowly than binary arithmetic, it has two distinct advantages:

- Conversion from string format before performing arithmetic is not necessary.
- Using an assumed decimal point permits operations on real numbers without danger of the roundoff errors that occur with floating-point numbers.

ASCII addition and subtraction permit operands to be in ASCII format or unpacked decimal format. Only unpacked decimal numbers can be used for multiplication and division.

7.6.1 AAA Instruction

The AAA (ASCII adjust after addition) instruction adjusts the binary result of an ADD or ADC instruction. Assuming that AL contains a binary value produced by adding two ASCII digits, AAA converts AL to two unpacked decimal digits and stores them in AH and AL. Once in unpacked format, AH and AL can easily be converted to ASCII by ORing them with 30h.

The following example shows how to add the ASCII digits 8 and 2 correctly, using the AAA instruction. You must clear AH to zero before performing the addition or it will influence the result returned by AAA. The last instruction converts AH and AL to ASCII digits:

```
mov  ah,0
mov  al,'8'          ; AX = 0038h
add  al,'2'          ; AX = 006Ah
aaa                  ; AX = 0100h (ASCII adjust result)
or   ax,3030h        ; AX = 3130h = '10' (convert to ASCII)
```

Multibyte Addition Using AAA

Let's look at a procedure that adds ASCII decimal values with implied decimal points. The implementation is a bit more complex than one would imagine because the carry from each digit addition must be propagated to the next highest position. In the following pseudocode, the name *acc* refers to an 8-bit accumulator register:

```
esi (index) = length of first_number - 1
edi (index) = length of first_number
ecx = length of first_number
set carry value to 0
Loop
    acc = first_number[esi]
    add previous carry to acc
    save carry in carry1
    acc += second_number[esi]
    OR the carry with carry1
    sum[edi] = acc
    dec edi
Until ecx == 0
Store last carry digit in sum
```

The carry digit must always be converted to ASCII. When you add the carry digit to the first operand, you must adjust the result with AAA. Here is the listing:

```
TITLE ASCII Addition                      (ASCII_add.asm)

; Perform ASCII arithmetic on strings having
; an implied fixed decimal point.
```

```
        INCLUDE Irvine32.inc

        DECIMAL_OFFSET = 5              ; offset from right of string
        .data
        decimal_one BYTE "100123456789765"   ; 1001234567.89765
        decimal_two BYTE "900402076502015"   ; 9004020765.02015
        sum BYTE (SIZEOF decimal_one + 1) DUP(0),0

        .code
        main PROC
        ; Start at the last digit position.
            mov    esi,SIZEOF decimal_one - 1
            mov    edi,SIZEOF decimal_one
            mov    ecx,SIZEOF decimal_one
            mov    bh,0                 ; set carry value to zero

        L1: mov    ah,0                 ; clear AH before addition
            mov    al,decimal_one[esi]  ; get the first digit
            add    al,bh                ; add the previous carry
            aaa                         ; adjust the sum (AH = carry)
            mov    bh,ah                ; save the carry in carry1
            or     bh,30h               ; convert it to ASCII
            add    al,decimal_two[esi]  ; add the second digit
            aaa                         ; adjust the sum (AH = carry)
            or     bh,ah                ; OR the carry with carry1
            or     bh,30h               ; convert it to ASCII
            or     al,30h               ; convert AL back to ASCII
            mov    sum[edi],al          ; save it in the sum
            dec    esi                  ; back up one digit
            dec    edi
            loop   L1
            mov    sum[edi],bh          ; save last carry digit

        ; Display the sum as a string.
            mov    edx,OFFSET sum
            call   WriteString
            call   Crlf

            exit
        main ENDP
        END main
```

Here is the program's output, showing the sum without a decimal point:

| 1000525533291780 |

7.6.2 AAS Instruction

The AAS (ASCII adjust after subtraction) instruction follows a SUB or SBB instruction that has subtracted one unpacked decimal value from another and stored the result in AL. It makes the result in AL consistent with ASCII digit representation. Adjustment is necessary only when the subtraction generates a negative result. For example, the following statements subtract ASCII 9 from 8:

```
.data
val1 BYTE '8'
val2 BYTE '9'
.code
mov ah,0
mov al,val1                     ; AX = 0038h
sub al,val2                     ; AX = 00FFh
aas                             ; AX = FF09h
pushf                           ; save the Carry flag
or  al,30h                      ; AX = FF39h
popf                            ; restore the Carry flag
```

After the SUB instruction, AX equals 00FFh. The AAS instruction converts AL to 09h and subtracts 1 from AH, setting it to FFh and setting the Carry flag.

7.6.3   AAM Instruction

The AAM (ASCII adjust after multiplication) instruction converts the binary product produced by MUL to unpacked decimal. The multiplication can only use unpacked decimals. In the following example, we multiply 5 by 6 and adjust the result in AX. After adjustment, AX = 0300h, the unpacked decimal representation of 30:

```
.data
AscVal BYTE 05h,06h
.code
mov bl,ascVal                   ; first operand
mov al,[ascVal+1]               ; second operand
mul bl                          ; AX = 001Eh
aam                             ; AX = 0300h
```

7.6.4   AAD Instruction

The AAD (ASCII adjust before division) instruction converts an unpacked decimal dividend in AX to binary in preparation for executing the DIV instruction. The following example converts unpacked 0307h to binary, then divides it by 5. DIV produces a quotient of 07h in AL and a remainder of 02h in AH:

```
.data
quotient  BYTE ?
remainder BYTE ?
.code
mov  ax,0307h                   ; dividend
aad                             ; AX = 0025h
mov  bl,5                       ; divisor
div  bl                         ; AX = 0207h
mov  quotient,al
mov  remainder,ah
```

7.6.5 Section Review

1. Write a single instruction that converts a two-digit unpacked decimal integer in AX to ASCII decimal.

2. Write a single instruction that converts a two-digit ASCII decimal integer in AX to unpacked decimal format.

3. Write a two-instruction sequence that converts a two-digit ASCII decimal number in AX to binary.

4. Write a single instruction that converts an unsigned binary integer in AX to unpacked decimal.

5. *Challenge:* Write a procedure that displays an unsigned 8-bit binary value in decimal format. Pass the binary value in AL. The input range is limited 0 to 99, decimal. The only procedure you can call from the book's link library is WriteChar. The procedure should contain no more than eight instructions. Here is a sample call:

```
mov  al,65                    ; range limit: 0 to 99
call showDecimal8
```

6. *Challenge:* Suppose AX contains 0072h and the Auxiliary Carry flag is set as a result of adding two unknown ASCII decimal digits. Use the Intel Instruction Set Reference Manual to determine what output the AAA instruction would produce. Explain your answer.

7.7   Packed Decimal Arithmetic

Packed decimal integers store two decimal digits per byte. Each digit is represented by 4 bits. If there is an odd number of digits, the highest nybble is filled with a zero. Storage sizes may vary:

```
bcd1 QWORD 2345673928737285h    ; 2,345,673,928,737,285 decimal
bcd2 DWORD 12345678h            ; 12,345,678 decimal
bcd3 DWORD 08723654h            ; 8,723,654 decimal
bcd4 WORD 9345h                 ; 9,345 decimal
bcd5 WORD 0237h                 ; 237 decimal
bcd6 BYTE 34h                   ; 34 decimal
```

Packed decimal storage has at least two strengths:

• The numbers can have almost any number of significant digits. This makes it possible to perform calculations with a great deal of accuracy.

• Conversion of packed decimal numbers to ASCII (and vice versa) is relatively simple.

Two instructions, DAA (decimal adjust after addition) and DAS (decimal adjust after subtraction), adjust the result of an addition or subtraction operation on packed decimals. Unfortunately, no such instructions exist for multiplication and division. In those cases, the number must be unpacked, multiplied or divided, and repacked.

7.7.1   DAA Instruction

The DAA (decimal adjust after addition) instruction converts a binary sum produced by ADD or ADC in AL to packed decimal format. For example, the following instructions add packed decimals 35 and 48. The binary sum (7Dh) is adjusted to 83h, the packed decimal sum of 35 and 48.

```
mov  al,35h
add  al,48h                      ; AL = 7Dh
daa                              ; AL = 83h (adjusted result)
```

The internal logic of DAA is documented in the Intel Instruction Set Reference Manual.

Example   The following program adds two 16-bit packed decimal integers and stores the sum in a packed doubleword. Addition requires the sum variable to contain space for one more digit than the operands:

```
TITLE Packed Decimal Example    (AddPacked.asm)

; Demonstrate packed decimal addition.
INCLUDE Irvine32.inc

.data
packed_1 WORD 4536h
packed_2 WORD 7207h
sum DWORD ?

.code
main PROC
; Initialize sum and index.
    mov  sum,0
    mov  esi,0

; Add low bytes.
    mov    al,BYTE PTR packed_1[esi]
    add    al,BYTE PTR packed_2[esi]
    daa
    mov    BYTE PTR sum[esi],al

; Add high bytes, include carry.
    inc    esi
    mov    al,BYTE PTR packed_1[esi]
    adc    al,BYTE PTR packed_2[esi]
    daa
    mov    BYTE PTR sum[esi],al

; Add final carry, if any.
    inc    esi
    mov    al,0
    adc    al,0
    mov    BYTE PTR sum[esi],al

; Display the sum in hexadecimal.
    mov    eax,sum
    call   WriteHex
    call   Crlf
    exit
main ENDP
END main
```

Needless to say, the program contains repetitive code that suggests using a loop. One of the chapter exercises will ask you to create a procedure that adds packed decimal integers of any size.

7.7.2 DAS Instruction

The DAS (decimal adjust after subtraction) instruction converts the binary result of a SUB or SBB instruction in AL to packed decimal format. For example, the following statements subtract packed decimal 48 from 85 and adjust the result:

```
mov  bl,48h
mov  al,85h
sub  al,bl                    ; AL = 3Dh
das                           ; AL = 37h   (adjusted result)
```

The internal logic of DAS is documented in the Intel Instruction Set Reference Manual.

7.7.3 Section Review

1. Under what circumstances does DAA instruction set the Carry flag? Give an example.

2. Under what circumstances does DAS instruction set the Carry flag? Give an example.

3. When adding two packed decimal integers of length n bytes, how many storage bytes must be reserved for the sum?

4. *Challenge:* Suppose AL contains 3Dh, AF = 0, and CF = 0. Using the Intel Instruction Set Reference Manual as a guide, explain the steps used by the DAS instruction to convert AL to packed decimal (37h).

7.8 Chapter Summary

Along with the bitwise instructions from the preceding chapter, shift instructions are among the most characteristic of assembly language. To *shift* a number means to move its bits right or left.

The SHL (shift left) instruction shifts each bit in a destination operand to the left, filling the lowest bit with 0. One of the best uses of SHL is for performing high-speed multiplication by powers of 2. Shifting any operand left by n bits multiplies the operand by 2^n. The SHR (shift right) instruction shifts each bit to the right, replacing the highest bit with a 0. Shifting any operand right by n bits divides the operand by 2^n.

SAL (shift arithmetic left) and SAR (shift arithmetic right) are shift instructions specifically designed for shifting signed numbers.

The ROL (rotate left) instruction shifts each bit to the left and copies the highest bit to both the Carry flag and the lowest bit position. The ROR (rotate right) instruction shifts each bit to the right and copies the lowest bit to both the Carry flag and the highest bit position.

The RCL (rotate carry left) instruction shifts each bit to the left and copies the highest bit into the Carry flag, which is first copied into the lowest bit of the result. The RCR (rotate carry right) instruction shifts each bit to the right and copies the lowest bit into the Carry flag. The Carry flag is copied into the highest bit of the result.

The SHLD (shift left double) and SHRD (shift right double) instructions, available on x86 processors, are particularly effective for shifting bits in large integers.

The MUL instruction multiplies an 8-, 16-, or 32-bit operand by AL, AX, or EAX. The IMUL instruction performs signed integer multiplication. It has three formats: single operand, double operand, and three operand.

The DIV instruction performs 8-bit, 16-bit, and 32-bit division on unsigned integers. The IDIV instruction performs signed integer division, using the same operands as the DIV instruction.

The CBW (convert byte to word) instruction extends the sign bit of AL into the AH register. The CDQ (convert doubleword to quadword) instruction extends the sign bit of EAX into the EDX register. The CWD (convert word to doubleword) instruction extends the sign bit of AX into the DX register.

Extended addition and subtraction refers to adding and subtracting integers of arbitrary size. The ADC and SBB instructions can be used to implement such addition and subtraction. The ADC (add with carry) instruction adds both a source operand and the contents of the Carry flag to a destination operand. The SBB (subtract with borrow) instruction subtracts both a source operand and the value of the Carry flag from a destination operand.

ASCII decimal integers store one digit per byte, encoded as an ASCII digit. The AAA (ASCII adjust after addition) instruction converts the binary result of an ADD or ADC instruction to ASCII decimal. The AAS (ASCII adjust after subtraction) instruction converts the binary result of a SUB or SBB instruction to ASCII decimal.

Unpacked decimal integers store one decimal digit per byte, as a binary value. The AAM (ASCII adjust after multiplication) instruction converts the binary product of a MUL instruction to unpacked decimal. The AAD (ASCII adjust before division) instruction converts an unpacked decimal dividend to binary in preparation for the DIV instruction.

Packed decimal integers store two decimal digits per byte. The DAA (decimal adjust after addition) instruction converts the binary result of an ADD or ADC instruction to packed decimal. The DAS (decimal adjust after subtraction) instruction converts the binary result of a SUB or SBB instruction to packed decimal.

7.9   Programming Exercises

★   **1.   Extended Addition Procedure**
Modify the **Extended_Add** procedure in Section 7.5.2 to add two 256-bit (32-byte) integers.

★★   **2.   Extended Subtraction Procedure**
Create and test a procedure named **Extended_Sub** that subtracts two binary integers of arbitrary size. Restrictions: The storage size of the two integers must be the same, and their size must be a multiple of 32 bits.

★★   **3.   ShowFileTime**
The time stamp of a MS-DOS file directory entry uses bits 0 through 4 for the number of 2-second increments, bits 5 through 10 for the minutes, and bits 11 through 15 for the hours (24-hour clock). For example, the following binary value indicates a time of 02:16:14, in *hh:mm:ss* format:

```
00010 010000 00111
```

Write a procedure named **ShowFileTime** that receives a binary file time value in the AX register and displays the time in *hh:mm:ss* format.

★★ **4. Encryption Using Rotate Operations**

Write a program that performs simple encryption by rotating each plaintext byte a varying number of positions in different directions. For example, in the following array that represents the encryption key, a negative value indicates a rotation to the left and a positive value indicates a rotation to the right. The integer in each position indicates the magnitude of the rotation:

```
key BYTE -2, 4, 1, 0, -3, 5, 2, -4, -4, 6
```

Your program should loop through a plaintext message and align the key to the first 10 bytes of the message. Rotate each plaintext byte by the amount indicated by its matching key array value. Then, align the key to the next 10 bytes of the message and repeat the process. *(A VideoNote for this exercise is posted on the Web site.)*

★★★ **5. Bitwise Multiplication**

Write a procedure named **BitwiseMultiply** that multiplies any unsigned 32-bit integer by EAX, using only shifting and addition. Pass the integer to the procedure in the EBX register, and return the product in the EAX register. Write a short test program that calls the procedure and displays the product. (We will assume that the product is never larger than 32 bits.) This is a fairly challenging program to write. One possible approach is to use a loop to shift the multiplier to the right, keeping track of the number of shifts that occur before the Carry flag is set. The resulting shift count can then be applied to the SHR instruction, using the multiplicand as the destination operand. Then, the same process must be repeated until you find the next highest bit in the multiplier. *(A VideoNote for this exercise is posted on the Web site.)*

★★ **6. Greatest Common Divisor (GCD)**

The greatest common divisor (GCD) of two integers is the largest integer that will evenly divide both integers. The GCD algorithm involves integer division in a loop, described by the following C++ code:

```
int GCD(int x, int y)
{
    x = abs(x);                    // absolute value
    y = abs(y);
    do {
      int n = x % y;
      x = y;
      y = n;
    } while (y > 0);
    return x;
}
```

Implement this function in assembly language and write a test program that calls the function several times, passing it different values. Display all results on the screen.

★★ **7. Prime Number Program**

Write a procedure named **IsPrime** that sets the Zero flag if the 32-bit integer passed in the EAX register is prime. Optimize the program's loop to run as efficiently as possible. Write a test program that prompts the user for an integer, calls **IsPrime**, and displays a message indicating whether or not the value is prime. Continue prompting the user for integers and calling **IsPrime** until the user enters −1.

★ **8.   Packed Decimal Conversion**

Write a procedure named **PackedToAsc** that converts a 4-byte packed decimal integer to a string of ASCII decimal digits. Pass the packed integer and the address of a buffer holding the ASCII digits to the procedure. Write a short test program that displays several converted integers.

★★ **9.   AscAdd Procedure**

Convert the code for multidigit ASCII addition presented in Section 7.6.1 to a procedure named **AscAdd** with the following parameters: ESI points to the first number, EDI points to the second number, EDX points to the sum, and ECX contains the number of digits in the operands. Write a program that calls AscAdd and calls WriteString to show that the addition worked correctly.

★ **10.   Display ASCII Decimal**

Write a procedure named WriteScaled that outputs a decimal ASCII number with an implied decimal point. Suppose the following number were defined as follows, where DECIMAL_OFFSET indicates that the decimal point must be inserted five positions from the right side of the number:

```
DECIMAL_OFFSET = 5
.data
decimal_one BYTE "100123456789765"
```

WriteScaled would display the number like this:

```
1001234567.89765
```

When calling WriteScaled, pass the number's offset in EDX, the number length in ECX, and the decimal offset in EBX. Write a test program that displays three numbers of different sizes.

★★★ **11.   Add Packed Integers**

Using the code in Section 7.7.1, write a procedure named AddPacked that adds two packed decimal integers of arbitrary size (both must be the same). Write a test program that passes AddPacked several pairs of integers: 4-byte, 8-byte, and 16-byte. Display the sums in hexadecimal. Use the following registers to pass information:

```
ESI - pointer to the first number
EDI - pointer to the second number
EDX - pointer to the sum
ECX - number of bytes to add
```

(A VideoNote for this exercise is posted on the Web site.)

8

Advanced Procedures

8.1 Introduction

8.2 Stack Frames
    8.2.1 Stack Parameters
    8.2.2 Accessing Stack Parameters
    8.2.3 Local Variables
    8.2.4 ENTER and LEAVE Instructions
    8.2.5 LOCAL Directive
    8.2.6 Section Review

8.3 Recursion
    8.3.1 Recursively Calculating a Sum
    8.3.2 Calculating a Factorial
    8.3.3 Section Review

8.4 INVOKE, ADDR, PROC, and PROTO
    8.4.1 INVOKE Directive
    8.4.2 ADDR Operator
    8.4.3 PROC Directive
    8.4.4 PROTO Directive
    8.4.5 Parameter Classifications
    8.4.6 Example: Exchanging Two Integers

8.4.7 Debugging Tips
8.4.8 WriteStackFrame Procedure
8.4.9 Section Review

8.5 Creating Multimodule Programs
    8.5.1 Hiding and Exporting Procedure Names
    8.5.2 Calling External Procedures
    8.5.3 Using Variables and Symbols across Module Boundaries
    8.5.4 Example: ArraySum Program
    8.5.5 Creating the Modules Using Extern
    8.5.6 Creating the Modules Using INVOKE and PROTO
    8.5.7 Section Review

8.6 Java Bytecodes
    8.6.1 Java Virtual Machine (JVM)
    8.6.2 Instruction Set
    8.6.3 Java Disassembly Examples

8.7 Chapter Summary

8.8 Programming Exercises

8.1 Introduction

In this chapter, we focus on the underlying structure of subroutines and subroutine calls. There is a natural tendency to look for universal concepts that make learning easier, so we will use this chapter to show how all procedures work, using assembly language as a low-level programming tool. In other words, what you learn here is often discussed in midlevel programming courses in

C++ and Java and in a core computer science course called *programming languages*. The following topics, discussed in this chapter, are basic programming language concepts:

- Stack frames
- Variable scope and lifetime
- Stack parameters
- Passing arguments by value and by reference
- Creating and initializing local variables on the stack
- Recursion
- Writing multimodule programs
- Memory models and language specifiers

The following optional topics demonstrate high-level directives included in MASM designed to aid application programmers:

- INVOKE, PROC, and PROTO directives
- USES and ADDR operators

Above all, your knowledge of assembly language makes it possible for you to peek into the mind of the compiler writer as he or she produces the low-level code that makes a program run.

Terminology   Programming languages use different terms to refer to subroutines. In C and C++, for example, subroutines are called *functions*. In Java, subroutines are called *methods*. In MASM, subroutines are called *procedures*. Our purpose in this chapter is to show low-level implementations of typical subroutine calls as they might appear in C and C++. At the beginning of this chapter, when referring to general principles, we will use the general term *subroutine*. Later in the chapter, when concentrating on specific MASM directives (such as PROC and PROTO), we will use the specific term *procedure*.

Values passed to a subroutine by a calling program are called *arguments*. When the values are received by the called subroutine, they are called *parameters*.

8.2   Stack Frames

The procedures in the Irvine32 and Irvine16 libraries require you to pass parameters in registers. In this chapter, we show how subroutines can declare parameters that are located on the runtime stack.

A *stack frame* (or *activation record*) is the area of the stack set aside for passed arguments, subroutine return address, local variables, and saved registers. The stack frame is created by the following sequential steps:

- Passed arguments, if any, are pushed on the stack.
- The subroutine is called, causing the subroutine return address to be pushed on the stack.
- As the subroutine begins to execute, EBP is pushed on the stack.
- EBP is set equal to ESP. From this point on, EBP acts as a base reference for all of the subroutine parameters.
- If there are local variables, ESP is decremented to reserve space for the variables on the stack.
- If any registers need to be saved, they are pushed on the stack.

The structure of a stack frame is directly affected by a program's memory model and its choice of argument passing convention.

There's a good reason to learn about passing arguments on the stack; nearly all high-level languages use them. If you want to call functions in the MS-Windows Application Programmer Interface (API), for example, you must pass arguments on the stack.

8.2.1 Stack Parameters

Up to this point in the book, we have only used registers to pass arguments to procedures. We can say that the procedures used *register parameters*. Register parameters are optimized for program execution speed and they are easy to use. Unfortunately, register parameters tend to create code clutter in calling programs. Existing register contents often must be saved before they can be loaded with argument values. Such is the case when calling **DumpMem** from the Irvine32 library, for example:

```
pushad
mov    esi,OFFSET array          ; starting OFFSET
mov    ecx,LENGTHOF array        ; size, in units
mov    ebx,TYPE array            ; doubleword format
call   DumpMem                   ; display memory
popad
```

Stack parameters offer a more flexible approach. Just before the subroutine call, the arguments are pushed on the stack. For example, if **DumpMem** used stack parameters, we would call it using the following code:

```
push   TYPE array
push   LENGTHOF array
push   OFFSET array
call   DumpMem
```

Two general types of arguments are pushed on the stack during subroutine calls:

- Value arguments (values of variables and constants)
- Reference arguments (addresses of variables)

Passing by Value   When an argument is passed *by value*, a copy of the value is pushed on the stack. Suppose we call a subroutine named **AddTwo**, passing it two 32-bit integers:

```
.data
val1    DWORD 5
val2    DWORD 6
.code
push    val2
push    val1
call    AddTwo
```

Following is a picture of the stack just prior to the CALL instruction:

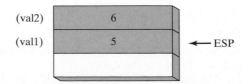

An equivalent function call written in C++ would be

```
int sum = AddTwo( val1, val2 );
```

Observe that the arguments are pushed on the stack in reverse order, which is the norm for the C and C++ languages.

Passing by Reference   An argument passed by reference consists of the address (offset) of an object. The following statements call **Swap**, passing the two arguments by reference:

```
push    OFFSET val2
push    OFFSET val1
call    Swap
```

Following is a picture of the stack just prior to the call to Swap:

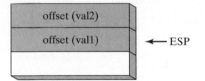

The equivalent function call in C/C++ would pass the addresses of the val1 and val2 arguments:

```
Swap( &val1, &val2 );
```

Passing Arrays   High-level languages always pass arrays to subroutines by reference. That is, they push the address of an array on the stack. The subroutine can then get the address from the stack and use it to access the array. It's easy to see why one would not want to pass an array by value, because doing so would require each array element to be pushed on the stack separately. Such an operation would be very slow and it would use up precious stack space. The following statements do it the right way by passing the offset of array to a subroutine named **ArrayFill:**

```
.data
array DWORD 50 DUP(?)
.code
push    OFFSET array
call    ArrayFill
```

8.2.2   Accessing Stack Parameters

High-level languages have various ways of initializing and accessing parameters during function calls. We will use the C and C++ languages as an example. They begin with a *prologue* consisting of statements that save the EBP register and point EBP to the top of the stack. Optionally, they may push certain registers on the stack whose values will be restored when the function returns. The end of the function consists of an *epilogue* in which the EBP register is restored and the RET instruction returns to the caller.

AddTwo Example   The following **AddTwo** function, written in C, receives two integers passed by value and returns their sum:

```
int AddTwo( int x, int y )
{
    return x + y;
}
```

Let's create an equivalent implementation in assembly language. In its prologue, **AddTwo** pushes EBP on the stack to preserve its existing value:

```
AddTwo PROC
      push  ebp
```

Next, EBP is set to the same value as ESP, so EBP can be the base pointer for AddTwo's stack frame:

```
AddTwo PROC
      push  ebp
      mov   ebp,esp
```

After the two instructions execute, the following figure shows the contents of the stack frame. A function call such as AddTwo(5, 6) would cause the second parameter to be pushed on the stack, followed by the first parameter:

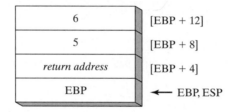

AddTwo could push additional registers on the stack without altering the offsets of the stack parameters from EBP. ESP would change value, but EBP would not.

Base-Offset Addressing   We will use base-offset addressing to access stack parameters. EBP is the base register and the offset is a constant. 32-bit values are usually returned in EAX. The following implementation of AddTwo adds the parameters and returns their sum in EAX:

```
AddTwo PROC
      push  ebp
      mov   ebp,esp              ; base of stack frame
      mov   eax,[ebp + 12]       ; second parameter
      add   eax,[ebp + 8]        ; first parameter
      pop   ebp
      ret
AddTwo ENDP
```

Explicit Stack Parameters

When stack parameters are referenced with expressions such as [ebp + 8], we call them *explicit stack parameters*. The reason for this term is that the assembly code explicitly states the offset of the parameter as a constant value. Some programmers define symbolic constants to represent the explicit stack parameters, to make their code easier to read:

```
y_param EQU [ebp + 12]
x_param EQU [ebp + 8]

AddTwo PROC
      push  ebp
```

```
        mov     ebp,esp
        mov     eax,y_param
        add     eax,x_param
        pop     ebp
        ret
AddTwo ENDP
```

Cleaning Up the Stack

There must be a way for parameters to be removed from the stack when a subroutine returns. Otherwise, a memory leak would result, and the stack would become corrupted. For example, suppose the following statements in **main** call **AddTwo**:

```
    push    6
    push    5
    call    AddTwo
```

Assuming that AddTwo leaves the two parameters on the stack, the following illustration shows the stack after returning from the call:

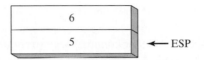

Inside main, we might try to ignore the problem and hope that the program terminates normally. But if we were to call AddTwo from a loop, the stack could overflow. Each call uses 12 bytes of stack space—4 bytes for each parameter, plus 4 bytes for the CALL instruction's return address. A more serious problem could result if we called **Example1** from main, which in turn calls AddTwo:

```
main PROC
     call   Example1
     exit
main ENDP

Example1 PROC
     push   6
     push   5
     call   AddTwo
     ret                      ; stack is corrupted!
Example1 ENDP
```

When the RET instruction in Example1 is about to execute, ESP points to the integer 5 rather than the return address that would take it back to main:

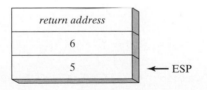

The RET instruction loads the value 5 into the instruction pointer and attempts to transfer control to memory address 5. Assuming that this address is outside the program's code boundary, the processor issues a runtime exception, which tells the OS to terminate the program.

The C Calling Convention   A simple way to remove parameters from the runtime stack is to add a value to ESP equal to the combined sizes of the parameters. Then, ESP will point to the stack location that contains the subroutine's return address. Using the current code example, we can follow the CALL with an ADD:

```
Example1 PROC
    push  6
    push  5
    call  AddTwo
    add   esp,8                 ; remove arguments from the stack
    ret
Example1 ENDP
```

Just as we have done here, programs written in C/C++ always remove arguments from the stack in the calling program after a subroutine has returned.

STDCALL Calling Convention   Another common way to remove parameters from the stack is to use a convention named STDCALL. In the following AddTwo procedure, we supply an integer parameter to the RET instruction, which in turn adds 8 to EBP after returning to the calling procedure. The integer must equal the number of bytes of stack space consumed by the subroutine parameters:

```
AddTwo  PROC
    push  ebp
    mov   ebp,esp              ; base of stack frame
    mov   eax,[ebp + 12]       ; second parameter
    add   eax,[ebp + 8]        ; first parameter
    pop   ebp
    ret   8                    ; clean up the stack
AddTwo  ENDP
```

It should be pointed out that STDCALL, like C, pushes arguments onto the stack in reverse order. By having a parameter in the RET instruction, STDCALL reduces the amount of code generated for subroutine calls (by one instruction) and ensures that calling programs will never forget to clean up the stack. The C calling convention, on the other hand, permits subroutines to declare a variable number of parameters. The caller can decide how many arguments it will pass. An example is the **printf** function from the C programming language, whose number of arguments depends on the number of format specifiers in the initial string argument:

```
int x = 5;
float y = 3.2;
char z = 'Z';
printf("Printing values: %d, %f, %c", x, y, z);
```

A C compiler pushes arguments on the stack in reverse order, followed by a count argument indicating the number of actual arguments. The function gets the argument count and accesses the arguments one by one. The function implementation has no convenient way of encoding a constant in the RET instruction to clean up the stack, so the responsibility is left to the caller.

The Irvine32 library uses the STDCALL calling convention in order to be compatible with the MS-Windows API library. The Irvine16 library uses the same convention to be consistent with the Irvine32 library.

> From this point forward, we assume STDCALL is used in all procedure examples, unless explicitly stated otherwise. We will also refer to subroutines as procedures because our examples are written in assembly language.

Passing 8-Bit and 16-Bit Arguments on the Stack

When passing stack arguments to procedures in protected mode, it's best to push 32-bit operands. Though you can push 16-bit operands on the stack, doing so prevents ESP from being aligned on a doubleword boundary. A page fault may occur and runtime performance may be degraded. You should expand them to 32 bits before pushing them on the stack.

The following **Uppercase** procedure receives a character argument and returns its uppercase equivalent in AL:

```
Uppercase PROC
      push  ebp
      mov   ebp,esp
      mov   al,[esp+8]           ; AL = character
      cmp   al,'a'               ; less than 'a'?
      jb    L1                   ; yes: do nothing
      cmp   al,'z'               ; greater than 'z'?
      ja    L1                   ; yes: do nothing
      sub   al,32                ; no: convert it
L1:   pop   ebp
      ret   4                    ; clean up the stack
Uppercase ENDP
```

If we pass a character literal to Uppercase, the PUSH instruction automatically expands the character to 32 bits:

```
      push  'x'
      call  Uppercase
```

Passing a character variable requires more care because the PUSH instruction does not permit 8-bit operands:

```
.data
charVal BYTE 'x'
.code
      push  charVal              ; syntax error!
      call  Uppercase
```

Instead, we use MOVZX to expand the character into EAX:

```
        movzx eax,charVal              ; move with extension
        push  eax
        call  Uppercase
```

16-Bit Argument Example   Suppose we want to pass two 16-bit integers to the AddTwo procedure shown earlier. The procedure expects 32-bit values, so the following call would cause an error:

```
    .data
    word1 WORD 1234h
    word2 WORD 4111h
    .code
        push  word1
        push  word2
        call  AddTwo                   ; error!
```

Instead, we can zero-extend each argument before pushing it on the stack. The following code correctly calls AddTwo:

```
        movzx eax,word1
        push  eax
        movzx eax,word2
        push  eax
        call  AddTwo                   ; sum is in EAX
```

> The caller of a procedure must ensure the arguments it passes are consistent with the parameters expected by the procedure. In the case of stack parameters, the order and size of the parameters are important!

Passing Multiword Arguments

When passing multiword integers to procedures using the stack, you may want to push the high-order part first, working your way down to the low-order part. Doing so places the integer into the stack in *little endian* order (low-order byte at the lowest address). The following **WriteHex64** procedure receives a 64-bit integer on the stack and displays it in hexadecimal:

```
    WriteHex64 PROC
        push  ebp
        mov   ebp,esp
        mov   eax,[ebp+12]             ; high doubleword
        call  WriteHex
        mov   eax,[ebp+8]              ; low doubleword
        call  WriteHex
        pop   ebp
        ret   8
    WriteHex64 ENDP
```

The call to WriteHex64 pushes the upper half of **longVal**, followed by the lower half:

```
    .data
    longVal DQ 1234567800ABCDEFh
    .code
        push  DWORD PTR longVal + 4    ; high doubleword
        push  DWORD PTR longVal        ; low doubleword
        call  WriteHex64
```

FIGURE 8–1   Stack Frame after Pushing EBP.

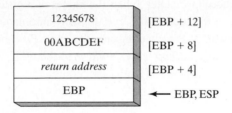

Figure 8–1 shows a picture of the stack frame inside WriteHex64 just after EBP was pushed on the stack and ESP was copied to EBP:

Saving and Restoring Registers

Subroutines often save the current contents of registers on the stack before modifying them so the original values can be restored just before returning. Ideally, the registers in question should be pushed on the stack just after setting EBP to ESP, and just before reserving space for local variables. This helps us to avoid changing offsets of existing stack parameters. For example, assume that the following **MySub** procedure has one stack parameter. It pushes ECX and EDX after setting EBP to the base of the stack frame and loads the stack parameter into EAX:

```
MySub PROC
      push  ebp                ; save base pointer
      mov   ebp,esp            ; base of stack frame
      push  ecx
      push  edx                ; save EDX
      mov   eax,[ebp+8]        ; get the stack parameter
       .
       .
      pop   edx                ; restore saved registers
      pop   ecx
      pop   ebp                ; restore base pointer
      ret                      ; clean up the stack
MySub ENDP
```

After it is initialized, EBP's contents remain fixed throughout the subroutine. Pushing ECX and EDX does not affect the displacement from EBP of parameters already on the stack because the stack grows below EBP (see Figure 8–2).

FIGURE 8–2   Stack Frame for the MySub Procedure.

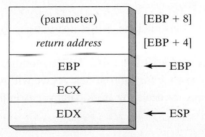

Stack Affected by the USES Operator

The USES operator, introduced in Chapter 5, lists the names of registers to save at the beginning of a procedure and restore at the procedure's end. MASM automatically generates appropriate PUSH and POP instructions for each named register. *Caution: Procedures that reference parameters using constant offsets such as [ebp + 8] should avoid the USES operator.* Let's look at an example that shows why. The following **MySub1** procedure employs the USES operator to save and restore ECX and EDX:

```
MySub1 PROC USES ecx edx
    ret
MySub1 ENDP
```

The following code is generated by MASM when it assembles **MySub1**:

```
push  ecx
push  edx
pop   edx
pop   ecx
ret
```

Suppose we combine USES with a stack parameter, as does the following **MySub2** procedure. Its parameter is expected to be located on the stack at EBP+8:

```
MySub2 PROC USES ecx edx
    push  ebp                 ; save base pointer
    mov   ebp,esp             ; base of stack frame
    mov   eax,[ebp+8]         ; get the stack parameter
    pop   ebp                 ; restore base pointer
    ret   4                   ; clean up the stack
MySub2 ENDP
```

Here is the corresponding code generated by MASM for **MySub2**:

```
push  ecx
push  edx
push  ebp
mov   ebp,esp
mov   eax,dword ptr [ebp+8]; wrong location!
pop   ebp
pop   edx
pop   ecx
ret   4
```

An error results because MASM inserted the PUSH instructions for ECX and EDX at the beginning of the procedure, altering the offset of the stack parameter. Figure 8–3 shows how the stack parameter must now be referenced as [EBP + 16]. USES modifies the stack before saving EBP, going against standard prologue code for subroutines. As we will see in Section 8.4.3, the PROC directive has a high-level syntax for declaring stack parameters. In that context, the USES operator causes no problems.

FIGURE 8–3   Stack Frame of the MySub2 Procedure.

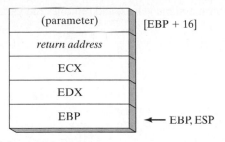

Procedures using explicit stack parameters should avoid the USES operator.

8.2.3 Local Variables

In high-level language programs, variables created, used, and destroyed within a single subroutine are called *local variables*. A local variable has distinct advantages over variables declared outside subroutines:

- Only statements within a local variable's enclosing subroutine can view or modify the variable. This characteristic helps to prevent program bugs caused by modifying variables from many different locations in a program's source code.
- Storage space used by local variables is released when the subroutine ends.
- A local variable can have the same name as a local variable in another subroutine without creating a name clash. This characteristic is useful in large programs when the chance of two variables having the same name is likely.
- Local variables are essential when writing recursive subroutines, as well as subroutines executed by multiple execution threads.

Local variables are created on the runtime stack, usually below the base pointer (EBP). Although they cannot be assigned default values at assembly time, they can be initialized at runtime. We can create local variables in assembly language by using the same techniques as C and C++.

Example   The following C++ function declares local variables X and Y:

```
void MySub()
{
    int X = 10;
    int Y = 20;
}
```

We can use the compiled C++ program as a guide, showing how local variables are allocated by the C++ compiler. Each stack entry defaults to 32 bits, so each variable's storage size is rounded upward to a multiple of 4. A total of 8 bytes is reserved for the two local variables:

Variable	Bytes	Stack Offset
X	4	EBP − 4
Y	4	EBP − 8

The following disassembly (shown by a debugger) of the MySub function shows how a C++ program creates local variables, assigns values, and removes the variables from the stack. It uses the C calling convention:

```
MySub PROC
    push  ebp
    mov   ebp,esp
    sub   esp,8                 ; create locals
    mov   DWORD PTR [ebp-4],10  ; X
    mov   DWORD PTR [ebp-8],20  ; Y
    mov   esp,ebp               ; remove locals from stack
    pop   ebp
    ret
MySub ENDP
```

Figure 8–4 shows the function's stack frame after the local variables are initialized.

Figure 8–4   Stack Frame after Creating Local Variables.

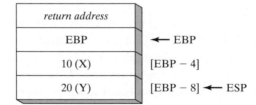

Before finishing, the function resets the stack pointer by assigning it the value of EBP. The effect is to release the local variables from the stack:

```
    mov   esp,ebp               ; remove locals from stack
```

If this step is omitted, the POP EBP instruction would set EBP to 20 and the RET instruction would branch to memory location 10, causing the program to halt with a processor exception. Such is the case in the following version of MySub:

```
MySub PROC
    push  ebp
    mov   ebp,esp
    sub   esp,8                 ; create locals
    mov   DWORD PTR [ebp-4],10  ; X
    mov   DWORD PTR [ebp-8],20  ; Y
    pop   ebp
    ret                         ; return to invalid address!
MySub ENDP
```

Local Variable Symbols   In the interest of making programs easier to read, you can define a symbol for each local variable's offset and use the symbol in your code:

```
X_local  EQU DWORD PTR [ebp-4]
Y_local  EQU DWORD PTR [ebp-8]

MySub PROC
    push  ebp
```

```
        mov     ebp,esp
        sub     esp,8               ; reserve space for locals
        mov     X_local,10          ; X
        mov     Y_local,20          ; Y
        mov     esp,ebp             ; remove locals from stack
        pop     ebp
        ret
MySub ENDP
```

Accessing Reference Parameters

Reference parameters are usually accessed by subroutines using base-offset addressing (from EBP). Because each reference parameter is a pointer, it is usually loaded into a register for use as an indirect operand. Suppose, for example, that a pointer to an array is located at stack address [ebp+12]. The following statement copies the pointer into ESI:

```
    mov esi,[ebp+12]                ; points to the array
```

ArrayFill Example   The **ArrayFill** procedure, which we are about to show, fills an array with a pseudorandom sequence of 16-bit integers. It receives two arguments: a pointer to the array and the array length. The first is passed by reference and the second is passed by value. Here is a sample call:

```
    .data
    count = 100
    array WORD count DUP(?)

    .code
    push    OFFSET array
    push    count
    call    ArrayFill
```

Inside **ArrayFill**, the following prologue code initializes the stack frame pointer (EBP):

```
    ArrayFill PROC
        push    ebp
        mov     ebp,esp
```

Now the stack frame contains the array offset, count, return address, and saved EBP:

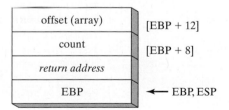

ArrayFill saves the general-purpose registers, retrieves the parameters, and fills the array:

```
    ArrayFill PROC
        push    ebp
        mov     ebp,esp
        pushad                      ; save registers
```

```
        mov    esi,[ebp+12]        ; offset of array
        mov    ecx,[ebp+8]         ; array length
        cmp    ecx,0               ; ECX == 0?
        je     L2                  ; yes: skip over loop
    L1:
        mov    eax,10000h          ; get random 0 — FFFFh
        call   RandomRange         ; from the link library
        mov    [esi],ax            ; insert value in array
        add    esi,TYPE WORD       ; move to next element
        loop   L1
    L2: popad                      ; restore registers
        pop    ebp
        ret    8                   ; clean up the stack
    ArrayFill ENDP
```

LEA Instruction

The LEA instruction returns the effective address of an indirect operand. Because indirect operands contain one or more registers, their offsets are calculated at runtime. To show how LEA can
be used, let's look at the following C++ program, which declares a local array of char and references **myString** when assigning values:

```
void makeArray( )
{
    char myString[30];
    for( int i = 0; i < 30; i++ )
        myString[i] = '*';
}
```

The equivalent code in assembly language allocates space for myString on the stack and assigns
the address to ESI, an indirect operand. Although the array is only 30 bytes, ESP is decremented
by 32 to keep it aligned on a doubleword boundary. Note how LEA is used to assign the array's
address to ESI:

```
    makeArray PROC
        push   ebp
        mov    ebp,esp
        sub    esp,32              ; myString is at EBP−30
        lea    esi,[ebp−30]        ; load address of myString
        mov    ecx,30              ; loop counter
    L1: mov    BYTE PTR [esi],'*'  ; fill one position
        inc    esi                 ; move to next
        loop   L1                  ; continue until ECX = 0
        add    esp,32              ; remove the array (restore ESP)
        pop    ebp
        ret
    makeArray ENDP
```

It is not possible to use OFFSET to get the address of a stack parameter because OFFSET only
works with addresses known at compile time. The following statement would not assemble:

```
        mov    esi,OFFSET [ebp−30]          ; error
```

8.2.4   ENTER and LEAVE Instructions

The ENTER instruction automatically creates a stack frame for a called procedure. It reserves stack space for local variables and saves EBP on the stack. Specifically, it performs three actions:

- Pushes EBP on the stack (*push ebp*)
- Sets EBP to the base of the stack frame (*mov ebp, esp*)
- Reserves space for local variables (*sub esp,numbytes*)

ENTER has two operands: The first is a constant specifying the number of bytes of stack space to reserve for local variables and the second specifies the lexical nesting level of the procedure.

```
ENTER  numbytes, nestinglevel
```

Both operands are immediate values. *Numbytes* is always rounded up to a multiple of 4 to keep ESP on a doubleword boundary. *Nestinglevel* determines the number of stack frame pointers copied into the current stack frame from the stack frame of the calling procedure. In our programs, *nestinglevel* is always zero. The Intel manuals explain how the ENTER instruction supports nesting levels in block-structured languages.

Example 1   The following example declares a procedure with no local variables:

```
MySub PROC
      enter 0,0
```

It is equivalent to the following instructions:

```
MySub PROC
      push  ebp
      mov   ebp,esp
```

Example 2   The ENTER instruction reserves 8 bytes of stack space for local variables:

```
MySub PROC
      enter 8,0
```

It is equivalent to the following instructions:

```
MySub PROC
      push  ebp
      mov   ebp,esp
      sub   esp,8
```

Figure 8–5 shows the stack before and after ENTER has executed.

FIGURE 8–5   Stack Frame before and after ENTER Has Executed.

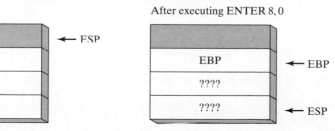

> If you use the ENTER instruction, it is strongly advised that you also use the LEAVE instruction at the end of the same procedure. Otherwise, the stack space you create for local variables might not be released. This would cause the RET instruction to pop the wrong return address off the stack.

LEAVE Instruction   The LEAVE instruction terminates the stack frame for a procedure. It reverses the action of a previous ENTER instruction by restoring ESP and EBP to the values they were assigned when the procedure was called. Using the **MySub** procedure example again, we can write the following:

```
MySub PROC
      enter 8,0
        .
        .
      leave
      ret
MySub ENDP
```

The following equivalent set of instructions reserves and discards 8 bytes of space for local variables:

```
MySub PROC
      push   ebp
      mov    ebp,esp
      sub    esp,8
        .
        .
      mov    esp,ebp
      pop    ebp
      ret
MySub ENDP
```

8.2.5 LOCAL Directive

We can guess that Microsoft created the LOCAL directive as a high-level substitute for the ENTER instruction. LOCAL declares one or more local variables by name, assigning them size attributes. (ENTER, on the other hand, only reserves a single unnamed block of stack space for local variables.) If used, LOCAL must appear on the line immediately following the PROC directive. Its syntax is

```
LOCAL varlist
```

varlist is a list of variable definitions, separated by commas, optionally spanning multiple lines. Each variable definition takes the following form:

```
label:type
```

The label may be any valid identifier, and type can either be a standard type (WORD, DWORD, etc.) or a user-defined type. (Structures and other user-defined types are described in Chapter 10.)

Examples   The **MySub** procedure contains a local variable named **var1** of type BYTE:

```
MySub PROC
      LOCAL var1:BYTE
```

The **BubbleSort** procedure contains a doubleword local variable named **temp** and a variable named **SwapFlag** of type BYTE:

```
BubbleSort PROC
      LOCAL temp:DWORD, SwapFlag:BYTE
```

The **Merge** procedure contains a PTR WORD local variable named **pArray**, which is a pointer to a 16-bit integer:

```
Merge PROC
      LOCAL pArray:PTR WORD
```

The local variable **TempArray** is an array of 10 doublewords. Note the use of brackets to show the array size:

```
LOCAL TempArray[10]:DWORD
```

MASM Code Generation

It's a good idea to look at the code generated by MASM when the LOCAL directive is used, by looking at a disassembly. The following **Example1** procedure has a single doubleword local variable:

```
Example1 PROC
      LOCAL temp:DWORD

      mov    eax,temp
      ret
Example1 ENDP
```

MASM generates the following code for Example1, showing how ESP is decremented by 4 to leave space for the doubleword variable:

```
push  ebp
mov   ebp,esp
add   esp,0FFFFFFFCh            ; add −4 to ESP
mov   eax,[ebp−4]
leave
ret
```

Here is a diagram of Example1's stack frame:

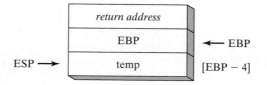

Non-Doubleword Local Variables

The LOCAL directive has interesting behavior when you declare local variables of differing sizes. Each is allocated space according to its size: An 8-bit variable is assigned to the next available byte, a 16-bit variable is assigned to the next even address (word-aligned), and a 32-bit variable is allocated the next doubleword aligned boundary.

Let's look at a few examples. First, the **Example1** procedure contains a local variable named
var1 of type BYTE:

```
Example1 PROC
    LOCAL var1:BYTE

    mov   al,var1              ; [EBP − 1]
    ret
Example1 ENDP
```

Because stack offsets default to 32 bits, one might expect **var1** to be located at EBP −4. Instead, as
shown in Figure 8–6, MASM decrements ESP by 4 and places **var1** at EBP −1, leaving the three
bytes below it unused (marked by the letters *nu*, which indicate *not used.*). In the figure, each block
represents a single byte.

FIGURE 8–6   Creating Space for Local Variables (Example 1 Procedure).

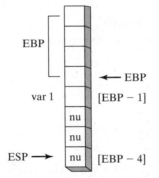

The **Example2** procedure contains a doubleword followed by a byte:

```
Example2 PROC
    LOCAL temp:DWORD, SwapFlag:BYTE
    ;
    ret
Example2 ENDP
```

The following code is generated by MASM for Example2. The ADD instruction adds −8 to ESP,
creating an opening in the stack between ESP and EBP for the two local variables:

```
push  ebp
mov   ebp,esp
add   esp,0FFFFFFF8h       ; add −8 to ESP
mov   eax,[ebp−4]          ; temp
mov   bl,[ebp−5]           ; SwapFlag
leave
ret
```

Though **SwapFlag** is only a byte, ESP is rounded downward to the next doubleword stack location.
A detailed view of the stack, shown as individual bytes in Figure 8–7, shows the exact location of
SwapFlag and the unused space below it (labeled *nu*). In the figure, each block equals a single byte.

Reserving Extra Stack Space   If you plan to create arrays larger than a few hundred bytes
as local variables, be sure to reserve adequate space for the runtime stack, using the STACK

FIGURE 8–7   Creating Space in Example 2 for Local Variables.

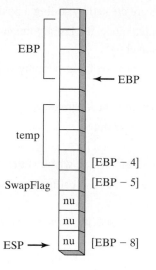

directive. In the **Irvine32.inc** library file, for example, we reserve 4096 bytes of stack space:

```
.STACK 4096
```

If procedure calls are nested, the runtime stack must be large enough to hold the sum of all local variables active at any point in the program's execution. For example, suppose **Sub1** calls **Sub2** and **Sub2** calls **Sub3**. Each might have a local array variable:

```
Sub1 PROC
     LOCAL array1[50]:DWORD      ; 200 bytes
.
.
.
Sub2 PROC
     LOCAL array2[80]:WORD       ; 160 bytes
.
.
.
Sub3 PROC
     LOCAL array3[300]:BYTE      ; 300 bytes
```

When the program enters **Sub3,** the runtime stack holds local variables from **Sub1**, **Sub2**, and **Sub3**. The stack will require 660 bytes used by local variables, plus the two procedure return addresses (8 bytes), plus any registers that might have been pushed on the stack within the procedures. If a procedure is called recursively, the stack space it uses will be approximately the size of its local variables and parameters multiplied by the estimated depth of the recursion. We discuss recursion in Section 8.3.

8.2.6   Section Review

1. *(True/False):* A subroutine's stack frame always contains the caller's return address and the subroutine's local variables.

2. *(True/False):* Arrays are passed by reference to avoid copying them onto the stack.

3. *(True/False):* A procedure's prologue code always pushes EBP on the stack.

4. *(True/False):* Local variables are created by adding a positive value to the stack pointer.

5. *(True/False):* In 32-bit protected mode, the last argument to be pushed on the stack in a procedure call is stored at location ebp+8.

6. *(True/False):* Passing by reference requires popping a parameter's offset from the stack inside the called procedure.

7. What are the two common types of stack parameters?

8. Which statements belong in a procedure's epilogue when the procedure has stack parameters and local variables?

9. When a C function returns a 32-bit integer, where is the return value stored?

10. How does a program using the STDCALL calling convention clean up the stack after a procedure call?

11. Here is a calling sequence for a procedure named **AddThree** that adds three doublewords (assume STDCALL):

```
push 10h
push 20h
push 30h
call AddThree
```

Draw a picture of the procedure's stack frame immediately after EBP has been pushed on the stack.

12. How is the LEA instruction more powerful than the OFFSET operator?

13. In the C++ example shown in Section 8.2.3, how much stack space is used by a variable of type *int*?

14. Write statements in the **AddThree** procedure (from question 11) that calculate the sum of the three stack parameters.

15. How is an 8-bit character argument passed to a procedure that expects a 32-bit integer parameter?

16. Declare a local variable named **pArray** that is a pointer to an array of doublewords.

17. Declare a local variable named **buffer** that is an array of 20 bytes.

18. Declare a local variable named **pwArray** that points to a 16-bit unsigned integer.

19. Declare a local variable named **myByte** that holds an 8-bit signed integer.

20. Declare a local variable named **myArray** that is an array of 20 doublewords.

21. *Discussion:* What advantages might the C calling convention have over the STDCALL calling convention?

8.3 Recursion

A *recursive* subroutine is one that calls itself, either directly or indirectly. *Recursion*, the practice of calling recursive subroutines, can be a powerful tool when working with data structures that have repeating patterns. Examples are linked lists and various types of connected graphs where a program must retrace its path.

Endless Recursion   The most obvious type of recursion occurs when a subroutine calls itself. The following program, for example, has a procedure named **Endless** that calls itself repeatedly without ever stopping:

```
TITLE Endless Recursion                    (Endless.asm)

INCLUDE Irvine32.inc
.data
endlessStr BYTE "This recursion never stops",0
.code
main PROC
    call  Endless
    exit
main ENDP

Endless PROC
    mov   edx,OFFSET endlessStr
    call  WriteString
    call  Endless
    ret                          ; never executes
Endless ENDP
END main
```

Of course, this example doesn't have any practical value. Each time the procedure calls itself, it uses up 4 bytes of stack space when the CALL instruction pushes the return address. The RET instruction is never executed.

> If you have access to a performance-monitoring utility such as the Windows Task manager, open it and have it display the current CPU usage. Then build and run the *Endless.asm* program from the chapter examples. The program will use a large percentage of CPU resources, overflow the runtime stack, and halt.

8.3.1   Recursively Calculating a Sum

Useful recursive subroutines always contain a terminating condition. When the terminating condition becomes true, the stack unwinds when the program executes all pending RET instructions. To illustrate, let's consider the recursive procedure named **CalcSum**, which sums the integers 1 to n, where n is an input parameter passed in ECX. CalcSum returns the sum in EAX:

```
TITLE Sum of Integers             (CSum.asm)

INCLUDE Irvine32.inc
.code
main PROC
    mov   ecx,5              ; count = 5
    mov   eax,0              ; holds the sum
    call CalcSum             ; calculate sum
L1: call WriteDec            ; display EAX
    call Crlf                ; new line
    exit
main ENDP
;--------------------------------------------------------
CalcSum PROC
; Calculates the sum of a list of integers
```

```
; Receives: ECX = count
; Returns:  EAX = sum
;--------------------------------------------------
      cmp    ecx,0              ; check counter value
      jz     L2                 ; quit if zero
      add    eax,ecx            ; otherwise, add to sum
      dec    ecx                ; decrement counter
      call   CalcSum            ; recursive call
L2:   ret
CalcSum ENDP
end Main
```

The first two lines of **CalcSum** check the counter and exit the procedure when ECX = 0. The code bypasses further recursive calls. When the RET instruction is reached for the first time, it returns to the previous call to CalcSum, which returns to *its* previous call, and so on. Table 8-1 shows the return addresses (as labels) pushed on the stack by the CALL instruction, along with the concurrent values of ECX (counter) and EAX (sum).

Table 8-1   Stack Frame and Registers (CalcSum).

Pushed on Stack	Value in ECX	Value in EAX
L1	5	0
L2	4	5
L2	3	9
L2	2	12
L2	1	14
L2	0	15

Even a simple recursive procedure makes ample use of the stack. At the very minimum, four bytes of stack space are used up each time a procedure call takes place because the return address must be saved on the stack.

8.3.2   Calculating a Factorial

Recursive subroutines often store temporary data in stack parameters. When the recursive calls unwind, the data saved on the stack can be useful. The next example we will look at calculates the factorial of an integer n. The *factorial* algorithm calculates $n!$, where n is an unsigned integer. The first time the **factorial** function is called, the parameter n is the starting number, shown here programmed in C/C++/Java syntax:

```
int function factorial(int n)
{
    if(n == 0)
      return 1;
    else
      return n * factorial(n-1);
}
```

Given any number n, we assume we can calculate the factorial of $n - 1$. If so, we can continue to reduce n until it equals zero. By definition, 0! equals 1. In the process of backing up to the original expression $n!$, we accumulate the product of each multiplication. For example, to calculate 5!, the recursive algorithm descends along the left column of Figure 8–8 and backs up along the right column.

FIGURE 8–8   Recursive Calls to the Factorial Function.

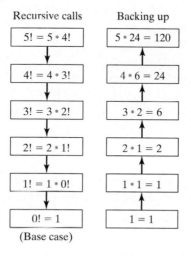

Example Program   The following assembly language program contains a procedure named **Factorial** that uses recursion to calculate a factorial. We pass n (an unsigned integer between 0 and 12) on the stack to the **Factorial** procedure, and a value is returned in EAX. Because EAX is a 32-bit register, the largest factorial it can hold is 12! (479,001,600).

```
TITLE Calculating a Factorial (Fact.asm)

INCLUDE Irvine32.inc
.code
main PROC
      push 5                        ; calc 5!
      call  Factorial               ; calculate factorial (EAX)
      call  WriteDec                ; display it
      call  Crlf
      exit
main ENDP

;---------------------------------------------------
Factorial PROC
; Calculates a factorial.
; Receives: [ebp+8] = n, the number to calculate
; Returns: eax = the factorial of n
;---------------------------------------------------
      push  ebp
      mov   ebp,esp
```

```
        mov    eax, [ebp+8]          ; get n
        cmp    eax, 0                ; n > 0?
        ja     L1                    ; yes: continue
        mov    eax, 1                ; no: return 1 as the value of 0!
        jmp    L2                    ; and return to the caller
L1:     dec    eax
        push   eax                   ; Factorial(n−1)
        call   Factorial
; Instructions from this point on execute when each
; recursive call returns.
ReturnFact:
        mov    ebx, [ebp+8]          ; get n
        mul    ebx                   ; EDX:EAX = EAX * EBX
L2:     pop    ebp                   ; return EAX
        ret    4                     ; clean up stack
Factorial ENDP
END main
```

Let's examine the Factorial procedure more closely by tracking a call to it with an initial value of N = 3. As documented in its specifications, Factorial assigns its return value to the EAX register:

```
push 3
call Factorial                       ; EAX = 3!
```

The Factorial procedure receives one stack parameter, N, which is the starting value that determines which factorial to calculate. The calling program's return address is automatically pushed on the stack by the CALL instruction. The first thing Factorial does is to push EBP on the stack, to save the base pointer to the calling program's stack:

```
Factorial PROC
      push  ebp
```

Next, it must set EBP to the beginning of the current stack frame:

```
      mov   ebp, esp
```

Now that EBP and ESP both point to the top of the stack, the runtime stack contains the following stack frame. It contains the parameter N, the caller's return address, and the saved value of EBP:

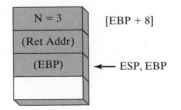

The same diagram shows that in order to retrieve the value of N from the stack and load it into EAX, the code must add 8 to the value of EBP, using base-offset addressing:

```
      mov   eax, [ebp+8]            ; get n
```

Next, the code checks the *base case*, the condition that stops the recursion. If N (currently in EAX) equals zero, the function returns 1, defined as 0!

```
cmp    eax,0                    ; is n > 0?
ja     L1                       ; yes: continue
mov    eax,1                    ; no: return 1 as the value of 0!
jmp    L2                       ; and return to the caller
```

(We will examine the code at label L2 later.) Since the value in EAX is currently equal to 3, Factorial will call itself recursively. First, it subtracts 1 from N and pushes the new value on the stack. This value is the parameter that is passed with the new call to Factorial:

```
L1:    dec    eax
       push   eax                ; Factorial(n - 1)
       call   Factorial
```

Execution now transfers to the first line of Factorial, with a new value of N:

```
Factorial PROC
       push   ebp
       mov    ebp,esp
```

The runtime stack now holds a second stack frame, with N equal to 2:

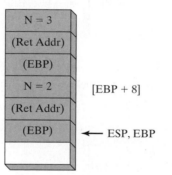

The value of N, which is now 2, is loaded into EAX and compared to zero.

```
mov    eax,[ebp+8]              ; N = 2 at this point
cmp    eax,0                    ; compare N to zero
ja     L1                       ; still greater than zero
mov    eax,1                    ; not executed
jmp    L2                       ; not executed
```

It is greater than zero, so execution continues at label L1.

> *Tip:* You may have observed that the previous value of EAX, assigned during the first call to Factorial, was just overwritten by a new value. This illustrates an important point: when making recursive calls to a procedure, you should take careful note of which registers are overwritten. If you need to save any of these register values, push them on the stack before making the recursive call, and then pop them back off the stack after returning from the call. Fortunately, in the current situation we are not concerned with saving the contents of EAX across recursive procedure calls.

At L1, we are about to use a recursive procedure call to get the factorial of N − 1. The code subtracts 1 from EAX, pushes it on the stack, and calls Factorial:

```
L1:   dec   eax                 ; N = 1
      push  eax                 ; Factorial(1)
      call  Factorial
```

Now, entering Factorial a third time, three stack frames are active:

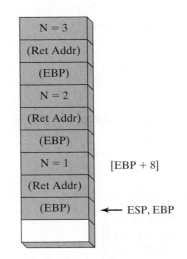

The Factorial procedure compares N to 0, and on finding that N is greater than zero, calls Factorial one more time with N = 0. The runtime stack now contains its fourth stack frame as it enters the Factorial procedure for the last time:

When Factorial is called with N = 0, things get interesting. The following statements cause a branch to label L2. The value 1 is assigned to EAX because 0! = 1, and EAX must be assigned Factorial's return value:

```
        mov    eax,[ebp+8]          ; EAX = 0
        cmp    eax,0                ; is n > 0?
        ja     L1                   ; yes: continue
        mov    eax,1                ; no: return 1 as the value of 0!
        jmp    L2                   ; and return to the caller
```

The following statements at label L2 cause Factorial to return to where it was last called:

```
L2:    pop    ebp                   ; return EAX
       ret    4                     ; clean up stack
```

At this point, the following figure shows that the most recent frame is no longer in the runtime stack, and EAX contains 1 (the factorial of Zero):

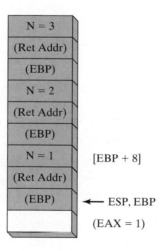

The following lines are the return point from the call to Factorial. They take the current value of N (stored on the stack at EBP+8), multiply it against EAX (the value returned by the call to Factorial). The product in EAX is now the return value of this iteration of Factorial:

```
ReturnFact:
        mov    ebx,[ebp+8]          ; get n
        mul    ebx                  ; EAX = EAX * EBX
L2:     pop    ebp                   ; return EAX
        ret    4                     ; clean up stack
Factorial ENDP
```

(The upper half of the product in EDX is all zeros, and is ignored.) Therefore, the first time the foregoing lines are reached, EAX is assigned the product of the expression 1 × 1. As the RET statement executes, another frame is removed from the stack:

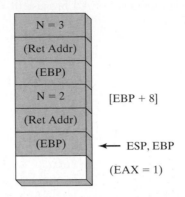

Again, the statements following the CALL instruction execute, multiplying N (which now equals 2) by the value in EAX (equal to 1):

```
ReturnFact:
      mov    ebx,[ebp+8]          ; get n
      mul    ebx                  ; EDX:EAX = EAX * EBX
L2:   pop    ebp                  ; return EAX
      ret    4                    ; clean up stack
Factorial ENDP
```

With EAX now equal to 2, the RET statement removes another frame from the stack:

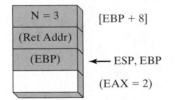

Finally, the statements following the CALL instruction execute one last time, multiplying N (equal to 3) by the value in EAX (equal to 2):

```
ReturnFact:
      mov    ebx,[ebp+8]          ; get n
      mul    ebx                  ; EDX:EAX = EAX * EBX
L2:   pop    ebp                  ; return EAX
      ret    4                    ; clean up stack
Factorial ENDP
```

The return value in EAX, 6, is the computed value of 3 factorial. This was the calculation we sought when first calling Factorial. The last stack frame disappears when the RET statement executes.

8.3.3 Section Review

1. *(True/False):* Given the same task to accomplish, a recursive subroutine usually uses less memory than a nonrecursive one.

2. In the Factorial function, what condition terminates the recursion?

3. Which instructions in the assembly language Factorial procedure execute after each recursive call has finished?

4. What would happen to the Factorial program's output if you tried to calculate 13!?

5. *Challenge:* How many bytes of stack space would be used by the Factorial procedure when calculating 5!?

6. *Challenge:* Write pseudocode for a recursive algorithm that generates 20 consecutive integers of the Fibonacci series, beginning with 1 (1, 1, 2, 3, 5, 8, 13, 21, . . .).

8.4   INVOKE, ADDR, PROC, and PROTO

The INVOKE, ADDR, PROC, and PROTO directives provide powerful tools for defining and calling procedures. In many ways, they approach the convenience offered by high-level programming languages. From a pedagogical point of view, their use is controversial because they mask the underlying structure of the runtime stack. Students learning computer fundamentals are best served by developing a detailed understanding of the low-level mechanics involved in subroutine calls.

There is a situation in which using advanced procedure directives leads to better programming—when your program executes procedure calls across module boundaries. In such cases, the PROTO directive helps the assembler to validate procedure calls by checking argument lists against procedure declarations. This feature encourages advanced assembly language programmers to take advantage of the convenience offered by advanced MASM directives.

8.4.1   INVOKE Directive

The INVOKE directive pushes arguments on the stack (in the order specified by the MODEL directive's language specifier) and calls a procedure. INVOKE is a convenient replacement for the CALL instruction because it lets you pass multiple arguments using a single line of code. Here is the general syntax:

```
INVOKE procedureName [, argumentList]
```

ArgumentList is an optional comma-delimited list of arguments passed to the procedure. Using the CALL instruction, for example, we could call a procedure named DumpArray after executing several PUSH instructions:

```
push  TYPE array
push  LENGTHOF array
push  OFFSET array
call  DumpArray
```

The equivalent statement using INVOKE is reduced to a single line in which the arguments are listed in reverse order (assuming STDCALL is in effect):

```
INVOKE DumpArray, OFFSET array, LENGTHOF array, TYPE array
```

INVOKE permits almost any number of arguments, and individual arguments can appear on separate source code lines. The following INVOKE statement includes helpful comments:

```
INVOKE DumpArray,              ; displays an array
       OFFSET array,           ; points to the array
```

```
        LENGTHOF array,              ; the array length
        TYPE array                  ; array component size
```

Argument types are listed in Table 8-2.

Table 8-2   Argument Types Used with INVOKE.

Type	Examples
Immediate value	10, 3000h, OFFSET mylist, TYPE array
Integer expression	(10 * 20), COUNT
Variable	myList, array, myWord, myDword
Address expression	[myList+2], [ebx + esi]
Register	eax, bl, edi
ADDR name	ADDR myList
OFFSET name	OFFSET myList

EAX, EDX Overwritten   If you pass arguments smaller than 32 bits to a procedure, INVOKE frequently causes the assembler to overwrite EAX and EDX when it widens the arguments before pushing them on the stack. You can avoid this behavior by always passing 32-bit arguments to INVOKE, or you can save and restore EAX and EDX before and after the procedure call.

8.4.2   ADDR Operator

The ADDR operator can be used to pass a pointer argument when calling a procedure using INVOKE. The following INVOKE statement, for example, passes the address of **myArray** to the **FillArray** procedure:

```
    INVOKE FillArray, ADDR myArray
```

The argument passed to ADDR must be an assembly time constant. The following is an error:

```
    INVOKE mySub, ADDR [ebp+12]      ; error
```

The ADDR operator can only be used in conjunction with INVOKE. The following is an error:

```
    mov  esi, ADDR myArray           ; error
```

Example   The following INVOKE directive calls **Swap**, passing it the addresses of the first two elements in an array of doublewords:

```
    .data
    Array DWORD 20 DUP(?)
    .code
    ...
    INVOKE Swap,
        ADDR  Array,
        ADDR  [Array+4]
```

Here is the corresponding code generated by the assembler, assuming STDCALL is in effect:

```
    push  OFFSET Array+4
    push  OFFSET Array
    call  Swap
```

8.4.3 PROC Directive

Syntax of the PROC Directive

The PROC directive has the following basic syntax:

```
label PROC [attributes] [USES reglist], parameter_list
```

Label is a user-defined label following the rules for identifiers explained in Chapter 3. *Attributes* refers to any of the following:

```
[distance] [langtype] [visibility] [prologue]
```

Table 8-3 describes each of the attributes.

Table 8-3   Attributes Field in the PROC Directive.

Attribute	Description
distance	NEAR or FAR. Indicates the type of RET instruction (RET or RETF) generated by the assembler.
langtype	Specifies the calling convention (parameter passing convention) such as C, PASCAL, or STDCALL. Overrides the language specified in the .MODEL directive.
visibility	Indicates the procedure's visibility to other modules. Choices are PRIVATE, PUBLIC (default), and EXPORT. If the visibility is EXPORT, the linker places the procedure's name in the export table for segmented executables. EXPORT also enables PUBLIC visibility.
prologue	Specifies arguments affecting generation of prologue and epilogue code. See the section entitled "User-Defined Prologue and Epilogue Code" in the MASM 6.1 Programmers Guide, Chapter 7.

Parameter Lists

The PROC directive permits you to declare a procedure with a comma-separated list of named parameters. Your implementation code can refer to the parameters by name rather than by calculated stack offsets such as [ebp+8]:

```
label PROC [attributes] [USES reglist],
    parameter_1,
    parameter_2,
    .
    .
    parameter_n
```

The comma following PROC can be omitted if the parameter list appears on the same line:

```
label PROC [attributes], parameter_1, parameter_2, ..., parameter_n
```

A single parameter has the following syntax:

```
paramName: type
```

ParamName is an arbitrary name you assign to the parameter. Its scope is limited to the current procedure (called *local scope*). The same parameter name can be used in more than one procedure, but it cannot be the name of a global variable or code label. *Type* can be one of the following:

BYTE, SBYTE, WORD, SWORD, DWORD, SDWORD, FWORD, QWORD, or TBYTE. It can also be a *qualified type*, which may be a pointer to an existing type. Following are examples of qualified types:

PTR BYTE	PTR SBYTE
PTR WORD	PTR SWORD
PTR DWORD	PTR SDWORD
PTR QWORD	PTR TBYTE

Though it is possible to add NEAR and FAR attributes to these expressions, they are relevant only in more specialized applications. Qualified types can also be created using the TYPEDEF and STRUCT directives, which we explain in Chapter 10.

Example 1   The AddTwo procedure receives two doubleword values and returns their sum in EAX:

```
AddTwo PROC,
     val1:DWORD,
     val2:DWORD
     mov   eax,val1
     add   eax,val2
     ret
AddTwo ENDP
```

The assembly language generated by MASM when assembling AddTwo shows how the parameter names are translated into offsets from EBP. A constant operand is appended to the RET instruction because STDCALL is in effect:

```
AddTwo PROC
     push  ebp
     mov   ebp, esp
     mov   eax,dword ptr [ebp+8]
     add   eax,dword ptr [ebp+0Ch]
     leave
     ret   8
AddTwo ENDP
```

Note: It would be just as correct to substitute the ENTER 0,0 instruction in place of the following statements in the AddTwo procedure:

```
push  ebp
mov   ebp,esp
```

> *Tip:* The complete details of MASM-generated procedure code do not appear in listing files (.LST extension). Instead, open your program with a debugger and view the Disassembly window.

Example 2   The FillArray procedure receives a pointer to an array of bytes:

```
FillArray PROC,
     pArray:PTR BYTE
     . . .
FillArray ENDP
```

Example 3   The Swap procedure receives two pointers to doublewords:

```
Swap PROC,
     pValX:PTR DWORD,
     pValY:PTR DWORD
     . . .
Swap ENDP
```

Example 4   The Read_File procedure receives a byte pointer named **pBuffer**. It has a local doubleword variable named **fileHandle**, and it saves two registers on the stack (EAX and EBX):

```
Read_File PROC USES eax ebx,
     pBuffer:PTR BYTE
     LOCAL fileHandle:DWORD

     mov    esi,pBuffer
     mov    fileHandle,eax
     .
     .
     ret
Read_File ENDP
```

The MASM-generated code for Read_File shows how space is reserved on the stack for the local variable (fileHandle) before pushing EAX and EBX (specified in the USES clause):

```
Read_File PROC
     push  ebp
     mov   ebp,esp
     add   esp,0FFFFFFFCh          ; create fileHandle
     push  eax                     ; save EAX
     push  ebx                     ; save EBX
     mov   esi,dword ptr [ebp+8]   ; pBuffer
     mov   dword ptr [ebp-4],eax   ; fileHandle
     pop   ebx
     pop   eax
     leave
     ret   4
Read_File ENDP
```

Note: Although Microsoft chose not to do so, another way to begin the generated code for Read_File would have been this:

```
Read_File PROC
     enter  4,0
     push   eax
     (etc.)
```

The ENTER instruction saves EBP, sets it to the value of the stack pointer, and reserves space for the local variable.

RET Instruction Modified by PROC   When PROC is used with one or more parameters and STDCALL is the default protocol, MASM generates the following entry and exit code, assuming PROC has *n* parameters:

```
push   ebp
mov    ebp,esp
   .
   .
   .
leave
ret    (n*4)
```

The constant appearing in the RET instruction is the number of parameters multiplied by 4 (because each parameter is a doubleword). The STDCALL convention is the default when you INCLUDE Irvine32.inc, and it is the calling convention used for all Windows API function calls.

Specifying the Parameter Passing Protocol

A program might call Irvine32 library procedures and in turn contain procedures that can be called from C++ programs. To provide this flexibility, the *attributes* field of the PROC directive lets you specify the language convention for passing parameters. It overrides the default language convention specified in the .MODEL directive. The following example declares a procedure with the C calling convention:

```
Example1 PROC C,
      parm1:DWORD, parm2:DWORD
```

If we execute Example1 using INVOKE, the assembler generates code consistent with the C calling convention. Similarly, if we declare Example1 using STDCALL, INVOKE generates consistent with that language convention:

```
Example1 PROC STDCALL,
      parm1:DWORD, parm2:DWORD
```

8.4.4   PROTO Directive

The PROTO directive creates a prototype for an existing procedure. A *prototype* declares a procedure's name and parameter list. It allows you to call a procedure before defining it and to verify that the number and types of arguments match the procedure definition. (The C and C++ languages use function prototypes to validate function calls at compile time.)

MASM requires a prototype for each procedure called by INVOKE. PROTO must appear first before INVOKE. In other words, the standard ordering of these directives is

```
MySub PROTO                        ; procedure prototype
   .
INVOKE MySub                       ; procedure call
   .
MySub PROC                         ; procedure implementation
   .
   .
MySub ENDP
```

An alternative scenario is possible: The procedure implementation can appear in the program prior to the location of the INVOKE statement for that procedure. In that case, PROC acts as its own prototype:

```
MySub PROC                         ; procedure definition
   .
```

```
          .
MySub ENDP
          .
INVOKE MySub                            ; procedure call
```

Assuming you have already written a particular procedure, you can easily create its prototype by copying the PROC statement and making the following changes:

• Change the word PROC to PROTO.
• Remove the USES operator if any, along with its register list.

For example, suppose we have already created the **ArraySum** procedure:

```
ArraySum PROC USES esi ecx,
      ptrArray:PTR DWORD,               ; points to the array
      szArray:DWORD                     ; array size
      ; (remaining lines omitted...)
ArraySum ENDP
```

This is a matching PROTO declaration:

```
ArraySum PROTO,
      ptrArray:PTR DWORD,               ; points to the array
      szArray:DWORD                     ; array size
```

The PROTO directive lets you override the default parameter passing protocol in the .MODEL directive. It must be consistent with the procedure's PROC declaration:

```
Example1 PROTO C,
      parm1:DWORD, parm2:DWORD
```

Assembly Time Argument Checking

The PROTO directive helps the assembler compare a list of arguments in a procedure call to the procedure's definition. The error checking is not as precise as you would find in languages like C and C++. Instead, MASM checks for the correct number of parameters, and to a limited extent, matches argument types to parameter types. Suppose, for example, the prototype for **Sub1** is declared thus:

```
Sub1 PROTO, p1:BYTE, p2:WORD, p3:PTR BYTE
```

We will define the following variables:

```
.data
byte_1  BYTE  10h
word_1  WORD  2000h
word_2  WORD  3000h
dword_1 DWORD 12345678h
```

The following is a valid call to Sub1:

```
INVOKE Sub1, byte_1, word_1, ADDR byte_1
```

The code generated by MASM for this INVOKE shows arguments pushed on the stack in reverse order:

```
push  404000h                          ; ptr to byte_1
sub   esp,2                            ; pad stack with 2 bytes
push  word ptr ds:[00404001h]          ; value of word_1
```

```
mov   al,byte ptr ds:[00404000h]  ; value of byte_1
push  eax
call  00401071
```

EAX is overwritten, and the **sub esp,2** instruction pads the subsequent stack entry to 32 bits.

Errors Detected by MASM   If an argument exceeds the size of a declared parameter, MASM generates an error:

```
INVOKE Sub1, word_1, word_2, ADDR byte_1; arg 1 error
```

MASM generates errors if we invoke Sub1 using too few or too many arguments:

```
INVOKE Sub1, byte_1, word_2        ; error: too few arguments
INVOKE Sub1, byte_1,               ; error: too many arguments
    word_2, ADDR byte_1, word_2
```

Errors Not Detected by MASM   If an argument's type is smaller than a declared parameter, MASM does not detect an error:

```
INVOKE Sub1, byte_1, byte_1, ADDR byte_1
```

Instead, MASM expands the smaller argument to the size of the declared parameter. In the following code generated by our INVOKE example, the second argument (byte_1) is expanded into EAX before pushing it on the stack:

```
push   404000h                     ; addr of byte_1
mov    al,byte ptr ds:[00404000h]  ; value of byte_1
movzx  eax,al                      ; expand into EAX
push   eax                         ; push on stack
mov    al,byte ptr ds:[00404000h]  ; value of byte_1
push   eax                         ; push on stack
call   00401071                    ; call Sub1
```

If a doubleword is passed when a pointer was expected, no error is detected. This type of error usually leads to a runtime error when the subroutine tries to use the stack parameter as a pointer:

```
INVOKE Sub1, byte_1, word_2, dword_1       ; no error detected
```

ArraySum Example

Let's review the **ArraySum** procedure from Chapter 5, which calculates the sum of an array of doublewords. Originally, we passed arguments in registers; now we can use the PROC directive to declare stack parameters:

```
ArraySum PROC USES esi ecx,
    ptrArray:PTR DWORD,            ; points to the array
    szArray:DWORD                  ; array size

    mov   esi,ptrArray            ; address of the array
    mov   ecx,szArray             ; size of the array
    mov   eax,0                   ; set the sum to zero
    cmp   ecx,0                   ; length = zero?
    je    L2                      ; yes: quit
```

```
L1:  add    eax,[esi]            ; add each integer to sum
     add    esi,4                ; point to next integer
     loop  L1                    ; repeat for array size
L2:  ret                         ; sum is in EAX
ArraySum ENDP
```

The INVOKE statement calls **ArraySum**, passing the address of an array and the number of elements in the array:

```
.data
array DWORD 10000h,20000h,30000h,40000h,50000h
theSum DWORD   ?
.code
main PROC
    INVOKE ArraySum,
        ADDR array,            ; address of the array
        LENGTHOF array         ; number of elements
    mov theSum,eax             ; store the sum
```

8.4.5 Parameter Classifications

Procedure parameters are usually classified according to the direction of data transfer between the calling program and the called procedure:

- *Input:* An input parameter is data passed by a calling program to a procedure. The called procedure is not expected to modify the corresponding parameter variable, and even if it does, the modification is confined to the procedure itself.
- *Output:* An output parameter is created when a calling program passes the address of a variable to a procedure. The procedure uses the address to locate and assign data to the variable. The Win32 Console Library, for example, has a function named **ReadConsole** that reads a string of characters from the keyboard. The calling program passes a pointer to a string buffer, into which ReadConsole stores text typed by the user:

```
.data
buffer BYTE 80 DUP(?)
inputHandle DWORD ?
.code
INVOKE ReadConsole, inputHandle, ADDR buffer,
    (etc.)
```

- *Input-Output:* An input-output parameter is identical to an output parameter, with one exception: The called procedure expects the variable referenced by the parameter to contain some data. The procedure is also expected to modify the variable via the pointer.

8.4.6 Example: Exchanging Two Integers

The following program exchanges the contents of two 32-bit integers. The Swap procedure has two input-output parameters named **pValX** and **pValY**, which contain the addresses of data to be exchanged:

```
TITLE Swap Procedure Example                    (Swap.asm)

INCLUDE Irvine32.inc
Swap PROTO, pValX:PTR DWORD, pValY:PTR DWORD
```

```
    .data
    Array DWORD 10000h,20000h

    .code
    main PROC
        ; Display the array before the exchange:
        mov   esi,OFFSET Array
        mov   ecx,2                   ; count = 2
        mov   ebx,TYPE Array
        call  DumpMem                 ; dump the array values

        INVOKE Swap, ADDR Array, ADDR [Array+4]

        ; Display the array after the exchange:
        call  DumpMem
        exit
    main ENDP

;----------------------------------------------------------
Swap PROC USES eax esi edi,
        pValX:PTR DWORD,              ; pointer to first integer
        pValY:PTR DWORD               ; pointer to second integer
;
; Exchange the values of two 32-bit integers
; Returns: nothing
;----------------------------------------------------------
        mov   esi,pValX               ; get pointers
        mov   edi,pValY
        mov   eax,[esi]               ; get first integer
        xchg  eax,[edi]               ; exchange with second
        mov   [esi],eax               ; replace first integer
        ret                           ; PROC generates RET 8 here
Swap ENDP
END main
```

The two parameters in the Swap procedure, **pValX** and **pValY**, are input-output parameters. Their existing values are *input* to the procedure, and their new values are also *output* from the procedure. Because we're using PROC with parameters, the assembler changes the RET instruction at the end of Swap to **RET 8** (assuming STDCALL is the calling convention).

8.4.7   Debugging Tips

In this section, we call attention to a few common errors encountered when passing arguments to procedures in assembly language. We hope you never make these mistakes.

Argument Size Mismatch

Array addresses are based on the sizes of their elements. To address the second element of a doubleword array, for example, one adds 4 to the array's starting address. Suppose we call **Swap** from Section 8.4.6, passing pointers to the first two elements of **DoubleArray**. If we incorrectly calculate the address of the second element as **DoubleArray + 1**, the resulting hexadecimal values in **DoubleArray** after calling **Swap** are incorrect:

```
.data
DoubleArray DWORD 10000h,20000h
.code
INVOKE Swap, ADDR [DoubleArray + 0], ADDR [DoubleArray + 1]
```

Passing the Wrong Type of Pointer

When using INVOKE, remember that the assembler does not validate the type of pointer you pass to a procedure. For example, the **Swap** procedure from Section 8.4.6 expects to receive two doubleword pointers. Suppose we inadvertently pass it pointers to bytes:

```
.data
ByteArray BYTE 10h,20h,30h,40h,50h,60h,70h,80h
.code
INVOKE Swap, ADDR [ByteArray + 0], ADDR [ByteArray + 1]
```

The program will assemble and run, but when ESI and EDI are dereferenced, 32-bit values are exchanged.

Passing Immediate Values

If a procedure has a reference parameter, do not pass an immediate argument. Consider the following procedure, which has a single reference parameter:

```
Sub2 PROC, dataPtr:PTR WORD
    mov   esi,dataPtr        ; get the address
    mov   WORD PTR [esi],0    ; dereference, assign zero
    ret
Sub2 ENDP
```

The following INVOKE statement assembles but causes a runtime error. The **Sub2** procedure receives 1000h as a pointer value and dereferences memory location 1000h:

```
INVOKE  Sub2, 1000h
```

The example is likely to cause a general protection fault, because memory location 1000h is not within the program's data segment.

8.4.8 WriteStackFrame Procedure

The book's link library contains a useful procedure named WriteStackFrame that displays the contents of the current procedure's stack frame. It shows the procedure's stack parameters, return address, local variables, and saved registers. It was generously provided by Professor James Brink of Pacific Lutheran University. Here is the prototype:

```
WriteStackFrame PROTO,
    numParam:DWORD,          ; number of passed parameters
    numLocalVal: DWORD,      ; number of DWordLocal variables
    numSavedReg: DWORD       ; number of saved registers
```

Here's an excerpt from a program that demonstrates WriteStackFrame:

```
main PROC
      mov eax, 0EAEAEAEAh
      mov ebx, 0EBEBEBEBh
      INVOKE myProc, 1111h, 2222h ; pass two integer arguments
      exit
main ENDP

myProc PROC USES eax ebx,
      x: DWORD, y: DWORD
      LOCAL a:DWORD, b:DWORD

      PARAMS = 2
      LOCALS = 2
      SAVED_REGS = 2
      mov a,0AAAAh
      mov b,0BBBBh
      INVOKE WriteStackFrame, PARAMS, LOCALS, SAVED_REGS
```

The following sample output was produced by the call:

```
Stack Frame

00002222 ebp+12 (parameter)
00001111 ebp+8 (parameter)
00401083 ebp+4 (return address)
0012FFF0 ebp+0 (saved ebp) <--- ebp
0000AAAA ebp-4 (local variable)
0000BBBB ebp-8 (local variable)
EAEAEAEA ebp-12 (saved register)
EBEBEBEB ebp-16 (saved register) <--- esp
```

A second procedure, named WriteStackFrameName, has an additional parameter that holds the name of the procedure owning the stack frame:

```
WriteStackFrameName PROTO,
      numParam:DWORD,              ; number of passed parameters
      numLocalVal:DWORD,           ; number of DWORD local variables
      numSavedReg:DWORD,           ; number of saved registers
      procName:PTR BYTE            ; null-terminated string
```

See the Chapter 8 example program named *Test_WriteStackFrame.asm* for examples and documentation relating to this procedure. In addition, the source code (in \Lib32\Irvine32.asm) contains detailed documentation.

8.4.9 Section Review

1. *(True/False):* The CALL instruction cannot include procedure arguments.

2. *(True/False):* The INVOKE directive can include up to a maximum of three arguments.

3. *(True/False):* The INVOKE directive can only pass memory operands, but not register values.

4. *(True/False):* The PROC directive can contain a USES operator, but the PROTO directive cannot.

5. *(True/False):* When using the PROC directive, all parameters must be listed on the same line.

6. *(True/False):* If you pass a variable containing the offset of an array of bytes to a procedure that expects a pointer to an array of words, the assembler will not catch your error.

7. *(True/False):* If you pass an immediate value to a procedure that expects a reference parameter, you can generate a general-protection fault (in protected mode).

8. Declare a procedure named **MultArray** that receives two pointers to arrays of doublewords, and a third parameter indicating the number of array elements.

9. Create a PROTO directive for the procedure in the preceding exercise.

10. Did the **Swap** procedure from Section 8.4.6 use input parameters, output parameters, or input-output parameters?

11. In the **ReadConsole** procedure from Section 8.4.5, is **buffer** an input parameter or an output parameter?

8.5 Creating Multimodule Programs

Large source files are hard to manage and slow to assemble. You could break a single file into multiple include files, but a modification to any source file would still require a complete assembly of all the files. A better approach is to divide up a program into *modules* (assembled units). Each module is assembled independently, so a change to one module's source code only requires reassembling the single module. The linker combines all assembled modules (OBJ files) into a single executable file rather quickly. Linking large numbers of object modules requires far less time than assembling the same number of source code files.

There are two general approches to creating multimodule programs: The first is the traditional one, using the EXTERN directive, which is more or less portable across different 80x86 assemblers. The second approach is to use Microsoft's advanced INVOKE and PROTO directives, which simplify procedure calls and hide some low-level details. We will demonstrate both approaches and let you decide which you want to use.

8.5.1 Hiding and Exporting Procedure Names

By default, MASM makes all procedures public, permitting them to be called from any other module in the same program. You can override this behavior using the PRIVATE qualifier:

```
mySub PROC PRIVATE
```

By making procedures private, you use the principle of *encapsulation* to hide procedures inside modules and avoid potential name clashes when procedures in different modules have the same names.

OPTION PROC:PRIVATE Directive   Another way to hide procedures inside a source module is to place the OPTION PROC:PRIVATE directive at the top of the file. All procedures become private by default. Then, you use the PUBLIC directive to identify any procedures you want to export:

```
OPTION PROC:PRIVATE
PUBLIC mySub
```

The PUBLIC directive takes a comma-delimited list of names:

```
PUBLIC sub1, sub2, sub3
```

Alternatively, you can designate individual procedures as public:

```
mySub PROC PUBLIC
    .
mySub ENDP
```

If you use OPTION PROC:PRIVATE in your program's startup module, be sure to designate your startup procedure (usually main) as PUBLIC, or the operating system's loader will not be able to find it. For example,

```
main PROC PUBLIC
```

8.5.2   Calling External Procedures

The EXTERN directive, used when calling a procedure outside the current module, identifies the procedure's name and stack frame size. The following program example calls **sub1**, located in an external module:

```
INCLUDE Irvine32.inc
EXTERN sub1@0:PROC
.code
main PROC
     call   sub1@0
     exit
main ENDP
END main
```

When the assembler discovers a missing procedure in a source file (identified by a CALL instruction), its default behavior is to issue an error message. Instead, EXTERN tells the assembler to create a blank address for the procedure. The linker resolves the missing address when it creates the program's executable file.

The @**n** suffix at the end of a procedure name identifies the total stack space used by declared parameters (see the extended PROC directive in Section 8.4). If you're using the basic PROC directive with no declared parameters, the suffix on each procedure name in EXTERN will be @**0**. If you declare a procedure using the extended PROC directive, add 4 bytes for every parameter. Suppose we declare **AddTwo** with two doubleword parameters:

```
AddTwo PROC,
     val1:DWORD,
     val2:DWORD
     . . .
AddTwo ENDP
```

The corresponding EXTERN directive is **EXTERN AddTwo@8:PROC**. If you plan to call AddTwo using INVOKE (Section 8.4), use the PROTO directive in place of EXTERN:

```
AddTwo PROTO,
     val1:DWORD,
     val2:DWORD
```

8.5.3 Using Variables and Symbols across Module Boundaries

Exporting Variables and Symbols

Variables and symbols are, by default, private to their enclosing modules. You can use the PUBLIC directive to export specific names, as in the following example:

```
PUBLIC count, SYM1
SYM1 = 10
.data
count DWORD 0
```

Accessing External Variables and Symbols

You can use the EXTERN directive to access variables and symbols defined in external modules:

```
EXTERN name : type
```

For symbols (defined with EQU and =), *type* should be ABS. For variables, *type* can be a data-definition attribute such as BYTE, WORD, DWORD, and SDWORD, including PTR. Here are examples:

```
EXTERN one:WORD, two:SDWORD, three:PTR BYTE, four:ABS
```

Using an INCLUDE File with EXTERNDEF

MASM has a useful directive named EXTERNDEF that takes the place of both PUBLIC and EXTERN. It can be placed in a text file and copied into each program module using the INCLUDE directive. For example, let's define a file named *vars.inc* containing the following declaration:

```
; vars.inc
EXTERNDEF count:DWORD, SYM1:ABS
```

Next, we create a source file named *sub1.asm* containing **count** and **SYM1**, an INCLUDE statement that copies vars.inc into the compile stream.

```
TITLE sub1.asm
.386
.model flat,STDCALL
INCLUDE vars.inc
SYM1 = 10
.data
count DWORD 0
END
```

Because this is not the program startup module, we omit a program entry point label in the END directive, and we do not need to declare a runtime stack.

Next, we create a startup module named *main.asm* that includes *vars.inc* and makes references to count and SYM1.

```
TITLE main.asm
INCLUDE Irvine32.inc
INCLUDE vars.inc
```

```
      .code
      main PROC
            mov    count,2000h
            mov    eax,SYM1
            exit
      main ENDP
      END main
```

This module does contain a runtime stack, declared with the .STACK directive inside Irvine32.inc. It also defines the program entry point in the END directive.

8.5.4   Example: ArraySum Program

The *ArraySum* program, first presented in Chapter 5, is an easy program to separate into modules. For a quick review of the program's design, let's review the structure chart (Figure 8–9). Shaded rectangles refer to procedures in the book's link library. The **main** procedure calls **PromptForIntegers**, which in turn calls **WriteString** and **ReadInt**. It's usually easiest to keep track of the various files in a multimodule program by creating a separate disk directory for the files. That's what we did for the *ArraySum* program, to be shown in the next section.

FIGURE 8–9   Structure Chart, ArraySum Program.

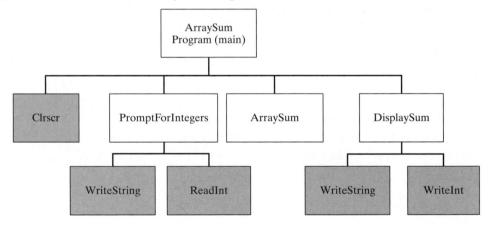

8.5.5   Creating the Modules Using Extern

We will show two versions of the multimodule ArraySum program. This section will use the traditional EXTERN directive to reference functions in separate modules. Later, in Section 8.5.6, we will implement the same program using the advanced capabilities of INVOKE, PROTO, and PROC.

PromptForIntegers   *_prompt.asm* contains the source code file for the PromptForIntegers procedure. It displays prompts asking the user to enter three integers, inputs the values by calling ReadInt, and inserts them in an array:

```
      TITLE Prompt For Integers          (_prompt.asm)
      INCLUDE Irvine32.inc
      .code
```

```
;-------------------------------------------------------
PromptForIntegers PROC

; Prompts the user for an array of integers and fills
; the array with the user's input.
; Receives:
;    ptrPrompt:PTR BYTE                    ; prompt string
;    ptrArray:PTR DWORD                    ; pointer to array
;    arraySize:DWORD                       ; size of the array
; Returns:  nothing
;-------------------------------------------------------
arraySize EQU [ebp+16]
ptrArray  EQU [ebp+12]
ptrPrompt EQU [ebp+8]

      enter 0,0
      pushad                               ; save all registers

      mov   ecx,arraySize
      cmp   ecx,0                          ; array size <= 0?
      jle   L2                             ; yes: quit
      mov   edx,ptrPrompt                  ; address of the prompt
      mov   esi,ptrArray

L1:   call  WriteString                    ; display string
      call  ReadInt                        ; read integer into EAX
      call  Crlf                           ; go to next output line
      mov   [esi],eax                      ; store in array
      add   esi,4                          ; next integer
      loop  L1

L2:   popad                                ; restore all registers
      leave
      ret   12                             ; restore the stack
PromptForIntegers ENDP
END
```

ArraySum   The _arraysum.asm module contains the ArraySum procedure, which calculates the sum of the array elements and returns a result in EAX:

```
TITLE ArraySum Procedure                 (_arrysum.asm)

INCLUDE Irvine32.inc
.code
ArraySum PROC
;
; Calculates the sum of an array of 32-bit integers.
; Receives:
;    ptrArray                             ; pointer to array
;    arraySize                            ; size of array (DWORD)
; Returns:  EAX = sum
;-------------------------------------------------------
ptrArray EQU [ebp+8]
arraySize EQU [ebp+12]
```

```
            enter 0,0
            push  ecx                    ; don't push EAX
            push  esi

            mov   eax,0                  ; set the sum to zero
            mov   esi,ptrArray
            mov   ecx,arraySize
            cmp   ecx,0                  ; array size <= 0?
            jle   L2                     ; yes: quit

    L1: add   eax,[esi]                  ; add each integer to sum
        add   esi,4                      ; point to next integer
        loop  L1                         ; repeat for array size

    L2: pop   esi
        pop   ecx                        ; return sum in EAX
        leave
        ret   8                          ; restore the stack
    ArraySum ENDP
    END
```

DisplaySum The _display.asm_ module contains the DisplaySum procedure, which displays a label, followed by the array sum:

```
    TITLE DisplaySum Procedure       (_display.asm)

    INCLUDE Irvine32.inc
    .code
    ;-------------------------------------------------------
    DisplaySum PROC
    ; Displays the sum on the console.
    ; Receives:
    ;    ptrPrompt                   ; offset of prompt string
    ;    theSum                      ; the array sum (DWORD)
    ; Returns: nothing
    ;-------------------------------------------------------

    theSum    EQU [ebp+12]
    ptrPrompt EQU [ebp+8]
        enter 0,0
        push  eax
        push  edx

        mov   edx,ptrPrompt          ; pointer to prompt
        call  WriteString
        mov   eax,theSum
        call  WriteInt               ; display EAX
        call  Crlf

        pop   edx
        pop   eax
        leave
        ret   8                      ; restore the stack
    DisplaySum ENDP
    END
```

Startup Module   The *Sum_main.asm* module contains the startup procedure (main). It contains EXTERN directives for the three external procedures. To make the source code more user-friendly, the EQU directive redefines the procedure names:

```
ArraySum            EQU ArraySum@0
PromptForIntegers   EQU PromptForIntegers@0
DisplaySum          EQU DisplaySum@0
```

Just before each procedure call, a comment describes the parameter order. This program uses the STDCALL parameter passing convention:

```
TITLE Integer Summation Program (Sum_main.asm)

; Multimodule example:
; This program inputs multiple integers from the user,
; stores them in an array, calculates the sum of the
; array, and displays the sum.

INCLUDE Irvine32.inc

EXTERN PromptForIntegers@0:PROC
EXTERN ArraySum@0:PROC, DisplaySum@0:PROC

; Redefine external symbols for convenience
ArraySum            EQU ArraySum@0
PromptForIntegers   EQU PromptForIntegers@0
DisplaySum          EQU DisplaySum@0

; modify Count to change the size of the array:
Count = 3

.data
prompt1 BYTE "Enter a signed integer: ",0
prompt2 BYTE "The sum of the integers is: ",0
array   DWORD  Count DUP(?)
sum     DWORD  ?

.code
main PROC
    call  Clrscr

; PromptForIntegers( addr prompt1, addr array, Count )
    push  Count
    push  OFFSET array
    push  OFFSET prompt1
    call  PromptForIntegers

; sum = ArraySum( addr array, Count )
    push  Count
    push  OFFSET array
    call  ArraySum
    mov   sum,eax

; DisplaySum( addr prompt2, sum )
    push  sum
    push  OFFSET prompt2
```

```
        call   DisplaySum
        call   Crlf
        exit
main ENDP
END main
```

The source files for this program are stored in the example programs directory in a folder named ch08\ModSum32_traditional.

Next, we will see how this program would change if it were built using Microsoft's INVOKE and PROTO directives.

8.5.6   Creating the Modules Using INVOKE and PROTO

Multimodule programs may be created using Microsoft's advanced INVOKE, PROTO, and extended PROC directives (Section 8.4). Their primary advantage over the more traditional use of CALL and EXTERN is their ability to match up argument lists passed by INVOKE to corresponding parameter lists declared by PROC.

Let's recreate the ArraySum program, using the INVOKE, PROTO, and advanced PROC directives. A good first step is to create an include file containing a PROTO directive for each external procedure. Each module will include this file (using the INCLUDE directive) without incurring any code size or runtime overhead. If a module does not call a particular procedure, the corresponding PROTO directive is ignored by the assembler. The source code for this program is located in the \ch08\ModSum32_advanced folder.

The sum.inc Include File   Here is the *sum.inc* include file for our program:

```
; (sum.inc)
INCLUDE Irvine32.inc

PromptForIntegers PROTO,
    ptrPrompt:PTR BYTE,            ; prompt string
    ptrArray:PTR DWORD,            ; points to the array
    arraySize:DWORD                ; size of the array

ArraySum PROTO,
    ptrArray:PTR DWORD,            ; points to the array
    arraySize:DWORD                ; size of the array

DisplaySum PROTO,
    ptrPrompt:PTR BYTE,            ; prompt string
    theSum:DWORD                   ; sum of the array
```

The _ prompt Module   The *_prompt.asm* file uses the PROC directive to declare parameters for the PromptForIntegers procedure. It uses an INCLUDE to copy *sum.inc* into this file:

```
TITLE Prompt For Integers          (_prompt.asm)

INCLUDE sum.inc                    ; get procedure prototypes
.code
;----------------------------------------------------
PromptForIntegers PROC,
  ptrPrompt:PTR BYTE,              ; prompt string
```

```
        ptrArray:PTR DWORD,            ; pointer to array
        arraySize:DWORD               ; size of the array
;
; Prompts the user for an array of integers and fills
; the array with the user's input.
; Returns:  nothing
;------------------------------------------------------
        pushad                        ; save all registers

        mov   ecx,arraySize
        cmp   ecx,0                   ; array size <= 0?
        jle   L2                      ; yes: quit
        mov   edx,ptrPrompt           ; address of the prompt
        mov   esi,ptrArray

L1:   call WriteString                ; display string
        call ReadInt                  ; read integer into EAX
        call Crlf                     ; go to next output line
        mov   [esi],eax               ; store in array
        add   esi,4                   ; next integer
        loop  L1

L2:   popad                           ; restore all registers
        ret
PromptForIntegers ENDP
END
```

Compared to the previous version of PromptForIntegers, the statements **enter 0, 0** and **leave** are now missing because they will be generated by MASM when it encounters the PROC directive with declared parameters. Also, the RET instruction needs no constant parameter (PROC takes care of that).

The _arraysum Module   Next, the *_arrysum.asm* file contains the ArraySum procedure:

```
TITLE ArraySum Procedure                    (_arrysum.asm)

INCLUDE sum.inc
.code
;------------------------------------------------------
ArraySum PROC,
        ptrArray:PTR DWORD,           ; pointer to array
        arraySize:DWORD               ; size of array
;
; Calculates the sum of an array of 32-bit integers.
; Returns:  EAX = sum
;------------------------------------------------------
        push ecx                      ; don't push EAX
        push esi

        mov   eax,0                   ; set the sum to zero
        mov   esi,ptrArray
        mov   ecx,arraySize
        cmp   ecx,0                   ; array size <= 0?
        jle   L2                      ; yes: quit
```

```
L1: add  eax,[esi]                ; add each integer to sum
    add  esi,4                    ; point to next integer
    loop L1                       ; repeat for array size

L2: pop  esi
    pop  ecx                      ; return sum in EAX
    ret
ArraySum ENDP
END
```

The _display Module

The *_display.asm* file contains the DisplaySum procedure:

```
TITLE DisplaySum Procedure       (_display.asm)

INCLUDE Sum.inc
.code
;------------------------------------------------------
DisplaySum PROC,
    ptrPrompt:PTR BYTE,           ; prompt string
    theSum:DWORD                  ; the array sum
;
; Displays the sum on the console.
; Returns:  nothing
;------------------------------------------------------
    push eax
    push edx

    mov  edx,ptrPrompt                ; pointer to prompt
    call WriteString
    mov  eax,theSum
    call WriteInt                     ; display EAX
    call Crlf

    pop  edx
    pop  eax
    ret
DisplaySum ENDP
END
```

The Sum_main Module

The *Sum_main.asm* (startup module) contains main and calls each of the other procedures. It uses INCLUDE to copy in the procedure prototypes from *sum.inc*:

```
TITLE Integer Summation Program (Sum_main.asm)

INCLUDE sum.inc
Count = 3
.data
prompt1 BYTE "Enter a signed integer: ",0
prompt2 BYTE "The sum of the integers is: ",0
array   DWORD  Count DUP(?)
sum     DWORD  ?

.code
main PROC
```

```
        call Clrscr

        INVOKE PromptForIntegers, ADDR prompt1, ADDR array, Count
        INVOKE ArraySum, ADDR array, Count
        mov   sum,eax
        INVOKE DisplaySum, ADDR prompt2, sum

        call  Crlf
        exit
    main ENDP
    END main
```

Summary   We have shown two ways of creating multimodule programs—first, using the more conventional EXTERN directive, and second, using the advanced capabilities of INVOKE, PROTO, and PROC. The latter directives simplify many details and are optimized for calling Windows API functions. They also hide a number of details, so you may prefer to use explicit stack parameters along with CALL and EXTERN.

8.5.7   Section Review

1. *(True/False):* Linking OBJ modules is much faster than assembling ASM source files.

2. *(True/False):* Separating a large program into short modules makes a program more difficult to maintain.

3. *(True/False):* In a multimodule program, an END statement with a label occurs only once, in the startup module.

4. *(True/False):* PROTO directives use up memory, so you must be careful not to include a PROTO directive for a procedure unless the procedure is actually called.

8.6   Java Bytecodes

8.6.1   Java Virtual Machine

The *Java Virtual Machine* (JVM) is the software that executes compiled Java bytecodes. It is an important part of the Java Platform, which encompasses programs, specifications, libraries, and data structures working together. *Java bytecodes* is the name given to the machine language inside compiled Java programs.

While this book teaches native assembly language on x86 processors, it is also instructive to learn how other machine architectures work. The JVM is the foremost example of a stack-based machine. Rather than using registers to hold operands (as the x86 does), the JVM uses a stack for data movement, arithmetic, comparison, and branching operations.

The compiled programs executed by a JVM contain *Java bytecodes*. Every Java source program must be compiled into Java bytecodes (in the form of a .class file) before it can execute. The same program containing Java bytecodes will execute on any computer system that has Java runtime software installed.

A Java source file named *Account.java*, for example, is compiled into a file named *Account.class*. Inside this class file is a stream of bytecodes for each method in the class. The JVM might optionally use a technique called *just-in-time compilation* to compile the class byte-codes into the computer's native machine language.

When a Java method executes, it has its own stack frame, which is divided into separate areas: (1) an area for local variables, (2) an area for operands, and (3) an area for the execution environment. The operand area of the stack is actually at the top of the stack, so values pushed there are immediately available as arithmetic operators, logical operators, and arguments passed to class methods.

Before local variables can be used in instructions that involve arithmetic or comparison, they must be pushed onto the operand area of the stack frame. From this point forward, we will refer to this area as the *operand stack*.

In Java bytecodes, each instruction contains a 1-byte opcode, followed by zero or more operands. When displayed by a Java disassembler utility, the opcodes have names, such as iload, istore, imul, and goto. Each stack entry is 4 bytes (32 bits).

Viewing Disassembled Bytecodes

The *Java Development Kit* (JDK) contains a utility named *javap.exe* that displays the byte codes in a java .class file. We call this a *disassembly* of the file. The command-line syntax is:

```
javap -c classname
```

For example, if your class file were named Account.class, the appropriate *javap* command line would be

```
javap -c Account
```

You can find the javap.exe utility in the \bin folder of your installed Java Development Kit.

8.6.2   Instruction Set

Primitive Data Types

There are seven primitive data types recognized by the JVM, shown in Table 8-4. All signed integers are in two's complement format, just like x86 integers. But they are stored in big-endian order, with the high-order byte at the starting address of each integer (x86 integers are stored in little-endian order). The IEEE real formats are described in Chapter 12.

Table 8-4   Java Primitive Data Types

Data Type	Bytes	Format
char	2	Unicode character
byte	1	signed integer
short	2	signed integer
int	4	signed integer
long	8	signed integer
float	4	IEEE single-precision real
double	8	IEEE double-precision real

Comparison Instructions

Comparison instructions pop two operands off the top of the operand stack, compare them, and push the result of the comparison back on the stack. Let's assume the operands are pushed in the following order:

(top of stack)

The following table shows the value pushed on the stack after comparing *op1* and *op2*:

Results of Comparing op1 and op2	Value Pushed on the Operand Stack
op1 > op2	1
op1 = op2	0
op1 < op2	−1

The *dcmp* instruction compares doubles, and *fcmp* compares float values.

Branching Instructions

Branching instructions can be categorized as either conditional branches or unconditional branches. Examples of unconditional branches in Java bytecode are *goto* and *jsr*.

The *goto* instruction unconditionally branches to a label:

```
goto label
```

The *jsr* instruction calls a subroutine identified by a label. Its syntax is:

```
jsr label
```

A conditional branch instruction usually inspects the value that it pops from the top of the operand stack. Then, based on the value, the instruction decides whether or not to branch to a given label. For example, the *ifle* instruction branches to a label if the popped value is less than or equal to zero. Its syntax is:

```
ifle label
```

Similarly, the *ifgt* instruction branches to a label if the popped value is greater than zero. Its syntax is:

```
ifgt label
```

8.6.3   Java Disassembly Examples

In order to help you better understand how Java bytecodes work, we will present a series of short code examples written in Java. In the examples that follow, you should know that details in the bytecode listings may vary slightly between different releases of Java.

Example: Adding Two Integers

The following Java source code lines add two integers and place their sum in a third variable:

```
int A = 3;
int B = 2;
int sum = 0;
sum = A + B;
```

Following is a disassembly of the Java code:

```
0:   iconst_3
1:   istore_0
2:   iconst_2
3:   istore_1
4:   iconst_0
5:   istore_2
6:   iload_0
7:   iload_1
8:   iadd
9:   istore_2
```

Each numbered line represents the byte offset of a Java bytecode instruction. In the current example, we can tell that each instruction is only one byte long because the instruction offsets are numbered consecutively.

Although bytecode disassemblies usually do not contain comments, we will add our own. Local variables have their own reserved area on the runtime stack. There is another stack called the *operand stack* that is used by instructions when performing arithmetic and moving of data. To avoid confusion between these two stacks, we will refer to variable locations with index values 0, 1, 2, and so on.

Now we will analyze the bytecodes in detail. The first two instructions push a constant value onto the operand stack and pop the same value into the local variable at location 0:

```
0:   iconst_3         // push constant (3) onto operand stack
1:   istore_0         // pop into local variable 0
```

The next four lines push two more constants on the operand stack and pop them into local variables at locations 1 and 2:

```
2:   iconst_2         // push constant (2) onto stack
3:   istore_1         // pop into local variable 1
4:   iconst_0         // push constant (0) onto stack
5:   istore_2         // pop into local variable 2
```

Having seen the Java source code from which this bytecode was generated, it is now clear that the following table shows the location indexes of the three variables:

Location Index	Variable Name
0	A
1	B
2	sum

Next, in order to perform addition, the two operands must be pushed on the operand stack. The *iload_0* instruction pushes the variable A onto the stack. The *iload_1* instruction does the same for the variable B:

```
6:   iload_0          // push A onto the stack
7:   iload_1          // push B onto the stack
```

The operand stack now contains two values:

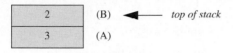

We are not concerned with actual machine representation in these examples, so the runtime stack is shown as growing in the upward direction. The uppermost value in each stack diagram is the top of stack.

The *iadd* instruction adds the two values at the top of the stack and pushes the sum back on the stack:

```
8:    iadd
```

The operand stack contains the sum of A and B:

```
5    (A + B)
```

The *istore_2* instruction pops the stack into location 2, which is the variable named *sum*:

```
9:    istore_2
```

The operand stack is now empty.

Example: Adding Two Doubles

The following Java snippet adds two variables of type double and saves them in a sum. It performs the same operations as our *Adding Two Integers* example, so we will focus on the differences between processing integers and doubles:

```
double A = 3.1;
double B = 2;
double sum = A + B;
```

Following are the disassembled bytecodes for our example. The comments shown at the right were inserted by the *javap* utility program:

```
0:    ldc2_w #20;            // double 3.1d
3:    dstore_0
4:    ldc2_w #22;            // double 2.0d
7:    dstore_2
8:    dload_0
9:    dload_2
10:   dadd
11:   dstore_4
```

We will discuss this code in steps. The *ldc2_w* instruction at offset 0 pushes a floating-point constant (3.1) from the constant pool onto the operand stack. The *ldc2* instruction always includes a 2-byte index into the constant pool area:

```
0:    ldc2_w #20;            // double 3.1d
```

The *dstore* instruction at offset 3 pops a double from the operand stack into the local variable at location 0. The instruction's starting offset (3) reflects the number of bytes used by the first instruction (opcode, plus 2-byte index):

```
3:   dstore_0                      // save in A
```

The next two instructions at offsets 4 and 7 follow suit, initializing the variable B:

```
4:   ldc2_w #22;                   // double 2.0d
7:   dstore_2                      // save in B
```

The *dload_0* and *dload_2* instructions push the local variables onto the stack. The indexes refer to 64-bit locations (two variable stack entries) because the doubleword values are 8 bytes long:

```
8:   dload_0
9:   dload_2
```

The next instruction (*dadd*) adds the two double values at the top of the stack and pushes their sum back onto the stack:

```
10:  dadd
```

The final *dstore_4* instruction pops the stack into the local variable at location 4:

```
11:  dstore_4
```

Example: Conditional Branch

An important part of understanding Java bytecodes relates to how the JVM handles conditional branching. Comparison operations always pop the top two items off the stack, compare them, and push an integer result value back onto the stack. Conditional branching instructions, which often follow comparison operations, use the integer value at the top of the stack to decide whether or not to branch to a target label. For example, the following Java code contains a simple IF statement that assigns one of two values to a boolean variable:

```
double A = 3.0;
boolean result = false;

if( A > 2.0 )
    result = false;
else
    result = true;
```

Following is the corresponding disassembly of the Java code:

```
0:   ldc2_w #26;                   // double 3.0d
3:   dstore_0                      // pop into A
4:   iconst_0                      // false = 0
5:   istore_2                      // store in result
6:   dload_0
7:   ldc2_w #22;                   // double 2.0d
10:  dcmpl
11:  ifle  19                      // if A <= 2.0, goto 19
14:  iconst_0                      // false
```

```
15:  istore_2                  // result = false
16:  goto  21                  // skip next two statements
19:  iconst_1                  // true
20:  istore_2                  // result = true
```

The first two instructions copy 3.0 from the constant pool onto the runtime stack, and then pop it from the stack into the variable A:

```
0:   ldc2_w #26;               // double 3.0d
3:   dstore_0                  // pop into A
```

The next two instructions copy the boolean value *false* (equal to 0) from the constant area onto the stack, and then pop it into the variable named *result*:

```
4:   iconst_0                  // false = 0
5:   istore_2                  // store in result
```

The value of A (location 0) is pushed onto the operand stack, followed by the value 2.0:

```
6:   dload_0                   // push A onto the stack
7:   ldc2_w #22;               // double 2.0d
```

The operand stack now contains two values:

```
+-----------+
|    2.0    |
+-----------+
|    3.0    |  (A)
+-----------+
```

The *dcmpl* instruction pops two doubles from the stack and compares them. Since the value at the top of the stack (2.0) is less than the value just below it (3.0), the integer 1 is pushed on the stack.

```
10:  dcmpl
```

The *ifle* instruction branches to a given offset if the value it pops from the stack is less than or equal to zero:

```
11:  ifle  19                  // if stack.pop() <= 0 goto 19
```

Here, we should recall that our starting Java source code example assigned a value of false if A > 2.0:

```
if( A > 2.0 )
    result = false;
else
    result = true;
```

The Java bytecode turns this IF statement around by jumping to offset 19 if A ≤ 2.0. At offset 19, *result* is assigned the value *true*. Meanwhile, if the branch to offset 19 is not taken, *result* is assigned the value *false* by the next few instructions:

```
14:  iconst_0                  // false
15:  istore_2                  // result = false
16:  goto  21                  // skip next two statements
```

The *goto* instruction at offset 16 skips over the next two lines, which are responsible for assigning *true* to *result*:

```
19:  iconst_1                  // true
20:  istore_2                  // result = true
```

Conclusion

The Java Virtual Machine has a markedly different instruction set than that of the x86 processor family. Its stack-oriented approach to calculations, comparisons, and branching contrasts sharply to the constant use of registers and memory operands in x86 instructions. While the symbolic disassembly of bytecodes is not as easy to read as x86 assembly language, bytecodes are fairly easy for the compiler to generate. Each operation is atomic, meaning that it performs just one operation. In cases where a just-in-time compiler is used by a JVM, the Java bytecodes are translated into native machine language just before execution. In this respect, Java bytecodes have a great deal in common with machine languages based on the Reduced Instruction Set (RISC) model.

8.7 Chapter Summary

There are two basic types of procedure parameters: register parameters and stack parameters. The Irvine32 and Irvine16 libraries use register parameters, which are optimized for program execution speed. Unfortunately, they tend to create code clutter in calling programs. Stack parameters are the alternative. The procedure arguments must be pushed on the stack by a calling program.

A stack frame (or activation record) is the area of the stack set aside for a procedure's return address, passed parameters, local variables, and saved registers. The stack frame is created when the running program begins to execute a procedure.

When a copy of a procedure argument is pushed on the stack, it is *passed by value*. When an argument's address is pushed on the stack, it is *passed by reference*; the procedure can modify the variable via its address. Arrays should be passed by reference, to avoid having to push all array elements on the stack.

Procedure parameters can be accessed using indirect addressing with the EBP register. Expressions such as [ebp+8] give you a high level of control over stack parameter addressing. The LEA instruction returns the offset of any type of indirect operand. LEA is ideally suited for use with stack parameters.

The ENTER instruction completes the stack frame by saving EBP on the stack and reserving space for local variables. The LEAVE instruction terminates the stack frame for a procedure by reversing the action of a preceding ENTER instruction.

A recursive procedure is one that calls itself, either directly or indirectly. Recursion, the practice of calling recursive procedures, can be a powerful tool when working with data structures that have repeating patterns.

The LOCAL directive declares one or more local variables inside a procedure. It must be placed on the line immediately following a PROC directive. Local variables have distinct advantages over global variables:

- Access to the name and contents of a local variable can be restricted to its containing procedure. Local variables help when debugging programs because only a limited number of program statements are capable of modifying the local variables.
- A local variable's lifetime is limited to the execution scope of its enclosing procedure. Local variables make efficient use of memory because the same storage space can be used for other variables.

- The same variable name may be used in more than one procedure without causing a naming clash.
- Local variables can be used in recursive procedures to store values on the stack. If global variables were used instead, their values would be overwritten each time the procedure called itself.

The INVOKE directive is a more powerful replacement for the CALL instruction that lets you pass multiple arguments. The ADDR operator can be used to pass a pointer when calling a procedure with the INVOKE directive.

The PROC directive declares a procedure name with a list of named parameters. The PROTO directive creates a prototype for an existing procedure. A prototype declares a procedure's name and parameter list.

An application program of any size is difficult to manage when all of its source code is in the same file. It is more convenient to break the program up into multiple source code files (called modules), making each file easy to view and edit.

Java Bytecodes   *Java bytecodes* is the name given to the machine language inside compiled Java programs. The Java Virtual Machine (JVM) is the software that executes compiled Java bytecodes. In Java bytecodes, each instruction contains a 1-byte opcode, followed by zero or more operands. The JVM uses a stack-oriented model for performing arithmetic, data movement, comparison, and branching. The Java Development Kit (JDK) contains a utility named *javap.exe* that displays a disassembly of the byte codes in a java .class file.

8.8   Programming Exercises

★ **1.   SetColor and WriteColorChar**
Create two procedures: (1) **SetColor** receives two byte parameters: *forecolor* and *backcolor*. It calls the SetTextColor procedure from the Irvine32 library. (2) **WriteColorChar** receives three byte parameters: *char*, *forecolor*, and *backcolor*. It displays a single character, using the color attributes specified in forecolor and backcolor. It calls the SetColor procedure, and it also calls WriteChar from the Irvine32 library. Both SetColor and WriteColorChar must contain declared parameters. Write a short test program that tests both procedures. Be sure to create PROTO declarations for SetColor and WriteColorChar.

★ **2.   Square with Stripes**
This exercise extends Exercise 1. Write a test program that uses INVOKE to call WriteColorChar, and displays a color square (10 rows by 20 columns) with alternating pairs of blue and white vertical bars. Call a separate procedure when printing each row of the square.

★ **3.   DumpMemory Procedure**
Write a procedure named **DumpMemory** that encapsulates the DumpMem procedure in the Irvine32 library. Use declared parameters and the USES directive. The following is an example of how it should be called:

```
INVOKE DumpMemory,OFFSET array,LENGTHOF array,TYPE array
```

Write a test program that calls your procedure several times, using a variety of data types.

★★★ **4.   Nonrecursive Factorial**

Write a nonrecursive version of the **Factorial** procedure (Section 8.3.2) that uses a loop. *(A VideoNote for this exercise is posted on the Web site.)* Write a short program that interactively tests your Factorial procedure. Let the user enter the value of n. If overflow occurs in your loop when calculating each factorial value, your program should display an error message. If no overflow occurs, display the calculated factorial. Following is a sample of the interaction between the user and the program:

```
Enter the value of n to calculate the factorial (-1 to quit): 0
The factorial is: 1
Enter the value of n to calculate the factorial (-1 to quit): 1
The factorial is: 1
Enter the value of n to calculate the factorial (-1 to quit): 5
The factorial is: 120
Enter the value of n to calculate the factorial (-1 to quit): 12
The factorial is: 479001600
Enter the value of n to calculate the factorial (-1 to quit): 13
Error: Calculated value cannot fit into 32 bits
Enter the value of n to calculate the factorial (-1 to quit): -1
```

★★ **5.   Factorial Comparison**

Write a program that compares the runtime speeds of both the recursive **Factorial** procedure from Section 8.4.2 and the nonrecursive Factorial procedure written for Exercise 4. Use the **GetMseconds** procedure from the book's link library to measure and display the number of milliseconds required to call each Factorial procedure several thousand times in a row.

★★ **6.   Greatest Common Divisor**

Write a recursive implementation of Euclid's algorithm for finding the greatest common divisor (GCD) of two integers. Descriptions of this algorithm are available in algebra books and on the Web. (Note: A nonrecursive version of the GCD problem was given in the programming exercises for Chapter 7.) Write a test program that calls your GCD procedure five times, using the following pairs of integers: (5,20), (24,18), (11,7), (432,226), (26,13). After each procedure call, display the GCD.

★★★ **7.   Show Procedure Parameters**

Write a procedure named **ShowParams** that displays the address and hexadecimal value of the 32-bit parameters on the runtime stack of the procedure that called it. The parameters are to be displayed in order from the lowest address to the highest. Input to the procedure will be a single integer that indicates the number of parameters to display. For example, suppose the following statement in main calls MySample, passing three arguments:

```
INVOKE MySample, 1234h, 5000h, 6543h
```

Next, inside MySample, we make a call to ShowParams, passing the number of parameters:

```
MySample PROC first:DWORD, second:DWORD, third:DWORD
    paramCount = 3

call ShowParams, paramCount
```

Suggestion: Run the program in Debug mode and examine the Disassembly window. The following is a sample of the expected output:

```
Stack parameters:
---------------------------
Address  0012FF80 = 00001234
Address  0012FF84 = 00005000
Address  0012FF88 = 00006543
```

★★★ **8.   Exchanging Integers**

Create an array of randomly ordered integers. Using the Swap procedure from Section 8.4.6 as a tool, write a loop that exchanges each consecutive pair of integers in the array. *(A VideoNote for this exercise is posted on the Web site.)*

★★ **9.   Chess Board**

Write a program that draws an 8 × 8 chess board, with alternating gray and white squares. You can use the SetTextColor and Gotoxy procedures from the Irvine32 library. Avoid the use of global variables, and use declared parameters in all procedures. Use short procedures that are focused on a single task. *(A VideoNote for this exercise is posted on the Web site.)*

★★★ **10.   Chess Board with Alternating Colors**

This exercise extends Exercise 9. Every 500 milliseconds, change the color of the colored squares and redisplay the board. Continue until you have shown the board 16 times, using all possible 4-bit background colors. (The white squares remain white throughout.)

9

Strings and Arrays

9.1   Introduction

9.2   String Primitive Instructions
    9.2.1   MOVSB, MOVSW, and MOVSD
    9.2.2   CMPSB, CMPSW, and CMPSD
    9.2.3   SCASB, SCASW, and SCASD
    9.2.4   STOSB, STOSW, and STOSD
    9.2.5   LODSB, LODSW, and LODSD
    9.2.6   Section Review

9.3   Selected String Procedures
    9.3.1   Str_compare Procedure
    9.3.2   Str_length Procedure
    9.3.3   Str_copy Procedure
    9.3.4   Str_trim Procedure
    9.3.5   Str_ucase Procedure
    9.3.6   String Library Demo Program
    9.3.7   Section Review

9.4   Two-Dimensional Arrays
    9.4.1   Ordering of Rows and Columns
    9.4.2   Base-Index Operands
    9.4.3   Base-Index-Displacement Operands
    9.4.4   Section Review

9.5   Searching and Sorting Integer Arrays
    9.5.1   Bubble Sort
    9.5.2   Binary Search
    9.5.3   Section Review

9.6   Java Bytecodes: String Processing

9.7   Chapter Summary

9.8   Programming Exercises

9.1   Introduction

If you learn to efficiently process strings and arrays, you can master the most common area of code optimization. Studies have shown that most programs spend 90% of their running time executing 10% of their code. No doubt the 10% occurs frequently in loops, and loops are required when processing strings and arrays. In this chapter, we will show techniques for string and array processing, with the goal of writing efficient code.

We will begin with the optimized string primitive instructions designed for moving, comparing, loading, and storing blocks of data. Next, we will introduce several string-handling procedures in

Irvine32 (or Irvine16) library. Their implementations are fairly similar to the code you might see in an implementation of the standard C string library. The third part of the chapter shows how to manipulate two-dimensional arrays, using advanced indirect addressing modes: base-index and base-index-displacement. Simple indirect addressing was introduced in Section 4.4.

Section 9.5, *Searching and Sorting Integer Arrays*, is the most interesting. You will see how easy it is to implement two of the most common array processing algorithms in computer science: bubble sort and binary search. It's a great idea to study these algorithms in Java or C++, as well as assembly language.

9.2   String Primitive Instructions

The x86 instruction set has five groups of instructions for processing arrays of bytes, words, and doublewords. Although they are called *string primitives*, they are not limited to character arrays. Each instruction in Table 9-1 implicitly uses ESI, EDI, or both registers to address memory. References to the accumulator imply the use of AL, AX, or EAX, depending on the instruction data size. String primitives execute efficiently because they automatically repeat and increment array indexes.

Table 9-1   String Primitive Instructions.

Instruction	Description
MOVSB, MOVSW, MOVSD	**Move string data:** Copy data from memory addressed by ESI to memory addressed by EDI.
CMPSB, CMPSW, CMPSD	**Compare strings:** Compare the contents of two memory locations addressed by ESI and EDI.
SCASB, SCASW, SCASD	**Scan string:** Compare the accumulator (AL, AX, or EAX) to the contents of memory addressed by EDI.
STOSB, STOSW, STOSD	**Store string data:** Store the accumulator contents into memory addressed by EDI.
LODSB, LODSW, LODSD	**Load accumulator from string:** Load memory addressed by ESI into the accumulator.

In protected mode programs, ESI is automatically an offset in the segment addressed by DS, and EDI is automatically an offset in the segment addressed by ES. DS and ES are always set to the same value and you cannot change them. (In real-address mode, on the other hand, ES and DS are often manipulated by ASM programmers.)

In real-address mode, string primitives use the SI and DI registers to address memory. SI is an offset from DS, and DI is an offset from ES. Usually you will set ES to the same segment value as DS at the beginning of main:

```
main PROC
     mov    ax,@data       ; get addr of data seg
     mov    ds,ax          ; initialize DS
     mov    es,ax          ; initialize ES
```

Using a Repeat Prefix   By itself, a string primitive instruction processes only a single memory value or pair of values. If you add a *repeat prefix*, the instruction repeats, using ECX as a counter. The repeat prefix permits you to process an entire array using a single instruction.

The following repeat prefixes are used:

REP	Repeat while ECX > 0
REPZ, REPE	Repeat while the Zero flag is set and ECX > 0
REPNZ, REPNE	Repeat while the Zero flag is clear and ECX > 0

Example: Copy a String   In the following example, MOVSB moves 10 bytes from **string1** to **string2**. The repeat prefix first tests ECX > 0 before executing the MOVSB instruction. If ECX = 0, the instruction is ignored and control passes to the next line in the program. If ECX > 0, ECX is decremented and the instruction repeats:

```
cld                               ; clear direction flag
mov    esi,OFFSET string1         ; ESI points to source
mov    edi,OFFSET string2         ; EDI points to target
mov    ecx,10                     ; set counter to 10
rep    movsb                      ; move 10 bytes
```

ESI and EDI are automatically incremented when MOVSB repeats. This behavior is controlled by the CPU's Direction flag.

Direction Flag   String primitive instructions increment or decrement ESI and EDI based on the state of the Direction flag (see Table 9-2). The Direction flag can be explicitly modified using the CLD and STD instructions:

```
CLD        ; clear Direction flag (forward direction)
STD        ; set Direction flag (reverse direction)
```

Forgetting to set the Direction flag before a string primitive instruction can be a major headache, since the ESI and EDI registers may not increment or decrement as intended.

Table 9-2   Direction Flag Usage in String Primitive Instructions.

Value of the Direction Flag	Effect on ESI and EDI	Address Sequence
Clear	Incremented	Low-high
Set	Decremented	High-low

9.2.1   MOVSB, MOVSW, and MOVSD

The MOVSB, MOVSW, and MOVSD instructions copy data from the memory location pointed to by ESI to the memory location pointed to by EDI. The two registers are either incremented or decremented automatically (based on the value of the Direction flag):

MOVSB	Move (copy) bytes
MOVSW	Move (copy) words
MOVSD	Move (copy) doublewords

You can use a repeat prefix with MOVSB, MOVSW, and MOVSD. The Direction flag determines whether ESI and EDI will be incremented or decremented. The size of the increment/decrement is shown in the following table:

Instruction	Value Added or Subtracted from ESI and EDI
MOVSB	1
MOVSW	2
MOVSD	4

Example: Copy Doubleword Array   Suppose we want to copy 20 doubleword integers from **source** to **target**. After the array is copied, ESI and EDI point one position (4 bytes) beyond the end of each array:

```
.data
source DWORD 20 DUP(0FFFFFFFFh)
target DWORD 20 DUP(?)
.code
cld                                ; direction = forward
mov    ecx,LENGTHOF source         ; set REP counter
mov    esi,OFFSET source           ; ESI points to source
mov    edi,OFFSET target           ; EDI points to target
rep    movsd                       ; copy doublewords
```

9.2.2   CMPSB, CMPSW, and CMPSD

The CMPSB, CMPSW, and CMPSD instructions each compare a memory operand pointed to by ESI to a memory operand pointed to by EDI:

CMPSB	Compare bytes
CMPSW	Compare words
CMPSD	Compare doublewords

You can use a repeat prefix with CMPSB, CMPSW, and CMPSD. The Direction flag determines the incrementing or decrementing of ESI and EDI.

Example: Comparing Doublewords   Suppose you want to compare a pair of doublewords using CMPSD. In the following example, **source** has a smaller value than **target**, so the JA instruction will not jump to label L1.

```
.data
source DWORD 1234h
target DWORD 5678h
.code
mov    esi,OFFSET source
mov    edi,OFFSET target
cmpsd                              ; compare doublewords
ja     L1                          ; jump if source > target
```

To compare multiple doublewords, clear the Direction flag (forward direction), initialize ECX as a counter, and use a repeat prefix with CMPSD:

```
mov    esi,OFFSET source
mov    edi,OFFSET target
cld                              ; direction = forward
mov    ecx,LENGTHOF source       ; repetition counter
repe   cmpsd                     ; repeat while equal
```

The REPE prefix repeats the comparison, incrementing ESI and EDI automatically until ECX equals zero or a pair of doublewords is found to be different.

9.2.3   SCASB, SCASW, and SCASD

The SCASB, SCASW, and SCASD instructions compare a value in AL/AX/EAX to a byte, word, or doubleword, respectively, addressed by EDI. The instructions are useful when looking for a single value in a string or array. Combined with the REPE (or REPZ) prefix, the string or array is scanned while ECX > 0 and the value in AL/AX/EAX matches each subsequent value in memory. The REPNE prefix scans until either AL/AX/EAX matches a value in memory or ECX = 0.

Scan for a Matching Character   In the following example we search the string **alpha**, looking for the letter F. If the letter is found, EDI points one position beyond the matching character. If the letter is not found, JNZ exits:

```
.data
alpha BYTE "ABCDEFGH",0
.code
mov    edi,OFFSET alpha          ; EDI points to the string
mov    al,'F'                    ; search for the letter F
mov    ecx,LENGTHOF alpha        ; set the search count
cld                              ; direction = forward
repne scasb                      ; repeat while not equal
jnz    quit                      ; quit if letter not found
dec    edi                       ; found: back up EDI
```

JNZ was added after the loop to test for the possibility that the loop stopped because ECX = 0 and the character in AL was not found.

9.2.4   STOSB, STOSW, and STOSD

The STOSB, STOSW, and STOSD instructions store the contents of AL/AX/EAX, respectively, in memory at the offset pointed to by EDI. EDI is incremented or decremented based on the state of the Direction flag. When used with the REP prefix, these instructions are useful for filling all elements of a string or array with a single value. For example, the following code initializes each byte in **string1** to 0FFh:

```
.data
Count = 100
string1 BYTE Count DUP(?)
.code
mov    al,0FFh                   ; value to be stored
mov    edi,OFFSET string1        ; EDI points to target
```

```
    mov    ecx,Count                    ; character count
    cld                                 ; direction = forward
    rep    stosb                        ; fill with contents of AL
```

9.2.5   LODSB, LODSW, and LODSD

The LODSB, LODSW, and LODSD instructions load a byte or word from memory at ESI into AL/AX/EAX, respectively. ESI is incremented or decremented based on the state of the Direction flag. The REP prefix is rarely used with LODS because each new value loaded into the accumulator overwrites its previous contents. Instead, LODS is used to load a single value. In the next example, LODSB substitutes for the following two instructions (assuming the Direction flag is clear):

```
    mov    al,[esi]                     ; move byte into AL
    inc    esi                          ; point to next byte
```

Array Multiplication Example   The following program multiplies each element of a double-word array by a constant value. LODSD and STOSD work together:

```
    TITLE Multiply an Array                        (Mult.asm)

    ; This program multiplies each element of an array
    ; of 32-bit integers by a constant value.

    INCLUDE Irvine32.inc
    .data
    array DWORD 1,2,3,4,5,6,7,8,9,10       ; test data
    multiplier DWORD 10                    ; test data

    .code
    main PROC
        cld                               ; direction = forward
        mov    esi,OFFSET array           ; source index
        mov    edi,esi                    ; destination index
        mov    ecx,LENGTHOF array         ; loop counter

    L1: lodsd                             ; load [ESI] into EAX
        mul    multiplier                 ; multiply by a value
        stosd                             ; store EAX into [EDI]
        loop   L1

        exit
    main ENDP
    END main
```

9.2.6   Section Review

1. In reference to string primitives, which 32-bit register is known as the *accumulator*?

2. Which instruction compares a 32-bit integer in the accumulator to the contents of memory, pointed to by EDI?

3. Which index register is used by the STOSD instruction?

4. Which instruction copies data from the memory location addressed by ESI into AX?

5. What does the REPZ prefix do for a CMPSB instruction?

6. Which Direction flag value causes index registers to move backward through memory when executing string primitives?

7. When a repeat prefix is used with STOSW, what value is added to or subtracted from the index register?

8. In what way is the CMPS instruction ambiguous?

9. *Challenge:* When the Direction flag is clear and SCASB has found a matching character, where does EDI point?

10. *Challenge:* When scanning an array for the first occurrence of a particular character, which repeat prefix would be best?

9.3   Selected String Procedures

In this section, we will demonstrate several procedures from the Irvine32 and Irvine16 libraries that manipulate null-terminated strings. The procedures are clearly similar to functions in the standard C library:

```
; Copy a source string to a target string.
Str_copy PROTO,
    source:PTR BYTE,
    target:PTR BYTE

; Return the length of a string (excluding the null byte) in EAX.
Str_length PROTO,
    pString:PTR BYTE

; Compare string1 to string2. Set the Zero and
; Carry flags in the same way as the CMP instruction.
Str_compare PROTO,
    string1:PTR BYTE,
    string2:PTR BYTE

; Trim a given trailing character from a string.
; The second argument is the character to trim.
Str_trim PROTO,
    pString:PTR BYTE,
    char:BYTE

; Convert a string to upper case.
Str_ucase PROTO,
    pString:PTR BYTE
```

9.3.1   Str_compare Procedure

The **Str_compare** procedure compares two strings. The calling format is

```
INVOKE Str_compare, ADDR string1, ADDR string2
```

It compares the strings in forward order, starting at the first byte. The comparison is case sensitive because ASCII codes are different for uppercase and lowercase letters. The procedure does not return a value, but the Carry and Zero flags can be interpreted as shown in Table 9-3, using the *string1* and *string2* arguments.

Table 9-3   Flags Affected by the Str_compare Procedure.

Relation	Carry Flag	Zero Flag	Branch If True
string1 < string2	1	0	JB
string1 = string2	0	1	JE
string1 > string2	0	0	JA

See Section 6.2.8 for an explanation of how CMP sets the Carry and Zero flags. The following is a listing of the **Str_compare** procedure. See the *Compare.asm* program for a demonstration:

```
Str_compare PROC USES eax edx esi edi,
     string1:PTR BYTE,
     string2:PTR BYTE
;
; Compare two strings.
; Returns nothing, but the Zero and Carry flags are affected
; exactly as they would be by the CMP instruction.
;-----------------------------------------------------
     mov   esi,string1
     mov   edi,string2

L1:  mov   al,[esi]
     mov   dl,[edi]
     cmp   al,0                    ; end of string1?
     jne   L2                      ; no
     cmp   dl,0                    ; yes: end of string2?
     jne   L2                      ; no
     jmp   L3                      ; yes, exit with ZF = 1

L2:  inc   esi                     ; point to next
     inc   edi
     cmp   al,dl                   ; chars equal?
     je    L1                      ; yes: continue loop
                                   ; no: exit with flags set
L3:  ret
Str_compare ENDP
```

We could have used the CMPSB instruction when implementing Str_compare, but it would have required knowing the length of the longer string. Two calls to the **Str_length** procedure would be required. In this particular case, it is easier to check for the null terminators in both strings within the same loop. CMPSB is most effective when dealing with large strings or arrays of known length.

9.3.2   Str_length Procedure

The **Str_length** procedure returns the length of a string in the EAX register. When you call it, pass the string's offset. For example:

```
INVOKE Str_length, ADDR myString
```

Here is the procedure implementation:

```
Str_length PROC USES edi,
      pString:PTR BYTE              ; pointer to string
      mov edi,pString
      mov eax,0                     ; character count

L1: cmp BYTE PTR[edi],0             ; end of string?
      je  L2                        ; yes: quit
      inc edi                       ; no: point to next
      inc eax                       ; add 1 to count
      jmp L1
L2: ret
Str_length ENDP
```

See the *Length.asm* program for a demonstration of this procedure.

9.3.3   Str_copy Procedure

The **Str_copy** procedure copies a null-terminated string from a source location to a target location. Before calling this procedure, you must make sure the target operand is large enough to hold the copied string. The syntax for calling Str_copy is

```
INVOKE Str_copy, ADDR source, ADDR target
```

No values are returned by the procedure. Here is the implementation:

```
Str_copy PROC USES eax ecx esi edi,
      source:PTR BYTE,             ; source string
      target:PTR BYTE              ; target string
;
; Copy a string from source to target.
; Requires: the target string must contain enough
;           space to hold a copy of the source string.
;-------------------------------------------------
      INVOKE Str_length,source     ; EAX = length source
      mov   ecx,eax                ; REP count
      inc   ecx                    ; add 1 for null byte
      mov   esi,source
      mov   edi,target
      cld                          ; direction = forward
      rep   movsb                  ; copy the string
      ret
Str_copy ENDP
```

See the *CopyStr.asm* program for a demonstration of this procedure.

9.3.4   Str_trim Procedure

The **Str_trim** procedure removes all occurrences of a selected trailing character from a null-terminated string. The syntax for calling it is

```
INVOKE Str_trim, ADDR string, char_to_trim
```

The logic for this procedure is interesting because you have to check a number of possible cases (shown here with # as the trailing character):

1. The string is empty.
2. The string contains other characters followed by one or more trailing characters, as in "Hello##".
3. The string contains only one character, the trailing character, as in "#".
4. The string contains no trailing character, as in "Hello" or "H".
5. The string contains one or more trailing characters followed by one or more nontrailing characters, as in "#H" or "###Hello".

You can use Str_trim to remove all spaces (or any other repeated character) from the end of a string. The easiest way to truncate characters from a string is to insert a null byte just after the characters you want to retain. Any characters after the null byte become insignificant.

Table 9-4 lists some useful test cases. For each case, assuming that the # character is to be trimmed from the string, the expected output is shown.

Let's look at some code that tests the Str_trim procedure. The INVOKE statement passes the address of a string to Str_trim:

```
.data
string_1 BYTE "Hello##",0
.code
INVOKE Str_trim,ADDR string_1,'#'
INVOKE ShowString,ADDR string_1
```

The ShowString procedure, not shown here, displays the trimmed string with brackets on either side. Here's an example of its output:

```
[Hello]
```

For more examples, see *Trim.asm* in the Chapter 9 examples. The implementation of Str_trim, shown below, inserts a null byte just after the last character we want to keep in the string. Any characters following the null byte are universally ignored by string processing functions.

```
;------------------------------------------------------
Str_trim PROC USES eax ecx edi,
    pString:PTR BYTE,               ; points to string
    char:BYTE                       ; char to remove
;
; Remove all occurrences of a given delimiter character from
; the end of a string.
; Returns: nothing
;------------------------------------------------------
    mov  edi,pString                ; prepare to call Str_length
    INVOKE Str_length,edi           ; returns the length in EAX
    cmp  eax,0                       ; is the length equal to zero?
    je   L3                          ; yes: exit now
    mov  ecx,eax                     ; no: ECX = string length
    dec  eax
    add  edi,eax                     ; point to last character
```

```
L1:  mov  al,[edi]              ; get a character
     cmp  al,char               ; is it the delimiter?
     jne  L2                    ; no: insert null byte
     dec  edi                   ; yes: keep backing up
     loop L1                    ; until beginning reached
L2:  mov  BYTE PTR [edi+1],0    ; insert a null byte
L3:  ret
Stmr_trim ENDP
```

Table 9-4   Testing the Str_trim Procedure with a # Delimiter Character

Input String	Expected Modified String
"Hello##"	"Hello"
"#"	"" (empty string)
"Hello"	"Hello"
"H"	"H"
"#H"	"#H"

Detailed Description

Let us carefully examine *Str_trim*. The algorithm starts at the end of the string and scans backwards, looking for the first nondelimiter character. When it finds one, a null byte is inserted into the string just after the character position:

```
ecx = length(str)
if length(str) > 0 then
    edi = length - 1
    do while ecx > 0
      if str[edi] ≠ delimiter then
          str[edi+1] = null
          break
      else
          edi = edi - 1
      end if
      ecx = ecx - 1
    end do
else
    str[edi+1] = null
```

Next, let's look at the code implementation, line by line. First, *pString* contains the address of the string to be trimmed. We need to know the length of the string, and the Str_length procedure receives its input in the EDI register:

```
mov   edi,pString        ; prepare to call Str_length
INVOKE Str_length,edi    ; returns the length in EAX
```

The *Str_length* procedure returns the length of the string in the EAX register, so the following lines compare it to zero and skip the rest of the code if the string is empty:

```
cmp   eax,0              ; is the length equal to zero?
je    L3                 ; yes: exit now
```

From this point forward, we assume that the string is not empty. ECX will be the loop counter, so it is assigned a copy of the string length. Then, since we want EDI to point to the last character in the string, EAX (containing the string length) is decreased by 1 and added to EDI:

```
mov  ecx,eax              ; no: ECX = string length
dec  eax
add  edi,eax              ; point to last character
```

With EDI now pointing at the last character in the string, we copy the character into the AL register and compare it to the delimiter character:

```
L1: mov  al,[edi]         ; get a character
    cmp  al,char          ; is it the delimiter?
```

If the character is not the delimiter, we exit the loop, knowing that a null byte will be inserted at label L2:

```
jne  L2                   ; no: insert null byte
```

Otherwise, if the delimiter character is found, the loop continues to search backward through the string. This is done by moving EDI backward one position, and repeating the loop:

```
dec  edi                  ; yes: keep backing up
loop L1                   ; until beginning reached
```

If the entire string is filled with only delimiter characters, the loop will count down to zero and execution will continue on the next line after the loop. This is, of course, the code at label L2, which inserts a null byte in the string:

```
L2: mov  BYTE PTR [edi+1],0      ; insert a null byte
```

If control arrives at this point because the loop counted down to zero, EDI points one position prior to the beginning of the string. That is why the expression [edi+1] points to the first string position.

Execution reaches label L2 in two different ways: either by finding a nontrim character in the string, or by running the loop down to zero. Label L2 is followed by a RET instruction at label L3 that ends the procedure:

```
L3:  ret
Str_trim ENDP
```

9.3.5 Str_ucase Procedure

The **Str_ucase** procedure converts a string to all uppercase characters. It returns no value. When you call it, pass the offset of a string:

```
INVOKE Str_ucase, ADDR myString
```

Here is the procedure implementation:

```
Str_ucase PROC USES eax esi,
    pString:PTR BYTE
; Converts a null-terminated string to uppercase.
; Returns: nothing
;------------------------------------------------
    mov  esi,pString
```

```
L1:
       mov    al,[esi]                      ; get char
       cmp    al,0                          ; end of string?
       je     L3                            ; yes: quit
       cmp    al,'a'                        ; below "a"?
       jb     L2
       cmp    al,'z'                        ; above "z"?
       ja     L2
       and    BYTE PTR [esi],11011111b      ; convert the char
L2:    inc    esi                           ; next char
       jmp    L1

L3:    ret
Str_ucase ENDP
```

(See the *Ucase.asm* program for a demonstration of this procedure.)

9.3.6 String Library Demo Program

The following program (*StringDemo.asm*) shows examples of calling the Str_trim, Str_ucase, Str_compare, and Str_length procedures from the book's library:

```
TITLE String Library Demo        (StringDemo.asm)

; This program demonstrates the string-handling procedures in
; the book's link library.

INCLUDE Irvine32.inc

.data
string_1 BYTE "abcde////",0
string_2 BYTE "ABCDE",0
msg0     BYTE "string_1 in upper case: ",0
msg1     BYTE "string1 and string2 are equal",0
msg2     BYTE "string_1 is less than string_2",0
msg3     BYTE "string_2 is less than string_1",0
msg4     BYTE "Length of string_2 is ",0
msg5     BYTE "string_1 after trimming: ",0

.code
main PROC

     call   trim_string
     call   upper_case
     call   compare_strings
     call   print_length

     exit
main ENDP

trim_string PROC
; Remove trailing characters from string_1.

     INVOKE Str_trim, ADDR string_1, '/'
```

```
        mov     edx,OFFSET msg5
        call    WriteString
        mov     edx,OFFSET string_1
        call    WriteString
        call    Crlf

        ret
trim_string ENDP

upper_case PROC
; Convert string_1 to upper case.

        mov     edx,OFFSET msg0
        call    WriteString
        INVOKE Str_ucase, ADDR string_1
        mov     edx,OFFSET string_1
        call    WriteString
        call    Crlf

        ret
upper_case ENDP

compare_strings PROC
; Compare string_1 to string_2.

        INVOKE Str_compare, ADDR string_1, ADDR string_2
        .IF ZERO?
        mov     edx,OFFSET msg1
        .ELSEIF CARRY?
        mov     edx,OFFSET msg2         ; string 1 is less than...
        .ELSE
        mov     edx,OFFSET msg3         ; string 2 is less than...
        .ENDIF
        call    WriteString
        call    Crlf

        ret
compare_strings  ENDP

print_length PROC
; Display the length of string_2.

        mov     edx,OFFSET msg4
        call    WriteString
        INVOKE Str_length, ADDR string_2
        call    WriteDec
        call    Crlf

        ret
print_length ENDP
END main
```

Trailing characters are removed from string_1 by the call to Str_trim. The string is converted to uppercase by calling the Str_ucase procedure.

Program Output   Here is the String Library Demo program's output:

```
string_1 after trimming: abcde
string_1 in upper case: ABCDE
string1 and string2 are equal
Length of string_2 is 5
```

9.3.7 Section Review

1. *(True/False):* The **Str_compare** procedure stops when the null terminator of the longer string is reached.

2. *(True/False):* The **Str_compare** procedure does not need to use ESI and EDI to access memory.

3. *(True/False):* The **Str_length** procedure uses SCASB to find the null terminator at the end of the string.

4. *(True/False):* The **Str_copy** procedure prevents a string from being copied into too small a memory area.

5. What Direction flag setting is used in the **Str_trim** procedure?

6. Why does the **Str_trim** procedure use the JNE instruction?

7. What happens in the **Str_ucase** procedure if the target string contains a digit?

8. *Challenge:* If the **Str_length** procedure used SCASB, which repeat prefix would be most appropriate?

9. *Challenge:* If the **Str_length** procedure used SCASB, how would it calculate and return the string length?

9.4   Two-Dimensional Arrays

9.4.1   Ordering of Rows and Columns

From an assembly language programmer's perspective, a two-dimensional array is a high-level abstraction of a one-dimensional array. High-level languages select one of two methods of arranging the rows and columns in memory: *row-major order* and *column-major order*, as shown in Figure 9–1. When row-major order (most common) is used, the first row appears at the beginning of the memory block. The last element in the first row is followed in memory by the first element of the second row. When column-major order is used, the elements in the first column appear at the beginning of the memory block. The last element in the first column is followed in memory by the first element of the second column.

   If you implement a two-dimensional array in assembly language, you can choose either ordering method. In this chapter, we will use row-major order. If you write assembly language subroutines for a high-level language, you will follow the ordering specified in their documentation.

   The x86 instruction set includes two operand types, base-index and base-index-displacement, both suited to array applications. We will examine both and show examples of how they can be used effectively.

Figure 9–1   Row-Major and Column-Major Ordering.

Logical arrangement:

10	20	30	40	50
60	70	80	90	A0
B0	C0	D0	E0	F0

Row-major order

| 10 | 20 | 30 | 40 | 50 | 60 | 70 | 80 | 90 | A0 | B0 | C0 | D0 | E0 | F0 |

Column-major order

| 10 | 60 | B0 | 20 | 70 | C0 | 30 | 80 | D0 | 40 | 90 | E0 | 50 | A0 | F0 |

9.4.2   Base-Index Operands

A base-index operand adds the values of two registers (called *base* and *index*), producing an offset address:

```
[base + index]
```

The square brackets are required. In 32-bit mode, any 32-bit general-purpose registers may be used as base and index registers. In 16-bit mode, the base register must be BX or BP, and the index register must be SI or DI. (Usually, we avoid using BP or EBP except when addressing the stack.) The following are examples of various combinations of base and index operands in 32-bit mode:

```
.data
array WORD 1000h,2000h,3000h
.code
mov    ebx,OFFSET array
mov    esi,2
mov    ax,[ebx+esi]              ; AX = 2000h

mov    edi,OFFSET array
mov    ecx,4
mov    ax,[edi+ecx]              ; AX = 3000h

mov    ebp,OFFSET array
mov    esi,0
mov    ax,[ebp+esi]             ; AX = 1000h
```

Two-Dimensional Array   When accessing a two-dimensional array in row-major order, the row offset is held in the base register and the column offset is in the index register. The following table, for example, has three rows and five columns:

```
tableB BYTE    10h,  20h,  30h,  40h,  50h
Rowsize = ($  - tableB)
       BYTE    60h,  70h,  80h,  90h, 0A0h
       BYTE   0B0h, 0C0h, 0D0h, 0E0h, 0F0h
```

The table is in row-major order and the constant Rowsize is calculated by the assembler as the number of bytes in each table row. Suppose we want to locate a particular entry in the table using row and column coordinates. Assuming that the coordinates are zero based, the entry at row 1, column 2 contains 80h. We set EBX to the table's offset, add (Rowsize * row_index) to calculate the row offset, and set ESI to the column index:

```
row_index = 1
column_index = 2
mov   ebx,OFFSET tableB        ; table offset
add   ebx,RowSize * row_index  ; row offset
mov   esi,column_index
mov   al,[ebx + esi]           ; AL = 80h
```

Suppose the array is located at offset 0150h. Then the effective address represented by EBX + ESI is 0157h. Figure 9–2 shows how adding EBX and ESI produces the offset of the byte at tableB[1, 2]. If the effective address points outside the program's data region, a general protection fault occurs.

Figure 9–2   Addressing an Array with a Base-Index Operand.

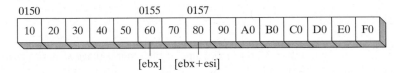

Calculating a Row Sum

Base index addressing simplifies many tasks associated with two-dimensional arrays. We might, for example, want to sum the elements in a row belonging to an integer matrix. The following calc_row_sum procedure (see *RowSum.asm*) calculates the sum of a selected row in a matrix of 8-bit integers:

```
calc_row_sum PROC uses ebx ecx edx esi
;
; Calculates the sum of a row in a byte matrix.
; Receives: EBX = table offset, EAX = row index,
;           ECX = row size, in bytes.
; Returns:  EAX holds the sum.
;------------------------------------------------------------
      mul   ecx                    ; row index * row size
      add   ebx,eax                ; row offset
      mov   eax,0                  ; accumulator
      mov   esi,0                  ; column index
L1:   movzx edx,BYTE PTR[ebx + esi] ; get a byte
      add   eax,edx                ; add to accumulator
      inc   esi                    ; next byte in row
      loop  L1

      ret
calc_row_sum ENDP
```

BYTE PTR was needed to clarify the operand size in the MOVZX instruction.

Scale Factors

If you're writing code for an array of WORD, multiply the index operand by a scale factor of 2. The following example locates the value at row 1, column 2:

```
tableW  WORD    10h,  20h,  30h,  40h,  50h
RowsizeW = ($ - tableW)
        WORD    60h,  70h,  80h,  90h,  0A0h
        WORD  0B0h, 0C0h, 0D0h, 0E0h, 0F0h
.code
row_index = 1
column_index = 2
mov     ebx,OFFSET tableW              ; table offset
add     ebx,RowSizeW * row_index       ; row offset
mov     esi,column_index
mov     ax,[ebx + esi*TYPE tableW]     ; AX = 0080h
```

The scale factor used in this example (TYPE tableW) is equal to 2. Similarly, you must use a scale factor of 4 if the array contains doublewords:

```
tableD DWORD 10h, 20h, ...etc.
.code
mov     eax,[ebx + esi*TYPE tableD]
```

9.4.3   Base-Index-Displacement Operands

A base-index-displacement operand combines a displacement, a base register, an index register, and an optional scale factor to produce an effective address. Here are the formats:

```
[base + index + displacement]
displacement[base + index]
```

Displacement can be the name of a variable or a constant expression. In 32-bit mode, any general-purpose 32-bit registers may be used for the base and index. In 16-bit mode, the base operand may be BX or BP and the index operand may be SI or DI. Base-index-displacement operands are well suited to processing two-dimensional arrays. The displacement can be an array name, the base operand can hold the row offset, and the index operand can hold the column offset.

Doubleword Array Example   The following two-dimensional array holds three rows of five doublewords:

```
tableD DWORD    10h,  20h,  30h,  40h,  50h
Rowsize = ($ - tableD)
        DWORD   60h,  70h,  80h,  90h,  0A0h
        DWORD  0B0h, 0C0h, 0D0h, 0E0h, 0F0h
```

Rowsize is equal to 20 (14h). Assuming that the coordinates are zero based, the entry at row 1, column 2 contains 80h. To access this entry, we set EBX to the row index and ESI to the column index:

```
mov     ebx,Rowsize                ; row index
mov     esi,2                      ; column index
mov     eax,tableD[ebx + esi*TYPE tableD]
```

Suppose **tableD** begins at offset 0150h. Figure 9–3 shows the positions of EBX and ESI relative to the array. Offsets are in hexadecimal.

FIGURE 9–3   Base-Index-Displacement Example.

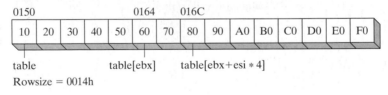

9.4.4   Section Review

1. In 32-bit mode, which registers can be used in a base-index operand?

2. Show an example of a base-index operand in 32-bit mode.

3. Show an example of a base-index-displacement operand in 32-bit mode.

4. Suppose a two-dimensional array of doublewords has three logical rows and four logical columns. If ESI is used as the row index, what value is added to ESI to move from one row to the next?

5. Suppose a two-dimensional array of doublewords has three logical rows and four logical columns. Write an expression using ESI and EDI that addresses the third column in the second row. (Numbering for rows and columns starts at zero.)

6. In 16-bit mode, should you use BP to address an array?

7. In 32-bit mode, should you use EBP to address an array?

9.5   Searching and Sorting Integer Arrays

A great deal of time and energy has been expended by computer scientists in finding better ways to search and sort massive data sets. It has been proven that choosing the best algorithm for a particular application is far more useful than buying a faster computer. Most students study searching and sorting using high-level languages such as C++ and Java. Assembly language lends a different perspective to the study of algorithms by letting you see low-level implementation details. It's interesting to note that one of the most noted algorithm authors of the twentieth century, Donald Knuth, used assembly language for his published program examples.[1]

Searching and sorting gives you a chance to try out the addressing modes introduced in this chapter. In particular, base-indexed addressing turns out to be useful because you can point one register (such as EBX) to the base of an array and use another register (such as ESI) to index into any other array location.

9.5.1   Bubble Sort

A bubble sort compares pairs of array values, beginning in positions 0 and 1. If the compared values are in reverse order, they are exchanged. Figure 9–4 shows the progress of one pass through an integer array.

FIGURE 9–4 First Pass through an Array (Bubble Sort).

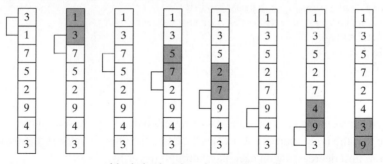

(shaded values have been exchanged)

After one pass, the array is still not sorted, but the largest value is now in the highest index position. The outer loop starts another pass through the array. After $n - 1$ passes, the array is guaranteed to be sorted.

The bubble sort works well for small arrays, but it becomes tremendously inefficient for larger ones. When computer scientists measure the relative efficiency of an algorithm, they often use what is known as "big-oh" notation that describes how the average running time increases in relation to increases in the number of items to be processed. The bubble sort is known as an $O(n^2)$ algorithm, meaning that its running time increases quadratically in relation to the number of array elements (n). Suppose, for example, that it takes 0.1 second to sort 1000 elements. As the number of elements increases by a factor of 10, the time required to sort the array increases by a factor of 10^2 (100). The following table shows sort times for various array sizes, assuming that 1000 array elements can be sorted in 0.1 second:

Array Size	Time (seconds)
1,000	0.1
10,000	10.0
100,000	1000
1,000,000	100,000 (27.78 hours)

A bubble sort would not be effective for an array of 1 million integers because it would take too long to finish! But it would be efficient enough to process a few hundred integers.

Pseudocode It's useful to create a simplified version of the bubble sort, using pseudocode that is similar to assembly language. We will use **N** to represent the size of the array, **cx1** to represent the outer loop counter, and **cx2** to represent the inner loop counter:

```
cx1 = N - 1
while( cx1 > 0 )
{
  esi = addr(array)
  cx2 = cx1
  while( cx2 > 0 )
```

```
    {
      if( array[esi] < array[esi+4] )
        exchange( array[esi], array[esi+4] )
      add esi,4
      dec cx2
    }
    dec cx1
  }
```

Mechanical concerns, such as saving and restoring the outer loop counter, have purposely been left out. Note that the inner loop count (**cx2**) is based on the current value of the outer loop count (**cx1**), which in turn decreases with each pass through the array.

Assembly Language   From pseudocode, we can easily generate a matching implementation in assembly language, placing it in a procedure with parameters and local variables:

```
;------------------------------------------------------------
BubbleSort PROC USES eax ecx esi,
    pArray:PTR DWORD,           ; pointer to array
    Count:DWORD                 ; array size
;
; Sort an array of 32-bit signed integers in ascending
; order, using the bubble sort algorithm.
; Receives: pointer to array, array size
; Returns: nothing
;------------------------------------------------------------
      mov     ecx,Count
      dec     ecx                 ; decrement count by 1

L1:   push    ecx                 ; save outer loop count
      mov     esi,pArray          ; point to first value

L2:   mov     eax,[esi]           ; get array value
      cmp     [esi+4],eax         ; compare a pair of values
      jg      L3                  ; if [ESI] <= [ESI+4], no exchange
      xchg    eax,[esi+4]         ; exchange the pair
      mov     [esi],eax

L3:   add     esi,4               ; move both pointers forward
      loop    L2                  ; inner loop

      pop     ecx                 ; retrieve outer loop count
      loop    L1                  ; else repeat outer loop

L4:   ret
BubbleSort ENDP
```

9.5.2 Binary Search

Array searches are some of the most common operations in everyday programming. For a small array (1000 elements or less), it's easy to do a *sequential search*, where you start at the beginning of the array and examine each element in sequence until a matching one is found. For any array of n elements, a sequential search requires an average of $n/2$ comparisons. If a small array is searched, the execution time is minimal. On the other hand, searching an array of 1 million elements can require a more significant amount of processing time.

The *binary search* algorithm is particularly effective when searching for a single item in a large array. It has one important precondition: The array elements must be arranged in ascending or descending order. The following algorithm assumes the elements are in ascending order:

Before beginning the search, ask the user to enter an integer, which we will call *searchVal*.

1. The range of the array to be searched is indicated by the subscripts named *first* and *last*. If *first* > *last*, exit the search, indicating failure to find a match.
2. Calculate the midpoint of the array between array subscripts *first* and *last*.
3. Compare *searchVal* to the integer at the midpoint of the array:
   - If the values are equal, return from the procedure with the midpoint in EAX. This return value indicates that a match has been found in the array.
   - On the other hand, if *searchVal* is larger than the number at the midpoint, reset *first* to one position higher than the midpoint.
   - Or, if *searchVal* is smaller than the number at the midpoint, reset *last* to one position below the midpoint.
4. Return to Step 1.

The binary search algorithm is spectacularly efficient because it uses a divide and conquer strategy. The range of values is divided in half with each iteration of the loop. In general, it is described as an O(log *n*) algorithm, meaning that as the number of array elements increases by a factor of *n*, the average search time increases by only a factor of log *n*. To help you get a feel for how efficient the binary search is, Table 9–5 lists the maximum number of comparisons that would be required to perform both a sequential search and a binary search on arrays of several sample sizes. These numbers represent a worst-case scenario—in actual practice, matching values might be found after fewer comparisons.

Table 9-5   Maximum Comparisons for Sequential and Binary Search

Array Size	Sequential Search	Binary Search
64	64	6
1,024	1,024	10
65,536	65,536	17
1,048,576	1,048,576	21
4,294, 967,296	4,294, 967,296	33

Following is a C++ implementation of a binary search function designed to work with an array of signed integers:

```
int BinSearch( int values[], const int searchVal, int count )
{
  int first = 0;
  int last = count - 1;

  while( first <= last )
  {
    int mid = (last + first) / 2;
```

```
    if( values[mid] < searchVal )
      first = mid + 1;
    else if( values[mid] > searchVal )
      last = mid - 1;
    else
      return mid;          // success
  }
  return -1;               // not found
}
```

The following listing shows an assembly language implementation of the sample C++ code:

```
;------------------------------------------------------------
BinarySearch PROC USES ebx edx esi edi,
    pArray:PTR DWORD,          ; pointer to array
    Count:DWORD,               ; array size
    searchVal:DWORD            ; search value
LOCAL first:DWORD,             ; first position
    last:DWORD,                ; last position
    mid:DWORD                  ; midpoint
;
; Searches an array of signed integers for a single value.
; Receives: Pointer to array, array size, search value.
; Returns: If a match is found, EAX = the array position of the
; matching element; otherwise, EAX = -1.
;------------------------------------------------------------
    mov    first,0             ; first = 0
    mov    eax,Count           ; last = (count - 1)
    dec    eax
    mov    last,eax
    mov    edi,searchVal       ; EDI = searchVal
    mov    ebx,pArray          ; EBX points to the array

L1:  ; while first <= last
    mov    eax,first
    cmp    eax,last
    jg     L5                  ; exit search
; mid = (last + first) / 2
    mov    eax,last
    add    eax,first
    shr    eax,1
    mov    mid,eax
; EDX = values[mid]
    mov    esi,mid
    shl    esi,2               ; scale mid value by 4
    mov    edx,[ebx+esi]       ; EDX = values[mid]
; if ( EDX < searchval(EDI) )
    cmp    edx,edi
    jge    L2
;    first = mid + 1
```

```
           mov    eax,mid
           inc    eax
           mov    first,eax
           jmp    L4
      ; else if( EDX > searchVal(EDI) )
      L2: cmp    edx,edi               ; optional
           jle    L3
      ;      last = mid - 1
           mov    eax,mid
           dec    eax
           mov    last,eax
           jmp    L4

      ; else return mid
      L3: mov    eax,mid               ; value found
           jmp    L9                    ; return (mid)

      L4: jmp    L1                    ; continue the loop

      L5: mov    eax,-1                ; search failed
      L9: ret
      BinarySearch ENDP
```

Test Program

To demonstrate the bubble sort and binary search functions presented in this chapter, let's write a short test program that performs the following steps, in sequence:

• Fills an array with random integers
• Displays the array
• Sorts the array using a bubble sort
• Redisplays the array
• Asks the user to enter an integer
• Performs a binary search for the user's integer (in the array)
• Displays the results of the binary search

The individual procedures have been placed in separate source files to make it easier to locate and edit source code. Table 9-6 lists each module and its contents. Most professionally written programs are divided into separate code modules.

Table 9-6   Modules in the Bubble Sort/Binary Search Program.

Module	Contents
B_main.asm	Main module: Contains the main, **ShowResults**, and **AskForSearchVal** procedures. Contains the program entry point and manages the overall sequence of tasks.
Bsort.asm	**BubbleSort** procedure: Performs a bubble sort on a 32-bit signed integer array.
Bsearch.asm	**BinarySearch** procedure: Performs a binary search on a 32-bit signed integer array.
FillArry.asm	**FillArray** procedure: Fills a 32-bit signed integer array with a range of random values.
PrtArry.asm	**PrintArray** procedure: Writes the contents of a 32-bit signed integer array to standard output.

The procedures in all modules except *B_main* are written in such a way that it would be easy to use them in other programs without making any modifications. This is highly desirable because we might save time in the future by reusing existing code. The same approach is used in the Irvine32 and Irvine16 link libraries. Following is an include file (*Bsearch.inc*) containing prototypes of the procedures called from the main module:

```
; Bsearch.inc - prototypes for procedures used in
; the BubbleSort / BinarySearch program.

; Searches for an integer in an array of 32-bit signed
; integers.
BinarySearch PROTO,
     pArray:PTR DWORD,            ; pointer to array
     Count:DWORD,                 ; array size
     searchVal:DWORD              ; search value

; Fills an array with 32-bit signed random integers
FillArray PROTO,
     pArray:PTR DWORD,            ; pointer to array
     Count:DWORD,                 ; number of elements
     LowerRange:SDWORD,           ; lower limit of random values
     UpperRange:SDWORD            ; upper limit of random values

; Writes a 32-bit signed integer array to standard output
PrintArray PROTO,
     pArray:PTR DWORD,
     Count:DWORD

; Sorts the array in ascending order
BubbleSort PROTO,
     pArray:PTR DWORD,
     Count:DWORD
```

Following is a listing of *B_main.asm*, the main module:

```
TITLE Bubble Sort and Binary Search          B_main.asm)

; Bubble sort an array of signed integers, and perform
; a binary search.
; Main module, calls Bsearch.asm, Bsort.asm, FillArry.asm,
; and PrtArry.asm

INCLUDE Irvine32.inc
INCLUDE Bsearch.inc                ; procedure prototypes

LOWVAL = -5000                     ; minimum value
HIGHVAL = +5000                    ; maximum value
ARRAY_SIZE = 50                    ; size of the array

.data
array DWORD ARRAY_SIZE DUP(?)

.code
main PROC
    call Randomize
```

```
            ; Fill an array with random signed integers
            INVOKE FillArray, ADDR array, ARRAY_SIZE, LOWVAL, HIGHVAL

            ; Display the array
            INVOKE PrintArray, ADDR array, ARRAY_SIZE
            call WaitMsg

            ; Perform a bubble sort and redisplay the array
            INVOKE BubbleSort, ADDR array, ARRAY_SIZE
            INVOKE PrintArray, ADDR array, ARRAY_SIZE

            ; Demonstrate a binary search
            call AskForSearchVal         ; returned in EAX
            INVOKE BinarySearch,
              ADDR array, ARRAY_SIZE, eax
            call ShowResults

            exit
main ENDP

;-----------------------------------------------------------
AskForSearchVal PROC
;
; Prompt the user for a signed integer.
; Receives: nothing
; Returns: EAX = value input by user
;-----------------------------------------------------------
.data
prompt BYTE "Enter a signed decimal integer "
       BYTE "in the range of -5000 to +5000 "
       BYTE "to find in the array: ",0
.code
    call  Crlf
    mov   edx,OFFSET prompt
    call  WriteString
    call  ReadInt
    ret
AskForSearchVal ENDP

;-----------------------------------------------------------
ShowResults PROC
;
; Display the resulting value from the binary search.
; Receives: EAX = position number to be displayed
; Returns: nothing
;-----------------------------------------------------------
.data
msg1 BYTE "The value was not found.",0
msg2 BYTE "The value was found at position ",0
.code
.IF eax == -1
    mov   edx,OFFSET msg1
```

```
        call  WriteString
.ELSE
        mov   edx,OFFSET msg2
        call  WriteString
        call  WriteDec
.ENDIF
        call  Crlf
        call  Crlf
        ret
ShowResults ENDP
END main
```

PrintArray   Following is a listing of the module containing the PrintArray procedure:

```
TITLE PrintArray Procedure (PrtArry.asm)

INCLUDE Irvine32.inc

.code
;---------------------------------------------------------------
PrintArray PROC USES eax ecx edx esi,
        pArray:PTR DWORD,             ; pointer to array
        Count:DWORD                   ; number of elements
;
; Writes an array of 32-bit signed decimal integers to
; standard output, separated by commas
; Receives: pointer to array, array size
; Returns: nothing
;---------------------------------------------------------------
.data
comma BYTE ", ",0
.code
        mov   esi,pArray
        mov   ecx,Count
        cld                           ; direction = forward

L1: lodsd                             ; load [ESI] into EAX
        call  WriteInt                ; send to output
        mov   edx,OFFSET comma
        call  Writestring             ; display comma
        loop  L1

        call  Crlf
        ret
PrintArray ENDP
END
```

FillArray   Following is a listing of the module containing the FillArray procedure:

```
TITLE FillArray Procedure                  (FillArry.asm)

INCLUDE Irvine32.inc

.code
;---------------------------------------------------------------
FillArray PROC USES eax edi ecx edx,
```

```
        pArray:PTR DWORD,           ; pointer to array
        Count:DWORD,                ; number of elements
        LowerRange:SDWORD,          ; lower range
        UpperRange:SDWORD           ; upper range
    ;
    ; Fills an array with a random sequence of 32-bit signed
    ; integers between LowerRange and (UpperRange - 1).
    ; Returns: nothing
    ;----------------------------------------------------------
        mov    edi,pArray           ; EDI points to the array
        mov    ecx,Count            ; loop counter
        mov    edx,UpperRange
        sub    edx,LowerRange       ; EDX = absolute range (0..n)
        cld                         ; clear direction flag

    L1: mov    eax,edx              ; get absolute range
        call   RandomRange
        add    eax,LowerRange       ; bias the result
        stosd                       ; store EAX into [edi]
        loop   L1

        ret
    FillArray ENDP
    END
```

9.5.3 Section Review

1. If an array were already in sequential order, how many times would the outer loop of the **BubbleSort** procedure in Section 9.5.1 execute?

2. In the **BubbleSort** procedure, how many times does the inner loop execute on the first pass through the array?

3. In the **BubbleSort** procedure, does the inner loop always execute the same number of times?

4. If it were found (through testing) that an array of 500 integers could be sorted in 0.5 seconds, how many seconds would it take to bubble sort an array of 5000 integers?

5. What is the maximum number of comparisons needed by the binary search algorithm when an array contains 1,024 elements?

6. In the FillArray procedure from the Binary Search example, why must the Direction flag be cleared by the CLD instruction?

7. *Challenge:* In the **BinarySearch** procedure (Section 9.5.2), why could the statement at label **L2** be removed without affecting the outcome?

8. *Challenge:* In the **BinarySearch** procedure, how might the statement at label **L4** be eliminated?

9.6 Java Bytecodes: String Processing

In Chapter 8, we introduced Java bytecodes and showed how you can disassemble java .class files into a readable bytecode format. In this section, we show how Java handles strings and methods that work on strings.

Example: Finding a Substring

The following Java code defines a string variable containing an employee ID and last name. Then, it calls the substring method to place the account number in a second string variable:

```
String empInfo = "10034Smith";
String id = empInfo.substring(0,5);
```

The following bytecodes are displayed when this Java code is disassembled:

```
0: ldc #32;                  // String 10034Smith
2: astore_0
3: aload_0
4: iconst_0
5: iconst_5
6: invokevirtual #34;        // Method java/lang/String.substring
9: astore_1
```

Now we will study the code in steps, adding our own comments. The *ldc* instruction loads a reference to a string literal from the constant pool onto the operand stack. Then, the *astore_0* instruction pops the string reference from the runtime stack and stores it in the local variable named *empInfo*, at index 0 in the local variables area:

```
0: ldc  #32;                 // load literal string: 10034Smith
2: astore_0                  // store into empInfo (index 0)
```

Next, the *aload_0* instruction pushes a reference to *empinfo* onto the operand stack:

```
3: aload_0                   // load empinfo onto the stack
```

Next, before calling the *substring* method, its two arguments (0 and 5) must be pushed onto the operand stack. This is accomplished by the *iconst_0* and *iconst_5* instructions:

```
4: iconst_0
5: iconst_5
```

The *invokevirtual* instruction invokes the substring method, which has a reference ID number of 34:

```
6: invokevirtual #34;        // Method java/lang/String.substring
```

The substring method creates a new string and pushes the string's reference on the operand stack. The following *astore_1* instruction stores this string into index position 1 in the local variables area. This is where the variable named *id* is located:

```
9: astore_1
```

9.7   Chapter Summary

String primitive instructions are unusual in that they require no register operands and are optimized for high-speed memory access. They are

- MOVS: Move string data
- CMPS: Compare strings
- SCAS: Scan string
- STOS: Store string data
- LODS: Load accumulator from string

Each string primitive instruction has a suffix of B, W, or D when manipulating bytes, words, and doublewords, respectively.

The repeat prefix REP repeats a string primitive instruction with automatic incrementing or decrementing of index registers. For example, when REPNE is used with SCASB, it scans memory bytes until a value in memory pointed to by EDI matches the contents of the AL register. The Direction flag determines whether the index register is incremented or decremented during each iteration of a string primitive instruction.

Strings and arrays are practically the same. Traditionally, a string consisted of an array of single-byte ASCII values, but now strings can contain 16-bit Unicode characters. The only important difference between a string and an array is that a string is usually terminated by a single null byte (containing zero).

Array manipulation is computationally intensive because it usually involves a looping algorithm. Most programs spend 80 to 90 percent of their running time executing small fraction of their code. As a result, you can speed up your software by reducing the number and complexity of instructions inside loops. Assembly language is a great tool for code optimization because you can control every detail. You might optimize a block of code, for example, by substituting registers for memory variables. Or you might use one of the string-processing instructions shown in this chapter rather than MOV and CMP instructions.

Several useful string-processing procedures were introduced in this chapter: The **Str_copy** procedure copies one string to another. **Str_length** returns the length of a string. **Str_compare** compares two strings. **Str_trim** removes a selected character from the end of a string. **Str_ucase** converts a string to uppercase letters.

Base-index operands assist in manipulating two-dimensional arrays (tables). You can set a base register to the address of a table row, and point an index register to the offset of a column within the selected row. In 32-bit mode, any general-purpose 32-bit registers can be used as base and index registers. In 16-bit mode, base registers must be BX and BP; index registers must be SI and DI. Base-index-displacement operands are similar to base-index operands, except that they also include the name of the array:

```
[ebx + esi]                          ; base-index
array[ebx + esi]                     ; base-index-displacement
```

We presented assembly language implementations of a bubble sort and a binary search. A bubble sort orders the elements of an array in ascending or descending order. It is effective for arrays having no more than a few hundred elements, but inefficient for larger arrays. A binary search permits rapid searching for a single value in an ordered array. It is easy to implement in assembly language.

9.8   Programming Exercises

The following exercises can be done in either 32-bit mode or 16-bit mode. Each string-handling procedure assumes the use of null-terminated strings. Even when not explicitly requested, write a short driver program for each exercise solution that tests your new procedure.

★ **1. Improved Str_copy Procedure**

The **Str_copy** procedure shown in this chapter does not limit the number of characters to be copied. Create a new version (named **Str_copyN**) that receives an additional input parameter indicating the maximum number of characters to be copied.

★★ **2. Str_concat Procedure**

Write a procedure named **Str_concat** that concatenates a source string to the end of a target string. Sufficient space must exist in the target string to accommodate the new characters. Pass pointers to the source and target strings. Here is a sample call:

```
.data
targetStr BYTE "ABCDE",10 DUP(0)
sourceStr BYTE "FGH",0
.code
INVOKE Str_concat, ADDR targetStr, ADDR sourceStr
```

★★ **3. Str_remove Procedure**

Write a procedure named **Str_remove** that removes *n* characters from a string. Pass a pointer to the position in the string where the characters are to be removed. Pass an integer specifying the number of characters to remove. The following code, for example, shows how to remove "xxxx" from **target**:

```
.data
target BYTE "abcxxxxdefghijklmop",0
.code
INVOKE Str_remove, ADDR [target+3], 4
```

★★★ **4. Str_find Procedure**

Write a procedure named **Str_find** that searches for the first matching occurrence of a source string inside a target string and returns the matching position. *(A VideoNote for this exercise is posted on the Web site.)* The input parameters should be a pointer to the source string and a pointer to the target string. If a match is found, the procedure sets the Zero flag and EAX points to the matching position in the target string. Otherwise, the Zero flag is clear and EAX is undefined. The following code, for example, searches for "ABC" and returns with EAX pointing to the "A" in the target string:

```
.data
target BYTE "123ABC342432",0
source BYTE "ABC",0
pos    DWORD ?
.code
INVOKE Str_find, ADDR source, ADDR target
jnz notFound
mov pos,eax                      ; store the position value
```

★★ **5. Str_nextword Procedure**

Write a procedure called **Str_nextword** that scans a string for the first occurrence of a certain delimiter character and replaces the delimiter with a null byte. There are two input parameters: a pointer to the string, and the delimiter character. After the call, if the delimiter was found, the Zero flag is set and EAX contains the offset of the next character beyond the delimiter. Otherwise, the

Zero flag is clear and EAX is undefined. The following example code passes the address of **target** and a comma as the delimiter:

```
.data
target BYTE "Johnson,Calvin",0
.code
INVOKE Str_nextword, ADDR target, ','
jnz notFound
```

In Figure 9–5, after calling **Str_nextword**, EAX points to the character following the position where the comma was found (and replaced).

FIGURE 9–5   Str_nextword Example.

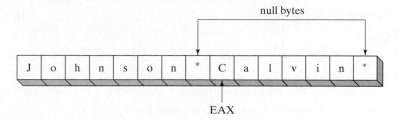

★★ 6.   **Constructing a Frequency Table**

Write a procedure named **Get_frequencies** that constructs a character frequency table. Input to the procedure should be a pointer to a string and a pointer to an array of 256 doublewords initialized to all zeros. Each array position is indexed by its corresponding ASCII code. When the procedure returns, each entry in the array contains a count of how many times the corresponding character occurred in the string. For example,

```
.data
target BYTE "AAEBDCFBBC",0
freqTable DWORD 256 DUP(0)
.code
INVOKE Get_frequencies, ADDR target, ADDR freqTable
```

Figure 9–6 shows a picture of the string and entries 41 (hexadecimal) through 4B in the frequency table. Position 41 contains the value 2 because the letter A (ASCII code 41h) occurred twice in the string. Similar counts are shown for other characters. Frequency tables are useful in data compression and other applications involving character processing. The *Huffman encoding algorithm*, for example, stores the most frequently occurring characters in fewer bits than other characters that occur less often.

FIGURE 9–6   Sample Character Frequency Table.

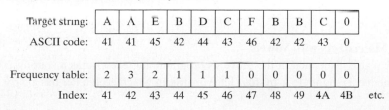

★★★ **7. Sieve of Eratosthenes**

The *Sieve of Eratosthenes,* invented by the Greek mathematician of the same name, provides a quick way to find all prime numbers within a given range. The algorithm involves creating an array of bytes in which positions are "marked" by inserting 1's in the following manner: Beginning with position 2 (which is a prime number), insert a 1 in each array position that is a multiple of 2. Then do the same thing for multiples of 3, the next prime number. Find the next prime number after 3, which is 5, and mark all positions that are multiples of 5. Proceed in this manner until all multiples of primes have been found. The remaining positions of the array that are unmarked indicate which numbers are prime. For this program, create a 65,000-element array and display all primes between 2 and 65,000. Declare the array in an uninitialized data segment (see Section 3.4.11) and use STOSB to fill it with zeros. In 32-bit mode, your array can be much larger. *(A VideoNote for this exercise is posted on the Web site.)*

★ **8. Bubble Sort**

Add a variable to the **BubbleSort** procedure in Section 9.5.1 that is set to 1 whenever a pair of values is exchanged within the inner loop. Use this variable to exit the sort before its normal completion if you discover that no exchanges took place during a complete pass through the array. (This variable is commonly known as an *exchange flag*.)

★★ **9. Binary Search**

Rewrite the binary search procedure shown in this chapter by using registers for mid, first, and last. Add comments to clarify the registers' usage.

★★★ **10. Letter Matrix**

Create a procedure that generates a four-by-four matrix of randomly chosen capital letters. *(A VideoNote for this exercise is posted on the Web site.)* When choosing the letters, there must be a 50% probability that the chosen letter is a vowel. Write a test program with a loop that calls your procedure five times and displays each matrix in the console window. Following is sample output for the first three matrices:

```
D W A L
S I V W
U I O L
L A I I

K X S V
N U U O
O R Q O
A U U T

P O A Z
A E A U
G K A E
I A G D
```

★★★★ **11. Letter Matrix/Sets with Vowels**

Use the letter matrix generated in the previous programming exercise as a starting point for this program. Generate a random four-by-four letter matrix in which each letter has a 50% probability of being a vowel. Traverse each matrix row, column, and diagonal, generating sets of letters. Display only four-letter sets containing exactly two vowels. Suppose, for example, the following matrix was generated:

```
P O A Z
A E A U
G K A E
I A G D
```

Then the four-letter sets displayed by the program would be POAZ, GKAE, IAGD, PAGI, ZUED, PEAD, and ZAKI. The order of letters within each set is unimportant.

★★★★ **12.   Calculating the Sum of an Array Row**

Write a procedure named **calc_row_sum** that calculates the sum of a single row in a two-dimensional array of bytes, words, or doublewords. The procedure should have the following stack parameters: array offset, row size, array type, row index. It must return the sum in EAX. Use explicit stack parameters, not INVOKE or extended PROC. Write a program that tests your procedure with arrays of byte, word, and doubleword. Prompt the user for the row index, and display the sum of the selected row.

End Note

1. Donald, Knuth, *The Art of Computer Programming,* Volume I: *Fundamental Algorithms,* Addison-Wesley, 1997.

10

Structures and Macros

10.1 Structures

    10.1.1 Defining Structures
    10.1.2 Declaring Structure Variables
    10.1.3 Referencing Structure Variables
    10.1.4 Example: Displaying the System Time
    10.1.5 Structures Containing Structures
    10.1.6 Example: Drunkard's Walk
    10.1.7 Declaring and Using Unions
    10.1.8 Section Review

10.2 Macros

    10.2.1 Overview
    10.2.2 Defining Macros
    10.2.3 Invoking Macros
    10.2.4 Additional Macro Features
    10.2.5 Using the Book's Macro Library
    10.2.6 Example Program: Wrappers
    10.2.7 Section Review

10.3 Conditional-Assembly Directives

    10.3.1 Checking for Missing Arguments

    10.3.2 Default Argument Initializers
    10.3.3 Boolean Expressions
    10.3.4 IF, ELSE, and ENDIF Directives
    10.3.5 The IFIDN and IFIDNI Directives
    10.3.6 Example: Summing a Matrix Row
    10.3.7 Special Operators
    10.3.8 Macro Functions
    10.3.9 Section Review

10.4 Defining Repeat Blocks

    10.4.1 WHILE Directive
    10.4.2 REPEAT Directive
    10.4.3 FOR Directive
    10.4.4 FORC Directive
    10.4.5 Example: Linked List
    10.4.6 Section Review

10.5 Chapter Summary

10.6 Programming Exercises

10.1 Structures

A structure is a template or pattern given to a logically related group of variables. The variables in a structure are called *fields*. Program statements can access the structure as a single entity, or they can access individual fields. Structures often contain fields of different types. A union also groups together multiple identifiers, but the identifiers overlap the same area in memory. Unions will be covered in Section 10.1.7.

Structures provide an easy way to cluster data and pass it from one procedure to another. Suppose input parameters for a procedure consisted of 20 different units of data relating to a disk drive. Calling such a procedure would be error-prone, since one might mix up the order of arguments, or pass the incorrect number of arguments. Instead, you could place all of the input data in a structure and pass the address of the structure to the procedure. Minimal stack space would be used (one address), and the called procedure could modify the contents of the structure.

Structures in assembly language are essentially the same as structures in C and C++. With a small effort at translation, you can take any structure from the MS-Windows API library and make it work in assembly language. Most debuggers can display individual structure fields.

COORD Structure   The COORD structure defined in the Windows API identifies X and Y screen coordinates. The field X has an offset of zero relative to the beginning of the structure, and the field Y's offset is 2:

```
COORD STRUCT
    X WORD ?                         ; offset 00
    Y WORD ?                         ; offset 02
COORD ENDS
```

Using a structure involves three sequential steps:

1. Define the structure.
2. Declare one or more variables of the structure type, called *structure variables*.
3. Write runtime instructions that access the structure fields.

10.1.1 Defining Structures

A structure is defined using the STRUCT and ENDS directives. Inside the structure, fields are defined using the same syntax as for ordinary variables. Structures can contain virtually any number of fields:

```
name STRUCT
    field-declarations
name ENDS
```

Field Initializers   When structure fields have initializers, the values are assigned when structure variables are created. You can use various types of field initializers:

- *Undefined:* The ? operator leaves the field contents undefined.
- *String literals:* Character strings enclosed in quotation marks.
- *Integers:* Integer constants and integer expressions.
- *Arrays:* The DUP operator can initialize array elements.

The following **Employee** structure describes employee information, with fields such as ID number, last name, years of service, and an array of salary history values. The following definition must appear prior to the declaration of **Employee** variables:

```
Employee STRUCT
    IdNum     BYTE "000000000"
    LastName BYTE 30 DUP(0)
    Years     WORD 0
    SalaryHistory DWORD 0,0,0,0
Employee ENDS
```

This is a linear representation of the structure's memory layout:

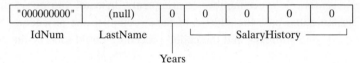

Years

Aligning Structure Fields

For best memory I/O performance, structure members should be aligned to addresses matching their data types. Otherwise, the CPU will require more time to access the members. For example, a doubleword member should be aligned on a doubleword boundary. Table 10-1 lists the alignments used by the Microsoft C and C++ compilers and by Win32 API functions. In assembly language, the ALIGN directive sets the address alignment of the next field or variable:

```
ALIGN datatype
```

The following, for example, aligns **myVar** to a doubleword boundary:

```
.data
ALIGN DWORD
myVar DWORD ?
```

Let's correctly define the Employee structure, using ALIGN to put **Years** on a WORD boundary and **SalaryHistory** on a DWORD boundary. Field sizes appear as comments.

```
Employee STRUCT
     IdNum      BYTE "000000000"          ;  9
     LastName BYTE 30 DUP(0)              ; 30
     ALIGN      WORD                      ;  1 byte added
     Years      WORD 0                    ;  2
     ALIGN      DWORD                     ;  2 bytes added
     SalaryHistory DWORD 0,0,0,0          ; 16
Employee ENDS                            ; 60 total
```

Table 10-1   Alignment of Structure Members.

Member Type	Alignment
BYTE, SBYTE	Align on 8-bit (byte) boundary
WORD, SWORD	Align on 16-bit (word) boundary
DWORD, SDWORD	Align on 32-bit (doubleword) boundary
QWORD	Align on 64-bit (quadword) boundary
REAL4	Align on 32-bit (doubleword) boundary
REAL8	Align on 64-bit (quadword) boundary
structure	Largest alignment requirement of any member
union	Alignment requirement of the first member

10.1.2   Declaring Structure Variables

Structure variables can be declared and optionally initialized with specific values. This is the syntax, in which *structureType* has already been defined using the STRUCT directive:

```
identifier structureType < initializer-list >
```

The *identifier* follows the same rules as other variable names in MASM. The *initializer-list* is optional, but if used, is a comma-separated list of assembly-time constants that match the data types of specific structure fields:

```
initializer [, initializer] . . .
```

Empty angle brackets < > cause the structure to contain the default field values from the structure definition. Alternatively, you can insert new values in selected fields. The values are inserted into the structure fields in order from left to right, matching the order of the fields in the structure declaration. Examples of both approaches are shown here, using the **COORD** and **Employee** structures:

```
.data
point1 COORD <5,10>                ; X = 5, Y = 10
point2 COORD <20>                  ; X = 20, Y = ?
point3 COORD <>                    ; X = ?, Y = ?
worker Employee <>                 ; (default initializers)
```

It is possible to override only selected field initializers. The following declaration overrides only the **IdNum** field of the **Employee** structure, assigning the remaining fields default values:

```
person1 Employee <"555223333">
```

An alternative notational form uses curly braces {. . .} rather than angle brackets:

```
person2 Employee {"555223333"}
```

When the initializer for a string field is shorter than the field, the remaining positions are padded with spaces. A null byte is not automatically inserted at the end of a string field. You can skip over structure fields by inserting commas as place markers. For example, the following statement skips the **IdNum** field and initializes the **LastName** field:

```
person3 Employee <,"dJones">
```

For an array field, use the DUP operator to initialize some or all of the array elements. If the initializer is shorter than the field, the remaining positions are filled with zeros. In the following, we initialize the first two **SalaryHistory** values and set the rest to zero:

```
person4 Employee <,,,2 DUP(20000)>
```

Array of Structures   Use the DUP operator to create an array of structures. In the following, the X and Y fields of each element in **AllPoints** are initialized to zeros:

```
NumPoints = 3
AllPoints COORD NumPoints DUP(<0,0>)
```

Aligning Structure Variables

For best processor performance, align structure variables on memory boundaries equal to the largest structure member. The Employee structure contains DWORD fields, so the following definition uses that alignment:

```
.data
ALIGN DWORD
person Employee <>
```

10.1.3 Referencing Structure Variables

References to structure variables and structure names can be made using the TYPE and SIZEOF operators. For example, let's return to the **Employee** structure we saw earlier:

```
Employee STRUCT
    IdNum     BYTE "000000000"         ; 9
    LastName BYTE 30 DUP(0)            ; 30
    ALIGN     WORD                     ; 1 byte added
    Years     WORD 0                   ; 2
    ALIGN     DWORD                    ; 2 bytes added
    SalaryHistory DWORD 0,0,0,0        ; 16
Employee ENDS                         ; 60 total
```

Given the data definition

```
.data
worker Employee <>
```

each of the following expressions returns the same value:

```
TYPE Employee               ; 60
SIZEOF Employee             ; 60
SIZEOF worker               ; 60
```

The TYPE operator (Section 4.4) returns the number of bytes used by the identifier's storage type (BYTE, WORD, DWORD, etc.) The LENGTHOF operator returns a count of the number of elements in an array. The SIZEOF operator multiplies LENGTHOF by TYPE.

References to Members

References to named structure members require a structure variable as a qualifier. The following constant expressions can be generated at assembly time, using the **Employee** structure:

```
TYPE Employee.SalaryHistory      ; 4
LENGTHOF Employee.SalaryHistory  ; 4
SIZEOF Employee.SalaryHistory    ; 16
TYPE Employee.Years              ; 2
```

The following are runtime references to **worker**, an Employee:

```
.data
worker Employee <>
.code
mov  dx,worker.Years
mov  worker.SalaryHistory,20000       ; first salary
mov  [worker.SalaryHistory+4],30000   ; second salary
```

Using the OFFSET Operator   You can use the OFFSET operator to obtain the address of a field within a structure variable:

```
mov  edx,OFFSET worker.LastName
```

Indirect and Indexed Operands

Indirect operands permit the use of a register (such as ESI) to address structure members. Indirect addressing provides flexibility, particularly when passing a structure address to a procedure or when using an array of structures. The PTR operator is required when referencing indirect operands:

```
mov  esi,OFFSET worker
mov  ax,(Employee PTR [esi]).Years
```

The following statement does not assemble because **Years** by itself does not identify the structure it belongs to:

```
mov  ax,[esi].Years              ; invalid
```

Indexed Operands   We can use indexed operands to access arrays of structures. Suppose **department** is an array of five Employee objects. The following statements access the **Years** field of the employee in index position 1:

```
.data
department Employee 5 DUP(<>)
.code
mov  esi,TYPE Employee           ; index = 1
mov  department[esi].Years, 4
```

Looping through an Array   A loop can be used with indirect or indexed addressing to manipulate an array of structures. The following program (*AllPoints.asm*) assigns coordinates to the **AllPoints** array:

```
TITLE Loop Through Array          (AllPoints.asm)

INCLUDE Irvine32.inc
NumPoints = 3
.data
ALIGN WORD
AllPoints COORD NumPoints DUP(<0,0>)

.code
main PROC
     mov   edi,0                  ; array index
     mov   ecx,NumPoints          ; loop counter
     mov   ax,1                   ; starting X, Y values

L1:  mov   (COORD PTR AllPoints[edi]).X,ax
     mov   (COORD PTR AllPoints[edi]).Y,ax
     add   edi,TYPE COORD
     inc   ax
     loop  L1

     exit
main ENDP
END main
```

Performance of Aligned Structure Members

We have asserted that the processor can more efficiently access properly aligned structure members. How much impact do misaligned fields have on performance? Let's perform a simple test, using the two versions of the Employee structure presented in this chapter. We will rename the first version so both structures may be used in the same program:

```
EmployeeBad STRUCT
     IdNum     BYTE "000000000"
     LastName BYTE 30 DUP(0)
     Years     WORD 0
     SalaryHistory DWORD 0,0,0,0
EmployeeBad ENDS

Employee STRUCT
     IdNum     BYTE "000000000"
     LastName BYTE 30 DUP(0)
     ALIGN     WORD
     Years     WORD 0
     ALIGN     DWORD
     SalaryHistory DWORD 0,0,0,0
Employee ENDS
```

The following code gets the system time, executes a loop that accesses structure fields, and calculates the elapsed time. The variable emp can be declared as an Employee or EmployeeBad object:

```
.data
ALIGN DWORD
startTime DWORD ?                     ; align startTime
emp Employee <>                       ; or: emp EmployeeBad <>
.code
     call  GetMSeconds                ; get starting time
     mov   startTime,eax

     mov   ecx,0FFFFFFFFh             ; loop counter
L1:  mov   emp.Years,5
     mov   emp.SalaryHistory,35000
     loop  L1

     call  GetMSeconds               ; get starting time
     sub   eax,startTime
     call  WriteDec                  ; display elapsed time
```

In our simple test program (*Struct1.asm*), the execution time using the properly aligned Employee structure was 6141 milliseconds. The execution time when using the EmployeeBad structure was 6203 milliseconds. The timing difference was small (62 milliseconds), perhaps because the processor's internal memory cache minimized the alignment problems.

10.1.4   Example: Displaying the System Time

MS-Windows provides console functions that set the screen cursor position and get the system time. To use these functions, create instances of two predefined structures—COORD and SYSTEMTIME:

```
COORD STRUCT
     X WORD ?
     Y WORD ?
COORD ENDS
```

```
SYSTEMTIME STRUCT
    wYear WORD ?
    wMonth WORD ?
    wDayOfWeek WORD ?
    wDay WORD ?
    wHour WORD ?
    wMinute WORD ?
    wSecond WORD ?
    wMilliseconds WORD ?
SYSTEMTIME ENDS
```

Both structures are defined in *SmallWin.inc*, a file located in the assembler's INCLUDE directory and referenced by *Irvine32.inc*. To get the system time (adjusted for your local time zone), call the MS-Windows **GetLocalTime** function and pass it the address of a SYSTEMTIME structure:

```
.data
sysTime SYSTEMTIME <>
.code
INVOKE GetLocalTime, ADDR sysTime
```

Next, we retrieve the appropriate values from the SYSTEMTIME structure:

```
movzx eax,sysTime.wYear
call WriteDec
```

> The *SmallWin.inc* file, created by the author, contains structure definitions and function prototypes adapted from the Microsoft Windows header files for C and C++ programmers. It represents a small subset of the possible functions that can be called by application programs.

When a Win32 program produces screen output, it calls the MS-Windows **GetStdHandle** function to retrieve the standard console output handle (an integer):

```
.data
consoleHandle DWORD ?
.code
INVOKE GetStdHandle, STD_OUTPUT_HANDLE
mov consoleHandle,eax
```

(The constant STD_OUTPUT_HANDLE is defined in *SmallWin.inc*.)

To set the cursor position, call the MS-Windows **SetConsoleCursorPosition** function, passing it the console output handle and a COORD structure variable containing X, Y character coordinates:

```
.data
XYPos COORD <10,5>
.code
INVOKE SetConsoleCursorPosition, consoleHandle, XYPos
```

Program Listing   The following program (*ShowTime.asm*) retrieves the system time and displays it at a selected screen location. It runs only in protected mode:

```
TITLE Structures                          (ShowTime.ASM)

INCLUDE Irvine32.inc
```

```
    .data
    sysTime SYSTEMTIME <>
    XYPos COORD <10,5>
    consoleHandle DWORD ?
    colonStr BYTE ":",0

    .code
    main PROC
    ; Get the standard output handle for the Win32 Console.
        INVOKE GetStdHandle, STD_OUTPUT_HANDLE
        mov consoleHandle,eax

    ; Set the cursor position and get the system time.
        INVOKE SetConsoleCursorPosition, consoleHandle, XYPos
        INVOKE GetLocalTime, ADDR sysTime

    ; Display the system time (hh:mm:ss).
        movzx  eax,sysTime.wHour        ; hours
        call   WriteDec
        mov    edx,OFFSET colonStr      ; ":"
        call   WriteString
        movzx  eax,sysTime.wMinute      ; minutes
        call   WriteDec
        call   WriteString
        movzx  eax,sysTime.wSecond      ; seconds
        call   WriteDec
        call   Crlf
        call   WaitMsg                  ; "Press any key..."
        exit
    main ENDP
    END main
```

The following definitions were used by this program from *SmallWin.inc* (automatically included by *Irvine32.inc*):

```
    STD_OUTPUT_HANDLE EQU -11

    SYSTEMTIME STRUCT ...

    COORD STRUCT ...

    GetStdHandle PROTO,
        nStdHandle:DWORD

    GetLocalTime PROTO,
        lpSystemTime:PTR SYSTEMTIME

    SetConsoleCursorPosition PROTO,
        nStdHandle:DWORD,
        coords:COORD
```

Following is a sample program output, taken at 12:16 p.m.:

```
12:16:35
Press any key to continue...
```

10.1.5 Structures Containing Structures

Structures can contain instances of other structures. For example, a **Rectangle** can be defined in terms of its upper-left and lower-right corners, both COORD structures:

```
Rectangle STRUCT
    UpperLeft COORD <>
    LowerRight COORD <>
Rectangle ENDS
```

Rectangle variables can be declared without overrides or by overriding individual COORD fields. Alternative notational forms are shown:

```
rect1 Rectangle < >
rect2 Rectangle { }
rect3 Rectangle { {10,10}, {50,20} }
rect4 Rectangle < <10,10>, <50,20> >
```

The following is a direct reference to a structure field:

```
mov rect1.UpperLeft.X, 10
```

You can access a structure field using an indirect operand. The following example moves 10 to the Y coordinate of the upper-left corner of the structure pointed to by ESI:

```
mov esi,OFFSET rect1
mov (Rectangle PTR [esi]).UpperLeft.Y, 10
```

The OFFSET operator can return pointers to individual structure fields, including nested fields:

```
mov edi,OFFSET rect2.LowerRight
mov (COORD PTR [edi]).X, 50
mov edi,OFFSET rect2.LowerRight.X
mov WORD PTR [edi], 50
```

10.1.6 Example: Drunkard's Walk

Programming textbooks often contain a version of the "Drunkard's Walk" exercise, in which the program simulates the path taken by a not-too-sober professor on his or her way to class. Using a random number generator, you can choose a direction for each step the professor takes. Usually, you check to make sure the person hasn't veered off into a campus lake, but we won't bother. Suppose the professor begins at the center of an imaginary grid in which each square represents a step in a north, south, east, or west direction. The person follows a random path through the grid (Figure 10–1).

Our program will use a COORD structure to keep track of each step along the path taken by the professor. The steps are stored in an array of COORD objects:

```
WalkMax = 50
DrunkardWalk STRUCT
    path COORD WalkMax DUP(<0,0>)
    pathsUsed WORD 0
DrunkardWalk ENDS
```

FIGURE 10–1   Drunkard's Walk, Example Path.

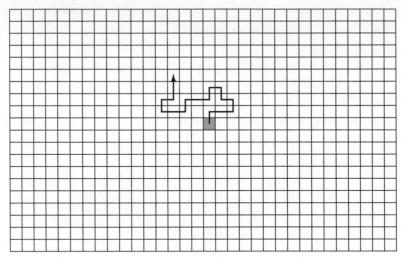

Walkmax is a constant that determines the total number of steps taken by the professor in the simulation. The **pathsUsed** field indicates, when the program loop ends, how many steps were taken by the professor. As the professor takes each step, his or her position is stored in a COORD object and inserted in the next available position in the **path** array. The program displays the coordinates on the screen. Here is the complete program listing:

```
TITLE Drunkard's Walk            (Walk.asm)

; Drunkard's walk program. The professor starts at
; coordinates 25, 25 and wanders around the immediate area.

INCLUDE Irvine32.inc
WalkMax = 50
StartX = 25
StartY = 25

DrunkardWalk STRUCT
    path COORD WalkMax DUP(<0,0>)
    pathsUsed WORD 0
DrunkardWalk ENDS

DisplayPosition PROTO currX:WORD, currY:WORD

.data
aWalk DrunkardWalk <>

.code
main PROC
    mov   esi,OFFSET aWalk
    call  TakeDrunkenWalk
    exit
main ENDP
```

```
;----------------------------------------------------------
TakeDrunkenWalk PROC
LOCAL currX:WORD, currY:WORD
;
; Take a walk in random directions (north, south, east,
; west).
; Receives: ESI points to a DrunkardWalk structure
; Returns:  the structure is initialized with random values
;----------------------------------------------------------
    pushad

; Use the OFFSET operator to obtain the address of the
; path, the array of COORD objects, and copy it to EDI.
    mov   edi,esi
    add   edi,OFFSET DrunkardWalk.path
    mov   ecx,WalkMax                ; loop counter
    mov   currX,StartX               ; current X-location
    mov   currY,StartY               ; current Y-location
Again:
    ; Insert current location in array.
    mov   ax,currX
    mov   (COORD PTR [edi]).X,ax
    mov   ax,currY
    mov   (COORD PTR [edi]).Y,ax

    INVOKE DisplayPosition, currX, currY

    mov   eax,4                      ; choose a direction (0-3)
    call RandomRange

    .IF eax == 0                     ; North
      dec currY
    .ELSEIF eax == 1                 ; South
      inc currY
    .ELSEIF eax == 2                 ; West
      dec currX
    .ELSE                            ; East (EAX = 3)
      inc currX
    .ENDIF

    add   edi,TYPE COORD             ; point to next COORD
    loop Again
Finish:
    mov   (DrunkardWalk PTR [esi]).pathsUsed, WalkMax
    popad
    ret
TakeDrunkenWalk ENDP

;----------------------------------------------------------
DisplayPosition PROC currX:WORD, currY:WORD
; Display the current X and Y positions.
;----------------------------------------------------------
```

```
.data
commaStr BYTE ",",0
.code
    pushad
    movzx eax,currX              ; current X position
    call  WriteDec
    mov   edx,OFFSET commaStr    ; "," string
    call  WriteString
    movzx eax,currY              ; current Y position
    call  WriteDec
    call  Crlf
    popad
    ret
DisplayPosition ENDP
END main
```

TakeDrunkenWalk Procedure   Let's take a closer look at the **TakeDrunkenWalk** procedure. It receives a pointer (ESI) to a **DrunkardWalk** structure. Using the OFFSET operator, it
calculates the offset of the **path** array and copies it to EDI:

```
mov  edi,esi
add  edi,OFFSET DrunkardWalk.path
```

The initial X and Y positions (StartX and StartY) of the professor are set to 25, at the center of
an imaginary 50-by-50 grid. The loop counter is initialized:

```
mov  ecx, WalkMax                ; loop counter
mov  currX,StartX                ; current X-location
mov  currY,StartY                ; current Y-location
```

At the beginning of the loop, the first entry in the **path** array is initialized:

```
Again:
    ; Insert current location in array.
    mov    ax,currX
    mov    (COORD PTR [edi]).X,ax
    mov    ax,currY
    mov    (COORD PTR [edi]).Y,ax
```

At the end of the walk, a counter is inserted into the **pathsUsed** field, indicating how many steps
were taken:

```
Finish:
    mov (DrunkardWalk PTR [esi]).pathsUsed, WalkMax
```

In the current version of the program, **pathsUsed** is always equal to **WalkMax**, but that could
change if we checked for hazards such as lakes and buildings. Then the loop would terminate
before **WalMax** was reached.

10.1.7   Declaring and Using Unions

Whereas each field in a structure has an offset relative to the first byte of the structure, all
the fields in a *union* start at the same offset. The storage size of a union is equal to the length

of its longest field. When not part of a structure, a union is declared using the UNION and ENDS directives:

```
unionname UNION
    union-fields
unionname ENDS
```

If the union is nested inside a structure, the syntax is slightly different:

```
structname STRUCT
    structure-fields
    UNION unionname
        union-fields
    ENDS
structname ENDS
```

The field declarations in a union follow the same rules as for structures, except that each field can have only a single initializer. For example, the **Integer** union has three different size attributes for the same data and initializes all fields to zero:

```
Integer UNION
    D DWORD 0
    W WORD  0
    B BYTE  0
Integer ENDS
```

Be Consistent Initializers, if used, must have consistent values. Suppose Integer were declared with different initializers:

```
Integer UNION
    D DWORD 1
    W WORD  5
    B BYTE  8
Integer ENDS
```

Then we declared an Integer variable named **myInt** using default initializers:

```
.data
myInt Integer <>
```

The values of myInt.D, myInt.W, and myInt.B would all equal 1. The declared initializers for fields W and B would be ignored by the assembler.

Structure Containing a Union You can nest a union inside a structure by using the union name in a declaration, as we have done here for the **FileID** field inside the **FileInfo** structure,

```
FileInfo STRUCT
    FileID Integer <>
    FileName BYTE 64 DUP(?)
FileInfo ENDS
```

or you can declare a union directly inside the structure, as we have done here for the **FileID** field:

```
FileInfo STRUCT
  UNION FileID
```

```
        D DWORD ?
        W WORD ?
        B BYTE ?
    ENDS
    FileName BYTE 64 DUP(?)
FileInfo ENDS
```

Declaring and Using Union Variables   A union variable is declared and initialized in much the same way as a structure variable, with one important difference: No more than one initializer is permitted. The following are examples of Integer-type variables:

```
val1 Integer <12345678h>
val2 Integer <100h>
val3 Integer <>
```

To use a union variable in an executable instruction, you must supply the name of one of the variant fields. In the following example, we assign register values to **Integer** union fields. Note the flexibility we have in being able to use different operand sizes:

```
mov   val3.B, al
mov   val3.W, ax
mov   val3.D, eax
```

Unions can also contain structures. The following INPUT_RECORD structure is used by some MS-Windows console input functions. It contains a union named **Event**, which selects among several predefined structure types. The **EventType** field indicates which type of record appears in the union. Each structure has a different layout and size, but only one is used at a time:

```
INPUT_RECORD STRUCT
    EventType WORD ?
    ALIGN DWORD
    UNION Event
      KEY_EVENT_RECORD <>
      MOUSE_EVENT_RECORD <>
      WINDOW_BUFFER_SIZE_RECORD <>
      MENU_EVENT_RECORD <>
      FOCUS_EVENT_RECORD <>
    ENDS
INPUT_RECORD ENDS
```

The Win32 API often includes the word RECORD when naming structures.[1] This is the definition of a KEY_EVENT_RECORD structure:

```
KEY_EVENT_RECORD STRUCT
    bKeyDown            DWORD ?
    wRepeatCount        WORD  ?
    wVirtualKeyCode     WORD  ?
    wVirtualScanCode    WORD  ?
    UNION uChar
      UnicodeChar       WORD  ?
      AsciiChar         BYTE  ?
    ENDS
    dwControlKeyState DWORD ?
KEY_EVENT_RECORD ENDS
```

The remaining STRUCT definitions from INPUT_RECORD can be found in the Small-Win.inc file.

10.1.8 Section Review

1. What is the purpose of the STRUCT directive?

2. Create a structure named **MyStruct** containing two fields: **field1**, a single word, and **field2**, an array of 20 doublewords. The initial values of the fields may be left undefined.

The structure created in Exercise 2 (MyStruct) will be used in Exercises 3 through 11:

3. Declare a **MyStruct** variable with default values.

4. Declare a **MyStruct** variable that initializes the first field to zero.

5. Declare a **MyStruct** variable and initialize the second field to an array containing all zeros.

6. Declare a variable as an array of 20 **MyStruct** objects.

7. Using the **MyStruct** array from the preceding exercise, move **field1** of the first array element to AX.

8. Using the **MyStruct** array from the preceding exercise, use ESI to index to the third array element and move AX to **field1**. *Hint:* Use the PTR operator.

9. What value does the expression **TYPE MyStruct** return?

10. What value does the expression **SIZEOF MyStruct** return?

11. Write an expression that returns the number of bytes in **field2** of **MyStruct**.

The following exercises are not related to MyStruct:

12. Assume that the following structure has been defined:

```
RentalInvoice STRUCT
    invoiceNum BYTE 5 DUP(' ')
    dailyPrice WORD ?
    daysRented WORD ?
RentalInvoice ENDS
```

State whether or not each of the following declarations is valid:

```
a. rentals RentalInvoice <>
b. RentalInvoice rentals <>
c. march RentalInvoice <'12345',10,0>
d. RentalInvoice <,10,0>
e. current RentalInvoice <,15,0,0>
```

13. Write a statement that retrieves the **wHour** field of a SYSTEMTIME structure.

14. Using the following **Triangle** structure, declare a structure variable and initialize its vertices to (0,0), (5, 0), and (7,6):

```
Triangle STRUCT
      Vertex1 COORD <>
      Vertex2 COORD <>
      Vertex3 COORD <>
Triangle ENDS
```

15. Declare an array of **Triangle** structures. Write a loop that initializes **Vertex1** of each triangle to random coordinates in the range (0..10, 0..10).

10.2 Macros

10.2.1 Overview

A *macro procedure* is a named block of assembly language statements. Once defined, it can be invoked (called) as many times in a program as you wish. When you *invoke* a macro procedure, a copy of its code is inserted directly into the program at the location where it was invoked. This type of automatic code insertion is also known as *inline expansion*. It is customary to refer to *calling* a macro procedure, although technically there is no CALL instruction involved.

> The term *macro procedure* is used in the Microsoft Assembler manual to identify macros that do not return a value. There are also *macro functions* that return a value. Among programmers, the word *macro* is usually understood to mean the same thing as *macro procedure*. From this point on, we will use the shorter form.

Declaring   Macros are defined directly at the beginning of a source program, or they are placed in a separate file and copied into a program by an INCLUDE directive. Macros are expanded during the assembler's *preprocessing* step. In this step, the preprocessor reads a macro definition and scans the remaining source code in the program. At every point where the macro is called, the assembler inserts a copy of the macro's source code into the program. A macro definition must be found by the assembler before trying to assemble any calls of the macro. If a program defines a macro but never calls it, the macro code does not appear in the compiled program.

In the following example, a macro named **PrintX** calls the **WriteChar** procedure from Irvine32 or Irvine16. This definition would normally be placed just before the data segment:

```
PrintX MACRO
    mov    al,'X'
    call   WriteChar
ENDM
```

Next, in the code segment, we call the macro:

```
.code
PrintX
```

When the preprocessor scans this program and discovers the call to **PrintX**, it replaces the macro call with the following statements:

```
mov  al,'X'
call WriteChar
```

Text substitution has taken place. Although the macro is somewhat inflexible, we will soon show how to pass arguments to macros, making them far more useful.

10.2.2 Defining Macros

A macro is defined using the MACRO and ENDM directives. The syntax is

```
macroname MACRO parameter-1, parameter-2...
    statement-list
ENDM
```

There is no fixed rule regarding indentation, but we recommend that you indent statements between *macroname* and ENDM. You might also want to prefix macro names with the letter m, creating recognizable names such as **mPutChar, mWriteString,** and **mGotoxy.** The statements between the MACRO and ENDM directives are not assembled until the macro is called. There can be any number of parameters in the macro definition, separated by commas.

Parameters Macro parameters are named placeholders for text arguments passed to the caller. The arguments may in fact be integers, variable names, or other values, but the preprocessor treats them as text. Parameters are not typed, so the preprocessor does not check argument types to see whether they are correct. If a type mismatch occurs, it is caught by the assembler after the macro has been expanded.

mPutchar Example The following **mPutchar** macro receives a single input parameter called **char** and displays it on the console by calling **WriteChar** from the book's link library:

```
mPutchar MACRO char
    push  eax
    mov   al,char
    call  WriteChar
    pop   eax
ENDM
```

10.2.3 Invoking Macros

A macro is called (invoked) by inserting its name in the program, possibly followed by macro arguments. The syntax for calling a macro is

```
macroname argument-1, argument-2, ...
```

Macroname must be the name of a macro defined prior to this point in the source code. Each argument is a text value that replaces a parameter in the macro. The order of arguments must correspond to the order of parameters, but the number of arguments does not have to match the number of parameters. If too many arguments are passed, the assembler issues a warning. If too few arguments are passed to a macro, the unfilled parameters are left blank.

Invoking mPutchar In the previous section, we defined the **mPutChar** macro. When invoking mPutchar, we can pass any character or ASCII code. The following statement invokes mPutchar and passes it the letter A:

```
mPutchar 'A'
```

The assembler's preprocessor expands the statement into the following code, shown in the listing file:

```
1    push  eax
1    mov   al,'A'
1    call  WriteChar
1    pop   eax
```

The 1 in the left column indicates the macro expansion level, which increases when you call other macros from within a macro. The following loop displays the first 20 letters of the alphabet:

```
    mov   al,'A'
    mov   ecx,20
```

```
L1:
        mPutchar al              ; macro call
        inc  al
        loop L1
```

Our loop is expanded by the preprocessor into the following code (visible in the source listing file). The macro call is shown just before its expansion:

```
        mov  al,'A'
        mov  ecx,20
L1:
        mPutchar al                      ; macro call
1       push eax
1       mov  al,al
1       call WriteChar
1       pop  eax
        inc  al
        loop L1
```

> In general, macros execute more quickly than procedures because procedures have the extra overhead of CALL and RET instructions. There is, however, one disadvantage to using macros: repeated use of large macros tends to increase a program's size because each call to a macro inserts a new copy of the macro's statements in the program.

Debugging Programs That Contain Macros

Debugging a program that uses macros can be a special challenge. After assembling a program, check its listing file (extension.LST) to make sure each macro is expanded the way you intended. Next, start the program in a debugger (such as Visual Studio .NET). Trace the program in a disassembly window, using the *show source code* option if it is supported by the debugger. Each macro call will be followed by the code generated by the macro. Here is an example:

```
mWriteAt 15,10,"Hi there"
        push  edx
        mov   dh,0Ah
        mov   dl,0Fh
        call  _Gotoxy@0 (401551h)
        pop   edx
        push  edx
        mov   edx,offset ??0000 (405004h)
        call  _WriteString@0 (401D64h)
        pop   edx
```

[The function names begin with underscore (_) because the Irvine32 library uses the STDCALL calling convention. See Section 8.4.1 for details.]

10.2.4   Additional Macro Features

Required Parameters

Using the REQ qualifier, you can specify that a macro parameter is required. If the macro is called without an argument to match the required parameter, the assembler displays an error message. If a macro has multiple required parameters, each one must include the REQ qualifier. In the following **mPutchar** macro, the **char** parameter is required:

```
mPutchar MACRO char:REQ
      push  eax
      mov   al,char
      call  WriteChar
      pop   eax
ENDM
```

Macro Comments

Ordinary comment lines appearing in a macro definition appear each time the macro is expanded. If you want to have comments in the macro that will not appear in macro expansions, begin them with a double semicolon (;;):

```
mPutchar MACRO char:REQ
      push  eax                            ;; reminder: char must contain 8 bits
      mov   al,char
      call  WriteChar
      pop   eax
ENDM
```

ECHO Directive

The ECHO directive displays a message on the console as the program is assembled. In the following version of **mPutchar**, the message "Expanding the mPutchar macro" appears on the console during assembly:

```
mPutchar MACRO char:REQ
      ECHO  Expanding the mPutchar macro
      push  eax
      mov   al,char
      call  WriteChar
      pop   eax
ENDM
```

LOCAL Directive

Macro definitions often contain labels and self-reference those labels in their code. The following **makeString** macro, for example, declares a variable named **string** and initializes it with a character array:

```
makeString MACRO text
      .data
      string BYTE text,0
ENDM
```

Suppose we invoke the macro twice:

```
makeString "Hello"
makeString "Goodbye"
```

An error results because the assembler will not let the **string** label be redefined:

```
        makeString "Hello"
1       .data
1       string BYTE "Hello",0
        makeString "Goodbye"
1       .data
1       string BYTE "Goodbye",0     ; error!
```

Using LOCAL   To avoid problems caused by label redefinitions, you can apply the LOCAL directive to labels inside a macro definition. When a label is marked LOCAL, the preprocessor converts the label's name to a unique identifier each time the macro is expanded. Here's a new version of **makeString** that uses LOCAL:

```
makeString MACRO text
    LOCAL string
    .data
    string BYTE text,0
ENDM
```

If we invoke the macro twice as before, the code generated by the preprocessor replaces each occurrence of **string** with a unique identifier:

```
        makeString "Hello"
1       .data
1       ??0000 BYTE "Hello",0
        makeString "Goodbye"
1       .data
1       ??0001 BYTE "Goodbye",0
```

The label names produced by the assembler take the form *??nnnn*, where *nnnn* is a unique integer. The LOCAL directive should also be used for code labels in macros.

Macros Containing Code and Data

Macros often contain both code and data. The following **mWrite** macro, for example, displays a literal string on the console:

```
mWrite MACRO text
    LOCAL string              ;; local label
    .data
    string BYTE text,0        ;; define the string
    .code
    push  edx
    mov   edx,OFFSET string
    call  WriteString
    pop   edx
ENDM
```

The following statements invoke the macro twice, passing it different string literals:

```
mWrite "Please enter your first name"
mWrite "Please enter your last name"
```

The expansion of the two statements by the assembler shows that each string is assigned a unique label, and the **mov** instructions are adjusted accordingly:

```
        mWrite "Please enter your first name"
1    .data
1    ??0000 BYTE "Please enter your first name",0
1    .code
1    push edx
1    mov   edx,OFFSET ??0000
1    call WriteString
1    pop   edx
        mWrite "Please enter your last name"
1    .data
1    ??0001 BYTE "Please enter your last name",0
1    .code
1    push edx
1    mov   edx,OFFSET ??0001
1    call WriteString
1    pop   edx
```

Nested Macros

A macro invoked from another macro is called a *nested macro*. When the assembler's preprocessor encounters a call to a nested macro, it expands the macro in place. Parameters passed to an enclosing macro are passed directly to its nested macros.

> Use a modular approach when creating macros. Keep them short and simple so they can be combined into more complex macros. Doing this helps to reduce the amount of duplicate code in your programs.

mWriteln Example   The following **mWriteln** macro writes a string literal to the console and appends an end of line. It invokes the **mWrite** macro and calls the **Crlf** procedure:

```
mWriteln MACRO text
    mWrite text
    call   Crlf
ENDM
```

The **text** parameter is passed directly to **mWrite**. Suppose the following statement invokes mWriteln:

```
mWriteln "My Sample Macro Program"
```

In the resulting code expansion, the nesting level (2) next to the statements indicates a nested macro has been invoked:

```
        mWriteln "My Sample Macro Program"
2    .data
2    ??0002 BYTE "My Sample Macro Program",0
2    .code
2    push edx
2    mov   edx,OFFSET ??0002
2    call WriteString
2    pop   edx
1    call Crlf
```

10.2.5 Using the Book's Macro Library

The sample programs supplied with this book include a small but useful macro library, which you can enable simply by adding the following line to your programs just after the INCLUDE you already have:

```
INCLUDE Macros.inc
```

Some of the macros are wrappers around existing procedures in the Irvine32 and Irvine16 libraries, making it easier to pass parameters. Other macros provide new functionality. Table 10-2 describes each macro in detail. The example code can be found in *MacroTest.asm*.

Table 10-2   Macros in the Macros.inc Library.

Macro Name	Parameters	Description
mDump	varName, useLabel	Displays a variable, using its name and default attributes.
mDumpMem	address, itemCount, componentSize	Displays a range of memory.
mGotoxy	X, Y	Sets the cursor position in the console window buffer.
mReadString	varName	Reads a string from the keyboard.
mShow	itsName, format	Displays a variable or register in various formats.
mShowRegister	regName, regValue	Displays a 32-bit register's name and contents in hexadecimal.
mWrite	text	Writes a string literal to the console window.
mWriteSpace	count	Writes one or more spaces to the console window.
mWriteString	buffer	Writes a string variable's contents to the console window.

mDumpMem

The mDumpMem macro displays a block of memory in the console window. Pass it a constant, register, or variable containing the offset of the memory you want displayed. The second argument should be the number of memory components to be displayed, and the third argument is the size of each memory component. (The macro calls the DumpMem library procedure, assigning the three arguments to ESI, ECX, and EBX, respectively.) Let's assume the following data definition:

```
.data
array DWORD 1000h,2000h,3000h,4000h
```

The following statement displays the array using its default attributes:

```
mDumpMem OFFSET array, LENGTHOF array, TYPE array
```

Output:

```
Dump of offset 00405004
-------------------------------
00001000  00002000  00003000  00004000
```

The following displays the same array as a byte sequence:

```
mDumpMem OFFSET array, SIZEOF array, TYPE BYTE
```

Output:

```
Dump of offset 00405004
-------------------------------
00 10 00 00 00 20 00 00 00 30 00 00 00 40 00 00
```

The following code pushes three values on the stack, sets the values of EBX, ECX, and ESI, and uses mDumpMem to display the stack:

```
mov     eax,0AAAAAAAAh
push    eax
mov     eax,0BBBBBBBBh
push    eax
mov     eax,0CCCCCCCCh
push    eax
mov     ebx,1
mov     ecx,2
mov     esi,3
mDumpMem esp, 8, TYPE DWORD
```

The resulting stack dump shows the macro has pushed EBX, ECX, and ESI on the stack. Following those values are the three integers we pushed on the stack before invoking mDumpMem:

```
Dump of offset 0012FFAC
-------------------------------
00000003  00000002  00000001  CCCCCCCC  BBBBBBBB  AAAAAAAA  7C816D4F
0000001A
```

Implementation   Here is the macro's code listing:

```
mDumpMem MACRO address:REQ, itemCount:REQ, componentSize:REQ
;
; Displays a dump of memory, using the DumpMem procedure.
; Receives: memory offset, count of the number of items
;      to display, and the size of each memory component.
; Avoid passing EBX, ECX, and ESI as arguments.
;------------------------------------------------------------
     push   ebx
     push   ecx
     push   esi
     mov    esi,address
     mov    ecx,itemCount
     mov    ebx,componentSize
     call   DumpMem
     pop    esi
     pop    ecx
     pop    ebx
ENDM
```

mDump

The mDump macro displays the address and contents of a variable in hexadecimal. Pass it the name of a variable and (optionally) a character indicating that a label should be displayed next to the variable. The display format automatically matches the variable's size attribute (BYTE,

WORD, or DWORD). The following example shows two calls to mDump:

```
.data
diskSize DWORD 12345h
.code
mDump   diskSize                     ; no label
mDump   diskSize,Y                   ; show label
```

The following output is produced when the code executes:

```
Dump of offset 00405000
-------------------------------
00012345

Variable name: diskSize
Dump of offset 00405000
-------------------------------
00012345
```

Implementation Here is a listing of the mDump macro, which in turn calls mDumpMem. It uses a new directive named IFNB (*if not blank*) to find out if the caller has passed an argument into the second parameter (see Section 10.3):

```
;-----------------------------------------------------
mDump MACRO varName:REQ, useLabel
;
; Displays a variable, using its known attributes.
; Receives: varName, the name of a variable.
;    If useLabel is nonblank, the name of the
;    variable is displayed.
;-----------------------------------------------------
    call Crlf
    IFNB <useLabel>
      mWrite "Variable name: &varName"
    ENDIF
    mDumpMem OFFSET varName, LENGTHOF varName, TYPE varName
ENDM
```

The & in **&varName** is a *substitution operator*, which permits the **varName** parameter's value to be inserted into the string literal. See Section 10.3.7 for more details.

mGotoxy

The **mGotoxy** macro locates the cursor at a specific column and row location in the console window's buffer. You can pass it 8-bit immediate values, memory operands, and register values:

```
mGotoxy   10,20                      ; immediate values
mGotoxy   row,col                    ; memory operands
mGotoxy   ch,cl                      ; register values
```

Implementation Here is a source listing of the macro:

```
;-----------------------------------------------------
mGotoxy MACRO X:REQ, Y:REQ
;
```

```
; Sets the cursor position in the console window.
; Receives: X and Y coordinates (type BYTE). Avoid
;     passing DH and DL as arguments.
;--------------------------------------------------------
      push  edx
      mov   dh,Y
      mov   dl,X
      call  Gotoxy
      pop   edx
ENDM
```

Avoiding Register Conflicts   When macro arguments are registers, they can sometimes conflict with registers used internally by macros. If we call **mGotoxy** using DH and DL, for example, it does not generate correct code. To see why, let's inspect the expanded code after such parameters have been substituted:

```
1     push  edx
2     mov   dh,dl          ;; row
3     mov   dl,dh          ;; column
4     call  Gotoxy
5     pop   edx
```

Assuming that DL is passed as the Y value and DH is the X value, line 2 replaces DH before we have a chance to copy the column value to DL on line 3.

> Whenever possible, macro definitions should specify which registers cannot be used as arguments.

mReadString

The **mReadString** macro inputs a string from the keyboard and stores the string in a buffer. Internally, it encapsulates a call to the **ReadString** library procedure. Pass it the name of the buffer:

```
.data
firstName BYTE 30 DUP(?)
.code
mReadString  firstName
```

Here is the macro's source code:

```
;--------------------------------------------------------
mReadString MACRO varName:REQ
;
; Reads from standard input into a buffer.
; Receives: the name of the buffer. Avoid passing
;     ECX and EDX as arguments.
;--------------------------------------------------------
      push  ecx
      push  edx
      mov   edx,OFFSET varName
      mov   ecx,SIZEOF varName
      call  ReadString
      pop   edx
      pop   ecx
ENDM
```

mShow

The mShow macro displays any register or variable's name and contents in a caller-selected format. Pass it the name of the register, followed by an optional sequence of letters identifying the desired format. Use the following codes: H = hexadecimal, D = unsigned decimal, I = signed decimal, B = binary, and N = append a newline. Multiple output formats can be combined, and multiple newlines can be specified. The default format is "HIN". mShow is a useful debugging aid, and is used extensively by the DumpRegs library procedure. You can insert calls to mShow in any program, displaying the values of important registers or variables.

Example   The following statements display the AX register in hexadecimal, signed decimal, unsigned decimal, and binary:

```
mov     ax,4096
mShow AX                     ; default options: HIN
mShow AX,DBN                  ; unsigned decimal, binary, newline
```

Here is the output:

```
AX = 1000h +4096d
AX = 4096d  0001 0000 0000 0000b
```

Example   The following statements display AX, BX, CX, and DX in unsigned decimal, on the same output line:

```
; Insert some test values and show four registers:
mov       ax,1
mov       bx,2
mov       cx,3
mov       dx,4
mShow     AX,D
mShow     BX,D
mShow     CX,D
mShow     DX,DN
```

Here is the corresponding output:

```
AX = 1d     BX = 2d     CX = 3d     DX = 4d
```

Example   The following call to mShow displays the contents of **mydword** in unsigned decimal, followed by a newline:

```
.data
mydword DWORD ?
.code
mShow  mydword,DN
```

Implementation   The implementation of mShow is too long to include here, but may be found in the Macros.inc file. When implementing mShow, we had to be careful to show the current register values before they were modified by statements inside the macro itself.

mShowRegister

The mShowRegister macro displays the name and contents of a single 32-bit register in hexadecimal. Pass it the register's name as you want it displayed, followed by the register itself.

The following macro invocation specifies the displayed name as EBX:

```
mShowRegister EBX, ebx
```

The following output is produced:

```
EBX=7FFD9000
```

The following invocation uses angle brackets around the label because it contains an embedded space:

```
mShowRegister <Stack Pointer>, esp
```

The following output is produced:

```
Stack Pointer=0012FFC0
```

Implementation   Here is the macro's source code:

```
;----------------------------------------------------
mShowRegister MACRO regName, regValue
LOCAL tempStr
;
; Displays a register's name and contents.
; Receives: the register name, the register value.
;----------------------------------------------------
.data
tempStr BYTE " &regName=",0
.code
    push eax

; Display the register name
    push edx
    mov  edx,OFFSET tempStr
    call WriteString
    pop  edx

; Display the register contents
    mov  eax,regValue
    call WriteHex
    pop  eax
ENDM
```

mWriteSpace

The mWriteSpace macro writes one or more spaces to the console window. You can optionally pass it an integer parameter specifying the number of spaces to write (the default is one). The following statement, for example, writes five spaces:

```
mWriteSpace 5
```

Implementation   Here is the source code for mWriteSpace:

```
;-------------------------------------------------------
mWriteSpace MACRO count:=<1>
;
; Writes one or more spaces to the console window.
```

```
; Receives: an integer specifying the number of spaces.
; Default value of count is 1.
;-----------------------------------------------------
LOCAL spaces
.data
spaces BYTE count DUP(' '),0
.code
    push  edx
    mov   edx,OFFSET spaces
    call  WriteString
    pop   edx
ENDM
```

Section 10.3.2 explains how to use default initializers for macro parameters.

mWriteString

The **mWriteString** macro writes the contents of a string variable to the console window. Internally, it simplifies calls to **WriteString** by letting you pass the name of a string variable on the same statement line. For example:

```
.data
str1 BYTE "Please enter your name: ",0
.code
mWriteString str1
```

Implementation   The following **mWriteString** implementation saves EDX on the stack, fills EDX with the string's offset, and pops EDX from the stack after the procedure call:

```
;-----------------------------------------------------
mWriteString MACRO buffer:REQ
;
; Writes a string variable to standard output.
; Receives: string variable name.
;-----------------------------------------------------
    push  edx
    mov   edx,OFFSET buffer
    call  WriteString
    pop   edx
ENDM
```

10.2.6   Example Program: Wrappers

Let's create a short program named *Wraps.asm* that shows off the macros we've already introduced as procedure wrappers. Because each macro hides a lot of tedious parameter passing, the program is surprisingly compact. We will assume that all of the macros shown so far are located inside the *Macros.inc* file:

```
TITLE Procedure Wrapper Macros           (Wraps.asm)

; This program demonstrates macros as wrappers
; for library procedures. Contents: mGotoxy, mWrite,
; mWriteString, mReadString, and mDumpMem.
```

```
      INCLUDE Irvine32.inc
      INCLUDE Macros.inc                  ; macro definitions
      .data
      array DWORD 1,2,3,4,5,6,7,8
      firstName BYTE 31 DUP(?)
      lastName  BYTE 31 DUP(?)

      .code
      main PROC
          mGotoxy 0,0
          mWrite <"Sample Macro Program",0dh,0ah>

      ; Input the user's name.
          mGotoxy 0,5
          mWrite "Please enter your first name: "
          mReadString firstName
          call Crlf

          mWrite "Please enter your last name: "
          mReadString lastName
          call Crlf

      ; Display the user's name.
          mWrite "Your name is "
          mWriteString firstName
          mWriteSpace
          mWriteString lastName
          call Crlf

      ; Display the array of integers.
          mDumpMem OFFSET array, LENGTHOF array, TYPE array
          exit
      main ENDP
      END main
```

Program Output   The following is a sample of the program's output:

```
Sample Macro Program
Please enter your first name: Joe
Please enter your last name: Smith
Your name is Joe Smith
Dump of offset 00404000
-------------------------------
00000001   00000002   00000003   00000004   00000005
00000006   00000007   00000008
```

10.2.7   Section Review

1. (*True/False*): When a macro is invoked, the CALL and RET instructions are automatically inserted into the assembled program.

2. (*True/False*): Macro expansion is handled by the assembler's preprocessor.

3. What is the primary advantage to using macros with parameters versus macros without them?

4. (*True/False*): As long as it is in the code segment, a macro definition may appear either before or after statements that invoke the macro.

5. (*True/False*): Replacing a long procedure with a macro containing the procedure's code will typically increase the compiled code size of a program if the macro is invoked multiple times.

6. (*True/False*): A macro cannot contain data definitions.

7. What is the purpose of the LOCAL directive?

8. Which directive displays a message on the console during the assembly step?

9. Write a macro named **mPrintChar** that displays a single character on the screen. It should have two parameters: this first specifies the character to be displayed, the second specifies how many times the character should be repeated. Here is a sample call:

```
mPrintChar 'X',20
```

10. Write a macro named **mGenRandom** that generates a random integer between 0 and $n - 1$. Let n be the only parameter.

11. Write a macro named **mPromptInteger** that displays a prompt and inputs an integer from the user. Pass it a string literal and the name of a doubleword variable. Sample call:

```
.data
minVal DWORD ?
.code
mPromptInteger "Enter the minimum value", minVal
```

12. Write a macro named **mWriteAt** that locates the cursor and writes a string literal to the console window. *Suggestion:* Invoke the **mGotoxy** and **mWrite** macros.

13. Show the expanded code produced by the following statement that invokes the **mWriteString** macro from Section 10.2.5:

```
mWriteStr namePrompt
```

14. Show the expanded code produced by the following statement that invokes the **mRead-String** macro from Section 10.2.5:

```
mReadStr customerName
```

15. *Challenge:* Write a macro named **mDumpMemx** that receives a single parameter, the name of a variable. Your macro must call the **mDumpMem** macro, passing it the variable's offset, number of units, and unit size. Demonstrate a call to the mDumpMemx macro.

10.3 Conditional-Assembly Directives

A number of different conditional-assembly directives can be used in conjunction with macros to make them more flexible. The general syntax for conditional-assembly directives is

```
IF condition
    statements
[ELSE
    statements]
ENDIF
```

The constant directives shown in this chapter should not be confused with runtime directives such as .IF and .ENDIF introduced in Section 6.7. The latter evaluated expressions based on runtime values stored in registers and variables.

Table 10-3 lists the more common conditional-assembly directives. When the descriptions say that a directive *permits assembly*, it means that any subsequent statements are assembled up to the next ELSE or ENDIF directive. It must be emphasized that the directives listed in the table are evaluated at assembly time, not at runtime.

Table 10-3   Conditional-Assembly Directives.

Directive	Description
IF *expression*	Permits assembly if the value of *expression* is true (nonzero). Possible relational operators are LT, GT, EQ, NE, LE, and GE.
IFB <*argument*>	Permits assembly if *argument* is blank. The argument name must be enclosed in angle brackets (<>).
IFNB <*argument*>	Permits assembly if *argument* is not blank. The argument name must be enclosed in angle brackets (<>).
IFIDN <*arg1*>,<*arg2*>	Permits assembly if the two arguments are equal (identical). Uses a case-sensitive comparison.
IFIDNI <*arg1*>,<*arg2*>	Permits assembly if the two arguments are equal. Uses a case-insensitive comparison.
IFDIF <*arg1*>,<*arg2*>	Permits assembly if the two arguments are unequal. Uses a case-sensitive comparison.
IFDIFI <*arg1*>,<*arg2*>	Permits assembly if the two arguments are unequal. Uses a case-insensitive comparison.
IFDEF *name*	Permits assembly if *name* has been defined.
IFNDEF *name*	Permits assembly if *name* has not been defined.
ENDIF	Ends a block that was begun using one of the conditional-assembly directives.
ELSE	Terminates assembly of the previous statements if the condition is true. If the condition is false, ELSE assembles statements up to the next ENDIF.
ELSEIF *expression*	Assembles all statements up to ENDIF if the condition specified by a previous conditional directive is false and the value of the current expression is true.
EXITM	Exits a macro immediately, preventing any following macro statements from being expanded.

10.3.1   Checking for Missing Arguments

A macro can check to see whether any of its arguments are blank. Often, if a blank argument is received by a macro, invalid instructions result when the macro is expanded by the preprocessor. For example, if we invoke the **mWriteString** macro without passing an argument, the macro expands with an invalid instruction when moving the string offset to EDX. The following are statements generated by the assembler, which detects the missing operand and issues an error message:

```
   mWriteString
1     push edx
1     mov  edx,OFFSET
```

```
Macro2.asm(18) : error A2081: missing operand after unary operator
1    call WriteString
1    pop  edx
```

To prevent errors caused by missing operands, you can use the IFB (*if blank*) directive, which returns true if a macro argument is blank. Or, you can use the IFNB (*if not blank*) operator, which returns true if a macro argument is not blank. Let's create an alternate version of **mWriteString** that displays an error message during assembly:

```
mWriteString MACRO string
    IFB <string>
      ECHO ---------------------------------------------
      ECHO *  Error: parameter missing in mWriteString
      ECHO *  (no code generated)
      ECHO ---------------------------------------------
      EXITM
    ENDIF
    push  edx
    mov   edx,OFFSET string
    call  WriteString
    pop   edx
ENDM
```

(Recall from Section 10.2.2 that the ECHO directive writes a message to the console while a program is being assembled.) The EXITM directive tells the preprocessor to exit the macro and to not expand any more statements from the macro. The following shows the screen output when assembling a program with a missing parameter:

```
 Assembling: Macro2.asm

------------------------------------------
*  Error: parameter missing in mWriteString

*  (no code generated)

------------------------------------------
```

10.3.2 Default Argument Initializers

Macros can have default argument initializers. If a macro argument is missing when the macro is called, the default argument is used instead. The syntax is

```
paramname := < argument >
```

(Spaces before and after the operators are optional.) For example, the **mWriteln** macro can supply a string containing a single space as its default argument. If it is called with no arguments, it still prints a space followed by an end of line:

```
mWriteln MACRO text:=<" ">
    mWrite text
    call Crlf
ENDM
```

The assembler issues an error if a null string (" ") is used as the default argument, so you have to insert at least one space between the quotes.

10.3.3   Boolean Expressions

The assembler permits the following relational operators to be used in constant boolean expressions containing IF and other conditional directives:

```
LT    Less than
GT    Greater than
EQ    Equal to
NE    Not equal to
LE    Less than or equal to
GE    Greater than or equal to
```

10.3.4   IF, ELSE, and ENDIF Directives

The IF directive must be followed by a constant boolean expression. The expression can contain integer constants, symbolic constants, or constant macro arguments, but it cannot contain register or variable names. One syntax format uses just IF and ENDIF:

```
IF expression
    statement-list
ENDIF
```

Another format uses IF, ELSE, and ENDIF:

```
IF expression
    statement-list
ELSE
    statement-list
ENDIF
```

Example: mGotoxyConst Macro   The **mGotoxyConst** macro uses the LT and GT operators to perform range checking on the arguments passed to the macro. The arguments X and Y must be constants. Another constant symbol named ERRS counts the number of errors found. Depending on the value of X, we may set ERRS to 1. Depending on the value of Y, we may add 1 to ERRS. Finally, if ERRS is greater than zero, the EXITM directive exits the macro:

```
;-------------------------------------------------------
mGotoxyConst MACRO X:REQ, Y:REQ
;
; Sets the cursor position at column X, row Y.
; Requires X and Y coordinates to be constant expressions
; in the ranges 0 <= X < 80 and 0 <= Y < 25.
;-------------------------------------------------------
    LOCAL ERRS                    ;; local constant
    ERRS = 0
    IF (X LT 0) OR (X GT 79)
        ECHO Warning: First argument to mGotoxy (X) is out of range.
        ECHO  **********************************************************
        ERRS = 1
```

```
        ENDIF
        IF (Y LT 0) OR (Y GT 24)
            ECHO Warning: Second argument to mGotoxy (Y) is out of range.
            ECHO ********************************************************
            ERRS = ERRS + 1
        ENDIF
        IF ERRS GT 0                    ;; if errors found,
            EXITM                       ;; exit the macro
        ENDIF
        push    edx
        mov     dh,Y
        mov     dl,X
        call    Gotoxy
        pop     edx
    ENDM
```

10.3.5   The IFIDN and IFIDNI Directives

The IFIDNI directive performs a case-insensitive match between two symbols (including macro parameter names) and returns true if they are equal. The IFIDN directive performs a case-sensitive match. The latter is useful when you want to make sure the caller of your macro has not used a register argument that might conflict with register usage inside the macro. The syntax for IFIDNI is

```
    IFIDNI <symbol>, <symbol>
        statements
    ENDIF
```

The syntax for IFIDN is identical. In the following **mReadBuf** macro, for example, the second argument cannot be EDX because it will be overwritten when the offset of **buffer** is moved into EDX. The following revised version of the macro displays a warning message if this requirement is not met:

```
    ;--------------------------------------------------------
mReadBuf MACRO bufferPtr, maxChars
    ;
    ; Reads from the keyboard into a buffer.
    ; Receives: offset of the buffer, count of the maximum
    ;     number of characters that can be entered. The
    ;     second argument cannot be edx or EDX.
    ;--------------------------------------------------------
        IFIDNI <maxChars>,<EDX>
            ECHO Warning: Second argument to mReadBuf cannot be EDX
            ECHO ************************************************
            EXITM
        ENDIF
        push    ecx
        push    edx
        mov     edx,bufferPtr
        mov     ecx,maxChars
```

```
        call  ReadString
        pop   edx
        pop   ecx
ENDM
```

The following statement causes the macro to generate a warning message because EDX is the second argument:

```
mReadBuf OFFSET buffer,edx
```

10.3.6   Example: Summing a Matrix Row

Section 9.4.2 showed how to calculate the sum of a single row in a byte matrix. A programming exercise in Chapter 9 asked you to generalize the procedure for word and doubleword matrices. Although the solution to that exercise is somewhat lengthy, let us see if we can use a macro to simplify the task. First, here is the original **calc_row_sum** procedure shown in Chapter 9:

```
calc_row_sum PROC USES ebx ecx esi
;
; Calculates the sum of a row in a byte matrix.
; Receives: EBX = table offset, EAX = row index,
;           ECX = row size, in bytes.
; Returns:  EAX holds the sum.
;------------------------------------------------------------
        mul   ecx                       ; row index * row size
        add   ebx,eax                   ; row offset
        mov   eax,0                     ; accumulator
        mov   esi,0                     ; column index
L1:  movzx edx,BYTE PTR[ebx + esi]      ; get a byte
        add   eax,edx                   ; add to accumulator
        inc   esi                       ; next byte in row
        loop  L1
        ret
calc_row_sum ENDP
```

We start by changing PROC to MACRO, remove the RET instruction, and change ENDP to ENDM. There is no macro equivalent to the USES directive, so we insert PUSH and POP instructions:

```
mCalc_row_sum MACRO
        push  ebx                       ; save changed regs
        push  ecx
        push  esi
        mul   ecx                       ; row index * row size
        add   ebx,eax                   ; row offset
        mov   eax,0                     ; accumulator
        mov   esi,0                     ; column index
L1:  movzx edx,BYTE PTR[ebx + esi]      ; get a byte
        add   eax,edx                   ; add to accumulator
        inc   esi                       ; next byte in row
```

```
        loop  L1
        pop   esi                           ; restore changed regs
        pop   ecx
        pop   ebx
    ENDM
```

Next, we substitute macro parameters for register parameters and initialize the registers inside the macro:

```
    mCalc_row_sum MACRO index, arrayOffset, rowSize
        push  ebx                           ; save changed regs
        push  ecx
        push  esi

    ; set up the required registers
        mov   eax,index
        mov   ebx,arrayOffset
        mov   ecx,rowSize

        mul   ecx                           ; row index * row size
        add   ebx,eax                       ; row offset
        mov   eax,0                         ; accumulator
        mov   esi,0                         ; column index

    L1: movzx edx,BYTE PTR[ebx + esi]       ; get a byte
        add   eax,edx                       ; add to accumulator
        inc   esi                           ; next byte in row
        loop  L1
        pop   esi                           ; restore changed regs
        pop   ecx
        pop   ebx
    ENDM
```

We now add a parameter named **eltType** that specifies the array type (BYTE, WORD, or DWORD):

```
    mCalc_row_sum MACRO index, arrayOffset, rowSize, eltType
```

The rowSize parameter, copied into ECX, currently indicates the number of bytes in each row. If we are to use it as a loop counter, it must contain the number of *elements* in each row. Therefore, we divide ECX by 2 for 16-bit arrays and by 4 for doubleword arrays. A fast way to accomplish this is to divide **eltType** by 2 and use it as a shift counter, shifting ECX to the right:

```
    shr ecx,(TYPE eltType / 2)              ; byte=0, word=1, dword=2
```

TYPE eltType becomes the scale factor in the base-index operand of the MOVZX instruction:

```
    movzx edx,eltType PTR[ebx + esi*(TYPE eltType)]
```

MOVZX will not assemble if the right-hand operand is a doubleword, so we must use the IFIDNI operator to create a separate MOV instruction when eltType equals DWORD:

```
    IFIDNI <eltType>,<DWORD>
        mov edx,eltType PTR[ebx + esi*(TYPE eltType)]
    ELSE
        movzx edx,eltType PTR[ebx + esi*(TYPE eltType)]
    ENDIF
```

At last, we have the finished macro, remembering to designate label L1 as LOCAL:

```
;------------------------------------------------------------
mCalc_row_sum MACRO index, arrayOffset, rowSize, eltType
; Calculates the sum of a row in a two-dimensional array.
;
; Receives: row index, offset of the array, number of bytes
; in each table row, and the array type (BYTE, WORD, or DWORD).
; Returns:  EAX = sum.
;------------------------------------------------------------
LOCAL L1
     push   ebx                        ; save changed regs
     push   ecx
     push   esi

; set up the required registers
     mov    eax,index
     mov    ebx,arrayOffset
     mov    ecx,rowSize

; calculate the row offset.
     mul    ecx                        ; row index * row size
     add    ebx,eax                    ; row offset

; prepare the loop counter.
     shr    ecx,(TYPE eltType / 2)     ; byte=0, word=1, dword=2

; initialize the accumulator and column indexes
     mov    eax,0                      ; accumulator
     mov    esi,0                      ; column index

L1:
     IFIDNI <eltType>, <DWORD>
       mov      edx,eltType PTR[ebx + esi*(TYPE eltType)]
     ELSE
       movzx    edx,eltType PTR[ebx + esi*(TYPE eltType)]
     ENDIF
     add    eax,edx                    ; add to accumulator
     inc    esi
     loop   L1

     pop    esi                        ; restore changed regs
     pop    ecx
     pop    ebx
ENDM
```

Following are sample calls to the macro, using arrays of byte, word, and doubleword. See the
rowsum.asm program:

```
.data
tableB   BYTE   10h,  20h,  30h,  40h,  50h
RowSizeB = ($ - tableB)
         BYTE   60h,  70h,  80h,  90h,  0A0h
         BYTE   0B0h, 0C0h, 0D0h, 0E0h, 0F0h
```

```
tableW    WORD    10h,   20h,   30h,   40h,   50h
RowSizeW = ($ - tableW)
          WORD    60h,   70h,   80h,   90h,   0A0h
          WORD    0B0h,  0C0h,  0D0h,  0E0h,  0F0h

tableD    DWORD   10h,   20h,   30h,   40h,   50h
RowSizeD = ($ - tableD)
          DWORD   60h,   70h,   80h,   90h,   0A0h
          DWORD   0B0h,  0C0h,  0D0h,  0E0h,  0F0h

index DWORD ?
.code
mCalc_row_sum index, OFFSET tableB, RowSizeB, BYTE
mCalc_row_sum index, OFFSET tableW, RowSizeW, WORD
mCalc_row_sum index, OFFSET tableD, RowSizeD, DWORD
```

10.3.7 Special Operators

There are four assembler operators that make macros more flexible:

&	Substitution operator
<>	Literal-text operator
!	Literal-character operator
%	Expansion operator

Substitution Operator (&)

The *substitution* (&) operator resolves ambiguous references to parameter names within a macro. The **mShowRegister** macro (Section 10.2.5) displays the name and hexadecimal contents of a 32-bit register. The following is a sample call:

```
.code
mShowRegister ECX
```

Following is a sample of the output generated by the call to mShowRegister:

```
ECX=00000101
```

A string variable containing the register name could be defined inside the macro:

```
mShowRegister MACRO regName
.data
tempStr BYTE " regName=",0
```

But the preprocessor would assume **regName** was part of a string literal and would not replace it with the argument value passed to the macro. Instead, if we add the & operator, it forces the preprocessor to insert the macro argument (such as ECX) into the string literal. The following shows how to define **tempStr**:

```
mShowRegister MACRO regName
.data
tempStr BYTE " &regName=",0
```

Expansion Operator (%)

The *expansion* operator (%) expands text macros or converts constant expressions into their text representations. It does this in several different ways. When used with TEXTEQU, the % operator evaluates a constant expression and converts the result to an integer. In the following example, the % operator evaluates the expression (5 + count) and returns the integer 15 (as text):

```
count = 10
sumVal TEXTEQU %(5 + count)      ; = "15"
```

If a macro requires a constant integer argument, the % operator gives you the flexibility of passing an integer expression. The expression is evaluated to its integer value, which is then passed to the macro. For example, when invoking **mGotoxyConst**, the expressions here evaluate to 50 and 7:

```
mGotoxyConst %(5 * 10), %(3 + 4)
```

The preprocessor produces the following statements:

```
1     push   edx
1     mov    dh,7
1     mov    dl,50
1     call   Gotoxy
1     pop    edx
```

% at Beginning of Line   When the expansion operator (%) is the first character on a source code line, it instructs the preprocessor to expand all text macros and macro functions found on the same line. Suppose, for example, we wanted to display the size of an array on the screen during assembly. The following attempts would not produce the intended result:

```
.data
array DWORD 1,2,3,4,5,6,7,8
.code
ECHO The array contains (SIZEOF array) bytes
ECHO The array contains %(SIZEOF array) bytes
```

The screen output would be useless:

```
The array contains (SIZEOF array) bytes
The array contains %(SIZEOF array) bytes
```

Instead, if we use TEXTEQU to create a text macro containing (SIZEOF array), the macro can be expanded on the next line:

```
TempStr TEXTEQU %(SIZEOF array)
%     ECHO The array contains TempStr bytes
```

The following output is produced:

```
The array contains 32 bytes
```

Displaying the Line Number   The following **Mul32** macro multiplies its first two arguments together and returns the product in the third argument. Its parameters can be registers, memory operands, and immediate operands (except for the product):

```
Mul32 MACRO op1, op2, product
     IFIDNI <op2>,<EAX>
        LINENUM TEXTEQU %(@LINE)
        ECHO ----------------------------------------------------
%       ECHO *  Error on line LINENUM: EAX cannot be the second
        ECHO *   argument when invoking the MUL32 macro.
        ECHO ----------------------------------------------------
     EXITM
     ENDIF
     push eax
     mov  eax,op1
     mul  op2
     mov  product,eax
     pop  eax
ENDM
```

Mul32 checks one important requirement: EAX cannot be the second argument. What is interesting about the macro is that it displays the line number from where the macro was called, to make it easier to track down and fix the problem. The Text macro LINENUM is defined first. It references @LINE, a predefined assembler operator that returns the current source code line number:

```
LINENUM TEXTEQU %(@LINE)
```

Next, the expansion operator (%) in the first column of the line containing the ECHO statement causes LINENUM to be expanded:

```
%       ECHO * Error on line LINENUM: EAX cannot be the second
```

Suppose the following macro call occurs in a program on line 40:

```
MUL32 val1,eax,val3
```

Then the following message is displayed during assembly:

```
     ----------------------------------------------------

     *   Error on line 40: EAX cannot be the second

     *   argument when invoking the MUL32 macro.

     ----------------------------------------------------
```

You can view a test of the **Mul32** macro in the program named *Macro3.asm*.

Literal-Text Operator (<>)

The *literal-text* operator (<>) groups one or more characters and symbols into a single text literal. It prevents the preprocessor from interpreting members of the list as separate arguments. This operator is particularly useful when a string contains special characters, such as commas, percent signs (%), ampersands (&), and semicolons (;), that would otherwise be interpreted as delimiters or other operators. For example, the **mWrite** macro presented earlier in this chapter receives a string literal as its only argument. If we were to pass it the following string, the preprocessor would interpret it as three separate macro arguments:

```
mWrite "Line three", 0dh, 0ah
```

Text after the first comma would be discarded because the macro expects only one argument. On the other hand, if we surrounded the string with the literal-text operator, the preprocessor considers all text between the brackets to be a single macro argument:

```
mWrite <"Line three", 0dh, 0ah>
```

Literal-Character Operator (!)

The *literal-character* operator (!) was invented for much the same purpose as the literal-text operator: It forces the preprocessor to treat a predefined operator as an ordinary character. In the following TEXTEQU definition, the ! operator prevents the > symbol from being a text delimiter:

```
BadYValue TEXTEQU <Warning: Y-coordinate is !> 24>
```

Warning Message Example   The following example helps to show how the %, &, and ! operators work together. Let's assume we have defined the **BadYValue** symbol. We can create a macro named **ShowWarning** that receives a text argument, encloses it in quotes, and passes the literal to the **mWrite** macro. Note the use of the substitution (&) operator:

```
ShowWarning MACRO message
    mWrite "&message"
ENDM
```

Next, we invoke **ShowWarning**, passing it the expression %BadYValue. The % operator evaluates (dereferences) **BadYValue** and produces its equivalent string:

```
.code
ShowWarning %BadYValue
```

As you might expect, the program runs and displays the warning message:

```
Warning: Y-coordinate is > 24
```

10.3.8   Macro Functions

A macro function is similar to a macro procedure in that it assigns a name to a list of assembly language statements. It is different in that it always returns a constant (integer or string) via the EXITM directive. In the following example, the **IsDefined** macro returns true (-1) if a given symbol has been defined; otherwise, it returns false (0):

```
IsDefined MACRO symbol
    IFDEF symbol
      EXITM <-1>              ;; True
    ELSE
      EXITM <0>               ;; False
    ENDIF
ENDM
```

The EXITM (exit macro) directive halts all further expansion of the macro.

Calling a Macro Function   When you call a macro function, its argument list must be enclosed in parentheses. For example, we can call the **IsDefined** macro, passing it **RealMode**, the name of a symbol which may or may not have been defined:

```
IF IsDefined( RealMode )
    mov    ax,@data
    mov    ds,ax
ENDIF
```

If the assembler has already encountered a definition of **RealMode** before this point in the assembly process, it assembles the two instructions:

```
mov ax,@data
mov ds,ax
```

The same IF directive can be placed inside a macro named **Startup**:

```
Startup MACRO
    IF IsDefined( RealMode )
      mov    ax,@data
      mov    ds,ax
    ENDIF
ENDM
```

A macro such as **IsDefined** can be useful when you design programs for multiple memory models. For example, we can use it to determine which include file to use:

```
IF IsDefined( RealMode )
    INCLUDE Irvine16.inc
ELSE
    INCLUDE Irvine32.inc
ENDIF
```

Defining the RealMode Symbol   All that remains is to find a way to define the **RealMode** symbol. One way is to put the following line at the beginning of a program:

```
RealMode = 1
```

Alternatively, the assembler's command line has an option for defining symbols, using the –D switch. The following ML command defines the RealMode symbol and assigns it a value of 1:

```
ML -c -DRealMode=1 myProg.asm
```

The corresponding ML command for protected mode programs does not define the RealMode symbol:

```
ML -c myProg.asm
```

HelloNew Program   The following program (*HelloNew.asm*) uses the macros we have just described, displaying a message on the screen:

```
TITLE Macro Functions                   (HelloNew.asm)

INCLUDE Macros.inc
IF IsDefined( RealMode )
    INCLUDE Irvine16.inc
```

```
    ELSE
        INCLUDE Irvine32.inc
    ENDIF

    .code
    main PROC
        Startup
        mWrite <"This program can be assembled to run ",0dh,0ah>
        mWrite <"in both Real mode and Protected mode.",0dh,0ah>
        exit
    main ENDP
    END main
```

This program can be assembled in real-address mode, using *makeHello16.bat*.

10.3.9   Section Review

1. What is the purpose of the IFB directive?

2. What is the purpose of the IFIDN directive?

3. Which directive stops all further expansion of a macro?

4. How is IFIDNI different from IFIDN?

5. What is the purpose of the IFDEF directive?

6. Which directive marks the end of a conditional block of statements?

7. Show an example of a macro parameter having a default argument initializer.

8. List all the relational operators that can be used in constant boolean expressions.

9. Write a short example that uses the IF, ELSE, and ENDIF directives.

10. Write a statement using the IF directive that checks the value of the constant macro parameter Z; if Z is less than zero, display a message during assembly indicating that Z is invalid.

11. What is the purpose of the & operator in a macro definition?

12. What is the purpose of the ! operator in a macro definition?

13. What is the purpose of the % operator in a macro definition?

14. Write a short macro that demonstrates the use of the & operator when the macro parameter is embedded in a literal string.

15. Assume the following **mLocate** macro definition:

```
mLocate MACRO xval,yval
    IF xval LT 0                    ;; xval < 0?
      EXITM                        ;; if so, exit
    ENDIF
    IF yval LT 0                    ;; yval < 0?
      EXITM                        ;; if so, exit
    ENDIF
    mov   bx,0                      ;; video page 0
    mov   ah,2                      ;; locate cursor
    mov   dh,yval
    mov   dl,xval
    int   10h                       ;; call the BIOS
ENDM
```

Show the source code generated by the preprocessor when the macro is expanded by each of the following statements:

```
.data
row BYTE 15
col BYTE 60
.code
mLocate  -2,20
mLocate  10,20
mLocate  col,row
```

10.4   Defining Repeat Blocks

MASM has a number of looping directives for generating repeated blocks of statements: WHILE, REPEAT, FOR, and FORC. Unlike the LOOP instruction, these directives work only at assembly time, using constant values as loop conditions and counters:

• The WHILE directive repeats a statement block based on a boolean expression.
• The REPEAT directive repeats a statement block based on the value of a counter.
• The FOR directive repeats a statement block by iterating over a list of symbols.
• The FORC directive repeats a statement block by iterating over a string of characters.

Each is demonstrated in an example program named *Repeat.asm*.

10.4.1   WHILE Directive

The WHILE directive repeats a statement block as long as a particular constant expression is true. The syntax is

```
WHILE constExpression
    statements
ENDM
```

The following code shows how to generate Fibonacci numbers between 1 and F0000000h as a series of assembly-time constants:

```
.data
val1  = 1
val2  = 1
DWORD val1                           ; first two values
DWORD val2
val3 = val1 + val2
WHILE val3 LT 0F0000000h
    DWORD val3
    val1 = val2
    val2 = val3
    val3 = val1 + val2
ENDM
```

The values generated by this code can be viewed in a listing (.LST) file.

10.4.2   REPEAT Directive

The REPEAT directive repeats a statement block a fixed number of times at assembly time. The syntax is

```
REPEAT constExpression
   statements
ENDM
```

ConstExpression, an unsigned constant integer expression, determines the number of repetitions.

REPEAT can be used in a similar way as DUP to create an array. In the following example, the WeatherReadings struct contains a location string, followed by an array of rainfall and humidity readings:

```
WEEKS_PER_YEAR = 52

WeatherReadings STRUCT
     location BYTE 50 DUP(0)
     REPEAT WEEKS_PER_YEAR
       LOCAL rainfall, humidity
       rainfall DWORD ?
       humidity DWORD ?
     ENDM
WeatherReadings ENDS
```

The LOCAL directive was used to avoid errors caused by redefining rainfall and humidity when the loop was repeated at assembly time.

10.4.3   FOR Directive

The FOR directive repeats a statement block by iterating over a comma-delimited list of symbols. Each symbol in the list causes one iteration of the loop. The syntax is

```
FOR parameter,<arg1,arg2,arg3,...>
     statements
ENDM
```

On the first loop iteration, *parameter* takes on the value of *arg1*; on the second iteration, *parameter* takes on the value of *arg2*; and so on through the last argument in the list.

Student Enrollment Example   Let's create a student enrollment scenario in which we have a COURSE structure containing a course number and number of credits. A SEMESTER structure contains an array of six courses and a counter named **NumCourses**:

```
COURSE STRUCT
     Number  BYTE 9 DUP(?)
     Credits BYTE ?
COURSE ENDS

; A semester contains an array of courses.
SEMESTER STRUCT
     Courses COURSE 6 DUP(<>)
     NumCourses WORD ?
SEMESTER ENDS
```

We can use a FOR loop to define four SEMESTER objects, each having a different name selected from the list symbols between angle brackets:

```
.data
FOR semName,<Fall1999,Spring2000,Summer2000,Fall2000>
     semName SEMESTER <>
ENDM
```

If we inspect the listing file, we find the following variables:

```
.data
Fall1999 SEMESTER <>
Spring2000 SEMESTER <>
Summer2000 SEMESTER <>
Fall2000 SEMESTER <>
```

10.4.4 FORC Directive

The FORC directive repeats a statement block by iterating over a string of characters. Each character in the string causes one iteration of the loop. The syntax is

```
FORC parameter, <string>
      statements
ENDM
```

On the first loop iteration, *parameter* is equal to the first character in the string; on the second iteration, *parameter* is equal to the second character in the string; and so on, to the end of the string. The following example creates a character lookup table consisting of several nonalphabetic characters. Note that < and > must be preceded by the literal-character (!) operator to prevent them from violating the syntax of the FORC directive:

```
Delimiters LABEL BYTE
FORC code,<@#$%^&*!<!>>
      BYTE "&code"
ENDM
```

The following data table is generated, which you can view in the listing file:

```
00000000   40   1 BYTE "@"
00000001   23   1 BYTE "#"
00000002   24   1 BYTE "$"
00000003   25   1 BYTE "%"
00000004   5E   1 BYTE "^"
00000005   26   1 BYTE "&"
00000006   2A   1 BYTE "*"
00000007   3C   1 BYTE "<"
00000008   3E   1 BYTE ">"
```

10.4.5 Example: Linked List

It is fairly simple to combine a structure declaration with the REPEAT directive to instruct the assembler to create a linked list data structure. Each node in a linked list contains a data area and a link area:

In the data area, one or more variables can hold data unique to each node. In the link area, a pointer contains the address of the next node in the list. The link part of the final node usually contains a null pointer. Let's create a program that creates and displays a simple linked list. First, the program defines a list node having a single integer (data) and a pointer to the next node:

```
ListNode STRUCT
    NodeData DWORD ?              ; the node's data
    NextPtr  DWORD ?              ; pointer to next node
ListNode ENDS
```

Next, the REPEAT directive creates multiple instances of **ListNode** objects. For testing purposes, the **NodeData** field contains an integer constant ranging from 1 to 15. Inside the loop, we increment the counter and insert values into the ListNode fields:

```
TotalNodeCount = 15
NULL = 0
Counter = 0

.data
LinkedList LABEL PTR ListNode
REPEAT TotalNodeCount
    Counter = Counter + 1
    ListNode <Counter, ($ + Counter * SIZEOF ListNode)>
ENDM
```

The expression ($ + Counter * SIZEOF ListNode) tells the assembler to multiply the counter by the **ListNode** size and add their product to the current location counter. The value is inserted into the **NextPtr** field in the structure. [It's interesting to note that the location counter's value ($) remains fixed at the first node of the list.] The list is given a *tail node* marking its end, in which the **NextPtr** field contains null (0):

```
ListNode <0,0>
```

When the program traverses the list, it uses the following statements to retrieve the **NextPtr** field and compare it to NULL so the end of the list can be detected:

```
mov   eax,(ListNode PTR [esi]).NextPtr
cmp   eax,NULL
```

Program Listing   The following is a complete program listing. In main, a loop traverses the list and displays all the node values. Rather than using a fixed counter for the loop, the program checks for the null pointer in the tail node and stops looping when it is found:

```
TITLE Creating a Linked List              (List.asm)

INCLUDE Irvine32.inc

ListNode STRUCT
  NodeData DWORD ?
  NextPtr  DWORD ?
ListNode ENDS

TotalNodeCount = 15
NULL = 0
Counter = 0

.data
LinkedList LABEL PTR ListNode
```

```
     REPEAT TotalNodeCount
         Counter = Counter + 1
         ListNode <Counter, ($ + Counter * SIZEOF ListNode)>
     ENDM
     ListNode <0,0>                    ; tail node

     .code
     main PROC
         mov   esi,OFFSET LinkedList

     ; Display the integers in the NodeData fields.
     NextNode:
         ; Check for the tail node.
         mov   eax,(ListNode PTR [esi]).NextPtr
         cmp   eax,NULL
         je    quit

         ; Display the node data.
         mov   eax,(ListNode PTR [esi]).NodeData
         call  WriteDec
         call  Crlf

         ; Get pointer to next node.
         mov   esi,(ListNode PTR [esi]).NextPtr
         jmp   NextNode

     quit:
         exit
     main ENDP
     END main
```

10.4.6   Section Review

1. Briefly describe the WHILE directive.

2. Briefly describe the REPEAT directive.

3. Briefly describe the FOR directive.

4. Briefly describe the FORC directive.

5. Which looping directive would be the best tool to generate a character lookup table?

6. Write the statements generated by the following macro:

```
FOR val,<100,20,30>
    BYTE 0,0,0,val
ENDM
```

7. Assume the following **mRepeat** macro has been defined:

```
mRepeat MACRO char,count
    LOCAL L1
    mov   cx,count
L1: mov   ah,2
    mov   dl,char
    int   21h
    loop  L1
ENDM
```

Write the code generated by the preprocessor when the **mRepeat** macro is expanded by each of the following statements (a, b, and c):

```
mRepeat 'X',50            ; a
mRepeat AL,20             ; b
mRepeat byteVal,countVal  ; c
```

8. *Challenge:* In the Linked List example program (Section 10.4.5), what would be the result if the REPEAT loop were coded as follows?

```
REPEAT TotalNodeCount
    Counter = Counter + 1
    ListNode <Counter, ($ + SIZEOF ListNode)>
ENDM
```

10.5 Chapter Summary

A *structure* is a template or pattern used when creating user-defined types. Many structures are already defined in the MS-Windows API library and are used for the transfer of data between application programs and the library. Structures can contain a diverse set of field types. Each field declaration may use a field-initializer, which assigns a default value to the field.

Structures themselves take up no memory, but structure variables do. The SIZEOF operator returns the number of bytes used by the variable.

The dot operator (.) references a structure field by using either a structure variable or an indirect operand such as [esi]. When an indirect operand references a structure field, you must use the PTR operator to identify the structure type, as in (COORD PTR [esi]).X.

Structures can contain fields that are also structures. An example was shown in the Drunkard's Walk program (Section 10.1.6), where the **DrunkardWalk** structure contained an array of COORD structures.

Macros are usually defined at the beginning of a program, before the data and code segments. Then, when a macro is called, the preprocessor inserts a copy of the macro's code into the program at the calling location.

Macros can be effectively used as *wrappers* around procedure calls to simplify parameter passing and saving registers on the stack. Macros such as **mGotoxy, mDumpMem**, and **mWriteString** are examples of wrappers because they call procedures from the book's link library.

A *macro procedure* (or *macro*) is a named block of assembly language statements. A *macro function* is similar, except that it also returns a constant value.

Conditional-assembly directives such as IF, IFNB, and IFIDNI can be used to detect arguments that are out of range, missing, or of the wrong type. The ECHO directive displays error messages during assembly, making it possible to alert the programmer to errors in arguments passed to macros.

The substitution operator (&) resolves ambiguous references to parameter names. The expansion operator (%) expands text macros and converts constant expressions to text. The literal-text operator (< >) groups diverse characters and text into a single literal. The literal-character operator (!) forces the preprocessor to treat predefined operators as ordinary characters.

Repeat block directives can reduce the amount of repetitive code in programs. The directives are as follows:

- WHILE repeats a statement block based on a boolean expression.
- REPEAT repeats a statement block based on the value of a counter.
- FOR repeats a statement block by iterating over a list of symbols.
- FORC repeats a statement block by iterating over a string of characters.

10.6   Programming Exercises

★ 1.   mReadkey Macro

Create a macro that waits for a keystroke and returns the key that was pressed. The macro should include parameters for the ASCII code and keyboard scan code. *Hint:* Call ReadKey from the book's link library. Write a program that tests your macro. For example, the following code waits for a key; when it returns, the two arguments contain the ASCII code and scan code:

```
.data
ascii BYTE ?
scan BYTE ?
.code
mReadkey ascii, scan
```

★ 2.   mWritestringAttr Macro

(Requires reading Section 15.3.3 or Section 11.1.11.) Create a macro that writes a null-terminated string to the console with a given text color. The macro parameters should include the string name and the color. *Hint:* Call SetTextColor from the book's link library. Write a program that tests your macro with several strings in different colors. Sample call:

```
.data
myString db "Here is my string",0
.code
mWritestring myString, white
```

★ 3.   mMove32 Macro

Write a macro named **mMove32** that receives two 32-bit memory operands. The macro should move the source operand to the destination operand. Write a program that tests your macro.

★ 4.   mMult32 Macro

Create a macro named **mMult32** that multiplies two 32-bit memory operands and produces a 32-bit product. Write a program that tests your macro.

★★ 5.   mReadInt Macro

Create a macro named **mReadInt** that reads a 16- or 32-bit signed integer from standard input and returns the value in an argument. Use conditional operators to allow the macro to adapt to the size of the desired result. Write a program that calls the macro, passing it operands of various sizes.

★★ 6.   mWriteInt Macro

Create a macro named **mWriteInt** that writes a signed integer to standard output by calling the **WriteInt** library procedure. The argument passed to the macro can be a byte, word, or doubleword. Use conditional operators in the macro so it adapts to the size of the argument. Write a program that tests the macro, passing it arguments of different sizes.

★★ **7.   mScroll Macro**

(Requires reading Section 15.3.3.) Create a macro named **mScroll** that displays a color rectangle in the console window. Include the following parameters in the macro definition. If **attrib** is blank, assume a color of light gray characters on a black background:

ULrow	Upper-left window row
ULcol	Upper-left window column
LRrow	Lower-right window row
LRcol	Lower-right window column
attrib	Color of scrolled lines

Write a program that tests your macro.

★★★ **8.   Drunkard's Walk**

When testing the Drunkard Walk program, you may have noticed that the professor doesn't seem to wander very far from the starting point. This is no doubt caused by an equal probability of the professor moving in any direction. Modify the program so there is a 50% probability the professor will continue to walk in the same direction as he or she did when taking the previous step. There should be a 10% probability that he or she will reverse direction and a 20% probability that he or she will turn either right or left. Assign a default starting direction before the loop begins.

★★★★ **9.   Shifting Multiple Doublewords**

Create a macro that shifts an array of 32-bit integers a variable number of bits in either direction, using the SHRD instruction. Write a test program that tests your macro by shifting the same array in both directions and displaying the resulting values. You can assume that the array is in little-endian order. Here is a sample macro declaration:

```
mShiftDoublewords MACRO arrayName, direction, numberOfBits

Parameters:
   arrayName      Name of the array
   direction      Right (R) or Left (L)
   numberOfBits   Number of bit positions to shift
```

★★ **10.   Three-Operand Instructions**

Some computer instruction sets permit arithmetic instructions with three operands. Such operations sometimes appear in simple virtual assemblers used to introduce students to the concept of assembly language or using intermediate language in compilers. In the following macros, assume EAX is reserved for macro operations and is not preserved. Other registers modified by the macro must be preserved. All parameters are signed memory doublewords. Write macros that simulate the following operations:

```
a. add3 destination, source1, source2
b. sub3 destination, source1, source2 (destination = source1 − source2)
c. mul3 destination, source1, source2
d. div3 destination, source1, source2 (destination = source1 / source2)
```

For example, the following macro calls implement the expression **x = (w + y) * z**:

```
.data
temp DWORD ?
.code
add3 temp, w, y                    ; temp = w + y
mul3 x, temp, z                    ; x = temp * z
```

Write a program that tests your macros by implementing four arithmetic expressions, each involving multiple operations.

End Note

1. Probably because RECORD is the term used in the old COBOL programming language, familiar to the designers of Windows NT.

11

MS-Windows Programming

11.1 Win32 Console Programming
    11.1.1   Background Information
    11.1.2   Win32 Console Functions
    11.1.3   Displaying a Message Box
    11.1.4   Console Input
    11.1.5   Console Output
    11.1.6   Reading and Writing Files
    11.1.7   File I/O in the Irvine32 Library
    11.1.8   Testing the File I/O Procedures
    11.1.9   Console Window Manipulation
    11.1.10 Controlling the Cursor
    11.1.11 Controlling the Text Color
    11.1.12 Time and Date Functions
    11.1.13 Section Review
11.2 Writing a Graphical Windows Application
    11.2.1   Necessary Structures
    11.2.2   The MessageBox Function

    11.2.3   The WinMain Procedure
    11.2.4   The WinProc Procedure
    11.2.5   The ErrorHandler Procedure
    11.2.6   Program Listing
    11.2.7   Section Review
11.3 Dynamic Memory Allocation
    11.3.1   HeapTest Programs
    11.3.2   Section Review
11.4 x86 Memory Management
    11.4.1   Linear Addresses
    11.4.2   Page Translation
    11.4.3   Section Review
11.5 Chapter Summary
11.6 Programming Exercises

11.1 Win32 Console Programming

Some of the following questions should have been in the back of your mind while reading this book:

- How do 32-bit programs handle text input-output?
- How are colors handled in 32-bit console mode?
- How does the Irvine32 link library work?
- How are times and dates handled in MS-Windows?
- How can I use MS-Windows functions to read and write data files?

- Is it possible to write a graphical Windows application in assembly language?
- How do protected mode programs translate segments and offsets to physical addresses?
- I've heard that virtual memory is good. But why is that so?

This chapter will answer these questions and more, as we show you the basics of 32-bit programming under Microsoft Windows. Most of the information here is oriented toward 32-bit console mode text applications because they are reasonably easy to program, given a knowledge of structures and procedure parameters. The Irvine32 link library is completely built on Win32 console functions, so you can compare its source code to the information in this chapter. Find its source code in the \Examples\Lib32 directory of the sample programs accompanying this book.

Why not write graphical applications for MS-Windows? If written in assembly language or C, graphical programs are long and detailed. For years, C and C++ programmers have labored over technical details such as graphical device handles, message posting, font metrics, device bitmaps, and mapping modes, with the help of excellent authors. There is a devoted group of assembly language programmers with excellent Web sites who do graphical Windows programming. See the link to *Assembly Language Sources* from this book's home page (*www.asmirvine.com*).

To provide some interest to graphical programmers, Section 11.2 introduces 32-bit graphical programming in a generic sort of way. It's only a start, but you might be inspired to go further into the topic. A list of recommended books for further study is given in the summary at the end of this chapter.

On the surface, 32-bit console mode programs look and behave like 16-bit MS-DOS programs running in text mode. There are differences, however: The former runs in 32-bit protected mode, whereas MS-DOS programs run in real-address mode. They use different function libraries. Win32 programs call functions from the same library used by graphical Windows applications. MS-DOS programs use BIOS and MS-DOS interrupts that have existed since the introduction of the IBM-PC.

An *Application Programming Interface* (API) is a collection of types, constants, and functions that provide a way to directly manipulate objects through programming. Therefore, the Win32 API lets you tap into the functions in the 32-bit version of MS-Windows.

Win32 Platform SDK   Closely related to the Win32 API is the Microsoft *Platform SDK (Software Development Kit)*, a collection of tools, libraries, sample code, and documentation for creating MS-Windows applications. Complete documentation is available online at Microsoft's Web site. Search for "Platform SDK" at www.msdn.microsoft.com. The Platform SDK is a free download.

Tip: The Irvine32 library is compatible with Win32 API functions, so you can call both from the same program.

11.1.1 Background Information

When a Windows application starts, it creates either a console window or a graphical window. We have been using the following option with the LINK command in our project files. It tells the linker to create a console-based application:

```
/SUBSYSTEM:CONSOLE
```

A console program looks and behaves like an MS-DOS window, with some enhancements, which we will see later. The console has a single input buffer and one or more screen buffers:

- The *input buffer* contains a queue of *input records*, each containing data about an input event. Examples of input events are keyboard input, mouse clicks, and the user's resizing of the console window.
- A *screen buffer* is a two-dimensional array of character and color data that affects the appearance of text in the console window.

Win32 API Reference Information

Functions Throughout this section, we will introduce you to a subset of Win32 API functions and provide a few simple examples. Many details cannot be covered here because of space limitations. To find out more, click on Help inside Microsoft Visual C++ Express, or visit the Microsoft MSDN Web site (currently located at www.msdn.microsoft.com). When searching for functions or identifiers, set the *Filtered by* parameter to **Platform SDK**. Also, in the sample programs supplied with this book, the kernel32.txt and user32.txt files provide comprehensive lists of function names in the kernel32.lib and user32.lib libraries.

Constants Often when reading documentation for Win32 API functions, you will come across constant names, such as TIME_ZONE_ID_UNKNOWN. In a few cases, the constant will already be defined in SmallWin.inc. But if you can't find it there, look on our book's Web site. A header file named *WinNT.h*, for example, defines TIME_ZONE_ID_UNKNOWN along with related constants:

```
#define TIME_ZONE_ID_UNKNOWN   0
#define TIME_ZONE_ID_STANDARD  1
#define TIME_ZONE_ID_DAYLIGHT  2
```

Using this information, you would add the following to *SmallWin.h* or your own include file:

```
TIME_ZONE_ID_UNKNOWN  = 0
TIME_ZONE_ID_STANDARD = 1
TIME_ZONE_ID_DAYLIGHT = 2
```

Character Sets and Windows API Functions

Two types of character sets are used when calling functions in the Win32 API: the 8-bit ASCII/ ANSI character set and the 16-bit Unicode set (available in Windows NT, 2000, Vista, and XP). Win32 functions dealing with text are usually supplied in two versions, one ending in the letter A (for 8-bit ANSI characters) and the other ending in W (for *wide* character sets, including Unicode). One of these is WriteConsole:

- WriteConsoleA
- WriteConsoleW

Function names ending in W are not supported by Windows 95 or 98. In Windows NT, 2000, Vista, and XP, on the other hand, Unicode is the native character set. If you call a function such as **WriteConsoleA**, for example, the operating system converts the characters from ANSI to Unicode and calls **WriteConsoleW**.

In the Microsoft MSDN Library documentation for functions such as WriteConsole, the trailing A or W is omitted from the name. In the include file for the programs in this book, we redefine function names such as **WriteConsoleA**:

```
WriteConsole EQU <WriteConsoleA>
```

This definition makes it possible to call WriteConsole using its generic name.

High-Level and Low-Level Access

There are two levels of access to the console, permitting tradeoffs between simplicity and complete control:

- High-level console functions read a stream of characters from the console's input buffer. They write character data to the console's screen buffer. Both input and output can be redirected to read from or write to text files.
- Low-level console functions retrieve detailed information about keyboard and mouse events and user interactions with the console window (dragging, resizing, etc.). These functions also permit detailed control of the window size and position, as well as text colors.

Windows Data Types

Win32 functions are documented using function declarations for C/C++ programmers. In these declarations, the types of all function parameters are based either on standard C types or on one of the MS-Windows predefined types (a partial list is in Table 11-1). It is important to distinguish data values from pointers to values. A type name that begins with the letters LP is a *long pointer* to some other object.

SmallWin.inc Include File

SmallWin.inc, created by the author, is an include file containing constant definitions, text equates, and function prototypes for Win32 API programming. It is automatically included in programs by Irvine32.inc, which we have been using throughout the book. The file is located in the \Examples\Lib32 folder where you installed the sample programs from this book. Most of the constants can be found in Windows.h, a header file used for programming in C and C++. Despite its name, SmallWin.inc is rather large, so we'll just show highlights:

```
DO_NOT_SHARE = 0
NULL = 0
TRUE = 1
FALSE = 0

; Win32 Console handles
STD_INPUT_HANDLE EQU -10
STD_OUTPUT_HANDLE EQU -11
STD_ERROR_HANDLE EQU -12
```

The HANDLE type, an alias for DWORD, helps our function prototypes to be more consistent with the Microsoft Win32 documentation:

```
HANDLE TEXTEQU <DWORD>
```

Table 11-1   Translating MS-Windows Types to MASM.

MS-Windows Type	MASM Type	Description
BOOL, BOOLEAN	DWORD	A boolean value (TRUE or FALSE)
BYTE	BYTE	An 8-bit unsigned integer
CHAR	BYTE	An 8-bit Windows ANSI character
COLORREF	DWORD	A 32-bit value used as a color value
DWORD	DWORD	A 32-bit unsigned integer
HANDLE	DWORD	Handle to an object
HFILE	DWORD	Handle to a file opened by OpenFile
INT	SDWORD	A 32-bit signed integer
LONG	SDWORD	A 32-bit signed integer
LPARAM	DWORD	Message parameter, used by window procedures and callback functions
LPCSTR	PTR BYTE	A 32-bit pointer to a constant null-terminated string of 8-bit Windows (ANSI) characters
LPCVOID	DWORD	Pointer to a constant of any type
LPSTR	PTR BYTE	A 32-bit pointer to a null-terminated string of 8-bit Windows (ANSI) characters
LPCTSTR	PTR WORD	A 32-bit pointer to a constant character string that is portable for Unicode and double-byte character sets
LPTSTR	PTR WORD	A 32-bit pointer to a character string that is portable for Unicode and double-byte character sets
LPVOID	DWORD	A 32-bit pointer to an unspecified type
LRESULT	DWORD	A 32-bit value returned from a window procedure or callback function
SIZE_T	DWORD	The maximum number of bytes to which a pointer can point
UINT	DWORD	A 32-bit unsigned integer
WNDPROC	DWORD	A 32-bit pointer to a window procedure
WORD	WORD	A 16-bit unsigned integer
WPARAM	DWORD	A 32-bit value passed as a parameter to a window procedure or callback function

SmallWin.inc also includes structure definitions used in Win32 calls. Two are shown here:

```
COORD STRUCT
    X WORD ?
    Y WORD ?
COORD ENDS

SYSTEMTIME STRUCT
    wYear WORD ?
    wMonth WORD ?
    wDayOfWeek WORD ?
    wDay WORD ?
```

```
        wHour WORD ?
        wMinute WORD ?
        wSecond WORD ?
        wMilliseconds WORD ?
    SYSTEMTIME ENDS
```

Finally, SmallWin.inc contains function prototypes for all Win32 functions documented in this chapter.

Console Handles

Nearly all Win32 console functions require you to pass a handle as the first argument. A *handle* is a 32-bit unsigned integer that uniquely identifies an object such as a bitmap, drawing pen, or any input/output device:

```
    STD_INPUT_HANDLE      standard input
    STD_OUTPUT_HANDLE     standard output
    STD_ERROR_HANDLE      standard error output
```

The latter two handles are used when writing to the console's active screen buffer.

The **GetStdHandle** function returns a handle to a console stream: input, output, or error output. You need a handle in order to do any input/output in a console-based program. Here is the function prototype:

```
    GetStdHandle PROTO,
        nStdHandle:HANDLE             ; handle type
```

nStdHandle can be STD_INPUT_HANDLE, STD_OUTPUT_HANDLE, or STD_ERROR_HANDLE. The function returns the handle in EAX, which should be copied into a variable for safekeeping. Here is a sample call:

```
    .data
    inputHandle HANDLE ?
    .code
        INVOKE GetStdHandle, STD_INPUT_HANDLE
        mov inputHandle,eax
```

11.1.2   Win32 Console Functions

Table 11-2 contains a quick reference to the complete set of Win32 console functions.[1] You can find a complete description of each function in the MSDN library at www.msdn.microsoft.com.

> **Tip:** Win32 API functions do not preserve EAX, EBX, ECX, and EDX, so you should push and pop those registers yourself.

Table 11-2   Win32 Console Functions.

Function	Description
AllocConsole	Allocates a new console for the calling process.
CreateConsoleScreenBuffer	Creates a console screen buffer.
ExitProcess	Ends a process and all its threads.
FillConsoleOutputAttribute	Sets the text and background color attributes for a specified number of character cells.

Table 11-2   *(Continued)*

Function	Description
FillConsoleOutputCharacter	Writes a character to the screen buffer a specified number of times.
FlushConsoleInputBuffer	Flushes the console input buffer.
FreeConsole	Detaches the calling process from its console.
GenerateConsoleCtrlEvent	Sends a specified signal to a console process group that shares the console associated with the calling process.
GetConsoleCP	Retrieves the input code page used by the console associated with the calling process.
GetConsoleCursorInfo	Retrieves information about the size and visibility of the cursor for the specified console screen buffer.
GetConsoleMode	Retrieves the current input mode of a console's input buffer or the current output mode of a console screen buffer.
GetConsoleOutputCP	Retrieves the output code page used by the console associated with the calling process.
GetConsoleScreenBufferInfo	Retrieves information about the specified console screen buffer.
GetConsoleTitle	Retrieves the title bar string for the current console window.
GetConsoleWindow	Retrieves the window handle used by the console associated with the calling process.
GetLargestConsoleWindowSize	Retrieves the size of the largest possible console window.
GetNumberOfConsoleInputEvents	Retrieves the number of unread input records in the console's input buffer.
GetNumberOfConsoleMouseButtons	Retrieves the number of buttons on the mouse used by the current console.
GetStdHandle	Retrieves a handle for the standard input, standard output, or standard error device.
HandlerRoutine	An application-defined function used with the SetConsoleCtrlHandler function.
PeekConsoleInput	Reads data from the specified console input buffer without removing it from the buffer.
ReadConsole	Reads character input from the console input buffer and removes it from the buffer.
ReadConsoleInput	Reads data from a console input buffer and removes it from the buffer.
ReadConsoleOutput	Reads character and color attribute data from a rectangular block of character cells in a console screen buffer.
ReadConsoleOutputAttribute	Copies a specified number of foreground and background color attributes from consecutive cells of a console screen buffer.
ReadConsoleOutputCharacter	Copies a number of characters from consecutive cells of a console screen buffer.
ScrollConsoleScreenBuffer	Moves a block of data in a screen buffer.
SetConsoleActiveScreenBuffer	Sets the specified screen buffer to be the currently displayed console screen buffer.
SetConsoleCP	Sets the input code page used by the console associated with the calling process.
SetConsoleCtrlHandler	Adds or removes an application-defined HandlerRoutine from the list of handler functions for the calling process.

Table 11-2   *(Continued)*

Function	Description
SetConsoleCursorInfo	Sets the size and visibility of the cursor for the specified console screen buffer.
SetConsoleCursorPosition	Sets the cursor position in the specified console screen buffer.
SetConsoleMode	Sets the input mode of a console's input buffer or the output mode of a console screen buffer.
SetConsoleOutputCP	Sets the output code page used by the console associated with the calling process.
SetConsoleScreenBufferSize	Changes the size of the specified console screen buffer.
SetConsoleTextAttribute	Sets the foreground (text) and background color attributes of characters written to the screen buffer.
SetConsoleTitle	Sets the title bar string for the current console window.
SetConsoleWindowInfo	Sets the current size and position of a console screen buffer's window.
SetStdHandle	Sets the handle for the standard input, standard output, or standard error device.
WriteConsole	Writes a character string to a console screen buffer beginning at the current cursor location.
WriteConsoleInput	Writes data directly to the console input buffer.
WriteConsoleOutput	Writes character and color attribute data to a specified rectangular block of character cells in a console screen buffer.
WriteConsoleOutputAttribute	Copies a number of foreground and background color attributes to consecutive cells of a console screen buffer.
WriteConsoleOutputCharacter	Copies a number of characters to consecutive cells of a console screen buffer.

11.1.3   Displaying a Message Box

One of the easiest ways to generate output in a Win32 application is to call the **MessageBoxA** function:

```
MessageBoxA PROTO,
     hWnd:DWORD,              ; handle to window (can be null)
     lpText:PTR BYTE,         ; string, inside of box
     lpCaption:PTR BYTE,      ; string, dialog box title
     uType:DWORD              ; contents and behavior
```

In console-based applications, you can set *hWnd* to NULL, indicating that the message box is not associated with a containing or parent window. The *lpText* parameter is a pointer to the null-terminated string that you want to put in the message box. The *lpCaption* parameter points to a null-terminated string for the dialog box title. The *uType* parameter specifies the dialog box contents and behavior.

Contents and Behavior   The *uType* parameter holds a bit-mapped integer combining three types of options: buttons to display, icons, and default button choice. Several button combinations are possible:

- MB_OK
- MB_OKCANCEL
- MB_YESNO
- MB_YESNOCANCEL
- MB_RETRYCANCEL
- MB_ABORTRETRYIGNORE
- MB_CANCELTRYCONTINUE

Default Button   You can choose which button will be automatically selected if the user presses the Enter key. The choices are MB_DEFBUTTON1 (the default), MB_DEFBUTTON2, MB_DEFBUTTON3, and MB_DEFBUTTON4. Buttons are numbered from the left, starting with 1.

Icons   Four icon choices are available. Sometimes more than one constant produces the same icon:

- Stop-sign: MB_ICONSTOP, MB_ICONHAND, or MB_ICONERROR
- Question mark (?): MB_ICONQUESTION
- Information symbol (i): MB_ICONINFORMATION, MB_ICONASTERISK
- Exclamation point (!): MB_ICONEXCLAMATION, MB_ICONWARNING

Return Value   If MessageBoxA fails, it returns zero. Otherwise, it returns an integer specifying which button the user clicked when closing the box. The choices are IDABORT, IDCANCEL, IDCONTINUE, IDIGNORE, IDNO, IDOK, IDRETRY, IDTRYAGAIN, and IDYES. All are defined in Smallwin.inc.

SmallWin.inc redefines **MessageBoxA** as **MessageBox**, which seems a more user-friendly name.

If you want your message box window to float above all other windows on your desktop, add the MB_SYSTEMMODAL option to the values you pass to the last argument (the uType parameter).

Demonstration Program

We will demonstrate a short program that demonstrates some capabilities of the MessageBoxA function. The first function call displays a warning message:

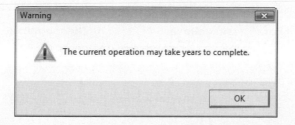

The second function call displays a question icon and Yes/No buttons. If the user selects the Yes button, the program could use the return value to select a course of action:

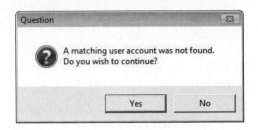

The third function call displays an information icon with three buttons:

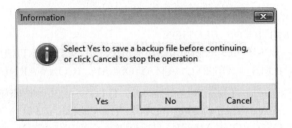

The fourth function call displays a stop icon with an OK button:

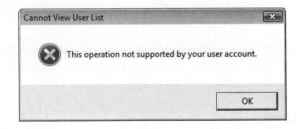

Program Listing

Following is a complete listing of a MessageBox demonstration program. The function named MessageBox is an alias for the MessageBoxA function, so we will use the simpler name:

```
TITLE Demonstrate MessageBoxA                (MessageBox.asm)

INCLUDE Irvine32.inc
.data
captionW      BYTE "Warning",0
warningMsg    BYTE "The current operation may take years "
              BYTE "to complete.",0
```

```
captionQ        BYTE "Question",0
questionMsg     BYTE "A matching user account was not found."
                BYTE 0dh,0ah,"Do you wish to continue?",0

captionC        BYTE "Information",0
infoMsg         BYTE "Select Yes to save a backup file "
                BYTE "before continuing,",0dh,0ah
                BYTE "or click Cancel to stop the operation",0

captionH        BYTE "Cannot View User List",0
haltMsg         BYTE "This operation not supported by your "
                BYTE "user account.",0

.code
main PROC

; Display Exclamation icon with OK button
    INVOKE MessageBox, NULL, ADDR warningMsg,
            ADDR captionW,
            MB_OK + MB_ICONEXCLAMATION

; Display Question icon with Yes/No buttons
    INVOKE MessageBox, NULL, ADDR questionMsg,
            ADDR captionQ, MB_YESNO + MB_ICONQUESTION

    ; interpret the button clicked by the user
    cmp     eax,IDYES               ; YES button clicked?

; Display Information icon with Yes/No/Cancel buttons
    INVOKE MessageBox, NULL, ADDR infoMsg,
        ADDR captionC, MB_YESNOCANCEL + MB_ICONINFORMATION \
            + MB_DEFBUTTON2

; Display stop icon with OK button
    INVOKE MessageBox, NULL, ADDR haltMsg,
            ADDR captionH,
            MB_OK + MB_ICONSTOP

    exit
main ENDP
END main
```

11.1.4   Console Input

By now, you have used the ReadString and ReadChar procedures from the book's link library quite a few times. They were designed to be simple and straightforward, so you could concentrate on other issues. Both procedures are wrappers around ReadConsole, a Win32 function. (A *wrapper* procedure hides some of the details of another procedure.)

Console Input Buffer   The Win32 console has an input buffer containing an array of input event records. Each input event, such as a keystroke, mouse movement, or mouse-button click, creates an input record in the console's input buffer. High-level input functions such as ReadConsole filter and process the input data, returning only a stream of characters.

ReadConsole Function

The **ReadConsole** function provides a convenient way to read text input and put it in a buffer.
Here is the prototype:

```
ReadConsole PROTO,
    hConsoleInput:HANDLE,                ; input handle
    lpBuffer:PTR BYTE,                   ; pointer to buffer
    nNumberOfCharsToRead:DWORD,          ; number of chars to read
    lpNumberOfCharsRead:PTR DWORD,       ; ptr to num bytes read
    lpReserved:DWORD                     ; (not used)
```

hConsoleInput is a valid console input handle returned by the **GetStdHandle** function. The
lpBuffer parameter is the offset of a character array. *nNumberOfCharsToRead* is a 32-bit integer
specifying the maximum number of characters to read. *lpNumberOfCharsRead* is a pointer to a
doubleword that permits the function to fill in, when it returns, a count of the number of characters placed in the buffer. The last parameter is not used, so pass the value zero.

When calling ReadConsole, include two extra bytes in your input buffer to hold the end-of-
line characters. If you want the input buffer to contain a null-terminated string, replace the byte
containing 0Dh with a null byte. This is exactly what is done by the ReadString procedure from
Irvine32.lib.

Note: Win32 API functions do not preserve the EAX, EBX, ECX, and EDX registers.

Example Program   To read characters entered by the user, call **GetStdHandle** to get the console's standard input handle and call **ReadConsole**, using the same input handle. The following
ReadConsole program demonstrates the technique. Notice that Win32 API calls are compatible
with the Irvine32 library, so we are able to call DumpRegs at the same time we call Win32
functions:

```
TITLE Read From the Console            (ReadConsole.asm)

INCLUDE Irvine32.inc
BufSize = 80

.data
buffer BYTE BufSize DUP(?),0,0
stdInHandle HANDLE ?
bytesRead   DWORD ?

.code
main PROC
    ; Get handle to standard input
    INVOKE GetStdHandle, STD_INPUT_HANDLE
    mov stdInHandle,eax

    ; Wait for user input
    INVOKE ReadConsole, stdInHandle, ADDR buffer,
      BufSize, ADDR bytesRead, 0

    ; Display the buffer
    mov   esi,OFFSET buffer
```

```
        mov    ecx,bytesRead
        mov    ebx,TYPE buffer
        call   DumpMem

        exit
main ENDP
END main
```

If the user enters "abcdefg", the program generates the following output. Nine bytes are inserted in the buffer: "abcdefg" plus 0Dh and 0Ah, the end-of-line characters inserted when the user pressed the Enter key. **bytesRead** equals 9:

```
Dump of offset 00404000
-------------------------------
61 62 63 64 65 66 67 0D 0A
```

Checking for Errors

If a Windows API function returns an error value (such as NULL), you can call the **GetLastError** API function to get more information about the error. It returns a 32-bit integer error code in EAX:

```
.data
messageId DWORD ?
.code
call GetLastError
mov  messageId,eax
```

MS-Windows has a large number of error codes, so you'll probably want to obtain a message string explaining the error. To do that, call the **FormatMessage** function:

```
FormatMessage PROTO,                ; format a message
    dwFlags:DWORD,                  ; formatting options
    lpSource:DWORD,                 ; location of message def
    dwMsgID:DWORD,                  ; message identifier
    dwLanguageID:DWORD,             ; language identifier
    lpBuffer:PTR BYTE,              ; ptr to buffer receiving string
    nSize:DWORD,                    ; buffer size
    va_list:DWORD                   ; pointer to list of arguments
```

Its parameters are somewhat complicated, so you will have to read the SDK documentation to get the full picture. Following is a brief listing of the values we find most useful. All are input parameters except *lpBuffer*, an output parameter:

- *dwFlags,* doubleword integer that holds formatting options, including how to interpret the lpSource parameter. It specifies how to handle line breaks, as well as the maximum width of a formatted output line. The recommended values are FORMAT_MESSAGE_ALLOCATE_BUFFER FORMAT_MESSAGE_FROM_SYSTEM
- *lpSource*, a pointer to the location of the message definition. Given the dwFlags setting we recommend, set lpSource to NULL (0).
- *dwMsgID*, the integer doubleword returned by calling GetLastError.

- *dwLanguageID*, a language identifier. If you set it to zero, the message will be language neutral, or it will correspond to the user's default locale.
- *lpBuffer (output parameter)*, a pointer to a buffer that receives the null-terminated message string. Because we use the FORMAT_MESSAGE_ALLOCATE_BUFFER option, the buffer is allocated automatically.
- *nSize*, which can be used to specify a buffer to hold the message string. You can set this parameter to 0 if you use the options for dwFlags suggested above.
- *va_list*, a pointer to an array of values that can be inserted in a formatted message. Because we are not formatting error messages, this parameter can be NULL (0).

Following is a sample call to FormatMessage:

```
.data
messageId DWORD ?
pErrorMsg DWORD ?                    ; points to error message
.code
call GetLastError
mov messageId,eax
INVOKE FormatMessage, FORMAT_MESSAGE_ALLOCATE_BUFFER + \
    FORMAT_MESSAGE_FROM_SYSTEM, NULL, messageID, 0,
    ADDR pErrorMsg, 0, NULL
```

After calling FormatMessage, call **LocalFree** to release the storage allocated by FormatMessage:

```
INVOKE LocalFree, pErrorMsg
```

WriteWindowsMsg   The Irvine32 library contains the following **WriteWindowsMsg** procedure, which encapsulates the message handling details:

```
;----------------------------------------------------
WriteWindowsMsg PROC USES eax edx
;
; Displays a string containing the most recent error
; generated by MS-Windows.
; Receives: nothing
; Returns: nothing
;----------------------------------------------------
.data
WriteWindowsMsg_1 BYTE "Error ",0
WriteWindowsMsg_2 BYTE ": ",0
pErrorMsg DWORD ?                    ; points to error message
messageId DWORD ?
.code
    call  GetLastError
    mov   messageId,eax

; Display the error number.
    mov   edx,OFFSET WriteWindowsMsg_1
    call  WriteString
    call  WriteDec
    mov   edx,OFFSET WriteWindowsMsg_2
```

```
      call  WriteString

; Get the corresponding message string.
      INVOKE FormatMessage, FORMAT_MESSAGE_ALLOCATE_BUFFER + \
         FORMAT_MESSAGE_FROM_SYSTEM, NULL, messageID, NULL,
         ADDR pErrorMsg, NULL, NULL

; Display the error message generated by MS-Windows.
      mov   edx,pErrorMsg
      call  WriteString

; Free the error message string.
      INVOKE LocalFree, pErrorMsg

      ret
WriteWindowsMsg ENDP
```

Single-Character Input

Single-character input in console mode is a little tricky. MS-Windows provides a device driver for the currently installed keyboard. When a key is pressed, an 8-bit *scan code* is transmitted to the computer's keyboard port. When the key is released, a second scan code is transmitted. MS-Windows uses a device driver program to translate the scan code into a 16-bit *virtual-key code*, a device-independent value defined by MS-Windows that identifies the key's purpose. A message is created by MS-Windows containing the scan code, the virtual-key code, and other related information. The message is placed in the MS-Windows message queue, eventually finding its way to the currently executing program thread (which we identify by the console input handle). If you would like to learn more about the keyboard input process, read the *About Keyboard Input* topic in the Platform SDK documentation. For a list of virtual key constants, see the *VirtualKeys.inc* file in the book's \Examples\ch11 directory.

Irvine32 Keyboard Procedures   The Irvine32 library has two related procedures:

- **ReadChar** waits for an ASCII character to be typed at the keyboard and returns the character in AL.
- The **ReadKey** procedure performs a no-wait keyboard check. If no key is waiting in the console input buffer, the Zero flag is set. If a key is found, the Zero flag is clear and AL contains either zero or an ASCII code. The upper halves of EAX and EDX are overwritten.

In ReadKey, if AL contains zero, the user may have pressed a special key (function key, cursor arrow, etc.). The AH register contains the keyboard scan code, which you can match to the list of keyboard keys on the facing page inside the front cover of this book. DX contains the virtual-key code, and EBX contains state information about the states of the keyboard control keys. See Table 11-3 for a list of control key values. After calling ReadKey, you can use the TEST instruction to check for various key values. The implementation of ReadKey is somewhat long, so we will not show it here. You can view it in the Irvine32.asm file in the book's \Examples\Lib32 folder.

ReadKey Test Program   The following program tests ReadKey by waiting for a keypress and then reporting whether or not the CapsLock key is down. As we mentioned in Chapter 5, you must include a delay factor when calling ReadKey to allow time for MS-Windows to

Table 11-3   Keyboard Control Key State Values.

Value	Meaning
CAPSLOCK_ON	The CAPS LOCK light is on.
ENHANCED_KEY	The key is enhanced.
LEFT_ALT_PRESSED	The left ALT key is pressed.
LEFT_CTRL_PRESSED	The left CTRL key is pressed.
NUMLOCK_ON	The NUM LOCK light is on.
RIGHT_ALT_PRESSED	The right ALT key is pressed.
RIGHT_CTRL_PRESSED	The right CTRL key is pressed.
SCROLLLOCK_ON	The SCROLL LOCK light is on.
SHIFT_PRESSED	The SHIFT key is pressed.

process its message loop:

```
TITLE Testing ReadKey                (TestReadkey.asm)
INCLUDE Irvine32.inc
INCLUDE Macros.inc
.code
main PROC
L1: mov   eax,10                ; delay for msg processing
    call  Delay
    call  ReadKey               ; wait for a keypress
    jz    L1

    test  ebx,CAPSLOCK_ON
    jz    L2
    mWrite <"CapsLock is ON",0dh,0ah>
    jmp   L3
L2: mWrite <"CapsLock is OFF",0dh,0ah>

L3: exit
main ENDP
END main
```

Getting the Keyboard State

You can test the state of individual keyboard keys to find out which are currently pressed. Call the **GetKeyState** API function.

```
GetKeyState PROTO, nVirtKey:DWORD
```

Pass it a virtual key value, such as the ones identified by Table 11-4. Your program must test the value returned in EAX, as indicated by the same table.

The following example program demonstrates GetKeyState by checking the states of the Num-Lock and Left Shift keys:

```
TITLE Keyboard Toggle Keys               (Keybd.asm)

INCLUDE Irvine32.inc
```

```
INCLUDE Macros.inc

; GetKeyState sets bit 0 in EAX if a toggle key is
; currently on (CapsLock, NumLock, ScrollLock).
; It sets the high bit of EAX if the specified key is
; currently down.

.code
main PROC

    INVOKE GetKeyState, VK_NUMLOCK
    test al,1
    .IF !Zero?
      mWrite <"The NumLock key is ON",0dh,0ah>
    .ENDIF

    INVOKE GetKeyState, VK_LSHIFT
    test eax,80000000h
    .IF !Zero?
      mWrite <"The Left Shift key is currently DOWN",0dh,0ah>
    .ENDIF

    exit
main ENDP
END main
```

Table 11-4   Testing Keys with GetKeyState.

Key	Virtual Key Symbol	Bit to Test in EAX
NumLock	VK_NUMLOCK	0
Scroll Lock	VK_SCROLL	0
Left Shift	VK_LSHIFT	15
Right Shift	VK_tRSHIFT	15
Left Ctrl	VK_LCONTROL	15
Right Ctrl	VK_RCONTROL	15
Left Menu	VK_LMENU	15
Right Menu	VK_RMENU	15

11.1.5   Console Output

In earlier chapters we tried to make console output as simple as possible. As far back as Chapter 5, the **WriteString** procedure in the Irvine32 link library required only a single argument, the offset of a string in EDX. It turns out that WriteString is actually a wrapper around a more detailed call to a Win32 function named **WriteConsole**.

In this chapter, however, you learn how to make direct calls to Win32 functions such as WriteConsole and WriteConsoleOutputCharacter. Direct calls require you to learn more details, but they also offer you more flexibility than the Irvine32 library procedures.

Data Structures

Several of the Win32 console functions use predefined data structures, including COORD and SMALL_RECT. The COORD structure holds the coordinates of a character cell in the console screen buffer. The origin of the coordinate system (0,0) is at the top left cell:

```
COORD STRUCT
      X WORD ?
      Y WORD ?
COORD ENDS
```

The SMALL_RECT structure holds the upper left and lower right corners of a rectangle. It specifies screen buffer character cells in the console window:

```
SMALL_RECT STRUCT
    Left    WORD ?
    Top     WORD ?
    Right   WORD ?
    Bottom  WORD ?
SMALL_RECT ENDS
```

WriteConsole Function

The **WriteConsole** function writes a string to the console window at the current cursor position and leaves the cursor just past the last character written. It acts upon standard ASCII control characters such as *tab*, *carriage return*, and *line feed*. The string does not have to be null-terminated. Here is the function prototype:

```
WriteConsole PROTO,
     hConsoleOutput:HANDLE,
     lpBuffer:PTR BYTE,
     nNumberOfCharsToWrite:DWORD,
     lpNumberOfCharsWritten:PTR DWORD,
     lpReserved:DWORD
```

hConsoleOutput is the console output stream handle; *lpBuffer* is a pointer to the array of characters you want to write; *nNumberOfCharsToWrite* holds the array length; *lpNumberOfCharsWritten* points to an integer assigned the number of bytes actually written when the function returns. The last parameter is not used, so set it to zero.

Example Program: Console1

The following program, *Console1.asm*, demonstrates the **GetStdHandle, ExitProcess,** and **WriteConsole** functions by writing a string to the console window:

```
TITLE Win32 Console Example #1                    (Console1.asm)

; This program calls the following Win32 Console functions:
; GetStdHandle, ExitProcess, WriteConsole

INCLUDE Irvine32.inc

.data
endl EQU <0dh,0ah>              ; end of line sequence
message LABEL BYTE
    BYTE "This program is a simple demonstration of"
```

```
        BYTE "console mode output, using the GetStdHandle"
        BYTE "and WriteConsole functions.",endl
messageSize DWORD ($ - message)

consoleHandle HANDLE 0           ; handle to standard output device
bytesWritten   DWORD ?           ; number of bytes written

.code
main PROC
  ; Get the console output handle:
      INVOKE GetStdHandle, STD_OUTPUT_HANDLE
      mov consoleHandle,eax

  ; Write a string to the console:
      INVOKE WriteConsole,
        consoleHandle,             ; console output handle
        ADDR message,              ; string pointer
        messageSize,               ; string length
        ADDR bytesWritten,         ; returns num bytes written
        0                          ; not used

      INVOKE ExitProcess,0
main ENDP
END main
```

The program produces the following output:

```
This program is a simple demonstration of console mode output, using
the GetStdHandle and WriteConsole functions.
```

WriteConsoleOutputCharacter Function

The **WriteConsoleOutputCharacter** function copies an array of characters to consecutive cells of the console screen buffer, beginning at a specified location. Here is the prototype:

```
WriteConsoleOutputCharacter PROTO,
      hConsoleOutput:HANDLE,             ; console output handle
      lpCharacter:PTR BYTE,              ; pointer to buffer
      nLength:DWORD,                     ; size of buffer
      dwWriteCoord:COORD,                ; first cell coordinates
      lpNumberOfCharsWritten:PTR DWORD   ; output count
```

If the text reaches the end of a line, it wraps around. The attribute values in the screen buffer are not changed. If the function cannot write the characters, it returns zero. ASCII control codes such as *tab*, *carriage return*, and *line feed* are ignored.

11.1.6   Reading and Writing Files

CreateFile Function

The **CreateFile** function either creates a new file or opens an existing file. If successful, it returns a handle to the open file; otherwise, it returns a special constant named INVALID_HANDLE_VALUE.

Here is the prototype:

```
CreateFile PROTO,                          ; create new file
    lpFilename:PTR BYTE,                   ; ptr to filename
    dwDesiredAccess:DWORD,                 ; access mode
    dwShareMode:DWORD,                     ; share mode
    lpSecurityAttributes:DWORD,            ; ptr security attrib
    dwCreationDisposition:DWORD,           ; file creation options
    dwFlagsAndAttributes:DWORD,            ; file attributes
    hTemplateFile:DWORD                    ; handle to template file
```

The parameters are described in Table 11-5. The return value is zero if the function fails.

Table 11-5   CreateFile Parameters.

Parameter	Description
lpFileName	Points to a null-terminated string containing either a partial or fully qualified filename (*drive*:*path**filename*).
dwDesiredAccess	Specifies how the file will be accessed (reading or writing).
dwShareMode	Controls the ability for multiple programs to access the file while it is open.
lpSecurityAttributes	Points to a security structure controlling security rights.
dwCreationDisposition	Specifies what action to take when a file exists or does not exist.
dwFlagsAndAttributes	Holds bit flags specifying file attributes such as archive, encrypted, hidden, normal, system, and temporary.
hTemplateFile	Contains an optional handle to a template file that supplies file attributes and extended attributes for the file being created; when not using this parameter, set it to zero.

dwDesiredAccess   The *dwDesiredAccess* parameter lets you specify read access, write access, read/write access, or device query access to the file. Choose from the values listed in Table 11-6 or from a large set of specific flag values not listed here. (Search for *CreateFile* in the Platform SDK documentation).

Table 11-6   dwDesiredAccess Parameter Options.

Value	Meaning
0	Specifies device query access to the object. An application can query device attributes without accessing the device, or it can check for the existence of a file.
GENERIC_READ	Specifies read access to the object. Data can be read from the file, and the file pointer can be moved. Combine with GENERIC_WRITE for read/write access.
GENERIC_WRITE	Specifies write access to the object. Data can be written to the file, and the file pointer can be moved. Combine with GENERIC_READ for read/write access.

CreationDisposition   The *dwCreationDisposition* parameter specifies which action to take on files that exist and which action to take when files do not exist. Select one of the values in Table 11-7.

Table 11-7   dwCreationDisposition Parameter Options.

Value	Meaning
CREATE_NEW	Creates a new file. Requires setting the dwDesiredAccess parameter to GENERIC_WRITE. The function fails if the file already exists.
CREATE_ALWAYS	Creates a new file. If the file exists, the function overwrites the file, clears the existing attributes, and combines the file attributes and flags specified by the *attributes* parameter with the predefined constant FILE_ATTRIBUTE_ARCHIVE. Requires setting the dwDesiredAccess parameter to GENERIC_WRITE.
OPEN_EXISTING	Opens the file. The function fails if the file does not exist. May be used for reading from and/or writing to the file.
OPEN_ALWAYS	Opens the file if it exists. If the file does not exist, the function creates the file as if *CreationDisposition* were CREATE_NEW.
TRUNCATE_EXISTING	Opens the file. Once opened, the file is truncated to size zero. Requires setting the dwDesiredAccess parameter to GENERIC_WRITE. This function fails if the file does not exist.

Table 11-8 lists the more commonly used values permitted in the *dwFlagsAndAttributes* parameter. (For a complete list, search for *CreateFile* in the Platform SDK documentation.) Any combination of the attributes is acceptable, except that all other file attributes override FILE_ATTRIBUTE_NORMAL. The values map to powers of 2, so you can use the assembly time OR operator or + operator to combine them into a single argument:

```
FILE_ATTRIBUTE_HIDDEN OR FILE_ATTRIBUTE_READONLY
FILE_ATTRIBUTE_HIDDEN + FILE_ATTRIBUTE_READONLY
```

Table 11-8   Selected FlagsAndAttributes Values.

Attribute	Meaning
FILE_ATTRIBUTE_ARCHIVE	The file should be archived. Applications use this attribute to mark files for backup or removal.
FILE_ATTRIBUTE_HIDDEN	The file is hidden. It is not to be included in an ordinary directory listing.
FILE_ATTRIBUTE_NORMAL	The file has no other attributes set. This attribute is valid only if used alone.
FILE_ATTRIBUTE_READONLY	The file is read only. Applications can read the file but cannot write to it or delete it.
FILE_ATTRIBUTE_TEMPORARY	The file is being used for temporary storage.

Examples   The following examples are for illustrative purposes only, to show how you might create and open files. See the online Microsoft MSDN documentation for **CreateFile** to learn about the many available options:

• Open an existing file for reading (input):

```
INVOKE CreateFile,
    ADDR filename,              ; ptr to filename
    GENERIC_READ,              ; read from the file
```

```
    DO_NOT_SHARE,                 ; share mode
    NULL,                         ; ptr to security attributes
    OPEN_EXISTING,                ; open an existing file
    FILE_ATTRIBUTE_NORMAL,        ; normal file attribute
    0                             ; not used
```

• Open an existing file for writing (output). Once the file is open, we could write over existing data or append new data to the file by moving the file pointer to the end (see SetFilePointer, Section 11.1.6):

```
INVOKE CreateFile,
    ADDR filename,
    GENERIC_WRITE,                ; write to the file
    DO_NOT_SHARE,
    NULL,
    OPEN_EXISTING,                ; file must exist
    FILE_ATTRIBUTE_NORMAL,
    0
```

• Create a new file with normal attributes, erasing any existing file by the same name:

```
INVOKE CreateFile,
    ADDR filename,
    GENERIC_WRITE,                ; write to the file
    DO_NOT_SHARE,
    NULL,
    CREATE_ALWAYS,                ; overwrite existing file
    FILE_ATTRIBUTE_NORMAL,
    0
```

• Create a new file if the file does not already exist; otherwise, open the existing file for output:

```
INVOKE CreateFile,
    ADDR filename,
    GENERIC_WRITE,                ; write to the file
    DO_NOT_SHARE,
    NULL,
    CREATE_NEW,                   ; don't erase existing file
    FILE_ATTRIBUTE_NORMAL,
    0
```

(The constants named DO_NOT_SHARE and NULL are defined in the *SmallWin.inc* include file, which is automatically included by *Irvine32.inc*.)

CloseHandle Function

The **CloseHandle** function closes an open object handle. Its prototype is

```
CloseHandle PROTO,
    hObject:HANDLE                ; handle to object
```

You can use CloseHandle to close a currently open file handle. The return value is zero if the function fails.

ReadFile Function

The **ReadFile** function reads text from an input file. Here is the prototype:

```
ReadFile PROTO,
    hFile:HANDLE,                       ; input handle
    lpBuffer:PTR BYTE,                  ; ptr to buffer
    nNumberOfBytesToRead:DWORD,         ; num bytes to read
    lpNumberOfBytesRead:PTR DWORD,      ; bytes actually read
    lpOverlapped:PTR DWORD              ; ptr to asynch info
```

The *hFile* parameter is an open file handle returned by **CreateFile**; *lpBuffer* points to a buffer that receives data read from the file; *nNumberOfBytesToRead* specifies the maximum number of bytes to read from the file; *lpNumberOfBytesRead* points to an integer indicating the number of bytes actually read when the function returns; *lpOverlapped* should be set to NULL (0) for synchronous reading (which we use). The return value is zero if the function fails.

If called more than once on the same open file handle, ReadFile remembers where it last finished reading and reads from that point on. In other words, it maintains an internal pointer to the current position in the file. ReadFile can also run in asynchronous mode, meaning that the calling program does not wait for the read operation to finish.

WriteFile Function

The **WriteFile** function writes data to a file, using an output handle. The handle can be the screen buffer handle, or it can be one assigned to a text file. The function starts writing data to the file at the position indicated by the file's internal position pointer. After the write operation has been completed, the file's position pointer is adjusted by the number of bytes actually written. Here is the function prototype:

```
WriteFile PROTO,
    hFile:HANDLE,                       ; output handle
    lpBuffer:PTR BYTE,                  ; pointer to buffer
    nNumberOfBytesToWrite:DWORD,        ; size of buffer
    lpNumberOfBytesWritten:PTR DWORD,   ; num bytes written
    lpOverlapped:PTR DWORD              ; ptr to asynch info
```

hFile is a handle to a previously opened file; *lpBuffer* points to a buffer holding the data written to the file; *nNumberOfBytesToWrite* specifies how many bytes to write to the file; *lpNumberOfBytesWritten* points to an integer that specifies the number of bytes actually written after the function executes; *lpOverlapped* should be set to NULL for synchronous operation. The return value is zero if the function fails.

SetFilePointer Function

The **SetFilePointer** function moves the position pointer of an open file. This function can be used to append data to a file or to perform random-access record processing:

```
SetFilePointer PROTO,
    hFile:HANDLE,                       ; file handle
    lDistanceToMove:SDWORD,             ; bytes to move pointer
    lpDistanceToMoveHigh:PTR SDWORD,    ; ptr bytes to move, high
    dwMoveMethod:DWORD                  ; starting point
```

The return value is zero if the function fails. *dwMoveMethod* specifies the starting point for moving the file pointer, which is selected from three predefined symbols: FILE_BEGIN, FILE_CURRENT, and FILE_END. The distance itself is a 64-bit signed integer value, divided into two parts:

• *lpDistanceToMove*: the lower 32 bits
• *pDistanceToMoveHigh:* a pointer to a variable containing the upper 32 bits

If *lpDistanceToMoveHigh* is null, only the value in *lpDistanceToMove* is used to move the file pointer. For example, the following code prepares to append to the end of a file:

```
INVOKE SetFilePointer,
    fileHandle,                     ; file handle
    0,                              ; distance low
    0,                              ; distance high
    FILE_END                        ; move method
```

See the *AppendFile.asm* program.

11.1.7 File I/O in the Irvine32 Library

The Irvine32 library contains a few simplified procedures for file input/output, which we documented in Chapter 5. The procedures are wrappers around the Win32 API functions we have described in the current chapter. The following source code lists CreateOutputFile, OpenFile, WriteToFile, ReadFromFile, and CloseFile:

```
;-------------------------------------------------------
CreateOutputFile PROC
;
; Creates a new file and opens it in output mode.
; Receives: EDX points to the filename.
; Returns: If the file was created successfully, EAX
;   contains a valid file handle. Otherwise, EAX
;   equals INVALID_HANDLE_VALUE.
;-------------------------------------------------------
    INVOKE CreateFile,
      edx, GENERIC_WRITE, DO_NOT_SHARE, NULL,
      CREATE_ALWAYS, FILE_ATTRIBUTE_NORMAL, 0
    ret
CreateOutputFile ENDP

;-------------------------------------------------------
OpenFile PROC
;
; Opens a new text file and opens for input.
; Receives: EDX points to the filename.
; Returns: If the file was opened successfully, EAX
; contains a valid file handle. Otherwise, EAX equals
; INVALID_HANDLE_VALUE.
;-------------------------------------------------------
    INVOKE CreateFile,
      edx, GENERIC_READ, DO_NOT_SHARE, NULL,
```

```
                   OPEN_EXISTING, FILE_ATTRIBUTE_NORMAL, 0
     ret
OpenFile ENDP

;------------------------------------------------------------
WriteToFile PROC
;
; Writes a buffer to an output file.
; Receives: EAX = file handle, EDX = buffer offset,
;    ECX = number of bytes to write
; Returns: EAX = number of bytes written to the file.
; If the value returned in EAX is less than the
; argument passed in ECX, an error likely occurred.
;------------------------------------------------------------
.data
WriteToFile_1 DWORD ?              ; number of bytes written
.code
    INVOKE WriteFile,              ; write buffer to file
        eax,                       ; file handle
        edx,                       ; buffer pointer
        ecx,                       ; number of bytes to write
        ADDR WriteToFile_1,        ; number of bytes written
        0                          ; overlapped execution flag
    mov eax,WriteToFile_1          ; return value
    ret
WriteToFile ENDP

;------------------------------------------------------------
ReadFromFile PROC
;
; Reads an input file into a buffer.
; Receives: EAX = file handle, EDX = buffer offset,
;    ECX = number of bytes to read
; Returns: If CF = 0, EAX = number of bytes read; if
;    CF = 1, EAX contains the system error code returned
;    by the GetLastError Win32 API function.
;------------------------------------------------------------
.data
ReadFromFile_1 DWORD ?             ; number of bytes read
.code
    INVOKE ReadFile,
        eax,                       ; file handle
        edx,                       ; buffer pointer
        ecx,                       ; max bytes to read
        ADDR ReadFromFile_1,       ; number of bytes read
        0                          ; overlapped execution flag
    mov eax,ReadFromFile_1
    ret
ReadFromFile ENDP
;------------------------------------------------------------
CloseFile PROC
```

```
;
; Closes a file using its handle as an identifier.
; Receives: EAX = file handle
; Returns: EAX = nonzero if the file is successfully
;   closed.
;--------------------------------------------------------

    INVOKE CloseHandle, eax
    ret
CloseFile ENDP
```

11.1.8   Testing the File I/O Procedures

CreateFile Program Example

The following program creates a file in output mode, asks the user to enter some text, writes the text to the output file, reports the number of bytes written, and closes the file. It checks for errors after attempting to create the file:

```
TITLE Creating a File               (CreateFile.asm)

INCLUDE Irvine32.inc

BUFFER_SIZE = 501
.data
buffer BYTE BUFFER_SIZE DUP(?)
filename     BYTE "output.txt",0
fileHandle   HANDLE ?
stringLength DWORD ?
bytesWritten DWORD ?
str1 BYTE "Cannot create file",0dh,0ah,0
str2 BYTE "Bytes written to file [output.txt]:",0
str3 BYTE "Enter up to 500 characters and press"
     BYTE "[Enter]: ",0dh,0ah,0

.code
main PROC
; Create a new text file.
    mov    edx,OFFSET filename
    call   CreateOutputFile
    mov    fileHandle,eax

; Check for errors.
    cmp    eax, INVALID_HANDLE_VALUE   ; error found?
    jne    file_ok                     ; no: skip
    mov    edx,OFFSET str1             ; display error
    call   WriteString
    jmp    quit
file_ok:

; Ask the user to input a string.
    mov    edx,OFFSET str3             ; "Enter up to ...."
    call   WriteString
    mov    ecx,BUFFER_SIZE             ; Input a string
    mov    edx,OFFSET buffer
```

```
        call   ReadString
        mov    stringLength,cax              ; counts chars entered
; Write the buffer to the output file.
        mov    eax,fileHandle
        mov    edx,OFFSET buffer
        mov    ecx,stringLength
        call   WriteToFile
        mov    bytesWritten,eax              ; save return value
        call   CloseFile
; Display the return value.
        mov    edx,OFFSET str2               ; "Bytes written"
        call   WriteString
        mov    eax,bytesWritten
        call   WriteDec
        call   Crlf
quit:
        exit
main ENDP
END main
```

ReadFile Program Example

The following program opens a file for input, reads its contents into a buffer, and displays the buffer. All procedures are called from the Irvine32 library:

```
TITLE Reading a File                        (ReadFile.asm)

; Opens, reads, and displays a text file using
; procedures from Irvine32.lib.

INCLUDE Irvine32.inc
INCLUDE macros.inc
BUFFER_SIZE = 5000

.data
buffer BYTE BUFFER_SIZE DUP(?)
filename    BYTE 80 DUP(0)
fileHandle  HANDLE ?

.code
main PROC

; Let user input a filename.
        mWrite "Enter an input filename: "
        mov    edx,OFFSET filename
        mov    ecx,SIZEOF filename
        call   ReadString

; Open the file for input.
        mov    edx,OFFSET filename
        call   OpenInputFile
        mov    fileHandle,eax
; Check for errors.
```

```
        cmp    eax,INVALID_HANDLE_VALUE    ; error opening file?
        jne    file_ok                      ; no: skip
        mWrite <"Cannot open file",0dh,0ah>
        jmp    quit                         ; and quit
file_ok:

; Read the file into a buffer.
        mov    edx,OFFSET buffer
        mov    ecx,BUFFER_SIZE
        call   ReadFromFile
        jnc    check_buffer_size            ; error reading?
        mWrite "Error reading file. "       ; yes: show error message
        call   WriteWindowsMsg
        jmp    close_file

check_buffer_size:
        cmp    eax,BUFFER_SIZE              ; buffer large enough?
        jb     buf_size_ok                  ; yes
        mWrite <"Error: Buffer too small for the file",0dh,0ah>
        jmp    quit                         ; and quit

buf_size_ok:
        mov    buffer[eax],0                ; insert null terminator
        mWrite "File size: "
        call   WriteDec                     ; display file size
        call   Crlf

; Display the buffer.
        mWrite <"Buffer:",0dh,0ah,0dh,0ah>
        mov    edx,OFFSET buffer            ; display the buffer
        call   WriteString
        call   Crlf

close_file:
        mov    eax,fileHandle
        call   CloseFile

quit:
        exit
main ENDP
END main
```

The program reports an error if the file cannot be opened:

```
Enter an input filename: crazy.txt
Cannot open file
```

It reports an error if it cannot read from the file. Suppose, for example, a bug in the program used the wrong file handle when reading the file:

```
Enter an input filename: infile.txt
Error reading file. Error 6: The handle is invalid.
```

The buffer might be too small to hold the file:

```
Enter an input filename: infile.txt
Error: Buffer too small for the file
```

11.1.9   Console Window Manipulation

The Win32 API provides considerable control over the console window and its buffer. Figure 11–1 shows that the screen buffer can be larger than the number of lines currently displayed in the console window. The console window acts as a "viewport," showing part of the buffer.

FIGURE 11–1   Screen Buffer and Console Window.

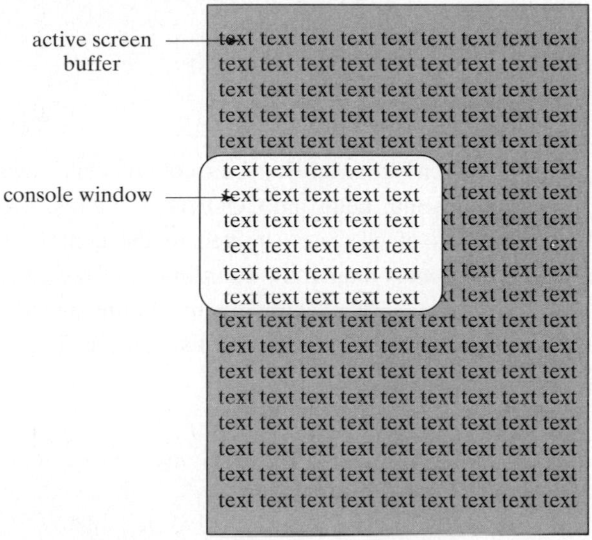

Several functions affect the console window and its position relative to the screen buffer:

- **SetConsoleWindowInfo** sets the size and position of the console window relative to the screen buffer.
- **GetConsoleScreenBufferInfo** returns (among other things) the rectangle coordinates of the console window relative to the screen buffer.
- **SetConsoleCursorPosition** sets the cursor position to any location within the screen buffer; if that area is not visible, the console window is shifted to make the cursor visible.
- **ScrollConsoleScreenBuffer** moves some or all of the text within the screen buffer, which can affect the displayed text in the console window.

SetConsoleTitle

The **SetConsoleTitle** function lets you change the console window's title. An example is

```
.data
titleStr BYTE "Console title",0
.code
INVOKE SetConsoleTitle, ADDR titleStr
```

GetConsoleScreenBufferInfo

The **GetConsoleScreenBufferInfo** function returns information about the current state of the console window. It has two parameters: a handle to the console screen, and a pointer to a structure that is filled in by the function:

```
GetConsoleScreenBufferInfo PROTO,
    hConsoleOutput:HANDLE,
    lpConsoleScreenBufferInfo:PTR CONSOLE_SCREEN_BUFFER_INFO
```

The following is the CONSOLE_SCREEN_BUFFER_INFO structure:

```
CONSOLE_SCREEN_BUFFER_INFO STRUCT
    dwSize                  COORD <>
    dwCursorPosition        COORD <>
    wAttributes             WORD ?
    srWindow                SMALL_RECT <>
    dwMaximumWindowSize     COORD <>
CONSOLE_SCREEN_BUFFER_INFO ENDS
```

dwSize returns the size of the screen buffer, in character columns and rows. *dwCursorPosition* returns the location of the cursor. Both fields are COORD structures. *wAttributes* returns the foreground and background colors of characters written to the console by functions such as **WriteConsole** and **WriteFile**. *srWindow* returns the coordinates of the console window relative to the screen buffer. *drMaximumWindowSize* returns the maximum size of the console window, based on the current screen buffer size, font, and video display size. The following is a sample call to the function:

```
.data
consoleInfo CONSOLE_SCREEN_BUFFER_INFO <>
outHandle HANDLE ?
.code
INVOKE GetConsoleScreenBufferInfo, outHandle,
    ADDR consoleInfo
```

Figure 11–2 shows a sample of the structure data shown by the Microsoft Visual Studio debugger.

SetConsoleWindowInfo Function

The **SetConsoleWindowInfo** function lets you set the size and position of the console window relative to its screen buffer. Following is its function prototype:

```
SetConsoleWindowInfo PROTO,
    hConsoleOutput:HANDLE,              ; screen buffer handle
    bAbsolute:DWORD,                    ; coordinate type
    lpConsoleWindow:PTR SMALL_RECT      ; ptr to window rectangle
```

bAbsolute indicates how the coordinates in the structure pointed to by *lpConsoleWindow* are to be used. If *bAbsolute* is true, the coordinates specify the new upper left and lower right corners of the console window. If *bAbsolute* is false, the coordinates will be added to the current window coordinates.

Figure 11–2   CONSOLE_SCREEN_BUFFER_INFO Structure.

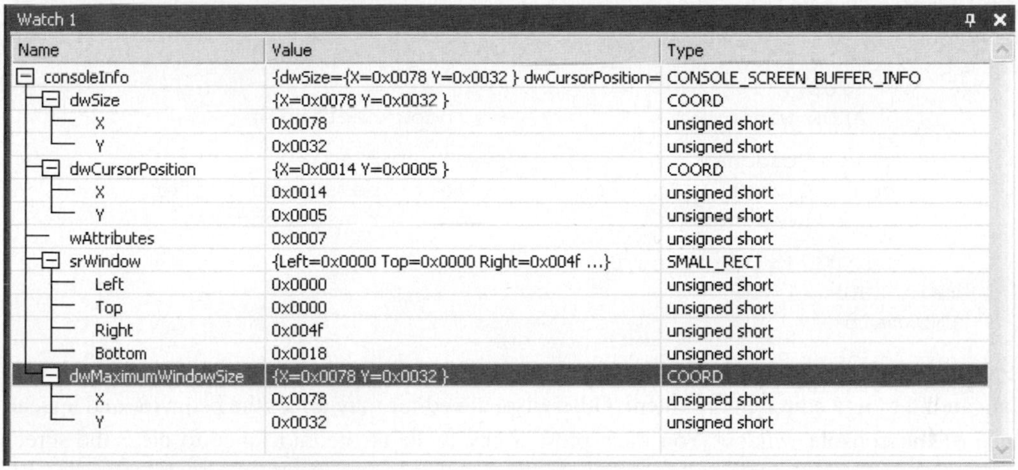

Watch 1		⊼ ✕
Name	**Value**	**Type**
⊟ consoleInfo	{dwSize={X=0x0078 Y=0x0032 } dwCursorPosition=	CONSOLE_SCREEN_BUFFER_INFO
├─⊟ dwSize	{X=0x0078 Y=0x0032 }	COORD
│ ├─ X	0x0078	unsigned short
│ └─ Y	0x0032	unsigned short
├─⊟ dwCursorPosition	{X=0x0014 Y=0x0005 }	COORD
│ ├─ X	0x0014	unsigned short
│ └─ Y	0x0005	unsigned short
├─ wAttributes	0x0007	unsigned short
├─⊟ srWindow	{Left=0x0000 Top=0x0000 Right=0x004f ...}	SMALL_RECT
│ ├─ Left	0x0000	unsigned short
│ ├─ Top	0x0000	unsigned short
│ ├─ Right	0x004f	unsigned short
│ └─ Bottom	0x0018	unsigned short
├─⊟ dwMaximumWindowSize	{X=0x0078 Y=0x0032 }	COORD
│ ├─ X	0x0078	unsigned short
│ └─ Y	0x0032	unsigned short

The following *Scroll.asm* program writes 50 lines of text to the screen buffer. It then resizes and repositions the console window, effectively scrolling the text backward. It uses the **SetConsoleWindowInfo** function:

```
TITLE Scrolling the Console Window                   (Scroll.asm)

INCLUDE Irvine32.inc

.data
message BYTE ":  This line of text was written "
        BYTE "to the screen buffer",0dh,0ah
messageSize DWORD ($-message)

outHandle       HANDLE 0          ; standard output handle
bytesWritten    DWORD ?           ; number of bytes written
lineNum         DWORD 0
windowRect      SMALL_RECT <0,0,60,11> ; left,top,right,bottom

.code
main PROC
    INVOKE GetStdHandle, STD_OUTPUT_HANDLE
    mov outHandle,eax

.REPEAT
    mov   eax,lineNum
    call  WriteDec            ; display each line number
    INVOKE WriteConsole,
      outHandle,              ; console output handle
      ADDR message,           ; string pointer
      messageSize,            ; string length
      ADDR bytesWritten,      ; returns num bytes written
      0                       ; not used
    inc   lineNum             ; next line number
.UNTIL lineNum > 50
```

```
        ; Resize and reposition the console window relative to the
        ; screen buffer.
            INVOKE SetConsoleWindowInfo,
              outHandle,
              TRUE,
              ADDR windowRect              ; window rectangle

            call  Readchar                 ; wait for a key
            call  Clrscr                   ; clear the screen buffer
            call  Readchar                 ; wait for a second key

            INVOKE ExitProcess,0
    main ENDP
    END main
```

It is best to run this program directly from MS-Windows Explorer or a command prompt rather than an integrated editor environment. Otherwise, the editor may affect the behavior and appearance of the console window. You must press a key twice at the end: once to clear the screen buffer and a second time to end the program.

SetConsoleScreenBufferSize Function

The **SetConsoleScreenBufferSize** function lets you set the screen buffer size to X columns by Y rows. Here is the prototype:

```
    SetConsoleScreenBufferSize PROTO,
        hConsoleOutput:HANDLE,         ; handle to screen buffer
        dwSize:COORD                   ; new screen buffer size
```

11.1.10   Controlling the Cursor

The Win32 API provides functions to set the cursor size, visibility, and screen location. An important data structure related to these functions is CONSOLE_CURSOR_INFO, which contains information about the console's cursor size and visibility:

```
    CONSOLE_CURSOR_INFO STRUCT
        dwSize    DWORD ?
        bVisible  DWORD ?
    CONSOLE_CURSOR_INFO ENDS
```

dwSize is the percentage (1 to 100) of the character cell filled by the cursor. *bVisible* equals TRUE (1) if the cursor is visible.

GetConsoleCursorInfo Function

The **GetConsoleCursorInfo** function returns the size and visibility of the console cursor. Pass it a pointer to a CONSOLE_CURSOR_INFO structure:

```
    GetConsoleCursorInfo PROTO,
        hConsoleOutput:HANDLE,
        lpConsoleCursorInfo:PTR CONSOLE_CURSOR_INFO
```

By default, the cursor size is 25, indicating that the character cell is 25% filled by the cursor.

SetConsoleCursorInfo Function

The **SetConsoleCursorInfo** function sets the size and visibility of the cursor. Pass it a pointer to a CONSOLE_CURSOR_INFO structure:

```
SetConsoleCursorInfo PROTO,
    hConsoleOutput:HANDLE,
    lpConsoleCursorInfo:PTR CONSOLE_CURSOR_INFO
```

SetConsoleCursorPosition

The **SetConsoleCursorPostion** function sets the X, Y position of the cursor. Pass it a COORD structure and the console output handle:

```
SetConsoleCursorPosition PROTO,
    hConsoleOutput:DWORD,              ; input mode handle
    dwCursorPosition:COORD             ; screen X,Y coordinates
```

11.1.11   Controlling the Text Color

There are two ways to control the color of text in a console window. You can change the current text color by calling **SetConsoleTextAttribute**, which affects all subsequent text output to the console. Alternatively, you can set the attributes of specific cells by calling **WriteConsoleOutputAttribute**. The **GetConsoleScreenBufferInfo** function (Section 11.1.9) returns the current screen colors, along with other console information.

SetConsoleTextAttribute Function

The **SetConsoleTextAttribute** function lets you set the foreground and background colors for all subsequent text output to the console window. Here is its prototype:

```
SetConsoleTextAttribute PROTO,
    hConsoleOutput:HANDLE,             ; console output handle
    wAttributes:WORD                   ; color attribute
```

The color value is stored in the low-order byte of the *wAttributes* parameter. Colors are created using the same method as for the VIDEO BIOS, which is shown in Section 15.3.2.

WriteConsoleOutputAttribute Function

The **WriteConsoleOutputAttribute** function copies an array of attribute values to consecutive cells of the console screen buffer, beginning at a specified location. Here is the prototype:

```
WriteConsoleOutputAttribute PROTO,
    hConsoleOutput:DWORD,              ; output handle
    lpAttribute:PTR WORD,              ; write attributes
    nLength:DWORD,                     ; number of cells
    dwWriteCoord:COORD,                ; first cell coordinates
    lpNumberOfAttrsWritten:PTR DWORD   ; output count
```

lpAttribute points to an array of attributes in which the low-order byte of each contains the color; *nLength* is the length of the array; *dwWriteCoord* is the starting screen cell to receive the attributes; and *lpNuumberOfAttrsWritten* points to a variable that will hold the number of cells written.

Example: Writing Text Colors

To demonstrate the use of colors and attributes, the *WriteColors.asm* program creates an array of characters and an array of attributes, one for each character. It calls **WriteConsoleOutputAttribute** to copy the attributes to the screen buffer and **WriteConsoleOutputCharacter** to copy the characters to the same screen buffer cells:

```
TITLE Writing Text Colors                    (WriteColors.asm)
INCLUDE Irvine32.inc
.data
outHandle    HANDLE ?
cellsWritten DWORD ?
xyPos COORD <10,2>

; Array of character codes:
buffer BYTE 1,2,3,4,5,6,7,8,9,10,11,12,13,14,15
       BYTE 16,17,18,19,20
BufSize DWORD ($-buffer)

; Array of attributes:
attributes WORD 0Fh,0Eh,0Dh,0Ch,0Bh,0Ah,9,8,7,6
           WORD 5,4,3,2,1,0F0h,0E0h,0D0h,0C0h,0B0h
.code
main PROC
; Get the Console standard output handle:
    INVOKE GetStdHandle,STD_OUTPUT_HANDLE
    mov outHandle,eax

; Set the colors of adjacent cells:
    INVOKE WriteConsoleOutputAttribute,
       outHandle, ADDR attributes,
       BufSize, xyPos, ADDR cellsWritten

; Write character codes 1 through 20:
    INVOKE WriteConsoleOutputCharacter,
       outHandle, ADDR buffer, BufSize,
       xyPos, ADDR cellsWritten

    INVOKE ExitProcess,0          ; end program
main ENDP
END main
```

Figure 11–3 shows a snapshot of the program's output, in which character codes 1 through 20 are displayed as graphic characters. Each character is in a different color, although the printed page appears in grayscale.

FIGURE 11–3   Output from the WriteColors Program.

11.1.12   Time and Date Functions

The Win32 API provides a fairly large selection of time and date functions. Most commonly, you may want to use them to get and set the current date and time. We can only discuss a small subset of the functions here, but you can look up the Platform SDK documentation for the Win32 functions listed in Table 11-9.

Table 11-9   Win32 DateTime Functions.

Function	Description
CompareFileTime	Compares two 64-bit file times.
DosDateTimeToFileTime	Converts MS-DOS date and time values to a 64-bit file time.
FileTimeToDosDateTime	Converts a 64-bit file time to MS-DOS date and time values.
FileTimeToLocalFileTime	Converts a UTC (*universal coordinated time*) file time to a local file time.
FileTimeToSystemTime	Converts a 64-bit file time to system time format.
GetFileTime	Retrieves the date and time that a file was created, last accessed, and last modified.
GetLocalTime	Retrieves the current local date and time.
GetSystemTime	Retrieves the current system date and time in UTC format.
GetSystemTimeAdjustment	Determines whether the system is applying periodic time adjustments to its time-of-day clock.
GetSystemTimeAsFileTime	Retrieves the current system date and time in UTC format.
GetTickCount	Retrieves the number of milliseconds that have elapsed since the system was started.
GetTimeZoneInformation	Retrieves the current time-zone parameters.
LocalFileTimeToFileTime	Converts a local file time to a file time based on UTC.
SetFileTime	Sets the date and time that a file was created, last accessed, or last modified.
SetLocalTime	Sets the current local time and date.
SetSystemTime	Sets the current system time and date.
SetSystemTimeAdjustment	Enables or disables periodic time adjustments to the system's time-of-day clock.
SetTimeZoneInformation	Sets the current time-zone parameters.
SystemTimeToFileTime	Converts a system time to a file time.
SystemTimeToTzSpecificLocalTime	Converts a UTC time to a specified time zone's corresponding local time.

Source: Microsoft MSDN Windows SDK documentation.

SYSTEMTIME Structure   The SYSTEMTIME structure is used by date- and time-related Windows API functions:

```
SYSTEMTIME STRUCT
    wYear WORD ?                        ; year (4 digits)
    wMonth WORD ?                       ; month (1-12)
```

```
        wDayOfWeek WORD ?            ; day of week (0-6)
        wDay WORD ?                  ; day (1-31)
        wHour WORD ?                 ; hours (0-23)
        wMinute WORD ?               ; minutes (0-59)
        wSecond WORD ?               ; seconds (0-59)
        wMilliseconds WORD ?         ; milliseconds (0-999)
    SYSTEMTIME ENDS
```

The *wDayOfWeek* field value begins with Sunday = 0, Monday = 1, and so on. The value in *wMilliseconds* is not exact because the system can periodically refresh the time by synchronizing with a time source.

GetLocalTime and SetLocalTime

The **GetLocalTime** function returns the date and current time of day, according to the system clock. The time is adjusted for the local time zone. When calling it, pass a pointer to a SYSTEM-TIME structure:

```
    GetLocalTime PROTO,
        lpSystemTime:PTR SYSTEMTIME
```

The following is a sample call to the GetLocalTime function:

```
    .data
    sysTime SYSTEMTIME <>
    .code
    INVOKE GetLocalTime, ADDR sysTime
```

The **SetLocalTime** function sets the system's local date and time. When calling it, pass a pointer to a SYSTEMTIME structure containing the desired date and time:

```
    SetLocalTime PROTO,
        lpSystemTime:PTR SYSTEMTIME
```

If the function executes successfully, it returns a nonzero integer; if it fails, it returns zero.

GetTickCount Function

The **GetTickCount** function returns the number of milliseconds that have elapsed since the system was started:

```
    GetTickCount PROTO                  ; return value in EAX
```

Because the returned value is a doubleword, the time will wrap around to zero if the system is run continuously for 49.7 days. You can use this function to monitor the elapsed time in a loop and break out of the loop when a certain time limit has been reached.

The following *Timer.asm* program measures the elapsed time between two calls to GetTick-Count. It attempts to verify that the timer count has not rolled over (beyond 49.7 days). Similar code could be used in a variety of programs:

```
    TITLE Calculate Elapsed Time                  (Timer.asm)

    ; Demonstrate a simple stopwatch timer, using
    ; the Win32 GetTickCount function.
```

```
        INCLUDE Irvine32.inc
        INCLUDE macros.inc

        .data
        startTime DWORD ?

        .code
        main PROC
            INVOKE GetTickCount        ; get starting tick count
            mov    startTime,eax        ; save it

            ; Create a useless calculation loop.
            mov    ecx,10000100h
        L1: imul   ebx
            imul   ebx
            imul   ebx
            loop   L1

            INVOKE GetTickCount        ; get new tick count
            cmp    eax,startTime        ; lower than starting one?
            jb     error                ; it wrapped around

            sub    eax,startTime        ; get elapsed milliseconds
            call   WriteDec             ; display it
            mWrite <" milliseconds have elapsed",0dh,0ah>
            jmp    quit

        error:
            mWrite "Error: GetTickCount invalid--system has"
            mWrite <"been active for more than 49.7 days",0dh,0ah>
        quit:
            exit
        main ENDP
        END main
```

Sleep Function

Programs sometimes need to pause or delay for short periods of time. Although one could construct a calculation loop or busy loop that keeps the processor busy, the loop's execution time would vary from one processor to the next. In addition, the busy loop would needlessly tie up the processor, slowing down other programs executing at the same time. The Win32 **Sleep** function suspends the currently executing thread for a specified number of milliseconds:

```
Sleep PROTO,
    dwMilliseconds:DWORD
```

(Because our assembly language programs are single-threaded, we will assume a thread is the same as a program.) A thread uses no processor time while it is sleeping.

GetDateTime Procedure

The **GetDateTime** procedure in the Irvine32 library returns the number of 100-nanosecond time intervals that have elapsed since January 1, 1601. This may seem a little odd, in that computers were unknown at the time. In any event, Microsoft uses this value to keep track of file dates and times. The following steps are recommended by the Win32 SDK when you want to prepare a system date/time value for date arithmetic:

1. Call a function such as **GetLocalTime** that fills in a SYSTEMTIME structure.
2. Convert the SYSTEMTIME structure to a FILETIME structure by calling the **SystemTime-ToFileTime** function.
3. Copy the resulting FILETIME structure to a 64-bit quadword.

A FILETIME structure divides a 64-bit quadword into two doublewords:

```
FILETIME STRUCT
    loDateTime DWORD ?
    hiDateTime DWORD ?
FILETIME ENDS
```

The following **GetDateTime** procedure receives a pointer to a 64-bit quadword variable. It stores the current date and time in the variable, in Win32 FILETIME format:

```
;---------------------------------------------------
GetDateTime PROC,
    pStartTime:PTR QWORD
    LOCAL sysTime:SYSTEMTIME, flTime:FILETIME
;
; Gets and saves the current local date/time as a
; 64-bit integer (in the Win32 FILETIME format).
;---------------------------------------------------
; Get the system local time
    INVOKE GetLocalTime,
      ADDR sysTime

; Convert the SYSTEMTIME to FILETIME
    INVOKE SystemTimeToFileTime,
      ADDR sysTime,
      ADDR flTime

; Copy the FILETIME to a 64-bit integer
    mov    esi,pStartTime
    mov    eax,flTime.loDateTime
    mov    DWORD PTR [esi],eax
    mov    eax,flTime.hiDateTime
    mov    DWORD PTR [esi+4],eax
    ret
GetDateTime ENDP
```

Because a SYSTEMTIME is a 64-bit integer, you can use the extended precision arithmetic techniques shown in Section 7.5 to perform date arithmetic.

11.1.13 Section Review

1. What is the linker command that specifies that the target program is for the Win32 console?
2. *(True/False):* A function ending with the letter W (such as WriteConsoleW) is designed to work with a wide (16-bit) character set such as Unicode.
3. *(True/False):* Unicode is the native character set for Windows 98.
4. *(True/False):* The **ReadConsole** function reads mouse information from the input buffer.

5. *(True/False):* Win32 console input functions can detect when the user has resized the console window.

6. Name the MASM data type that matches each of the following standard MS-Windows types:

   ```
   BOOL
   COLORREF
   HANDLE
   LPSTR
   WPARAM
   ```

7. Which Win32 function returns a handle to standard input?

8. Which Win32 function reads a string of text from the keyboard and places the string in a buffer?

9. Show an example call to the **ReadConsole** function.

10. Describe the COORD structure.

11. Show an example call to the **WriteConsole** function.

12. Show an example call to the **CreateFile** function that will open an existing file for reading.

13. Show an example call to the **CreateFile** function that will create a new file with normal attributes, erasing any existing file by the same name.

14. Show an example call to the **ReadFile** function.

15. Show an example call to the **WriteFile** function.

16. Which Win32 function moves the file pointer to a specified offset relative to the beginning of a file?

17. Which Win32 function changes the title of the console window?

18. Which Win32 function lets you change the dimensions of the screen buffer?

19. Which Win32 function lets you change the size of the cursor?

20. Which Win32 function lets you change the color of subsequent text output?

21. Which Win32 function lets you copy an array of attribute values to consecutive cells of the console screen buffer?

22. Which Win32 function lets you pause a program for a specified number of milliseconds?

11.2 Writing a Graphical Windows Application

In this section, we will show how to write a simple graphical application for Microsoft Windows. The program creates and displays a main window, displays message boxes, and responds to mouse events. The information provided here is only a brief introduction; it would require at least an entire chapter to describe the workings of even the simplest MS-Windows application. If you want more information, see the Platform SDK documentation. Another great source is Charles Petzold's book, *Programming Windows*.

Table 11-10 lists the various libraries and includes files used when building this program. Use the Visual Studio project file located in the book's Examples\Ch11\WinApp folder to build and run the program.

Table 11-10   Files Required When Building the WinApp Program.

Filename	Description
WinApp.asm	Program source code
GraphWin.inc	Include file containing structures, constants, and function prototypes used by the program
kernel32.lib	Same MS-Windows API library used earlier in this chapter
user32.lib	Additional MS-Windows API functions

/SUBSYSTEM:WINDOWS replaces the /SUBSYSTEM:CONSOLE we used in previous chapters. The program calls functions from two standard MS-Windows libraries: kernel32.lib and user32.lib.

Main Window   The program displays a main window which fills the screen. It is reduced in size here to make it fit on the printed page (Figure 11–4).

Figure 11–4   Main Startup Window, WinApp Program.

11.2.1 Necessary Structures

The **POINT** structure specifies the X and Y coordinates of a point on the screen, measured in pixels. It can be used, for example, to locate graphic objects, windows, and mouse clicks:

```
POINT STRUCT
    ptX    DWORD ?
    ptY    DWORD ?
POINT ENDS
```

The **RECT** structure defines the boundaries of a rectangle. The **left** member contains the X-coordinate of the left side of the rectangle. The **top** member contains the Y-coordinate of the top of the rectangle. Similar values are stored in the **right** and **bottom** members:

```
RECT STRUCT
    left       DWORD ?
    top        DWORD ?
    right      DWORD ?
    bottom     DWORD ?
RECT ENDS
```

The **MSGStruct** structure defines the data needed for an MS-Windows message:

```
MSGStruct STRUCT
        msgWnd         DWORD  ?
        msgMessage     DWORD  ?
        msgWparam      DWORD  ?
        msgLparam      DWORD  ?
        msgTime        DWORD  ?
        msgPt          POINT  <>
MSGStruct ENDS
```

The **WNDCLASS** structure defines a window class. Each window in a program must belong to a class, and each program must define a window class for its main window. This class is registered with the operating system before the main window can be shown:

```
WNDCLASS STRUC
   style           DWORD  ?          ; window style options
   lpfnWndProc     DWORD  ?          ; pointer to WinProc function
   cbClsExtra      DWORD  ?          ; shared memory
   cbWndExtra      DWORD  ?          ; number of extra bytes
   hInstance       DWORD  ?          ; handle to current program
   hIcon           DWORD  ?          ; handle to icon
   hCursor         DWORD  ?          ; handle to cursor
   hbrBackground   DWORD  ?          ; handle to background brush
   lpszMenuName    DWORD  ?          ; pointer to menu name
   lpszClassName   DWORD  ?          ; pointer to WinClass name
WNDCLASS ENDS
```

Here's a quick summary of the parameters:

- *style* is a conglomerate of different style options, such as WS_CAPTION and WS_BORDER, that control the window's appearance and behavior.
- *lpfnWndProc* is a pointer to a function (in our program) that receives and processes event messages triggered by the user.
- *cbClsExtra* refers to shared memory used by all windows belonging to the class. Can be null.
- *cbWndExtra* specifies the number of extra bytes to allocate following the window instance.
- *hInstance* holds a handle to the current program instance.
- *hIcon* and *hCursor* hold handles to icon and cursor resources for the current program.
- *hbrBackground* holds a handle to a background (color) brush.
- *lpszMenuName* points to a menu name.
- *lpszClassName* points to a null-terminated string containing the window's class name.

11.2.2   The MessageBox Function

The easiest way for a program to display text is to put it in a message box that pops up and waits for the user to click on a button. The **MessageBox** function from the Win32 API library displays a simple message box. Its prototype is shown here:

```
MessageBox PROTO,
        hWnd:DWORD,
        lpText:PTR BYTE,
        lpCaption:PTR BYTE,
        uType:DWORD
```

hWnd is a handle to the current window. *lpText* points to a null-terminated string that will appear inside the box. *lpCaption* points to a null-terminated string that will appear in the box's caption bar. *style* is an integer that describes both the dialog box's icon (optional) and the buttons (required). Buttons are identified by constants such as MB_OK and MB_YESNO. Icons are also identified by constants such as MB_ICONQUESTION. When a message box is displayed, you can add together the constants for the icon and buttons:

```
INVOKE MessageBox, hWnd, ADDR QuestionText,
       ADDR QuestionTitle, MB_OK + MB_ICONQUESTION
```

11.2.3 The WinMain Procedure

Every Windows application needs a startup procedure, usually named **WinMain**, which is responsible for the following tasks:

- Get a handle to the current program.
- Load the program's icon and mouse cursor.
- Register the program's main window class and identify the procedure that will process event messages for the window.
- Create the main window.
- Show and update the main window.
- Begin a loop that receives and dispatches messages. The loop continues until the user closes the application window.

WinMain contains a message processing loop that calls **GetMessage** to retrieve the next available message from the program's message queue. If GetMessage retrieves a WM_QUIT message, it returns zero, telling WinMain that it's time to halt the program. For all other messages, WinMain passes them to the **DispatchMessage** function, which forwards them to the program's WinProc procedure. To read more about messages, search for *Windows Messages* in the Platform SDK documentation.

11.2.4 The WinProc Procedure

The **WinProc** procedure receives and processes all event messages relating to a window. Most events are initiated by the user by clicking and dragging the mouse, pressing keyboard keys, and so on. This procedure's job is to decode each message, and if the message is recognized, to carry out application-oriented tasks relating to the message. Here is the declaration:

```
WinProc PROC,
      hWnd:DWORD,                    ; handle to the window
      localMsg:DWORD,                ; message ID
      wParam:DWORD,                  ; parameter 1 (varies)
      lParam:DWORD                   ; parameter 2 (varies)
```

The content of the third and fourth parameters will vary, depending on the specific message ID. When the mouse is clicked, for example, *lParam* contains the X- and Y-coordinates of the point clicked. In the upcoming example program, the **WinProc** procedure handles three specific messages:

- WM_LBUTTONDOWN, generated when the user presses the left mouse button
- WM_CREATE, indicates that the main window was just created
- WM_CLOSE, indicates that the application's main window is about to close

For example, the following lines (from the procedure) handle the WM_LBUTTONDOWN message by calling **MessageBox** to display a popup message to the user:

```
.IF eax == WM_LBUTTONDOWN
  INVOKE MessageBox, hWnd, ADDR PopupText,
    ADDR PopupTitle, MB_OK
  jmp WinProcExit
```

The resulting message seen by the user is shown in Figure 11–5. Any other messages that we don't wish to handle are passed on to **DefWindowProc**, the default message handler for MS-Windows.

FIGURE 11–5   Popup Window, WinApp Program.

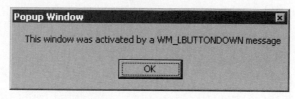

11.2.5   The ErrorHandler Procedure

The **ErrorHandler** procedure, which is optional, is called if the system reports an error during the registration and creation of the program's main window. For example, the RegisterClass function returns a nonzero value if the program's main window was successfully registered. But if it returns zero, we call ErrorHandler (to display a message) and quit the program:

```
INVOKE RegisterClass, ADDR MainWin
.IF eax == 0
  call ErrorHandler
  jmp Exit_Program
.ENDIF
```

The **ErrorHandler** procedure has several important tasks to perform:

- Call **GetLastError** to retrieve the system error number.
- Call **FormatMessage** to retrieve the appropriate system-formatted error message string.
- Call **MessageBox** to display a popup message box containing the error message string.
- Call **LocalFree** to free the memory used by the error message string.

11.2.6   Program Listing

Don't be distressed by the length of this program. Much of it is code that would be identical in any MS-Windows application:

```
TITLE Windows Application                (WinApp.asm)

; This program displays a resizable application window and
; several popup message boxes. Special thanks to Tom Joyce
; for the first version of this program.

.386
.model flat,STDCALL
INCLUDE GraphWin.inc
```

```
;==================== DATA ========================
.data
AppLoadMsgTitle BYTE "Application Loaded",0
AppLoadMsgText  BYTE "This window displays when the WM_CREATE "
                BYTE "message is received",0

PopupTitle   BYTE "Popup Window",0
PopupText    BYTE "This window was activated by a "
             BYTE "WM_LBUTTONDOWN message",0

GreetTitle   BYTE "Main Window Active",0
GreetText    BYTE "This window is shown immediately after "
             BYTE "CreateWindow and UpdateWindow are called.",0

CloseMsg     BYTE "WM_CLOSE message received",0

ErrorTitle   BYTE "Error",0
WindowName   BYTE "ASM Windows App",0
className    BYTE "ASMWin",0

; Define the Application's Window class structure.
MainWin WNDCLASS <NULL,WinProc,NULL,NULL,NULL,NULL,NULL, \
     COLOR_WINDOW,NULL,className>

msg        MSGStruct <>
winRect    RECT <>
hMainWnd   DWORD ?
hInstance  DWORD ?

;==================== CODE ==========================
.code
WinMain PROC

; Get a handle to the current process.
    INVOKE GetModuleHandle, NULL
    mov    hInstance, eax
    mov    MainWin.hInstance, eax

; Load the program's icon and cursor.
    INVOKE LoadIcon, NULL, IDI_APPLICATION
    mov    MainWin.hIcon, eax
    INVOKE LoadCursor, NULL, IDC_ARROW
    mov    MainWin.hCursor, eax

; Register the window class.
    INVOKE RegisterClass, ADDR MainWin
    .IF eax == 0
      call ErrorHandler
      jmp Exit_Program
    .ENDIF

; Create the application's main window.
    INVOKE CreateWindowEx, 0, ADDR className,
      ADDR WindowName,MAIN_WINDOW_STYLE,
      CW_USEDEFAULT,CW_USEDEFAULT,CW_USEDEFAULT,
      CW_USEDEFAULT,NULL,NULL,hInstance,NULL
```

```
    ; If CreateWindowEx failed, display a message and exit.
        .IF eax == 0
            call ErrorHandler
            jmp  Exit_Program
        .ENDIF

    ; Save the window handle, show and draw the window.
        mov hMainWnd,eax
        INVOKE ShowWindow, hMainWnd, SW_SHOW
        INVOKE UpdateWindow, hMainWnd

    ; Display a greeting message.
        INVOKE MessageBox, hMainWnd, ADDR GreetText,
           ADDR GreetTitle, MB_OK

    ; Begin the program's continuous message-handling loop.
    Message_Loop:
        ; Get next message from the queue.
        INVOKE GetMessage, ADDR msg, NULL,NULL,NULL

        ; Quit if no more messages.
        .IF eax == 0
          jmp Exit_Program
        .ENDIF

        ; Relay the message to the program's WinProc.
        INVOKE DispatchMessage, ADDR msg
        jmp Message_Loop

    Exit_Program:
        INVOKE ExitProcess,0
    WinMain ENDP
```

In the previous loop, the **msg** structure is passed to the **GetMessage** function. It fills in the structure, which is then passed to the MS-Windows **DispatchMessage** function.

```
    ;------------------------------------------------------
    WinProc PROC,
        hWnd:DWORD, localMsg:DWORD, wParam:DWORD, lParam:DWORD
    ;
    ; The application's message handler, which handles
    ; application-specific messages. All other messages
    ; are forwarded to the default Windows message
    ; handler.
    ;------------------------------------------------------
        mov eax, localMsg

        .IF eax == WM_LBUTTONDOWN            ; mouse button?
          INVOKE MessageBox, hWnd, ADDR PopupText,
            ADDR PopupTitle, MB_OK
          jmp WinProcExit
        .ELSEIF eax == WM_CREATE             ; create window?
```

```
            INVOKE MessageBox, hWnd, ADDR AppLoadMsgText,
              ADDR AppLoadMsgTitle, MB_OK
            jmp WinProcExit
         .ELSEIF eax == WM_CLOSE              ; close window?
            INVOKE MessageBox, hWnd, ADDR CloseMsg,
              ADDR WindowName, MB_OK
            INVOKE PostQuitMessage,0
            jmp WinProcExit
         .ELSE                                ; other message?
            INVOKE DefWindowProc, hWnd, localMsg, wParam, lParam
            jmp WinProcExit
         .ENDIF

WinProcExit:
    ret
WinProc ENDP

;----------------------------------------------------
ErrorHandler PROC
; Display the appropriate system error message.
;----------------------------------------------------
.data
pErrorMsg  DWORD ?              ; ptr to error message
messageID  DWORD ?
.code
    INVOKE GetLastError         ; Returns message ID in EAX
    mov    messageID,eax

    ; Get the corresponding message string.
    INVOKE FormatMessage, FORMAT_MESSAGE_ALLOCATE_BUFFER + \
      FORMAT_MESSAGE_FROM_SYSTEM,NULL,messageID,NULL,
      ADDR pErrorMsg,NULL,NULL

    ; Display the error message.
    INVOKE MessageBox,NULL, pErrorMsg, ADDR ErrorTitle,
      MB_ICONERROR+MB_OK

    ; Free the error message string.
    INVOKE LocalFree, pErrorMsg
    ret
ErrorHandler ENDP
END WinMain
```

Running the Program

When the program first loads, the following message box displays:

When the user clicks on OK to close the **Application Loaded** message box, another message box displays:

This window is shown immediately after CreateWindow and UpdateWindow are called.

Main Window Active message box with OK button.

When the user closes the **Main Window Active** message box, the program's main window displays:

ASM Windows App main window.

When the user clicks the mouse anywhere inside the main window, the following message box displays:

This window was activated by a WM_LBUTTONDOWN message

Popup Window message box with OK button.

When the user closes this message box and then clicks on the X in the upper-right corner of the main window, the following message displays just before the window closes:

WM_CLOSE message received

ASM Windows App message box with OK button.

When the user closes this message box, the program ends.

11.2.7 Section Review

1. Describe a **POINT** structure.
2. How is the **WNDCLASS** structure used?
3. In a **WNDCLASS** structure, what is the meaning of the *lpfnWndProc* field?
4. In a **WNDCLASS** structure, what is the meaning of the *style* field?
5. In a **WNDCLASS** structure, what is the meaning of the *hInstance* field?

6. When **CreateWindowEx** is called, how is the window's appearance information transmitted to the function?

7. Show an example of calling the **MessageBox** function.

8. Name two button constants that can be used when calling the **MessageBox** function.

9. Name two icon constants that can be used when calling the **MessageBox** function.

10. Name at least three tasks performed by the **WinMain** (startup) procedure.

11. Describe the role of the **WinProc** procedure in the example program.

12. Which messages are processed by the **WinProc** procedure in the example program?

13. Describe the role of the **ErrorHandler** procedure in the example program.

14. Does the message box activated immediately after calling **CreateWindow** appear before or after the application's main window?

15. Does the message box activated by WM_CLOSE appear before or after the main window closes?

11.3 Dynamic Memory Allocation

Dynamic memory allocation, also known as *heap allocation*, is a tool programming languages have for reserving memory when objects, arrays, and other structures are created. In Java, for example, a statement such as the following causes memory to be reserved for a String object:

```
String str = new String("abcde");
```

Similarly, in C++ you might want to allocate space for an array of integers, using a size attribute from a variable:

```
int size;
cin >> size;                        // user inputs the size
int array[] = new int[size];
```

C, C++, and Java have built-in runtime heap managers that handle programmatic requests for storage allocation and deallocation. Heap managers generally allocate a large block of memory from the operating system when the program starts up. They create a *free list* of pointers to storage blocks. When an allocation request is received, the heap manager marks an appropriately sized block of memory as reserved and returns a pointer to the block. Later, when a delete request for the same block is received, the heap frees up the block, returning it to the free list. Each time a new allocation request is received, the heap manager scans the free list, looking for the first available block large enough to grant the request.

Assembly language programs can perform dynamic allocation in a couple of ways. First, they can make system calls to get blocks of memory from the operating system. Second, they can implement their own heap managers that serve requests for smaller objects. In this section, we show how to implement the first method. The example program is a 32-bit protected mode application.

You can request multiple blocks of memory of varying sizes from MS-Windows, using several Windows API functions listed in Table 11-11. All of these functions overwrite the general-purpose registers, so you may want to create wrapper procedures that push and pop important

Table 11-11   Heap-Related Functions.

Function	Description
GetProcessHeap	Returns a 32-bit integer handle to the program's existing heap area in EAX. If the function succeeds, it returns a handle to the heap in EAX. If it fails, the return value in EAX is NULL.
HeapAlloc	Allocates a block of memory from a heap. If it succeeds, the return value in EAX contains the address of the memory block. If it fails, the returned value in EAX is NULL.
HeapCreate	Creates a new heap and makes it available to the calling program. If the function succeeds, it returns a handle to the newly created heap in EAX. If it fails, the return value in EAX is NULL.
HeapDestroy	Destroys the specified heap object and invalidates its handle. If the function succeeds, the return value in EAX is nonzero.
HeapFree	Frees a block of memory previously allocated from a heap, identified by its address and heap handle. If the block is freed successfully, the return value is nonzero.
HeapReAlloc	Reallocates and resizes a block of memory from a heap. If the function succeeds, the return value is a pointer to the reallocated memory block. If the function fails and you have not specified HEAP_GENERATE_EXCEPTIONS, the return value is NULL.
HeapSize	Returns the size of a memory block previously allocated by a call to HeapAlloc or HeapReAlloc. If the function succeeds, EAX contains the size of the allocated memory block, in bytes. If the function fails, the return value is SIZE_T − 1. (SIZE_T equals the maximum number of bytes to which a pointer can point.)

registers. To learn more about memory management, search for *Memory Management Reference* in the Platform SDK documentation.

GetProcessHeap   GetProcessHeap is sufficient if you're content to use the default heap owned by the current program. It has no parameters, and the return value in EAX is the heap handle:

```
GetProcessHeap PROTO
```

Sample call:

```
.data
hHeap HANDLE ?
.code
INVOKE GetProcessHeap
.IF eax == NULL                       ; cannot get handle
  jmp    quit
.ELSE
  mov    hHeap,eax                    ; handle is OK
.ENDIF
```

HeapCreate   HeapCreate lets you create a new private heap for the current program:

```
HeapCreate PROTO,
    flOptions:DWORD,                  ; heap allocation options
    dwInitialSize:DWORD,              ; initial heap size, in bytes
    dwMaximumSize:DWORD               ; maximum heap size, in bytes
```

Set *flOptions* to NULL. Set *dwInitialSize* to the initial heap size, in bytes. The value is rounded up to the next page boundary. When calls to HeapAlloc exceed the initial heap size, it will grow as large as the value you specify in the *dwMaximumSize* parameter (rounded up to the next page boundary). After calling it, a null return value in EAX indicates the heap was not created. The following is a sample call to HeapCreate:

```
HEAP_START =   2000000          ;    2 MB
HEAP_MAX   =  400000000         ;  400 MB
.data
hHeap HANDLE ?                  ; handle to heap
.code
INVOKE HeapCreate, 0, HEAP_START, HEAP_MAX
.IF eax == NULL                 ; heap not created
  call WriteWindowsMsg          ; show error message
  jmp   quit
.ELSE
  mov   hHeap,eax               ; handle is OK
.ENDIF
```

HeapDestroy   HeapDestroy destroys an existing private heap (one created by HeapCreate). Pass it a handle to the heap:

```
HeapDestroy PROTO,
     hHeap:DWORD                ; heap handle
```

If it fails to destroy the heap, EAX equals NULL. Following is a sample call, using the WriteWindowsMsg procedure described in Section 11.1.4:

```
.damta
hHeap HANDLE ?                  ; handle to heap
.code
INVOKE HeapDestroy, hHeap
.IF eax == NULL
  call WriteWindowsMsg          ; show error message
.ENDIF
```

HeapAlloc   HeapAlloc allocates a memory block from an existing heap:

```
HeapAlloc PROTO,
     hHeap:HANDLE,              ; handle to private heap block
     dwFlags:DWORD,             ; heap allocation control flags
     dwBytes:DWORD              ; number of bytes to allocate
```

Pass the following arguments:

- *hHeap*, a 32-bit handle to a heap that was initialized by GetProcessHeap or HeapCreate.
- *dwFlags*, a doubleword containing one or more flag values. You can optionally set it to HEAP_ZERO_MEMORY, which sets the memory block to all zeros.
- *dwBytes*, a doubleword indicating the size of the heap, in bytes.

If HeapAlloc succeeds, EAX contains a pointer to the new storage; if it fails, the value returned in EAX is NULL. The following statements allocate a 1000-byte array from the heap identified by **hHeap** and set its values to all zeros:

```
.data
hHeap HANDLE ?                      ; heap handle
pArray DWORD ?                      ; pointer to array
.code
INVOKE HeapAlloc, hHeap, HEAP_ZERO_MEMORY, 1000
.IF eax == NULL
  mWrite "HeapAlloc failed"
  jmp  quit
.ELSE
  mov  pArray,eax
.ENDIF
```

HeapFree   The HeapFree function frees a block of memory previously allocated from a heap, identified by its address and heap handle:

```
HeapFree PROTO,
      hHeap:HANDLE,
      dwFlags:DWORD,
      lpMem:DWORD
```

The first argument is a handle to the heap containing the memory block; the second argument is usually zero; the third argument is a pointer to the block of memory to be freed. If the block is freed successfully, the return value is nonzero. If the block cannot be freed, the function returns zero. Here is a sample call:

```
INVOKE HeapFree, hHeap, 0, pArray
```

Error Handling   If you encounter an error when calling HeapCreate, HeapDestroy, or GetProcessHeap, you can get details by calling the **GetLastError** API function. Or, you can call the **WriteWindowsMsg** function from the Irvine32 library. Following is an example that calls HeapCreate:

```
INVOKE HeapCreate, 0,HEAP_START, HEAP_MAX

.IF eax == NULL                 ; failed?
  call  WriteWindowsMsg         ; show error message
.ELSE
  mov   hHeap,eax               ; success
.ENDIF
```

The **HeapAlloc** function, on the other hand, does not set a system error code when it fails, so you cannot call GetLastError or WriteWindowsMsg.

11.3.1 HeapTest Programs

The following example (*Heaptest1.asm*) uses dynamic memory allocation to create and fill a 1000-byte array:

```
Title Heap Test #1                                  (Heaptest1.asm)

INCLUDE Irvine32.inc

; This program uses dynamic memory allocation to allocate and
; fill an array of bytes.
```

```
        .data
        ARRAY_SIZE = 1000
        FILL_VAL EQU 0FFh

        hHeap    HANDLE ?                ; handle to the process heap
        pArray   DWORD ?                 ; pointer to block of memory
        newHeap DWORD ?                  ; handle to new heap
        str1 BYTE "Heap size is: ",0

        .code
        main PROC
            INVOKE GetProcessHeap        ; get handle prog's heap
            .IF eax == NULL              ; if failed, display message
            call  WriteWindowsMsg
            jmp   quit
            .ELSE
            mov   hHeap,eax              ; success
            .ENDIF

            call  allocate_array
            jnc   arrayOk                ; failed (CF = 1)?
            call  WriteWindowsMsg
            call  Crlf
            jmp quit
        arrayOk:                         ; ok to fill the array
            call  fill_array
            call  display_array
            call  Crlf

            ; free the array
            INVOKE HeapFree, hHeap, 0, pArray

        quit:
            exit
        main ENDP

        ;----------------------------------------------------------
        allocate_array PROC USES eax
        ;
        ; Dynamically allocates space for the array.
        ; Receives: EAX = handle to the program heap
        ; Returns: CF = 0 if the memory allocation succeeds.
        ;----------------------------------------------------------
            INVOKE HeapAlloc, hHeap, HEAP_ZERO_MEMORY, ARRAY_SIZE

            .IF eax == NULL
              stc                        ; return with CF = 1
            .ELSE
              mov  pArray,eax            ; save the pointer
              clc                        ; return with CF = 0
            .ENDIF

            ret
        allocate_array ENDP
```

```
;--------------------------------------------------------
fill_array PROC USES ecx edx esi
;
; Fills all array positions with a single character.
; Receives: nothing
; Returns: nothing
;--------------------------------------------------------
     mov    ecx,ARRAY_SIZE            ; loop counter
     mov    esi,pArray                ; point to the array

L1:  mov    BYTE PTR [esi],FILL_VAL   ; fill each byte
     inc    esi                       ; next location
     loop   L1

     ret
fill_array ENDP

;--------------------------------------------------------
display_array PROC USES eax ebx ecx esi
;
; Displays the array
; Receives: nothing
; Returns: nothing
;--------------------------------------------------------
     mov    ecx,ARRAY_SIZE            ; loop counter
     mov    esi,pArray                ; point to the array

L1:  mov    al,[esi]                  ; get a byte
     mov    ebx,TYPE BYTE
     call   WriteHexB                 ; display it
     inc    esi                       ; next location
     loop   L1

     ret
display_array ENDP

END main
```

The following example (*Heaptest2.asm*) uses dynamic memory allocation to repeatedly allocate large blocks of memory until the heap size is exceeded.

```
Title Heap Test #2                    (Heaptest2.asm)

INCLUDE Irvine32.inc

.data
HEAP_START =    2000000             ;    2 MB
HEAP_MAX   =  400000000             ; 400 MB
BLOCK_SIZE =     500000             ;  .5 MB

hHeap HANDLE ?                      ; handle to the heap
pData DWORD ?                       ; pointer to block

str1 BYTE 0dh,0ah,"Memory allocation failed",0dh,0ah,0

.code
main PROC
```

```
        INVOKE HeapCreate, 0,HEAP_START, HEAP_MAX
        .IF eax == NULL              ; failed?
        call  WriteWindowsMsg
        call  Crlf
        jmp   quit
        .ELSE
        mov   hHeap,eax              ; success
        .ENDIF

        mov   ecx,2000               ; loop counter
L1:  call allocate_block            ; allocate a block
        .IF Carry?                   ; failed?
        mov   edx,OFFSET str1        ; display message
        call  WriteString
        jmp   quit
        .ELSE                        ; no: print a dot to
        mov   al,'.'                 ; show progress
        call  WriteChar
        .ENDIF

        ;call free_block             ; enable/disable this line
        loop  L1
quit:
     INVOKE HeapDestroy, hHeap    ; destroy the heap
     .IF eax == NULL              ; failed?
     call  WriteWindowsMsg        ; yes: error message
     call  Crlf
     .ENDIF

     exit
main ENDP


allocate_block PROC USES ecx
     ; allocate a block and fill with all zeros.
     INVOKE HeapAlloc, hHeap, HEAP_ZERO_MEMORY, BLOCK_SIZE

     .IF eax == NULL
        stc                       ; return with CF = 1
     .ELSE
        mov   pData,eax           ; save the pointer
        clc                       ; return with CF = 0
     .ENDIF

     ret
allocate_block ENDP


free_block PROC USES ecx

     INVOKE HeapFree, hHeap, 0, pData
     ret
free_block ENDP
END main
```

11.3.2   Section Review

1. What is another term for *heap allocation*, in the context of C, C++, and Java?

2. Describe the GetProcessHeap function.

3. Describe the HeapAlloc function.

4. Show a sample call to the HeapCreate function.

5. When calling HeapDestroy, how do you identify the memory block being destroyed?

11.4   x86 Memory Management

When Microsoft Windows was first released, there was a great deal of interest among programmers about the switch from real-address mode to protected mode. (Anyone who wrote programs for Windows 2.x will recall how difficult it was to work with only 640K in real-address mode!) With Windows protected mode (and soon after, Virtual mode), whole new possibilities seemed to open up. One must not forget that it was the Intel386 processor (the first of the IA-32 family) that made all of this possible. What we now take for granted was a gradual evolution from the unstable Windows 3.0 to the sophisticated (and stable) versions of Windows and Linux offered today.

This section will focus on two primary aspects of memory management:

• Translating logical addresses into linear addresses
• Translating linear addresses into physical addresses (paging)

Let's briefly review some of the x86 memory-management terms introduced in Chapter 2, beginning with the following:

• *Multitasking* permits multiple programs (or tasks) to run at the same time. The processor divides its time among all of the running programs.
• *Segments* are variable-sized areas of memory used by a program containing either code or data.
• *Segmentation* provides a way to isolate memory segments from each other. This permits multiple programs to run simultaneously without interfering with each other.
• A *segment descriptor* is a 64-bit value that identifies and describes a single memory segment: It contains information about the segment's base address, access rights, size limit, type, and usage.

Now we will add two new terms to the list:

• A *segment selector* is a 16-bit value stored in a segment register (CS, DS, SS, ES, FS, or GS).
• A *logical address* is a combination of a segment selector and a 32-bit offset.

Segment registers have been ignored throughout this book because they are never modified directly by user programs. We have only been concerned with 32-bit data offsets. From a system programmer's point of view, however, segment registers are important because they contain indirect references to memory segments.

11.4.1   Linear Addresses

Translating Logical Addresses to Linear Addresses

A multitasking operating system allows several programs (tasks) to run in memory at the same time. Each program has its own unique area for data. Suppose three programs each had a variable at offset 200h; how could the three variables be separate from each other without being shared? The answer to this is that x86 processors use a one- or two-step process to convert each variable's offset into a unique memory location.

The first step combines a segment value with a variable's offset to create a *linear address*. This linear address could be the variable's physical address. But operating systems such as MS-Windows and Linux employ a feature called *paging* to permit programs to use more linear memory than is physically available in the computer. They must use a second step called *page translation* to convert a linear address to a physical address. We will explain page translation in Section 11.4.2.

First, let's look at the way the processor uses a segment and offset to determine the linear address of a variable. Each segment selector points to a segment descriptor (in a descriptor table), which contains the base address of a memory segment. The 32-bit offset from the logical address is added to the segment's base address, generating a 32-bit *linear address*, as shown in Figure 11–6.

FIGURE 11–6   Converting a Logical Address into a Linear Address.

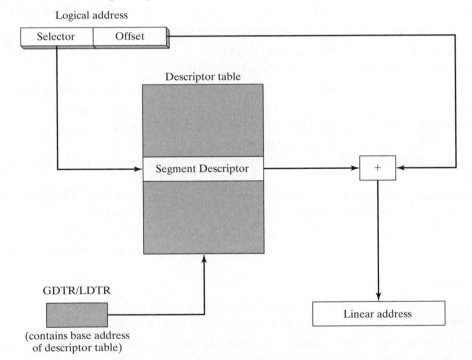

Linear Address   A *linear address* is a 32-bit integer ranging between 0 and FFFFFFFFh, which refers to a memory location. The linear address may also be the physical address of the target data if a feature called *paging* is disabled.

Paging
Paging is an important feature of the x86 processor that makes it possible for a computer to run a combination of programs that would not otherwise fit into memory. The processor does this

by initially loading only part of a program in memory while keeping the remaining parts on disk. The memory used by the program is divided into small units called *pages*, typically 4 KByte each. As each program runs, the processor selectively unloads inactive pages from memory and loads other pages that are immediately required.

The operating system maintains a *page directory* and a set of *page tables* to keep track of the pages used by all programs currently in memory. When a program attempts to access an address somewhere in the linear address space, the processor automatically converts the linear address into a physical address. This conversion is called *page translation*. If the requested page is not currently in memory, the processor interrupts the program and issues a *page fault*. The operating system copies the required page from disk into memory before the program can resume. From the point of view of an application program, page faults and page translation happen automatically.

You can activate a Microsoft Windows utility named *Task Manager* and see the difference between physical memory and virtual memory. Figure 11–7 shows a computer with 256 MByte of physical memory. The total amount of virtual memory currently in use is in the *Commit Charge* frame of the Task Manager. The virtual memory limit is 633 MByte, considerably larger than the computer's physical memory size.

FIGURE 11–7   Windows Task Manager Example.

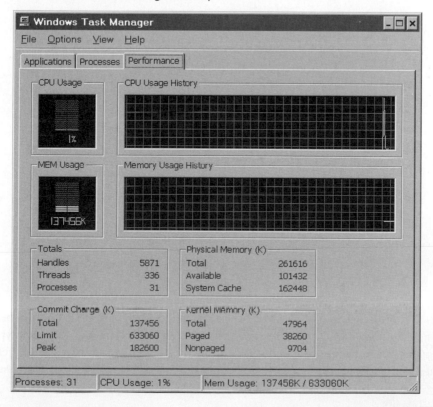

Descriptor Tables

Segment descriptors can be found in two types of tables: *global descriptor tables* and *local descriptor tables*.

Global Descriptor Table (GDT)   A single GDT is created when the operating system switches the processor into protected mode during boot up. Its base address is held in the GDTR (global descriptor table register). The table contains entries (called *segment descriptors*) that point to segments. The operating system has the option of storing the segments used by all programs in the GDT.

Local Descriptor Tables (LDT)   In a multitasking operating system, each task or program is usually assigned its own table of segment descriptors, called an LDT. The LDTR register contains the address of the program's LDT. Each segment descriptor contains the base address of a segment within the linear address space. This segment is usually distinct from all other segments, as in Figure 11–8. Three different logical addresses are shown, each selecting a different entry in the LDT. In this figure we assume that paging is disabled, so the linear address space is also the physical address space.

FIGURE 11–8   Indexing into a Local Descriptor Table.

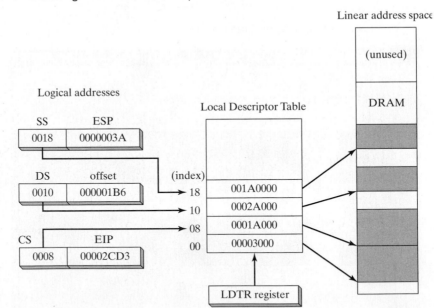

Segment Descriptor Details

In addition to the segment's base address, the segment descriptor contains bit-mapped fields specifying the segment limit and segment type. An example of a read-only segment type is the code segment. If a program tries to modify a read-only segment, a processor fault is generated. Segment descriptors can contain protection levels that protect operating system data from access by application programs. The following are descriptions of individual selector fields:

Base address: A 32-bit integer that defines the starting location of the segment in the 4 GByte linear address space.

Privilege level: Each segment can be assigned a privilege level between 0 and 3, where 0 is the most privileged, usually for operating system kernel code. If a program with a higher-numbered privilege level tries to access a segment having a lower-numbered privilege level, a processor fault is generated.

Segment type: Indicates the type of segment and specifies the type of access that can be made to the segment and the direction the segment can grow (up or down). Data (including Stack) segments can be read-only or read/write and can grow either up or down. Code segments can be execute-only or execute/read-only.

Segment present flag: This bit indicates whether the segment is currently present in physical memory.

Granularity flag: Determines the interpretation of the Segment limit field. If the bit is clear, the segment limit is interpreted in byte units. If the bit is set, the segment limit is interpreted in 4096-byte units.

Segment limit: This 20-bit integer specifies the size of the segment. It is interpreted in one of the following two ways, depending on the Granularity flag:

• The number of bytes in the segment, ranging from 1 to 1 MByte.
• The number of 4096-byte units, permitting the segment size to range from 4 KByte to 4 GByte.

11.4.2   Page Translation

When paging is enabled, the processor must translate a 32-bit linear address into a 32-bit physical address.[2] There are three structures used in the process:

• Page directory: An array of up to 1024 32-bit page-directory entries.
• Page table: An array of up to 1024 32-bit page-table entries.
• Page: A 4 KByte or 4 MByte address space.

To simplify the following discussion, we will assume that 4 KByte pages are used:

A linear address is divided into three fields: a pointer to a page-directory entry, a pointer to a page-table entry, and an offset into a page frame. Control register (CR3) contains the starting address of the page directory. The following steps are carried out by the processor when translating a linear address to a physical address, as shown in Figure 11–9:

1. The *linear address* references a location in the linear address space.
2. The 10-bit *directory* field in the linear address is an index to a page-directory entry. The page-directory entry contains the base address of a page table.
3. The 10-bit *table* field in the linear address is an index into the page table identified by the page-directory entry. The page-table entry at that position contains the base location of a *page* in physical memory.
4. The 12-bit *offset* field in the linear address is added to the base address of the page, generating the exact physical address of the operand.

Figure 11–9   Translating Linear Address to Physical Address.

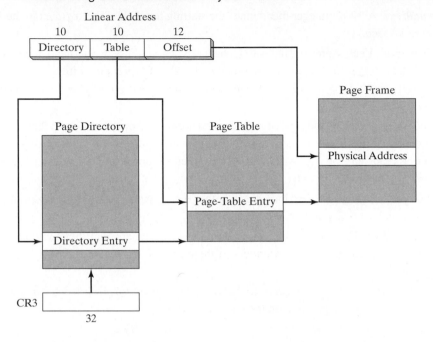

The operating system has the option of using a single page directory for all running programs and tasks, or one page directory per task, or a combination of the two.

MS-Windows Virtual Machine Manager

Now that we have a general idea of how the IA-32 manages memory, it might be interesting to see how memory management is handled by MS-Windows. The following passage is paraphrased from the Platform SDK documentation:

> The Virtual Machine Manager (VMM) is the 32-bit protected mode operating system at the core of MS-Windows. It creates, runs, monitors, and terminates virtual machines. It manages memory, processes, interrupts, and exceptions. It works with *virtual devices*, allowing them to intercept interrupts and faults that control access to hardware and installed software. The VMM and virtual devices run in a single 32-bit flat model address space at privilege level 0. The system creates two global descriptor table entries (segment descriptors), one for code and the other for data. The segments are fixed at linear address 0. The VMM provides multithreaded, preemptive multitasking. It runs multiple applications simultaneously by sharing CPU time between the virtual machines in which the applications run.

In the foregoing passage, we can interpret the term *virtual machine* to be what Intel calls a *process* or *task*. It consists of program code, supporting software, memory, and registers. Each virtual machine is assigned its own address space, I/O port space, interrupt vector table, and local descriptor table. Applications running in virtual-8086 mode run at privilege level 3. In MS-Windows, protected-mode programs run at privilege levels 0 and 3.

11.4.3   Section Review

1. Define the following terms:
   a. Multitasking
   b. Segmentation
2. Define the following terms:
   a. Segment selector
   b. Logical address
3. *(True/False):* A segment selector points to an entry in a segment descriptor table.
4. *(True/False):* A segment descriptor contains the base location of a segment.
5. *(True/False):* A segment selector is 32 bits.
6. *(True/False):* A segment descriptor does not contain segment size information.
7. Describe a linear address.
8. How does paging relate to linear memory?
9. If paging is disabled, how does the processor translate a linear address to a physical address?
10. What advantage does paging offer?
11. Which register contains the base location of a local descriptor table?
12. Which register contains the base location of a global descriptor table?
13. How many global descriptor tables can exist?
14. How many local descriptor tables can exist?
15. Name at least four fields in a segment descriptor.
16. Which structures are involved in the paging process?
17. What structure contains the base address of a page table?
18. What structure contains the base address of a page frame?

11.5   Chapter Summary

On the surface, 32-bit console mode programs look and behave like 16-bit MS-DOS programs running in text mode. Both types of programs read from standard input and write to standard output, they support command-line redirection, and they can display text in color. Beneath the surface, however, Win32 consoles and MS-DOS programs are quite different. Win32 runs in 32-bit protected mode, whereas MS-DOS runs in real-address mode. Win32 programs can call functions from the same function library used by graphical Windows applications. MS-DOS programs are limited to a smaller set of BIOS and MS-DOS interrupts that have existed since the introduction of the IBM-PC.

Types of character sets are used in Windows API functions: the 8-bit ASCII/ANSI character set and a 16-bit version of the Unicode character set.

Standard MS-Windows data types used in the API functions must be translated to MASM data types (see Table 11-1).

Console handles are 32-bit integers used for input/output in console windows. The **GetStdHandle** function retrieves a console handle. For high-level console input, call the

ReadConsole function; for high-level output, call **WriteConsole**. When creating or opening a file, call **CreateFile**. When reading from a file, call **ReadFile**, and when writing, call **WriteFile**. **CloseHandle** closes a file. To move a file pointer, call **SetFilePointer**.

To manipulate the console screen buffer, call **SetConsoleScreenBufferSize**. To change the text color, call **SetConsoleTextAttribute**. The WriteColors program in this chapter demonstrated the **WriteConsoleOutputAttribute** and **WriteConsoleOutputCharacter** functions.

To get the system time, call **GetLocalTime**; to set the time, call **SetLocalTime**. Both functions use the SYSTEMTIME structure. The **GetDateTime** function example in this chapter returns the date and time as a 64-bit integer, specifying the number of 100-nanosecond intervals that have occurred since January 1, 1601. The **TimerStart** and **TimerStop** functions can be used to create a simple stopwatch timer.

When creating a graphical MS-Windows application, fill in a WNDCLASS structure with information about the program's main window class. Create a **WinMain** procedure that gets a handle to the current process, loads the icon and mouse cursor, registers the program's main window, creates the main window, shows and updates the main windows, and begins a message loop that receives and dispatches messages.

The **WinProc** procedure is responsible for handling incoming Windows messages, often activated by user actions such as a mouse click or keystroke. Our example program processes a WM_LBUTTONDOWN message, a WM_CREATE message, and a WM_CLOSE message. It displays popup messages when these events are detected.

Dynamic memory allocation, or heap allocation, is a tool you can use to reserve memory and free memory for use by your program. Assembly language programs can perform dynamic allocation in a couple of ways. First, they can make system calls to get blocks of memory from the operating system. Second, they can implement their own heap managers that serve requests for smaller objects. Following are the most important Win32 API calls for dynamic memory allocation:

• GetProcessHeap returns a 32-bit integer handle to the program's existing heap area.
• HeapAlloc allocates a block of memory from a heap.
• HeapCreate creates a new heap.
• HeapDestroy destroys a heap.
• HeapFree frees a block of memory previously allocated from a heap.
• HeapReAlloc reallocates and resizes a block of memory from a heap.
• HeapSize returns the size of a previously allocated memory block.

The memory management section of this chapter focuses on two main topics: translating logical addresses into linear addresses and translating linear addresses into physical addresses.

The selector in a logical address points to an entry in a segment descriptor table, which in turn points to a segment in linear memory. The segment descriptor contains information about the segment, including its size and type of access. There are two types of descriptor tables: a single global descriptor table (GDT) and one or more local descriptor tables (LDT).

Paging is an important feature of the IA-32 processor that makes it possible for a computer to run a combination of programs that would not otherwise fit into memory. The processor does this by initially loading only part of a program in memory, while keeping the remaining parts on disk.

The processor uses a page directory, page table, and page frame to generate the physical location of data. A page directory contains pointers to page tables. A page table contains pointers to pages.

Reading   For further reading about Windows programming, the following books may be helpful:

- Mark Russinovich and David Solomon, *Microsoft Windows Internals 4th Ed.,* Microsoft Press, 2004.
- Barry Kauler, *Windows Assembly Language and System Programming*, CMP Books, 1997.
- Charles Petzold, *Programming Windows, 5th Ed.,* Microsoft Press, 1998.

11.6   Programming Exercises

★★ **1.   ReadString**

Implement your own version of the **ReadString** procedure, using stack parameters. Pass it a pointer to a string and an integer indicating the maximum number of characters to be entered. Return a count (in EAX) of the number of characters actually entered. The procedure must input a string from the console and insert a null byte at the end of the string (in the position occupied by 0Dh). See Section 11.1.4 for details on the Win32 **ReadConsole** function. Write a short program that tests your procedure.

★★★ **2.   String Input/Output**

Write a program that inputs the following information from the user, using the Win32 **Read-Console** function: first name, last name, age, phone number. Redisplay the same information with labels and attractive formatting, using the Win32 **WriteConsole** function. Do not use any procedures from the Irvine32 library.

★★ **3.   Clearing the Screen**

Write your own version of the link library's **Clrscr** procedure that clears the screen.

★★ **4.   Random Screen Fill**

Write a program that fills each screen cell with a random character in a random color. *Extra:* Assign a 50% probability that the color of any character will be red.

★★ **5.   DrawBox**

Draw a box on the screen using line-drawing characters from the character set listed on the inside back cover of the book. *Hint:* Use the **WriteConsoleOutputCharacter** function.

★★★ **6.   Student Records**

Write a program that creates a new text file. Prompt the user for a student identification number, last name, first name, and date of birth. Write this information to the file. Input several more records in the same manner and close the file. *(A VideoNote for this exercise is posted on the Web site.)*

★★ **7.   Scrolling Text Window**

Write a program that writes 50 lines of text to the console screen buffer. Number each line. Move the console window to the top of the buffer, and begin scrolling the text upward at a steady rate (two lines per second). Stop scrolling when the console window reaches the end of the buffer.

★★★ **8. Block Animation**

Write a program that draws a small square on the screen using several blocks (ASCII code DBh) in color. Move the square around the screen in randomly generated directions. Use a fixed delay value of 50 milliseconds. *Extra:* Use a randomly generated delay value between 10 and 100 milliseconds. *(A VideoNote for this exercise is posted on the Web site.)*

★★ **9. Last Access Date of a File**

Write a procedure named **LastAccessDate** that fills a SYSTEMTIME structure with the date and time stamp information of a file. Pass the offset of a filename in EDX, and pass the offset of a SYSTEMTIME structure in ESI. If the function fails to find the file, set the Carry flag. When you implement this function, you will need to open the file, get its handle, pass the handle to **GetFileTime**, pass its output to **FileTimeToSystemTime**, and close the file. Write a test program that calls your procedure and prints out the date when a particular file was last accessed. Sample:

```
ch11_09.asm was last accessed on: 6/16/2005
```

★★ **10. Reading a Large File**

Modify the ReadFile.asm program in Section 11.1.8 so that it can read files larger than its input buffer. Reduce the buffer size to 1024 bytes. Use a loop to continue reading and displaying the file until it can read no more data. If you plan to display the buffer with WriteString, remember to insert a null byte at the end of the buffer data.

★★★ **11. Linked List**

Advanced: Implement a singly linked list, using the dynamic memory allocation functions presented in this chapter. Each link should be a structure named Node (see Chapter 10) containing an integer value and a pointer to the next link in the list. Using a loop, prompt the user for as many integers as they want to enter. As each integer is entered, allocate a Node object, insert the integer in the Node, and append the Node to the linked list. When a value of 0 is entered, stop the loop. Finally, display the entire list from beginning to end. *This project should only be attempted if you have previously created linked lists in a high-level language. (A VideoNote for this exercise is posted on the Web site.)*

End Notes

1. Source: Microsoft MSDN Documentation.

2. The Pentium Pro and later processors permit a 36-bit address option, but it will not be covered here.

12

FLOATING-POINT PROCESSING AND INSTRUCTION ENCODING

12.1 Floating-Point Binary Representation
  12.1.1 IEEE Binary Floating-Point Representation
  12.1.2 The Exponent
  12.1.3 Normalized Binary Floating-Point Numbers
  12.1.4 Creating the IEEE Representation
  12.1.5 Converting Decimal Fractions to Binary Reals
  12.1.6 Section Review
12.2 Floating-Point Unit
  12.2.1 FPU Register Stack
  12.2.2 Rounding
  12.2.3 Floating-Point Exceptions
  12.2.4 Floating-Point Instruction Set
  12.2.5 Arithmetic Instructions
  12.2.6 Comparing Floating-Point Values
  12.2.7 Reading and Writing Floating-Point Values

  12.2.8 Exception Synchronization
  12.2.9 Code Examples
  12.2.10 Mixed-Mode Arithmetic
  12.2.11 Masking and Unmasking Exceptions
  12.2.12 Section Review
12.3 x86 Instruction Encoding
  12.3.1 Instruction Format
  12.3.2 Single-Byte Instructions
  12.3.3 Move Immediate to Register
  12.3.4 Register-Mode Instructions
  12.3.5 Processor Operand-Size Prefix
  12.3.6 Memory-Mode Instructions
  12.3.7 Section Review
12.4 Chapter Summary
12.5 Programming Exercises

12.1 Floating-Point Binary Representation

A floating-point decimal number contains three components: a sign, a significand, and an exponent. In the number -1.23154×10^5 for example, the sign is negative, the significand is 1.23154, and the exponent is 5. (Although slightly less correct, the term *mantissa* is sometimes substituted for *significand*.)

> **Finding the Intel x86 Documentation.** To get the most out of this chapter, get free electronic copies of the *Intel 64 and IA-32 Architectures Software Developer's Manual*, Vols. 1 and 2. Point your Web browser to www.intel.com, and search for *IA-32 manuals*.

12.1.1   IEEE Binary Floating-Point Representation

x86 processors use three floating-point binary storage formats specified in the *Standard 754-1985 for Binary Floating-Point Arithmetic* produced by the IEEE organization. Table 12-1 describes their characteristics.[1]

Table 12-1   IEEE Floating-Point Binary Formats.

Single Precision	32 bits: 1 bit for the sign, 8 bits for the exponent, and 23 bits for the fractional part of the significand. Approximate normalized range: 2^{-126} to 2^{127}. Also called a *short real*.
Double Precision	64 bits: 1 bit for the sign, 11 bits for the exponent, and 52 bits for the fractional part of the significand. Approximate normalized range: 2^{-1022} to 2^{1023}. Also called a *long real*.
Double Extended Precision	80 bits: 1 bit for the sign, 16 bits for the exponent, and 63 bits for the fractional part of the significand. Approximate normalized range: 2^{-16382} to 2^{16383}. Also called an *extended real*.

Because the three formats are so similar, we will focus on the single-precision (SP) format (Figure 12–1). The 32 bits are arranged with the most significant bit (MSB) on the left. The segment marked *fraction* indicates the fractional part of the significand. As you might expect, the individual bytes are stored in memory in little endian order [least significant bit (LSB) at the starting address].

Figure 12–1   Single-Precision Format.

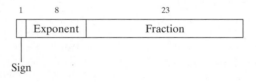

The Sign

If the sign bit is 1, the number is negative; if the bit is 0, the number is positive. Zero is considered positive.

The Significand

In the floating-point number represented by the expression $m * b^e$, m is called the significand, or mantissa; b is the base; and e is the exponent. The *significand* (or mantissa) of a floating-point number consists of the decimal digits to the left and right of the decimal point. In Chapter 1 we introduced the concept of weighted positional notation when explaining the binary, decimal, and hexadecimal numbering systems. The same concept can be extended to include the fractional part of a floating-point number. For example, the decimal value 123.154 is represented by the following sum:

$$123.154 = (1 \times 10^2) + (2 \times 10^1) + (3 \times 10^0) + (1 \times 10^{-1}) + (5 \times 10^{-2}) + (4 \times 10^{-3})$$

All digits to the left of the decimal point have positive exponents, and all digits to the right side have negative exponents.

Binary floating-point numbers also use weighted positional notation. The floating-point binary value 11.1011 is expressed as

$$11.1011 = (1 \times 2^1) + (1 \times 2^0) + (1 \times 2^{-1}) + (0 \times 2^{-2}) + (1 \times 2^{-3}) + (1 \times 2^{-4})$$

Another way to express the values to the right of the binary point is to list them as a sum of fractions whose denominators are powers of 2. In our sample, the sum is 11/16 (or 0.6875):

.1011 = 1/2 + 0/4 + 1/8 + 1/16 = 11/16

Generating the decimal fraction is fairly intuitive. The decimal numerator (11) represents the binary bit pattern 1011. If e is the number of significant bits to the right of the binary point, the decimal denominator is 2^e. In our example, $e = 4$, so $2^e = 16$. Table 12-2 shows additional examples of translating binary floating-point notation to base-10 fractions. The last entry in the table contains the smallest fraction that can be stored in a 23-bit normalized significand. For quick reference, Table 12-3 lists examples of binary floating-point numbers alongside their equivalent decimal fractions and decimal values.

Table 12-2   Examples: Translating Binary Floating-Point to Fractions.

Binary Floating-Point	Base-10 Fraction
11.11	3 3/4
101.0011	5 3/16
1101.100101	13 37/64
0.00101	5/32
1.011	1 3/8
0.00000000000000000000001	1/8388608

Table 12-3   Binary and Decimal Fractions.

Binary	Decimal Fraction	Decimal Value
.1	1/2	.5
.01	1/4	.25
.001	1/8	.125
.0001	1/16	.0625
.00001	1/32	.03125

The Significand's Precision

The entire continuum of real numbers cannot be represented in any floating-point format having a finite number of bits. Suppose, for example, a simplified floating-point format had 5-bit significands. There would be no way to represent values falling between 1.1111 and 10.000 binary. The binary value 1.11111, for example, requires a more precise significand. Extending this idea to the IEEE double-precision format, we see that its 53-bit significand cannot represent a binary value requiring 54 or more bits.

12.1.2   The Exponent

SP exponents are stored as 8-bit unsigned integers with a bias of 127. The number's actual exponent must be added to 127. Consider the binary value 1.101×2^5: After the actual exponent (5) is added to 127, the biased exponent (132) is stored in the number's representation. Table 12-4 shows examples of exponents in signed decimal, then biased decimal, and finally unsigned binary. The biased exponent is always positive, between 1 and 254. As stated earlier, the actual exponent range is from -126 to $+127$. The range was chosen so the smallest possible exponent's reciprocal cannot cause an overflow.

Table 12-4   Sample Exponents Represented in Binary.

Exponent (E)	Biased (E + 127)	Binary
+5	132	10000100
0	127	01111111
−10	117	01110101
+127	254	11111110
−126	1	00000001
−1	126	01111110

12.1.3 Normalized Binary Floating-Point Numbers

Most floating-point binary numbers are stored in *normalized* form so as to maximize the precision of the significand. Given any floating-point binary number, you can normalize it by shifting the binary point until a single "1" appears to the left of the binary point. The exponent expresses the number of positions the binary point is moved left (positive exponent) or right (negative exponent). Here are examples:

Denormalized	Normalized
1110.1	1.1101×2^3
.000101	1.01×2^{-4}
1010001.	1.010001×2^6

Denormalized Values   To reverse the normalizing operation is to *denormalize* (or unnormalize) a binary floating-point number. Shift the binary point until the exponent is zero. If the exponent is positive n, shift the binary point n positions to the right; if the exponent is negative n, shift the binary point n positions to the left, filling leading zeros if necessary.

12.1.4 Creating the IEEE Representation

Real Number Encodings

Once the sign bit, exponent, and significand fields are normalized and encoded, it's easy to generate a complete binary IEEE short real. Using Figure 12–1 as a reference, we can place the sign bit first, the exponent bits next, and the fractional part of the significand last. For example, binary 1.101×2^0 is represented as follows:

- Sign bit: 0
- Exponent: 01111111
- Fraction: 10100000000000000000000

The biased exponent (01111111) is the binary representation of decimal 127. All normalized significands have a 1 to the left of the binary point, so there is no need to explicitly encode the bit. Additional examples are shown in Table 12-5.

Table 12-5   Examples of SP Bit Encodings.

Binary Value	Biased Exponent	Sign, Exponent, Fraction		
-1.11	127	1	01111111	11000000000000000000000
+1101.101	130	0	10000010	10110100000000000000000
-.00101	124	1	01111100	01000000000000000000000
+100111.0	132	0	10000100	00111000000000000000000
+.0000001101011	120	0	01111000	10101100000000000000000

The IEEE specification includes several real-number and non-number encodings.

- Positive and negative zero
- Denormalized finite numbers
- Normalized finite numbers
- Positive and negative infinity
- Non-numeric values (NaN, known as *Not a Number*)
- Indefinite numbers

Indefinite numbers are used by the floating-point unit (FPU) as responses to some invalid floating-point operations.

Normalized and Denormalized   *Normalized finite numbers* are all the nonzero finite values that can be encoded in a normalized real number between zero and infinity. Although it would seem that all finite nonzero floating-point numbers should be normalized, it is not possible when their values are close to zero. This happens when the FPU cannot shift the binary point to a normalized position, given the limitation posed by the range of the exponent. Suppose the FPU computes a result of $1.0101111 \times 2^{-129}$, which has an exponent that is too small to be stored in a SP number. An underflow exception condition is generated, and the number is gradually denormalized by shifting the binary point left 1 bit at a time until the exponent reaches a valid range:

```
1.0101111000000000000001111 x 2⁻¹²⁹
0.1010111100000000000000111 x 2⁻¹²⁸
0.0101011110000000000000011 x 2⁻¹²⁷
0.0010101111000000000000001 x 2⁻¹²⁶
```

In this example, some loss of precision occurred in the significand as a result of the shifting of the binary point.

Positive and Negative Infinity   Positive infinity ($+\infty$) represents the maximum positive real number, and negative infinity ($-\infty$) represents the maximum negative real number. You can compare infinities to other values: $-\infty$ is less than $+\infty$, $-\infty$ is less than any finite number, and $+\infty$ is greater than any finite number. Either infinity may represent a floating-point overflow condition. The result of a computation cannot be normalized because its exponent would be too large to be represented by the available number of exponent bits.

NaNs   *NaNs* are bit patterns that do not represent any valid real number. The x86 includes two types of NaNs: A *quiet NaN* can propagate through most arithmetic operations without causing an exception. A *signaling NaN* can be used to generate a floating-point invalid operation exception. A compiler might fill an uninitialized array with signaling NaN values so that any attempt to perform calculations on the array will generate an exception. A quiet NaN can be used to hold diagnostic information created during debugging sessions. A program is free to encode any information in a NaN it wishes. The FPU does not attempt to perform operations on NaNs. The Intel manuals contain a set of rules that determine instruction results when combinations of the two types of NaNs are used as operands.[2]

Specific Encodings   There are several specific encodings for values often encountered in floating-point operations, listed in Table 12-6. Bit positions marked with the letter x can be either 1 or 0. QNaN is a quiet NaN, and SNaN is a signaling NaN.

Table 12-6   Specific SP Encodings.

Value	Sign, Exponent, Significand		
Positive zero	0	00000000	00000000000000000000000
Negative zero	1	00000000	00000000000000000000000
Positive infinity	0	11111111	00000000000000000000000
Negative infinity	1	11111111	00000000000000000000000
QNaN	x	11111111	1xxxxxxxxxxxxxxxxxxxxxx
SNaN	x	11111111	0xxxxxxxxxxxxxxxxxxxxxx[a]

[a] SNaN significand field begins with 0, but at least one of the remaining bits must be 1.

12.1.5   Converting Decimal Fractions to Binary Reals

When a decimal fraction can be represented as a sum of fractions in the form $(1/2 + 1/4 + 1/8 + \ldots)$, it is fairly easy for you to discover the corresponding binary real. In Table 12-7, most of the fractions in the left column are not in a form that translates easily to binary. They can, however, be written as in the second column.

Many real numbers, such as 1/10 (0.1) or 1/100 (.01), cannot be represented by a finite number of binary digits. Such a fraction can only be approximated by a sum of fractions whose denominators are powers of 2. Imagine how currency values such as $39.95 are affected!

Alternate Method, Using Binary Long Division   When small decimal values are involved, an easy way to convert decimal fractions into binary is to first convert the numerator and denominator to binary and then perform long division. For example, decimal 0.5 is represented as the fraction 5/10. Decimal 5 is binary 0101, and decimal 10 is binary 1010. Performing the binary long division, we find that the quotient is 0.1 binary:

$$
\begin{array}{r}
.1 \\
1010 \overline{\left)\ 0\,1\,0\,1.0\right.} \\
-1\,0\,1\,0 \\
\hline
0
\end{array}
$$

TABLE 12-7   Examples of Decimal Fractions and Binary Reals.

Decimal Fraction	Factored As...	Binary Real
1/2	1/2	.1
1/4	1/4	.01
3/4	1/2 + 1/4	.11
1/8	1/8	.001
7/8	1/2 + 1/4 + 1/8	.111
3/8	1/4 + 1/8	.011
1/16	1/16	.0001
3/16	1/8 + 1/16	.0011
5/16	1/4 + 1/16	.0101

When 1010 binary is subtracted from the dividend the remainder is zero, and the division stops. Therefore, the decimal fraction 5/10 equals 0.1 binary. We will call this approach the *binary long division method*.[3]

Representing 0.2 in Binary   Let's convert decimal 0.2 (2/10) to binary using the binary long division method. First, we divide binary 10 by binary 1010 (decimal 10):

$$
\begin{array}{r}
.0\,0\,1\,1\,0\,0\,1\,1\ (\text{etc.}) \\
1010 \overline{\left)\ 1\,0.0\,0\,0\,0\,0\,0\,0\,0\right.} \\
1\,0\,1\,0 \\
\hline
1\,1\,0\,0 \\
1\,0\,1\,0 \\
\hline
1\,0\,0\,0\,0 \\
1\,0\,1\,0 \\
\hline
1\,1\,0\,0 \\
1\,0\,1\,0 \\
\hline
\text{etc.}
\end{array}
$$

The first quotient large enough to use is 10000. After dividing 1010 into 10000, the remainder is 110. Appending another zero, the new dividend is 1100. After dividing 1010 into 1100, the remainder is 10. After appending three zeros, the new dividend is 10000. This is the same dividend we started with. From this point on, the sequence of the bits in the quotient repeats (0011. . .), so we know that an exact quotient will not be found and 0.2 cannot be represented by a finite number of bits. The SP encoded significand is 00110011001100110011001.

Converting Single-Precision Values to Decimal

The following are suggested steps when converting a IEEE SP value to decimal:

1. If the MSB is 1, the number is negative; otherwise, it is positive.

2. The next 8 bits represent the exponent. Subtract binary 01111111 (decimal 127), producing the unbiased exponent. Convert the unbiased exponent to decimal.

3. The next 23 bits represent the significand. Notate a "1.", followed by the significand bits. Trailing zeros can be ignored. Create a floating-point binary number, using the significand, the sign determined in step 1, and the exponent calculated in step 2.

4. Denormalize the binary number produced in step 3. (Shift the binary point the number of places equal to the value of the exponent. Shift right if the exponent is positive, or left if the exponent is negative.)

5. From left to right, use weighted positional notation to form the decimal sum of the powers of 2 represented by the floating-point binary number.

Example: **Convert IEEE (0 10000010 01011000000000000000000) to Decimal**

1. The number is positive.

2. The unbiased exponent is binary 00000011, or decimal 3.

3. Combining the sign, exponent, and significand, the binary number is $+1.01011 \times 2^3$.

4. The denormalized binary number is $+1010.11$.

5. The decimal value is $+10\ 3/4$, or $+10.75$.

12.1.6   Section Review

1. Why doesn't the single-precision real format permit an exponent of -127?

2. Why doesn't the single-precision real format permit an exponent of $+128$?

3. In the IEEE double-precision format, how many bits are reserved for the fractional part of the significand?

4. In the IEEE single-precision format, how many bits are reserved for the exponent?

5. Express the binary floating-point value 1101.01101 as a sum of decimal fractions.

6. Explain why decimal 0.2 cannot be represented exactly by a finite number of bits.

7. Normalize the binary value 11011.01011.

8. Normalize the binary value 0000100111101.1.

9. Show the IEEE single-precision encoding of binary $+1110.011$.

10. What are the two types of *NaN*s?

11. Convert the fraction 5/8 to a binary real.

12. Convert the fraction 17/32 to a binary real.

13. Convert the decimal value $+10.75$ to IEEE single-precision real.

14. Convert the decimal value -76.0625 to IEEE single-precision real.

12.2   Floating-Point Unit

The Intel 8086 processor was designed to handle only integer arithmetic. This turned out to be a problem for graphics and calculation-intensive software using floating-point calculations. It was possible to emulate floating-point arithmetic purely through software, but the performance penalty was severe. Programs such as *AutoCad* (by Autodesk) demanded a more powerful way to perform floating-point math. Intel sold a separate floating-point coprocessor chip named the 8087, and upgraded it along with each processor generation. With the advent of the Intel486, floating-point hardware was integrated into the main CPU and called the FPU.

12.2.1   FPU Register Stack

The FPU does not use the general-purpose registers (EAX, EBX, etc.). Instead, it has its own set of registers called a *register stack*. It loads values from memory into the register stack, performs calculations, and stores stack values into memory. FPU instructions evaluate mathematical expressions in *postfix* format, in much the same way as Hewlett-Packard calculators. The following, for example, is called an *infix expression*: (5 * 6) + 4. The postfix equivalent is

```
5  6  *  4  +
```

The infix expression **(A + B) * C** requires parentheses to override the default precedence rules (multiplication before addition). The equivalent postfix expression does not require parentheses:

```
A  B + C *
```

Expression Stack   A stack holds intermediate values during the evaluation of postfix expressions. Figure 12–2 shows the steps required to evaluate the postfix expression **5 6 * 4 –**. The stack entries are labeled ST(0) and ST(1), with ST(0) indicating where the stack pointer would normally be pointing.

Figure 12–2   Evaluating the Postfix Expression 5 6 * 4 – .

Left to Right	Stack		Action
5	5	ST (0)	push 5
5 6	5	ST (1)	push 6
	6	ST (0)	
5 6 *	30	ST (0)	Multiply ST(1) by ST(0) and pop ST(0) off the stack.
5 6 * 4	30	ST (1)	push 4
	4	ST (0)	
5 6 * 4 -	26	ST (0)	Subtract ST(0) from ST(1) and pop ST(0) off the stack.

Commonly used methods for translating infix expressions to postfix are well documented in introductory computer science texts and on the Internet, so we will skip them here. Table 12-8 contains a few examples of equivalent expressions.

Table 12-8   Infix to Postfix Examples.

Infix	Postfix
A + B	A B +
(A - B) / D	A B - D /
(A + B) * (C + D)	A B + C D + *
((A + B) / C) * (E - F)	A B + C / E F - *

FPU Data Registers

The FPU has eight individually addressable 80-bit data registers named R0 through R7 (see Figure 12–3). Together, they are called a *register stack*. A three-bit field named TOP in the FPU status word identifies the register number that is currently the top of the stack. In Figure 12–3, for example, TOP equals binary 011, identifying R3 as the top of the stack. This stack location is also known as ST(0) (or simply ST) when writing floating-point instructions. The last register is ST(7).

FIGURE 12–3   Floating-Point Data Register Stack.

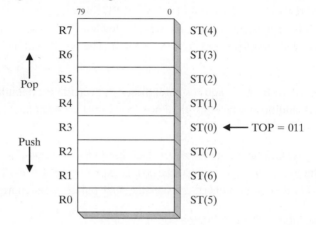

As we might expect, a *push* operation (also called *load*) decrements TOP by 1 and copies an operand into the register identified as ST(0). If TOP equals 0 before a push, TOP wraps around to register R7. A *pop* operation (also called *store*) copies the data at ST(0) into an operand, then adds 1 to TOP. If TOP equals 7 before the pop, it wraps around to register R0. If loading a value into the stack would result in overwriting existing data in the register stack, a *floating-point exception* is generated. Figure 12–4 shows the same stack after 1.0 and 2.0 have been pushed (loaded) on the stack.

FIGURE 12–4   FPU Stack after Pushing 1.0 and 2.0.

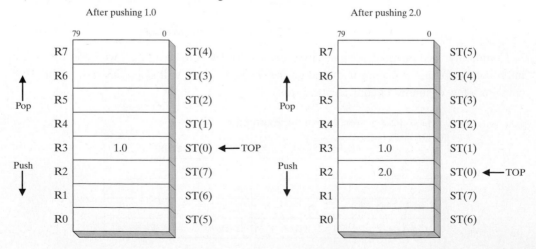

Although it is interesting to understand how the FPU implements the stack using a limited set of registers, we need only focus on the ST(*n*) notation, where ST(0) is always the top of stack. From this point forward, we refer to stack registers as ST(0), ST(1), and so on. Instruction operands cannot refer directly to register numbers.

Floating-point values in registers use the IEEE 10-byte *extended real* format (also known as *temporary real*). When the FPU stores the result of an arithmetic operation in memory, it translates the result into one of the following formats: integer, long integer, single precision (short real), double precision (long real), or packed binary-coded decimal (BCD).

Special-Purpose Registers

The FPU has six *special-purpose* registers (see Figure 12–5):

- **Opcode register:** stores the opcode of the last noncontrol instruction executed.
- **Control register:** controls the precision and rounding method used by the FPU when performing calculations. You can also use it to mask out (hide) individual floating-point exceptions.
- **Status register:** contains the top-of-stack pointer, condition codes, and warnings about exceptions.
- **Tag register:** indicates the contents of each register in the FPU data-register stack. It uses two bits per register to indicate whether the register contains a valid number, zero, or a special value (NaN, infinity, denormal, or unsupported format) or is empty.
- **Last instruction pointer register:** stores a pointer to the last noncontrol instruction executed.
- **Last data (operand) pointer register:** stores a pointer to a data operand, if any, used by the last instruction executed.

FIGURE 12–5   FPU Special-Purpose Registers.

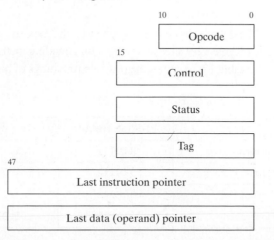

The special-purpose registers are used by operating systems to preserve state information when switching between tasks. We mentioned state preservation in Chapter 2 when explaining how the CPU performs multitasking.

12.2.2   Rounding

The FPU attempts to generate an infinitely accurate result from a floating-point calculation. In many cases this is impossible because the destination operand may not be able to accurately represent the calculated result. For example, suppose a certain storage format would only permit three fractional bits. It would permit us to store values such as 1.011 or 1.101, but not 1.0101. Suppose the precise result of a calculation produced +1.0111 (decimal 1.4375). We could either round the number up to the next higher value by adding .0001 or round it downward to by subtracting .0001:

```
(a)  1.0111 --> 1.100
(b)  1.0111 --> 1.011
```

If the precise result were negative, adding –.0001 would move the rounded result closer to –∞. Subtracting –.0001 would move the rounded result closer to both zero and +∞:

```
(a)  -1.0111 --> -1.100
(b)  -1.0111 --> -1.011
```

The FPU lets you select one of four rounding methods:

- *Round to nearest even*: The rounded result is the closest to the infinitely precise result. If two values are equally close, the result is an even value (LSB = 0).
- *Round down toward* −∞: The rounded result is less than or equal to the infinitely precise result.
- *Round up toward* +∞: The rounded result is greater than or equal to the infinitely precise result.
- *Round toward zero*: (also known as *truncation*): The absolute value of the rounded result is less than or equal to the infinitely precise result.

FPU Control Word   The FPU control word contains two bits named the *RC field* that specify which rounding method to use. The field values are as follows:

- 00 binary: Round to nearest even (default).
- 01 binary: Round down toward negative infinity.
- 10 binary: Round up toward positive infinity.
- 11 binary: Round toward zero (truncate).

Round to nearest even is the default, and is considered to be the most accurate and appropriate for most application programs. Table 12-9 shows how the four rounding methods would be applied to binary +1.0111. Similarly, Table 12-10 shows the possible roundings of binary –1.0111.

Table 12-9   Example: Rounding +1.0111.

Method	Precise Result	Rounded
Round to nearest even	1.0111	1.100
Round down toward −∞	1.0111	1.011
Round toward +∞	1.0111	1.100
Round toward zero	1.0111	1.011

Table 12-10   Example: Rounding –1.0111.

Method	Precise Result	Rounded
Round to nearest (even)	-1.0111	-1.100
Round toward −∞	-1.0111	-1.100
Round toward +∞	-1.0111	-1.011
Round toward zero	-1.0111	-1.011

12.2.3 Floating-Point Exceptions

In every program, things can go wrong, and the FPU has to deal with the results. Consequently, it recognizes and detects six types of exception conditions: Invalid operation (#I), Divide by zero (#Z), Denormalized operand (#D), Numeric overflow (#O), Numeric underflow (#U), and Inexact precision (#P). The first three (#I, #Z, and #D) are detected before any arithmetic operation occurs. The latter three (#O, #U, and #P) are detected after an operation occurs.

Each exception type has a corresponding flag bit and mask bit. When a floating-point exception is detected, the processor sets the matching flag bit. For each exception flagged by the processor, there are two courses of action:

- If the corresponding mask bit is **set**, the processor handles the exception automatically and lets the program continue.
- If the corresponding mask bit is **clear**, the processor invokes a software exception handler.

The processor's masked (automatic) responses are generally acceptable for most programs. Custom exception handlers can be used in cases where specific responses are required by the application. A single instruction can trigger multiple exceptions, so the processor keeps an ongoing record of all exceptions occurring since the last time exceptions were cleared. After a sequence of calculations completes, you can check to see if any exceptions occurred.

12.2.4 Floating-Point Instruction Set

The FPU instruction set is somewhat complex, so we will attempt here to give you an overview of its capabilities, along with specific examples that demonstrate code typically generated by compilers. In addition, we will see how you can exercise control over the FPU by changing its rounding mode. The instruction set contains the following basic categories of instructions:

- Data transfer
- Basic arithmetic
- Comparison
- Transcendental
- Load constants (specialized predefined constants only)
- x87 FPU control
- x87 FPU and SIMD state management

Floating-point instruction names begin with the letter F to distinguish them from CPU instructions. The second letter of the instruction mnemonic (often B or I) indicates how a memory operand is to be interpreted: B indicates a BCD operand, and I indicates a binary integer operand. If neither is specified, the memory operand is assumed to be in real-number format. For example, FBLD operates on BCD numbers, FILD operates on integers, and FLD operates on real numbers.

Table B-3 in Appendix B contains a reference listing of x86 floating-point instructions.

Operands   A floating-point instruction can have zero operands, one operand, or two operands. If there are two operands, one must be a floating-point register. There are no immediate operands, but certain predefined constants (such as 0.0, π, and $\log_2 10$) can be loaded into the stack. General-purpose registers such as EAX, EBX, ECX, and EDX cannot be operands. (The only exception is FSTSW, which stores the FPU status word in AX.) Memory-to-memory operations are not permitted.

Integer operands must be loaded into the FPU from memory (never from CPU registers); they are automatically converted to floating-point format. Similarly, when storing floating-point values into integer memory operands, the values are automatically truncated or rounded into integers.

Initialization (FINIT)

The FINIT instruction initializes the FPU. It sets the FPU control word to 037Fh, which masks (hides) all floating-point exceptions, sets rounding to nearest even, and sets the calculation precision to 64 bits. We recommend calling FINIT at the beginning of your programs, so you know the starting state of the processor.

Floating-Point Data Types

Let's quickly review the floating-point data types supported by MASM (QWORD, TBYTE, REAL4, REAL8, and REAL10), listed in Table 12-11. You will need to use these types when defining memory operands for FPU instructions. For example, when loading a floating-point variable into the FPU stack, the variable is defined as REAL4, REAL8, or REAL10:

```
.data
bigVal REAL10 1.212342342234234243E+864
.code
fld bigVal                    ; load variable into stack
```

Table 12-11   Intrinsic Data Types.

Type	Usage
QWORD	64-bit integer
TBYTE	80-bit (10-byte) integer
REAL4	32-bit (4-byte) IEEE short real
REAL8	64-bit (8-byte) IEEE long real
REAL10	80-bit (10-byte) IEEE extended real

Load Floating-Point Value (FLD)

The FLD (load floating-point value) instruction copies a floating-point operand to the top of the FPU stack [known as ST(0)]. The operand can be a 32-bit, 64-bit, or 80-bit memory operand (REAL4, REAL8, REAL10) or another FPU register:

```
FLD m32fp
FLD m64fp
FLD m80fp
FLD ST(i)
```

Memory Operand Types   FLD supports the same memory operand types as MOV. Here are examples:

```
.data
array REAL8 10 DUP(?)
```

```
.code
fld  array                        ; direct
fld  [array+16]                   ; direct-offset
fld  REAL8 PTR[esi]               ; indirect
fld  array[esi]                   ; indexed
fld  array[esi*8]                 ; indexed, scaled
fld  array[esi*TYPE array]        ; indexed, scaled
fld  REAL8 PTR[ebx+esi]           ; base-index
fld  array[ebx+esi]               ; base-index-displacement
fld  array[ebx+esi*TYPE array]    ; base-index-displacement, scaled
```

Example   The following example loads two direct operands on the FPU stack:

```
.data
dblOne   REAL8 234.56
dblTwo   REAL8 10.1
.code
fld  dblOne                   ; ST(0) = dblOne
fld  dblTwo                   ; ST(0) = dblTwo, ST(1) = dblOne
```

The following figure shows the stack contents after executing each instruction:

fld dblOne	ST(0)	234.56

fld dblTwo	ST(1)	234.56
	ST(0)	10.1

When the second FLD executes, TOP is decremented, causing the stack element previously labeled ST(0) to become ST(1).

FILD   The FILD (load integer) instruction coverts a 16-, 32-, or 64-bit signed integer source operand to double-precision floating point and loads it into ST(0). The source operand's sign is preserved. We will demonstrate its use in Section 12.2.10 (Mixed-Mode Arithmetic). FILD supports the same memory operand types as MOV (indirect, indexed, base-indexed, etc.).

Loading Constants   The following instructions load specialized constants on the stack. They have no operands:

- The FLD1 instruction pushes 1.0 onto the register stack.
- The FLDL2T instruction pushes $\log_2 10$ onto the register stack.
- The FLDL2E instruction pushes $\log_2 e$ onto the register stack.
- The FLDPI instruction pushes π onto the register stack.
- The FLDLG2 instruction pushes $\log_{10} 2$ onto the register stack.
- The FLDLN2 instruction pushes $\log_e 2$ onto the register stack.
- The FLDZ (load zero) instruction pushes 0.0 on the FPU stack.

Store Floating-Point Value (FST, FSTP)
The FST (store floating-point value) instruction copies a floating-point operand from the top of the FPU stack into memory. FST supports the same memory operand types as FLD. The operand

can be a 32-bit, 64-bit, or 80-bit memory operand (REAL4, REAL8, REAL10) or it can be another FPU register:

```
FST    m32fp                       FST    m80fp
FST    m64fp                       FST    ST(i)
```

FST does not pop the stack. The following instructions store ST(0) into memory. Let's assume ST(0) equals 10.1 and ST(1) equals 234.56:

```
fst    dblThree                    ; 10.1
fst    dblFour                     ; 10.1
```

Intuitively, we might have expected dblFour to equal 234.56. But the first FST instruction left 10.1 in ST(0). If our intention is to copy ST(1) into dblFour, we must use the FSTP instruction.

FSTP   The FSTP (store floating-point value and pop) instruction copies the value in ST(0) to memory and pops ST(0) off the stack. Let's assume ST(0) equals 10.1 and ST(1) equals 234.56 before executing the following instructions:

```
fstp   dblThree                    ; 10.1
fstp   dblFour                     ; 234.56
```

After execution, the two values have been logically removed from the stack. Physically, the TOP pointer is incremented each time FSTP executes, changing the location of ST(0).

The FIST (store integer) instruction converts the value in ST(0) to signed integer and stores the result in the destination operand. Values can be stored as words or doublewords. We will demonstrate its use in Section 12.2.10 (Mixed-Mode Arithmetic). FIST supports the same memory operand types as FST.

12.2.5 Arithmetic Instructions

The basic arithmetic operations are listed in Table 12-12. Arithmetic instructions all support the same memory operand types as FLD (load) and FST (store), so operands can be indirect, indexed, base-index, and so on.

Table 12-12   Basic Floating-Point Arithmetic Instructions.

FCHS	Change sign
FADD	Add source to destination
FSUB	Subtract source from destination
FSUBR	Subtract destination from source
FMUL	Multiply source by destination
FDIV	Divide destination by source
FDIVR	Divide source by destination

FCHS and FABS

The FCHS (change sign) instruction reverses the sign of the floating-point value in ST(0). The FABS (absolute value) instruction clears the sign of the number in ST(0) to create its absolute value. Neither instruction has operands:

```
FCHS
FABS
```

FADD, FADDP, FIADD

The FADD (add) instruction has the following formats, where *m32fp* is a REAL4 memory operand, *m64fp* is a REAL8 operand, and *i* is a register number:

```
FADD⁴
FADD  m32fp
FADD  m64fp
FADD  ST(0), ST(i)
FADD  ST(i), ST(0)
```

No Operands   If no operands are used with FADD, ST(0) is added to ST(1). The result is temporarily stored in ST(1). ST(0) is then popped from the stack, leaving the result on the top of the stack. The following figure demonstrates FADD, assuming that the stack already contains two values:

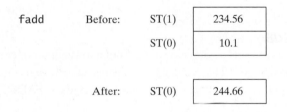

Register Operands   Starting with the same stack contents, the following illustration demonstrates adding ST(0) to ST(1):

	fadd st(1), st(0)	Before:	ST(1)	234.56
			ST(0)	10.1
		After:	ST(1)	244.66
			ST(0)	10.1

Memory Operand   When used with a memory operand, FADD adds the operand to ST(0). Here are examples:

```
fadd  mySingle              ; ST(0) += mySingle
fadd  REAL8 PTR[esi]        ; ST(0) += [esi]
```

FADDP   The FADDP (add with pop) instruction pops ST(0) from the stack after performing the addition operation. MASM supports the following format:

```
FADDP ST(i),ST(0)
```

The following figure shows how FADDP works:

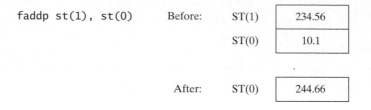

FIADD   The FIADD (add integer) instruction converts the source operand to double extended-precision floating-point format before adding the operand to ST(0). It has the following syntax:

```
FIADD   m16int
FIADD   m32int
```

Example:

```
.data
myInteger DWORD 1
.code
fiadd  myInteger                    ; ST(0) += myInteger
```

FSUB, FSUBP, FISUB

The FSUB instruction subtracts a source operand from a destination operand, storing the difference in the destination operand. The destination is always an FPU register, and the source can be either an FPU register or memory. It accepts the same operands as FADD:

```
FSUB⁵
FSUB    m32fp
FSUB    m64fp
FSUB    ST(0), ST(i)
FSUB    ST(i), ST(0)
```

FSUB's operation is similar to that of FADD, except that it subtracts rather than adds. For example, the no-operand form of FSUB subtracts ST(0) from ST(1). The result is temporarily stored in ST(1). ST(0) is then popped from the stack, leaving the result on the top of the stack. FSUB with a memory operand subtracts the memory operand from ST(0) and does not pop the stack.

Examples:

```
fsub   mySingle                 ; ST(0) -= mySingle
fsub   array[edi*8]             ; ST(0) -= array[edi*8]
```

FSUBP   The FSUBP (subtract with pop) instruction pops ST(0) from the stack after performing the subtraction. MASM supports the following format:

```
FSUBP ST(i),ST(0)
```

FISUB   The FISUB (subtract integer) instruction converts the source operand to double extended-precision floating-point format before subtracting the operand from ST(0):

```
FISUB   m16int
FISUB   m32int
```

FMUL, FMULP, FIMUL

The FMUL instruction multiplies a source operand by a destination operand, storing the product in the destination operand. The destination is always an FPU register, and the source can be a register or memory operand. It uses the same syntax as FADD and FSUB:

```
FMUL[6]
FMUL  m32fp
FMUL  m64fp
FMUL  ST(0), ST(i)
FMUL  ST(i), ST(0)
```

FMUL's operation is similar to that of FADD, except it multiplies rather than adds. For example, the no-operand form of FMUL multiplies ST(0) by ST(1). The product is temporarily stored in ST(1). ST(0) is then popped from the stack, leaving the product on the top of the stack. Similarly, FMUL with a memory operand multiplies ST(0) by the memory operand:

```
fmul  mySingle                ; ST(0) *= mySingle
```

FMULP The FMULP (multiply with pop) instruction pops ST(0) from the stack after performing the multiplication. MASM supports the following format:

```
FMULP ST(i),ST(0)
```

FIMUL is identical to FIADD, except that it multiplies rather than adds:

```
FIMUL m16int
FIMUL m32int
```

FDIV, FDIVP, FIDIV

The FDIV instruction divides a destination operand by a source operand, storing the dividend in the destination operand. The destination is always a register, and the source operand can be either a register or memory. It has the same syntax as FADD and FSUB:

```
FDIV[7]
FDIV  m32fp
FDIV  m64fp
FDIV  ST(0), ST(i)
FDIV  ST(i), ST(0)
```

FDIV's operation is similar to that of FADD, except that it divides rather than adds. For example, the no-operand form of FDIV divides ST(1) by ST(0). ST(0) is popped from the stack, leaving the dividend on the top of the stack. FDIV with a memory operand divides ST(0) by the memory operand. The following code divides **dblOne** by **dblTwo** and stores the quotient in **dblQuot**:

```
.data
dblOne    REAL8   1234.56
dblTwo    REAL8   10.0
dblQuot   REAL8   ?
.code
fld    dblOne                 ; load into ST(0)
fdiv   dblTwo                 ; divide ST(0) by dblTwo
fstp   dblQuot                ; store ST(0) to dblQuot
```

If the source operand is zero, a divide-by-zero exception is generated. A number of special cases apply when operands equal to positive or negative infinity, zero, and *NaN* are divided. For details, see the Intel Instruction Set Reference manual.

FIDIV   The FIDIV instruction converts an integer source operand to double extended-precision floating-point format before dividing it into ST(0). Syntax:

```
FIDIV   m16int
FIDIV   m32int
```

12.2.6   Comparing Floating-Point Values

Floating-point values cannot be compared using the CMP instruction—the latter uses integer subtraction to perform comparisons. Instead, the FCOM instruction must be used. After executing FCOM, special steps must be taken before using conditional jump instructions (JA, JB, JE, etc.) in logical IF statements. Since all floating-point values are implicitly signed, FCOM performs a signed comparison.

FCOM, FCOMP, FCOMPP   The FCOM (compare floating-point values) instruction compares ST(0) to its source operand. The source can be a memory operand or FPU register. Syntax:

Instruction	Description
FCOM	Compare ST(0) to ST(1)
FCOM *m32fp*	Compare ST(0) to *m32fp*
FCOM *m64fp*	Compare ST(0) to *m64fp*
FCOM ST(*i*)	Compare ST(0) to ST(*i*)

The FCOMP instruction carries out the same operations with the same types of operands, and ends by popping ST(0) from the stack. The FCOMPP instruction is the same as that of FCOMP, except it pops the stack one more time.

Condition Codes   Three FPU condition code flags, C3, C2, and C0, indicate the results of comparing floating-point values (Table 12-13). The column headings show equivalent CPU status flags because C3, C2, and C0 are similar in function to the Zero, Parity, and Carry flags, respectively.

Table 12-13   Condition Codes Set by FCOM, FCOMP, FCOMPP.

Condition	C3 (Zero Flag)	C2 (Parity Flag)	C0 (Carry Flag)	Conditional Jump to Use
ST(0) > SRC	0	0	0	JA, JNBE
ST(0) < SRC	0	0	1	JB, JNAE
ST(0) = SRC	1	0	0	JE, JZ
Unordered[a]	1	1	1	(*None*)

[a]If an invalid arithmetic operand exception is raised (because of invalid operands) and the exception is masked, C3, C2, and C0 are set according to the row marked *Unordered*.

The primary challenge after comparing two values and setting FPU condition codes is to find a way to branch to a label based on the conditions. Two steps are involved:

- Use the FNSTSW instruction to move the FPU status word into AX.
- Use the SAHF instruction to copy AH into the EFLAGS register.

Once the condition codes are in EFLAGS, you can use conditional jumps based on the Zero, Parity, and Carry flags. Table 12-13 showed the appropriate conditional jump for each combination of flags. We can infer additional jumps: The JAE instruction causes a transfer of control if CF = 0. JBE causes a transfer of control if CF = 1 or ZF = 1. JNE transfers if ZF = 0.

Example   Start with the following C++ code:

```
double X = 1.2;
double Y = 3.0;
int N = 0;
if( X < Y )
    N = 1;
```

The following assembly language code is equivalent:

```
.data
X REAL8   1.2
Y REAL8   3.0
N DWORD 0
.code
; if( X < Y )
;    N = 1
    fld    X              ; ST(0) = X
    fcomp  Y              ; compare ST(0) to Y
    fnstsw ax             ; move status word into AX
    sahf                  ; copy AH into EFLAGS
    jnb    L1             ; X not < Y? skip
    mov    N,1            ; N = 1
L1:
```

P6 Processor Improvements   One point to be made about the foregoing example is that floating-point comparisons incur more runtime overhead than integer comparisons. With this in mind, Intel's P6 family introduced the FCOMI instruction. It compares floating-point values and sets the Zero, Parity, and Carry flags directly. (The P6 family started with the Pentium Pro and Pentium II processors.) FCOMI has the following syntax:

```
FCOMI ST(0),ST(i)
```

Let's rewrite our previous code example (comparing X and Y) using FCOMI:

```
.code
; if( X < Y )
;    N = 1
    fld    Y              ; ST(0) = Y
    fld    X              ; ST(0)= X,  ST(1)= Y
    fcomi  ST(0),ST(1)    ; compare ST(0) to ST(1)
    jnb    L1             ; ST(0) not < ST(1)? skip
    mov    N,1            ; N = 1
L1:
```

The FCOMI instruction took the place of three instructions in the previous version, but required one more FLD. The FCOMI instruction does not accept memory operands.

Comparing for Equality

Almost every beginning programming textbook warns readers not to compare floating-point values for equality because of rounding errors that occur during calculations. We can demonstrate the problem by calculating the following expression: $(sqrt(2.0) * sqrt(2.0)) - 2.0$. Mathematically, it should equal zero, but the results are quite different (approximately 4.4408921E-016). We will use the following data, and show the FPU stack after every step in Table 12-14:

```
val1 REAL8 2.0
```

Table 12-14   Calculating (sqrt(2.0) * sqrt(2.0)) – 2.0.

Instruction	FPU Stack
fld val1	ST(0): +2.0000000E+000
fsqrt	ST(0): +1.4142135E+000
fmul ST(0),ST(0)	ST(0): +2.0000000E+000
fsub val1	ST(0): +4.4408921E-016

The proper way to compare floating-point values x and y is to take the absolute value of their difference, $|x - y|$, and compare it to a small user-defined value called *epsilon*. Here's code in assembly language that does it, using epsilon as the maximum difference they can have and still be considered equal:

```
.data
epsilon REAL8 1.0E-12
val2 REAL8 0.0                  ; value to compare
val3 REAL8 1.001E-13            ; considered equal to val2

.code
; if( val2 == val3 ), display "Values are equal".
    fld    epsilon
    fld    val2
    fsub   val3
    fabs
    fcomi  ST(0),ST(1)
    ja     skip
    mWrite <"Values are equal",0dh,0ah>
skip:
```

Table 12-15 tracks the program's progress, showing the stack after each of the first four instructions execute.

If we redefined val3 as being larger than epsilon, it would not be equal to val2:

```
    val3 REAL8 1.001E-12            ; not equal
```

12.2.7 Reading and Writing Floating-Point Values

Included in the book's link libraries are two procedures for floating-point input-output, created by William Barrett of San Jose State University:

• **ReadFloat**: Reads a floating-point value from the keyboard and pushes it on the floating-point stack.

Table 12-15   Calculating a Dot Product (6.0 * 2.0) + (4.5 * 3.2).

Instruction	FPU Stack
fld epsilon	ST(0): +1.0000000E-012
fld val2	ST(0): +0.0000000E+000
	ST(1): +1.0000000E-012
fsub val3	ST(0): -1.0010000E-013
	ST(1): +1.0000000E-012
fabs	ST(0): +1.0010000E-013
	ST(1): +1.0000000E-012
fcomi ST(0),ST(1)	ST(0) < ST(1), so CF=1, ZF=0

- **WriteFloat**: Writes the floating-point value at ST(0) to the console window in exponential format.

ReadFloat accepts a wide variety of floating-point formats. Here are examples:

```
35
+35.
-3.5
.35
3.5E5
3.5E005
-3.5E+5
3.5E-4
+3.5E-4
```

ShowFPUStack   Another useful procedure, written by James Brink of Pacific Lutheran University, displays the FPU stack. Call it with no parameters:

```
call ShowFPUStack
```

Example Program   The following example program pushes two floating-point values on the FPU stack, displays it, inputs two values from the user, multiplies them, and displays their product:

```
TITLE 32-bit Floating-Point I/O Test   (floatTest32.asm)

INCLUDE Irvine32.inc
INCLUDE macros.inc

.data
first  REAL8 123.456
second REAL8 10.0
third  REAL8 ?

.code
main PROC
    finit                          ; initialize FPU

; Push two floats and display the FPU stack.
    fld   first
    fld   second
    call  ShowFPUStack
```

```
; Input two floats and display their product.
      mWrite "Please enter a real number: "
      call  ReadFloat

      mWrite "Please enter a real number: "
      call  ReadFloat

      fmul  ST(0),ST(1)              ; multiply

      mWrite "Their product is: "
      call  WriteFloat
      call  Crlf

      exit
main ENDP
END main
```

Sample input/output (user input shown in bold type):

```
------ FPU Stack ------

ST(0): +1.0000000E+001

ST(1): +1.2345600E+002

Please enter a real number: 3.5

Please enter a real number: 4.2

Their product is: +1.4700000E+001
```

12.2.8 Exception Synchronization

The integer (CPU) and FPU are separate units, so floating-point instructions can execute at the same time as integer and system instructions. This capability, named *concurrency*, can be a potential problem when unmasked floating-point exceptions occur. Masked exceptions, on the other hand, are not a problem because the FPU always completes the current operation and stores the result.

When an unmasked exception occurs, the current floating-point instruction is interrupted and the FPU signals the exception event. When the next floating-point instruction or the FWAIT (WAIT) instruction is about to execute, the FPU checks for pending exceptions. If any are found, it invokes the floating-point exception hander (a subroutine).

What if the floating-point instruction causing the exception is followed by an integer or system instruction? Unfortunately, such instructions do not check for pending exceptions—they execute immediately. If the first instruction is supposed to store its output in a memory operand and the second instruction modifies the same memory operand, the exception handler cannot execute properly. Here's an example:

```
.data
intVal DWORD 25
.code
fild intVal                        ; load integer into ST(0)
inc  intVal                        ; increment the integer
```

The WAIT and FWAIT instructions were created to force the processor to check for pending, unmasked floating-point exceptions before proceeding to the next instruction. Either one solves our potential synchronization problem, preventing the INC instruction from executing until the exception handler has a chance to finish:

```
fild intVal                     ; load integer into ST(0)
fwait                           ; wait for pending exceptions
inc  intVal                     ; increment the integer
```

12.2.9   Code Examples

In this section, we look at a few short examples that demonstrate floating-point arithmetic instructions. An excellent way to learn is to code expressions in C++, compile them, and inspect the code produced by the compiler.

Expression

Let's code the expression valD = −valA + (valB * valC). A possible step-by-step solution is: Load valA on the stack and negate it. Load valB into ST(0), moving valA down to ST(1). Multiply ST(0) by valC, leaving the product in ST(0). Add ST(1) and ST(0) and store the sum in valD:

```
.data
valA REAL8 1.5
valB REAL8 2.5
valC REAL8 3.0
valD REAL8 ?; +6.0
.code
fld  valA                       ; ST(0) = valA
fchs                            ; change sign of ST(0)
fld  valB                       ; load valB into ST(0)
fmul valC                       ; ST(0) *= valC
fadd                            ; ST(0) += ST(1)
fstp valD                       ; store ST(0) to valD
```

Sum of an Array

The following code calculates and displays the sum of an array of double-precision reals:

```
ARRAY_SIZE = 20
.data
sngArray   REAL8   ARRAY_SIZE DUP(?)
.code
      mov   esi,0               ; array index
      fldz                      ; push 0.0 on stack
      mov   ecx,ARRAY_SIZE
L1:   fld   sngArray[esi]       ; load mem into ST(0)
      fadd                      ; add ST(0), ST(1), pop
      add   esi,TYPE REAL8      ; move to next element
      loop  L1

      call  WriteFloat          ; display the sum in ST(0)
```

Sum of Square Roots

The FSQRT instruction replaces the number in ST(0) with its square root. The following code calculates the sum of two square roots:

```
.data
valA REAL8 25.0
valB REAL8 36.0
.code
fld valA              ; push valA
fsqrt                 ; ST(0) = sqrt(valA)
fld valB              ; push valB
fsqrt                 ; ST(0) = sqrt(valB)
fadd                  ; add ST(0), ST(1)
```

Array Dot Product

The following code calculates the expression (array[0] * array[1]) + (array[2] * array[3]). The calculation is sometimes referred to as a *dot product*. Table 12-16 displays the FPU stack after each instruction executes. Here is the input data:

```
.data
array REAL4 6.0, 2.0, 4.5, 3.2
```

Table 12-16   Calculating a Dot Product (6.0 * 2.0) + (4.5 * 3.2).

Instruction	FPU Stack
`fld    array`	`ST(0): +6.0000000E+000`
`fmul [array+4]`	`ST(0): +1.2000000E+001`
`fld  [array+8]`	`ST(0): +4.5000000E+000`
	`ST(1): +1.2000000E+001`
`fmul [array+12]`	`ST(0): +1.4400000E+001`
	`ST(1): +1.2000000E+001`
`fadd`	`ST(0): +2.6400000E+001`

12.2.10   Mixed-Mode Arithmetic

Up to this point, we have performed arithmetic operations involving only reals. Applications often perform mixed-mode arithmetic, combining integers and reals. Integer arithmetic instructions such as ADD and MUL cannot handle reals, so our only choice is to use floating-point instructions. The Intel instruction set provides instructions that promote integers to reals and load the values onto the floating-point stack.

Example   The following C++ code adds an integer to a double and stores the sum in a double. C++ automatically promotes the integer to a real before performing the addition:

```
int N = 20;
double X = 3.5;
double Z = N + X;
```

Here is the equivalent assembly language:

```
.data
N SDWORD 20
X REAL8 3.5
```

```
Z REAL8 ?
.code
fild N                                    ; load integer into ST(0)
fadd X                                    ; add mem to ST(0)
fstp Z                                    ; store ST(0) to mem
```

Example   The following C++ program promotes N to a double, evaluates a real expression, and stores the result in an integer variable:

```
int N = 20;
double X = 3.5;
int Z = (int) (N + X);
```

The code generated by Visual C++ calls a conversion function (ftol) before storing the truncated result in Z. If we code the expression in assembly language using FIST, we can avoid the function call, but Z is (by default) rounded upward to 24:

```
fild N                                    ; load integer into ST(0)
fadd X                                    ; add mem to ST(0)
fist Z                                    ; store ST(0) to mem int
```

Changing the Rounding Mode   The RC field of the FPU control word lets you specify the type of rounding to be performed. We can use FSTCW to store the control word in a variable, modify the RC field (bits 10 and 11), and use the FLDCW instruction to load the variable back into the control word:

```
fstcw   ctrlWord                          ; store control word
or      ctrlWord,110000000000b            ; set RC = truncate
fldcw   ctrlWord                          ; load control word
```

Then we perform calculations requiring truncation, producing Z = 23:

```
fild N                                    ; load integer into ST(0)
fadd X                                    ; add mem to ST(0)
fist Z                                    ; store ST(0) to mem int
```

Optionally, we reset the rounding mode to its default (*round to nearest even*):

```
fstcw   ctrlWord                          ; store control word
and     ctrlWord,001111111111b            ; reset rounding to default
fldcw   ctrlWord                          ; load control word
```

12.2.11   Masking and Unmasking Exceptions

Exceptions are masked by default (Section 12.2.3), so when a floating-point exception is generated, the processor assigns a default value to the result and continues quietly on its way. For example, dividing a floating-point number by zero produces infinity without halting the program:

```
.data
val1    DWORD 1
val2    REAL8 0.0
.code
fild    val1                              ; load integer into ST(0)
fdiv    val2                              ; ST(0) = positive infinity
```

If you unmask the exception in the FPU control word, the processor tries to execute an appropriate exception handler. Unmasking is accomplished by clearing the appropriate bit in the FPU control word (Table 12-17). Suppose we want to unmask the divide by Zero exception. Here are the required steps:

1. Store the FPU control word in a 16-bit variable.
2. Clear bit 2 (divide by zero flag).
3. Load the variable back into the control word.

Table 12-17   Fields in the FPU Control Word.

Bit(s)	Description
0	Invalid operation exception mask
1	Denormal operand exception mask
2	Divide by zero exception mask
3	Overflow exception mask
4	Underflow exception mask
5	Precision exception mask
8–9	Precision control
10–11	Rounding control
12	Infinity control

The following code unmasks floating-point exceptions:

```
.data
ctrlWord WORD ?
.code
fstcw  ctrlWord                  ; get the control word
and    ctrlWord,1111111111111011b; unmask divide by zero
fldcw  ctrlWord                  ; load it back into FPU
```

Now, if we execute code that divides by zero, an unmasked exception is generated:

```
fild val1
fdiv val2                        ; divide by zero
fst  val2
```

As soon as the FST instruction begins to execute, MS-Windows displays the following dialog:

Masking Exceptions To mask an exception, set the appropriate bit in the FPU control word. The following code masks divide by zero exceptions:

```
.data
ctrlWord WORD ?
.code
fstcw   ctrlWord            ; get the control word
or      ctrlWord,100b       ; mask divide by zero
fldcw   ctrlWord            ; load it back into FPU
```

12.2.12 Section Review

1. Write an instruction that loads a duplicate of ST(0) onto the FPU stack.
2. If ST(0) is positioned at absolute register R6 in the register stack, what is the position of ST(2)?
3. Name at least three FPU special-purpose registers.
4. When the second letter of a floating-point instruction is B, what type of operand is indicated?
5. Which instructions accept immediate operands?
6. What is the largest data type permitted by the FLD instruction, and how many bits does it contain?
7. How is the FSTP instruction different from FST?
8. Which instruction changes the sign of a floating-point number?
9. What types of operands may be used with the FADD instruction?
10. How is the FISUB instruction different from FSUB?
11. In processors prior to the P6 family, which instruction compares two floating-point values?
12. Write a two-instruction sequence that moves the FPU status flags into the EFLAGS register.
13. Which instruction loads an integer operand into ST(0)?
14. Which field in the FPU control word lets you change the processor's rounding mode?
15. Given a precise result of 1.010101101, round it to an 8-bit significand using the FPU's default rounding method.
16. Given a precise result of −1.010101101, round it to an 8-bit significand using the FPU's default rounding method.
17. Write instructions that implement the following C++ code:

```
double B = 7.8;
double M = 3.6;
double N = 7.1;
double P = -M * (N + B);
```

18. Write instructions that implement the following C++ code:

```
int B = 7;
double N = 7.1;
double P = sqrt(N) + B;
```

12.3　x86 Instruction Encoding

To fully understand assembly language operation codes and operands, you need to spend some time looking at the way assembly instructions are translated into machine language. The topic is quite complex because of the rich variety of instructions and addressing modes available in the Intel instruction set. We will begin with the 8086/8088 processor as an illustrative example, running in real-address mode. Later, we will show some of the changes made when Intel introduced 32-bit processors.

The Intel 8086 processor was the first in a line of processors using a *Complex Instruction Set Computer* (CISC) design. The instruction set includes a wide variety of memory-addressing, shifting, arithmetic, data movement, and logical operations. Compared to RISC (*Reduced Instruction Set Computer*) instructions, Intel instructions are somewhat tricky to encode and decode. To *encode* an instruction means to convert an assembly language instruction and its operands into machine code. To *decode* an instruction means to convert a machine code instruction into assembly language. If nothing else, our walk-through of the encoding and decoding of Intel instructions will help to give you an appreciation for the hard work done by MASM's authors.

12.3.1　Instruction Format

The general x86 machine instruction format (Figure 12–6) contains an instruction prefix byte, opcode, Mod R/M byte, scale index byte (SIB), address displacement, and immediate data. Instructions are stored in little endian order, so the prefix byte is located at the instruction's starting address. Every instruction has an opcode, but the remaining fields are optional. Few instructions contain all fields; on average, most instructions are 2 or 3 bytes. Here is a quick summary of the fields:

- The **instruction prefix** overrides default operand sizes.
- The **opcode** (operation code) identifies a specific variant of an instruction. The ADD instruction, for example, has nine different opcodes, depending on the parameter types used.
- The **Mod R/M** field identifies the addressing mode and operands. The notation "R/M" stands for *register* and *mode*. Table 12-18 describes the Mod field, and Table 12-19 describes the R/M field for 16-bit applications when Mod = 10 binary.
- The **scale index byte** (SIB) is used to calculate offsets of array indexes.

Figure 12–6　x86 Instruction Format.

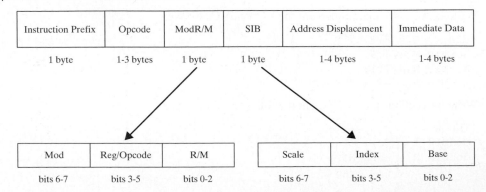

• The **address displacement** field holds an operand's offset, or it can be added to base and index registers in addressing modes such as base-displacement or base-index-displacement.
• The **immediate data** field holds constant operands.

Table 12-18   Mod Field Values.

Mod	Displacement
00	DISP = 0, disp-low and disp-high are absent (unless r/m = 110).
01	DISP = disp-low sign-extended to 16 bits; disp-high is absent.
10	DISP = disp-high and disp-low are used.
11	R/M field contains a register number.

Table 12-19   16-Bit R/M Field Values (for Mod = 10).

R/M	Effective Address
000	[BX + SI] + D16[a]
001	[BX + DI] + D16
010	[BP + SI] + D16
011	[BP + DI] + D16
100	[SI] + D16
101	[DI] + D16
110	[BP] + D16
111	[BX] + D16

[a]D16 indicates a 16-bit displacement.

12.3.2   Single-Byte Instructions

The simplest type of instruction is one with either no operand or an implied operand. Such instructions require only the opcode field, the value of which is predetermined by the processor's instruction set. Table 12-20 lists a few common single-byte instructions. It might appear that the INC DX instruction slipped into the table by mistake, but the designers of the instruction set decided to supply unique opcodes for certain commonly used instructions. As a consequence, register increments are optimized for code size and execution speed.

Table 12-20   Single-Byte Instructions.

Instruction	Opcode
AAA	37
AAS	3F
CBW	98
LODSB	AC
XLAT	D7
INC DX	42

12.3.3 Move Immediate to Register

Immediate operands (constants) are appended to instructions in little endian order (lowest byte first). We will focus first on instructions that move immediate values to registers, avoiding the complications of memory-addressing modes for the moment. The encoding format of a MOV instruction that moves an immediate word into a register is **B8 +rw dw**, where the opcode byte value is **B8 + rw**, indicating that a register number (0 through 7) is added to B8; *dw* is the immediate word operand, low byte first. (Register numbers used in opcodes are listed in Table 12-21.) All numeric values in the following examples are hexadecimal.

Table 12-21   Register Numbers (8/16 bit).

Register	Code
AX/AL	0
CX/CL	1
DX/DL	2
BX/BL	3
SP/AH	4
BP/CH	5
SI/DH	6
DI/BH	7

Example: PUSH CX   The machine instruction is **51**. The encoding steps are as follows:

1. The opcode for PUSH with a 16-bit register operand is **50.**
2. The register number for CX is 1, so add 1 to 50, producing opcode **51.**

Example: MOV AX,1   The machine instruction is **B8 01 00** (hexadecimal). Here's how it is encoded:

1. The opcode for moving an immediate value to a 16-bit register is **B8**.
2. The register number for AX is 0, so 0 is added to B8 (refer to Table 12-21).
3. The immediate operand (0001) is appended to the instruction in little endian order (01, 00).

Example: MOV BX, 1234h   The machine instruction is **BB 34 12**. The encoding steps are as follows:

1. The opcode for moving an immediate value to a 16-bit register is **B8**.
2. The register number for BX is 3, so add 3 to B8, producing opcode **BB**.
3. The immediate operand bytes are **34 12**.

For practice, we suggest you hand-assemble a few MOV immediate instructions to improve your skills, and then check your results by inspecting the code generated by MASM in a source listing file.

12.3.4 Register-Mode Instructions

In instructions using register operands, the Mod R/M byte contains a 3-bit identifier for each register operand. Table 12-22 lists the bit encodings for registers. The choice of 8-bit or 16-bit register depends on bit 0 of the opcode field: 1 indicates a 16-bit register, and 0 indicates an 8-bit register.

Table 12-22   Identifying Registers in the Mod R/M Field.

R/M	Register	R/M	Register
000	AX or AL	100	SP or AH
001	CX or CL	101	BP or CH
010	DX or DL	110	SI or DH
011	BX or BL	111	DI or BH

For example, the machine language for **MOV AX, BX** is **89 D8**. The Intel encoding of a 16-bit MOV from a register to any other operand is **89/r**, where /r indicates that a Mod R/M byte follows the opcode. The Mod R/M byte is made up of three fields (mod, reg, and r/m). A Mod R/M value of D8, for example, contains the following fields:

mod	reg	r/m
11	011	000

- Bits 6 to 7 are the *mod* field, which identifies the addressing mode. The mod field is 11, indicating that the r/m field contains a register number.
- Bits 3 to 5 are the *reg* field, which identifies the source operand. In our example, BX is register 011.
- Bits 0 to 2 are the *r/m* field, which identifies the destination operand. In our example, AX is register 000.

Table 12-23 lists a few more examples that use 8-bit and 16-bit register operands.

Table 12-23   Sample MOV Instruction Encodings, Register Operands.

Instruction	Opcode	mod	reg	r/m
mov ax,dx	8B	11	000	010
mov al,dl	8A	11	000	010
mov cx,dx	8B	11	001	010
mov cl,dl	8A	11	001	010

12.3.5   Processor Operand-Size Prefix

Let us now turn our attention to instruction encoding for x86 processors (IA-32). Some instructions begin with an operand-size prefix (66h) that overrides the default segment attribute for the instruction it modifies. The question is, why have an instruction prefix? When the 8088/8086 instruction set was created, almost all 256 possible opcodes were used to handle instructions using 8- and 16-bit operands. When Intel introduced 32-bit processors, they had to find a way to invent new opcodes to handle 32-bit operands, yet retain compatibility with older processors. For programs targeting 16-bit processors, they added a prefix byte to any instruction that used 32-bit operands. For programs targeting 32-bit processors, 32-bit operands were the default, so a prefix byte was added to any instruction using 16-bit operands. Eight-bit operands need no prefix.

Example: 16-Bit Operands We can see how prefix bytes work in 16-bit mode by assembling the MOV instructions listed earlier in Table 12-23. The .286 directive indicates the target processor for the compiled code, assuring (for one thing) that no 32-bit registers are used. Alongside each MOV instruction, we show its instruction encoding:

```
.model small
.286
.stack 100h
.code
main PROC
     mov    ax,dx              ; 8B C2
     mov    al,dl              ; 8A C2
```

(We did not use the *Irvine16.inc* file because it targets the 386 processor.)

Let's assemble the same instructions for a 32-bit processor, using the .386 directive; the default operand size is 32 bits. We will include both 16-bit and 32-bit operands. The first MOV instruction (EAX, EDX) needs no prefix because it uses 32-bit operands. The second MOV (AX, DX) requires an operand-size prefix (66) because it uses 16-bit operands:

```
.model small
.386
.stack 100h
.code
main PROC
     mov    eax,edx            ; 8B C2
     mov    ax,dx              ; 66 8B C2
     mov    al,dl              ; 8A C2
```

12.3.6 Memory-Mode Instructions

If the Mod R/M byte were only used for identifying register operands, Intel instruction encoding would be relatively simple. In fact, Intel assembly language has a wide variety of memory-addressing modes, causing the encoding of the Mod R/M byte to be fairly complex. (The instruction set's complexity is a common source of criticism by proponents of reduced instruction set computer designs.)

Exactly 256 different combinations of operands can be specified by the Mod R/M byte. Table 12-24 lists the Mod R/M bytes (in hexadecimal) for Mod 00. (The complete table can be found in the *Intel 64 and IA-32 Architectures Software Developer's Manual*, Vol. 2A.) Here's how the encoding of Mod R/M bytes works: The two bits in the **Mod** column indicate groups of addressing modes. Mod 00, for example, has eight possible **R/M** values (000 to 111 binary) that identify operand types listed in the **Effective Address** column.

Suppose we want to encode **MOV AX,[SI]**; the Mod bits are 00, and the R/M bits are 100 binary. We know from Table 12-19 that AX is register number 000 binary, so the complete Mod R/M byte is 00 000 100 binary or 04 hexadecimal:

mod	reg	r/m
00	000	100

The hexadecimal byte 04 appears in the column marked AX, in row 5 of Table 12-24.

The Mod R/M byte for **MOV [SI],AL** is the same (04h) because register AL is also register number 000. Let's encode the instruction **MOV [SI],AL**. The opcode for a move from an 8-bit register is **88**. The Mod R/M byte is 04h, and the machine instruction is **88 04**.

Table 12-24   Partial List of Mod R/M Bytes (16-bit Segments).

Byte:		AL	CL	DL	BL	AH	CH	DH	BH	
Word:		**AX**	**CX**	**DX**	**BX**	**SP**	**BP**	**SI**	**DI**	
Register ID:		**000**	**001**	**010**	**011**	**100**	**101**	**110**	**111**	
Mod	**R/M**				Mod R/M Value					**Effective Address**
00	000	00	08	10	18	20	28	30	38	[BX + SI]
	001	01	09	11	19	21	29	31	39	[BX + DI]
	010	02	0A	12	1A	22	2A	32	3A	[BP + SI]
	011	03	0B	13	1B	23	2B	33	3B	[BP + DI]
	100	04	0C	14	1C	24	2C	34	3C	[SI]
	101	05	0D	15	1D	25	2D	35	3D	[DI]
	110	06	0E	16	1E	26	2E	36	3E	16-bit displacement
	111	07	0F	17	1F	27	2F	37	3F	[BX]

MOV Instruction Examples

All the instruction formats and opcodes for 8-bit and 16-bit MOV instructions are shown in Table 12-25. Tables 12-26 and 12-27 provide supplemental information about abbreviations used in Table 12-25. Use these tables as references when hand-assembling MOV instructions. (For more details, refer to the Intel manuals.)

Table 12-25   MOV Instruction Opcodes.

Opcode	Instruction	Description
88/r	MOV eb,rb	Move byte register into EA byte
89/r	MOV ew,rw	Move word register into EA word
8A/r	MOV rb,eb	Move EA byte into byte register
8B/r	MOV rw,ew	Move EA word into word register
8C/0	MOV ew,ES	Move ES into EA word
8C/1	MOV ew,CS	Move CS into EA word
8C/2	MOV ew,SS	Move SS into EA word
8C/3	MOV DS,ew	Move DS into EA word
8E/0	MOV ES,mw	Move memory word into ES
8E/0	MOV ES,rw	Move word register into ES

Table 12-25   *(Continued)*

Opcode	Instruction	Description
8E/2	MOV SS,mw	Move memory word into SS
8E/2	MOV SS,rw	Move register word into SS
8E/3	MOV DS,mw	Move memory word into DS
8E/3	MOV DS,rw	Move word register into DS
A0 dw	MOV AL,xb	Move byte variable (offset dw) into AL
A1 dw	MOV AX,xw	Move word variable (offset dw) into AX
A2 dw	MOV xb,AL	Move AL into byte variable (offset dw)
A3 dw	MOV xw,AX	Move AX into word register (offset dw)
B0 +rb db	MOV rb,db	Move immediate byte into byte register
B8 +rw dw	MOV rw,dw	Move immediate word into word register
C6 /0 db	MOV eb,db	Move immediate byte into EA byte
C7 /0 dw	MOV ew,dw	Move immediate word into EA word

Table 12-26   Key to Instruction Opcodes.

/n:	A Mod R/M byte follows the opcode, possibly followed by immediate and displacement fields. The digit n (0–7) is the value of the reg field of the Mod R/M byte.
/r:	A Mod R/M byte follows the opcode, possibly followed by immediate and displacement fields.
db:	An immediate byte operand follows the opcode and Mod R/M bytes.
dw:	An immediate word operand follows the opcode and Mod R/M bytes.
+rb:	A register code (0–7) for an 8-bit register, which is added to the preceding hexadecimal byte to form an 8-bit opcode.
+rw:	A register code (0–7) for a 16-bit register, which is added to the preceding hexadecimal byte to form an 8-bit opcode.

Table 12-27   Key to Instruction Operands.

db	A signed value between −128 and +127. If combined with a word operand, this value is sign-extended.
dw	An immediate word value that is an operand of the instruction.
eb	A byte-sized operand, either register or memory.
ew	A word-sized operand, either register or memory.
rb	An 8-bit register identified by the value (0–7).
rw	A 16-bit register identified by the value (0–7).
xb	A simple byte memory variable without a base or index register.
xw	A simple word memory variable without a base or index register.

Table 12-28 contains a few additional examples of MOV instructions that you can assemble by hand and compare to the machine code shown in the table. We assume that **myWord** begins at offset 0102h.

Table 12-28   Sample MOV Instructions, with Machine Code.

Instruction	Machine Code	Addressing Mode
mov ax,myWord	A1 02 01	direct (optimized for AX)
mov myWord,bx	89 1E 02 01	direct
mov [di],bx	89 1D	indexed
mov [bx+2],ax	89 47 02	base-disp
mov [bx+si],ax	89 00	base-indexed
mov word ptr [bx+di+2],1234h	C7 41 02 34 12	base-indexed-disp

12.3.7   Section Review

1. Provide opcodes for the following MOV instructions:

```
.data
myByte BYTE ?
myWord WORD ?
.code
mov  ax,@data
mov  ds,ax           ; a.
mov  ax,bx           ; b.
mov  bl,al           ; c.
mov  al,[si]         ; d.
mov  myByte,al       ; e.
mov  myWord,ax       ; f.
```

2. Provide opcodes for the following MOV instructions:

```
.data
myByte BYTE ?
myWord WORD ?
.code
mov  ax,@data
mov  ds,ax
mov  es,ax           ; a.
mov  dl,bl           ; b.
mov  bl,[di]         ; c.
mov  ax,[si+2]       ; d.
mov  al,myByte       ; e.
mov  dx,myWord       ; f.
```

3. Provide Mod R/M bytes for the following MOV instructions:

```
.data
array WORD 5 DUP(?)
.code
```

```
mov  ax,@data
mov  ds,ax                    ; a.
mov  dl,bl                    ; b.
mov  bl,[di]                  ; c.
mov  ax,[si+2]                ; d.
mov  ax,array[si]             ; e.
mov  array[di],ax             ; f.
```

4. Provide Mod R/M bytes for the following MOV instructions:

```
.data
array WORD 5 DUP(?)
.code
mov  ax,@data
mov  ds,ax
mov  BYTE PTR array,5         ; a.
mov  dx,[bp+5]                ; b.
mov  [di],bx                  ; c.
mov  [di+2],dx                ; d.
mov  array[si+2],ax           ; e.
mov  array[bx+di],ax          ; f.
```

5. Assemble the following instructions by hand and write the hexadecimal machine language bytes for each labeled instruction. Assume that **val1** is located at offset 0. Where 16-bit values are used, the bytes must appear in little endian order:

```
.data
val1  BYTE   5
val2  WORD   256
.code
mov  ax,@data
mov  ds,ax                    ; a.
mov  al,val1                  ; b.
mov  cx,val2                  ; c.
mov  dx,OFFSET val1           ; d.
mov  dl,2                     ; e.
mov  bx,1000h                 ; f.
```

12.4 Chapter Summary

A binary floating-point number contains three components: a sign, a significand, and an exponent. Intel processors use three floating-point binary storage formats specified in the Standard 754-1985 for Binary Floating-Point Arithmetic produced by the IEEE organization:

- A 32-bit single precision value uses 1 bit for the sign, 8 bits for the exponent, and 23 bits for the fractional part of the significand.
- A 64-bit double-precision value uses 1 bit for the sign, 11 bits for the exponent, and 52 bits for the fractional part of the significand.
- An 80-bit double extended-precision value uses 1 bit for the sign, 16 bits for the exponent, and 63 bits for the fractional part of the significand.

If the sign bit equals 1, the number is negative; if the bit is 0, the number is positive.

The significand of a floating-point number consists of the decimal digits to the left and right of the decimal point.

Not all real numbers between 0 and 1 can be represented by floating-point numbers in a computer because there are only a finite number of available bits.

Normalized finite numbers are all the nonzero finite values that can be encoded in a normalized real number between zero and infinity. Positive infinity ($+\infty$) represents the maximum positive real number, and negative infinity ($-\infty$) represents the maximum negative real number. *NaNs* are bit patterns that do not represent valid floating-point numbers.

The Intel 8086 processor was designed to handle only integer arithmetic, so Intel produced a separate 8087 *floating-point coprocessor* chip that was inserted on the computer's motherboard along with the 8086. With the advent of the Intel486, floating-point operations were integrated into the main CPU and renamed the *Floating-Point Unit* (FPU) .

The FPU has eight individually addressable 80-bit registers, named R0 through R7, arranged in the form of a register stack. Floating-point operands are stored in the FPU stack in extended real format while being used in calculations. Memory operands are also used in calculations. When the FPU stores the result of an arithmetic operation in memory, it translates the result into one of the following formats: integer, long integer, single precision, double precision, or binary-coded decimal.

Intel floating-point instruction mnemonics begin with the letter F to distinguish them from CPU instructions. The second letter of an instruction (often B or I) indicates how a memory operand is to be interpreted: B indicates a binary-coded decimal (BCD) operand, and I indicates a binary integer operand. If neither is specified, the memory operand is assumed to be in real-number format.

The Intel 8086 processor was the first in a line of processors using a *Complex Instruction Set Computer* (CISC) design. The instruction set is large, and includes a wide variety of memory-addressing, shifting, arithmetic, data movement, and logical operations.

To *encode* an instruction means to convert an assembly language instruction and its operands into machine code. To *decode* an instruction means to convert a machine code instruction into an assembly language instruction and its operands.

The x86 machine instruction format contains an optional prefix byte, an opcode, a optional Mod R/M byte, optional immediate bytes, and optional memory displacement bytes. Few instructions contain all of the fields. The prefix byte overrides the default operand size for the target processor. The opcode byte contains the instruction's unique operation code. The Mod R/M field identifies the addressing mode and operands. In instructions using register operands, the Mod R/M byte contains a 3-bit identifier for each register operand.

12.5 Programming Exercises

★ 1. **Floating-Point Comparison**

Implement the following C++ code in assembly language. Substitute calls to WriteString for the printf() function calls:

```
double X;
double Y;
if( X < Y )
```

```
        printf("X is lower\n");
    else
        printf("X is not lower\n");
```

(Use Irvine32 library routines for console output, rather than calling the Standard C library's printf function.) Run the program several times, assigning a range of values to X and Y that test your program's logic.

★★★ **2. Display Floating-Point Binary**

(A VideoNote for this exercise is posted on the Web site.) Write a procedure that receives a single-precision floating-point binary value and displays it in the following format: sign: display + or −; significand: binary floating-point, prefixed by "**1**."; exponent: display in decimal, unbiased, preceded by the letter E and the exponent's sign. Sample:

```
    .data
    sample REAL4 -1.75
```

Displayed output:

```
-1.11000000000000000000000 E+0
```

★★ **3. Set Rounding Modes**

(Requires knowledge of macros.) Write a macro that sets the FPU rounding mode. The single input parameter is a two-letter code:

• RE: Round to nearest even
• RD: Round down toward negative infinity
• RU: Round up toward positive infinity
• RZ: Round toward zero (truncate)

Sample macro calls (case should not matter):

```
    mRound Re
    mRound rd
    mRound RU
    mRound rZ
```

Write a short test program that uses the FIST (store integer) instruction to test each of the possible rounding modes.

★★ **4. Expression Evaluation**

Write a program that evaluates the following arithmetic expression:

$$((A + B) / C) * ((D − A) + E)$$

Assign test values to the variables and display the resulting value.

★ **5. Area of a Circle**

Write a program that prompts the user for the radius of a circle. Calculate and display the circle's area. Use the ReadFloat and WriteFloat procedures from the book's library. Use the FLDPI instruction to load π onto the register stack.

★★★ 6.   Quadratic Formula

Prompt the user for coefficients a, b, and c of a polynomial in the form $ax^2 + bx + c = 0$. Calculate and display the real roots of the polynomial using the *quadratic formula*. If any root is imaginary, display an appropriate message. *(A VideoNote for this exercise is posted on the Web site.)*

★★ 7.   Showing Register Status Values

The Tag register (Section 12.2.1) indicates the type of contents in each FPU register, using 2 bits for each (Figure 12–7). You can load the Tag word by calling the FSTENV instruction, which fills in the following protected-mode structure (defined in *Irvine32.inc*):

```
FPU_ENVIRON STRUCT
      controlWord      WORD ?
      ALIGN DWORD
      statusWord       WORD ?
      ALIGN DWORD
      tagWord          WORD ?
      ALIGN DWORD
      instrPointerOffset       DWORD ?
      instrPointerSelector     DWORD ?
      operandPointerOffset     DWORD ?
      operandPointerSelector WORD ?
      WORD ?                          ; not used
   FPU_ENVIRON ENDS
```

(A structure by the same name is defined *Irvine16.inc* with a slightly different format for real-address mode programming.)

Write a program that pushes two or more values on the FPU stack, displays the stack by calling ShowFPUStack, displays the Tag value of each FPU data register, and displays the register number that corresponds to ST(0). (For the latter, call the FSTSW instruction to save the status word in a 16-bit integer variable, and extract the stack TOP indicator from bits 11 through 13.) Use the following sample output as a guide:

```
------ FPU Stack ------
ST(0): +1.5000000E+000
ST(1): +2.0000000E+000
R0   is empty
R1   is empty
R2   is empty
R3   is empty
R4   is empty
R5   is empty
R6   is valid
R7   is valid
ST(0) = R6
```

From the sample output, we can see that ST(0) is R6, and therefore ST(1) is R7. Both contain valid floating-point numbers.

Figure 12–7   Tag Word Values.

```
15                                        0
| R7 | R6 | R5 | R4 | R3 | R2 | R1 | R0 |
```

TAG values:
00 = valid
01 = zero
10 = special (NaN, unsupported, infinity, or denormal)
11 = empty

End Notes

1. *Intel 64 and IA-32 Architectures Software Developer's Manual*, Vol. 1, Chapter 4. See also http://grouper.ieee.org/groups/754/

2. *Intel 64 and IA-32 Architectures Software Developer's Manual*, Vol. 1, Section 4.8.3.

3. From Harvey Nice of DePaul University.

4. MASM uses a no-parameter FADD to perform the same operation as Intel's no-parameter FADDP.

5. MASM uses a no-parameter FSUB to perform the same operation as Intel's no-parameter FSUBP.

6. MASM uses a no-parameter FMUL to perform the same operation as Intel's no-parameter FMULP.

7. MASM uses a no-parameter FDIV to perform the same operation as Intel's no-parameter FDIVP.

13

High-Level Language Interface

13.1 Introduction
    13.1.1 General Conventions
    13.1.2 .MODEL Directive
    13.1.3 Section Review
13.2 Inline Assembly Code
    13.2.1 __asm Directive in Microsoft Visual C++
    13.2.2 File Encryption Example
    13.2.3 Section Review
13.3 Linking to C/C++ in Protected Mode
    13.3.1 Using Assembly Language to Optimize C++ Code
    13.3.2 Calling C and C++ Functions

13.3.3 Multiplication Table Example
13.3.4 Calling C Library Functions
13.3.5 Directory Listing Program
13.3.6 Section Review
13.4 Linking to C/C++ in Real-Address Mode
    13.4.1 Linking to Borland C++
    13.4.2 ReadSector Example
    13.4.3 Example: Large Random Integers
    13.4.4 Section Review
13.5 Chapter Summary
13.6 Programming Exercises

13.1 Introduction

Most programmers do not write large-scale applications in assembly language, doing so would require too much time. Instead, high-level languages hide details that would otherwise slow down a project's development. Assembly language is still used widely, however, to configure hardware devices and optimize both the speed and code size of programs.

In this chapter, we focus on the *interface*, or connection, between assembly language and high-level programming languages. In the first section, we will show how to write inline assembly code in C++. In the next section, we will link separate assembly language modules to C++ programs. Examples are shown for both protected mode and real-address mode. Finally, we will show how to call C and C++ functions from assembly language.

13.1.1 General Conventions

There are a number of general considerations that must be addressed when calling assembly language procedures from high-level languages.

First, the *naming convention* used by a language refers to the rules or characteristics regarding the naming of variables and procedures. For example, we have to answer an important question: Does the assembler or compiler alter the names of identifiers placed in object files, and if so, how?

Second, *segment names* must be compatible with those used by the high-level language.

Third, the *memory model* used by a program (tiny, small, compact, medium, large, huge, or flat) determines the segment size (16 or 32 bits), and whether calls and references will be near (within the same segment) or far (between different segments).

Calling Convention   The *calling convention* refers to the low-level details about how procedures are called. The following details must be considered:

- Which registers must be preserved by called procedures
- The method used to pass arguments: in registers, on the stack, in shared memory, or by some other method
- The order in which arguments are passed by calling programs to procedures
- Whether arguments are passed by value or by reference
- How the stack pointer is restored after a procedure call
- How functions return values to calling programs

Naming Conventions and External Identifiers   When calling an assembly language procedure from a program written in another language, external identifiers must have compatible naming conventions (naming rules). *External identifiers* are names that have been placed in a module's object file in such a way that the linker can make the names available to other program modules. The linker resolves references to external identifiers, but can only do so if the naming conventions being used are consistent.

For example, suppose a C program named *Main.c* calls an external procedure named **Array-Sum**. As illustrated in the following diagram, the C compiler automatically preserves case and appends a leading underscore to the external name, changing it to **_ArraySum**:

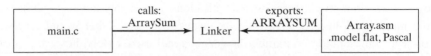

The *Array.asm* module, written in assembly language, exports the **ArraySum** procedure name as ARRAYSUM because the module uses the Pascal language option in its .MODEL directive. The linker fails to produce an executable program because the two exported names are different.

Compilers for older programming languages such as COBOL and PASCAL usually convert identifiers to all uppercase letters. More recent languages such as C, C++, and Java preserve the case of identifiers. In addition, languages that support function overloading (such as C++) use a technique known as *name decoration* that adds additional characters to function names. A function named *MySub(int n, double b)*, for example, might be exported as *MySub#int#double*.

In an assembly language module, you can control case sensitivity by choosing one of the language specifiers in the .MODEL directive (see Section 8.4.1 for details).

Segment Names   When linking an assembly language procedure to a program written in a high-level language, segment names must be compatible. In this chapter, we use the Microsoft simplified segment directives .CODE, .STACK, and .DATA because they are compatible with segment names produced by Microsoft C++ compilers.

Memory Models   A calling program and a called procedure must both use the same memory model. In real-address mode, for example, you can choose from the small, medium, compact, large, and huge models. In protected mode, you must use the flat model. We show examples of both modes in this chapter.

13.1.2   .MODEL Directive

MASM uses the .MODEL directive to determine several important characteristics of a program: its memory model type, procedure naming scheme, and parameter passing convention. The last two are particularly important when assembly language is called by programs written in other programming languages. The syntax of the .MODEL directive is

```
.MODEL memorymodel [,modeloptions]
```

MemoryModel   The *memorymodel* field can be one of the models described in Table 13-1. All of the modes, with the exception of flat, are used when programming in 16-bit real-address mode.

TABLE 13-1   Memory Models.

Model	Description
Tiny	A single segment, containing both code and data. This model is used by programs having a .com extension in their filenames.
Small	One code segment and one data segment. All code and data are near, by default.
Medium	Multiple code segments and a single data segment.
Compact	One code segment and multiple data segments.
Large	Multiple code and data segments.
Huge	Same as the large model, except that individual data items may be larger than a single segment.
Flat	Protected mode. Uses 32-bit offsets for code and data. All data and code (including system resources) are in a single 32-bit segment.

Most real-address mode programs use the small memory model because it keeps all code within a single code segment and all data (including the stack) within a single segment. As a result, we only have to manipulate code and data offsets, and the segments never change.

Protected mode programs use the flat memory model, in which offsets are 32 bits, and the code and data can be as large as 4 GByte. The Irvine32.inc file, for example, contains the following .MODEL directive:

```
.model flat,STDCALL
```

ModelOptions   The modeloptions field in the .MODEL directive can contain both a language specifier and a stack distance. The language specifier determines calling and naming conventions for procedures and public symbols. The stack distance can be NEARSTACK (the default) or FARSTACK.

Language Specifiers

Let's take a closer look at the language specifiers used in the .MODEL directive. The options
are C, BASIC, FORTRAN, PASCAL, SYSCALL, and STDCALL. The C, BASIC, FORTRAN,
and PASCAL specifiers enable assembly language programmers to create procedures that are
compatible with these languages. The SYSCALL and STDCALL specifiers are variations on the
other language specifiers.

In this book, we demonstrate the C and STDCALL specifiers. Each is shown here with the
flat memory model:

```
.model flat, C
.model flat, STDCALL
```

STDCALL is the language specifier used when calling MS-Windows functions. In this chapter
we use the C language specifier when linking assembly language code to C and C++ programs.

STDCALL

The STDCALL language specifier causes subroutine arguments to be pushed on the stack
in reverse order (last to first). Suppose we write the following function call in a high-level
language:

```
AddTwo( 5, 6 );
```

The following assembly language code is equivalent:

```
push 6
push 5
call AddTwo
```

Another important consideration is how arguments are removed from the stack after procedure
calls. STDCALL requires a constant operand to be supplied in the RET instruction. The constant
indicates the value added to ESP after the return address is popped from the stack by RET:

```
AddTwo PROC
    push    ebp
    mov     ebp,esp
    mov     eax,[ebp + 12]          ; first parameter
    add     eax,[ebp + 8]           ; second parameter
    pop     ebp
    ret     8                       ; clean up the stack
AddTwo ENDPP
```

By adding 8 to the stack pointer, we reset it to the value it had before the arguments were pushed
on the stack by the calling program.

Finally, STDCALL modifies exported (public) procedure names by storing them in the following format:

```
_name@nn
```

A leading underscore is added to the procedure name, and an integer follows the @ sign indicating the number of bytes used by the procedure parameters (rounded upward to a multiple of 4). For example, suppose the procedure **AddTwo** has two doubleword parameters. The name passed by the assembler to the linker is **_AddTwo@8**.

> The Microsoft link utility is case sensitive, so _MYSUB@8 is different from _MySub@8. To view all procedure names inside an OBJ file, use the DUMPBIN utility supplied in Visual Studio with the /SYMBOLS option.

C Specifier

The C language specifier requires procedure arguments to be pushed on the stack from last to first, like STDCALL. Regarding the removal of arguments from the stack after a procedure call, the C language specifier places responsibility on the caller. In the calling program, a constant is added to ESP, resetting it to the value it had before the arguments were pushed:

```
push  6                          ; second argument
push  5                          ; first argument
call  AddTwo
add   esp,8                      ; clean up the stack
```

The C language specifier appends a leading underscore character to external procedure names. For example:

```
_AddTwo
```

13.1.3   Section Review

1. What is meant by the *naming convention* used by a language?
2. Which memory models are available in real-address mode?
3. Will an assembly language procedure that uses the *Pascal* language specifier link to a C++ program?
4. When a procedure written in assembly language is called by a high-level language program, must the calling program and the procedure use the same memory model?
5. Why is case sensitivity important when calling assembly language procedures from C and C++ programs?
6. Does a language's calling convention include the preserving of certain registers by procedures?

13.2   Inline Assembly Code

13.2.1   __asm Directive in Microsoft Visual C++

Inline assembly code is assembly language source code that is inserted directly into high-level language programs. Most C and C++ compilers support this feature.

In this section, we demonstrate how to write inline assembly code for Microsoft Visual C++ running in 32-bit protected mode with the flat memory model. Other high-level language compilers support inline assembly code, but the exact syntax varies.

Inline assembly code is a straightforward alternative to writing assembly code in external modules. The primary advantage to writing inline code is simplicity because there are no external linking issues, naming problems, and parameter passing protocols to worry about.

The primary disadvantage to using inline assembly code is its lack of portability. This is an issue when a high-level language program must be compiled for different target platforms. Inline assembly code that runs on an Intel Pentium processor will not run on a RISC processor, for example. To some extent, the problem can be solved by inserting conditional definitions in the program's source code to enable different versions of functions for different target systems. It is easy to see, however, that maintenance is still a problem. A link library of external assembly language procedures, on the other hand, could easily be replaced by a similar link library designed for a different target machine.

The __asm Directive   In Visual C++, the **__asm** directive can be placed at the beginning of a single statement, or it can mark the beginning of a block of assembly language statements (called an *asm block*). The syntax is

```
__asm  statement

__asm {
  statement-1
  statement-2
  ...
  statement-n
}
```

(There are two underline characters before "asm.")

Comments   Comments can be placed after any statements in the asm block, using either assembly language syntax or C/C++ syntax. The Visual C++ manual suggests that you avoid assembler-style comments because they might interfere with C macros, which expand on a single logical line. Here are examples of permissible comments:

```
mov  esi,buf     ; initialize index register
mov  esi,buf     // initialize index register
mov  esi,buf     /* initialize index register */
```

Features   Here is what you can do when writing inline assembly code:
- Use most instructions in from the x86 instruction set.
- Use register names as operands.
- Reference function parameters by name.
- Reference code labels and variables that were declared outside the *asm* block. (This is important because local function variables must be declared outside the asm block.)
- Use numeric literals that incorporate either assembler-style or C-style radix notation. For example, 0A26h and 0xA26 are equivalent and can both be used.
- Use the PTR operator in statements such as **inc BYTE PTR [esi]**.
- Use the EVEN and ALIGN directives.

Limitations   You cannot do the following when writing inline assembly code:
- Use data definition directives such as DB (BYTE) and DW (WORD).
- Use assembler operators (other than PTR).
- Use STRUCT, RECORD, WIDTH, and MASK.

- Use macro directives, including MACRO, REPT, IRC, IRP, and ENDM, or macro operators (<>, !, &, %, and .TYPE).
- Reference segments by name. (You can, however, use segment register names as operands.)

Register Values   You cannot make any assumptions about register values at the beginning of an asm block. The registers may have been modified by code that executed just before the asm block. The **__fastcall** keyword in Microsoft Visual C++ causes the compiler to use registers to pass parameters. To avoid register conflicts, do not use **__fastcall** and **__asm** together.

In general, you can modify EAX, EBX, ECX, and EDX in your inline code because the compiler does not expect these values to be preserved between statements. If you modify too many registers, however, you may make it impossible for the compiler to fully optimize the C++ code in the same procedure because optimization requires the use of registers.

Although you cannot use the OFFSET operator, you can retrieve the offset of a variable using the LEA instruction. For example, the following instruction moves the offset of **buffer** to ESI:

```
lea esi,buffer
```

Length, Type, and Size   You can use the LENGTH, SIZE, and TYPE operators with the inline assembler. The LENGTH operator returns the number of elements in an array. The TYPE operator returns one of the following, depending on its target:

- The number of bytes used by a C or C++ type or scalar variable
- The number of bytes used by a structure
- For an array, the size of a single array element

The SIZE operator returns LENGTH * TYPE. The following program excerpt demonstrates the values returned by the inline assembler for various C++ types.

Microsoft Visual C++ inline assembler does not support the SIZEOF and LENGTHOF operators.

Using the LENGTH, TYPE, and SIZE Operators

The following program contains inline assembly code that uses the LENGTH, TYPE, and SIZE operators to evaluate C++ variables. The value returned by each expression is shown as a comment on the same line:

```
struct Package {
      long originZip;             // 4
      long destinationZip;        // 4
      float shippingPrice;        // 4
};

      char myChar;
      bool myBool;
      short myShort;
      int myInt;
      long myLong;
      float myFloat;
      double myDouble;
      Package myPackage;
```

```
        long double myLongDouble;
        long myLongArray[10];

    __asm {
        mov   eax,myPackage.destinationZip;

        mov   eax,LENGTH myInt;            // 1
        mov   eax,LENGTH myLongArray;      // 10

        mov   eax,TYPE myChar;             // 1
        mov   eax,TYPE myBool;             // 1
        mov   eax,TYPE myShort;            // 2
        mov   eax,TYPE myInt;              // 4
        mov   eax,TYPE myLong;             // 4
        mov   eax,TYPE myFloat;            // 4
        mov   eax,TYPE myDouble;           // 8
        mov   eax,TYPE myPackage;          // 12
        mov   eax,TYPE myLongDouble;       // 8
        mov   eax,TYPE myLongArray;        // 4

        mov   eax,SIZE myLong;             // 4
        mov   eax,SIZE myPackage;          // 12
        mov   eax,SIZE myLongArray;        // 40
    }
```

13.2.2   File Encryption Example

We will look at a short program that reads a file, encrypts it, and writes the output to another file. The **TranslateBuffer** function uses an **__asm** block to define statements that loop through a character array and XOR each character with a predefined value. The inline statements can refer to function parameters, local variables, and code labels. Because this example was compiled under Microsoft Visual C++ as a Win32 Console application, the unsigned integer data type is 32 bits:

```
    void TranslateBuffer( char * buf,
        unsigned count, unsigned char eChar )
    {
        __asm {
            mov   esi,buf
            mov   ecx,count
            mov   al,eChar
        L1:
            xor   [esi],al
            inc   esi
            loop  L1
        }   // asm
    }
```

C++ Module   The C++ startup program reads the names of the input and output files from the command line. It calls TranslateBuffer from a loop that reads blocks of data from a file, encrypts it, and writes the translated buffer to a new file:

```
    // ENCODE.CPP - Copy and encrypt a file.

    #include <iostream>
```

```
#include <fstream>
#include "translat.h"

using namespace std;

int main( int argcount, char * args[] )
{
    // Read input and output files from the command line.
    if( argcount < 3 ) {
        cout << "Usage: encode infile outfile" << endl;
        return -1;
    }

    const int BUFSIZE = 2000;
    char buffer[BUFSIZE];
    unsigned int count;            // character count

    unsigned char encryptCode;
    cout << "Encryption code [0-255]? ";
    cin >> encryptCode;

    ifstream infile( args[1], ios::binary );
    ofstream outfile( args[2], ios::binary );

    cout << "Reading" << args[1] << "and creating"
         << args[2] << endl;

    while (!infile.eof() )
    {
        infile.read(buffer, BUFSIZE);
        count = infile.gcount();
        TranslateBuffer(buffer, count, encryptCode);
        outfile.write(buffer, count);
    }
    return 0;
}
```

It's easiest to run this program from a command prompt, passing the names of the input and output files. For example, the following command line reads infile.txt and produces encoded.txt:

```
encode infile.txt encoded.txt
```

Header File   The *translat.h* header file contains a single function prototype for **Translate-Buffer**:

```
void TranslateBuffer(char * buf, unsigned count,
                     unsigned char eChar);
```

You can view this program in the book's *Examples\ch13\VisualCPP\Encode* folder.

Procedure Call Overhead

If you view the Disassembly window while debugging this program in a debugger, it is interesting to see exactly how much overhead can be involved in calling and returning from a procedure. The following statements push three arguments on the stack and call **TranslateBuffer**. In the Visual C++ Disassembly window, we activated the Show Source Code and Show

Symbol Names options:

```
; TranslateBuffer(buffer, count, encryptCode)
mov     al,byte ptr [encryptCode]
push    eax
mov     ecx,dword ptr [count]
push    ecx
lea     edx,[buffer]
push    edx
call    TranslateBuffer (4159BFh)
add     esp,0Ch
```

The following is a disassembly of **TranslateBuffer**. A number of statements were automatically inserted by the compiler to set up EBP and save a standard set of registers that are always preserved whether or not they are actually modified by the procedure:

```
push    ebp
mov     ebp,esp
sub     esp,40h
push    ebx
push    esi
push    edi

; Inline code begins here.
mov     esi,dword ptr [buf]
mov     ecx,dword ptr [count]
mov     al,byte ptr [eChar]
L1:
  xor   byte ptr [esi],al
  inc   esi
  loop L1 (41D762h)
; End of inline code.

pop     edi
pop     esi
pop     ebx
mov     esp,ebp
pop     ebp
ret
```

If we turn off the *Display Symbol Names* option in the debugger's Disassembly window, the three statements that move parameters to registers appear as

```
mov     esi,dword ptr [ebp+8]
mov     ecx,dword ptr [ebp+0Ch]
mov     al,byte ptr [ebp+10h]
```

The compiler was instructed to generate a *Debug* target, which is nonoptimized code suitable for interactive debugging. If we had selected a *Release* target, the compiler would have generated more efficient (but harder to read) code. In Section 13.3.1 we will show optimized compiler-generated code.

Omit the Procedure Call   The six inline instructions in the **TranslateBuffer** function shown at the beginning of this section required a total of 18 instructions to execute. If the function were called thousands of times, the required execution time might be measurable. To avoid this over-head, let's insert the inline code into the loop that called TranslateBuffer, creating a more efficient program:

```
while (!infile.eof() )
{
    infile.read(buffer, BUFSIZE );
    count = infile.gcount();
    __asm {
        lea esi,buffer
        mov ecx,count
        mov al,encryptCode
    L1:
        xor [esi],al
        inc  esi
        Loop L1
    } // asm
     outfile.write(buffer, count);
}
```

You can view this program in the book's *Examples\ch13\VisualCPP\Encode_Inline* folder.

13.2.3   Section Review

1. How is inline assembly code different from an inline C++ procedure?

2. What advantage does inline assembly code offer over the use of external assembly language procedures?

3. Show at least two ways of placing comments in inline assembly code.

4. *(Yes/no):* Can an inline statement refer to code labels outside the __asm block?

5. *(Yes/no):* Can both the EVEN and ALIGN directives be used in inline assembly code?

6. *(Yes/no):* Can the OFFSET operator be used in inline assembly code?

7. *(Yes/no):* Can variables be defined with both DW and the DUP operator in inline assembly code?

8. When using the __**fastcall** calling convention, what might happen if your inline assembly code modifies registers?

9. Rather than using the OFFSET operator, is there another way to move a variable's offset into an index register?

10. What value is returned by the LENGTH operator when applied to an array of 32-bit integers?

11. What value is returned by the SIZE operator when applied to an array of long integers?

13.3   Linking to C/C++ in Protected Mode

Programs written for x86 processors running in Protected mode can sometimes have bottlenecks that must be optimized for runtime efficiency. If they are embedded systems, they may have stringent memory size limitations. With such goals in mind, we will show how to write external procedures in assembly language that can be called from C and C++ programs running in

Protected mode. Such programs consist of at least two modules: The first, written in assembly language, contains the external procedure; the second module contains the C/C++ code that starts and ends the program. There are a few specific requirements and features of C/C++ that affect the way you write assembly code.

Arguments   Arguments are passed by C/C++ programs from right to left, as they appear in the argument list. After the procedure returns, the calling program is responsible for cleaning up the stack. This can be done by either adding a value to the stack pointer equal to the size of the arguments or popping an adequate number of values from the stack.

External Identifiers   In the assembly language source, specify the C calling convention in the .MODEL directive and create a prototype for each procedure called from an external C/C++ program:

```
.586
.model flat,C
AsmFindArray PROTO,
    srchVal:DWORD, arrayPtr:PTR DWORD, count:DWORD
```

Declaring the Function   In a C program, use the **extern** qualifier when declaring an external assembly language procedure. For example, this is how to declare **AsmFindArray**:

```
extern bool AsmFindArray( long n, long array[], long count );
```

If the procedure will be called from a C++ program, add a "C" qualifier to prevent C++ name decoration:

```
extern "C" bool AsmFindArray( long n, long array[], long count );
```

Name decoration is a standard C++ compiler technique that involves modifying a function name with extra characters that indicate the exact type of each function parameter. It is required in any language that supports function overloading (two functions having the same name, with different parameter lists). From the assembly language programmer's point of view, the problem with name decoration is that the C++ compiler tells the linker to look for the decorated name rather than the original one when producing the executable file.

13.3.1   Using Assembly Language to Optimize C++ Code

One of the ways you can use assembly language to optimize programs written in other languages is to look for speed bottlenecks. Loops are good candidates for optimization because any extra statements in a loop may be repeated enough times to have a noticeable effect on your program's performance.

Most C/C++ compilers have a command-line option that automatically generates an assembly language listing of the C/C++ program. In Microsoft Visual C++, for example, the listing file can contain any combination of C++ source code, assembly code, and machine code, shown by the options in Table 13-2. Perhaps the most useful is **/FAs**, which shows how C++ statements are translated into assembly language.

Table 13-2   Visual C++ Command-Line Options for ASM Code Generation.

Command Line	Contents of Listing File
/FA	Assembly-only listing
/FAc	Assembly with machine code
/FAs	Assembly with source code
/FAcs	Assembly, machine code, and source

FindArray Example

Let's create a program that shows how a sample C++ compiler generates code for a function named FindArray. Later, we will write an assembly language version of the function, attempting to write more efficient code than the C++ compiler. The following FindArray function (in C++) searches for a single value in an array of long integers:

```
bool FindArray( long searchVal, long array[], long count )
{
    for(int i = 0; i < count; i++)
    {
        if( array[i] == searchVal )
            return true;
    }
    return false;
}
```

FindArray Code Generated by Visual C++

Let's look at the assembly language source code generated by Visual C++ for the FindArray function, alongside the function's C++ source code. This procedure was compiled to a Release target with no code optimization in effect:

```
PUBLIC_FindArray
; Function compile flags: /Odtp

_TEXTSEGMENT
_i$2542 = -4                            ; size = 4
_searchVal$ = 8                         ; size = 4
_array$ = 12                            ; size = 4
_count$ = 16                            ; size = 4
_FindArray PROC

; 9    : {

    push    ebp
    mov     ebp, esp
    push    ecx

; 10   : for(int i = 0; i < count; i++)

    mov     DWORD PTR _i$2542[ebp], 0
    jmp     SHORT $LN4@FindArray
$LN3@FindArray:
    mov     eax, DWORD PTR _i$2542[ebp]
```

```
        add     eax, 1
        mov     DWORD PTR _i$2542[ebp], eax
$LN4@FindArray:
        mov     ecx, DWORD PTR _i$2542[ebp]
        cmp     ecx, DWORD PTR _count$[ebp]
        jge     SHORT $LN2@FindArray

; 11   : {
; 12   :     if( array[i] == searchVal )

        mov     edx, DWORD PTR _i$2542[ebp]
        mov     eax, DWORD PTR _array$[ebp]
        mov     ecx, DWORD PTR [eax+edx*4]
        cmp     ecx, DWORD PTR _searchVal$[ebp]
        jne     SHORT $LN1@FindArray

; 13   :             return true;

        mov     al, 1
        jmp     SHORT $LN5@FindArray
$LN1@FindArray:

; 14   : }

        jmp     SHORT $LN3@FindArray
$LN2@FindArray:

; 15   :
; 16   :             return false;

        xor     al, al
$LN5@FindArray:

; 17   : }

        mov     esp, ebp
        pop     ebp
        ret     0
_FindArray ENDP
```

Three 32-bit arguments were pushed on the stack in the following order: **count, array,** and **searchVal**. Of these three, **array** is the only one passed by reference because in C/C++, an array name is an implicit pointer to the array's first element. The procedure saves EBP on the stack and creates space for the local variable **i** by pushing an extra doubleword on the stack (Figure 13–1).

Figure 13–1   Stack Frame for the FindArray Function.

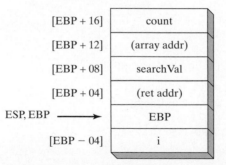

Inside the procedure, the compiler reserves local stack space for the variable **i** by pushing ECX (line 9). The same storage is released at the end when EBP is copied back into ESP (line 14). There are 14 instructions between the labels $L284 and $L285, which constitute the main body of the loop. We can easily write an assembly language procedure that is more efficient than the code shown here.

Linking MASM to Visual C++

Let's create a hand-optimized assembly language version of FindArray, named **AsmFindArray**. A few basic principles are applied to the code optimization:

• Move as much processing out of the loop as possible.
• Move stack parameters and local variables to registers.
• Take advantage of specialized string/array processing instructions (in this case, SCASD).

We will use Microsoft Visual C++ (Visual Studio) to compile the calling C++ program and Microsoft MASM to assemble the called procedure. Visual C++ generates 32-bit applications that run only in protected mode. We choose Win32 Console as the target application type for the examples shown here, although there is no reason why the same procedures would not work in ordinary MS-Windows applications. In Visual C++, functions return 8-bit values in AL, 16-bit values in AX, 32-bit values in EAX, and 64-bit values in EDX:EAX. Larger data structures (structure values, arrays, etc.) are stored in a static data location, and a pointer to the data is returned in EAX.

Our assembly language code is slightly more readable than the code generated by the C++ compiler because we can use meaningful label names and define constants that simplify the use of stack parameters. Here is the complete module listing:

```
TITLE AsmFindArray Procedure        (AsmFindArray.asm)

.586
.model flat,C

AsmFindArray PROTO,
     srchVal:DWORD, arrayPtr:PTR DWORD, count:DWORD

.code
;----------- ----------------------------------------
AsmFindArray PROC USES edi,
     srchVal:DWORD, arrayPtr:PTR DWORD, count:DWORD
;
; Performs a linear search for a 32-bit integer
; in an array of integers. Returns a boolean
; value in AL indicating if the integer was found.
;----------------------------------------------------
     true = 1
     false = 0

     mov    eax,srchVal         ; search value
     mov    ecx,count           ; number of items
     mov    edi,arrayPtr        ; pointer to array

     repne scasd                ; do the search
     jz     returnTrue          ; ZF = 1 if found
```

```
returnFalse:
    mov    al,false
    jmp    short exit

returnTrue:
    mov    al, true

exit:
    ret
AsmFindArray ENDP
END
```

Checking the Performance of FindArray

Test Program   It is interesting to check the performance of any assembly language code you write against similar code written in C++. To that end, the following C++ test program inputs a search value and gets the system time before and after executing a loop that calls FindArray one million times. The same test is performed on AsmFindArray. Here is a listing of the *findarr.h* header file, with function prototypes for the assembly language procedure and the C++ function:

```
// findarr.h

extern "C" {
    bool AsmFindArray( long n, long array[], long count );
    // Assembly language version

    bool FindArray( long n, long array[], long count );
    // C++ version
}
```

Main C++ Module   Here is a listing of *main.cpp*, the startup program that calls FindArray and AsmFindArray:

```
// main.cpp - Testing FindArray and AsmFindArray.

#include <iostream>
#include <time.h>
#include "findarr.h"
using namespace std;

int main()
{
    // Fill an array with pseudorandom integers.
    const unsigned ARRAY_SIZE = 10000;
    const unsigned LOOP_SIZE = 1000000;

    long array[ARRAY_SIZE];
    for(unsigned i = 0; i < ARRAY_SIZE; i++)
        array[i] = rand();

    long searchVal;
    time_t startTime, endTime;
    cout << "Enter value to find: ";
    cin >> searchVal;
```

```
        cout << "Please wait. This will take between 10 and 30
            seconds...\n";

    // Test the C++ function:
        time( &startTime );
        bool found = false;

        for( int n = 0; n < LOOP_SIZE; n++)
            found = FindArray( searchVal, array, ARRAY_SIZE );

        time( &endTime );
        cout << "Elapsed CPP time: " << long(endTime - startTime)
                << " seconds. Found = " << found << endl;

    // Test the Assembly language procedure:
        time( &startTime );
        found = false;

        for( int n = 0; n < LOOP_SIZE; n++)
            found = AsmFindArray( searchVal, array, ARRAY_SIZE );

        time( &endTime );
        cout << "Elapsed ASM time: " << long(endTime - startTime)
                << " seconds. Found = " << found << endl;

        return 0;
    }
```

Assembly Code versus Nonoptimized C++ Code   We compiled the C++ program to a Release (non-debug) target with code optimization turned off. Here is the output, showing the worst case (value not found):

```
Enter value to find: 55
Elapsed CPP time: 28 seconds. Found = 0
Elapsed ASM time: 14 seconds. Found = 0
```

Assembly Code versus Compiler Optimization   Next, we set the compiler to optimize the executable program for speed and ran the test program again. Here are the results, showing the assembly code is noticeably faster than the compiler-optimized C++ code:

```
Enter value to find: 55
Elapsed CPP time: 11 seconds. Found = 0
Elapsed ASM time: 14 seconds. Found = 0
```

Pointers versus Subscripts

Programmers using older C compilers observed that processing arrays with pointers was more efficient than using subscripts. For example, the following version of **FindArray** uses this approach:

```
    bool FindArray( long searchVal, long array[], long count )
    {
        long * p = array;
```

```
      for(int i = 0; i < count; i++, p++)
        if( searchVal == *p )
          return true;
      return false;
    }
```

Running this version of **FindArray** through the Visual C++ compiler produced virtually the same assembly language code as the earlier version using subscripts. Because modern compilers are good at code optimization, using a pointer variable is no more efficient than using a subscript. Here is the loop from the **FindArray** target code that was produced by the C++ compiler:

```
$L176:
    cmp   esi, DWORD PTR [ecx]
    je    SHORT $L184
    inc   eax
    add   ecx, 4
    cmp   eax, edx
    jl    SHORT $L176
```

Your time would be well spent studying the output produced by a C++ compiler to learn about optimization techniques, parameter passing, and object code implementation. In fact, many computer science students take a compiler-writing course that includes such topics. It is also important to realize that compilers take the general case because they usually have no specific knowledge about individual applications or installed hardware. Some compilers provide specialized optimization for a particular processor such as the Pentium, which can significantly improve the speed of compiled programs. Hand-coded assembly language can take advantage of string primitive instructions, as well as specialized hardware features of video cards, sound cards, and data acquisition boards.

13.3.2   Calling C and C++ Functions

You can write assembly language programs that call C++ functions. There are at least a couple of reasons for doing so:

- Input-output is more flexible under C++, with its rich iostream library. This is particularly useful when working with floating-point numbers.
- C++ has extensive math libraries.

When calling functions from the standard C library (or C++ library), you must start the program from a C or C++ main( ) procedure to allow library initialization code to run.

Function Prototypes

C++ functions called from assembly language code must be defined with the **"C"** and **extern** keywords. Here's the basic syntax:

```
extern "C" funcName( paramlist )
{ . . . }
```

Here's an example:

```
extern "C" int askForInteger( )
{
    cout << "Please enter an integer:";
    //...
}
```

Rather than modifying every function definition, it's easier to group multiple function prototypes inside a block. Then you can omit **extern** and **"C"** from the function implementations:

```
extern "C" {
    int askForInteger();
    int showInt( int value, unsigned outWidth );
    etc.
}
```

Assembly Language Module

Using the Irvine32's Link Library   If your assembly language module will be calling procedures from the Irvine32 link library, be aware that it uses the following .MODEL directive:

```
.model flat, STDCALL
```

Although STDCALL is compatible with the Win32 API, it does not match the calling convention used by C programs. Therefore, you must add the C qualifier to the PROTO directive when declaring external C or C++ functions to be called by the assembly module:

```
INCLUDE Irvine32.inc
askForInteger PROTO C
showInt PROTO C, value:SDWORD, outWidth:DWORD
```

The C qualifier is required because the linker must match up the function names and parameter lists to functions exported by the C++ module. In addition, the assembler must generate the right code to clean up the stack after the function calls, using the C calling convention (see Section 8.4.1).

Assembly language procedures called by the C++ program must use also the C qualifier so the assembler will use a naming convention the linker can recognize. The following **SetTextColor** procedure, for example, has a single doubleword parameter:

```
SetTextOutColor PROC C,
    color:DWORD
    .
    .
    .
SetTextOutColor ENDP
```

Finally, if your assembly code calls other assembly language procedures, the C calling convention requires you to remove parameters from the stack after each procedure call.

Using the .MODEL Directive   If your assembly language code does not call Irvine32 procedures, you can tell the .MODEL directive to use the C calling convention:

```
; (do not INCLUDE Irvine32.inc)
.586
.model flat,C
```

Now you no longer have to add the C qualifier to the PROTO and PROC directives:

```
askForInteger PROTO
showInt PROTO, value:SDWORD, outWidth:DWORD

SetTextOutColor PROC,
```

```
        color:DWORD
        .
        .
    SetTextOutColor ENDP
```

Function Return Values

The C++ language specification says nothing about code implementation details, so there is no standardized way for C++ functions to return values. When you write assembly language code that calls C++ functions, check your compiler's documentation to find out how their functions return values. The following list contains several, but by no means all, possibilities:

- Integers can be returned in a single register or combination of registers.
- Space for function return values can be reserved on the stack by the calling program. The function can insert the return values into the stack before returning.
- Floating-point values are usually pushed on the processor's floating-point stack before returning from the function.

The following list shows how Microsoft Visual C++ functions return values:

- **bool** and **char** values are returned in AL.
- **short int** values are returned in AX.
- **int** and **long int** values are returned in EAX.
- Pointers are returned in EAX.
- **float, double**, and **long double** values are pushed on the floating-point stack as 4-, 8-, and 10-byte values, respectively.

13.3.3   Multiplication Table Example

Let's write a simple application that prompts the user for an integer, multiplies it by ascending powers of 2 (from 2^1 to 2^{10}) using bit shifting, and redisplays each product with leading padded spaces. We will use C++ for the input-output. The assembly language module will contain calls to three functions written in C++. The program will be launched from C++.

Assembly Language Module

The assembly language module contains one function, named **DisplayTable**. It calls a C++ function named **askForInteger** that inputs an integer from the user. It uses a loop to repeatedly shift an integer named **intVal** to the left and display it by calling **showInt**.

```
; ASM function called from C++

INCLUDE Irvine32.inc

; External C++ functions:
askForInteger PROTO C
showInt PROTO C, value:SDWORD, outWidth:DWORD
newLine PROTO C

OUT_WIDTH = 8
ENDING_POWER = 10

.data
intVal DWORD ?
```

```
    .code
    ;-------------------------------------------------
    SetTextOutColor PROC C,
        color:DWORD
    ;
    ; Sets the text colors and clears the console
    ; window. Calls Irvine32 library functions.
    ;-------------------------------------------------
        mov    eax,color
        call   SetTextColor
        call   Clrscr
        ret
    SetTextOutColor ENDP

    ;-------------------------------------------------
    DisplayTable PROC C
    ;
    ; Inputs an integer n and displays a
    ; multiplication table ranging from n * 2^1
    ; to n * 2^10.
    ;-------------------------------------------------
        INVOKE askForInteger          ; call C++ function
        mov    intVal,eax             ; save the integer
        mov    ecx,ENDING_POWER       ; loop counter

    L1: push   ecx                    ; save loop counter
        shl    intVal,1               ; multiply by 2
        INVOKE showInt,intVal,OUT_WIDTH
        INVOKE newLine                ; output CR/LF
        pop    ecx                    ; restore loop counter
        loop   L1

        ret
    DisplayTable ENDP
    END
```

In DisplayTable, ECX must be pushed and popped before calling **showInt** and **newLine** because Visual C++ functions do not save and restore general-purpose registers. The **askForInteger** function returns its result in the EAX register.

DisplayTable is not required to use INVOKE when calling the C++ functions. The same result could be achieved using PUSH and CALL instructions. This is how the call to **showInt** would look:

```
    push   OUT_WIDTH               ; push last argument first
    push   intVal
    call   showInt                 ; call the function
    add    esp,8                   ; clean up stack
```

You must follow the C language calling convention, in which arguments are pushed on the stack in reverse order and the caller is responsible for removing arguments from the stack after the call.

C++ Startup Program

Let's look at the C++ module that starts the program. Its entry point is **main( )**, ensuring the execution of required C++ language initialization code. It contains function prototypes for the external assembly language procedure and the three exported functions:

```
// main.cpp

// Demonstrates function calls between a C++ program
// and an external assembly language module.

#include <iostream>
#include <iomanip>
using namespace std;

extern "C" {
    // external ASM procedures:
    void DisplayTable();
    void SetTextOutColor(unsigned color);

    // local C++ functions:
    int askForInteger();
    void showInt(int value, int width);
}

// program entry point
int main()
{
    SetTextOutColor( 0x1E );              // yellow on blue
    DisplayTable();                       // call ASM procedure
    return 0;
}

// Prompt the user for an integer.

int askForInteger()
{
    int n;
    cout << "Enter an integer between 1 and 90,000:";
    cin >> n;
    return n;
}

// Display a signed integer with a specified width.

void showInt( int value, int width )
{
    cout << setw(width) << value;
}
```

Building the Project   Our Web site (*www.asmirvine.com*) has a tutorial for building combined C++/Assembly Language projects in Visual Studio.

Program Output   Here is sample output generated by the Multiplication Table program when the user enters 90,000:

```
Enter an integer between 1 and 90,000: 90000
  180000
  360000
  720000
 1440000
 2880000
 5760000
11520000
23040000
46080000
92160000
```

Visual Studio Project Properties

If you're using Visual Studio to build programs that integrate C++ and assembly language and make calls to the Irvine32 library, you need to alter some project settings. We'll use the Multiplication_Table program as an example. Select *Properties* from the Project menu. Under *Configuration Properties* entry on the the left side of the window, select *Linker. In* the panel on the right side, enter **c:\Irvine** into the *Additional Library Directories* entry. An example is shown in Figure 13–2. Click on OK to close the Public Property Pages window. Now Visual Studio can find the Irvine32 library.

> The information here was tested in Visual Studio 2008, but is subject to change. Please see our Web site (www.asmirvine.com) for updates.

13.3.4   Calling C Library Functions

The C language has a standardized collection of functions named the *Standard C Library.* The same functions are available to C++ programs, and therefore to assembly language modules attached to C and C++ programs. Assembly language modules must contain a prototype for each C function they call. You can usually find C function prototypes by accessing the help system supplied with your C++ compiler. You must translate C function prototypes into assembly language prototypes before calling them from your program.

printf Function   The following is the C/C++ language prototype for the **printf** function, showing a pointer to character as its first parameter, followed by a variable number of parameters:

```
int printf(
   const char *format [, argument]...
);
```

Figure 13–2   Specifying the location of Irvine32.lib.

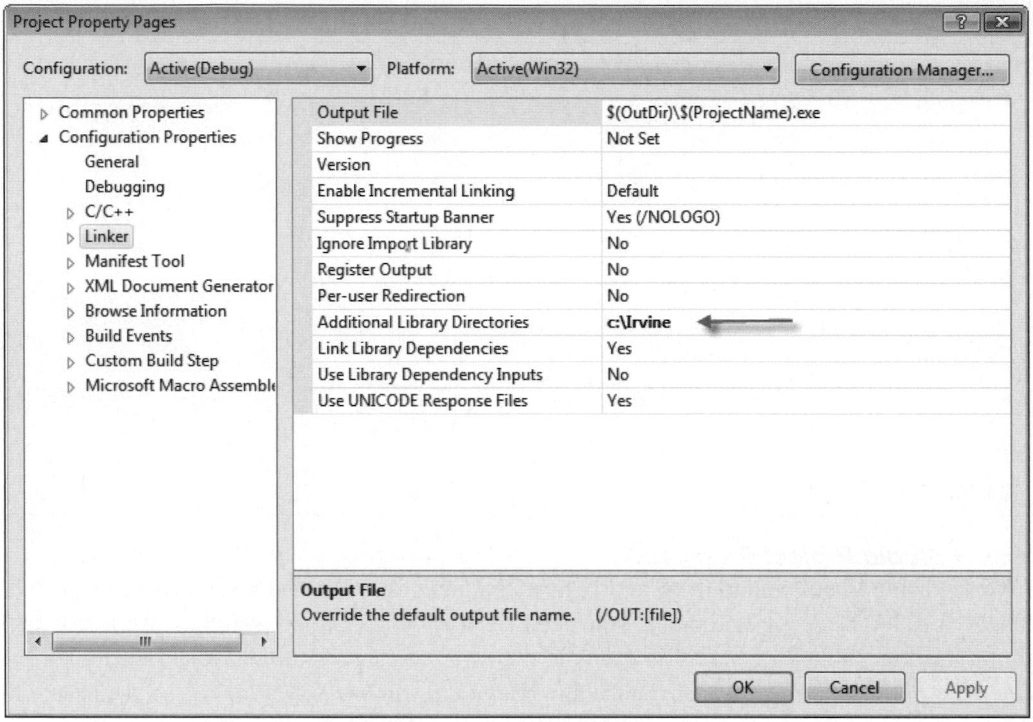

(Consult the C/C++ compiler's help library for documentation about the printf function.) The equivalent prototype in assembly language changes char * into PTR BYTE, and it changes the variable-length parameter list into the VARARG type:

```
printf PROTO C, pString:PTR BYTE, args:VARARG
```

Another useful function is **scanf**, which inputs characters, numbers, and strings from standard input (the keyboard) and assigns the input values to variables:

```
scanf PROTO C, format:PTR BYTE, args:VARARG
```

Displaying Formatted Reals with the `printf` Function

Writing assembly language functions that format and display floating point values is not easy. Rather than doing it yourself, you can take advantage of the C/C++ language **printf** function. You must create a startup module in C or C++ and link it to your assembly language code. Here's how to set up such a program in Visual C++ .NET:

1. Create a Win32 Console program in Visual C++. Create a file named *main.cpp* and insert a **main** function that calls **asmMain**:

```
extern "C" void asmMain( );

int main( )
```

```
            {
                    asmMain( );
                    return 0;
            }
```

2. In the same folder as main.cpp, create an assembly language module named *asmMain.asm*. It should contain a procedure named **asmMain**, declared with the C calling convention:

```
            TITLE asmMain.asm
            .386
            .model flat,stdcall
            .stack 2000
            .code
            asmMain PROC C

                    ret
            asmMain ENDP
            END
```

3. Assemble *asmMain.asm* (but do not link), producing *asmMain.obj*.
4. Add *asmMain.obj* to the C++ project.
5. Build and run the project. If you modify *asmMain.asm*, assemble it again and rebuild the project before running it again.

Once your program has been set up properly, you can add code to asmMain.asm that calls C/C++ language functions.

Displaying Double-Precision Values   The following assembly language code in **asmMain** prints a REAL8 by calling printf:

```
            .data
            double1 REAL8   1234567.890123
            formatStr BYTE "%.3f",0dh,0ah,0
            .code
            INVOKE printf, ADDR formatStr, double1
```

This is the corresponding output:

```
1234567.890
```

The format string passed to **printf** here is a little different than it would be in C++. Rather than embedding escape characters such as \n, you must insert ASCII codes (0dh, 0ah).

> Floating-point arguments passed to printf should be declared type REAL8. Although it is possible to pass values of type REAL4, a fair amount of clever programming is required. You can see how your C++ compiler does it by declaring a variable of type float and passing it to printf. Compile the program and trace the program's disassembled code with a debugger.

Multiple Arguments   The printf function accepts a variable number of arguments, so we can just as easily format and display two numbers in one function call:

```
            TAB = 9
            .data
```

```
formatTwo BYTE "%.2f",TAB,"%.3f",0dh,0ah,0
val1 REAL8 456.789
val2 REAL8 864.231
.code
INVOKE printf, ADDR formatTwo, val1, val2
```

This is the corresponding output:

```
456.79   864.231
```

(See the project named **Printf_Example** in the Examples\ch13\VisualCPP folder on the book's CD-ROM.)

Entering Reals with the `scanf` Function

You can call **scanf** to input floating-point values from the user. The following prototype is defined in SmallWin.inc (included by Irvine32.inc):

```
scanf PROTO C,
      format:PTR BYTE, args:VARARG
```

Pass it the offset of a format string and the offsets of one or more REAL4 or REAL8 variables to hold values entered by the user. Sample calls:

```
.data
strSingle BYTE "%f",0
strDouble BYTE "%lf",0
single1 REAL4 ?
double1 REAL8 ?
.code
INVOKE scanf, ADDR strSingle, ADDR single1
INVOKE scanf, ADDR strDouble, ADDR double1
```

You must invoke your assembly language code from a C or C++ startup program.

13.3.5 Directory Listing Program

Let's write a short program that clears the screen, displays the current disk directory, and asks the user to enter a filename. (You might want to extend this program so it opens and displays the selected file.)

C++ Stub Module   The C++ module contains only a call to **asm_main**, so we can call it a *stub module*:

```
// main.cpp
// stub module: launches assembly language program

extern "C" void asm_main();        // asm startup proc

void main()
{
    asm_main();
}
```

ASM Module   The assembly language module contains the function prototypes, several strings, and a **fileName** variable. It calls the **system** function twice, passing it "cls" and "dir" commands.

Then **printf** is called, displaying a prompt for a filename, and **scanf** is called so the user can input the name. It does not make any calls to the Irvine32 library, so we can set the .MODEL directive to the C language convention:

```
; ASM program launched from C++        (asmMain.asm)
.586
.MODEL flat,C

; Standard C library functions:
system PROTO, pCommand:PTR BYTE
printf PROTO, pString:PTR BYTE, args:VARARG
scanf  PROTO, pFormat:PTR BYTE,pBuffer:PTR BYTE, args:VARARG
fopen  PROTO, mode:PTR BYTE, filename:PTR BYTE
fclose PROTO, pFile:DWORD

BUFFER_SIZE = 5000
.data
str1 BYTE "cls",0
str2 BYTE "dir/w",0
str3 BYTE "Enter the name of a file:",0
str4 BYTE "%s",0
str5 BYTE "cannot open file",0dh,0ah,0
str6 BYTE "The file has been opened",0dh,0ah,0
modeStr BYTE "r",0

fileName BYTE 60 DUP(0)
pBuf  DWORD ?
pFile DWORD ?

.code
asm_main PROC

    ; clear the screen, display disk directory
    INVOKE system,ADDR str1
    INVOKE system,ADDR str2

    ; ask for a filename
    INVOKE printf,ADDR str3
    INVOKE scanf, ADDR str4, ADDR filename

    ; try to open the file
    INVOKE fopen, ADDR fileName, ADDR modeStr
    mov    pFile,eax

    .IF eax == 0                    ; cannot open file?
       INVOKE printf,ADDR str5
    jmp quit
    .ELSE
       INVOKE printf,ADDR str6
    .ENDIF
    .
    ; Close the file
    INVOKE fclose, pFile
```

```
quit:
      ret                              ; return to C++ main
asm_main ENDP
END
```

The **scanf** function requires two arguments: the first is a pointer to a format string ("%s"), and the second is a pointer to the input string variable (**fileName**). We will not take the time to explain standard C functions because there is ample documentation on the Web. An excellent reference is Brian W. Kernighan and Dennis M. Ritchie, *The C Programming Language,* 2nd Ed., Prentice Hall, 1988.

13.3.6 Section Review

1. Which two C++ keywords must be included in a function definition if the function will be called from an assembly language module?

2. In what way is the calling convention used by the Irvine32 library not compatible with the calling convention used by the C and C++ languages?

3. How do C++ functions usually return floating-point values?

4. How does a Microsoft Visual C++ function return a **short int**?

5. What is a valid assembly language PROTO declaration for the standard C printf( ) function?

6. When the following C language function is called, will the argument **x** be pushed on the stack first or last?

   ```
   void MySub( x, y, z );
   ```

7. What is the purpose of the "C" specifier in the *extern* declaration in procedures called from C++?

8. Why is name decoration important when calling external assembly language procedures from C++?

9. In this chapter, when an optimizing C++ compiler was used, what differences in code generation occurred between the loop coded with array subscripts and the loop coded with pointer variables?

13.4 Linking to C/C++ in Real-Address Mode

Many embedded systems applications continue to be written for 16-bit environments, using the Intel 8086 and 8088 processors. In addition, some applications use 32-bit processors running in real-address mode. It is important, therefore, for us to show examples of assembly language subroutines called from C and C++ in real-mode environments.

The sample programs in this section use the 16-bit version of Borland C++ 5.01 and select Windows 98 (MS-DOS window) as the target operating system with a small memory model. We will use Borland TASM 4.0 as the assembler for these examples because most users of Borland C++ are likely to use Turbo Assembler rather than MASM. We will also create 16-bit real mode applications using Borland C++ 5.01 and demonstrate both small and large memory model programs, showing how to call both near and far procedures.

13.4.1 Linking to Borland C++

Function Return Values In Borland C++, functions return 16-bit values in AX and 32-bit values in DX:AX. Larger data structures (structure values, arrays, etc.) are stored in a static data location, and a pointer to the data is returned in AX. (In medium, large, and huge memory model programs, a 32-bit pointer is returned in DX:AX.)

Setting Up a Project In the Borland C++ integrated development environment (IDE), create a new project. Create a source code module (CPP file), and enter the code for the main C++ program. Create the ASM file containing the procedure you plan to call. Use TASM to assemble the program into an object module, either from the DOS command line or from the Borland C++ IDE, using its transfer capability. The filename (minus the extension) must be eight characters or less; otherwise its name will not be recognized by the 16-bit linker.

If you have assembled the ASM module separately, add the object file created by the assembler to the C++ project. Invoke the MAKE or BUILD command from the menu. It compiles the CPP file, and if there are no errors, it links the two object modules to produce an executable program. Suggestion: Limit the name of the CPP source file to eight characters, otherwise the Turbo Debugger for DOS will not be able to find it when you debug the program.

Debugging The Borland C++ compiler does not allow the DOS debugger to be run from the IDE. Instead, you need to run Turbo Debugger for DOS either from the DOS prompt or from the Windows desktop. Using the debugger's File/Open menu command, select the executable file created by the C++ linker. The C++ source code file should immediately display, and you can begin tracing and running the program.

Saving Registers Assembly procedures called by Borland C++ must preserve the values of BP, DS, SS, SI, DI, and the Direction flag.

Storage Sizes A 16-bit Borland C++ program uses specific storage sizes for all its data types. These are unique to this particular implementation and must be adjusted for every C++ compiler. Refer to Table 13-3.

Table 13-3 Borland C++ Data Types in 16-Bit Applications.

C++ Type	Storage Bytes	ASM Type
char, unsigned char	1	byte
int, unsigned int, short int	2	word
enum	2	word
long, unsigned long	4	dword
float	4	dword
double	8	qword
long double	10	tbyte
near pointer	2	word
far pointer	4	dword

13.4.2 ReadSector Example

(Must be run under MS-DOS, Windows 95, 98, or Millenium.) Let's begin with a Borland C++ program that calls an external assembly language procedure called **ReadSector**. C++ compilers generally do not include library functions for reading disk sectors because such details are too hardware-dependent, and it would be impractical to implement libraries for all possible computers. Assembly language programs can easily read disk sectors by calling INT 21h Function 7305h (see Section 15.4 for details). Our present task, then, is to create the interface between assembly language and C++ that combines the strengths of both languages.

The **ReadSector** example requires the use of a 16-bit compiler because it involves calling MS-DOS interrupts. (Calling 16-bit interrupts from 32-bit programs is possible, but it is beyond the scope of this book.) The last version of Visual C++ to produce 16-bit programs was version 1.5. Other compilers that produce 16-bit code are Turbo C and Turbo Pascal, both by Borland.

Program Execution   First, we will demonstrate the program's execution. When the C++ program starts up, the user selects the drive number, starting sector, and number of sectors to read. For example, this user wants to read sectors 0 to 20 from drive A:

```
Sector display program.
Enter drive number [1=A, 2=B, 3=C, 4=D, 5=E,...]: 1
Starting sector number to read: 0
Number of sectors to read: 20
```

This information is passed to the assembly language procedure, which reads the sectors into a buffer. The C++ program begins to display the buffer, one sector at a time. As each sector is displayed, non-ASCII characters are replaced by dots. For example, the following is the program's display of sector 0 from drive A:

```
Reading sectors 0 - 20 from Drive 1
Sector 0 ------------------------------------------------------
.<.(P3j2IHC........@.................)Y...MYDISK    FAT12   .3.
....{...x..v..V.U."..~..N..........|.E...F..E.8N$}"....w.r...:f..
|f;..W.u.....V....s.3..F...f..F..V..F....v.`.F..V.. ....^...H...F
..N.a....#.r98-t.`....}..at9Nt... ;.r.....}.......t.<.t.........
..}....}.....^.f......}.}..E..N....F..V......r....p..B.-`fj.RP.Sj
.j...t...3..v...v.B...v.............V$...d.ar.@u.B.^.Iuw....'..I
nvalid system disk...Disk I/O error...Replace the disk, and then
press any key....IOSYSMSDOS    SYS...A....~...@...U.
```

Sectors continue to be displayed, one by one, until the entire buffer has been displayed.

C++ Program Calls ReadSector

We can now show the complete C++ program that calls the **ReadSector** procedure:

```cpp
// main.cpp -  Calls the ReadSector Procedure

#include <iostream.h>
#include <conio.h>
#include <stdlib.h>
const int SECTOR_SIZE = 512;
```

```cpp
extern "C" ReadSector( char * buffer, long startSector,
        int driveNum, int numSectors );

void DisplayBuffer( const char * buffer, long startSector,
    int numSectors )
{
  int n = 0;
  long last = startSector + numSectors;
  for(long sNum = startSector; sNum < last; sNum++)
  {
    cout << "\nSector " << sNum
        << " --------------------------"
        << "--------------------------\n";
    for(int i = 0; i < SECTOR_SIZE; i++)
    {
      char ch = buffer[n++];
      if( unsigned(ch) < 32 || unsigned(ch) > 127)
        cout << '.';
      else
        cout << ch;
    }
    cout << endl;
    getch();                // pause - wait for keypress
  }
}

int main()
{
  char * buffer;
  long startSector;
  int driveNum;
  int numSectors;

  system("CLS");
  cout << "Sector display program.\n\n"
      << "Enter drive number [1=A, 2=B, 3=C, 4=D, 5=E,...]:";
  cin >> driveNum;
  cout << "Starting sector number to read: ";
  cin >> startSector;
  cout << "Number of sectors to read:";
  cin >> numSectors;
  buffer = new char[numSectors * SECTOR_SIZE];

  cout << "\n\nReading sectors" << startSector << " - "
      << (startSector + numSectors) << "from Drive"
      << driveNum << endl;

  ReadSector( buffer, startSector, driveNum, numSectors );
  DisplayBuffer( buffer, startSector, numSectors );
  system("CLS");
  return 0;
}
```

At the top of the listing, we find the declaration, or prototype, of the **ReadSector** function:

```
extern "C" ReadSector( char buffer[], long startSector,
        int driveNum, int numSectors );
```

The first parameter, *buffer*, is a character array holding the sector data after it has been read from the disk. The second parameter, *startSector*, is the starting sector number to read. The third parameter, *driveNum*, is the disk drive number. The fourth parameter, *numSectors*, specifies the number of sectors to read. The first parameter is passed by reference, and all other parameters are passed by value.

In **main**, the user is prompted for the drive number, starting sector, and number of sectors. The program also dynamically allocates storage for the buffer that holds the sector data:

```
cout << "Sector display program.\n\n"
     << "Enter drive number [1=A, 2=B, 3=C, 4=D, 5=E,...]: ";
cin >> driveNum;
cout << "Starting sector number to read:";
cin >> startSector;
cout << "Number of sectors to read:";
cin >> numSectors;
buffer = new char[numSectors * SECTOR_SIZE];
```

This information is passed to the external **ReadSector** procedure, which fills the buffer with sectors from the disk:

```
ReadSector( buffer, startSector, driveNum, numSectors );
```

The buffer is passed to **DisplayBuffer**, a procedure in the C++ program that displays each sector in ASCII text format:

```
DisplayBuffer( buffer, startSector, numSectors );
```

Assembly Language Module

The assembly language module containing the **ReadSector** procedure is shown here. Because this is a real-mode application, the .386 directive must appear after the .MODEL directive to tell the assembler to create 16-bit segments:

```
TITLE Reading Disk Sectors          (ReadSec.asm)

; The ReadSector procedure is called from a 16-bit
; real-mode application written in Borland C++ 5.01.
; It can read FAT12, FAT16, and FAT32 disks under
; MS-DOS, Windows 95, Windows 98, and Windows Me.

Public _ReadSector
.model small
.386

DiskIO STRUC
      strtSector  DD ?              ; starting sector number
      nmSectors   DW 1              ; number of sectors
      bufferOfs   DW ?              ; buffer offset
      bufferSeg   DW ?              ; buffer segment
```

```
DiskIO ENDS
.data
diskStruct DiskIO <>
.code
;-------------------------------------------------------------
_ReadSector PROC NEAR C
 ARG bufferPtr:WORD, startSector:DWORD, driveNumber:WORD, \
    numSectors:WORD
;
; Read n sectors from a specified disk drive.
; Receives: pointer to buffer that will hold the sector,
;   data, starting sector number, drive number,
;   and number of sectors.
; Returns: nothing
;-------------------------------------------------------------
       enter 0,0
       pusha
       mov   eax,startSector
       mov   diskStruct.strtSector,eax
       mov   ax,numSectors
       mov   diskStruct.nmSectors,ax
       mov   ax,bufferPtr
       mov   diskStruct.bufferOfs,ax
       push ds
       pop  diskStruct.bufferSeg

       mov   ax,7305h              ; ABSDiskReadWrite
       mov   cx,0FFFFh             ; must be 0FFFFh
       mov   dx,driveNumber        ; drive number
       mov   bx,OFFSET diskStruct  ; sector number
       mov   si,0                  ; read mode
       int   21h                   ; read disk sector
       popa
       leave
       ret
_ReadSector ENDP
END
```

Because Borland Turbo Assembler was used to code this example, we use Borland's ARG keyword to specify the procedure arguments. The ARG directive allows you to specify the arguments in the same order as the corresponding C++ function declaration:

```
ASM:      _ReadSector PROC near C
          ARG bufferPtr:word, startSector:dword, \
             driveNumber:word, numSectors:word

C++:      extern "C" ReadSector(char buffer[],
             long startSector, int driveNum,
             int numSectors);
```

The arguments are pushed on the stack in reverse order, following the C calling convention. Farthest away from EBP is **numSectors**, the first parameter pushed on the stack, shown in the stack frame of Figure 13–3. **StartSector** is a 32-bit doubleword and occupies locations [bp+6] through [bp+09] on the stack. The program was compiled for the small memory model, so **buffer** is passed as a 16-bit near pointer.

Figure 13–3   ReadSector Procedure, Stack Frame.

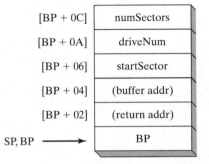

[BP + 0C]	numSectors
[BP + 0A]	driveNum
[BP + 06]	startSector
[BP + 04]	(buffer addr)
[BP + 02]	(return addr)
SP, BP →	BP

13.4.3   Example: Large Random Integers

To show a useful example of calling an external function from Borland C++, we can call **Long-Random**, an assembly language function that returns a pseudorandom unsigned 32-bit integer. This is useful because the standard rand() function in the Borland C++ library only returns an integer between 0 and RAND_MAX (32,767). Our procedure returns an integer between 0 and 4,294,967,295.

This program is compiled in the large memory model, allowing the data to be larger than 64K, and requiring that 32-bit values be used for the return address and data pointer values. The external function declaration in C++ is

```
extern "C" unsigned long LongRandom();
```

The listing of the main program is shown here. The program allocates storage for an array called **rArray**. It uses a loop to call **LongRandom**, inserts each number in the array, and writes the number to standard output:

```
// main.cpp

// Calls the external LongRandom function, written in
// assembly language, that returns an unsigned 32-bit
// random integer. Compile in the Large memory model.

#include <iostream.h>
extern "C" unsigned long LongRandom();
const int ARRAY_SIZE = 500;

int main()
{
  // Allocate array storage, fill with 32-bit
  // unsigned random integers, and display:

  unsigned long * rArray = new unsigned long[ARRAY_SIZE];
```

```
    for(unsigned i = 0; i < ARRAY_SIZE; i++)
    {
      rArray[i] = LongRandom();
      cout << rArray[i] << ',';
    }
    cout << endl;
    return 0;
}
```

The LongRandom Function   The assembly language module containing the **LongRandom** function is a simple adaptation of the **Random32** procedure from the book's link library:

```
; LongRandom procedure module                    (longrand.asm)
.model large
.386
Public _LongRandom
.data
seed  DWORD 12345678h

; Return an unsigned pseudorandom 32-bit integer
; in DX:AX, in the range 0 - FFFFFFFFh.
.code
_LongRandom  PROC far, C
      mov    eax, 343FDh
      mul    seed
      xor    edx,edx
      add    eax, 269EC3h
      mov    seed, eax          ; save the seed for next call
      ror    eax,8              ; rotate out the lowest digit
      shld   edx,eax,16         ; copy high 16 bits of EAX to DX
      ret
_LongRandom  ENDP
end
```

The ROR instruction helps to eliminate recurring patterns when small random integers are generated. Borland C++ expects the 32-bit function return value to be in the DX:AX registers, so we copy the high 16-bits from EAX into DX with the SHLD instruction, which seems conveniently designed for the task.

13.4.4   Section Review

1. Which registers and flags must be preserved by assembly language procedures called from Borland C++?

2. In Borland C++, how many bytes are used by the following types? 1) int, 2) enum, 3) float, 4) double.

3. In the ReadSector module in this section, if the ARG directive were not used, how would you code the following statement?

   ```
   mov   eax,startSector
   ```

4. In the **LongRandom** function shown in this section, what would happen to the output if the ROR instruction were eliminated?

13.5   Chapter Summary

Assembly language is the perfect tool for optimizing selected parts of a large application written in some high-level language. Assembly language is also a good tool for customizing certain procedures for specific hardware. These techniques require one of two approaches:

• Write inline assembly code embedded within high-level language code.

• Link assembly language procedures to high-level language code.

Both approaches have their merits and their limitations. In this chapter, we presented both approaches.

The naming convention used by a language refers to the way segments and modules are named, as well as rules or characteristics regarding the naming of variables and procedures. The memory model used by a program determines whether calls and references will be near (within the same segment) or far (between different segments).

When calling an assembly language procedure from a program written in another language, any identifiers that are shared between the two languages must be compatible. You must also use segment names in the procedure that are compatible with the calling program. The writer of a procedure uses the high-level language's calling convention to determine how to receive parameters. The calling convention affects whether the stack pointer must be restored by the called procedure or by the calling program.

In Visual C++, the __asm directive is used for writing inline assembly code in a C++ source program. In this chapter, a File Encryption program was used to demonstrate inline assembly language.

This chapter showed how to link assembly language procedures to Microsoft Visual C++ programs running in protected mode and Borland C++ programs running in real-address mode.

When calling functions from the Standard C (C++) library, create a stub program in C or C++ containing a main( ) function. When main( ) starts, the compiler's runtime library is automatically initialized. From main( ), you can call a startup procedure in the assembly language module. The assembly language module can call any function from the C Standard Library.

A procedure named **FindArray** was written in assembly language and called from a Visual C++ program. We compared the assembly language source file generated by the compiler to hand-assembled code in our efforts to learn more about code optimization techniques. The **ReadSector** program showed a Borland C++ program running in real-address mode that calls an assembly language procedure to read disk sectors.

13.6   Programming Exercises

★ 1.   MultArray Example

Use the FindArray example from Section 13.3.1 as a model for this exercise. Write an assembly language procedure named MultArray that multiplies a doubleword array by an integer. Write the same function in C++. Create a test program that calls both versions of MultArray from loops and compares their execution times.

★★ **2. ReadSector, Hexadecimal Display**

(Requires a 16-bit real-mode C++ compiler, running under MS-DOS, Windows 95, 98, or Millenium.) Add a new procedure to the C++ program in Section 13.4.2 that calls the **ReadSector** procedure. This new procedure should display each sector in hexadecimal. Use iomanip.setfill( ) to pad each output byte with a leading zero.

★★ **3. LongRandomArray Procedure**

Using the **LongRandom** procedure in Section 13.4.3 as a starting point, create a procedure called **LongRandomArray** that fills an array with 32-bit unsigned random integers. Pass an array pointer from a C or C++ program, along with a count indicating the number of array elements to be filled:

```
extern "C" void LongRandomArray( unsigned long * buffer,
     unsigned count );
```

★ **4. External TranslateBuffer Procedure**

Write an external procedure in assembly language that performs the same type of encryption shown in the inline **TranslateBuffer** procedure from Section 13.2.2. Run the compiled program in the debugger, and judge whether this version runs any faster than the *Encode.cpp* program from Section 13.2.2.

★★ **5. Prime Number Program**

Write an assembly language procedure that returns a value of 1 if the 32-bit integer passed in the EAX register is prime, and 0 if EAX is nonprime. Call this procedure from a high-level language program. Let the user input some very large numbers, and have your program display a message for each one indicating whether or not it is prime.

★★ **6. FindRevArray Procedure**

Modify the **FindArray** procedure from Section 13.3.1. Name your function **FindRevArray**, and let it search backward from the end of the array. Return the index of the first matching value, or if no match is found, return −1.

14

16-Bit MS-DOS Programming

14.1 MS-DOS and the IBM-PC
    14.1.1 Memory Organization
    14.1.2 Redirecting Input-Output
    14.1.3 Software Interrupts
    14.1.4 INT Instruction
    14.1.5 Coding for 16-Bit Programs
    14.1.6 Section Review

14.2 MS-DOS Function Calls (INT 21h)
    14.2.1 Selected Output Functions
    14.2.2 Hello World Program Example
    14.2.3 Selected Input Functions
    14.2.4 Date/Time Functions
    14.2.5 Section Review

14.3 Standard MS-DOS File I/O Services
    14.3.1 Create or Open File (716Ch)
    14.3.2 Close File Handle (3Eh)
    14.3.3 Move File Pointer (42h)
    14.3.4 Get File Creation Date and Time
    14.3.5 Selected Library Procedures
    14.3.6 Example: Read and Copy a Text File
    14.3.7 Reading the MS-DOS Command Tail
    14.3.8 Example: Creating a Binary File
    14.3.9 Section Review

14.4 Chapter Summary

14.5 Programming Exercises

> Ordinarily, 16-bit applications will run under all versions of MS-Windows. In more recent versions (XP, Vista, Windows 7), application programs cannot directly access computer hardware or restricted memory locations.

14.1 MS-DOS and the IBM-PC

IBM's PC-DOS was the first operating system to implement real-address mode on the IBM Personal Computer, using the Intel 8088 processor. Later, it evolved into Microsoft MS-DOS. Because of this history, it makes sense to use MS-DOS as the environment for explaining real-address mode programming. Real-address mode is also called *16-bit mode* because addresses are constructed from 16-bit values.

In this chapter, you will learn the basic memory organization of MS-DOS, how to activate MS-DOS function calls (called *interrupts*), and how to perform basic input-output operations at the operating system level. All of the programs in this chapter run in real-address mode because they use the INT instruction. Interrupts were originally designed to run under MS-DOS in real-address mode. It is possible to call interrupts in protected mode, but the techniques for doing so are beyond the scope of this book.

Real-address mode programs have the following characteristics:

• They can only address 1 megabyte of memory.
• Only one program can run at once (single tasking) in a single session.
• No memory boundary protection is possible, so any application program can overwrite memory used by the operating system.
• Offsets are 16 bits.

When it first appeared, the IBM-PC had a strong appeal because it was affordable and it ran Lotus 1-2-3, the electronic spreadsheet program that was instrumental in the PC's adoption by businesses. Computer hobbyists loved the PC because it was an ideal tool for learning how computers work. It should be noted that Digital Research CP/M, the most popular 8-bit operating system before PC-DOS, was only capable of addressing 64K of RAM. From this point of view, PC-DOS's 640K seemed like a gift from heaven.

Because of the obvious memory and speed limitations of the early Intel microprocessors, the IBM-PC was a single-user computer. There was no built-in protection against memory corruption by application programs. In contrast, the minicomputer systems available at the time could handle multiple users and prevented application programs from overwriting each other's data. Over time, more-robust operating systems for the PC have become available, making it a viable alternative to minicomputer systems, particularly when PCs are networked together.

14.1.1 Memory Organization

In real-address mode, the lowest 640K of memory is used by both the operating system and application programs. Following this is video memory and reserved memory for hardware controllers. Finally, locations F0000 to FFFFF are reserved for system ROM (read-only memory). Figure 14–1 shows a simple memory map. Within the operating system area of memory, the lowest 1024 bytes of memory (addresses 00000 to 003FF) contain a table of 32-bit addresses named the *interrupt vector table*. These addresses, called *interrupt vectors*, are used by the CPU when processing hardware and software interrupts.

Just above the vector table is the *BIOS and MS-DOS data area*. Next is the *software BIOS*, which includes procedures that manage most I/O devices, including the keyboard, disk drive, video display, serial, and printer ports. BIOS procedures are loaded from a hidden system file on an MS-DOS system (boot) disk. The MS-DOS kernel is a collection of procedures (called *services*) that are also loaded from a file on the system disk.

Grouped with the MS-DOS kernel are the file buffers and installable device drivers. Next highest in memory, the resident part of the *command processor* is loaded from an executable file named *command.com*. The command processor interprets commands typed at the MS-DOS prompt and loads and executes programs stored on disk. A second part of the command processor occupies high memory just below location A0000.

FIGURE 14–1   MS-DOS Memory Map.

Address		
FFFFF	ROM BIOS	
F0000		
	Reserved	
C0000		
	Video Text & Graphics	VRAM
B8000		
	Video Graphics	
A0000		
	⌐ ‾ ‾ ‾ ‾ ‾ ‾ ‾ ‾ ‾ ‾ ‾ ‾ ‾ ‾ ‾ ‾ ‾ ⌐	
	¦ Transient Command Processor ¦	
	⌐ _ _ _ _ _ _ _ _ _ _ _ _ _ _ _ _ ⌐	
	Transient Program Area	
	(available for application programs)	
	Resident Command Processor	640K RAM
	DOS Kernel, Device Drivers	
	Software BIOS	
	BIOS & DOS Data	
00400		
	Interrupt Vector Table	
00000		

Application programs can load into memory at the first address above the resident part of the command processor and can use memory all the way up to address 9FFFF. If the currently running program overwrites the transient command processor area, the latter is reloaded from the boot disk when the program exits.

Video Memory   The video memory area (VRAM) on an IBM-PC begins at location A0000, which is used when the video adapter is switched into graphics mode. When the video is in color text mode, memory location B8000 holds all text currently displayed on the screen. The screen is memory-mapped, so that each row and column on the screen corresponds to a 16-bit word in memory. When a character is copied into video memory, it immediately appears on the screen.

ROM BIOS   The *ROM BIOS*, at memory locations F0000 to FFFFF, is an important part of the computer's operating system. It contains system diagnostic and configuration software, as well as low-level input-output procedures used by application programs. The BIOS is stored in a static memory chip on the system board. Most systems follow a standardized BIOS specification modeled after IBM's original BIOS and use the BIOS data area from 00400 to 004FF.

14.1.2   Redirecting Input-Output

Throughout this chapter, references will be made to the *standard input device* and the *standard output device*. Both are collectively called the *console,* which involves the keyboard for input and the video display for output.

When running programs from the command prompt, you can redirect standard input so that it is read from a file or hardware port rather than the keyboard. Standard output can be redirected to a file, printer, or other I/O device. Without this capability, programs would have to be substantially revised before their input-output could be changed. For example, the operating system has a program named *sort.exe* that sorts an input file. The following command sorts a file named *myfile.txt* and displays the output:

```
sort < myfile.txt
```

The following command sorts *myfile.txt* and sends the output to *outfile.txt:*

```
sort < myfile.txt > outfile.txt
```

You can use the pipe (|) symbol to copy the output from the DIR command to the input of the *sort.exe* program. The following command sorts the current disk directory and displays the output on the screen:

```
dir | sort
```

The following command sends the output of the sort program to the default (non-networked) printer (identified by PRN):

```
dir | sort > prn
```

The complete set of device names is shown in Table 14-1.

Table 14-1   Standard MS-DOS Device Names.

Device Name	Description
CON	Console (video display or keyboard)
LPT1 or PRN	First parallel printer
LPT2, LPT3	Parallel ports 2 and 3
COM1, COM2	Serial ports 1 and 2
NUL	Nonexistent or dummy device

14.1.3   Software Interrupts

A *software interrupt* is a call to an operating system procedure. Most of these procedures, called *interrupt handlers*, provide input-output capability to application programs. They are used for such tasks as the following:

- Displaying characters and strings
- Reading characters and strings from the keyboard
- Displaying text in color
- Opening and closing files
- Reading data from files
- Writing data to files
- Setting and retrieving the system time and date

14.1.4   INT Instruction

The INT (*call to interrupt procedure*) instruction calls a system subroutine also known as an *interrupt handler*. Before the INT instruction executes, one or more parameters must be inserted in registers. At the very least, a number identifying the particular procedure must be moved to the AH register. Depending on the function, other values may have to be passed to the interrupt in registers. The syntax is

```
INT number
```

where *number* is an integer in the range 0 to FF hexadecimal.

Interrupt Vectoring

The CPU processes the INT instruction using the interrupt vector table, which, as we've mentioned, is a table of addresses in the lowest 1024 bytes of memory. Each entry in this table is a 32-bit segment-offset address that points to an interrupt handler. The actual addresses in this table vary from one machine to another. Figure 14–2 illustrates the steps taken by the CPU when the INT instruction is invoked by a program:

- **Step 1:** The operand of the INT instruction is multiplied by 4 to locate the matching interrupt vector table entry.
- **Step 2:** The CPU pushes the flags and a 32-bit segment/offset return address on the stack, disables hardware interrupts, and executes a far call to the address stored at location (10h * 4) in the interrupt vector table (F000:F065).
- **Step 3:** The interrupt handler at F000:F065 executes until it reaches an IRET (interrupt return) instruction.
- **Step 4:** The IRET instruction pops the flags and the return address off the stack, causing the processor to resume execution immediately following the INT 10h instruction in the calling program.

FIGURE 14–2   Interrupt Vectoring Process.

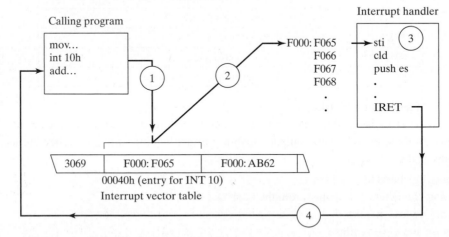

Common Interrupts

Software interrupts call *interrupt service routines* (ISRs) either in the BIOS or in DOS. Some frequently used interrupts are the following:

- *INT 10h Video Services*. Procedures that display routines that control the cursor position, write text in color, scroll the screen, and display video graphics.
- *INT 16h Keyboard Services*. Procedures that read the keyboard and check its status.

- *INT 17h Printer Services.* Procedures that initialize, print, and return the printer status.
- *INT 1Ah Time of Day.* Procedure that gets the number of clock ticks since the machine was turned on or sets the counter to a new value.
- *INT 1Ch User Timer Interrupt.* An empty procedure that is executed 18.2 times per second.
- *INT 21h MS-DOS Services.* Procedures that provide input-output, file handling, and memory management. Also known as *MS-DOS function calls.*

14.1.5   Coding for 16-Bit Programs

Programs designed for MS-DOS must be 16-bit applications running in real-address mode. Real-address mode applications use 16-bit segments and follow the segmented addressing scheme described in Section 2.3.1. If you're using a 32-bit processor, you can use the 32-bit general-purpose registers for data, even in real-address mode. Here is a summary of coding characteristics in 16-bit programs:

- The .MODEL directive specifies which memory model your program will use. We recommend the Small model, which keeps your code in one segment and your stack plus data in another segment:

  ```
  .MODEL small
  ```

- The .STACK directive allocates a small amount of local stack space for your program. Ordinarily, you rarely need more than 256 bytes of stack space. The following is particularly generous, with 512 bytes:

  ```
  .STACK 200h
  ```

- Optionally, you may want to enable the use of 32-bit registers. This can be done with the .386 directive:

  ```
  .386
  ```

- Two instructions are required at the beginning of main if your program references variables. They initialize the DS register to the starting location of the data segment, identified by the predefined MASM constant @**data**:

  ```
  mov  ax,@data
  mov  ds,ax
  ```

- Every program must include a statement that ends the program and returns to the operating system. One way to do this is to use the .EXIT directive:

  ```
  .EXIT
  ```

  Alternatively, you can call INT 21h, Function 4Ch:

  ```
  mov  ah,4ch                    ; terminate process
  int  21h                       ; MS-DOS interrupt
  ```

- You can assign values to segment registers using the MOV instruction, but do so only when assigning the address of a program segment.
- When assembling 16-bit programs, use the *make16.bat* (batch) file. It links to Irvine16.lib and executes the older Microsoft 16-bit linker (version 5.6).
- Real-address mode programs can only access hardware ports, interrupt vectors, and system memory when running under MS-DOS, Windows 95, 98, and Millenium. This type of access is not permitted under Windows NT, 2000, or XP.

- When the **Small** memory model is used, offsets (addresses) of data and code labels are 16 bits. The Irvine16 library uses the Small memory model, in which all code fits in a 16-bit segment and the program's data and stack fit into a 16-bit segment.
- In real-address mode, stack entries are 16 bits by default. You can still place a 32-bit value on the stack (it uses two stack entries).

You can simplify coding of 16-bit programs by including the Irvine16.inc file. It inserts the following statements into the assembly stream, which define the memory mode and calling convention, allocate stack space, enable 32-bit registers, and redefine the .EXIT directive as **exit**:

```
.MODEL small,stdcall
.STACK 200h
.386
exit EQU <.EXIT>
```

14.1.6 Section Review

1. What is the highest memory location into which you can load an application program?
2. What occupies the lowest 1024 bytes of memory?
3. What is the starting location of the BIOS and MS-DOS data area?
4. What is the name of the memory area containing low-level procedures used by the computer for input-output?
5. Show an example of redirecting a program's output to the printer.
6. What is the MS-DOS device name for the first parallel printer?
7. What is an interrupt service routine?
8. When the INT instruction executes, what is the first task carried out by the CPU?
9. What four steps are taken by the CPU when an INT instruction is invoked by a program? *Hint:* See Figure 14–2.
10. When an interrupt service routine finishes, how does an application program resume execution?
11. Which interrupt number is used for video services?
12. Which interrupt number is used for the time of day?
13. What offset within the interrupt vector table contains the address of the INT 21h interrupt handler?

14.2   MS-DOS Function Calls (INT 21h)

MS-DOS provides a lot of easy-to-use functions for displaying text on the console. They are all part of a group typically called *INT 21h MS-DOS Function calls*. There are about 200 different functions supported by this interrupt, identified by a *function number* placed in the AH register. An excellent, if somewhat outdated, source is Ray Duncan's book, *Advanced MS-DOS Programming,* 2nd Ed., Microsoft Press, 1988. A more comprehensive and up-to-date list, named *Ralf Brown's Interrupt List*, can be found on the Web. See the current book's Web site for details.

For each INT 21h function described in this chapter, we will list the necessary input parameters and return values, give notes about its use, and include a short code example that calls the function.

A number of functions require that the 32-bit address of an input parameter be stored in the DS:DX registers. DS, the data segment register, is usually set to your program's data area. If for some reason this is not the case, use the SEG operator to set DS to the segment containing the data passed to INT 21h. The following statements do this:

```
.data
inBuffer BYTE 80 DUP(?)
.code
mov    ax,SEG inBuffer
mov    ds,ax
mov    dx,OFFSET inBuffer
```

The very first Intel assembly language program I wrote (around 1983) displayed a "*" on the screen:

```
mov ah,2
mov dl,'*'
int 21h
```

People said assembly language was difficult, but this was encouraging! As it turned out, there were a few more details to learn before writing nontrivial programs.

INT 21h Function 4Ch: Terminate Process   INT 21h Function 4Ch terminates the current program (called a *process*). In the real-address mode programs presented in this book, we have relied on a macro definition in the Irvine16 library named **exit**. It is defined as

```
exit TEXTEQU <.EXIT>
```

In other words, **exit** is an alias, or substitute for .EXIT (the MASM directive that ends a program). The **exit** symbol was created so you could use a single command to terminate 16-bit and 32-bit programs. In 16-bit programs, the code generated by **.EXIT** is

```
mov    ah,4Ch                          ; terminate process
int    21h
```

If you supply an optional return code argument to the .EXIT macro, the assembler generates an additional instruction that moves the return code to AL:

```
.EXIT 0                                ; macro call
```

Generated code:

```
mov    ah,4Ch                          ; terminate process
mov    al,0                            ; return code
int    21h
```

The value in AL, called the *process return code*, is received by the calling process (including a batch file) to indicate the return status of your program. By convention, a return code of zero is considered successful completion. Other return codes between 1 and 255 can be used to indicate additional outcomes that have specific meaning for your program. For example, ML.EXE, the Microsoft Assembler, returns 0 if a program assembles correctly and a nonzero value if it does not.

Appendix D contains a fairly extensive list of BIOS and MS-DOS interrupts.

14.2.1   Selected Output Functions

In this section we present some of the most common INT 21h functions for writing characters and text. None of these functions alters the default current screen colors, so output will only be in color if you have previously set the screen color by other means. (For example, you can call video BIOS functions from Chapter 16.)

Filtering Control Characters   All of the functions in this section *filter*, or interpret ASCII control characters. If you write a backspace character to standard output, for example, the cursor moves one column to the left. Table 14-2 contains a list of control characters that you are likely to encounter.

Table 14-2   ASCII Control Characters.

ASCII Code	Description
08h	Backspace (moves one column to the left)
09h	Horizontal tab (skips forward *n* columns)
0Ah	Line feed (moves to next output line)
0Ch	Form feed (moves to next printer page)
0Dh	Carriage return (moves to leftmost output column)
1Bh	Escape character

The next several tables describe the important features of INT 21h Functions 2, 5, 6, 9, and 40h. INT 21h Function 2 writes a single character to standard output. INT 21h Function 5 writes a single character to the printer. INT 21h Function 6 writes a single unfiltered character to standard output. INT 21h Function 9 writes a string (terminated by a $ character) to standard output. INT 21h Function 40h writes an array of bytes to a file or device.

INT 21h Function 2	
Description	Write a single character to standard output and advance the cursor one column forward
Receives	AH = 2 DL = character value
Returns	Nothing

Sample call	```mov ah,2```
	```mov dl,'A'```
	```int 21h```

INT 21h Function 5	
Description	Write a single character to the printer
Receives	AH — 5 DL = character value
Returns	Nothing

Sample call	``` mov ah,5 ; select printer output ```
	 ``` mov dl,"Z" ; character to be printed ```
	 ``` int 21h ; call MS-DOS ```

Notes	MS-DOS waits until the printer is ready to accept the character. You can terminate the wait by pressing the Ctrl-Break keys. The default output is to the printer port for LPT1.

INT 21h Function 6	
Description	Write a character to standard output
Receives	AH = 6 DL = character value
Returns	If ZF = 0, AL contains the character's ASCII code

Sample call	``` mov ah,6 ```
	 ``` mov dl,"A" ```
	 ``` int 21h ```

Notes	Unlike other INT 21h functions, this one does not filter (interpret) ASCII control characters.

INT 21h Function 9	
Description	Write a $-terminated string to standard output
Receives	AH = 9 DS:DX = segment/offset of the string
Returns	Nothing

Sample call	``` .data ```
	 ``` string BYTE "This is a string$" ```
	 ``` .code ```
	 ``` mov ah,9 ```
	 ``` mov dx,OFFSET string ```
	 ``` int 21h ```

Notes	The string must be terminated by a dollar-sign character ($).

INT 21h Function 40h	
Description	Write an array of bytes to a file or device
Receives	AH = 40h BX = file or device handle (console = 1) CX = number of bytes to write DS:DX = address of array
Returns	AX = number of bytes written

Sample call	<pre>.data
	message "Hello, world"
	.code
	mov ah,40h
	mov bx,1
	mov cx,LENGTHOF message
	mov dx,OFFSET message
	int 21h</pre>

14.2.2 Hello World Program Example

The following is a simple program that displays a string on the screen using an MS-DOS function call:

```
TITLE Hello World Program          (Hello.asm)

.MODEL small
.STACK 100h
.386

.data
message BYTE "Hello, world!",0dh,0ah

.code
main PROC
    mov   ax,@data              ; initialize DS
    mov   ds,ax

    mov   ah,40h                ; write to file/device
    mov   bx,1                  ; output handle
    mov   cx,SIZEOF message     ; number of bytes
    mov   dx,OFFSET message     ; addr of buffer
    int   21h

    .EXIT
main ENDP
END main
```

Alternate Version   Another way to write Hello.asm is to use the predefined .STARTUP directive (which initializes the DS register). Doing so requires the removal of the label next to the

END directive:

```
TITLE Hello World Program              (Hello2.asm)
.MODEL small
.STACK 100h
.386
.data
message BYTE "Hello, world!",0dh,0ah
.code
main PROC
    .STARTUP
        mov     ah,40h               ; write to file/device
        mov     bx,1                 ; output handle
        mov     cx,SIZEOF message    ; number of bytes
        mov     dx,OFFSET message    ; addr of buffer
        int     21h
    .EXIT
main ENDP
END
```

14.2.3   Selected Input Functions

In this section, we describe a few of the most commonly used MS-DOS functions that read from standard input. For a more complete list, see Appendix D. As shown in the following table, INT 21h Function 1 reads a single character from standard input:

INT 21h Function 1	
Description	Read a single character from standard input
Receives	AH = 1
Returns	AL = character (ASCII code)

Sample call	`mov   ah,1`
	`int   21h`
	`mov   char,al`

Notes	If no character is present in the input buffer, the program waits. This function echoes the character to standard output.

INT 21h Function 6 reads a character from standard input if the character is waiting in the input buffer. If the buffer is empty, the function returns with the Zero flag set and no other action is taken:

INT 21h Function 6	
Description	Read a character from standard input without waiting
Receives	AH = 6 DL = FFh

INT 21h Function 6	
Returns	If ZF = 0, AL contains the character's ASCII code.
Sample call	```mov ah,6mov dl,0FFhint 21hjz skipmov char,ALskip:```
Notes	The interrupt only returns a character if one is already waiting in the input buffer. Does not echo the character to standard output and does not filter control characters.

INT 21h Function 0Ah reads a buffered string from standard input, terminated by the Enter key. When calling this function, pass a pointer to an input structure having the following format (**count** can be between 0 and 128):

```
count = 80
KEYBOARD STRUCT
    maxInput BYTE count          ; max chars to input
    inputCount BYTE ?            ; actual input count
    buffer BYTE count DUP(?)     ; holds input chars
KEYBOARD ENDS
```

The *maxInput* field specifies the maximum number of characters the user can input, including the Enter key. The backspace key can be used to erase characters and back up the cursor. The user terminates the input either by pressing the Enter key or by pressing Ctrl-Break. All non-ASCII keys, such as PageUp and F1, are filtered out and are not stored in the buffer. After the function returns, the *inputCount* field indicates how many characters were input, not counting the Enter key. The following table describes Function 0Ah:

INT 21h Function 0Ah	
Description	Read an array of buffered characters from standard input
Receives	AH = 0AhDS:DX = address of keyboard input structure
Returns	The structure is initialized with the input characters.
Sample call	```.datakybdData KEYBOARD <>.code mov ah,0Ah mov dx,OFFSET kybdData int 21h```

INT 21h Function 0Bh gets the status of the standard input buffer:

INT 21h Function 0Bh	
Description	Get the status of the standard input buffer
Receives	AH = 0Bh
Returns	If a character is waiting, AL = 0FFh; otherwise, AL = 0.
| Sample Call | ```
        mov    ah, 0Bh
        int    21h
        cmp    al, 0
        je     skip
        ; (input the character)
skip:
``` |
| Notes | Does not remove the character. |

Example: String Encryption Program

INT 21h Function 6 has the unique ability to read characters from standard input without pausing the program or filtering control characters. This can be put to good use if we run a program from the command prompt and redirect the input. That is, the input will come from a text file rather than the keyboard.

The following program (*Encrypt.asm*) reads each character from standard input, uses the XOR instruction to alter the character, and writes the altered character to standard output:

```
TITLE Encryption Program              (Encrypt.asm)

; This program uses MS-DOS function calls to
; read and encrypt a file. Run it from the
; command prompt, using redirection:
;     Encrypt < infile.txt > outfile.txt
; Function 6 is also used for output, to avoid
; filtering ASCII control characters.

INCLUDE Irvine16.inc
XORVAL = 239                          ; any value between 0-255
.code
main PROC
        mov    ax, @data
        mov    ds, ax

L1:
        mov    ah, 6                  ; direct console input
        mov    dl, 0FFh               ; don't wait for character
        int    21h                    ; AL = character
        jz     L2                     ; quit if ZF = 1 (EOF)
        xor    al, XORVAL
        mov    ah, 6                  ; write to output
```
```

```
        mov    dl,al
        int    21h
        jmp    L1                          ; repeat the loop
   L2:  exit
   main ENDP
   END  main
```

The choice of 239 as the encryption value is completely arbitrary. You can use any value between 0 and 255 in this context, although using 0 will not cause any encryption to occur. The encryption is weak, of course, but it might be enough to discourage the average user from trying to defeat the encryption. When you run the program at the command prompt, indicate the name of the input file (and output file, if any). The following are two examples:

`encrypt < infile.txt`	Input from file (infile.txt), output to console
`encrypt < infile.txt > outfile.txt`	Input from file (infile.txt), output to file (outfile.txt)

Int 21h Function 3Fh

INT 21h Function 3Fh, as shown in the following table, reads an array of bytes from a file or device. It can be used for keyboard input when the device handle in BX is equal to zero:

INT 21h Function 3Fh	
Description	Read an array of bytes from a file or device
Receives	AH = 3Fh BX = file/device handle (0 = keyboard) CX = maximum bytes to read DS:DX = address of input buffer
Returns	AX = number of bytes actually read

Sample Call	`.data`
	`inputBuffer BYTE 127 dup(0)`
	`bytesRead WORD ?`
	`.code`
	`mov   ah,3Fh`
	`mov   bx,0`
	`mov   cx,127`
	`mov   dx,OFFSET inputBuffer`
	`int   21h`
	`mov   bytesRead,ax`

Notes	If reading from the keyboard, input terminates when the Enter key is pressed, and the 0Dh, 0Ah, characters are appended to the input buffer.

If the user enters more characters than were requested by the function call, excess characters remain in the MS-DOS input buffer. If the function is called anytime later in the program, execution may not pause and wait for user input because the buffer already contains data (including the 0Dh, 0Ah, marking the end of the line). This can even occur between separate instances of program execution. To be absolutely sure your program works as intended, you need to flush the input buffer, one character at a time, after calling Function 3Fh. The following code does this (see the *Keybd.asm* program for a complete demonstration):

```
;------------------------------------------
FlushBuffer PROC
; Flush the standard input buffer.
; Receives: nothing. Returns: nothing
;------------------------------------------
.data
oneByte BYTE ?
.code
     pusha
L1:
     mov    ah,3Fh              ; read file/device
     mov    bx,0                ; keyboard handle
     mov    cx,1                ; one byte
     mov    dx,OFFSET oneByte   ; save it here
     int    21h                 ; call MS-DOS
     cmp    oneByte,0Ah         ; end of line yet?
     jne    L1                  ; no: read another
     popa
     ret
FlushBuffer ENDP
```

14.2.4 Date/Time Functions

Many popular software applications display the current date and time. Others retrieve the date and time and use it in their internal logic. A scheduling program, for example, can use the current date to verify that a user is not accidentally scheduling an appointment in the past.

As shown in the next series of tables, INT 21h Function 2Ah gets the system date, and INT 21h Function 2Bh sets the system date. INT 21h Function 2Ch gets the system time, and INT 21h Function 2Dh sets the system time.

INT 21h Function 2Ah	
Description	Get the system date
Receives	AH = 2Ah
Returns	CX = year DH, DL = month, day AL = day of week (Sunday = 0, Monday = 1, etc.)

INT 21h Function 2Ah

| Sample Call | ```
mov   ah,2Ah
int   21h
mov   year,cx
mov   month,dh
mov   day,dl
mov   dayOfWeek,al
``` |
|---|---|

INT 21h Function 2Bh

Description	Set the system date
Receives	AH = 2Bh CX = year DH = month DL = day
Returns	If the change was successful, AL = 0; otherwise, AL = FFh.
| Sample Call | ```
mov   ah,2Bh
mov   cx,year
mov   dh,month
mov   dl,day
int   21h
cmp   al,0
jne   failed
``` |
| Notes | Probably will not work if you are running Windows NT, 2000, or XP with a restricted user profile. |

INT 21h Function 2Ch

Description	Get the system time
Receives	AH = 2Ch
Returns	CH = hours (0 – 23) CL = minutes (0 – 59) DH = seconds (0 – 59) DL = hundredths of seconds (usually not accurate)
| Sample Call | ```
mov   ah,2Ch
int   21h
mov   hours,ch
mov   minutes,cl
mov   seconds,dh
``` |
```

INT 21h Function 2Dh	
Description	Set the system time
Receives	AH = 2Dh CH = hours (0 – 23) CL = minutes (0 – 59) DH = seconds (0 – 59)
Returns	If the change was successful, AL = 0; otherwise, AL = FFh.

Sample Call	```mov ah,2Dh```
	```mov ch,hours```
	```mov cl,minutes```
	```mov dh,seconds```
	```int 21h```
	```cmp al,0```
	```jne failed```

Notes	Does not work if you are running Windows with a restricted user profile.

Example: Displaying the Time and Date

The following program (*DateTime.asm*) displays the system date and time. The code is a little longer than one would expect because the program inserts leading zeros before the hours, minutes, and seconds:

```
TITLE Display the Date and Time       (DateTime.asm)

Include Irvine16.inc
Write PROTO char:BYTE
.data
str1 BYTE "Date: ",0
str2 BYTE ",  Time: ",0

.code
main PROC
    mov  ax,@data
    mov  ds,ax

; Display the date:
    mov      dx,OFFSET str1
    call     WriteString
    mov      ah,2Ah            ; get system date
    int      21h
    movzx    eax,dh            ; month
    call     WriteDec
    INVOKE   Write,'-'
    movzx    eax,dl            ; day
    call     WriteDec
```

```
        INVOKE  Write,'-'
        movzx   eax,cx                  ; year
        call    WriteDec

; Display the time:
        mov     dx,OFFSET str2
        call    WriteString
        mov     ah,2Ch                  ; get system time
        int     21h
        movzx   eax,ch                  ; hours
        call    WritePaddedDec
        INVOKE  Write,':'
        movzx   eax,cl                  ; minutes
        call    WritePaddedDec
        INVOKE  Write,':'
        movzx   eax,dh                  ; seconds
        call    WritePaddedDec
        call    Crlf

        exit
main ENDP


;------------------------------------------------
Write PROC char:BYTE
; Display a single character.
;------------------------------------------------
        push    eax
        push    edx
        mov     ah,2                    ; character output function
        mov     dl,char
        int     21h
        pop     edx
        pop     eax
        ret
Write ENDP


;------------------------------------------------
WritePaddedDec PROC
; Display unsigned integer in EAX, padding
; to two digit positions with a leading zero.
;------------------------------------------------
.IF eax < 10
        push    eax
        push    edx
        mov     ah,2                    ; display leading zero
        mov     dl,'0'
        int     21h
        pop     edx
        pop     eax
.ENDIF
```

```
        call    WriteDec              ; write unsigned decimal
        ret                           ; using value in EAX
    WritePaddedDec ENDP
    END main
```

Sample output:

```
Date: 12-8-2006,   Time: 23:01:23
```

14.2.5   Section Review

1. Which register holds the function number when calling INT 21h?
2. Which INT 21h function terminates a program?
3. Which INT 21h function writes a single character to standard output?
4. Which INT 21h function writes a string terminated by a $ character to standard output?
5. Which INT 21h function writes a block of data to a file or device?
6. Which INT 21h function reads a single character from standard input?
7. Which INT 21h function reads a block of data from the standard input device?
8. If you want to get the system date, display it, and then change it, which INT 21h functions are required?
9. Which INT 21h functions shown in this chapter probably will not work under Windows NT, 2000, or XP with a restricted user profile?
10. Which INT 21h function would you use to check the standard input buffer to see if a character is waiting to be processed?

14.3   Standard MS-DOS File I/O Services

INT 21h provides more file and directory I/O services that we can possibly show here. Table 14-3 shows a few of the functions you are likely to use.

Table 14-3   File- and Directory-Related INT 21h Functions.

Function	Description
716Ch	Create or open a file
3Eh	Close file handle
42h	Move file pointer
5706h	Get file creation date and time

File/Device Handles   MS-DOS and MS-Windows use 16-bit integers called *handles* to identify files and I/O devices. There are five predefined device handles. Each, except handle 2 (error output), supports redirection at the command prompt. The following handles are available all the time:

0	Keyboard (standard input)
1	Console (standard output)
2	Error output
3	Auxiliary device (asynchronous)
4	Printer

Each I/O function has a common characteristic: If it fails, the Carry flag is set, and an error code is returned in AX. You can use this error code to display an appropriate message. Table 14-4 contains a list of the error codes and their descriptions.

> Microsoft provides extensive documentation on MS-DOS function calls. Search the Platform SDK documentation for your version of Windows.

Table 14-4   MS-DOS Extended Error Codes.

Error Code	Description
01	Invalid function number
02	File not found
03	Path not found
04	Too many open files (no handles left)
05	Access denied
06	Invalid handle
07	Memory control blocks destroyed
08	Insufficient memory
09	Invalid memory block address
0A	Invalid environment
0B	Invalid format
0C	Invalid access code
0D	Invalid data
0E	Reserved
0F	Invalid drive was specified
10	Attempt to remove the current directory
11	Not same device
12	No more files
13	Diskette write-protected
14	Unknown unit
15	Drive not ready
16	Unknown command
17	Data error (CRC)
18	Bad request structure length
19	Seek error
1A	Unknown media type
1B	Sector not found
1C	Printer out of paper
1D	Write fault
1E	Read fault
1F	General failure

14.3.1   Create or Open File (716Ch)

INT 21h Function 716Ch can either create a new file or open an existing file. It permits the use of extended filenames and file sharing. As shown in the following table, the filename may optionally include a directory path.

INT 21h Function 716Ch	
Description	Create new file or open existing file
Receives	AX = 716Ch BX = access mode (0 = read, 1 = write, 2 = read/write) CX = attributes (0 = normal, 1 = read only, 2 = hidden, 3 = system, 8 = volume ID, 20h = archive) DX = action (1 = open, 2 = truncate, 10h = create) DS:SI = segment/offset of filename DI = alias hint (optional)
Returns	If the create/open was successful, CF = 0, AX = file handle, and CX = action taken. If create/open failed, CF = 1.

Sample Call	<pre>mov ax,716Ch ; extended open/create
	mov bx,0 ; read-only
	mov cx,0 ; normal attribute
	mov dx,1 ; open existing file
	mov si,OFFSET Filename
	int 21h
	jc failed
	mov handle,ax ; file handle
	mov actionTaken,cx ; action taken</pre>

Notes	The access mode in BX can optionally be combined with one of the following sharing mode values: OPEN_SHARE_COMPATIBLE, OPEN_SHARE_DENYREADWRITE, OPEN_SHARE_DENYWRITE, OPEN_SHARE_DENYREAD, OPEN_SHARE_DENYNONE. The action taken returned in CX can be one of the following values: ACTION_OPENED, ACTION_CREATED_OPENED, ACTION_REPLACED_OPENED. All are defined in Irvine16.inc.

Additional Examples   The following code either creates a new file or truncates an existing file having the same name:

```
mov   ax,716Ch          ; extended open/create
mov   bx,2              ; read-write
mov   cx,0              ; normal attribute
mov   dx,10h + 02h      ; action: create + truncate
mov   si,OFFSET Filename
int   21h
jc    failed
mov   handle,ax         ; file handle
mov   actionTaken,cx    ; action taken to open file
```

The following code attempts to create a new file. It fails (with the Carry flag set) if the file already exists:

```
mov     ax,716Ch              ; extended open/create
mov     bx,2                  ; read-write
mov     cx,0                  ; normal attribute
mov     dx,10h                ; action: create
mov     si,OFFSET Filename
int     21h
jc      failed
mov     handle,ax             ; file handle
mov     actionTaken,cx        ; action taken to open file
```

14.3.2   Close File Handle (3Eh)

INT 21h Function 3Eh closes a file handle. This function flushes the file's write buffer by copying any remaining data to disk, as shown in the following table:

INT 21h Function 3Eh	
Description	Close file handle
Receives	AH = 3Eh BX = file handle
Returns	If the file was closed successfully, CF = 0; otherwise, CF = 1.

Sample Call	.data
	filehandle WORD ?
	.code
	mov ah,3Eh
	mov bx,filehandle
	int 21h
	jc failed

Notes	If the file has been modified, its time stamp and date stamp are updated.

14.3.3   Move File Pointer (42h)

INT 21h Function 42h, as can be seen in the following table, moves the position pointer of an open file to a new location. When calling this function, the *method code* in AL identifies how the pointer will be set:

0	Offset from the beginning of the file
1	Offset from the current location
2	Offset from the end of the file

INT 21h Function 42h	
Description	Move file pointer
Receives	AH = 42h AL = method code BX = file handle CX:DX = 32-bit offset value
Returns	If the file pointer was moved successfully, CF = 0 and DX:AX returns the new file pointer offset; otherwise, CF = 1.

INT 21h Function 42h	
Sample Call	```mov ah,42h
mov   al,0   ; method: offset from beginning
mov   bx,handle
mov   cx,offsetHi
mov   dx,offsetLo
int   21h```
Notes	The returned file pointer offsct in DX:AX is always relative to the beginning of the file.

14.3.4   Get File Creation Date and Time

INT 21h Function 5706h, shown in the following table, obtains the date and time when a file was created. This is not necessarily the same date and time when the file was last modified or even accessed. To learn about MS-DOS packed date and time formats, see Section 15.3.7. To see an example of extracting date/time fields, see Section 7.3.4.

INT 21h Function 5706h	
Description	Get file creation date and time
Receives	AX = 5706h BX = file handle
Returns	If the function call was successful, CF = 0, DX = date (in MS-DOS packed format), CX = time, and SI = milliseconds. If the function failed, CF = 1.
Sample Call	```mov ax,5706h ; Get creation date/time
mov   bx,handle
int   21h
jc   error   ; quit if failed
mov   date,dx
mov   time,cx
mov   milliseconds,si```
Notes	The file must already be open. The *milliseconds* value indicates the number of 10-millisecond intervals to add to the MS-DOS time. Range is 0 to 199, indicating that the field can add as many as 2 seconds to the overall time.

14.3.5   Selected Library Procedures

Two procedures from the Irvine16 link library are shown here: **ReadString** and **WriteString**. **ReadString** is the trickiest of the two, since it must read one character at a time until it encounters the end of line character (0Dh). It reads the character, but does not copy it to the buffer.

ReadString

The **ReadString** procedure reads a string from standard input and places the characters in an input buffer as a null-terminated string. It terminates when the user presses the Enter key.:

```
;------------------------------------------------------------
ReadString PROC
; Receives: DS:DX points to the input buffer,
```

```
    ;                CX = maximum input size
    ; Returns:  AX = size of the input string
    ; Comments: Stops when the Enter key (0Dh) is pressed.
    ;------------------------------------------------------------
        push  cx                    ; save registers
        push  si
        push  cx                    ; save digit count again
        mov   si,dx                 ; point to input buffer
L1:     mov   ah,1                  ; function: keyboard input
        int   21h                   ; returns character in AL
        cmp   al,0Dh                ; end of line?
        je    L2                    ; yes: exit
        mov   [si],al               ; no: store the character
        inc   si                    ; increment buffer pointer
        loop  L1                    ; loop until CX=0
L2:     mov   byte ptr [si],0       ; end with a null byte
        pop   ax                    ; original digit count
        sub   ax,cx                 ; AX = size of input string
        pop   si                    ; restore registers
        pop   cx
        ret
ReadString ENDP
```

WriteString

The **WriteString** procedure writes a null-terminated string to standard output. It calls a helper procedure named **Str_length** that returns the number of bytes in a string:

```
    ;------------------------------------------------------------
WriteString PROC
    ; Writes a null-terminated string to standard output
    ; Receives: DS:DX = address of string
    ; Returns: nothing
    ;------------------------------------------------------------
        pusha
        push  ds                    ; set ES to DS
        pop   es
        mov   di,dx                 ; ES:DI = string ptr
        call  Str_length            ; AX = string length
        mov   cx,ax                 ; CX = number of bytes
        mov   ah,40h                ; write to file or device
        mov   bx,1                  ; standard output handle
        int   21h                   ; call MS-DOS
        popa
        ret
WriteString ENDP
```

14.3.6   Example: Read and Copy a Text File

We presented INT 21h Function 3Fh earlier in this chapter, in the context of reading from standard input. This function can also be used to read a file if the handle in BX identifies a file that has been opened for input. When Function 3Fh returns, AX indicates the number of bytes actually read from the file. When the end of the file is reached, the value returned in AX is less than the number of bytes requested (in CX).

We also presented INT 21h Function 40h earlier in this chapter in the context of writing to standard output (device handle 1). Instead, the handle in BX can refer to an open file. The function automatically updates the file's position pointer, so the next call to Function 40h begins writing where the previous call left off.

The *Readfile.asm* program we're about to present demonstrates several INT 21h functions presented in this section:

- Function 716Ch: Create new file or open existing file
- Function 3Fh: Read from file or device
- Function 40h: Write to file or device
- Function 3Eh: Close file handle

The following program opens a text file for input, reads no more than 5,000 bytes from the file, displays it on the console, creates a new file, and copies the data to a new file:

```
TITLE Read a text file           (Readfile.asm)

; Read, display, and copy a text file.
INCLUDE Irvine16.inc

.data
BufSize = 5000
infile    BYTE "my_text_file.txt",0
outfile   BYTE "my_output_file.txt",0
inHandle  WORD ?
outHandle WORD ?
buffer    BYTE BufSize DUP(?)
bytesRead WORD ?

.code
main PROC
      mov    ax,@data
      mov    ds,ax

; Open the input file
      mov    ax,716Ch           ; extended create or open
      mov    bx,0               ; mode = read-only
      mov    cx,0               ; normal attribute
      mov    dx,1               ; action: open
      mov    si,OFFSET infile
      int    21h                ; call MS-DOS
      jc     quit               ; quit if error
      mov    inHandle,ax

; Read the input file
      mov    ah,3Fh             ; read file or device
      mov    bx,inHandle        ; file handle
      mov    cx,BufSize         ; max bytes to read
      mov    dx,OFFSET buffer   ; buffer pointer
      int    21h
```

```
        jc     quit                    ; quit if error
        mov    bytesRead,ax

; Display the buffer
        mov    ah,40h                  ; write file or device
        mov    bx,1                    ; console output handle
        mov    cx,bytesRead            ; number of bytes
        mov    dx,OFFSET buffer        ; buffer pointer
        int    21h
        jc     quit                    ; quit if error

; Close the file
        mov    ah,3Eh                  ; function: close file
        mov    bx,inHandle             ; input file handle
        int    21h                     ; call MS-DOS
        jc     quit                    ; quit if error

; Create the output file
        mov    ax,716Ch                ; extended create or open
        mov    bx,1                    ; mode = write-only
        mov    cx,0                    ; normal attribute
        mov    dx,12h                  ; action: create/truncate
        mov    si,OFFSET outfile
        int    21h                     ; call MS-DOS
        jc     quit                    ; quit if error
        mov    outHandle,ax            ; save handle

; Write buffer to new file
        mov    ah,40h                  ; write file or device
        mov    bx,outHandle            ; output file handle
        mov    cx,bytesRead            ; number of bytes
        mov    dx,OFFSET buffer        ; buffer pointer
        int    21h
        jc     quit                    ; quit if error

; Close the file
        mov    ah,3Eh                  ; function: close file
        mov    bx,outHandle            ; output file handle
        int    21h                     ; call MS-DOS

quit:
        call   Crlf
        exit
main ENDP
END main
```

14.3.7   Reading the MS-DOS Command Tail

In the programs that follow, we will often pass information to programs on the command line. Suppose we needed to pass the name *file1.doc* to a program named *attr.exe*. The MS-DOS command line would be

```
attr file1.doc
```

When a program starts up, any additional text on its command line is automatically stored in the 128-byte *MS-DOS Command Tail* located in memory at offset 80h from the beginning of the segment address specified by the ES register. The memory area is named the *program segment prefix* (PSP). The program segment prefix is discussed in Section 17.3.1. Also see Section 2.3.1 for a discussion of how segmented addressing works in real-address mode.

The first byte contains the length of the command line. If its value is greater than zero, the second byte contains a space character. The remaining bytes contain the text typed on the command line. Using the example command line for the *attr.exe* program, the hexadecimal contents of the command tail would be the following:

Offset:	80	81	82	83	84	85	86	87	88	89	8A	8B
Contents:	0A	20	46	49	4C	45	31	2E	44	4F	43	0D
			F	I	L	E	1	.	D	O	C	

You can see the command tail bytes using the Microsoft CodeView debugger if you load the program and set the command-line arguments before running the program.

> To set command-line parameters in CodeView, choose *Set Runtime Arguments...* from the *Run* menu. Press F10 to execute the first program instruction, open a memory window, select *Memory* from the *Options* menu, and enter ES:0x80 into the *Address Expression* field.

There is one exception to the rule that MS-DOS stores all characters after the command or program name: It doesn't keep the file and device names used when redirecting input-output. For example, MS-DOS does not save any text in the command tail when the following command is typed because both *infile.txt* and PRN are used for redirection:

```
prog1 < infile.txt > prn
```

GetCommandTail Procedure   The **GetCommandTail** procedure from the Irvine16 library returns a copy of the running program's command tail under MS-DOS. When calling this procedure, set DX to the offset of the buffer where the command tail will be copied. Real-address mode programs often deal directly with segment registers so they can access data in different memory segments. For example, GetCommandTail saves the current value of ES on the stack, obtains the PSP segment using INT 21h Function 62h and copies it to ES:

```
push es
.
.
.
mov   ah,62h          ; get PSP segment address
int   21h             ; returned in BX
mov   es,bx           ; copied to ES
```

Next, it locates a byte inside the PSP. Because ES does not point to the program's default data segment, we must use a *segment override* (es:) to address data inside the program segment prefix:

```
mov   cl,es:[di-1]             ; get length byte
```

GetCommandTail skips over leading spaces with SCASB and sets the Carry flag if the command tail is empty. This makes it easy for the calling program to execute a JC (*jump carry*) instruction if nothing is typed on the command line:

```
        cld                         ; scan in forward direction
        mov     al,20h              ; space character
        repz    scasb               ; scan for non space
        jz      L2                  ; all spaces found
        .
        .
L2:     stc                         ; CF=1 means no command tail
```

SCASB automatically scans memory pointed to by the ES segment registers, so we had no choice but to set ES to the PSP segment at the beginning of GetCommandTail. Here's a complete listing:

```
GetCommandTail PROC
;
; Gets a copy of the MS-DOS command tail at PSP:80h.
; Receives: DX contains the offset of the buffer
;     that receives a copy of the command tail.
; Returns: CF=1 if the buffer is empty; otherwise,
;     CF=0.
;-----------------------------------------------------
SPACE = 20h
        push es
        pusha                       ; save general registers

        mov     ah,62h              ; get PSP segment address
        int     21h                 ; returned in BX
        mov     es,bx               ; copied to ES

        mov     si,dx               ; point to buffer
        mov     di,81h              ; PSP offset of command tail
        mov     cx,0                ; byte count
        mov     cl,es:[di-1]        ; get length byte
        cmp     cx,0                ; is the tail empty?
        je      L2                  ; yes: exit
        cld                         ; scan in forward direction
        mov     al,SPACE            ; space character
        repz    scasb               ; scan for non space
        jz      L2                  ; all spaces found
        dec     di                  ; non space found
        inc     cx
```

> By default, the assembler assumes that DI is an offset from the segment address in DS. The segment override (es:[di]) tells the CPU to use the segment address in ES instead.

```
L1:     mov     al,es:[di]          ; copy tail to buffer
        mov     [si],al             ; pointed to by DS:SI
        inc     si
        inc     di
        loop    L1
        clc                         ; CF=0 means tail found
        jmp     L3
```

```
L2:     stc                                 ; CF=1 means no command tail
L3:     mov     byte ptr [si],0             ; store null byte
        popa                                ; restore registers
        pop     es
        ret
GetCommandTail ENDP
```

14.3.8 Example: Creating a Binary File

A *binary file* is given its name because the data stored in the file is simply a binary image of program data. Suppose, for example, that your program created and filled an array of doublewords:

```
myArray DWORD 50 DUP(?)
```

If you wanted to write this array to a text file, you would have to convert each integer to a string and write it separately. A more efficient way to store this data would be to just write a binary image of **myArray** to a file. An array of 50 doublewords uses 200 bytes of memory, and that is exactly the amount of disk space the file would use.

The following *Binfile.asm* program fills an array with random integers, displays the integers on the screen, writes the integers to a binary file, and closes the file. It reopens the file, reads the integers, and displays them on the screen:

```
TITLE Binary File Program              (Binfile.asm)

; This program creates a binary file containing
; an array of doublewords. It then reads the file
; back in and displays the values.

INCLUDE Irvine16.inc

.data
myArray DWORD 50 DUP(?)

fileName    BYTE "binary array file.bin",0
fileHandle  WORD ?
commaStr    BYTE ", ",0

; Set CreateFile to zero if you just want to
; read and display the existing binary file.
CreateFile = 1

.code
main PROC
        mov     ax,@data
        mov     ds,ax

.IF CreateFile EQ 1
        call    FillTheArray
        call    DisplayTheArray
        call    CreateTheFile
        call    WaitMsg
        call    Crlf
.ENDIF
```

```
        call  ReadTheFile
        call  DisplayTheArray
quit:
        call  Crlf
        exit
main ENDP

;----------------------------------------------------------
ReadTheFile PROC
;
; Open and read the binary file.
; Receives: nothing.
; Returns: nothing
;----------------------------------------------------------
        mov   ax,716Ch          ; extended file open
        mov   bx,0              ; mode: read-only
        mov   cx,0              ; attribute: normal
        mov   dx,1              ; open existing file
        mov   si,OFFSET fileName ; filename
        int   21h              ; call MS-DOS
        jc    quit             ; quit if error
        mov   fileHandle,ax    ; save handle

; Read the input file, then close the file.
        mov   ah,3Fh           ; read file or device
        mov   bx,fileHandle    ; file handle
        mov   cx,SIZEOF myArray ; max bytes to read
        mov   dx,OFFSET myArray ; buffer pointer
        int   21h
        jc    quit             ; quit if error
        mov   ah,3Eh           ; function: close file
        mov   bx,fileHandle    ; output file handle
        int   21h              ; call MS-DOS
quit:
        ret
ReadTheFile ENDP

;----------------------------------------------------------
DisplayTheArray PROC
;
; Display the doubleword array.
; Receives: nothing.
; Returns: nothing
;----------------------------------------------------------
        mov   CX,LENGTHOF myArray
        mov   si,0
L1:
        mov   eax,myArray[si]   ; get a number
        call  WriteHex          ; display the number
        mov   edx,OFFSET commaStr ; display a comma
        call  WriteString
```

```
        add     si,TYPE myArray         ; next array position
        loop    L1
        ret
DisplayTheArray ENDP

;---------------------------------------------------------
FillTheArray PROC
;
; Fill the array with random integers.
; Receives: nothing.
; Returns: nothing
;---------------------------------------------------------
        mov     CX,LENGTHOF myArray
        mov     si,0
L1:
        mov     eax,1000                ; generate random integers
        call    RandomRange             ; between 0 - 999 in EAX
        mov     myArray[si],eax         ; store in the array
        add     si,TYPE myArray         ; next array position
        loop    L1
        ret
FillTheArray ENDP

;---------------------------------------------------------
CreateTheFile PROC
;
; Create a file containing binary data.
; Receives: nothing.
; Returns: nothing
;---------------------------------------------------------
        mov     ax,716Ch                ; create file
        mov     bx,1                    ; mode: write only
        mov     cx,0                    ; normal file
        mov     dx,12h                  ; action: create/truncate
        mov     si,OFFSET fileName      ; filename
        int     21h                     ; call MS-DOS
        jc      quit                    ; quit if error
        mov     fileHandle,ax           ; save handle

; Write the integer array to the file.
        mov     ah,40h                  ; write file or device
        mov     bx,fileHandle           ; output file handle
        mov     cx,SIZEOF myArray       ; number of bytes
        mov     dx,OFFSET myArray       ; buffer pointer
        int     21h
        jc      quit                    ; quit if error

; Close the file.
        mov     ah,3Eh                  ; function: close file
        mov     bx,fileHandle           ; output file handle
        int     21h                     ; call MS-DOS

quit:
```

```
        ret
CreateTheFile ENDP
END main
```

It is worth noting that writing the entire array is done with a single call to INT 21h Function 40h. There is no need for a loop:

```
mov  ah,40h                    ; write file or device
mov  bx,fileHandle             ; output file handle
mov  cx,SIZEOF myArray         ; number of bytes
mov  dx,OFFSET myArray         ; buffer pointer
int  21h
```

The same is true when reading the file back into the array. A single call to INT 21h Function 3Fh does the job:

```
mov  ah,3Fh                    ; read file or device
mov  bx,fileHandle             ; file handle
mov  cx,SIZEOF myArray         ; max bytes to read
mov  dx,OFFSET myArray         ; buffer pointer
int  21h
```

14.3.9 Section Review

1. Name the five standard MS-DOS device handles.

2. After calling an MS-DOS I/O function, which flag indicates that an error has occurred?

3. When you call Function 716Ch to create a file, what arguments are required?

4. Show an example of opening an existing file for input.

5. When you call Function 716Ch to read a binary array from a file that is already open, what argument values are required?

6. How do you check for end of file when reading an input file using INT 21h Function 3Fh?

7. When calling Function 3Fh, how is reading from a file different from reading from the keyboard?

8. If you wanted to read a random-access file, which INT 21h function would permit you to jump directly to a particular record in the middle of the file?

9. Write a short code segment that positions the file pointer 50 bytes from the beginning of a file. Assume that the file is already open, and BX contains the file handle.

14.4 Chapter Summary

In this chapter, you learned the basic memory organization of MS-DOS, how to activate MS-DOS function calls, and how to perform basic input-output operations at the operating system level.

The standard input device and the standard output device are collectively called the *console*, which involves the keyboard for input and the video display for output.

A *software interrupt* is a call to an operating system procedure. Most of these procedures, called *interrupt handlers*, provide input-output capability to application programs.

The INT (call to interrupt procedure) instruction pushes the CPU flags and 32-bit return address (CS and IP) on the stack, disables other interrupts, and calls an interrupt handler. The CPU processes the INT instruction using the *interrupt vector table*, a table containing 32-bit segment-offset addresses of interrupt handlers.

Programs designed for MS-DOS must be 16-bit applications running in real-address mode. Real-address mode applications use 16-bit segments and use segmented addressing.

The .MODEL directive specifies which memory model your program will use. The .STACK directive allocates a small amount of local stack space for your program. In real-address mode, stack entries are 16 bits by default. Enable the use of 32-bit registers using the .386 directive.

A 16-bit application containing variables must set DS to the location of the data segment before accessing the variables.

Every program must include a statement that ends the program and returns to the operating system. One way to do this is by using the .EXIT directive. Another way is by calling INT 21h Function 4Ch.

Any real-address mode program can access hardware ports, interrupt vectors, and system memory when running under MS-DOS, Windows 95, 98, and Millenium. On the other hand, this type of access is only granted to kernel mode and device driver programs in more recent versions of Windows.

When a program runs, any additional text on its command line is automatically stored in the 128-byte MS-DOS command tail area, at offset 80h in special memory segment named the *program segment prefix* (PSP). The **GetCommandTail** procedure from the Irvine16 library returns a copy of the command tail. The program segment prefix is discussed in Section 17.3.1.

Some frequently used BIOS interrupts are listed here:

- INT 10h Video Services: Procedures that display routines that control the cursor position, write text in color, scroll the screen, and display video graphics.
- INT 16h Keyboard Services: Procedures that read the keyboard and check its status.
- INT 17h Printer Services: Procedures that initialize, print, and return the printer status.
- INT 1Ah Time of Day: A procedure that gets the number of clock ticks since the machine was turned on or sets the counter to a new value.
- INT 1Ch User Timer Interrupt: An empty procedure that is executed 18.2 times per second.

A number of important MS-DOS (INT 21h) functions are listed here:

- INT 21h MS-DOS Services: Procedures that provide input-output, file handling, and memory management. Also known as MS-DOS function calls.
- About 200 different functions are supported by INT 21h, identified by a function number placed in the AH register.
- INT 21h Function 4Ch terminates the current program (called a process).
- INT 21h Functions 2 and 6 write a single character to standard output.
- INT 21h Function 5 writes a single character to the printer.
- INT 21h Function 9 writes a string to standard output.
- INT 21h Function 40h writes an array of bytes to a file or device.
- INT 21h Function 1 reads a single character from standard input.
- INT 21h Function 6 reads a character from standard input without waiting.
- INT 21h Function 0Ah reads a buffered string from standard input.

- INT 21h Function 0Bh gets the status of the standard input buffer.
- INT 21h Function 3Fh reads an array of bytes from a file or device.
- INT 21h Function 2Ah gets the system date.
- INT 21h Function 2Bh sets the system date.
- INT 21h Function 2Ch gets the system time.
- INT 21h Function 2Dh sets the system time.
- INT 21h Function 716Ch either creates a file or opens an existing file.
- INT 21h Function 3Eh closes a file handle.
- INT 21h Function 42h moves a file's position pointer.
- INT 21h Function 5706h obtains a file's creation date and time.
- INT 21h Function 62h returns the segment portion of the program segment prefix address.

The following sample programs showed how to apply MS-DOS functions:

- The *DateTime.asm* program displays the system date and time.
- The *Readfile.asm* program opens a text file for input, reads the file, displays it on the console, creates a new file, and copies the data to a new file.
- The *Binfile.asm* program fills an array with random integers, displays the integers on the screen, writes the integers to a binary file, and closes the file. It reopens the file, reads the integers, and displays them on the screen.

A binary file is given its name because the data stored in the file is a binary image of program data.

14.5 Programming Exercises

The following exercises must be done in real-address mode. Do not use any functions from the Irvine16 library. Use INT 21h function calls for all input-output, unless an exercise specifically says to do otherwise.

★★ **1. Read a Text File**

Open a file for input, read the file, and display its contents on the screen in hexadecimal. Make the input buffer small—about 256 bytes—so the program uses a loop to repeat the call to Function 3Fh as many times as necessary until the entire file has been processed.

★★ **2. Copy a Text File**

Modify the **Readfile** program in Section 14.3.6 so that it can read a file of any size. Assuming that the buffer is smaller than the input file, use a loop to read all data. Use a buffer size of 256 bytes. Display appropriate error messages if the Carry flag is set after any INT 21h function calls.

★ **3. Setting the Date**

Write a program that displays the current date and prompts the user for a new date. If a nonblank date is entered, use it to update the system date.

★ **4. Uppercase Conversion**

Write a program that uses INT 21h to input lowercase letters from the keyboard and convert them to uppercase. Display only the uppercase letters.

★ **5.   File Creation Date**

Write a procedure that displays the date when a file was created, along with its filename. Pass a pointer to the filename in the DX register. Write a test program that demonstrates the procedure with several different filenames, including extended filenames. If a file cannot be found, display an appropriate error message.

★★★ **6.   Text Matching Program**

Write a program that opens a text file containing up to 60K bytes and performs a case-insensitive search for a string. The string and the filename can be input by the user. Display each line from the file on which the string appears and prefix each line with a line number. Review the **Str_find** procedure from the programming exercises in Section 9.7. Your program must run in real-address mode. *(A VideoNote for this exercise is posted on the Web site.)*

★★ **7.   File Encryption Using XOR**

Enhance the file encryption program from Section 6.3.4 as follows:

• Prompt the user for the name of a plaintext file and a ciphertext file.
• Open the plaintext file for input, and open the cipher text file for output.
• Let the user enter a single integer encryption code (1 to 255).
• Read the plaintext file into a buffer, and exclusive-OR each byte with the encryption code.
• Write the buffer to the ciphertext file.

The only procedure you may call from the book's link library is **ReadInt**. All other input/output must be performed using INT 21h. The same code you write could also be used to decrypt the ciphertext file, producing the original plaintext file.

★★★ **8.   CountWords Procedure**

Write a program that counts the words in a text file. Prompt the user for a file name, and display the word count on the screen. The only procedure you may call from the book's link library is **WriteDec**. All other input/output must be performed using INT 21h. *(A VideoNote for this exercise is posted on the Web site.)*

MASM Reference

A.1   Introduction

A.2   MASM Reserved Words

A.3   Register Names

A.4   Microsoft Assembler (ML)

A.5   MASM Directives

A.6   Symbols

A.7   Operators

A.8   Runtime Operators

A.1   Introduction

The Microsoft MASM 6.11 manuals were last printed in 1992, and consisted of three volumes:

- Programmers Guide
- Reference
- Environment and Tools

Unfortunately, the printed manuals have not been available for many years, but Microsoft supplies electronic copies of the manuals (MS-Word files) in its *Platform SDK* package. The printed manuals are definitely collectors' items.

The information in this chapter was excerpted from Chapters 1 to 3 of the *Reference* manual, with updates from the MASM 6.14 *readme.txt* file. The Microsoft license agreement supplied with this book entitles the reader to a single copy of the software and accompanying documentation, which we have, in part, printed here.

Syntax Notation   Throughout this appendix, a consistent syntax notation is used. Words in all capital letters indicate a MASM reserved word that may appear in your program in either uppercase or lowercase letters. In the following example, DATA is a reserved word:

    .DATA

Words in italics indicate a defined term or category. In the following example, *number* refers to an integer constant:

>   ALIGN [[*number*]]

When double brackets [[..]] surround an item, the item is optional. In the following example, *text* is optional:

>   [[*text*]]

When a vertical separator | appears between items in a list of two or more items, you must select one of the items. The following example indicates a choice between NEAR and FAR:

>   NEAR | FAR

An ellipsis (. . .) indicates repetition of the last item in a list. In the next example, the comma followed by an *initializer* may repeat multiple times:

>   [[*name*]] BYTE *initializer* [[, *initializer*]] . . .

A.2   MASM Reserved Words

$	PARITY?
?	PASCAL
@B	QWORD
@F	REAL4
ADDR	REAL8
BASIC	REAL10
BYTE	SBYTE
C	SDWORD
CARRY?	SIGN?
DWORD	STDCALL
FAR	SWORD
FAR16	SYSCALL
FORTRAN	TBYTE
FWORD	VARARG
NEAR	WORD
NEAR16	ZERO?
OVERFLOW?	

A.3   Register Names

AH	CR0	DR1	EBX	SI
AL	CR2	DR2	ECX	SP
AX	CR3	DR3	EDI	SS
BH	CS	DR6	EDX	ST
BL	CX	DR7	ES	TR3

BP	DH	DS	ESI	TR4
BX	DI	DX	ESP	TR5
CH	DL	EAX	FS	TR6
CL	DR0	EBP	GS	TR7

A.4 Microsoft Assembler (ML)

The ML program (*ML.EXE*) assembles and links one or more assembly language source files. The syntax is

ML [[*options*]] *filename* [[[[*options*]] *filename*]]. . . [[**/link** *linkoptions*]]

The only required parameter is at least one *filename*, the name of a source file written in assembly language. The following command, for example, assembles the source file **AddSub.asm** and produces the object file *AddSub.obj*:

```
ML -c AddSub.asm
```

The *options* parameter consists of zero or more command-line options, each starting with a slash (/) or dash (–). Multiple options must be separated by at least one space. Table A-1 lists the complete set of command-line options. The command-line options are case sensitive.

Table A-1   ML Command-Line Options.

Option	Action
/AT	Enables tiny-memory-model support. Enables error messages for code constructs that violate the requirements for .COM format files. Note that this is not equivalent to the .MODEL TINY directive.
/Bl*filename*	Selects an alternate linker.
/c	Assembles only. Does not link.
/coff	Generates an object file in *Microsoft Common Object File Format*.
/Cp	Preserves case of all user identifiers.
/Cu	Maps all identifiers to uppercase.
/Cx	Preserves case in public and external symbols (default).
/D*symbol* [[=*value*]]	Defines a text macro with the given name. If *value* is missing, it is blank. Multiple tokens separated by spaces must be enclosed in quotation marks.
/EP	Generates a preprocessed source listing (sent to STDOUT). See /Sf.
/F*hexnum*	Sets stack size to *hexnum* bytes (this is the same as /link /STACK:*number*). The value must be expressed in hexadecimal notation. There must be a space between /F and *hexnum*.
/Fe*filename*	Names the executable file.
/Fl[[*filename*]]	Generates an assembled code listing. See /Sf.
/Fm[[*filename*]]	Creates a linker .MAP file.
/Fo*filename*	Names an object file.

Table A-1   *(Continued)*

Option	Action
/FPi	Generates emulator fixups for floating-point arithmetic (mixed-language only).
/Fr[[filename]]	Generates a Source Browser .SBR file.
/FR[[filename]]	Generates an extended form of a Source Browser .SBR file.
/Gc	Specifies use of FORTRAN- or Pascal-style function calling and naming conventions.
/Gd	Specifies use of C-style function calling and naming conventions.
/Gz	Use STDCALL calling connections.
/H number	Restricts external names to number significant characters. The default is 31 characters.
/help	Calls QuickHelp for help on ML.
/I pathname	Sets path for include file. A maximum of 10 /I options is allowed.
/link	Linker options and libraries.
/nologo	Suppresses messages for successful assembly.
/omf	Generate an OMF (Microsoft Object Module Format) file. This format is required by the older 16-bit Microsoft Linker (LINK16.EXE).
/Sa	Turns on listing of all available information.
/Sc	Adds instruction timings to listing file.
/Sf	Adds first-pass listing to listing file.
/Sg	Causes MASM-generated assembly code to appear in the source listing file. Use this, for example, if you want to see how .IF and .ELSE directives work.
/Sl width	Sets the line width of source listing in characters per line. Range is 60 to 255 or 0. Default is 0. Same as PAGE width.
/Sn	Turns off symbol table when producing a listing.
/Sp length	Sets the page length of source listing in lines per page. Range is 10 to 255 or 0. Default is 0. Same as PAGE length.
/Ss text	Specifies text for source listing. Same as SUBTITLE text.
/St text	Specifies title for source listing. Same as TITLE text.
/Sx	Turns on false conditionals in listing.
/Ta filename	Assembles source file whose name does not end with the .ASM extension.
/w	Same as /W0.
/Wlevel	Sets the warning level, where level = 0, 1, 2, or 3.
/WX	Returns an error code if warnings are generated.
/X	Ignore INCLUDE Environment path.
/Zd	Generates line-number information in object file.
/Zf	Makes all symbols public.

Table A-1   (Continued)

Option	Action
/Zi	Generates CodeView information in object file.
/Zm	Enables M510 option for maximum compatibility with MASM 5.1.
/Zp[[alignment]]	Packs structures on the specified byte boundary. The *alignment* may be 1, 2, or 4.
/Zs	Performs a syntax check only.
/?	Displays a summary of ML command-line syntax.
/error Report	Report internal assembler errors to Microsoft.

A.5   MASM Directives

name = expression

Assigns the numeric value of *expression* to *name*. The symbol may be redefined later.

.186

Enables assembly of instructions for the 80186 processor; disables assembly of instructions introduced with later processors. Also enables 8087 instructions.

.286

Enables assembly of nonprivileged instructions for the 80286 processor; disables assembly of instructions introduced with later processors. Also enables 80287 instructions.

.286P

Enables assembly of all instructions (including privileged) for the 80286 processor; disables assembly of instructions introduced with later processors. Also enables 80287 instructions.

.287

Enables assembly of instructions for the 80287 coprocessor; disables assembly of instructions introduced with later coprocessors.

.386

Enables assembly of nonprivileged instructions for the 80386 processor; disables assembly of instructions introduced with later processors. Also enables 80387 instructions.

.386P

Enables assembly of all instructions (including privileged) for the 80386 processor; disables assembly of instructions introduced with later processors. Also enables 80387 instructions.

.387

Enables assembly of instructions for the 80387 coprocessor.

.486

Enables assembly of nonprivileged instructions for the 80486 processor.

.486P

Enables assembly of all instructions (including privileged) for the 80486 processor.

.586

Enables assembly of nonprivileged instructions for the Pentium processor.

.586P
Enables assembly of all instructions (including privileged) for the Pentium processor.

.686
Enables assembly of nonprivileged instructions for the Pentium Pro processor.

.686P
Enables assembly of all instructions (including privileged) for the Pentium Pro processor.

.8086
Enables assembly of 8086 instructions (and the identical 8088 instructions); disables assembly of instructions introduced with later processors. Also enables 8087 instructions. This is the default mode for processors.

.8087
Enables assembly of 8087 instructions; disables assembly of instructions introduced with later coprocessors. This is the default mode for coprocessors.

ALIAS <alias> = <actual-name>
Maps an old function name to a new name. *Alias* is the alternate or alias name, and *actual-name* is the actual name of the function or procedure. The angle brackets are required. The ALIAS directive can be used for creating libraries that allow the linker (LINK) to map an old function to a new function.

ALIGN [[*number*]]
Aligns the next variable or instruction on a byte that is a multiple of *number*.

.ALPHA
Orders segments alphabetically.

ASSUME *segregister:name* [[, *segregister:name*]]. . .
ASSUME *dataregister:type* [[, *dataregister:type*]]. . .
ASSUME *register*:**ERROR** [[, *register*:**ERROR**]]. . .
ASSUME [[*register*:]] **NOTHING** [[, *register*:**NOTHING**]]. . .
Enables error-checking for register values. After an **ASSUME** is put into effect, the assembler watches for changes to the values of the given registers. **ERROR** generates an error if the register is used. **NOTHING** removes register error-checking. You can combine different kinds of assumptions in one statement.

.BREAK [[.IF *condition*]]
Generates code to terminate a **.WHILE** or **.REPEAT** block if *condition* is true.

[[*name*]] BYTE *initializer* [[, *initializer*]] . . .
Allocates and optionally initializes a byte of storage for each *initializer*. Can also be used as a type specifier anywhere a type is legal.

name CATSTR [[*textitem1* [[, *textitem2*]] . . .]]
Concatenates text items. Each text item can be a literal string, a constant preceded by a %, or the string returned by a macro function.

.CODE [[*name*]]
When used with **.MODEL**, indicates the start of a code segment called *name* (the default segment name is _TEXT for tiny, small, compact, and flat models, or *module*_TEXT for other models).

COMM *definition* [[*, definition*]] **...**

Creates a communal variable with the attributes specified in *definition*. Each *definition* has the following form:

    [[*langtype*]] [[**NEAR** | **FAR**]] *label:type*[[*:count*]]

The *label* is the name of the variable. The *type* can be any type specifier (**BYTE**, **WORD**, and so on) or an integer specifying the number of bytes. The *count* specifies the number of data objects (one is the default).

COMMENT *delimiter* [[*text*]]

    [[*text*]]

    [[*text*]] *delimiter* [[*text*]]

Treats all *text* between or on the same line as the delimiters as a comment.

.CONST

When used with **.MODEL**, starts a constant data segment (with segment name CONST). This segment has the read-only attribute.

.CONTINUE [[**.IF** *condition*]]

Generates code to jump to the top of a **.WHILE** or **.REPEAT** block if *condition* is true.

.CREF

Enables listing of symbols in the symbol portion of the symbol table and browser file.

.DATA

When used with **.MODEL**, starts a near data segment for initialized data (segment name _DATA).

.DATA?

When used with **.MODEL**, starts a near data segment for uninitialized data (segment name _BSS).

.DOSSEG

Orders the segments according to the MS-DOS segment convention: CODE first, then segments not in DGROUP, and then segments in DGROUP. The segments in DGROUP follow this order: segments not in BSS or STACK, then BSS segments, and finally STACK segments. Primarily used for ensuring CodeView support in MASM stand-alone programs. Same as **DOSSEG**.

DOSSEG

Identical to **.DOSSEG**, which is the preferred form.

DB

Can be used to define data like **BYTE**.

DD

Can be used to define data like **DWORD**.

DF

Can be used to define data like **FWORD**.

DQ

Can be used to define data like **QWORD**.

DT

Can be used to define data like **TBYTE**.

DW

Can be used to define data like **WORD**.

[[*name*]] **DWORD** *initializer* [[*, initializer*]]. . .

Allocates and optionally initializes a doubleword (4 bytes) of storage for each *initializer*. Can also be used as a type specifier anywhere a type is legal.

ECHO *message*

Displays *message* to the standard output device (by default, the screen). Same as **%OUT**.

.ELSE

See **.IF**.

ELSE

Marks the beginning of an alternate block within a conditional block. See **IF**.

ELSEIF

Combines **ELSE** and **IF** into one statement. See **IF**.

ELSEIF2

ELSEIF block evaluated on every assembly pass if **OPTION:SETIF2** is **TRUE**.

END [[*address*]]

Marks the end of a module and, optionally, sets the program entry point to *address*.

.ENDIF

See **.IF**.

ENDIF

See **IF**.

ENDM

Terminates a macro or repeat block. See **MACRO, FOR, FORC, REPEAT**, or **WHILE**.

name **ENDP**

Marks the end of procedure *name* previously begun with **PROC**. See **PROC**.

name **ENDS**

Marks the end of segment, structure, or union *name* previously begun with **SEGMENT, STRUCT, UNION**, or a simplified segment directive.

.ENDW

See **.WHILE**.

name **EQU** *expression*

Assigns numeric value of *expression* to *name*. The *name* cannot be redefined later.

name **EQU** *<text>*

Assigns specified *text* to *name*. The *name* can be assigned a different *text* later. See **TEXTEQU**.

.ERR [[*message*]]

Generates an error.

.ERR2 [[*message*]]

.ERR block evaluated on every assembly pass if **OPTION:SETIF2** is **TRUE**.

.ERRB *<textitem>* [[, *message*]]

Generates an error if *textitem* is blank.

.ERRDEF *name* [[, *message*]]

Generates an error if *name* is a previously defined label, variable, or symbol.

.ERRDIF[[I]] *<textitem1>*, *<textitem2>* [[, *message*]]

Generates an error if the text items are different. If **I** is given, the comparison is case insensitive.

.ERRE *expression* [[, *message*]]

Generates an error if *expression* is false (0).

.ERRIDN[[I]] *<textitem1>*, *<textitem2>* [[, *message*]]

Generates an error if the text items are identical. If **I** is given, the comparison is case insensitive.

.ERRNB *<textitem>* [[, *message*]]

Generates an error if *textitem* is not blank.

.ERRNDEF *name* [[, *message*]]

Generates an error if *name* has not been defined.

.ERRNZ *expression* [[, *message*]]

Generates an error if *expression* is true (nonzero).

EVEN

Aligns the next variable or instruction on an even byte.

.EXIT [[*expression*]]

Generates termination code. Returns optional *expression* to shell.

EXITM [[*textitem*]]

Terminates expansion of the current repeat or macro block and begins assembly of the next statement outside the block. In a macro function, *textitem* is the value returned.

EXTERN [[*langtype*]] *name* [[(*altid*)]] :*type* [[, [[*langtype*]] *name* [[(*altid*)]] :*type*]]. . .

Defines one or more external variables, labels, or symbols called *name* whose type is *type*. The *type* can be **ABS**, which imports *name* as a constant. Same as **EXTRN**.

EXTERNDEF [[*langtype*]] *name*:*type* [[, [[*langtype*]] *name*:*type*]]. . .

Defines one or more external variables, labels, or symbols called *name* whose type is *type*. If *name* is defined in the module, it is treated as **PUBLIC**. If *name* is referenced in the module, it is treated as **EXTERN**. If *name* is not referenced, it is ignored. The *type* can be **ABS**, which imports *name* as a constant. Normally used in include files.

EXTRN

See **EXTERN**.

.FARDATA [[*name*]]

When used with **.MODEL**, starts a far data segment for initialized data (segment name FAR_DATA or *name*).

.FARDATA? [[*name*]]

When used with **.MODEL**, starts a far data segment for uninitialized data (segment name FAR_BSS or *name*).

FOR parameter [[:REQ | :=default]] , <argument [[, argument]]. . . >
　statements
　ENDM

Marks a block that will be repeated once for each *argument*, with the current *argument* replacing *parameter* on each repetition. Same as **IRP**.

FORC
　parameter, <string> statements
　ENDM

Marks a block that will be repeated once for each character in *string*, with the current character replacing *parameter* on each repetition. Same as **IRPC**.

[[*name*]] **FWORD** *initializer* [[, *initializer*]]. . .

Allocates and optionally initializes 6 bytes of storage for each *initializer*. Also can be used as a type specifier anywhere a type is legal.

GOTO *macrolabel*

Transfers assembly to the line marked **:***macrolabel*. **GOTO** is permitted only inside **MACRO, FOR, FORC, REPEAT**, and **WHILE** blocks. The label must be the only directive on the line and must be preceded by a leading colon.

name **GROUP** *segment* [[, *segment*]]. . .

Add the specified *segments* to the group called *name*. This directive has no effect when used in 32-bit flat-model programming, and will result in error when used with the /coff command-line option.

.IF *condition1*
　statements
　[[**.ELSEIF** condition2
　　statements]]
　[[**.ELSE**
　　statements]]
　.ENDIF

Generates code that tests *condition1* (for example, AX > 7) and executes the *statements* if that condition is true. If an **.ELSE** follows, its statements are executed if the original condition was false. Note that the conditions are evaluated at runtime.

IF expression1
　ifstatements
　[[**ELSEIF** *expression2*
　　elseifstatements]]
　[[**ELSE**
　　elsestatements]]
　ENDIF

Grants assembly of *ifstatements* if *expression1* is true (nonzero) or *elseifstatements* if *expression1* is false (0) and *expression2* is true. The following directives may be substituted for **ELSEIF:**

ELSEIFB, ELSEIFDEF, ELSEIFDIF, ELSEIFDIFI, ELSEIFE, ELSEIFIDN, ELSE-IFIDNI, ELSEIFNB, and **ELSEIFNDEF**. Optionally, assembles *elsestatements* if the previous expression is false. Note that the expressions are evaluated at assembly time.

IF2 *expression*

IF block is evaluated on every assembly pass if **OPTION:SETIF2** is **TRUE**. See **IF** for complete syntax.

IFB *textitem*

Grants assembly if *textitem* is blank. See **IF** for complete syntax.

IFDEF *name*

Grants assembly if *name* is a previously defined label, variable, or symbol. See **IF** for complete syntax.

IFDIF⟦**I**⟧ *textitem1, textitem2*

Grants assembly if the text items are different. If **I** is given, the comparison is case insensitive. See **IF** for complete syntax.

IFE *expression*

Grants assembly if *expression* is false (0). See **IF** for complete syntax.

IFIDN⟦**I**⟧ *textitem1, textitem2*

Grants assembly if the text items are identical. If **I** is given, the comparison is case insensitive. See **IF** for complete syntax.

IFNB *textitem*

Grants assembly if *textitem* is not blank. See **IF** for complete syntax.

IFNDEF *name*

Grants assembly if *name* has not been defined. See **IF** for complete syntax.

INCLUDE *filename*

Inserts source code from the source file given by *filename* into the current source file during assembly. The *filename* must be enclosed in angle brackets if it includes a backslash, semicolon, greater-than symbol, less-than symbol, single quotation mark, or double quotation mark.

INCLUDELIB *libraryname*

Informs the linker that the current module should be linked with *libraryname*. The *libraryname* must be enclosed in angle brackets if it includes a backslash, semicolon, greater-than symbol, less-than symbol, single quotation mark, or double quotation mark.

name **INSTR** ⟦*position,*⟧ *textitem1, textitem2*

Finds the first occurrence of *textitem2* in *textitem1*. The starting *position* is optional. Each text item can be a literal string, a constant preceded by a %, or the string returned by a macro function.

INVOKE *expression* ⟦*, arguments*⟧

Calls the procedure at the address given by *expression*, passing the arguments on the stack or in registers according to the standard calling conventions of the language type. Each argument passed to the procedure may be an expression, a register pair, or an address expression (an expression preceded by **ADDR**).

IRP

See **FOR**.

IRPC

See **FORC**.

name **LABEL** *type*

Creates a new label by assigning the current location-counter value and the given *type* to *name*.

name **LABEL** [[**NEAR** | **FAR** | **PROC**]] **PTR** [[*type*]]

Creates a new label by assigning the current location-counter value and the given *type* to *name*.

.K3D

Enables assembly of K3D instructions.

.LALL

See **.LISTMACROALL**.

.LFCOND

See **.LISTIF**.

.LIST

Starts listing of statements. This is the default.

.LISTALL

Starts listing of all statements. Equivalent to the combination of **.LIST**, **.LISTIF**, and **.LIST-MACROALL**.

.LISTIF

Starts listing of statements in false conditional blocks. Same as **.LFCOND**.

.LISTMACRO

Starts listing of macro expansion statements that generate code or data. This is the default. Same as **.XALL**.

.LISTMACROALL

Starts listing of all statements in macros. Same as **.LALL**.

LOCAL *localname* [[*, localname*]]...

Within a macro, **LOCAL** defines labels that are unique to each instance of the macro.

LOCAL *label* [[[*count*]]] [[*:type*]] [[*, label* [[[*count*]]] [[*type*]]]]...

Within a procedure definition (**PROC**), **LOCAL** creates stack-based variables that exist for the duration of the procedure. The *label* may be a simple variable or an array containing *count* elements.

name **MACRO** [[*parameter* [[*:REQ* | *:=default* | *:VARARG*]]]]...

    statements
    ENDM [[*value*]]

Marks a macro block called *name* and establishes *parameter* placeholders for arguments passed when the macro is called. A macro function returns *value* to the calling statement.

.MMX

Enables assembly of MMX instructions.

.MODEL *memorymodel* [[, *langtype*]] [[, *stackoption*]]

Initializes the program memory model. The *memorymodel* can be **TINY, SMALL, COMPACT, MEDIUM, LARGE, HUGE**, or **FLAT**. The *langtype* can be **C, BASIC, FORTRAN, PASCAL, SYSCALL**, or **STDCALL**. The *stackoption* can be **NEARSTACK** or **FARSTACK**.

NAME *modulename*

Ignored.

.NO87

Disallows assembly of all floating-point instructions.

.NOCREF [[*name*[[, *name*]]. . .]]

Suppresses listing of symbols in the symbol table and browser file. If names are specified, only the given names are suppressed. Same as **.XCREF**.

.NOLIST

Suppresses program listing. Same as **.XLIST**.

.NOLISTIF

Suppresses listing of conditional blocks whose condition evaluates to false (0). This is the default. Same as **.SFCOND**.

.NOLISTMACRO

Suppresses listing of macro expansions. Same as **.SALL**.

OPTION *optionlist*

Enables and disables features of the assembler. Available options include **CASEMAP, DOTNAME, NODOTNAME, EMULATOR, NOEMULATOR, EPILOGUE, EXPR16, EXPR32, LANGUAGE, LJMP, NOLJMP, M510, NOM510, NOKEYWORD, NOSIGNEXTEND, OFFSET, OLDMACROS, NOOLDMACROS, OLDSTRUCTS, NOOLDSTRUCTS, PROC, PROLOGUE, READONLY, NOREADONLY, SCOPED, NOSCOPED, SEGMENT**, and **SETIF2**.

ORG *expression*

Sets the location counter to *expression*.

%OUT

See **ECHO**.

[[*name*]] **OWORD** *initializer* [[, *initializer*]]. . .

Allocates and optionally initializes an octalword (16 bytes) of storage for each *initializer*. Can also be used as a type specifier anywhere a type is legal. This data type is used primarily by Streaming SIMD instructions; it holds an array of four 4-byte reals.

PAGE [[[[*length*]], *width*]]

Sets line *length* and character *width* of the program listing. If no arguments are given, generates a page break.

PAGE[+]

Increments the section number and resets the page number to 1.

POPCONTEXT *context*

Restores part or all of the current *context* (saved by the **PUSHCONTEXT** directive). The *context* can be **ASSUMES, RADIX, LISTING, CPU**, or **ALL**.

label **PROC** [[*distance*]] [[*langtype*]] [[*visibility*]] [[*<prologuearg>*]]
    [[**USES** *reglist*]] [[, *parameter* [[:*tag*]]]]. . .
    statements
    label **ENDP**
        Marks start and end of a procedure block called *label*. The statements in the block can be
        called with the **CALL** instruction or **INVOKE** directive.

label **PROTO** [[*distance*]] [[*langtype*]] [[, [[*parameter*]]:*tag*]]. . .
    Prototypes a function.

PUBLIC [[*langtype*]] *name* [[, [[*langtype*]] *name*]]. . .
    Makes each variable, label, or absolute symbol specified as *name* available to all other mod-
    ules in the program.

PURGE *macroname* [[, *macroname*]]. . .
    Deletes the specified macros from memory.

PUSHCONTEXT *context*
    Saves part or all of the current *context*: segment register assumes, radix value, listing and cref
    flags, or processor/coprocessor values. The *context* can be **ASSUMES, RADIX, LISTING,
    CPU,** or **ALL.**

[[*name*]] **QWORD** *initializer* [[, *initializer*]]. . .
    Allocates and optionally initializes 8 bytes of storage for each *initializer*. Also can be used as
    a type specifier anywhere a type is legal.

.RADIX *expression*
    Sets the default radix, in the range 2 to 16, to the value of *expression*.

name **REAL4** *initializer* [[, *initializer*]]. . .
    Allocates and optionally initializes a single-precision (4-byte) floating-point number for each
    initializer.

name **REAL8** *initializer* [[, *initializer*]]. . .
    Allocates and optionally initializes a double-precision (8-byte) floating-point number for
    each *initializer*.

name **REAL10** *initializer* [[, *initializer*]]. . .
    Allocates and optionally initializes a 10-byte floating-point number for each *initializer*.

recordname **RECORD** *fieldname*:*width* [[= *expression*]]
    [[, *fieldname*:*width* [[= *expression*]]]]. . .
        Declares a record type consisting of the specified fields. The *fieldname* names the field,
        width specifies the number of bits, and *expression* gives its initial value.

.REPEAT
    statements
    .UNTIL *condition*
        Generates code that repeats execution of the block of *statements* until *condition* becomes
        true. **.UNTILCXZ,** which becomes true when CX is zero, may be substituted for
        .UNTIL. The *condition* is optional with **.UNTILCXZ.**

REPEAT *expression*
> *statements*
> **ENDM**
>> Marks a block that is to be repeated *expression* times. Same as **REPT**.

REPT
> See **REPEAT**.

.SALL
> See **.NOLISTMACRO**.

name **SBYTE** *initializer* [[, *initializer*]]. . .
> Allocates and optionally initializes a signed byte of storage for each *initializer*. Can also be used as a type specifier anywhere a type is legal.

name **SDWORD** *initializer* [[, *initializer*]]. . .
> Allocates and optionally initializes a signed doubleword (4 bytes) of storage for each *initializer*. Also can be used as a type specifier anywhere a type is legal.

name **SEGMENT** [[**READONLY**]] [[*align*]] [[*combine*]] [[*use*]] [[*'class'*]]
> *statements*
> *name* **ENDS**
>> Defines a program segment called *name* having segment attributes *align* (**BYTE, WORD, DWORD, PARA, PAGE**), *combine* (**PUBLIC, STACK, COMMON, MEMORY, AT** *address*, **PRIVATE**), *use* (**USE16, USE32, FLAT**), and *class*.

.SEQ
> Orders segments sequentially (the default order).

.SFCOND
> See **.NOLISTIF**.

name **SIZESTR** *textitem*
> Finds the size of a text item.

.STACK [[*size*]]
> When used with **.MODEL**, defines a stack segment (with segment name STACK). The optional *size* specifies the number of bytes for the stack (default 1024). The **.STACK** directive automatically closes the stack statement.

.STARTUP
> Generates program startup code.

STRUC
> See **STRUCT**.

name **STRUCT** [[*alignment*]] [[, **NONUNIQUE**]]
> *fielddeclarations*
> *name* **ENDS**
>> Declares a structure type having the specified *fielddeclarations*. Each field must be a valid data definition. Same as **STRUC**.

name **SUBSTR** *textitem, position* [[, *length*]]
> Returns a substring of *textitem*, starting at *position*. The *textitem* can be a literal string, a constant preceded by a %, or the string returned by a macro function.

SUBTITLE *text*

Defines the listing subtitle. Same as **SUBTTL**.

SUBTTL

See **SUBTITLE**.

name **SWORD** *initializer* [[, *initializer*]]. . .

Allocates and optionally initializes a signed word (2 bytes) of storage for each *initializer*. Can also be used as a type specifier anywhere a type is legal.

[[*name*]] **TBYTE** *initializer* [[, *initializer*]]. . .

Allocates and optionally initializes 10 bytes of storage for each *initializer*. Can also be used as a type specifier anywhere a type is legal.

name **TEXTEQU** [[*textitem*]]

Assigns *textitem* to *name*. The *textitem* can be a literal string, a constant preceded by a %, or the string returned by a macro function.

.TFCOND

Toggles listing of false conditional blocks.

TITLE *text*

Defines the program listing title.

name **TYPEDEF** *type*

Defines a new type called *name*, which is equivalent to *type*.

name **UNION** [[*alignment*]] [[, **NONUNIQUE**]]

   fielddeclarations

[[*name*]] **ENDS**

Declares a union of one or more data types. The *fielddeclarations* must be valid data definitions. Omit the **ENDS** *name* label on nested **UNION** definitions.

.UNTIL

See **.REPEAT**.

.UNTILCXZ

See **.REPEAT**.

.WHILE *condition*

   statements

   .ENDW

Generates code that executes the block of *statements* while *condition* remains true.

WHILE *expression*

   statements

   ENDM

Repeats assembly of block *statements* as long as *expression* remains true.

[[*name*]] **WORD** *initializer* [[, *initializer*]]. . .

Allocates and optionally initializes a word (2 bytes) of storage for each *initializer*. Can also be used as a type specifier anywhere a type is legal.

.XALL

See **.LISTMACRO**.

.XCREF

See **.NOCREF**.

.XLIST

See **.NOLIST**.

.XMM

Enables assembly of Internet Streaming SIMD Extension instructions.

A.6 Symbols

$

The current value of the location counter.

?

In data declarations, a value that the assembler allocates but does not initialize.

@@:

Defines a code label recognizable only between *label1* and *label2*, where *label1* is either start of code or the previous **@@:** label, and *label2* is either end of code or the next **@@:** label. See **@B** and **@F**.

@B

The location of the previous **@@:** label.

@CatStr(*string1* [[, *string2*. . .]] **)**

Macro function that concatenates one or more strings. Returns a string.

@code

The name of the code segment (text macro).

@CodeSize

0 for **TINY, SMALL, COMPACT**, and **FLAT** models, and 1 for **MEDIUM, LARGE**, and **HUGE** models (numeric equate).

@Cpu

A bit mask specifying the processor mode (numeric equate).

@CurSeg

The name of the current segment (text macro).

@data

The name of the default data group. Evaluates to DGROUP for all models except **FLAT**. Evaluates to **FLAT** under the **FLAT** memory model (text macro).

@DataSize

0 for **TINY, SMALL, MEDIUM**, and **FLAT** models, 1 for **COMPACT** and **LARGE** models, and 2 for **HUGE** model (numeric equate).

@Date

The system date in the format mm/dd/yy (text macro).

@Environ(*envvar* **)**

Value of environment variable *envvar* (macro function).

@F

The location of the next @@: label.

@fardata

The name of the segment defined by the **.FARDATA** directive (text macro).

@fardata?

The name of the segment defined by the **.FARDATA?** directive (text macro).

@FileCur

The name of the current file (text macro).

@FileName

The base name of the main file being assembled (text macro).

@InStr([[*position*]], *string1*, *string2*)

Macro function that finds the first occurrence of *string2* in *string1*, beginning at *position* within *string1*. If *position* does not appear, search begins at start of *string1*. Returns a position integer or 0 if *string2* is not found.

@Interface

Information about the language parameters (numeric equate).

@Line

The source line number in the current file (numeric equate).

@Model

1 for **TINY** model, 2 for **SMALL** model, 3 for **COMPACT** model, 4 for **MEDIUM** model, 5 for **LARGE** model, 6 for **HUGE** model, and 7 for **FLAT** model (numeric equate).

@SizeStr(*string*)

Macro function that returns the length of the given string. Returns an integer.

@stack

DGROUP for near stacks or STACK for far stacks (text macro).

@SubStr(*string*, *position* [[, *length*]])

Macro function that returns a substring starting at *position*.

@Time

The system time in 24-hour hh:mm:ss format (text macro).

@Version

610 in MASM 6.1 (text macro).

@WordSize

Two for a 16-bit segment or 4 for a 32-bit segment (numeric equate).

A.7   Operators

expression1 + *expression2*

Returns *expression1* plus *expression2*.

expression1 − *expression2*

Returns *expression1* minus *expression2*.

expression1 * expression2

Returns *expression1* times *expression2*.

expression1 / expression2

Returns *expression1* divided by *expression2*.

–expression

Reverses the sign of *expression*.

expression1 [expression2]

Returns *expression1* plus [*expression2*].

segment: expression

Overrides the default segment of *expression* with *segment*. The *segment* can be a segment register, group name, segment name, or segment expression. The *expression* must be a constant.

expression. field [[. field]] . . .

Returns *expression* plus the offset of *field* within its structure or union.

[register]. field [[. field]] . . .

Returns value at the location pointed to by *register* plus the offset of *field* within its structure or union.

<text>

Treats *text* as a single literal element.

"text"

Treats "*text*" as a string.

'text'

Treats '*text*' as a string.

!character

Treats *character* as a literal character rather than as an operator or symbol.

;text

Treats *text* as a comment.

;;text

Treats *text* as a comment in a macro that appears only in the macro definition. The listing does not show *text* where the macro is expanded.

%expression

Treats the value of *expression* in a macro argument as text.

&parameter&

Replaces *parameter* with its corresponding argument value.

ABS

See the **EXTERNDEF** directive.

ADDR

See the **INVOKE** directive.

expression1 AND expression2

Returns the result of a bitwise AND operation for *expression1* and *expression2*.

count DUP (*initialvalue* [[, *initialvalue*]]...)

Specifies *count* number of declarations of *initialvalue*.

expression1 EQ expression2

Returns true (-1) if *expression1* equals *expression2* and returns false (0) if it does not.

expression1 GE expression2

Returns true (-1) if *expression1* is greater than or equal to *expression2* and returns false (0) if it is not.

expression1 GT expression2

Returns true (-1) if *expression1* is greater than *expression2* and returns false (0) if it is not.

HIGH *expression*

Returns the high byte of *expression*.

HIGHWORD *expression*

Returns the high word of *expression*.

expression1 LE expression2

Returns true (-1) if *expression1* is less than or equal to *expression2* and returns false (0) if it is not.

LENGTH *variable*

Returns the number of data items in *variable* created by the first initializer.

LENGTHOF *variable*

Returns the number of data objects in *variable*.

LOW *expression*

Returns the low byte of *expression*.

LOWWORD *expression*

Returns the low word of *expression*.

LROFFSET *expression*

Returns the offset of *expression*. Same as **OFFSET**, but it generates a loader resolved offset, which allows Windows to relocate code segments.

expression1 LT expression2

Returns true (-1) if *expression1* is less than *expression2* and returns false (0) if it is not.

MASK { *recordfieldname* | *record* }

Returns a bit mask in which the bits in *recordfieldname* or *record* are set and all other bits are cleared.

expression1 MOD expression2

Returns the integer value of the remainder (modulo) when dividing *expression1* by *expression2*.

expression1 NE expression2

Returns true (-1) if *expression1* does not equal *expression2* and returns false (0) if it does.

NOT *expression*

Returns *expression* with all bits reversed.

OFFSET *expression*
> Returns the offset of *expression*.

OPATTR *expression*
> Returns a word defining the mode and scope of *expression*. The low byte is identical to the byte returned by **.TYPE**. The high byte contains additional information.

expression1 **OR** *expression2*
> Returns the result of a bitwise OR operation for *expression1* and *expression2*.

type **PTR** *expression*
> Forces the *expression* to be treated as having the specified *type.*

[[*distance*]] **PTR** *type*
> Specifies a pointer to *type*.

SEG *expression*
> Returns the segment of *expression*.

expression **SHL** *count*
> Returns the result of shifting the bits of *expression* left *count* number of bits.

SHORT *label*
> Sets the type of *label* to short. All jumps to *label* must be short (within the range –128 to +127 bytes from the jump instruction to *label*).

expression **SHR** *count*
> Returns the result of shifting the bits of *expression* right *count* number of bits.

SIZE *variable*
> Returns the number of bytes in *variable* allocated by the first initializer.

SIZEOF {*variable* | *type*}
> Returns the number of bytes in *variable* or *type*.

THIS *type*
> Returns an operand of specified *type* whose offset and segment values are equal to the current location-counter value.

.TYPE *expression*
> See **OPATTR**.

TYPE *expression*
> Returns the type of *expression*.

WIDTH {*recordfieldname* | *record*}
> Returns the width in bits of the current *recordfieldname* or *record*.

expression1 **XOR** *expression2*
> Returns the result of a bitwise XOR operation for *expression1* and *expression2*.

A.8 Runtime Operators

The following operators are used only within **.IF, .WHILE,** or **.REPEAT** blocks and are evaluated at runtime, not at assembly time:

expression1 == *expression2*
> Is equal to.

expression1 != *expression2*
>   Is not equal to.

expression1 > *expression2*
>   Is greater than.

expression1 >= *expression2*
>   Is greater than or equal to.

expression1 < *expression2*
>   Is less than.

expression1 <− *expression2*
>   Is less than or equal to.

expression1 || *expression2*
>   Logical OR.

expression1 && *expression2*
>   Logical AND.

expression1 & *expression2*
>   Bitwise AND.

!expression
>   Logical negation.

CARRY?
>   Status of Carry flag.

OVERFLOW?
>   Status of Overflow flag.

PARITY?
>   Status of Parity flag.

SIGN?
>   Status of Sign flag.

ZERO?
>   Status of Zero flag.

B

THE x86 INSTRUCTION SET

B.1 Introduction
    B.1.1 Flags
    B.1.2 Instruction Descriptions and Formats
B.2 Instruction Set Details (Non Floating-Point)
B.3 Floating-Point Instructions

B.1   Introduction

This appendix is a quick guide to the most commonly used x86 instructions. It does not cover system-mode instructions or instructions typically used only in operating system kernel code or protected-mode device drivers.

B.1.1   Flags (EFlags)

Each instruction description contains a series of boxes that describe how the instruction will affect the CPU status flags. Each flag is identified by a single letter:

O	Overflow	S	Sign	P	Parity
D	Direction	Z	Zero	C	Carry
I	Interrupt	A	Auxiliary Carry		

Inside the boxes, the following notation shows how each instruction will affect the flags:

1	Sets the flag.
0	Clears the flag.
?	May change the flag to an undetermined value.
(blank)	The flag is not changed.
*	Changes the flag according to specific rules associated with the flag.

620

For example, the following diagram of the CPU flags is taken from one of the instruction descriptions:

O	D	I	S	Z	A	P	C
?			?	?	*	?	*

From the diagram, we see that the Overflow, Sign, Zero, and Parity flags will be changed to unknown values. The Auxiliary Carry and Carry flags will be modified according to rules associated with the flags. The Direction and Interrupt flags will not be changed.

B.1.2 Instruction Descriptions and Formats

When a reference to source and destination operands is made, we use the natural order of operands in all x86 instructions, in which the first operand is the destination and the second is the source. In the MOV instruction, for example, the destination will be assigned a copy of the data in the source operand:

```
MOV destination, source
```

There may be several formats available for a single instruction. Table B-1 contains a list of symbols used in instruction formats. In the descriptions of individual instructions, we use the notation "x86" to indicate that an instruction or one of its variants is only available on processors in the 32-bit x86 family (Intel386 onward). Similarly, the notation "(80286)" indicates that at least an Intel 80286 processor must be used.

Register notations such as (E)CX, (E)SI, (E)DI, (E)SP, (E)BP, and (E)IP differentiate between x86 processors that use the 32-bit registers and all earlier processors that used 16-bit registers.

Table B-1   Symbols Used in Instruction Formats.

Symbol	Description
reg	An 8-, 16-, or 32-bit general register from the following list: AH, AL, BH, BL, CH, CL, DH, DL, AX, BX, CX, DX, SI, DI, BP, SP, EAX, EBX, ECX, EDX, ESI, EDI, EBP, and ESP.
reg8, reg16, reg32	A general register, identified by its number of bits.
segreg	A 16-bit segment register (CS, DS, ES, SS, FS, GS).
accum	AL, AX, or EAX.
mem	A memory operand, using any of the standard memory-addressing modes.
mem8, mem16, mem32	A memory operand, identified by its number of bits.
shortlabel	A location in the code segment within −128 to +127 bytes of the current location.
nearlabel	A location in the current code segment, identified by a label.
farlabel	A location in an external code segment, identified by a label.

Table B-1   (Continued)

Symbol	Description
imm	An immediate operand.
imm8, imm16, imm32	An immediate operand, identified by its number of bits.
instruction	An 80x86 assembly language instruction.

B.2   Instruction Set Details (Non Floating-Point)

AAA — ASCII Adjust After Addition

O	D	I	S	Z	A	P	C
?			?	?	*	?	*

Adjusts the result in AL after two ASCII digits have been added together. If AL > 9, the high digit of the result is placed in AH, and the Carry and Auxiliary Carry flags are set.
Instruction format:

        AAA

AAD — ASCII Adjust Before Division

O	D	I	S	Z	A	P	C
?			*	*	?	*	?

Converts unpacked BCD digits in AH and AL to a single binary value in preparation for the DIV instruction.
Instruction format:

        AAD

AAM — ASCII Adjust After Multiply

O	D	I	S	Z	A	P	C
?			*	*	?	*	?

Adjusts the result in AX after two unpacked BCD digits have been multiplied together.
Instruction format:

        AAM

AAS — ASCII Adjust After Subtraction

O	D	I	S	Z	A	P	C
?			?	?	*	?	*

Adjusts the result in AX after a subtraction operation. If AL > 9, AAS decrements AH and sets the Carry and Auxiliary Carry flags.

Instruction format:

    AAS

ADC — Add Carry

O	D	I	S	Z	A	P	C
*			*	*	*	*	*

Adds both the source operand and the Carry flag to the destination operand. Operands must be the same size.

Instruction formats:

    ADC   reg,reg   ADC   reg,imm
    ADC   mem,reg   ADC   mem,imm
    ADC   reg,mem   ADC   accum,imm

ADD — Add

O	D	I	S	Z	A	P	C
*			*	*	*	*	*

A source operand is added to a destination operand, and the sum is stored in the destination. Operands must be the same size.

Instruction formats:

    ADD   reg,reg   ADD   reg,imm
    ADD   mem,reg   ADD   mem,imm
    ADD   reg,mem   ADD   accum,imm

AND — Logical AND

O	D	I	S	Z	A	P	C
*			*	*	?	*	0

Each bit in the destination operand is ANDed with the corresponding bit in the source operand.

Instruction formats:

    AND   reg,reg   AND   reg,imm
    AND   mem,reg   AND   mem,imm
    AND   reg,mem   AND   accum,imm

BOUND

Check Array Bounds (80286)

O	D	I	S	Z	A	P	C

Verifies that a signed index value is within the bounds of an array. On the 80286 processor, the destination operand can be any 16-bit register containing the index to be checked. The source operand must be a 32-bit memory operand in which the high and low words contain the upper and lower bounds of the index value. On the x86 processor, the destination can be a 32-bit register and the source can be a 64-bit memory operand.

Instruction formats:

        BOUND   reg16,mem32   BOUND   r32,mem64

BSF, BSR

Bit Scan (x86)

O	D	I	S	Z	A	P	C
?			?	?	?	?	?

Scans an operand to find the first set bit. If the bit is found, the Zero flag is cleared, and the destination operand is assigned the bit number (index) of the first set bit encountered. If no set bit is found, ZF = 1. BSF scans from bit 0 to the highest bit, and BSR starts at the highest bit and scans toward bit 0.

Instruction formats (apply to both BSF and BSR):

        BSF reg16,r/m16   BSF reg32,r/m32

BSWAP

Byte Swap (x86)

O	D	I	S	Z	A	P	C

Reverses the byte order of a 32-bit destination register.

Instruction format:

        BSWAP reg32

BT, BTC, BTR, BTS

Bit Tests (x86)

O	D	I	S	Z	A	P	C
?			?	?	?	?	*

Copies a specified bit (n) into the Carry flag. The destination operand contains the value in which the bit is located, and the source operand indicates the bit's position within the destination. BT copies bit n to the Carry flag. BTC copies bit n to the Carry flag and complements bit n in the destination operand. BTR copies bit n to the Carry flag and clears bit n in the destination. BTS copies bit n to the Carry flag and sets bit n in the destination.

Instruction formats:

        BT r/m16,imm8   BT r/m16,r16
        BT r/m32,imm8   BT r/m32,r32

CALL	**Call a Procedure**
	O D I S Z A P C

	Pushes the location of the next instruction on the stack and transfers to the destination location. If the procedure is near (in the same segment), only the offset of the next instruction is pushed; otherwise, both the segment and the offset are pushed.
	 Instruction formats:
	     CALL *nearlabel* CALL *mem16*
	     CALL *farlabel* CALL *mem32*
	     CALL *reg*

CBW	**Convert Byte to Word**
	O D I S Z A P C
	Extends the sign bit in AL throughout the AH register. Instruction format: CBW

CDQ	**Convert Doubleword to Quadword (x86)**
	O D I S Z A P C
	Extends the sign bit in EAX throughout the EDX register. Instruction format: CDQ

CLC	**Clear Carry Flag**
	O D I S Z A P C 0
	Clears the Carry flag to zero. Instruction format: CLC

CLD   Clear Direction Flag

O	D	I	S	Z	A	P	C
	0						

Clears the Direction flag to zero. String primitive instructions will automatically increment (E)SI and (E)DI.

Instruction format:

```
CLD
```

CLI   Clear Interrupt Flag

O	D	I	S	Z	A	P	C
		0					

Clears the Interrupt flag to zero. This disables maskable hardware interrupts until an STI instruction is executed.

Instruction format:

```
CLI
```

CMC   Complement Carry Flag

O	D	I	S	Z	A	P	C
							*

Toggles the current value of the Carry flag.

Instruction format:

```
CMC
```

CMP   Compare

O	D	I	S	Z	A	P	C
*			*	*	*	*	*

Compares the destination to the source by performing an implied subtraction of the source from the destination.

Instruction formats:

```
CMP    reg,reg            CMP    reg,imm
CMP    mem,reg            CMP    mem,imm
CMP    reg,mem            CMP    accum,imm
```

CMPS, CMPSB, CMPSW, CMPSD

Compare Strings

O	D	I	S	Z	A	P	C
*			*	*	*	*	*

Compares strings in memory addressed by DS:(E)SI and ES:(E)DI. Carries out an implied subtraction of the destination from the source. CMPSB compares bytes, CMPSW compares words, and CMPSD compares doublewords (on x86 processors). (E)SI and (E)DI are increased or decreased according to the operand size and the status of the Direction flag. If the Direction flag is set, (E)SI and (E)DI are decreased; otherwise (E)SI and (E)DI are increased.

Instruction formats (formats using explicit operands have intentionally been omitted):

```
CMPSB                                          CMPSW
CMPSD
```

CMPXCHG

Compare and Exchange

O	D	I	S	Z	A	P	C
*			*	*	*	*	*

Compares the destination to the accumulator (AL, AX, or EAX). If they are equal, the source is copied to the destination. Otherwise, the destination is copied to the accumulator.

Instruction formats:

```
CMPXCHG reg,reg                                CMPXCHG mem,reg
```

CWD

Convert Word to Doubleword

O	D	I	S	Z	A	P	C

Extends the sign bit in AX into the DX register.

Instruction format:

```
CWD
```

DAA

Decimal Adjust After Addition

O	D	I	S	Z	A	P	C
?			*	*	*	*	*

Adjusts the binary sum in AL after two packed BCD values have been added. Converts the sum to two BCD digits in AL.

Instruction format:

```
DAA
```

DAS — Decimal Adjust After Subtraction

O	D	I	S	Z	A	P	C
?			*	*	*	*	*

Converts the binary result of a subtraction operation to two packed BCD digits in AL.
Instruction format:

```
DAS
```

DEC — Decrement

O	D	I	S	Z	A	P	C
*			*	*	*	*	

Subtracts 1 from an operand. Does not affect the Carry flag.
Instruction formats:

```
DEC  reg                      DEC  mem
```

DIV — Unsigned Integer Divide

O	D	I	S	Z	A	P	C
?			?	?	?	?	?

Performs either 8-, 16-, or 32-bit unsigned integer division. If the divisor is 8 bits, the dividend is AX, the quotient is AL, and the remainder is AH. If the divisor is 16 bits, the dividend is DX:AX, the quotient is AX, and the remainder is DX. If the divisor is 32 bits, the dividend is EDX:EAX, the quotient is EAX, and the remainder is EDX.
Instruction formats:

```
DIV  reg                      DIV  mem
```

ENTER — Make Stack Frame (80286)

O	D	I	S	Z	A	P	C

Creates a stack frame for a procedure that receives stack parameters and uses local stack variables. The first operand indicates the number of bytes to reserve for local stack variables. The second operand indicates the procedure nesting level (must be set to 0 for C, Basic, and FORTRAN).
Instruction format:

```
ENTER  imm16,imm8
```

HLT   Halt

O	D	I	S	Z	A	P	C

Stops the CPU until a hardware interrupt occurs. (*Note:* The Interrupt flag must be set with the STI instruction before hardware interrupts can occur.)

Instruction format:

```
HLT
```

IDIV   Signed Integer Divide

O	D	I	S	Z	A	P	C
?			?	?	?	?	?

Performs a signed integer division operation on EDX:EAX, DX:AX, or AX. If the divisor is 8 bits, the dividend is AX, the quotient is AL, and the remainder is AH. If the divisor is 16 bits, the dividend is DX:AX, the quotient is AX, and the remainder is DX. If the divisor is 32 bits, the dividend is EDX:EAX, the quotient is EAX, and the remainder is EDX. Usually the IDIV operation is prefaced by either CBW or CWD to sign-extend the dividend.

Instruction formats:

```
IDIV   reg                          IDIV   mem
```

IMUL   Signed Integer Multiply

O	D	I	S	Z	A	P	C
*			?	?	?	?	*

Performs a signed integer multiplication on AL, AX, or EAX. If the multiplier is 8 bits, the multiplicand is AL and the product is AX. If the multiplier is 16 bits, the multiplicand is AX and the product is DX:AX. If the multiplier is 32 bits, the multiplicand is EAX and the product is EDX:EAX. The Carry and Overflow flags are set if a 16-bit product extends into AH, or a 32-bit product extends into DX, or a 64-bit product extends into EDX.

Instruction formats:

Single operand:

```
IMUL   r/m8                         IMUL   r/m16
IMUL   r/m32
```

Two operands:

```
IMUL   r16,r/m16                    IMUL   r16,imm8
IMUL   r32,r/m32                    IMUL   r32,imm8
IMUL   r16,imm16                    IMUL   r32,imm32
```

Three operands:

```
IMUL   r16,r/m16,imm8               IMUL   r16,r/m16,imm16
IMUL   r32,r/m32,imm8               IMUL   r32,r/m32,imm32
```

IN	**Input From Port**

O   D   I   S   Z   A   P   C

Inputs a byte or word from a port into AL or AX. The source operand is a port address, expressed as either an 8-bit constant or a 16-bit address in DX. On x86 processors, a doubleword can be input from a port into EAX.

Instruction formats:

```
IN  accum,imm                      IN  accum,DX
```

INC	**Increment**

O   D   I   S   Z   A   P   C

*			*	*	*	*	

Adds 1 to a register or memory operand.

Instruction formats:

```
INC  reg                          INC  mem
```

INS, INSB, INSW, INSD	**Input from Port to String (80286)**

O   D   I   S   Z   A   P   C

Inputs a string pointed to by ES:(E)DI from a port. The port number is specified in DX. For each value received, (E)DI is adjusted in the same way as LODSB and similar string primitive instructions. The REP prefix may be used with this instruction.

Instruction formats:

```
INS dest,DX                       REP INSB dest,DX
REP INSW dest,DX                  REP INSD dest,DX
```

INT	**Interrupt**

O   D   I   S   Z   A   P   C

		0					

Generates a software interrupt, which in turn calls an operating system subroutine. Clears the Interrupt flag and pushes the flags, CS, and IP on the stack before branching to the interrupt routine.

Instruction formats:

```
INT  imm                          INT  3
```

INTO	Interrupt on Overflow

	O	D	I	S	Z	A	P	C
			*	*				

Generates internal CPU Interrupt 4 if the Overflow flag is set. No action is taken by MS-DOS if INT 4 is called, but a user-written routine may be substituted instead.
Instruction format:

```
INTO
```

IRET	Interrupt Return

	O	D	I	S	Z	A	P	C
	*	*	*	*	*	*	*	*

Returns from an interrupt handling routine. Pops the stack into (E)IP, CS, and the flags.
Instruction format:

```
IRET
```

Jcondition	Conditional Jump

	O	D	I	S	Z	A	P	C

Jumps to a label if a specified flag condition is true. When using a processor earlier than the x86, the label must be in the range of −128 to +127 bytes from the current location. On x86 processors, the label's offset can be a positive or negative 32-bit value. See Table B-2 for a list of mnemonics.
Instruction format:

```
Jcondition  label
```

Table B-2   Conditional Jump Mnemonics.

Mnemonic	Comment	Mnemonic	Comment
JA	Jump if above	JE	Jump if equal
JNA	Jump if not above	JNE	Jump if not equal
JAE	Jump if above or equal	JZ	Jump if zero
JNAE	Jump if not above or equal	JNZ	Jump if not zero
JB	Jump if below	JS	Jump if sign

Table B-2   *(Continued)*

Mnemonic	Comment	Mnemonic	Comment
JNB	Jump if not below	JNS	Jump if not sign
JBE	Jump if below or equal	JC	Jump if carry
JNBE	Jump if not below or equal	JNC	Jump if no carry
JG	Jump if greater	JO	Jump if overflow
JNG	Jump if not greater	JNO	Jump if no overflow
JGE	Jump if greater or equal	JP	Jump if parity
JNGE	Jump if not greater or equal	JPE	Jump if parity equal
JL	Jump if less	JNP	Jump if no parity
JNL	Jump if not less	JPO	Jump if parity odd
JLE	Jump if less or equal	JNLE	Jump if not less than or equal

---

JCXZ, JECXZ

Jump If CX Is Zero

O D I S Z A P C

Jump to a short label if the CX register is equal to zero. The short label must be in the range −128 to +127 bytes from the next instruction. On x86 processors, JECXZ jumps if ECX equals zero.

Instruction formats:

```
    JCXZ shortlabel                    JECXZ shortlabel
```

JMP

Jump Unconditionally to Label

O D I S Z A P C

Jump to a code label. A short jump is within −128 to +127 bytes from the current location. A near jump is within the same code segment, and a far jump is outside the current segment.

Instruction formats:

```
    JMP  shortlabel                    JMP  reg16
    JMP  nearlabel                     JMP  mem16
    JMP  farlabel                      JMP  mem32
```

LAHF — Load AH from Flags

O D I S Z A P C

The following flags are copied to AH: Sign, Zero, Auxiliary Carry, Parity, and Carry.
Instruction format:

    LAHF

LDS, LES, LFS, LGS, LSS — Load Far Pointer

O D I S Z A P C

Loads the contents of a doubleword memory operand into a segment register and the specified destination register. When using processors prior to the x86, LDS loads into DS, LES loads into ES. On the x86, LFS loads into FS, LGS loads into GS, and LSS loads into SS.
Instruction format (same for LDS, LES, LFS, LGS, LSS):

    LDS   reg,mem

LEA — Load Effective Address

O D I S Z A P C

Calculates and loads the 16-bit or 32-bit effective address of a memory operand. Similar to MOV..OFFSET, except that only LEA can obtain an address that is calculated at runtime.
Instruction format:

    LEA   reg,mem

LEAVE — High-Level Procedure Exit

O D I S Z A P C

Terminates the stack frame of a procedure. This reverses the action of the ENTER instruction at the beginning of a procedure by restoring (E)SP and (E)BP to their original values.
Instruction format:

    LEAVE

LOCK — Lock the System Bus

O	D	I	S	Z	A	P	C

Prevents other processors from executing during the next instruction. This instruction is used when another processor might modify a memory operand that is currently being accessed by the CPU. Instruction format:

```
LOCK instruction
```

LODS, LODSB, LODSW, LODSD — Load Accumulator from String

O	D	I	S	Z	A	P	C

Loads a memory byte or word addressed by DS:(E)SI into the accumulator (AL, AX, or EAX). If LODS is used, the memory operand must be specified. LODSB loads a byte into AL, LODSW loads a word into AX, and LODSD on the x86 loads a doubleword into EAX. (E)SI is increased or decreased according to the operand size and the status of the direction flag. If the Direction flag (DF) = 1, (E)SI is decreased; if DF = 0, (E)SI is increased.

Instruction formats:

```
LODS   mem                      LODSB
LODS   segreg:mem               LODSW
LODS
```

LOOP — Loop

O	D	I	S	Z	A	P	C

Decrements ECX and jumps to a short label if ECX is not equal to zero. The destination must be −128 to +127 bytes from the current location.

Instruction formats:

```
LOOP shortlabel                 LOOPW shortlabel
```

LOOPD — Loop (x86)

O	D	I	S	Z	A	P	C

Decrements ECX and jumps to a short label if ECX is not equal to zero. The destination must be −128 to +127 bytes from the current location.

Instruction format:

```
LOOPD shortlabel
```

LOOPE, LOOPZ

Loop If Equal (Zero)

O	D	I	S	Z	A	P	C

Decrements (E)CX and jumps to a short label if (E)CX > 0 and the Zero flag is set.
Instruction formats:

```
LOOPE shortlabel                    LOOPZ shortlabel
```

LOOPNE, LOOPNZ

Loop If Not Equal (Zero)

O	D	I	S	Z	A	P	C

Decrements (E)CX and jumps to a short label if (E)CX > 0 and the Zero flag is clear.
Instruction formats:

```
LOOPNE shortlabel                   LOOPNZ shortlabel
```

LOOPW

Loop with 16-bit Counter

O	D	I	S	Z	A	P	C

Decrements CX and jumps to a short label of CX is not equal to zero. The destination must be −128 to +127 bytes from the current location.
Instruction format:

```
LOOPW shortlabel
```

MOV

Move

O	D	I	S	Z	A	P	C

Copies a byte or word from a source operand to a destination operand.
Instruction formats:

```
MOV reg,reg                         MOV reg,imm
MOV mem,reg                         MOV mem,imm
MOV reg,mem                         MOV mem16,segreg
MOV reg16,segreg                    MOV segreg,mem16
MOV segreg,reg16
```

MOVS, MOVSB, MOVSW, MOVSD	**Move String**

O D I S Z A P C

Copies a byte or word from memory addressed by DS:(E)SI to memory addressed by ES:(E)DI. MOVS requires both operands to be specified. MOVSB copies a byte, MOVSW copies a word, and on the x86, MOVSD copies a doubleword. (E)SI and (E)DI are increased or decreased according to the operand size and the status of the direction flag. If the Direction flag (DF) = 1, (E)SI and (E)DI are decreased; if DF = 0, (E)SI and (E)DI are increased.

Instruction formats:

```
MOVSB
MOVSW
MOVSD
MOVS dest, source
MOVS ES:dest, segreg:source
```

MOVSX	**Move with Sign-Extend**

O D I S Z A P C

Copies a byte or word from a source operand to a destination register and sign-extends into the upper bits of the destination. This instruction is used to copy an 8-bit or 16-bit operand into a larger destination.

Instruction formats:

```
                              MOVSX reg32,reg8
MOVSX reg32,reg16             MOVSX reg32,mem16
MOVSX reg16,reg8              MOVSX reg16,m8
```

MOVZX	**Move with Zero-Extend**

O D I S Z A P C

Copies a byte or word from a source operand to a destination register and zero-extends into the upper bits of the destination. This instruction is used to copy an 8-bit or 16-bit operand into a larger destination.

Instruction formats:

```
                              MOVZX reg32,reg8
MOVSX reg32,reg16             MOVSX reg32,mem16
MOVSX reg16,reg8              MOVSX reg16,m8
```

MUL — Unsigned Integer Multiply

O	D	I	S	Z	A	P	C
*			?	?	?	?	*

Multiplies AL, AX, or EAX by a source operand. If the source is 8 bits, it is multiplied by AL and the product is stored in AX. If the source is 16 bits, it is multiplied by AX and the product is stored in DX:AX. If the source is 32 bits, it is multiplied by EAX and the product is stored in EDX:EAX.

Instruction formats:

```
MUL reg                          MUL mem
```

NEG — Negate

O	D	I	S	Z	A	P	C
*			*	*	*	*	*

Calculates the twos complement of the destination operand and stores the result in the destination.

Instruction formats:

```
NEG reg                          NEG mem
```

NOP — No Operation

O	D	I	S	Z	A	P	C

This instruction does nothing, but it may be used inside a timing loop or to align a subsequent instruction on a word boundary.

Instruction format:

```
NOP
```

NOT — Not

O	D	I	S	Z	A	P	C

Performs a logical NOT operation on an operand by reversing each of its bits.

Instruction formats:

```
NOT reg                          NOT mem
```

OR	**Inclusive OR**

O	D	I	S	Z	A	P	C
0			*	*	?	*	0

Performs a boolean (bitwise) OR operation between each matching bit in the destination operand and each bit in the source operand.

Instruction formats:

```
        OR   reg,reg                    OR   reg,imm
        OR   mem,reg                    OR   mem,imm
        OR   reg,mem                    OR   accum,imm
```

OUT	**Output to Port**

O	D	I	S	Z	A	P	C

When using processors prior to the x86, this instruction outputs a byte or word from the accumulator to a port. The port address may be a constant if in the range 0–FFh, or DX may contain a port address between 0 and FFFFh. On an x86 processor, a doubleword can be output to a port.

Instruction formats:

```
        OUT   imm8,accum               OUT   DX,accum
```

OUTS, OUTSB, OUTSW, OUTSD	**Output String to Port (80286)**

O	D	I	S	Z	A	P	C

Outputs a string pointed to by ES:(E)DI to a port. The port number is specified in DX. For each value output, (E)DI is adjusted in the same way as LODSB and similar string primitive instructions. The REP prefix may be used with this instruction.

Instruction formats:

```
        OUTS dest,DX                   REP OUTSB dest,DX
        REP OUTSW dest,DX              REP OUTSD dest,DX
```

POP	**Pop from Stack**

O	D	I	S	Z	A	P	C

Copies a word or doubleword at the current stack pointer location into the destination operand and adds 2 (or 4) to (E)SP.

Instruction formats:

```
        POP   reg16/r32                POP   segreg
        POP   mem16/mem32
```

POPA, POPAD

Pop All

O	D	I	S	Z	A	P	C

Pops 16 bytes from the top of the stack into the eight general-purpose registers, in the following order: DI, SI, BP, SP, BX, DX, CX, AX. The value for SP is discarded, so SP is not reassigned. POPA pops into 16-bit registers, and POPAD on an x86 pops into 32-bit registers.

Instruction formats:

    POPA   POPAD

POPF, POPFD

Pop Flags from Stack

O	D	I	S	Z	A	P	C
*	*	*	*	*	*	*	*

POPF pops the top of the stack into the 16-bit FLAGS register. POPFD on an x86 pops the top of the stack into the 32-bit EFLAGS register.

Instruction formats:

    POPF   POPFD

PUSH

Push on Stack

O	D	I	S	Z	A	P	C

If a 16-bit operand is pushed, 2 is subtracted from ESP. If a 32-bit operand is pushed, 4 is subtracted from ESP. Next, the operand is copied into the stack at the location pointed to by ESP.

Instruction formats:

    PUSH   reg16/reg32   PUSH   segreg
    PUSH   mem16/mem32   PUSH   imm16/imm32

PUSHA, PUSHAD

Push All (80286)

O	D	I	S	Z	A	P	C

Pushes the following 16-bit registers on the stack, in order: AX, CX, DX, BX, SP, BP, SI, and DI. The PUSHAD instruction for the x86 processor pushes EAX, ECX, EDX, EBX, ESP, EBP, ESI, and EDI.

Instruction formats:

    PUSHA   PUSHAD

PUSHF, PUSHFD

Push Flags

O	D	I	S	Z	A	P	C

PUSHF pushes the 16-bit FLAGS register onto the stack. PUSHFD pushes the 32-bit EFLAGS onto the stack (x86).

Instruction formats:

```
    PUSHF                              PUSHFD
```

PUSHW, PUSHD

Push on Stack

O	D	I	S	Z	A	P	C

PUSHW pushes a 16-bit word on the stack, and on the x86, PUSHD pushes a 32-bit double-word on the stack.

Instruction formats:

```
    PUSH   reg16/reg32              PUSH   segreg
    PUSH   mem16/mem32              PUSH   imm16/imm32
```

RCL

Rotate Carry Left

O	D	I	S	Z	A	P	C
*							*

Rotates the destination operand left, using the source operand to determine the number of rotations. The Carry flag is copied into the lowest bit, and the highest bit is copied into the Carry flag. The *imm8* operand must be a 1 when using the 8086/8088 processor.

Instruction formats:

```
    RCL   reg,imm8                  RCL   mem,imm8
    RCL   reg,CL                    RCL   mem,CL
```

RCR

Rotate Carry Right

O	D	I	S	Z	A	P	C
*							*

Rotates the destination operand right, using the source operand to determine the number of rotations. The Carry flag is copied into the highest bit, and the lowest bit is copied into the Carry flag. The *imm8* operand must be a 1 when using the 8086/8088 processor.

Instruction formats:

```
    RCR   reg,imm8                  RCR   mem,imm8
    RCR   reg,CL                    RCR   mem,CL
```

REP	**Repeat String**

O   D   I   S   Z   A   P   C

Repeats a string primitive instruction, using (E)CX as a counter. (E)CX is decremented each time the instruction is repeated, until (E)CX = 0.
Format (shown with MOVS):

```
REP MOVS dest,source
```

REP *condition*	**Repeat String Conditionally**

O   D   I   S   Z   A   P   C

Repeats a string primitive instruction until (E)CX = 0 and while a flag condition is true. REPZ (REPE) repeats while the Zero flag is set, and REPNZ (REPNE) repeats while the Zero flag is clear. Only SCAS and CMPS should be used with REP *condition*, because they are the only string primitives that modify the Zero flag.
Formats used with SCAS:

```
REPZ   SCAS   dest            REPNE   SCAS   dest
REPZ   SCASB                  REPNE   SCASB
REPE   SCASW                  REPNZ   SCASW
```

RET, **RETN,** **RETF**	**Return from Procedure**

O   D   I   S   Z   A   P   C

Pops a return address from the stack. RETN (return near) pops only the top of the stack into (E)IP. In real-address mode, RETF (return far) pops the stack first into (E)IP and then into CS. RET may be either near or far, depending on the attribute specified or implied by the PROC directive. An optional 8-bit immediate operand tells the CPU to add a value to (E)SP after popping the return address.
Instruction formats:

```
RET                           RET    imm8
RETN                          RETN   imm8
RETF                          RETF   imm8
```

ROL — Rotate Left

O	D	I	S	Z	A	P	C
*							*

Rotates the destination operand left, using the source operand to determine the number of rotations. The highest bit is copied into the Carry flag and moved into the lowest bit position. The *imm8* operand must be a 1 when using the 8086/8088 processor.

Instruction formats:

```
ROL    reg,imm8              ROL    mem,imm8
ROL    reg,CL                ROL    mem,CL
```

ROR — Rotate Right

O	D	I	S	Z	A	P	C
*							*

Rotates the destination operand right, using the source operand to determine the number of rotations. The lowest bit is copied into both the Carry flag and the highest bit position. The *imm8* operand must be a 1 when using the 8086/8088 processor.

Instruction formats:

```
ROR    reg,imm8              ROR    mem,imm8
ROR    reg,CL                ROR    mem,CL
```

SAHF — Store AH into Flags

O	D	I	S	Z	A	P	C
			*	*	*	*	*

Copies AH into bits 0 through 7 of the Flags register.

Instruction format:

```
SAHF
```

SAL — Shift Arithmetic Left

O	D	I	S	Z	A	P	C
*			*	*	?	*	*

Shifts each bit in the destination operand to the left, using the source operand to determine the number of shifts. The highest bit is copied into the Carry flag, and the lowest bit is filled with a zero. The *imm8* operand must be a 1 when using the 8086/8088 processor.

Instruction formats:

```
SAL    reg,imm8              SAL    mem,imm8
SAL    reg,CL                SAL    mem,CL
```

SAR — Shift Arithmetic Right

O	D	I	S	Z	A	P	C
*			*	*	?	*	*

Shifts each bit in the destination operand to the right, using the source operand to determine the number of shifts. The lowest bit is copied into the Carry flag, and the highest bit retains its previous value. This shift is often used with signed operands because it preserves the number's sign. The *imm8* operand must be a 1 when using the 8086/8088 processor.

Instruction formats:

```
SAR   reg,imm8            SAR   mem,imm8
SAR   reg,CL              SAR   mem,CL
```

SBB — Subtract with Borrow

O	D	I	S	Z	A	P	C
*			*	*	*	*	*

Subtracts the source operand from the destination operand and then subtracts the Carry flag from the destination.

Instruction formats:

```
SBB   reg,reg             SBB   reg,imm
SBB   mem,reg             SBB   mem,imm
SBB   reg,mem
```

SCAS, SCASB, SCASW, SCASD — Scan String

O	D	I	S	Z	A	P	C
*			*	*	*	*	*

Scans a string in memory pointed to by ES:(E)DI for a value that matches the accumulator. SCAS requires the operands to be specified. SCASB scans for an 8-bit value matching AL, SCASW scans for a 16-bit value matching AX, and SCASD scans for a 32-bit value matching EAX. (E)DI is increased or decreased according to the operand size and the status of the direction flag. If DF = 1, (E)DI is decreased; if DF = 0, (E)DI is increased.

Instruction formats:

```
SCASB                    SCASW
SCASD
SCAS dest
SCAS ES:dest
```

SET*condition*	**Set Conditionally**
	O D I S Z A P C
	If the given flag condition is true, the byte specified by the destination operand is assigned the value 1. If the flag condition is false, the destination is assigned a value of 0. The possible values for *condition* were listed in Table B-2.
	Instruction formats:
	`SETcond reg8` `SETcond mem8`

SHL	**Shift Left**
	O D I S Z A P C
	* * * ? * *
	Shifts each bit in the destination operand to the left, using the source operand to determine the number of shifts. The highest bit is copied into the Carry flag, and the lowest bit is filled with a zero (identical to SAL). The *imm8* operand must be a 1 when using the 8086/8088 processor.
	Instruction formats:
	`SHL  reg,imm8` `SHL  mem,imm8` `SHL  reg,CL` `SHL  mem,CL`

SHLD	**Double-Precision Shift Left (x86)**
	O D I S Z A P C
	* * * ? * *
	Shifts the bits of the second operand into the first operand. The third operand indicates the number of bits to be shifted. The positions opened by the shift are filled by the most significant bits of the second operand. The second operand must always be a register, and the third operand may be either an immediate value or the CL register.
	Instruction formats:

	`SHLD reg16,reg16,imm8` `SHLD mem16,reg16,imm8`
	`SHLD reg32,reg32,imm8` `SHLD mem32,reg32,imm8`
	`SHLD reg16,reg16,CL` `SHLD mem16,reg16,CL`
	`SHLD reg32,reg32,CL` `SHLD mem32,reg32,CL`

SHR — Shift Right

O	D	I	S	Z	A	P	C
*			*	*	?	*	*

Shifts each bit in the destination operand to the right, using the source operand to determine the number of shifts. The highest bit is filled with a zero, and the lowest bit is copied into the Carry flag. The *imm8* operand must be a 1 when using the 8086/8088 processor.

Instruction formats:

```
SHR   reg, imm8          SHR   mem, imm8
SHR   reg, CL            SHR   mem, CL
```

SHRD — Double-Precision Shift Right (x86)

O	D	I	S	Z	A	P	C
*			*	*	?	*	*

Shifts the bits of the second operand into the first operand. The third operand indicates the number of bits to be shifted. The positions opened by the shift are filled by the least significant bits of the second operand. The second operand must always be a register, and the third operand may be either an immediate value or the CL register.

Instruction formats:

```
SHRD  reg16, reg16, imm8     SHRD  mem16, reg16, imm8
SHRD  reg32, reg32, imm8     SHRD  mem32, reg32, imm8
SHRD  reg16, reg16, CL       SHRD  mem16, reg16, CL
SHRD  reg32, reg32, CL       SHRD  mem32, reg32, CL
```

STC — Set Carry Flag

O	D	I	S	Z	A	P	C
							1

Sets the Carry flag.

Instruction format:

```
STC
```

STD — Set Direction Flag

O	D	I	S	Z	A	P	C
	1						

Sets the Direction flag, causing (E)SI and/or (E)DI to be decremented by string primitive instructions. Thus, string processing will be from high addresses to low addresses.

Instruction format:

```
STD
```

STI — Set Interrupt Flag

O	D	I	S	Z	A	P	C
		1					

Sets the Interrupt flag, which enables maskable interrupts. Interrupts are automatically disabled when an interrupt occurs, so an interrupt handler procedure immediately reenables them, using STI.
Instruction format:

```
STI
```

STOS, STOSB, STOSW, STOSD — Store String Data

O	D	I	S	Z	A	P	C

Stores the accumulator in the memory location addressed by ES:(E)DI. If STOS is used, a destination operand must be specified. STOSB copies AL to memory, STOSW copies AX to memory, and STOSD for the x86 processor copies EAX to memory. (E)DI is increased or decreased according to the operand size and the status of the direction flag. If DF = 1, (E)DI is decreased; if DF = 0, (E)DI is increased.
Instruction formats:

```
STOSB                                    STOSW
STOSD
STOS mem
STOS ES:mem
```

SUB — Subtract

O	D	I	S	Z	A	P	C
*			*	*	*	*	*

Subtracts the source operand from the destination operand.
Instruction formats:

```
SUB   reg,reg                    SUB   reg,imm
SUB   mem,reg                    SUB   mem,imm
SUB   reg,mem                    SUB   accum,imm
```

TEST — Test

O	D	I	S	Z	A	P	C
0			*	*	?	*	0

Tests individual bits in the destination operand against those in the source operand. Performs a logical AND operation that affects the flags but not the destination operand.
Instruction formats:

```
TEST   reg,reg                   TEST   reg,imm
TEST   mem,reg                   TEST   mem,imm
TEST   reg,mem                   TEST   accum,imm
```

WAIT	**Wait for Coprocessor**
	O D I S Z A P C
	Suspends CPU execution until the coprocessor finishes the current instruction.
	Instruction format:
	`WAIT`

XADD	**Exchange and Add (Intel486)**
	O D I S Z A P C
	* * * * *
	Adds the source operand to the destination operand. At the same time, the original destination value is moved to the source operand.
	Instruction formats:
	`XADD  reg,reg` `XADD  mem,reg`

XCHG	**Exchange**
	O D I S Z A P C
	Exchanges the contents of the source and destination operands.
	Instruction formats:
	`XCH  reg,reg` `XCH  mem,reg`
	`XCH  reg,mem`

XLAT, XLATB	**Translate Byte**
	O D I S Z A P C
	Uses the value in AL to index into a table pointed to by DS:BX. The byte pointed to by the index is moved to AL. An operand may be specified in order to provide a segment override. XLATB may be substituted for XLAT.
	Instruction formats:
	`XLAT` `XLAT  segreg:mem`
	`XLAT  mem` `XLATB`

XOR	**Exclusive OR**

O	D	I	S	Z	A	P	C
0			*	*	?	*	0

Each bit in the source operand is exclusive ORed with its corresponding bit in the destination. The destination bit is a 1 only when the original source and destination bits are different. Instruction formats:

```
XOR    reg,reg                      XOR    reg,imm
XOR    mem,reg                      XOR    mem,imm
XOR    reg,mem                      XOR    accum,imm
```

B.3   Floating-Point Instructions

Table B-3 contains a list of all x86 floating-point instructions, with brief descriptions and operand formats. Instructions are usually grouped by function rather than strict alphabetical order. For example, the FIADD instruction immediately follows FADD and FADDP because it performs the same operation with integer conversion.

For complete information about floating-point instructions, consult the Intel Architecture Manuals. The word *stack* in this table refers to the FPU register stack. (Table B-1 lists many of the symbols used when describing the formats and operands of floating-point instructions.)

Table B-3   Floating-Point Instructions.

Instruction	Description
F2XM1	**Compute $2^x - 1$.** No operands.
FABS	**Absolute value.** Clears sign bit of ST(0). No operands.

FADD	**Add floating-point.** Adds destination and source operands, stores sum in destination operand. Formats:
	
	`FADD` `Add ST(0) to ST(1), and pop stack`
	`FADD   m32fp` `Add m32fp to ST(0)`
	`FADD   m64fp` `Add m64fp to ST(0)`
	`FADD   ST(0),ST(i)` `Add ST(i) to ST(0)`
	`FADD   ST(i),ST(0)` `Add ST(0) to ST(i)`

FADDP	**Add floating-point and pop.** Performs the same operation as FADD, then pops the stack. Format: `FADDP ST(i),ST(0)` `Add ST(0) to ST(i)`

FIADD	**Convert integer to floating-point and add.** Adds destination and source operands, stores sum in destination operand. Formats:
	
	`FIADD   m32int` `Add m32int to ST(0)`
	`FIADD   m16int` `Add m16int to ST(0)`

FBLD	**Load binary-coded decimal.** Converts BCD source operand into double extended-precision floating-point format and pushes it on the stack. Format: `FBLD m80bcd` `Push m80bcd onto register stack`

Table B-3   (Continued)

Instruction	Description
FBSTP	**Store BCD integer and pop.** Converts the value in the ST(0) register to an 18-digit packed BCD integer, stores the result in the destination operand, and pops the register stack. Format: FBSTP *m80bcd* Store ST(0) into *m80bcd*, and pop stack
FCHS	**Change sign.** Complements the sign of ST(0). No operands.
FCLEX	**Clear exceptions.** Clears the floating-point exception flags (PE, UE, OE, ZE, DE, and IE), the exception summary status flag (ES), the stack fault flag (SF), and the busy flag (B) in the FPU status word. No operands. FNCLEX performs the same operation without checking for pending unmasked floating-point exceptions.
FCMOV*cc*	**Floating-point conditional move.** Tests status flags in EFLAGS, moves source operand (second operand) to the destination operand (first operand) if the given test condition is true. Formats: FCMOVB ST(0),ST(i) Move if below FCMOVE ST(0),ST(i) Move if equal FCMOVBE ST(0),ST(i) Move if below or equal FCMOVU ST(0),ST(i) Move if unordered FCMOVNB ST(0),ST(i) Move if not below FCMOVNE ST(0),ST(i) Move if not equal FCMOVNBE ST(0),ST(i) Move if not below or equal FCMOVNU ST(0),ST(i) Move if not unordered
FCOM	**Compare floating-point values.** Compares ST(0) to the source operand and sets condition code flags C0, C2, and C3 in the FPU status word according to the results. Formats: FCOM *m32fp* Compare ST(0) to *m32fp* FCOM *m64fp* Compare ST(0) to *m64fp* FCOM ST(i) Compare ST(0) to ST(i) FCOM Compare ST(0) to ST(1) FCOMP performs the same operation as FCOM and then pops the stack. FCOMPP does the same task as FCOM and then pops the stack twice. FUCOM, FUCOMP, and FUCOMPP are the same as FCOM, FCOMP, and FCOMPP, respectively, except that they check for unordered values.
FCOMI	**Compare floating-point values and set EFLAGS.** Performs an unordered comparison of registers ST(0) and ST(i) and sets the status flags (ZF, PF, CF) in the EFLAGS register according to the results. Format: FCOMI ST(0),ST(i) Compare ST(0) to ST(i) FCOMIP does the same task as FCOMI and then pops the stack. FUCOMI and FUCOMIP check for unordered values.
FCOS	**Cosine.** Computes the cosine of ST(0) and stores the result in ST(0). Input must be in radians. No operands.
FDECSTP	**Decrement stack-top pointer.** Subtracts 1 from the TOP field of the FPU status word, effectively rotating the stack. No operands.
FDIV	**Divide floating-point and pop.** Divides the destination operand by the source operand and stores the result in the destination location. Formats: FDIV ST(1) = ST(1) / T(0), and pop stack FDIV *m32fp* ST(0) = ST(0) / *m32fp* FDIV *m64fp* ST(0) = ST(0) / *m64fp* FDIV ST(0),ST(i) ST(0) = ST(0) / ST(i) FDIV ST(i),ST(0) ST(i) = ST(i) / ST(0)

Table B-3   (Continued)

Instruction	Description
FDIVP	**Divide floating-point and pop.** Same as FDIV, then pops from the stack. Format: `FDIVP ST(i),ST(0)   ST(i) = ST(i) / ST(0)`, and pop stack

FIDIV	**Convert integer to floating-point and divide.** After converting, performs the same operation as FDIV. Formats:
	
	`FIDIV m32int      ST(0) = ST(0) / m32int`
	`FIDIV m16int      ST(0) = ST(0) / m16int`

FDIVR	**Reverse divide.** Divides the source operand by the destination operand and stores the result in the destination location. Formats:
	
	`FDIVR             ST(0) = ST(0) / ST(1)`, and pop stack
	`FDIVR m32fp       ST(0) = m32fp / ST(0)`
	`FDIVR m64fp       ST(0) = m64fp / ST(0)`
	`FDIVR ST(0),ST(i) ST(0) = ST(i) / ST(0)`
	`FDIVR ST(i),ST(0) ST(i) = ST(0) / ST(i)`

FDIVRP	**Reverse divide and pop.** Performs the same operation as FDIVR, then pops from the stack. Format: `FDIVRP ST(i),ST(0)  ST(i) = ST(0) / ST(i)`, and pop stack

FIDIVR	**Convert integer to float and perform reverse divide.** After converting, performs the same operation as FDIVR. Formats:
	
	`FIDIVR m32int     ST(0) = m32int / ST(0)`
	`FIDIVR m16int     ST(0) = m16int / ST(0)`

FFREE	**Free floating-point register.** Sets the register to empty, using Tag word. Format: `FFREE ST(i)       ST(i) = empty`

FICOM	**Compare integer.** Compares the value in ST(0) with an integer source operand and sets the condition code flags C0, C2, and C3 according to the results. The integer source operand is converted to floating-point before the comparison. Formats:
	
	`FICOM m32int      Compare ST(0) to m32int`
	`FICOM m16int      Compare ST(0) to m16int`
	FICOMP performs the same operation as FICOM, then pops from the stack.

FILD	**Convert integer to float and load onto register stack.** Formats:
	
	`FILD m16int       Push m16int onto register stack`
	`FILD m32int       Push m32int onto register stack`
	`FILD m64int       Push m64int onto register stack`

FINCSTP	**Increment stack-top pointer.** Adds 1 to the TOP field of the FPU status word. No operands.
FINIT	**Initialize floating-point unit.** Sets the control, status, tag, instruction pointer, and data pointer registers to their default states. The control word is set to 037FH (round to nearest, all exceptions masked, 64-bit precision). The status word is cleared (no exception flags set, TOP = 0). The data registers in the register stack are unchanged, but they are tagged as empty. No operands. FNINIT performs the same operation without checking for pending unmasked floating-point exceptions.

Table B-3 (Continued)

Instruction	Description
FIST	**Store integer in memory operand.** Stores ST(0) in a signed integer memory operand, rounding according to the RC field in the FPU control word. Formats: `FIST m16int` Store ST(0) in m16int `FIST m32int` Store ST(0) in m32int FISTP performs the same operation as FIST, then pops the register stack. It has one additional format: `FISTP m64int` Store ST(0) in m64int, and pop stack
FISTTP	**Store integer with truncation.** Performs same operation as FIST, but automatically truncates the integer and pops the stack. Formats: `FISTTP m16int` Store ST(0) in m16int, and pop stack `FISTTP m32int` Store ST(0) in m32int, and pop stack `FISTTP m64int` Store ST(0) in m64int, and pop stack
FLD	**Load floating-point value onto register stack.** Formats: `FLD m32fp` Push m32fp onto register stack `FLD m64fp` Push m64fp onto register stack `FLD m80fp` Push m80fp onto register stack `FLD ST(i)` Push ST(i) onto register stack
FLD1	**Load +1.0 onto register stack.** No operands.
FLDL2T	**Load $\log_2 10$ onto register stack.** No operands.
FLDL2E	**Load $\log_2 e$ onto register stack.** No operands.
FLDPI	**Load *pi* onto register stack.** No operands.
FLDLG2	**Load $\log_{10} 2$ onto register stack.** No operands.
FLDLN2	**Load $\log_e 2$ onto register stack.** No operands.
FLDZ	**Load +0.0 onto register stack.** No operands.
FLDCW	**Load FPU control word from 16-bit memory value.** Format: `FLDCW m2byte` Load FPU control word from m2byte
FLDENV	**Load FPU environment from memory into the FPU.** Format: `FLDENV m14/28byte` Load FPU environment from memory
FMUL	**Multiply floating-point.** Multiplies the destination and source operands and stores the product in the destination location. Formats: `FMUL` ST(1) = ST(1) * ST(0), and pop stack `FMUL m32fp` ST(0) = ST(0) * m32fp `FMUL m64fp` ST(0) = ST(0) * m64fp `FMUL ST(0),ST(i)` ST(0) = ST(0) * ST(i) `FMUL ST(i),ST(0)` ST(i) = ST(i) * ST(0)
FMULP	**Multiply floating-point and pop.** Performs the same operation as FMUL, then pops the stack. Format: `FMULP ST(i),ST(0)` ST(i) = ST(i) * ST(0), and pop stack

Table B-3   *(Continued)*

Instruction	Description

FIMUL	**Convert integer and multiply.** Converts the source operand to floating-point, multiplies it by ST(0), and stores the product in ST(0). Formats:
	
	`FIMUL m16int`
	`FIMUL m32int`

FNOP	**No operation.** No operands.
FPATAN	**Partial arctangent.** Replaces ST(1) with arctan(ST(1)/ST(0)) and pops the register stack. No operands.
FPREM	**Partial remainder.** Replaces ST(0) with the remainder obtained from dividing ST(0) by ST(1). No operands. FPREM1 is similar, replacing ST(0) with the IEEE remainder obtained from dividing ST(0) by ST(1).
FPTAN	**Partial tangent.** Replaces ST(0) with its tangent and pushes 1.0 onto the FPU stack. Input must be in radians. No operands.
FRNDINT	**Round to integer.** Rounds ST(0) to the nearest integer value. No operands.
FRSTOR	**Restore x87 FPU State.** Loads the FPU state (operating environment and register stack) from the memory area specified by the source operand. Format: `FRSTOR m94/108byte`
FSAVE	**Store x87 FPU State.** Stores the current FPU state (operating environment and register stack) in memory specified by the destination operand and then reinitializes the FPU. Format: `FSAVE m94/108byte` FNSAVE performs the same operation without checking for pending unmasked floating-point exceptions.
FSCALE	**Scale.** Truncates the value in ST(1) to an integral value and adds that value to the exponent of the destination operand ST(0). No operands.
FSIN	**Sine.** Replaces ST(0) with its sine. Input must be in radians. No operands.
FSINCOS	**Sine and cosine.** Computes the sine and cosine of ST(0). Input must be in radians. Replaces ST(0) with the sine and pushes the cosine on the register stack. No operands.
FSQRT	**Square root.** Replaces ST(0) with its square root. No operands.

FST	**Store floating-point value.** Formats:
	
	`FST m32fp` `Copy ST(0) to m32fp`
	`FST m64fp` `Copy ST(0) to m64fp`
	`FST ST(i)` `Copy ST(0) to ST(i)`
	
	FSTP performs the same operation as FST, then pops the stack. It has one additional format:
	
	`FSTP m80fp` `Copy ST(0) to m80fp, and pop stack`

FSTCW	**Store FPU control word.** Format: `FLDCW m2byte` `Store FPU control word to m2byte` FNSTCW performs the same operation without checking for pending unmasked floating-point exceptions.
FSTENV	**Store FPU environment.** Stores the FPU environment in a m14byte or m28byte structure, depending on whether the processor is in real mode or protected mode. Format: `FSTENV memop` `Store FPU environment to memop` FNSTENV performs the same operation without checking for pending unmasked floating-point exceptions.

Table B-3   (Continued)

Instruction	Description
FSTSW	**Store FPU status word.** Formats: `FSTSW m2byte` Store FPU status word to *m2byte* `FSTSW AX` Store FPU status word to AX register FNSTSW performs the same operation without checking for pending unmasked floating-point exceptions.

FSUB	**Subtract floating-point.** Subtracts the source operand from the destination operand and stores the difference in the destination location. Formats:
	
	`FSUB` `ST(0) = ST(1) - ST(0), and pop stack`
	`FSUB m32fp` `ST(0) = ST(0) - m32fp`
	`FSUB m64fp` `ST(0) = ST(0) - m64fp`
	`FSUB ST(0),ST(i)` `ST(0) = ST(0) - ST(i)`
	`FSUB ST(i),ST(0)` `ST(i) = ST(i) - ST(0)`

FSUBP	**Subtract floating-point and pop.** The FSUBP instruction performs the same operation as FSUB, then pops the stack. Format: `FSUBP ST(i),ST(0)` `ST(i) = ST(i) - ST(0), and pop stack`

FISUB	**Convert integer to floating-point and subtract.** Converts source operand to floating-point, subtracts it from ST(0), and stores the result in ST(0). Formats:
	
	`FISUB m16int` `ST(0) = ST(0) - m16int`
	`FISUB m32int` `ST(0) = ST(0) - m32int`

FSUBR	**Reverse subtract floating-point.** Subtracts the destination operand from the source operand and stores the difference in the destination location. Formats:
	
	`FSUBR` `ST(0) = ST(0) - ST(1), and pop stack`
	`FSUBR m32fp` `ST(0) = m32fp - ST(0)`
	`FSUBR m64fp` `ST(0) = m64fp - ST(0)`
	`FSUBR ST(0),ST(i)` `ST(0) = ST(i) - ST(0)`
	`FSUBR ST(i),ST(0)` `ST(i) = ST(0) - ST(i)`

FSUBRP	**Reverse subtract floating-point and pop.** The FSUBRP instruction performs the same operation as FSUB, then pops the stack. Format: `FSUBRP ST(i),ST(0)` `ST(i) = ST(0) - ST(i), and pop stack`

FISUBR	**Convert integer and reverse subtract floating-point.** After converting to floating-point, performs the same operation as FSUBR. Formats:
	
	`FISUBR m16int`
	`FISUBR m32int`

FTST	**Test.** Compares ST(0) to 0.0 and sets condition code flags in the FPU status word. No operands.
FWAIT	**Wait.** Waits for all pending floating-point exception handlers to complete. No operands.
FXAM	**Examine.** Examines ST(0) and sets condition code flags in the FPU status word. No operands.

FXCH	**Exchange register contents.** Formats:
	
	`FXCH ST(i)` Exchange `ST(0)` and `ST(i)`
	`FXCH` Exchange `ST(0)` and `ST(1)`

Table B-3   (Continued)

Instruction	Description
FXRSTOR	**Restore x87 FPU, MMX Technology, SSE, and SSE2 State.** Reloads the FPU, MMX technology, XMM, and MXCSR registers from the memory image specified in the source operand. Format: `FXRSTOR m512byte`
FXSAVE	**Save x87 FPU, MMX Technology, SSE, and SSE2 State.** Saves the current state of the FPU, MMX technology, XMM, and MXCSR registers to the memory image specified in the destination operand. Format: `FXRSAVE m512byte`
FXTRACT	**Extract exponent and significand.** Separates the source in ST(0) into its exponent and significand, stores the exponent in ST(0), and pushes the significand on the register stack. No operands.
FYL2X	**Compute y * $\log_2 x$.** Register ST(1) holds the value of y, and ST(0) holds the value of x. Stack is popped, so the result is left in ST(0). No operands.
FYL2XP1	**Compute y * $\log_2(x + 1)$.** Register ST(1) holds the value of y, and ST(0) holds the value of x. Stack is popped, so the result is left in ST(0). No operands.

C

Answers to Review Questions

1 Basic Concepts

1.1 Welcome to Assembly Language

1. An assembler converts source-code programs from assembly language into machine language. A linker combines individual files created by an assembler into a single executable program.

2. Assembly language is a good tool for learning how application programs communicate with the computer's operating system via interrupt handlers, system calls, and common memory areas. Assembly language programming also helps when learning how the operating system loads and executes application programs.

3. In a *one-to-many* relationship, a single statement expands into multiple assembly language or machine instructions.

4. A language whose source programs can be compiled and run on a wide variety of computer systems is said to be *portable*.

5. No. Each assembly language is based on either a processor family or a specific computer.

6. Some examples of embedded systems applications are automobile fuel and ignition systems, air-conditioning control systems, security systems, flight control systems, hand-held computers, modems, printers, and other intelligent computer peripherals.

7. *Device drivers* are programs that translate general operating system commands into specific references to hardware details that only the manufacturer knows.

8. C++ does not allow a pointer of one type to be assigned to a pointer of another type. Assembly language has no such restriction regarding pointers.

9. Applications suited to assembly language: hardware device driver and embedded systems and computer games requiring direct hardware access.

10. A high-level language may not provide for direct hardware access. Even if it does, awkward coding techniques must often be used, resulting in possible maintenance problems.

11. Assembly language has minimal formal structure, so structure must be imposed by programmers who have varying levels of experience. This leads to difficulties maintaining existing code.

12. Code for the expression X = (Y * 4) + 3:

```
mov    eax,Y            ; move Y to EAX
mov    ebx,4            ; move 4 to EBX
imul   ebx             ; EAX = EAX * EBX
add    eax,3            ; add 3 to EAX
mov    X,eax            ; move EAX to X
```

1.2   Virtual Machine Concept

1. Virtual machine concept: Computers are constructed in layers, so that each layer represents a translation layer from a higher-level instruction set to a lower-level instruction set.

2. Machine language: It is enormously detailed and consists purely of numbers. Hard for humans to understand.

3. True.

4. An entire L1 program is converted into an L0 program by an L0 program specifically designed for this purpose. Then the resulting L0 program is executed directly on the computer hardware.

5. Assembly language appears at Level 3.

6. The Java virtual machine (JVM) allows compiled Java programs to run on almost any computer.

7. Digital logic, instruction set architecture, assembly language, high-level language.

8. Machine language is difficult for humans to understand, since it provides no visual clues relating to the instruction syntax.

9. Instruction set architecture.

10. Level 2 (Instruction Set Architecture).

1.3   Data Representation

1. Least significant bit (bit 0).

2. Most significant bit (the highest numbered bit).

3. (a) 248   (b) 202   (c) 240

4. (a) 53   (b) 150   (c) 204

5. (a) 00010001   (b) 101000000   (c) 00011110

6. (a) 110001010   (b) 110010110   (c) 100100001

7. (a) 2   (b) 4   (c) 8

8. (a) 16   (b) 32   (c) 64

9. (a) 7   (b) 9   (c) 16

10. (a) 12   (b) 16   (c) 22

11. (a) CF57   (b) 5CAD   (c) 93EB

12. (a) 35DA   (b) CEA3   (c) FEDB

13. (a) 1110 0101 1011 0110 1010 1110 1101 0111
    (b) 1011 0110 1001 0111 1100 0111 1010 0001
    (c) 0010 0011 0100 1011 0110 1101 1001 0010

14. (a) 0000 0001 0010 0110 1111 1001 1101 0100
    (b) 0110 1010 1100 1101 1111 1010 1001 0101
    (c) 1111 0110 1001 1011 1101 1100 0010 1010

15. (a) 58   (b) 447   (c) 16534

16. (a) 98   (b) 457   (c) 27227

17. (a) FFE6   (b) FE3C

18. (a) FFE0   (b) FFC2

19. (a) +31915   (b) −16093

20. (a) +32667   (b) −32208

21. (a) −75   (b) +42   (c) −16

22. (a) −128   (b) −52   (c) −73

23. (a) 11111011   (b) 11011100   (c) 11110000

24. (a) 10111000   (b) 10011110   (c) 11100110

25. 58h and 88d.

26. 4Dh and 77d.

27. To handle international character sets that require more than 256 codes.

28. $2^{256} - 1$.

29. $+2^{255} - 1$.

1.4   Boolean Operations

1. (NOT X) OR Y.

2. X AND Y.

3. T.

4. F.

5. T.

6. Truth table:

A	B	A ∨ B	¬(A ∨ B)
F	F	F	T
F	T	T	F

A	B	A ∨ B	¬(A ∨ B)
T	F	T	F
T	T	T	F

7. Truth table:

A	B	¬A	¬B	¬A ∧ ¬B
F	F	T	T	T
F	T	T	F	F
T	F	F	T	F
T	T	F	F	F

8. 16, or (2^4).

9. 2 bits, producing the following values: 00, 01, 10, 11.

2   x86 Processor Architecture Details

2.1   General Concepts

1. Control Unit, Arithmetic Logic Unit, and the clock.

2. Data, Address, and Control buses.

3. Conventional memory is outside the CPU and it responds more slowly to access requests. Registers are hard-wired inside the CPU.

4. Fetch, decode, execute.

5. Fetch memory operands, store memory operands.

6. During the fetch step.

7. Section 2.1.4 mentions the filename, file size, and starting location on the disk. (Most directories also store the file's last modification date and time.)

8. The OS executes a branch (like a GOTO) to the first machine instruction in the program.

9. The CPU executes multiple tasks (programs) by rapidly switching from one program to the next. This gives the impression that all programs are executing at the same time.

10. The OS scheduler determines how much time to allot to each task, and it switches between tasks.

11. The program counter, the task's variables, and the CPU registers (including the status flags).

12. 3.33×10^{-10}, which is $1.0/3.0 \times 10^{9}$.

2.2   x86 Architecture Details

1. Real-address mode, Protected mode, and System Management mode.

2. EAX, EBX, ECX, EDX, ESI, EDI, ESP, EBP.

3. CS, DS, SS, ES, FS, GS.

4. Loop counter.

5. EBP.

6. Most common: Carry, Sign, Zero, Overflow. Less common: Auxiliary Carry, Parity.

7. Carry.

8. Overflow.

9. Sign.

10. Floating-Point Unit.

11. 80 bits.

12. The Intel 80386.

13. The Pentium.

14. The Pentium II.

15. CISC means *complex instruction set*: a large collection of instructions, some of which perform sophisticated operations that might be typical of a high-level language.

16. The term RISC stands for *reduced instruction set*: a small set of simple (atomic) instructions that may be combined into more complex operations.

2.3   x86 Memory Management

1. 4 GByte (0 to FFFFFFFFh).

2. 1 MByte (0 to FFFFFh).

3. Linear (absolute).

4. 09600h.

5. 0CFF0h.

6. 32 bits.

7. SS register.

8. Local descriptor table.

9. Global descriptor table.

10. The total size of all programs loaded into memory can exceed the amount of physical memory installed in the computer.

11. This is an open-ended question, of course. It is a fact that MS-DOS first had to run on the 8086/8088 processors, which only supported Real-address mode. When later processors came out that supported Protected mode, my guess is that Microsoft wanted MS-DOS to continue to run on the older processors. Otherwise, customers with older computers would refuse to upgrade to new versions of MS-DOS.

12. The following segment-offset addresses point to the same linear address: 0640:0100 and 0630:0200.

2.4   Components of a Typical x86 Computer

1. SRAM is an acronym for Static RAM, used in CPU cache memory.

2. VRAM (video ram) holds displayable video data. When CRT monitors are used, VRAM is dual ported, allowing one port to continuously refresh the display while another port writes data to the display.

3. Select any two features from the following list: (1) Intel Fast Memory Access uses an updated Memory Controller Hub (MCH). (2) I/O Controller Hub (Intel ICH8/R/DH) that supports serial ATA devices (disk drives). (3) Support for 10 USB ports, 6 PCI express slots, networking, and Intel Quiet System technology. (4) High definition audio chip.

4. Dynamic RAM, Static RAM, Video RAM, and CMOS RAM.

5. Static RAM.

6. The computer can query a device connected via USB to find out its name and device type and the type of driver it supports. The computer can also suspend power to individual devices. None of these capabilities is possible with serial and parallel ports.

7. The 8259 is the interrupt controller chip, sometimes called PIC, that schedules hardware interrupts and interrupts the CPU.

8. Bluetooth is a wireless communication protocol for exchanging small amounts of data over short distances. It is commonly used with mobile devices such as cell phones and PDAs. Wi-Fi devices operate at a greater speed and capacity than Bluetooth. Wi-Fi devices often communicate with each other when in the range of a wireless network.

2.5   Input-Output System

1. The application program level.

2. BIOS functions communicate directly with the system hardware. They are independent of the operating system.

3. New devices are invented all the time with capabilities that were often not anticipated when the BIOS was written.

4. The BIOS level.

5. The operating system, BIOS, and hardware levels.

6. Game programs often try to take advantage of the latest features in specialized sound cards. It should be noted that MS-DOS game applications were more prone to do this than games running under MS-Windows. In fact, Windows-NT, 2000, and XP all prevent applications from directly accessing system hardware.

7. No. The same BIOS would work for both operating systems. Many computer owners install two or three operating systems on the same computer. They would certainly not want to change the system BIOS every time they rebooted the computer!

3   Assembly Language Fundamentals

3.1   Basic Elements of Assembly Language

1. h, q, o, d, b, r, t, y.

2. No (a leading zero is required).

3. No (they have the same precedence).

4. Expression: 10 MOD 3.

5. Real number constant: +3.5E-02.

6. No, they can also be enclosed in double quotes.

7. Directives.

8. 247 characters.

9. True.

10. True.

11. False.

12. True.

13. Label, mnemonic, operand(s), comment.

14. True.

15. True.

16. Code example:

```
Comment !
      This is a comment
      This is also a comment
  !
```

17. Because the addresses coded in the instructions would have to be updated whenever new variables were inserted before existing ones.

3.2   Example: Adding and Subtracting Integers

1. The INCLUDE directive copies necessary definitions and setup information from the *Irvine32.inc* text file. The data from this file is inserted into the data stream read by the assembler.

2. The .CODE directive marks the beginning of the code segment.

3. code, data, and stack.

4. By calling the **DumpRegs** procedure.

5. The **exit** statement.

6. The PROC directive.

7. The ENDP directive.

8. It marks the last line of the program to be assembled, and the label next to END identifies the program's entry point (where execution begins).

9. PROTO declares the name of a procedure that is called by the current program.

3.3   Assembling, Linking, and Running Programs

1. Object (.OBJ) and listing (.LST) files.
2. True.
3. True.
4. Loader.
5. Executable (.EXE).

3.4   Defining Data

1. var1 SWORD ?
2. var2 BYTE ?
3. var3 SBYTE ?
4. var4 QWORD ?
5. SDWORD
6. var5 SDWORD −2147483648
7. wArray WORD 10, 20, 30
8. myColor BYTE "blue", 0
9. dArray DWORD 50 DUP(?)
10. myTestString BYTE 500 DUP("TEST")
11. bArray BYTE 20 DUP(0)
12. 21h, 43h, 65h, 87h

3.5   Symbolic Constants

1. BACKSPACE = 08h
2. SecondsInDay = 24 * 60 * 60
3. ArraySize = ($ − myArray)
4. ArraySize = ($ − myArray) / TYPE DWORD
5. PROCEDURE TEXTEQU <PROC>
6. Code example:

```
Sample TEXTEQU <"This is a string">
MyString BYTE Sample
```

7. SetupESI TEXTEQU <mov esi, OFFSET myArray>

4   Data Transfers, Addressing, and Arithmetic

4.1   Data Transfer Instructions

1. Register, immediate, and memory
2. False
3. False

4. True

5. A 32-bit register or memory operand

6. A 16-bit immediate (constant) operand

7. (a) not valid (b) valid (c) not valid (d) not valid (c) not valid (f) not valid (g) valid (h) not valid

8. (a) FCh (b) 01h

9. (a) 1000h (b) 3000h (c) FFF0h (d) 4000h

10. (a) 00000001h (b) 00001000h (c) 00000002h (d) FFFFFFFCh

4.2   Addition and Subtraction

1. inc val2

2. sub eax,val3

3. Code:

```
mov ax,val4
sub val2,ax
```

4. CF = 0, SF = 1.

5. OF = 1, SF = 1.

6. Write down the following flag values:
   (a) CF = 1, SF = 0, ZF = 1, OF = 0
   (b) CF = 0, SF = 1, ZF = 0, OF = 1
   (c) CF = 0, SF = 1, ZF = 0, OF = 0

7. Code example:

```
mov ax,val2
neg ax
add ax,bx
sub ax,val4
```

8. No.

9. Yes.

10. Yes (for example, mov al,−128 . . . followed by . . . neg al).

11. No.

12. Setting the Carry and Overflow flags at the same time:

```
mov al,80h
add al,80h
```

13. Setting the Zero flag after INC and DEC to indicate unsigned overflow:

```
mov al,0FFh
inc al
jz overflow_occurred
mov bl,1
dec bl
jz overflow_occurred
```

14. Subtracting 3 from 4 (unsigned). Carry out of MSB is inverted and placed in the Carry flag:

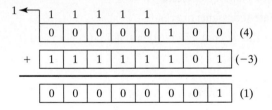

```
mov al,4
sub al,3      ; CF = 0
```

4.3   Data-Related Operators and Directives

1. False.

2. False.

3. True.

4. False.

5. True.

6. Data directive:

```
.data
ALIGN 2
myBytes BYTE 10h, 20h, 30h, 40h
etc.
```

7. (a) 1 (b) 4 (c) 4 (d) 2 (e) 4 (f) 8 (g) 5

8. mov dx, WORD PTR myBytes

9. mov al, BYTE PTR myWords+1

10. mov eax, DWORD PTR myBytes

11. Data directive:

```
myWordsD LABEL DWORD
myWords WORD 3 DUP(?),2000h
.code
mov eax,myWordsD
```

12. Data directive:

```
myBytesW LABEL WORD
myBytes BYTE 10h,20h,30h,40h
.code
mov ax,myBytesW
```

4.4   Indirect Addressing

1. False.

2. True.

3. False.

4. False.

5. True (the PTR operator is required).

6. True.

7. (a) 10h (b) 40h (c) 003Bh (d) 3 (e) 3 (f) 2

8. (a) 2010h (b) 003B008Ah (c) 0 (d) 0 (e) 0044h

4.5   JMP and LOOP Instructions

1. True.

2. False.

3. 4,294,967,296 times.

4. False.

5. True.

6. CX.

7. ECX.

8. False (-128 to $+127$ bytes from the current location).

9. This is a trick! The program does not stop, because the first LOOP instruction decrements ECX to zero. The second LOOP instruction decrements ECX to FFFFFFFFh, causing the outer loop to repeat.

10. Insert the following instruction at label L1: `push ecx`. Also insert the following instruction before the second LOOP instruction: `pop ecx`. (Once you have added these instructions, the final value of eax is 1Ch.)

5   Procedures

5.1   Introduction

No review questions.

5.2   Linking to an External Library

1. False (it contains object code).

2. Code example:

```
MyProc PROTO
```

3. Code example:

```
call MyProc
```

4. Irvine32.lib.

5. Kernel32.lib.

6. Kernel32.dll is a dynamic link library that is a fundamental part of the MS-Windows operating system.

5.3 The Book's Link Library

1. RandomRange procedure.

2. WaitMsg procedure.

3. Code example:

```
mov   eax,700
call Delay
```

4. WriteDec procedure.

5. Gotoxy procedure.

6. INCLUDE Irvine32.inc.

7. PROTO statements (procedure prototypes) and constant definitions. (There are also text macros, but they are not mentioned in this chapter.)

8. ESI contains the data's starting address, ECX contains the number of data units, and EBX contains the data unit size (byte, word, or doubleword).

9. EDX contains the offset of an array of bytes, and ECX contains the maximum number of characters to read.

10. Carry, Sign, Zero, Overflow, Auxiliary carry, and Parity.

11. Code example:

```
.data
str1 BYTE "Enter identification number: ",0
idStr BYTE 15 DUP(?)
.code
    mov   edx,OFFSET str1
    call WriteString
    mov   edx,OFFSET idStr
    mov   ecx,(SIZEOF idStr) - 1
    call ReadString
```

5.4 Stack Operations

1. ESP.

2. The runtime stack is the only type of stack that is managed directly by the CPU. For example, it holds the return addresses of called procedures.

3. LIFO stands for "last in, first out." The last value pushed into the stack is the first value popped out from the stack.

4. ESP is decremented by 4.

5. True.

6. False (you can push both 16-bit and 32-bit values).

7. True.

8. False (yes, it can, from the 80186 processor onward).

9. PUSHAD.

10. PUSHFD.

11. POPFD.

12. NASM's approach permits the programmer to be specific about which registers are to be pushed. PUSHAD, on the other hand, does not have that flexibility. This becomes important when a procedure needs to save several registers and at the same time return a value to its caller in the EAX register. In this type of situation, EAX cannot be pushed and popped because the return value would be lost.

13. Equivalent to PUSH EAX:

```
sub esp,4
mov [esp],eax
```

5.5   Defining and Using Procedures

1. True.

2. False.

3. Execution would continue beyond the end of the procedure, possibly into the beginning of another procedure. This type of programming bug is often difficult to detect!

4. *Receives* indicates the input parameters given to the procedure when it is called. *Returns* indicates what value, if any, the procedure produces when it returns it to its caller.

5. False (it pushes the offset of the instruction *following* the call).

6. True.

7. True.

8. False (there is no NESTED operator).

9. True.

10. False.

11. True (it also receives a count of the number of array elements).

12. True.

13. False.

14. False.

15. The following statements would have to be modified:

```
add eax,[esi]    becomes -->   add ax,[esi]
add esi,4        becomes -->   add esi,2
```

5.6   Program Design Using Procedures

1. Functional decomposition, or top-down design.

2. Clrscr, WriteString, ReadInt, and WriteInt.

3. A stub program contains all of its important procedures, but the procedures are either empty or nearly empty.

4. False (it receives a pointer to an array).

5. The following statements would have to be modified:

```
mov [esi],eax    becomes -->   mov [esi],ax
add esi,4        becomes -->   add esi,2
```

6. Flowchart of the PromptForIntegers procedure:

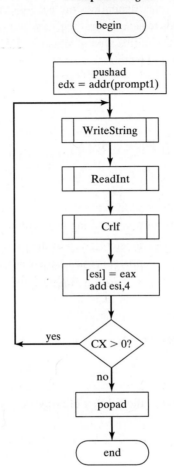

PromptForIntegers

6   Conditional Processing

6.1   Introduction

No review questions.

6.2   Boolean and Comparison Instructions

1. (a) 00101101   (b) 01001000   (c) 01101111   (d) 10100011
2. (a) 85h   (b) 34h   (c) BFh   (d) AEh
3. (a) CF=0, ZF=0, SF=0
   (b) CF=0, ZF=0, SF=0
   (c) CF=1, ZF=0, SF=1

4. `and ax,00FFh`

5. `or ax,0FF00h`

6. `xor eax,0FFFFFFFFh`

7. `test eax,1         ; (low bit set if eax is odd)`

8. `or al,00100000b`

9. `and al,00001111b`

10. Code example:

```
.data
memVal DWORD ?
.code
mov al,BYTE PTR memVal
xor al,BYTE PTR memVal+1
xor al,BYTE PTR memVal+2
xor al,BYTE PTR memVal+3
```

11. Find elements in SetX that are not found in SetY:

```
; Method 1: X - (X intersection Y)
mov   eax,SetX       ; X
mov   edx,eax        ; (X intersection Y)
and   edx,SetY
sub   eax,edx        ; X - (X intersection Y)

; Method 2: (X union Y) - Y
mov   eax,SetX
or    eax,SetY       ; X union Y
sub   eax,SetY       ; (X union Y) - Y
```

6.3 Conditional Loops

1. JA, JNBE, JAE, JNB, JB, JNAE, JBE, JNA

2. JG, JNLE, JGE, JNL, JL, JNGE, JLE, JNG

3. JECXZ

4. Yes, because they both depend on the flag combinations of CF = 0 and ZF = 0.

5. If JL is used after comparing 7FFFh to 8000h, the operands will be processed as signed values (+32,767 and −32,768), so the jump will not be taken. If JB is used instead, the values will be considered unsigned, and the jump will be taken.

6. JBE

7. JL

8. No (8109h is negative and 26h is positive).

9. Yes

10. Yes (the unsigned representation of −42 is compared to 26)

11. Code:

```
cmp dx,cx
jbe L1
```

12. Code:

```
cmp ax,cx
jg  L2
```

13. Code:

```
and al,11111100b
jz  L3
jmp L4
```

6.4 Conditional Loop Instructions

1. False.

2. True.

3. True.

4. Code example:

```
.data
array SWORD 3,5,14,-3,-6,-1,-10,10,30,40,4
sentinel SWORD 0
.code
main PROC
    mov esi,OFFSET array
    mov ecx,LENGTHOF array
next:
    test WORD PTR [esi],8000h   ; test sign bit
    pushfd                      ; push flags on stack
    add  esi,TYPE array
    popfd                       ; pop flags from stack
    loopz next                  ; continue loop while ZF=1
    jz   quit                   ; none found
    sub  esi,TYPE array         ; ESI points to value
```

5. If a matching value were not found, ESI would end up pointing beyond the end of the array. By pointing at an undefined memory location, a program runs the risk of causing a runtime error.

6.5 Conditional Structures

We will assume that all values are unsigned in this section.

1. Code example:

```
    cmp ebx,ecx
    jna next
    mov X,1
next:
```

2. Code example:

```
    cmp  edx,ecx
    jnbe L1
    mov  X,1
```

```
            jmp   next
    L1:   mov   X,2
    next:
```

3. Code example:

```
            cmp   val1,ecx
            jna   L1
            cmp   ecx,edx
            jna   L1
            mov   X,1
            jmp   next
    L1:   mov   X,2
    next:
```

4. Code example:

```
            cmp   ebx,ecx
            ja    L1
            cmp   ebx,val1
            ja    L1
            mov   X,2
            jmp   next
    L1:   mov   X,1
    next:
```

5. Code example:

```
            cmp   ebx,ecx              ; ebx > ecx?
            jna   L1                   ; no: try condition after OR
            cmp   ebx,edx              ; yes: is ebx > edx?
            jna   L1                   ; no: try condition after OR
            jmp   L2                   ; yes: set X to 1
    ;----------------OR(edx > eax) ----------------------
    L1:   cmp   edx,eax              ; edx > eax?
            jna   L3                   ; no: set X to 2
    L2:   mov   X,1                  ; yes:set X to 1
            jmp   next                 ; and quit
    L3:   mov   X,2                  ; set X to 2
    next:
```

6. Future changes to the table will alter the value of NumberOfEntries. We might forget to update the constant manually, but the assembler can correctly adjust a calculated value.

7. Code example:

```
    .data
    sum DWORD 0
    sample DWORD 50
    array DWORD 10,60,20,33,72,89,45,65,72,18
    ArraySize = ($ - Array) / TYPE array
    .code
        mov   eax,0                  ; sum
        mov   edx,sample
```

```
        mov   esi,0                        ; index
        mov   ecx,ArraySize
   L1:  cmp   esi,ecx
        jnl   L5
        cmp   array[esi*4],edx
        jng   L4
        add   eax,array[esi*4]
   L4:  inc   esi
        jmp   L1
   L5:  mov   sum,eax
```

6.6   Application: Finite-State Machines

1. A directed graph.

2. Each node is a state.

3. Each edge is a transition from one state to another, caused by some input.

4. State C.

5. An infinite number of digits.

6. The FSM enters an error state.

7. No. The proposed FSM would permit a signed integer to consist of only a plus (+) or minus (−) sign. The FSM in Section 6.6.2 would not permit that.

6.7   Conditional Control Flow Directives

No review questions.

7   Integer Arithmetic

7.1   Introduction

No review questions.

7.2   Shift and Rotate Instructions

1. ROL.

2. RCR.

3. First, shift EAX 16 bits to the left. Next, shift it arithmetically 16 bits to the right:

```
        shl eax,16
        sar eax,16
```

4. RCL.

5. Code example:

```
        shr al,1                         ; shift AL into Carry flag
        jnc next                         ; Carry flag set?
        or  al,80h                       ; yes: set highest bit
   next:                                 ; no: do nothing
```

6. The Carry flag receives the lowest bit of AX (before the shift).

7. ```
shl eax,4
```

8. ```
shr ebx,2
```

9. ```
ror dl,4   (or: rol dl,4)
```

10. ```
shld dx,ax,1
```

11. (a) 6Ah (b) EAh (c) FDh (d) A9h

12. (a) 9Ah (b) 6Ah (c) 0A9h (d) 3Ah

13. Code example:

```
        shr ax,1                    ; shift AX into Carry flag
        rcr bx,1                    ; shift Carry flag into BX
    ; Using SHRD:
        shrd bx,ax,1
```

14. Code example:

```
        mov ecx,32                  ; loop counter
        mov bl,0                    ; counts the '1' bits
    L1: shr eax,1                   ; shift into Carry flag
        jnc L2                      ; Carry flag set?
        inc bl                      ; yes: add to bit count
    L2: loop L1                     ; continue loop
    ; if BL is odd, clear the parity flag
    ; if BL is even, set the parity flag
        shr bl,1
        jc  odd
        mov bh,0
        or  bh,0                    ; PF = 1
        jmp next
odd:
        mov bh,1
        or  bh,1                    ; PF = 0
next:
```

15. Calculate x = n mod y, given n and y, where y is a power of 2:

```
.data
dividend DWORD 1000
divisor  DWORD 32                   ; must be a power of 2
answer   DWORD ?
.code
mov edx,divisor                     ; create a bit mask
sub edx,1
mov eax,dividend
and eax,edx                 ; clear high bits, low bits contain mod value
mov answer,eax
```

16. Calculate absolute value of EAX without using a conditional jump:

```
mov   edx,eax                       ; create a bit mask
sar   edx,31
```

```
add   eax,edx
xor   eax,edx
```

7.3   Shift and Rotate Applications

1. This problem requires us to start with the high-order byte and work our way down to the lowest byte:

```
byteArray BYTE 81h,20h,33h
.code
shr byteArray+2,1
rcr byteArray+1,1
rcr byteArray,1
```

2. This problem requires us to start with the low-order word and work our way up to the highest word:

```
wordArray WORD 810Dh,0C064h,93ABh
.code
shl wordArray,1
rcl wordArray+2,1
rcl wordArray+4,1
```

3. The multiplier (24) can be factored into 16 * 8:

```
mov ebx,eax              ; save a copy of eax
shl eax,4                ; multiply by 16
shl ebx,3                ; multiply by 8
add eax,ebx              ; add the products
```

4. As the hint explains, the multiplier (21) can be factored into 16 * 4 + 1:

```
mov ebx,eax              ; save a copy of eax
mov ecx,eax              ; save another copy of eax
shl eax,4                ; multiply by 16
shl ebx,2                ; multiply by 4
add eax,ebx              ; add the products
add eax,ecx              ; add original value of eax
```

5. Change the instruction at label L1 to `shr eax,1`

6. We will assume that the time stamp word is in the DX register:

```
shr dx,5
and dl,00111111b         ; (leading zeros optional)
mov bMinutes,dl          ; save in variable
```

7.4   Multiplication and Division Instructions

1. The product is stored in registers that are twice the size of the multiplier and multiplicand. If you multiply 0FFh by 0FFh, for example, the product (FE01h) easily fits within 16 bits.

2. When the product fits completely within the lower register of the product, IMUL sign-extends the product into the upper product register. MUL, on the other hand, zero-extends the product.

3. With IMUL, the Carry and Overflow flags are set when the upper half of the product is not a sign extension of the lower half of the product.

4. EAX.

5. AX.

6. AX.

7. Code example:

```
mov ax,dividendLow
cwd                          ; sign-extend dividend
mov bx,divisor
idiv bx
```

8. DX = 0002h, AX = 2200h.

9. AX = 0306h.

10. EDX = 0, EAX = 00012340h.

11. The DIV will cause a divide overflow, so the values of AX and DX cannot be determined.

12. Code example:

```
mov    ax,3
mov    bx,-5
imul   bx
mov    val1,ax              ; product

// alternative solution:
mov    al,3
mov    bl,-5
imul   bl
mov    val1,ax              ; product
```

13. Code example:

```
mov    ax,-276
cwd                         ; sign-extend AX into DX
mov    bx,10
idiv   bx
mov    val1,ax              ; quotient
```

14. Implement the unsigned expression val1 = (val2 * val3) / (val4 − 3):

```
mov    eax,val2
mul    val3
mov    ebx,val4
sub    ebx,3
div    ebx
mov    val1,eax
```

(You can substitute any 32-bit general-purpose register for EBX in this example.)

15. Implement the signed expression val1 = (val2 / val3) * (val1 + val2):

```
mov eax,val2
cdq                         ; extend EAX into EDX
```

```
idiv  val3                          ; EAX = quotient
mov   ebx,val1
add   ebx,val2
imul  ebx
mov   val1,eax                      ; lower 32 bits of product
```

(You can substitute any 32-bit general-purpose register for EBX in this example.)

7.5 Extended Addition and Subtraction

1. The ADC instruction adds both a source operand and the Carry flag to a destination operand.

2. The SBB instruction subtracts both a source operand and the Carry flag from a destination operand.

3. EAX = C0000000h, EDX = 00000010h.

4. EAX = F0000000h, EDX = 000000FFh.

5. DX = 0016h.

6. In correcting this example, it is easiest to reduce the number of instructions. You can use a single register (ESI) to index into all three variables. ESI should be set to zero before the loop because the integers are stored in little endian order with their low-order bytes occurring first:

```
      mov   ecx,8                   ; loop counter
      mov   esi,0                   ; use the same index reg
      clc                           ; clear Carry flag
top:
      mov   al,byte ptr val1[esi]   ; get first number
      sbb   al,byte ptr val2[esi]   ; subtract second
      mov   byte ptr result[esi],al ; store the result
      inc   esi                     ; move to next pair
      loop top
```

Of course, you could easily reduce the number of loop iterations by adding doublewords rather than bytes.

7.6 ASCII and Unpacked Decimal Arithmetic

1. Code example:
```
      or ax,3030h
```

2. Code example:
```
      and ax,0F0Fh
```

3. Code example:
```
      and ax,0F0Fh                  ; convert to unpacked
      aad
```

4. Code example:
```
      aam
```

5. Code example (displays binary value in AX):

```
out16PROC
      aam
      or     ax,3030h
      push   eax
      mov    al,ah
      call   WriteChar
      pop    eax
      call   WriteChar
      ret
out16ENDP
```

6. After AAA, AX would equal 0108h. First, if the lower digit of AL is greater than 9 or the AuxCarry flag is set, add 6 to AL and add 1 to AH. Then in all cases, AND AL with 0Fh. Pseudocode:

```
IF ((AL AND 0FH) > 9) OR (AuxCarry = 1) THEN
      add 6 to AL
      add 1 to AH
END IF
AND AL with 0FH;
```

7.7   Packed Decimal Arithmetic

1. When the sum of a packed decimal addition is greater than 99, DAA sets the Carry flag. For example,

```
      mov al,56h
      add al,92h              ; AL = E8h
      daa                     ; AL = 48h, CF=1
```

2. When a larger packed decimal integer is subtracted from a small one, DAS sets the Carry flag. For example,

```
      mov   al,56h
      sub   al,92h            ; AL = C4h
      das                     ; AL = 64h, CF=1
```

3. $n + 1$ bytes.

4. Suppose AL = 3Dh, AF = 0, and CF = 0. Because the lower digit (D) is > 9, we subtract 6 from D. AL now equals 37h. Because the upper digit (3) is ≤ 9 and CF = 0, no other adjustments are necessary. DAS produces AL = 37h.

8   Advanced Procedures

8.1   Introduction

No review questions.

8.2   Stack Frames

1. True.

2. True.

3. True.

4. False.

5. True.

6. True.

7. Value parameters and Reference parameters.

8. Code example:

```
mov   esp,ebp
pop   ebp
```

9. EAX

10. It passes an integer constant to the RET instruction. This constant is added to the stack pointer right after the RET instruction has popped the procedure's return address off the stack.

11. Stack frame diagram:

10h	[EBP + 16]
20h	[EBP + 12]
30h	[EBP + 8]
(return addr)	[EBP + 4]
EBP	<--ESP

12. LEA can return the offset of an indirect operand; it is particularly useful for obtaining the offset of a stack parameter.

13. Four bytes.

14. Code example:

```
AddThree PROC
; modeled after the AddTwo procedure
     push ebp
     mov  ebp,esp
     mov  eax,[ebp + 16]; 10h
     add  eax,[ebp + 12]; 20h
     add  eax,[ebp + 8] ; 30h
     pop  ebp
     ret  12
AddThree ENDP
```

15. It is zero-extended into EAX and pushed on the stack.

16. Declaration: LOCAL pArray:PTR DWORD

17. Declaration: LOCAL buffer[20]:BYTE

18. Declaration: LOCAL pwArray:PTR WORD

19. Declaration: LOCAL myByte:SBYTE

20. Declaration: LOCAL myArray[20]:DWORD

21. The C calling convention, because it specifies that arguments must be pushed on the stack in reverse order, makes it possible to create a procedure/function with a variable number of parameters. The last parameter pushed on the stack can be a count specifying the number of parameters already pushed on the stack. In the following diagram, for example, the count value is located at [EBP + 8]:

10h	[EBP + 20]
20h	[EBP + 16]
30h	[EBP + 12]
3	[EBP + 8]
(return addr)	[EBP + 4]
EBP	<--ESP

8.3 Recursion

1. False.

2. It terminates when n equals zero.

3. The following instructions execute after each recursive call has finished:

```
ReturnFact:
      mov ebx, [ebp+8]
      mul ebx
L2:   pop ebp
      ret 4
```

4. The calculated value would exceed the range of an unsigned doubleword, and would roll past zero. The output would appear to be smaller than 12 factorial.

5. 12! uses 156 bytes of stack space. *Rationale:* When $n = 0$, 12 stack bytes are used (3 stack entries, each equal to 4 bytes). When $n = 1$, 24 bytes are used. When $n = 2$, 36 bytes are used. Therefore, the amount of stack space required for n! is $(n + 1) \times 12$.

6. A recursive Fibonacci algorithm uses system resources inefficiently because each call to the Fibonacci function with a value of n generates function calls for all Fibonacci numbers between 1 and $n - 1$. Here is the pseudocode to generate the first 20 values:

```
for(int i = 1; i <= 20; i++)
  print( fibonacci(i) );

int fibonacci(int n)
{
    if( n == 1 )
          return 1;
    elseif( n == 2 )
          return 2;
    else
          return fibonacci(n-1) + fibonacci(n-2);
}
```

8.4   INVOKE, ADDR, PROC, and PROTO

1. True.

2. False.

3. False.

4. True.

5. False.

6. True.

7. True.

8. Declaration:

```
MultArray PROC ptr1:PTR DWORD,
    ptr2:PTR DWORD,
    count:DWORD                    ; (may be byte, word, or dword)
```

9. Declaration:

```
MultArray PROTO ptr1:PTR DWORD,
    ptr2:PTR DWORD,
    count:DWORD                    ; (may be byte, word, or dword)
```

10. It uses input-output parameters.

11. It is an output parameter.

8.5   Creating Multimodule Programs

1. True.

2. False.

3. True.

4. False.

9   Strings and Arrays

9.1   Introduction

No review questions.

9.2   String Primitive Instructions

1. EAX.

2. SCASD.

3. (E)DI.

4. LODSW.

5. Repeat while ZF = 1.

6. 1 (set).

7. 2.

8. Regardless of which operands are used, CMPS still compares the contents of memory pointed to by ESI to the memory pointed to by EDI.

9. 1 byte beyond the matching character.

10. REPNE (REPNZ).

9.3 Selected String Procedures

1. False (it stops when the null terminator of the shorter string is reached).

2. True.

3. False.

4. False.

5. 1 (set).

6. JNE is used to exit the loop and insert a null byte into the string when no more characters are to be trimmed.

7. The digit is unchanged.

8. REPNE (REPNZ).

9. The length would be $(EDI_{final} - EDI_{initial}) - 1$.

9.4 Two-Dimensional Arrays

1. Any general-purpose 32-bit registers.

2. [ebx + esi].

3. array[ebx + esi].

4. 16.

5. Code example:

```
mov esi,2                    ; row
mov edi,3                    ; column
mov eax,[esi*16 + edi*4]
```

6. BP points to the stack segment in Real-address mode.

7. No (the flat memory model uses the same segment for stack and data).

9.5 Searching and Sorting Integer Arrays

1. $n - 1$ times.

2. $n - 1$ times.

3. No. It decreases by 1 each.

4. $T(5000) = 0.5 * 10^2$

5. The maximum comparisons for 1,024 elements is 11.

6. The Direction flag is cleared so that the STOSD instruction will automatically increment the EDI register. Instead, if the flag were set, EDI would decrement and move backwards through the array.

7. EDX and EDI were already compared.

8. Change each JMP L4 instruction to JMP L1.

(Section 9.6 has no review questions.)

10   Structures and Macros

10.1   Structures

1. Structures are essential whenever you need to pass a large amount of data between procedures. One variable can be used to hold all the data.

2. Structure definition:

```
MyStruct STRUCT
      field1 WORD ?
      field2 DWORD 20 DUP(?)
MyStruct ENDS
```

3. `temp1 MyStruct <>`

4. `temp2 MyStruct <0>`

5. `temp3 MyStruct <, 20 DUP(0)>`

6. `array MyStruct 20 DUP(<>)`

7. `mov ax,array.field1`

8. Code example:

```
mov esi,OFFSET array
add esi,3 * (TYPE myStruct)
mov (MyStruct PTR[esi]).field1.ax
```

9. 82.

10. 82.

11. `TYPE MyStruct.field2 (or: SIZEOF Mystruct.field2)`

12. Multiple answers:

a. Yes.

b. No.

c. Yes.

d. Yes.

e. No.

13. Code example:

```
.data
time SYSTEMTIME <>
.code
mov ax,time.wHour
```

14. Code example:

```
myShape Triangle < <0,0>, <5,0>, <7,6> >
```

15. Code example (initializes an array of Triangle structures):

```
.data
ARRAY_SIZE = 5
triangles Triangle ARRAY_SIZE DUP(<>)
.code
      mov    ecx,ARRAY_SIZE
      mov    esi,0
L1:   mov    eax,11
      call   RandomRange
      mov    triangles[esi].Vertex1.X, ax
      mov    eax,11
      call   RandomRange
      mov    triangles[esi].Vertex1.Y, ax
      add    esi,TYPE Triangle
      loop   L1
```

10.2   Macros

1. False.

2. True.

3. Macros with parameters can be reused more easily.

4. False.

5. True.

6. False.

7. To permit the use of labels in a macro that is invoked more than once by the same program.

8. ECHO (also, the %OUT operator, which is shown later in the chapter).

9. Code example:

```
mPrintChar MACRO char,count
LOCAL temp
.data
temp BYTE count DUP(&char),0
.code
    push    edx
    mov     edx,OFFSET temp
    call    WriteString
    pop     edx
ENDM
```

10. Code example:

```
mGenRandom MACRO n
      mov  eax,n
      call RandomRange
ENDM
```

11. mPromptInteger:

```
mPromptInteger MACRO prompt,returnVal
    mWrite prompt
    call   ReadInt
    mov    returnVal,eax
ENDM
```

12. Code example:

```
mWriteAt MACRO X,Y,literal
    mGotoxy X,Y
    mWrite literal
ENDM
```

13. Code example:

```
mWriteStr namePrompt
1    push   edx
1    mov    edx,OFFSET namePrompt
1    call   WriteString
1    pop    edx
```

14. Code example:

```
mReadStr customerName
1    push   ecx
1    push   edx
1    mov    edx,OFFSET customerName
1    mov    ecx,(SIZEOF customerName) - 1
1    call   ReadString
1    pop    edx
1    pop    ecx
```

15. Code example:

```
;-----------------------------------------------
mDumpMemx MACRO varName
;
; Displays a variable in hexadecimal, using the
; variable's attributes to determine the number
; of units and unit size.
;-----------------------------------------------
    push   ebx
    push   ecx
    push   esi
    mov    esi,OFFSET varName
    mov    ecx,LENGTHOF varName
    mov    ebx,TYPE varName
    call   DumpMem
    pop    esi
    pop    ecx
    pop    ebx
ENDM
```

```
; Sample calls:
.data
array1 BYTE   10h,20h,30h,40h,50h
array2 WORD   10h,20h,30h,40h,50h
array3 DWORD  10h,20h,30h,40h,50h
.code
mDumpMemx array1
mDumpMemx array2
mDumpMemx array3
```

10.3   Conditional-Assembly Directives

1. The IFB directive is used to check for blank macro parameters.

2. The IFIDN directive compares two text values and returns true if they are identical. It performs a case-sensitive comparison.

3. EXITM.

4. IFIDNI is the case-insensitive version of IFIDN.

5. The IFDEF returns true if a symbol has already been defined.

6. ENDIF.

7. Code example:

```
mWriteLn MACRO text:=<" ">
     mWrite text
     call Crlf
ENDM
```

8. List of relational operators:
   LT   Less than
   GT   Greater than
   EQ   Equal to
   NE   Not equal to
   LE   Less than or equal to
   GE   Greater than or equal to

9. Code example:

```
mCopyWord MACRO intVal
     IF (TYPE intVal) EQ 2
       mov ax,intVal
     ELSE
       ECHO Invalid operand size
     ENDIF
ENDM
```

10. Code example:

```
mCheck MACRO Z
     IF Z LT 0
       ECHO **** Operand Z is invalid ****
     ENDIF
ENDM
```

11. The substitution (&) operator resolves ambiguous references to parameter names within a macro.

12. The literal-character operator (!) forces the preprocessor to treat a predefined operator as an ordinary character.

13. The expansion operator (%) expands text macros or converts constant expressions into their text representations.

14. Code example:

```
CreateString MACRO strVal
.data
temp BYTE "Var&strVal",0
.code
ENDM
```

15. Code example:

```
        mLocate -2,20
        ;(no code generated because xval < 0)
        mLocate 10,20
        1   mov bx,0
        1   mov ah,2
        1   mov dh,20
        1   mov dl,10
        1   int 10h
        mLocate col,row
        1   mov bx,0
        1   mov ah,2
        1   mov dh,row
        1   mov dl,col
        1   int 10h
```

10.4   Defining Repeat Blocks

1. The WHILE directive repeats a statement block based on a boolean expression.

2. The REPEAT directive repeats a statement block based on the value of a counter.

3. The FOR directive repeats a statement block by iterating over a list of symbols.

4. The FORC directive repeats a statement block by iterating over a string of characters.

5. FORC

6. Code example:

```
        BYTE 0,0,0,100
        BYTE 0,0,0,20
        BYTE 0,0,0,30
```

7. Code example:

```
mRepeat MACRO 'X',50
        mov   cx,50
??0000: mov ah,2
        mov   dl,'X'
```

```
        int   21h
        loop  ??0000
mRepeat MACRO AL,20
        mov   cx,20
??0001: mov ah,2
        mov   dl,AL
        int   21h
        loop  ??0001
mRepeat MACRO byteVal,countVal
        mov   cx,countVal
??0002: mov ah,2
        mov   dl,byteVal
        int   21h
        loop  ??0002
```

8. If we examine the linked list data (in the listing file), it is apparent that the **NextPtr** field of each **ListNode** always equals 00000008 (the address of the second node):

```
Offset     ListNode
----------------------------
00000000   00000001   NodeData
           00000008   NextPtr
00000008   00000002   NodeData
           00000008   NextPtr
00000010   00000003   NodeData
           00000008   NextPtr
00000018   00000004   NodeData
           00000008   NextPtr
00000020   00000005   NodeData
           00000008   NextPtr
00000028   00000006   NodeData
           00000008   NextPtr
```

We hinted at this in the text when we said "the location counter's value ($) remains fixed at the first node of the list."

11   MS-Windows Programming

11.1   Win32 Console Programming

1. /SUBSYSTEM:CONSOLE

2. True.

3. False.

4. False.

5. True.

6. BOOL = byte, COLORREF = DWORD, HANDLE = DWORD, LPSTR = PTR BYTE, WPARAM = DWORD.

7. GetStdHandle.

8. ReadConsole.

9. Example from the *ReadConsole.asm* program in Section 11.1.4:

```
INVOKE ReadConsole, stdInHandle, ADDR buffer,
    BufSize - 2, ADDR bytesRead, 0
```

10. The COORD structure contains X and Y screen coordinates in character measurements.

11. Example from the *Console1.asm* program in Section 11.1.5:

```
INVOKE WriteConsole,
        consoleHandle,              ; console output handle
        ADDR message,               ; string pointer
        messageSize,                ; string length
        ADDR bytesWritten,          ; returns num bytes written
        0                           ; not used
```

12. Calling **CreateFile** when reading an input file:

```
INVOKE CreateFile,
        ADDR filename,              ; ptr to filename
        GENERIC_READ,               ; access mode
        DO_NOT_SHARE,               ; share mode
        NULL,                       ; ptr to security attributes
        OPEN_EXISTING,              ; file creation options
        FILE_ATTRIBUTE_NORMAL,      ; file attributes
        0                           ; handle to template file
```

13. Calling **CreateFile** to create a new file:

```
INVOKE CreateFile,
        ADDR filename,
        GENERIC_WRITE,
        DO_NOT_SHARE,
        NULL,
        CREATE_ALWAYS,
        FILE_ATTRIBUTE_NORMAL,
        0
```

14. Calling **ReadFile**:

```
INVOKE ReadFile,                    ; read file into buffer
        fileHandle,
        ADDR buffer,
        bufSize,
        ADDR byteCount,
        0
```

15. Calling **WriteFile**:

```
INVOKE WriteFile,                   ; write text to file
        fileHandle,                 ; file handle
        ADDR buffer,                ; buffer pointer
        bufSize,                    ; number of bytes to write
        ADDR bytesWritten,          ; number of bytes written
        0                           ; overlapped execution flag
```

16. SetFilePointer.

17. SetConsoleTitle.

18. SetConsoleScreenBufferSize.

19. SetConsolcCursorInfo.

20. SetConsoleTextAttribute.

21. WriteConsoleOutputAttribute.

22. Sleep.

11.2   Writing a Graphical Windows Application

Note: Most of these questions can be answered by looking in *GraphWin.inc*, the include file supplied with this book's sample programs.

1. A POINT structure contains two fields, ptX and ptY, that describe the X- and Y-coordinates (in pixels) of a point on the screen.

2. The WNDCLASS structure defines a window class. Each window in a program must belong to a class, and each program must define a window class for its main window. This class is registered with the operating system before the main window can be shown.

3. *lpfnWndProc* is a pointer to a function in an application program that receives and processes event messages triggered by the user.

4. The *style* field is a combination of different style options, such as WS_CAPTION and WS_BORDER, that control a window's appearance and behavior.

5. *hInstance* holds a handle to the current program instance. Each program running under MS-Windows is automatically assigned a handle by the operating system when the program is loaded into memory.

6. (A program that calls CreatewindowEx is shown in Section 11.2.6.)

   The prototype for **CreateWindowEx** is located in the *GraphWin.inc* file:

```
CreateWindowEx PROTO,
     classexWinStyle:DWORD,
     className:PTR BYTE,
     winName:PTR BYTE,
     winStyle:DWORD,
     X:DWORD,
     Y:DWORD,
     rWidth:DWORD,
     rHeight:DWORD,
     hWndParent:DWORD,
     hMenu:DWORD,
     hInstance:DWORD,
     lpParam:DWORD
```

The fourth parameter, *winStyle*, determines the window's style characteristics. In the WinApp.asm program in Section 11.2.6, when we call CreateWindowEx, we pass it a combination of predefined style constants:

```
MAIN_WINDOW_STYLE = WS_VISIBLE + WS_DLGFRAME + WS_CAPTION
    + WS_BORDER + WS_SYSMENU + WS_MAXIMIZEBOX + WS_MINIMIZEBOX
    + WS_THICKFRAME
```

The window described here will be visible, and it will have a dialog box frame, a caption bar, a border, a system menu, a maximize icon, a minimize icon, and a thick surrounding frame.

7. Calling MessageBox:

```
INVOKE MessageBox, hMainWnd, ADDR GreetText,
    ADDR GreetTitle, MB_OK
```

8. Choose any two of the following (from *GraphWin.inc*):

```
MB_OK, MB_OKCANCEL, MB_ABORTRETRYIGNORE, MB_YESNOCANCEL, MB_YESNO,
MB_RETRYCANCEL, MB_CANCELTRYCONTINUE
```

9. Icon constants (choose any two):

```
MB_ICONHAND, MB_ICONQUESTION, MB_ICONEXCLAMATION, MB_ICONASTERISK
```

10. Tasks performed by **WinMain** (choose any three):
    • Get a handle to the current program.
    • Load the program's icon and mouse cursor.
    • Register the program's main window class and identify the procedure that will process event messages for the window.
    • Create the main window.
    • Show and update the main window.
    • Begin a loop that receives and dispatches messages.

11. The **WinProc** procedure receives and processes all event messages relating to a window. It decodes each message, and if the message is recognized, carries out application-oriented (or application-specific) tasks relating to the message.

12. The following messages are processed:
    • WM_LBUTTONDOWN, generated when the user presses the left mouse button.
    • WM_CREATE, indicates that the main window was just created.
    • WM_CLOSE, indicates that the application's main window is about to close.

13. The ErrorHandler procedure, which is optional, is called if the system reports an error during the registration and creation of the program's main window.

14. The message box is shown before the application's main window appears.

15. The message box appears before the main window closes.

11.3   Dynamic Memory Allocation

1. Dynamic memory allocation.
2. Returns a 32-bit integer handle to the program's existing heap area in EAX.
3. Allocates a block of memory from a heap.

4. HeapCreate example:

```
HEAP_START =   2000000                  ;   2 MB
HEAP_MAX   =  400000000                 ; 400 MB
.data
hHeap HANDLE ?                          ; handle to heap
.code
INVOKE HeapCreate, 0, HEAP_START, HEAP_MAX
```

5. Pass a pointer to the memory block (along with the heap handle).

11.4   x86 Memory Management

1. (a) Multitasking permits multiple programs (or tasks) to run at the same time. The processor divides up its time between all of the running programs.
   (b) Segmentation provides a way to isolate memory segments from each other. This permits multiple programs to run simultaneously without interfering with each other.

2. (a) A segment selector is a 16-bit value stored in a segment register (CS, DS, SS, ES, FS, or GS).
   (b) A logical address is a combination of a segment selector and a 32-bit offset.

3. True.

4. True.

5. False.

6. False.

7. A linear address is a 32-bit integer ranging between 0 and FFFFFFFFh, which refers to a memory location. The linear address may also be the physical address of the target data if a feature called paging is disabled.

8. When paging is enabled, the processor translates each 32-bit linear address into a 32-bit physical address. A linear address is divided into three fields: a pointer to a page directory entry, a pointer to a page table entry, and an offset into a page frame.

9. The linear address is automatically a 32-bit physical memory address.

10. Paging makes it possible for a computer to run a combination of programs that would not otherwise fit into memory. The processor does this by initially loading only part of a program in memory while keeping the remaining parts on disk.

11. The LDTR register.

12. The GDTR register.

13. One.

14. Many (each task or program has its own local descriptor table).

15. Choose any four from the following list: base address, privilege level, segment type, segment present flag, granularity flag, segment limit.

16. Page Directory, Page Table, and Page (page frame).

17. The Table field of a linear address (see Figure 11-4).

18. The Offset field of a linear address (see Figure 11-4).

12   Floating-Point Processing and Instruction Encoding

12.1   Floating-Point Binary Representation

1. Because the reciprocal of -127 is $+127$, which would generate an overflow.

2. Because adding $+128$ to the exponent bias (127) would generate a negative value.

3. 52 bits.

4. 8 bits.

5. $1101.01101 = 13/1 + 1/4 + 1/8 + 1/32$.

6. 0.2 generates an infinitely repeating bit pattern.

7. $11011.01011 = 1.101101011 \times 2^4$.

8. $0000100111101.1 = 1.001111011 \times 2^{-8}$.

9. $+1110.011 = 1.110011 \times 2^{-3}$, so the encoding is 0 01111100 11001100000000000000000.

10. Quiet NaN and Signaling NaN.

11. $5/8 = 0.101$ binary.

12. $17/32 = 0.10001$ binary.

13. $+10.75 = +1010.11 = +1.01011 \times 2^3$, encoded as 0 10000010 01011000000000000000000.

14. $-76.0625 = -01001100.0001 = -1.0011000001 \times 2^{-6}$, encoded as:
    1 10000101 00110000010000000000000

15. Positive or negative infinity, depending on the sign of the numerator.

12.2   Floating-Point Unit

1. fld st(0).

2. R0.

3. Choose from opcode, control, status, tag word, last instruction pointer, last data pointer.

4. Binary-coded decimal.

5. None.

6. REAL10 80 bits.

7. It pops ST(0) off the stack.

8. FCHS.

9. None, m32fp, m64fp, stack register.

10. FISUB converts the source operand from integer to floating-point.

11. FCOM, or FCOMP.

12. Code example:

```
fnstsw ax
lahf
```

13. FILD.

14. RC field.

15. 1.010101101 rounded to nearest even becomes 1.010101110.

16. 1.010101101 rounded to nearest even becomes 1.010101110.

17. Assembly language code:

```
.data
B REAL8 7.8
M REAL8 3.6
N REAL8 7.1
P REAL8 ?
.code
fld   M
fchs
fld   N
fadd  B
fmul
fst   P
```

18. Assembly language code:

```
.data
B DWORD 7
N REAL8 7.1
P REAL8 ?
.code
fld N
fsqrt
fiadd B
fst P
```

12.3   x86 Instruction Encoding

1. (a) 8E (b) 8B (c) 8A (d) 8A (e) A2 (f) A3

2. (a) 8E (b) 8A (c) 8A (d) 8B (e) A0 (f) 8B

3. (a) D8 (b) D3 (c) 1D (d) 44 (e) 84 (f) 85

4. (a) 06 (b) 56 (c) 1D (d) 55 (e) 84 (f) 81

5. Machine language bytes:

```
a. 8E D8
b. A0 00 00
c. 8B 0E 01 00
d. BA 00 00
e. B2 02
f. BB 00 10
```

13   High-Level Language Interface

13.1   Introduction

1. The naming convention used by a language refers to the rules or characteristics regarding the naming of variables and procedures.

2. Tiny, small, compact, medium, large, huge.

3. No, because the procedure name will not be found by the linker.

4. The memory model determines whether near or far calls are made. A near call pushes only the 16-bit offset of the return address on the stack. A far call pushes a 32-bit segment/offset address on the stack.

5. C and C++ are case sensitive, so they will only execute calls to procedures that are named in the same fashion.

6. Yes, many languages specify that EBP (BP), ESI (SI), and EDI (DI) must be preserved across procedure calls.

13.2   Inline Assembly Code

1. Inline assembly code is assembly language source code that is inserted directly into high-level language programs. The inline qualifier in C++, on the other hand, asks the C++ compiler to insert the body of a function directly into the program's compiled code to avoid the extra execution time it would take to call and return from the function. (Note: Answering this question requires some knowledge of the C++ language that is not covered in this book.)

2. The primary advantage to writing inline code is simplicity because there are no external linking issues, naming problems, and parameter passing protocols to worry about. Secondarily, inline code can execute more quickly because it avoids the extra execution time typically required by calling and returning from an assembly language procedure.

3. Examples of comments (select any two):

```
mov esi,buf                 ; initialize index register
mov esi,buf                 // initialize index register
mov esi,buf                 /* initialize index register */
```

4. Yes.

5. Yes.

6. No.

7. No.

8. A program bug might result because the __fastcall convention allows the compiler to use general-purpose registers as temporary variables.

9. Use the LEA instruction.

10. The LENGTH operator returns the number of elements in the array specified by the DUP operator. For example, the value placed in EAX by the LENGTH operator is 20:

```
myArray DWORD 20 DUP(?), 10, 20, 30
.code
mov eax,LENGTH myArray          ; 20
```

(Note that the LENGTHOF operator, introduced in Chapter 4, would return 23 when applied to myArray.)

11. The SIZE operator returns the product of TYPE (4) * LENGTH.

13.3   Linking to C++ in Protected Mode

1. The extern and "C" keywords must be used.

2. The Irvine32 library uses STDCALL, which is not the same as the C calling convention used by C and C++. The important difference is in how the stack is cleaned up after a function call.

3. Floating-point values are usually pushed on the processor's floating-point stack before returning from the function.

4. A short int is returned in the AX register.

5. printf PROTO C, pString:PTR BYTE, args:VARARG.

6. X will be pushed last.

7. To prevent the decoration (altering) of external procedure names by the C++ compiler. *Name decoration* (also called *name mangling*) is done by programming languages that permit function overloading, which permits multiple functions to have the same name.

8. If name decoration is in effect, an external function name generated by the C++ compiler will not be the same as the name of the called procedure written in assembly language. Understandably, the assembler does not have any knowledge of the name decoration rules used by C++ compilers.

9. Virtually no changes at all, showing that array subscripts can be just as efficient as pointers when manipulating arrays.

13.4   Linking to C/C++ in Real-Address Mode

1. Assembly procedures called by Borland C++ must preserve the values of BP, DS, SS, SI, DI, and the Direction flag.

2. INT = 2, enum = 1, float = 4, double = 8.

3. mov eax,[bp + 6].

4. The ror eax,8 statement rotates out the lowest digit of EAX, preventing a recurring pattern when generating sequences of small random numbers.

14   16-Bit MS-DOS Programming

14.1   MS-DOS and the IBM-PC

1. 9FFFFh.

2. Interrupt vector table.

3. 00400h.

4. The BIOS.

5. Suppose a program was named myProg.exe. The following would redirect its output to the default printer:

```
myProg > prn
```

6. LPT1.

7. An interrupt service routine (also called an *interrupt handler*) is an operating system procedure that (1) provides basic services to application programs and (2) handles hardware events. For more details, see Section 17.4.

8. Push the flags on the stack.

9. See the four steps in Section 14.1.4.

10. The interrupt handler executes an IRET instruction.

11. 10h.

12. 1Ah.

13. 21h * 4 = 0084h.

14.2   MS-DOS Function Calls (INT 21h)

1. AH.

2. Function 4Ch.

3. Functions 2 and 6 both write a single character.

4. Function 9.

5. Function 40h.

6. Functions 1 and 6.

7. Function 3Fh.

8. Functions 2Ah and 2Bh. To display the time, you would call the **WriteDec** procedure from the book's library. That procedure uses Function 2 to output digits to the console. (Look in the *Irvine16.asm* file for details, located in the \Examples\Lib16 directory.)

9. Functions 2Bh (set system date) and 2Dh (set system time).

10. Function 6.

14.3   Standard MS-DOS File I/O Services

1. Device Handles: 0 = Keyboard (standard input), 1 = Console (standard output), 2 = Error output, 3 = Auxiliary device (asynchronous), 4 = Printer.

2. Carry flag.

3. Parameters for function 716Ch:

```
AX = 716Ch
BX = access mode (0 = read, 1 = write, 2 = read/write)
CX = attributes (0 = normal, 1 = read only, 2 = hidden,
  3 = system, 8 = volume ID, 20h = archive)
DX = action (1 = open, 2 = truncate, 10h = create)
DS:SI = segment/offset of filename
DI = alias hint (optional)
```

4. Opening an existing file for input:

```
.data
infile BYTE "myfile.txt",0
inHandle WORD ?
```

```
.code
        mov     ax,716Ch                ; extended create or open
        mov     bx,0                    ; mode = read-only
        mov     cx,0                    ; normal attribute
        mov     dx,1                    ; action: open
        mov     si,OFFSET infile
        int     21h                     ; call MS-DOS
        jc      quit                    ; quit if error
        mov     inHandle,ax
```

5. Reading a binary array from a file is best done with INT 21h Function 3Fh. The following parameters are required:

```
AH = 3Fh
BX = open file handle
CX = maximum bytes to read
DS:DX = address of input buffer
```

6. After calling INT 21h, compare the return value in AX to the value that was placed in CX before the function call. If AX is smaller, the end of the file must have been reached.

7. The only difference is the value in BX. When reading from the keyboard, BX is set to the keyboard handle (0). When reading from a file, BX is set to the handle of the open file.

8. Function 42h.

9. Code example (BX already contains the file handle):

```
mov     ah,42h                  ; move file pointer
mov     al,0                    ; method: offset from beginning
mov     cx,0                    ; offset Hi
mov     dx,50                   ; offset Lo
int     21h
```

Index

A

__asm Directive (Visual
C++), 529–532
AAA (ASCII adjust after
addition) instruction,
261–262
AAD (ASCII adjust before
division) instruction, 263
AAM (ASCII adjust
after multiplication)
instruction, 263
AAS (ASCII adjust after
subtraction) instruction,
262–263
ADC (add with carry)
instruction, 230, 256
ADD instruction, 62, 67,
104–105
Addition and subtraction, 104
ADD instruction, 104–105
arithmetic expressions,
implementing, 106
example program
(AddSub3), 110–111
flags affected by,
106–110
INC and DEC
instruction, 104
NEG instruction, 105
SUB instruction, 105
Addition test, 109
Address, 44–45

Address bus, 33
Address space, 36–37
ADDR operator, 300
AddSub program, 68, 75, 76
adding variables to, 84
alternative version of,
69–70
AddSub2 program, 91
AddTwo procedure, 272,
273–274, 275, 302
Advanced Micro Devices
(AMD) Athaon, 1, 29
*Advanced MS-DOS
Programming,* 568
Advanced procedures, 270
recursion, 290–298
stack frames, 271–290
ALIGN directive, 113–114
Aligned structure members,
performance of, 371–372
AllocConsole function, 424
American National Standards
Institute (ANSI), 17
American Standard Code for
Information Interchange.
See ASCII
AND instruction, 182–183
AND (boolean operator), 22,
23
Application Programming
Interface (API), 52, 420
Arithmetic expressions,
implementing, 106, 253–255

Arithmetic instructions, 498
Arithmetic logic unit (ALU),
30
Arithmetic operators, 60
Arithmetic shifts versus
logical shifts, 230–231
ArrayFill procedure, 273, 283
ArraySum, 168, 175
calling, 169
procedure, 169, 170, 171,
306, 307, 315–316
program, 314
Arrays
calculating the sizes,
87–88
indirect operands,
119–120
looping through, 371
*The Art of Computer
Programming* (Knuth),
2
ASCII, 17
control characters, 18, 570
decimal and unpacked
decimal, 260–261
string, 18
unpacked decimal
arithmetic and, 260–264
askForInteger function, 545
asmMain, 548, 549
ASM module, 550–551
Assemble-link-execute cycle,
71

Assemblers, 2, 71
Assembly code, 207–208
    generating, 219
    versus compiler optimi-
        zation, 541
    versus nonoptimized
        C++ code, 541
Assembly language, 1–6, 8–9,
    29, 58, 94
    access levels, 54
    for addition and subtrac-
        tion of integers, 66–71
    applications of, 5–6
    definition, 2
    elements of, 58–66
    high-level languages
        and, 6
    to optimize C++ code,
        536–539
    portability of, 4
    program in, 59
    reasons for learning, 5
    relationship between
        machine and, 4
    rules in, 5
Assembly language module,
    544–545
ATA host adapters, 51
Auxiliary carry flag (AC), 39,
    107, 108–109

B

Base address, 477
Base-index-displacement
    operands, 349–350
Base-index operands,
    347–349
    calculating a Row Sum,
        348–349
    scale factors, 349
    two-dimensional array,
        347–348

Base-offset addressing, 274
Basic Input-Output System
    (BIOS), 53, 54, 55
Bignums, 230
Big O notation, 351
Binary addition, 11–12
Binary bits, displaying, 242
Binary file, creating, 591–594
Binary floating-point num-
    bers, normalized, 486
Binary integer, 9
    definition, 19
    signed, 10
    translating unsigned
        binary integers to
        decimal, 11
    translating unsigned
        decimal integers to
        binary, 11
    unsigned, 10
Binary multiplication, 241
Binary reals, converting deci-
    mal fraction to, 488–489
Binary search
    algorithm, 352–355
    test program for, 355–359
BIOS (Basic Input-Output
    System), 48, 53, 563
Bit-mapped sets, 184–186
Bit masking, 182
Bits, 9–10
Bit strings, 242
Bitwise instructions, 224
Block comments, 65
Block-structured IF state-
    ments, 202–204
Bluetooth, 52
Boole, George, 22
Boolean algebra, 22
Boolean and comparison
    instructions, 181
    AND instruction,
        182–183

bit-mapped sets, 184–186
    CMP instruction, 188–189
    CPU flags, 182
    NOT instruction, 187
    OR instruction, 183–184
    setting and clearing indi-
        vidual CPU flags, 189
    TEST instruction,
        187–188
    XOR instruction,
        186–187
Boolean expression, 22, 399
Boolean function
    definition, 24
    truth tables for, 24–26
Boolean operations, 22–26
    boolean expression,
        22–24
    boolean operations, truth
        tables for, 24–26
    operator precedence, 24
Borland C++, linking to, 553
Borland Turbo Assembler,
    557
Branching instructions, 323
.BREAK condition, 217
Brink, James, 309
Bubble sort, 350–352
    assembly language, 352
    pseudocode, 351–352
    test program, 355–359
BubbleSort procedure, 287
Bus, 30, 48
BYTE, 62, 78
Byte, 12

C

C++, 5
    assembly language and, 4
    module, 532–533
    startup program,
        546–547

stub module, 550
Cache memory, 34
CalcSum procedure, 291, 292
Calling convention, 526
CALL instruction, 165
CALL statement, 68
C and C++ functions, calling, 542
  assembly language module, 543–544
  function prototypes, 542–543
  function return values, 544
Carry flag, 39, 106
  addition and, 107–108
  subtraction and, 108
CBW (convert byte to word) instruction, 251
C language calling convention, 276–277
CDQ (convert doubleword to quadword) instruction, 251
Central Processor Unit (CPU), in microcomputer, 30
Character constant, 61
Character set, 17
Character storage, 17–19
Chipset, motherboard, 49
C language specifier, 529
C library functions, calling, 547–550
Clock, 30, 31
Clock cycle, 31
Close file handle (3Eh), 584
CloseFile procedure, 138
CloseHandle function, 440
Clrscr procedure, 138
CMOS RAM, 48
CMP instruction, 188–189
CMPSB instruction, 335–336

CMPSD instruction, 335, 336
CMPSW instruction, 335, 336
.CODE directive, 63, 67
Code examples
  array dot product, 508
  expression, 507
  sum of an array, 507
  sum of square roots, 508
Code label, 64
Code segment, 45, 68
Coding styles, 68–69
Command processor, 563
Command tail, MS-DOS, 588–591
Comments, 65
Comparison instructions, 323
Complex Instruction Set Computer (CISC) design, 42, 512
Compound expressions, 204–205, 220–223
Conditional and loop instructions, 200–201
  LOOPE (loop if equal) instruction, 200
  LOOPNE (loop if not equal) instruction, 201
  LOOPNZ (loop if not zero) instruction, 201
  LOOPZ (loop if zero) instruction, 200
Conditional-assembly directives, 396–410
  boolean expressions, 399
  default argument initializers, 398–399
  IF, ELSE, and ENDIF directives, 399–400
  IFIDN and IFIDNI directive, 400–401
  macro functions, 407–409

  matrix row, summing, 401–404
  missing arguments, checking for, 397–398
  special operators, 404–407
Conditional branching, 180
Conditional control flow directives, 217–224
  compound expressions, 220–223
  IF statements, creating, 218–219
  .REPEAT and .WHILE directives, 223–224
  signed and unsigned comparisons, 219–220
Conditional jump, 190
  applications, 195–199
  conditional structures, 190–191
  Jcond instruction, 191–192
  types of, 192–195
Conditional structures, 202–211
  block-structured IF statements, 202–204
  compound expressions, 204–205
  definition, 202
  WHILE loops, 206–208
Conditional transfer, 124
Condition codes (floating point), 502–503
Console input, 429–435
  console input buffer, 429–433
  getting keyboard state, 434–435
  single-character input, 433–434

Console output, 435–437
    data structures, 436
    WriteConsole function,
        436–437
    WriteConsoleOutput-
        Character function, 437
Console Window, 136, 447
.CONTINUE directive, 217
Control bus, 31
Control flags, 39
Control unit (CU), 30
COORD structure, 367, 436
Copy doubleword array, 335
Copying a string, 126–127
Core-Duo processor, 29
CPU flags, 182
CreateConsoleScreenBuffer
    function, 424
CreateFile function, 437–438
CreateFile parameters, 438
CreateFile program example,
    444–445
Create or open file (716Ch),
    583–584
CreateOutputFile procedure,
    138
Crlf procedure, 138
CR/LF (carriage-return
    line-feed), 80
Current location counter, 87
CWD (convert word to dou-
    bleword) instruction, 251

D

DAA (decimal adjust after
    addition) instruction,
    264–265
DAS (decimal adjust after sub-
    traction) instruction, 266
Data bus (DATA), 30–31
Data definition statement,
    77–78

BYTE and SBYTE data,
    78
data types in, 78
defining strings, 80
directive, 77
DUP operator
DWORD and SDWORD
    data, 81
initializer, 78
little endian order, 83
multiple initializers, 79
packed binary coded
    decimal (BCD), 82
real number data, 83
WORD and SWORD
    data, 80
.DATA directive, 63, 85
Data label, 63
Data-related operators and
    directives, 112
    align directive, 113–114
    offset operator, 112–113
Data representation, 9
    binary addition, 11–12
    binary integers, 9–11
    character storage, 17–19
    hexadecimal integers,
        13–15
    integer storage sizes,
        12–13
    signed integers, 15–17
Data segment, 45, 68
Data transfer, 94
    direct memory operands,
        96
    direct-offset operands,
        101–102
    example program, 102–103
    LAHF and SAHF
        instructions, 100
    MOV instruction, 96–98
    operand types, 95

XCHG instruction,
    100–101
zero/sign extension of
    integers, 98–100
Debugging tips
    argument size mismatch,
        308–309
    passing immediate
        values, 309
    passing wrong type of
        pointer, 309
Decimal real, 61
Declaring and using unions,
    378–381
    declaring and using union
        variables, 380–381
    structure containing
        union, 379–380
Default argument initializers,
    398–399
Delay procedure, 138
Descriptor table, 34, 476
Destination operand, 67, 96
Device drivers, 5, 53
Direct addressing, 117–118
Directed graph, 211
Direction flags, 39, 334
Directives, 62–63
Direct memory operands, 96
Direct-offset operands, 101–102
Directory listing program
    ASM module, 550–551
    C++ stub module, 550
DisplaySum procedure,
    175-176
Display_Sum procedure, 258
DIV instruction, 249–250
Doubleword (4bytes), 12, 101
DRAM. See Dynamic random-
    access memory (DRAM)
"Drunkard's Walk" exercise,
    375–378

Dual Core processor, 42
Dual processor system, 42
DumpMem procedure, 138–139, 272
DumpRegs procedure, 70, 76, 139
Duncan, Ray, 568
DUP operator, 80, 87
DWORD, 77, 81
Dynamic link library, 133
Dynamic memory allocation, 466–472
Dynamic random-access memory (DRAM), 50

E

EBP register, 38
ECHO directive, 385
EFLAGS register, 37, 38, 39
.ELSE directive, 217, 399
.ELSEIF condition, 217
Embedded programs, 5
Encoded reals, 61
END directive marks, 68
.ENDIF directive, 217, 399
Endless recursion, 291
ENDP directive marks, 68, 74
.ENDW directive, 217
ENTER instruction, 285–286
EPROM. *See* Erasable programmable read-only memory (EPROM)
Equal-sign directive, 86–87
EQU directive, 88–89
Erasable programmable read-only memory (EPROM), 50
ErrorHandler procedure, 461
Exabyte, 13
Exception synchronization, 506–507
Executable file, 71

EXITM (exit macro) directive, 407
ExitProcess function, 70, 163–164, 424
Exit statement, 68
Expansion operator (%), 405–406
Explicit stack parameters, 274–275
Expression stack, 491
Extended addition and subtraction, 256
    ADC instruction, 256
    extended addition example, 257–258
    SBB instruction, 258–259
Extended addition example, 257
Extended_Add procedure, 257r, 38
Extended Physical Addressing, 36
External identifiers, 536
External library, linking to, 132–134
EXTERNDEF directive, 313
EXTERN directive, 311, 312, 313

F

FABS (absolute value) instruction, 498–499
Factorial, calculating, 292–298
Factorial procedure, 293, 294, 296
FADD (add) instruction, 499
FADDP (add with pop) instruction, 499–500
Fast division (SHR), 233
Fast multiplication (SHL), 232

FCHS (change sign) instruction, 498–499
FCOM (compare floating-point values) instruction, 502
FDIV instruction, 501–502
FIADD (add integer) instruction, 500
Field initializers, 367–368
Fields, 366
FILD (load integer) instruction, 497
File/device handles, 581–582
File encryption example, 532–535
File I/O
    in the Irvine32 Library, 442–444
    testing procedures of, 444–447
FillArray procedure, 300, 302
FillConsoleOutputAttribute function, 424
FillConsoleOutputCharacter function, 425
    FindArray
    checking performance of, 540–541
    code generated by Visual C++, 537–539
Finite-state machine (FSM), 211
FINIT instruction, 496
FireWire, 51
FISUB (subtract integer) instruction, 500
    Flags
    addition and subtraction, 106–110
    attribute values and, 439
setting and clearing CPU, 189
Flat memory model, 45

Flat segmentation model, 45–46

Floating-point binary representation, 483
  converting decimal fractions to binary reals, 488–490
  creating IEEE representation, 486–488
  IEEE binary floating-point representation, 484–485
  normalized binary floating-point numbers, 486
  single-precision exponents, 485–486

Floating-point data type, 496

Floating-point decimal number, 483

Floating-point expressions, 495

Floating-point instruction set, 495–498

Floating-point unit (FPU), 39, 40, 48, 490
  arithmetic instructions, 498–502
  code examples, 507–508
  comparing floating-point values, 502–504
  exception synchronization, 506–507
  floating-point exceptions, 495
  instruction set, 495–498
  masking and unmasking exceptions, 509–511
  mixed-mode arithmetic, 508–509
  reading and writing floating-point values, 504–506
  register stack, 491–493
  rounding, 493–494

Flowcharts, 169

FlushConsoleInputBuffer function, 425

FMUL instruction, 501

FMULP (multiply with pop) instruction, 501

FORC directive, 410, 412

FOR directive, 410, 411–412

FPU stack, 505–506

FreeConsole function, 425

FST (store floating-point value) instruction, 497–498

FSTP (store floating-point value and pop) instruction, 498

FSUB instruction, 500

FSUBP (subtract with pop) instruction, 500

Functional decomposition. *See* Top-down design

Function prototypes, 542–543

Function return values, 544

G

General protection (GP) fault, 118

General-purpose registers, 37–38

GenerateConsoleCtrlEvent, 425

GetCommandTail procedure, 139–140, 589–591

GetConsoleCP function, 425

GetConsoleCursorInfo function, 425, 450

GetConsoleMode function, 425

GetConsoleOutputCP function, 425

GetConsoleScreenBufferInfo function, 425, 447

GetConsoleTitle function, 425

GetConsoleWindow function, 425

GetDateTime procedure, 455–456

Get file creation date and time, 585

GetKeyState function, 434

GetLargestConsoleWindow-Size function, 425

GetLastError API function, 431

GetLocalTime function, 454

GetMaxXY procedure, 140

GetMseconds procedure, 140, 154, 156, 247, 248

GetNumberOfConsole-InputEvents function, 425

GetNumberOfConsole-MouseButtons function, 425

GetProcessHeap, 467

GetStdHandle function, 424, 425

GetTickCount function, 454–455

Gigabyte, 12

Global descriptor table (GDT), 45, 476

GNU assembler, 1

Gotoxy procedure, 140–141

Granularity flag, 477

Graphical windows application, 457–466
  ErrorHandler procedure, 461
  MessageBox function, 459–460
  necessary structures, 458–459
  program listing, 461–465
  WinMain procedure, 460
  WinProc procedure, 460–461

H

HandlerRoutine function, 425
Hardware, detecting
    overflow, 109–110
HeapAlloc, 468–469
Heap allocation, 466
HeapCreate, 467–468
HcapDestroy, 468
HeapFree, 467, 469
HeapTest programs,
    469–472
Hello World program
    example, 572–573
Help-related functions, 457
Hexadecimal integers, 13
    converting unsigned
        hexadecimal to
        decimal, 14
    converting unsigned
        decimal to
        hexadecimal, 14–15
High-level console functions,
    422
High-level language, 9, 94–95
    assembly language and, 6
    functions, 52
High-level language
    interface, 525
    general convention,
        526–527
    inline assembly code,
        529–535
    linking to C/C++ in
        protected mode,
        535–552
    linking to C/C++ in
        real-address mode,
        552–559
    .MODEL directive,
        527–529
Horizontal retrace (video), 50
Hyperthreading (HT)
    technology, 42

I

IA-32e mode
    compatibility mode, 41
    64-bit mode, 41
IA-32 processor family (x86),
    40–41
IBM-PC and MS-DOS, 562
    coding for 16-bit
        programs, 567–568
    INT instruction, 565–567
    memory organization,
        563–564
    redirecting input-output,
        564–565
    software interrupts, 565
IBM's PC-DOS, 562
Identification number
    (process ID), 34
Identifier, 62
IDIV instruction, 251–253
IEEE floating-point binary
    formats, 484
IEEE representation, 486–488
IEEE single-precision (SP), 490
.IF condition, 217
IF directive, 399
IFIDN directive, 400
IFIDNI directive, 400
IF statements
    creating, 218–219
    loop containing, 224
    nested in loop, 206–207
IMUL instruction, 65,
    245–247
    bit string and, 248–249
    examples, 246–247
    one-operand formats, 245
    three-operand formats,
        246
    two-operand formats,
        245–246
    unsigned multiplication,
        246

INC and DEC instruction, 104
INC instruction, 65
INCLUDE dircctive, 67, 74,
    90, 163, 318
Indexed operands, 120–121,
    371
    displacements, adding,
        120
    scale factors in, 121
    16-bit registers in, 121
Indirect addressing, 117
    arrays, 119–120
    indexed operands, 120–121
    indirect operands, 118–119
    pointers, 121–123
Indirect operands, 118–119,
    371
Infix expression, 491
Inline assembly code, 529
    __asm directive in
        Microsoft Visual C++,
        529–532
    file encryption examplc,
        532–535
Inline expansion, 382
innerLoop procedure, 156
Input functions, MS-DOS,
    573
Input-output parameter, 307
Input-output system, 52–55
Input parameter, 307
Input string, validating,
    211–212
Instruction, 63
    comments, 65
    instruction mnemonic, 64
    label, 63–64
    operands, 64–65, 95, 518
Instruction execution cycle,
    31–33
    dccode, 31
    execute, 32
    fetch, 31

Instruction execution
cycle (*continued*)
fetch operands, 31
store output operand, 32
Instruction mnemonic, 64
Instruction operand notation, 95
Instruction pointer (EIP),
37, 38
Instruction set architecture
(ISA), 8
INT (call to interrupt
procedure) instruction,
565–566
common interrupts,
566–567
interrupt vectoring, 566
INT 1Ah time of day, 567
INT 1Ch user timer interrupt,
567
INT 10h video services, 566
INT 16h keyboard services,
566
INT 17h printer services, 567
INT 21h function 0Ah, 574
INT 21h function 0Bh, 575
INT 21h function 1, 573
INT 21h function 2, 570
INT 21h function 2Ah,
577–578
INT 21h function 2Bh, 577, 578
INT 21h function 2Ch, 577,
578
INT 21h function 2Dh, 577,
579
INT 21h function 3Eh, 584
INT 21h function 3Fh,
576–577, 586
INT 21h function 4Ch, 569
INT 21h function 5, 570, 571
INT 21h function 6, 570, 571,
573–574, 575–576
INT 21h function 9, 570, 571

INT 21h function 40h, 570,
572, 587
INT 21h function 42h,
584–585
INT 21h function 5706h, 585
INT 21h function 716Ch, 583
INT 21h MS-DOS function
calls, 568
INT 21h MS-DOS services, 567
Integer arithmetic, 229
ASCII and unpacked
decimal arithmetic,
260–264
extended addition and
subtraction, 256–260
multiplication and
division instructions,
243–256
packed decimal
arithmetic, 264–266
shift and rotate
applications, 239–243
shift and rotate
instructions, 230–239
Integer arrays, searching and
sorting, 350–359
binary search, 352–355
bubble sort, 350–352
test program, 355–358
Integer arrays, summing, 126
Integer constant, 59
Integer expressions, 60
Integers, adding and
subtracting, 66–70
Integer storage sizes, 12–13
Integer summation
implementation, 175–176
Integer summation program,
173–175
Integrated circuit (IC), 42
Intel64, 41
Intel486, 41

Intel 8086 processor, 40, 42
Intel 8088 processor, 40
Intel 80286 processor, 40
Intel 80386 processor, 1
Intel microprocessors, 39–42
Intel P965 Express chipset, 49
Intel Pentium, 1, 29
Intel Pentium 4, 1
Intel Pentium Core Duo, 1
Intel processor families, 41–42
Interrupt flags, 39
Interrupt handler, 565
Interrupt service routines
(ISRs), 566–567. *See also*
Interrupt handler
Interrupt vectoring, 566
Interrupt vector table, 563
Intrinsic data types, 77, 78
INVOKE directive, 164,
299–300, 318
I/O access, levels of, 52
BIOS, 53
high-level language
functions, 52
operating system, 52
Irvine16.lib, 133
Irvine32.lib, 133, 420
IsDefined macro, 408
IsDigit procedure, 141, 215,
216

J

Java, 5
assembly language and, 4
virtual machine concept
and, 8
Java bytecodes, 8
instruction set 322–323
Java disassembly
examples, 323–328
Java virtual machine
(JVM), 321–322

string processing and, 359–360

Java Development Kit (JDK), 322

Java disassembly examples, 323–328
adding two doubles, 325–326
adding two integers, 323–325
conditional branch, 326–327

Java HashSet, 184

Java primitive data types, 322

Java virtual machine (JVM), 8, 321–322

Jcond (conditional jump) instruction, 191
conditional jump applications, 195
equality comparisons, 192–193
signed comparisons, 193–195
unsigned comparisons, 193

JMP instruction, 124

K

Keyboard definition, 87

Kilobyte, 12

Knuth, Donald, 2, 350

L

Label, 63
code, 64
data, 63
directive, 112, 116–117

LAHF (load status flags into AH) instruction, 100

Large random integers, 558–559

LEA instruction, 284

Least significant bit (LSB), 10, 232

LEAVE instruction, 286

LENGTHOF operator, 112, 115–116

Library procedures, MS-DOS, 585–586

Library test program, 149–156
library test#1, 149–153
performance timing, 154–156
random integers, 153–154

LIFO (Last-In, First-Out) structure, 157, 162

Linear addresses, translating logical addresses to, 473–474

Linked list, 412–414

Linker command options, 133

Linkers, 2, 71

Linking 32-bit programs, 133–134

Link library, procedures in, 134–136

.LIST, 74

Listing file, 72–77

ListSize, 87–88

Literal-text operator (<>), 406–407

Literal-character operator (!), 407

Little-endian order, 83–84, 240

Load and execute process, 34

Loader, 71

Load floating-point value (FLD), 496–497

Local descriptor table (LDT), 46, 476

LOCAL directive, 286–289, 385

Local variables, 281–284

LODSB instruction, 337

LODSD instruction, 337

LODSW instruction, 337

Logical AND operator, 204–205

Logical OR operator, 205

Logical shifts versus arithmetic shifts, 230–231

LongRandom function, 558–559

Loop instruction, 124–125

LOOPE (loop if equal) instruction, 200

LOOPNE (loop if not equal) instruction, 201

LOOPNZ (loop if not zero) instruction, 201

LOOPZ (loop if zero) instruction, 200

Low-level console functions, 422

M

Machine language, relationship between assembly and, 4, 8

Macros
additional features of, 384–387
code and data in, 386–387
comments in macros, 385
debugging program that contains, 384
declaring, 382
defining, 382–383
functions, 407–409
invoking, 383–384
in library, 388–394
nested, 387

Macros (*continued*)
  parameters, 383, 384–385
  macro procedure, 383
  Wrappers example
    program, 394
Macros.inc library
  mDump, 389
  mDumpMem, 388
  mGotoxy, 390
  mReadString, 391
  mShow, 392
  mShowRegister, 392
  mWriteSpace, 393
  mWriteString, 394
  makeString macro,
    385–386
Masking and unmasking
  exceptions, 509–511
MASM
  code generation, 287
  linking to C++, 539–540
Matrix row, summing,
  401–404
  mDump macro, 389–390
  mDumpMem macro,
    388–389
Megabyte, 12
Memory, 50
  CMOS RAM, 48
  DRAM, 50
  dynamic allocation,
    48–55
  EPROM, 50
  management, 43-47
  models, 527
  operands, 64
  physical, 475
  reading from, 33
  ROM, 50
  segmented model, 40
  storage unit, 30
  SRAM, 50

  virtual, 41, 475
  VRAM, 50
Memory-mode instructions,
  516–519
Merge procedure, 287
Message box display in
  Win32 application,
  426–429
  contents and behavior,
    426–427
  demonstration program,
    427–428
  program listing, 428–429
MessageBox function, 459–460
mGotoxyConst macro, 399,
  405
mGotoxy macro, 390–391
Microcode, 42
Microcomputer, 30–31
Microsoft Macro Assembler
  (MASM), 1, 2, 3, 59, 62, 96
Mixed-mode arithmetic,
  508–509
MMX registers, 39
Mnemonic, 64
.MODEL directive, 69,
  527–529, 567
  C language specifier, 529
  language specifiers, 528
  STDCALL, 528–529
Most significant bit (MSB),
  10, 15, 232
Motherboard, 48–49
  chipset, 49–50
MOV instruction, 62, 65, 67,
  96–97
  opcodes, 517–518, 519
Move file pointer function,
  584–585
MOVSB instruction, 334–335
MOVSD instruction,
  334–335

MOVSW instruction,
  334–335
MOVSX (move with
  sign-extend) instruction,
  99–100
MOVZX (move with
  zero-extend) instruction,
  98–99
mPutchar macro, 383
mReadBuf macro, 400
mReadString macro, 391
MS-DOS
  device names, 565
  extended error codes, 582
  file date fields, 242–243
  function calls (INT 21h),
    568–581
  IBM-PC and, 562–568
  memory map, 564
MS-DOS file I/O services, 581
  close file handle (3Eh),
    584
  creating binary file,
    591–594
  create or open file
    (716Ch), 583–584
  get file creation date and
    time, 585
  move file pointer (42h),
    584–585
  read and copy a text file,
    586–588
  reading MS-DOS
    command tail, 588–591
  selected library procedures,
    585–586
MsgBoxAsk procedure,
  141–142
MsgBox procedure, 141
mShow macro, 392
mShowRegister macro,
  392–393, 404

MS-Windows virtual machine manager, 478
MUL (unsigned multiply) instruction, 62, 243
    bit shifting and, 248–249
    examples, 244–245
    operands, 244
Mul32 macro, 405–406
Multi-core, 42
Multimodule programs, 311
    ArraySum program, 314
    calling external procedures, 312
    creating modules using INVOKE and PROTO, 318–321
    creating modules using EXTERN directive, 314–318
    hiding and exporting procedure names, 311–312
    module boundaries, variables and symbols in, 313–314
Multiple shifts
    in SHL instruction, 232
    in SHR instruction, 233
Multiplexer, 26
Multiplication and division instructions in integer arithmetic, 243
    arithmetic expressions, implementing, 253–255
    DIV instruction, 249–250
    IMUL instruction, 244–247
    MUL instruction, 243–244
    signed integer division, 250–253

Multiplication table example, 544
    assembly language module, 544–545
    C++ startup program, 546–547
    visual studio project properties, 547
Multi-segment model, 46
Multitasking, 34–35
Multiword arguments, passing, 278–279
mWrite macro, 406–407
mWriteln macro, 387, 398
mWriteSpace macro, 393–394
mWriteString macro, 394
MySub procedure, 286

N

Name decorations in C++ programs, 536
Naming conventions, 526
NaNs (floating point), 488
Negative infinity, 487–488
NEG instruction, 105, 110
Nested loops, 125–126
Nested macros, 387
Nested procedure call, 166–167
Netwide Assembler (NASM), 1
.NOLIST directive, 74
Non-doubleword local variables, 287–289
NOP (No Operation) instruction, 65–66
Normalized finite numbers, 487
NOT (boolean operator), 22
NOT instruction, 187
Null-terminated string, 18, 80
Numeric data representation, terminology for, 19

Numeric strings, types of, 19

O

Object file, 71
OFFSET operator, 112–113, 122, 370
One's complement, 187
OpenInputFile procedure, 142
Operands, 64–65, 99
    direct memory, 96
    direct-offset, 101–102
    floating-point instruction set, 495–496
    instruction, 64–65, 95
    types, 95
Operating system (OS), 34, 52
Operator precedence, 60
Opteron processor, 29
OPTION PROC:PRIVATE directive, 311–312
OR (boolean operator), 22, 23–24
OR instruction, 183–184
OS. *See* Operating system (OS)
Output functions, MS-DOS, 570
    filing control characters, 570
Output parameter, 307
Overflow flag, 39, 106, 109, 236

P

Packed binary coded decimal (BCD), 82
Packed decimal arithmetic, 264
    DAA instructions, 264–265
    DAS instruction, 266
Page fault, 475
Paging, 46–47, 474

Page translation, 475, 477–478

Parallel port, 51

Parameter classifications, 307

Parity flag, 39, 107, 109, 186

ParseDecimal32 procedure, 142

ParseInteger32 procedure, 143

Passing arrays, 273

Passing by reference, 273

Passing by value, 272–273

Passing register arguments, 168

PCI (Peripheral Component Interconnect) bus, 49

PeekConsoleInput function, 425

Pentium processor, 41

Petabyte, 113

Pixels, 50

Pointers, 121–123
    compared to subscripts, 541–542

POINT structure, 458

POPAD instruction, 161

POPA instruction, 161

POPFD instruction, 160–161

POP instruction, 160–161

Pop operation, 159

Positive infinity, 487–488

Preemptive multitasking, 35
    printf function, 547–548, 551
    displaying formatted reals with, 548–550

PrintX macro, 382

PROC directive, 67, 163–165, 170, 301–304, 318
    parameter lists, 301–304
    parameter passing protocol, 304

RET instruction modified by, 303–304
    syntax of, 301

Procedure call overhead, 533–535

Procedures
    book's link library, 134–156
    checking for missing arguments, 397–398
    defining, 163
    calling external, 535-544
    labels in, 164
    linking to an external library, 132–134
    nested procedure calls, 166-167
    overhead of, 533-534
    program design using, 172–177

Processor clock (CLK), 33

Processor operand-size prefix, 515–516

Process return code, 569

Program execution times, measuring, 247–249

Programmable Interrupt Controller (PIC), 48

Programmable Interval Timer/Counter, 48

Programmable Parallel Port, 54

Programming at multiple levels, 54

Program segment prefix (PSP), 589

PromptForIntegers procedure, 175, 314–315, 318

Protected mode, 36, 45–47
    in indirect operands, 118
    linking to C/C++ in, 535–552

PROTO directive, 299, 304–307, 318
    assembly time argument checking, 305–306

PTR operator, 112, 114–115, 118–119

PUSHA instruction, 161

PUSHAD instruction, 161

PUSHFD instruction, 160–161

PUSH instruction, 160

Push operations, 158–159

Q

Quadword (8 bytes), 12

Quiet NaN (floating point), 488

QWORD data type, 81–82

R

Radix, 59

Ralf Brown's Interrupt List, 568

Random32 procedure, 143

Randomize procedure, 143

RandomRange procedure, 143–144

Range checking, 101

Raster scanning, 50

RCL (rotate carry left) instruction, 235

RCR (rotate carry right) instruction, 236

ReadChar procedure, 144

ReadConsole function, 425, 430–431

ReadConsoleInput function, 425

ReadConsoleOutput function, 425

ReadConsoleOutputAttribute function, 425

ReadConsoleOutputCharacter function, 425
ReadDec procedure, 144
ReadFile function, 441
ReadFile program example, 445–447
Read_File procedure, 303
ReadFloat procedure, 504–505
ReadFromFile procedure, 144–145
ReadHex procedure, 145
ReadInt procedure, 145
ReadKey procedure, 146, 196, 433–434
Read-only memory (ROM), 50
ReadSector example, 554–558
  assembly language module, 556–558
  C++ program calls, 554–556
  program execution, 554
ReadString procedure, 146, 585–586
REAL4 data type, 83
REAL8 data type, 83
REAL10 data type, 83
Real-address mode, linking to C/C++ in, 552
  large random integers, 558–559
  linking to Borland C++, 553
  ReadSector example, 554–558
Real-address mode programs, 36–37, 43–45, 90–91, 118
Real number constants, 61
Real number data, 83
Rect (rectangle) structure, 458
Recursion, 290–298
  factorial calculation, 292–298

recursively calculating a sum, 291–292
Redirection of standard input-output, 136–137
Reduced instruction set computer (RISC), 42, 512
References to named structure, 370
References to structure variables, 370
Register mode instructions, 514–515
Register parameters, 272
Registers, 37
  comparing, 220
  saving and restoring, 170, 279
Register stack, 491, 492
Repeat blocks, defining, 410–414
REPEAT directive, 410–411
.REPEAT directive, 217, 223
Repeat prefix, 333
Reserved words, 62
RET (return from procedure) instruction, 165, 166, 291
Reversing a string, 162
ROL instruction, 234
ROM. *See* Read-only memory (ROM)
ROM BIOS, 564
ROR instruction, 235
Rounding in FPU, 493–494
Round-robin scheduling, 35
Runtime relational and logical operators, 218
Runtime stack, 158

S

SAHF (store AH into status flags) instruction, 100

SAL (shift arithmetic left) instruction, 233–234
SAR (shift arithmetic right) instruction, 233, 234
SATA host adapter, 51
SBB (subtract with borrow) instruction, 258–259
SBYTE data type, 78
Scale factors, 349
scanf function, 550, 551–552
SCASB instruction, 336
SCASD instruction, 336
SCASW instruction, 336
ScrollConsoleScreenBuffer function, 425, 447
SDWORD data type, 81
Segment, 38, 44, 63, 68
Segment descriptor details, 476–477
Segment descriptor table, 45
Segmented memory, 44
Segment limit, 477
Segment names, 527
Segment-offset address, 45
Segment present flag, 477
Segment registers, 38
Selected string procedures, 338–346
Sequential search of array, 196–197
Serial port, 51–52
Set complement, 185
Set operations
  intersection, 185
  union, 185–186
SetConsoleActiveScreenBuffer function, 425
SetConsoleCP function, 425
SetConsoleCtrlHandler function, 425

SetConsoleCursorInfo
    function, 426, 451
SetConsoleCursorPosition
    function, 425, 447, 451
SetConsoleMode function,
    425
SetConsoleOutputCP
    function, 425
SetConsoleScreenBufferSize
    function, 425, 450
SetConsoleTextAttribute
    function, 425, 451
SetConsoleTitle function,
    425, 447
SetConsoleWindowInfo
    function, 425, 447, 448–450
SetCursorPosition procedure,
    221–222
SetFilePointer function,
    441–442
SetLocalTime function, 454
SetStdHandle function, 425
SetTextColor procedure,
    146–147
Shift and rotate applications,
    239
        binary multiplication,
            241
        displaying binary bits,
            242
        isolating MS-DOS file
            data fields, 242–243
        shifting multiple
            doublewords, 240–241
Shift and rotate instructions,
    229
Shifting multiple
    doublewords, 240–241
SHL (shift left) instruction,
    231–232
SHLD (shift left double)
    instruction, 236, 238

SHR (shift right) instruction,
    232–233
SHRD (shift right double)
    instruction, 237, 238
Signed and unsigned
    comparisons, 219–220
Signed division in SAL and
    SAR instruction, 234
Signed integer, 15
    comparing, 220
    converting signed binary
        to decimal, 16
    converting signed
        decimal to binary, 16
    converting signed decimal
        to hexadecimal, 16
    converting signed
        hexadecimal to
        decimal, 16–17
    maximum and minimum
        values, 17
    two's complement of
        hexadecimal value,
        15–16
    two's complement
        notation, 15
    validating, 212–216
Signed integer division,
    250–253
    divide overflow, 252–253
    IDIV instruction, 251–252
    sign extension
        instructions, 251
Signed overflow, 236
Sign flag (SF), 39, 106, 109
Significand (floating point), 484
    precision, 485
SIMD (Single-Instruction,
    Multiple-Data), 39
Single-byte instructions, 513
Single-character input,
    433–434

Single-line comments, 65
Single-precision bit
    encodings, 487
Single-precision exponents,
    485–486
16-bit argument, 278
16-bit parity, 187
16-bit programs, coding for,
    567
16-bit real-address mode
    programs, 3
16550 UART (Universal
    Asynchronous Receiver
    Transmitter), 52
SIZEOF operator, 112, 116
SMALL_RECT structure, 436
SmallWin.inc (include file),
    422–424
Software Development Kit
    (SDK), 133
Software interrupts, 565
Source operand, 67, 96
Special operators, 404
Special-purpose registers, 493
SRAM. See Static RAM
    (SRAM)
Stack abstract data type, 157
Stack applications, 159
Stack data structure, 157
STACK directive, 289–290
.STACK directive, 63, 567
Stack frames, 271–272
Stack parameters, 272–273
    accessing, 273–281
Stack operations, 157
    defining and using
        procedures, 163–171
    POP instruction,
        160–162
    program design using
        procedure, 172–177
    PUSH instruction, 160

runtime stack, 158–159
Stack segment, 38, 45
Static RAM (SRAM), 50
Status flags, 39
STC (set carry flag)
 instruction, 64
STDCALL calling
 convention, 276–277
STDCALL language
 specifier, 528–529
STOSB instruction, 336
STOSD instruction, 336
STOSW instruction, 336
Str_compare procedure,
 338–339
Str_copy procedure, 340
String, 18
 calculating the size of,
  87–88
 constant, 61
 copying a string,
  126–127, 334
 defining, 80
 encryption, 197–199
 reversing, 162
String encryption program,
 575–576
String library demo program,
 344–346
String primitive instructions,
 333–338
StrLength procedure, 147
Str_length procedure,
 339–340, 342–343
Str_trim procedure, 340–343
Str_ucase procedure,
 343–344
Structure, 366–367
 aligning structure fields,
  368
 aligning structure
  variables, 369

containing other
 structures, 375
declaring variables,
 368-369
defining, 367–368
indirect and index
 operands, 371
performance of aligned
 members, 371-372
references to members,
 370
referencing, 370–372
Structure chart, 173
*Structured Computer
Organization*
(Tanenbaum), 7
SUB instruction, 67, 105
Substitution operator, 390,
 404
SumOf procedure, 171
SwapFlag, 288
Swap procedure, 273, 300, 303
SWORD data type, 80
Symbolic constant, 86
System management mode
 (SMM), 36
SYSTEMTIME structure,
 453–454
System time, displaying,
 372–374

T

Table-driven selection,
 208–210
Task switching, 35
TBYTE data type, 82, 92
Terabyte, 12
Terminal state, 211
Testing status bits, 195
TEST instruction, 187–188
Text editor, 71
TEXTEQU directive, 89

Text macro, 89
32-bit integers, adding,
 119 120
32-bit protected mode
 programs, 3
Three integers, smallest of,
 195–196
Time and data functions,
 577 581
Time slice, 35
Title directive, 66, 67
Top-down design, 172
Trailing edges, 33
Transfer control, 124
Translate buffer function,
 532–535
Turbo Assembler (Borland
 TASM), 1
20-bit linear address
 calculation, 44–45
Two-dimensional arrays
 base-index displacement
  operands, 349–350
 base-index operands,
  347–349
 ordering of rows and
  columns, 346–347
Two integers
 exchanging, 307–308
 larger of, 195
TYPEDEF operator, 122–123
TYPE operator, 112, 115, 121

U

Unconditional transfer, 124
Unicode standard, 17–18
Uninitialized data, declaring,
 85
Universal serial bus (USB),
 48, 50
Unsigned integers, ranges of, 13
.UNTIL condition, 217, 223

.UNTILCXZ condition, 217
Uppercase procedure, 277
USES operator, 170–171, 280
UTF-8, 17
UTF-16, 18
UTF-32, 18

V

Vertical retrace, 50
Video memory area, 564
Video RAM (VRAM), 50
Virtual-8086 mode, 36
Virtual machine concept, 7
Virtual memory, 47
Virtual memory managers, 47
Visual studio project
    properties, 547

W

WaitMsg procedure, 147
Wait states, 31, 33
.WHILE condition, 217,
    223–224
WHILE directive, 410
WHILE loops, 206–208
White box testing, 203–204
Wi-Fi (wireless), 52
Win32 API Reference
    Information, 421
Win32 console functions,
    424–426
Win32 console programming,
    419–420
    background information,
        420–424
    console input, 429–435
    console output, 435–437
    console window
        manipulation,
        447–450

controlling cursor,
    450–451
controlling text color,
    451–453
displaying message box,
    426–429
file I/O in Irvine32
    library, 442–444
reading and writing files,
    437–442
testing file I/O
    procedures, 444–447
time and date functions,
    453–456
Win32 console functions,
    424–426
Win32 date time functions,
    453
Win32 Platform SDK, 420
Windows API functions,
    character sets and,
    421–422
Windows data types, 422
WinMain procedure, 460
WinProc procedure, 460–461
wireless Ethernet, 52
WNDCLASS structure, 459
WORD data type, 62, 80
Word (2 bytes), 12
    arrays of, 88, 101
WriteBinB procedure, 148
WriteBin procedure, 147–148
WriteChar procedure, 148,
    382
WriteColors program, 452–453
WriteConsole function, 425,
    436–437
WriteConsoleInput function,
    425
WriteConsoleOutputAttribute
    function, 425, 451

WriteConsoleOutputCharacter
    function, 425, 435, 437
WriteConsoleOutput
    function, 425
WriteDec procedure, 148
WriteFile function, 441
WriteFloat, 505
WriteHex procedure, 148
WriteHexB procedure, 148
WriteHex64 procedure, 278
WriteInt procedure, 59, 148
WriteStackFrame procedure,
    309–310
WriteString procedure, 133,
    148, 175, 586
WriteToFile procedure, 149
WriteWindowsMsg
    procedure, 149, 432

X

x86 computer, components
    of, 48
    input-output ports and
        device interfaces,
        50–52
    memory, 49
    motherboard, 48–49
    video output, 50
x86 instruction coding, 512
    instruction format,
        512–513
    memory-mode
        instructions, 516–519
    move immediate to
        register, 514
    processor operand-size
        prefix, 515–516
    register-mode
        instructions, 514–515
    single-byte instructions,
        513

x86 instruction format,
512–513
x86 memory management,
43–47, 473
linear addresses, 473–477
page transition, 477–478
protected mode, 45–47
real-address mode, 43–45
x86 processor, 1, 29
x86 processor architecture, 36
execution environment,
36–39

floating-point unit, 39
Intel microprocessors,
39–42
modes of operation, 36
XCHG instruction,
100–101
XMM registers, 39
XOR instruction, 186–187

Y

Yottabyte, 13

Z

Zero flag, 39, 106, 107
Zero/sign extension of
integers, 98
copying smaller values to
larger ones, 98
MOVSX instruction,
99–100
MOVZX instruction,
98–99
Zettabyte, 13

decimal ⇨	hexa-decimal	1	16	32	46	64	80	96	112
⇩		0	1	2	3	4	5	6	7
0	0	null	▶	space	0	@	P	`	p
1	1	☺	◀	!	1	A	Q	a	q
2	2	●	↕	"	2	B	R	b	r
3	3	♥	‼	#	3	C	S	c	s
4	4	♦	Π	$	4	D	T	d	t
5	5	♣	§	%	5	E	U	e	u
6	6	♠	■	&	6	F	V	f	v
7	7	•	↕	'	7	G	W	g	w
8	8	◘	^	(	8	H	X	h	x
9	9	○	↓	)	9	I	Y	i	y
10	A	◉	→	*	:	J	Z	j	z
11	B	♂	←	+	;	K	[	k	{
12	C	♀	∟	,	<	L	\	l		
13	D	♪	↔	–	=	M	]	m	}
14	E	♫	▲	.	>	N	^	n	~
15	F	☼	▼	/	?	O	_	o	Δ